The
Nautical
Institute

The Nautical Institute
on
COMMAND

A PRACTICAL GUIDE

THE NAUTICAL INSTITUTE ON COMMAND

A PRACTICAL GUIDE – 2nd edition

Published by The Nautical Institute
202 Lambeth Road, London SE1 7LQ, England
Telephone: +44 (0)20 7928 1351
Fax: +44 (0)20 7401 2817
Publications e-mail: pubs@nautinst.org
Worldwide web site: http://www.nautinst.org

First edition published 1986. Reprinted 1988
Second edition published 2000. Reprinted 2009

Although great care has been taken with the writing and production of this volume, neither The Nautical Institute nor the authors can accept any responsibility for errors, omissions or their consequences.

This book has been prepared to address the subject of ship command. This should not, however, be taken to mean that this document deals comprehensively with all of the concerns which will need to be addressed or even, where a particular matter is addressed, that this document sets out the only definitive view for all situations.

The opinions expressed are those of the authors only and are not necessarily to be taken as the policies or views of any organisation with which they have any connection.

Readers and students should make themselves aware of any local, national or international changes to bylaws, legislation, statutory and administrative requirements that have been introduced which might affect decisions taken on board.

All photographs and diagrams acknowledged

Printed in England by
O'Sullivan Printing Corporation
Trident Way, International Trading Estate, Brent Road
Southall, Middlesex UB2 5LF

ISBN 978 1 870077 55 2

Cover photograph supplied by Joachim Affeldt

CONTENTS

CONTENTS (continued)

CONTENTS (continued)

CONTENTS (continued)

FOREWORD

by Captain E.M. Scott RNR RD** FNI

Senior Vice President, The Nautical Institute

SHIPMASTERS TODAY AND THOSE IN COMMAND OF NAVAL VESSELS have unique authority which is different to that of the factory manager or civil servant. Ships, although under the jurisdiction of the Flag State, are treated in law as independent 'out-posts'. The master and commanding officer are expected to uphold the general rule of law and to ensure the safety of the crew and the ship using their best judgement.

Distress, search and rescue are mutual responsibilities and are shared between ships and shore coordination centres. Still, the oceans are too wide for any nation adequately to provide emergency coverage economically, so the principles of self-sufficiency are reinforced. But as every shipmaster is aware, the environment of command is changing. The old values are still expected but there are a growing number of restrictions which make command more difficult.

In commercial fleets, economics, efficiency and competition are a dominant influence. There are few overmanned cargo ships and seldom enough time or resources to meet all demands. The networks of trade sustained by shipping tend towards longer logistic supply lines as more products are manufactured in developing countries and consumed in the developed world. Under these terms, quality of service becomes ever more important.

With the growing trend towards free flags, ships are becoming increasingly exposed to port state and regional inspections. Unless they are on a regular trade, shipmasters never quite know what to expect when visiting ports in other countries.

Shipmasters are becoming more exposed to unlawful practices which are generally outside their control. The pressure on economic migrants is increasing and stowaways are becoming more numerous. Piracy shows no signs of being brought under control and ships continue to be used for traffic in narcotics.

Although ships may have a life expectancy in excess of twenty years the shipping industry, like all others, is taking advantage of new technology. There is thus a widening gap between the outfit and control of new and old ships. The crew, of course, have to interchange and are therefore exposed to a more varied spectrum of technology than ever before.

Few masters, except perhaps in coastal trades, would disagree that manning is now universally international. My own relatively small vessel currently has seven nationalities of crew and they all work well together as a team. However, for a shipping company, the problems of identifying the best personnel for command is becoming more difficult because those moving into the senior chief officer range now come from many different countries, backgrounds and cultures.

It cannot be assumed that the essence of command can just be picked up. Assuming authority and managing the voyage through the delegation of responsibility, whilst exercising good judgement to keep many often conflicting demands in balance whilst optimising the owner's return on the venture, is not a job for the uninitiated. Indeed, shipmasters today are exposed to an increasingly severe climate of financial penalties for injury, negligence, environmental damage and poor out-turns.

In my own current part of the industry, passenger safety and care for passengers even when not on board is my responsibility. A careless accident could cause my company to become involved in litigation costing millions of dollars.

Where people are concerned, the days are long since past when the role of the ship's staff was simply to take the ship safely from one location to another. There is significant competitive advantage in repeat passengers and we want to create an atmosphere where passengers will choose us again.

I want to emphasise that command, like all other aspects of management, is changing. Being a good chief navigator is essential but it is not enough. Shipmasters have to be able to contribute to the success of their companies and it is with this in mind that The Nautical Institute has developed the Command Partnership Programme and revised this book on Command.

The Nautical Institute has taken the view that if we as shipmasters want standards to improve we have to play our part in achieving this objective. The command book and scheme is our contribution to providing international industry-wide support to our future captains.

PREFACE

by Captain T.J. Bailey FNI, Chairman of the Command Book and Scheme Revision Group

WHEN THE FIRST EDITION OF *The Nautical Institute on Command* was published in 1986 my predecessors had the difficult task of distilling the best advice into a single publication. They did so with admirable skill and the book has sold in large numbers since that time.

But with the passage of time there have been significant changes to our industry, not only in terms of legislation and technology but also in the manner in which ships and shipping companies are operated, the background of the people involved and continuing changes in training and career development. Changes in technology –have taken us from steam power to 'cyber power' and the Internet. Many more ships are now owned by banks and finance companies; they are operated by ship management companies and more and more seafarers are employed on a contract basis – there is no longer the philosophy of a 'job for life'.

In trying to revise and review this fundamental work, it was necessary to reflect on these factors and to consider the parallel development of The Nautical Institute as an influential professional group.

Everywhere knowledge horizons are expanding and so it was felt necessary to provide a framework in which to structure the '*best advice*' into a format that would be most helpful to busy people who want to do the right thing and who want to avoid costly mistakes.

We took the model of the ISM Code as an underlying template. The functions of policy, procedures, implementation, review, audit and improvement are the elements of management. The master's role then becomes one of developing clarity of purpose, achieving results with least effort and encouraging positive participation from the crew.

The content of the book is not exhaustive and nor can it be: so much of the role of master/commander can only be learnt by experience. To cover every possible experience with written articles would be impossible and nonproductive – the prospective master/commander must learn for himself.

In this new edition the spread of authors is more international, reflecting the changes in Institute membership, ownership, registration and manning. The authors have provided an extraordinary richness of response which emphasises one crucial point behind the whole of this exercise. As masters we hold independent positions but no single master could have written this book on his own. Although often lonely, our position is not alone and the focus of our professional Institute can bring together a relevant collection of advice and guidance to build up that level of knowledge and awareness which provides 'good judgement'.

Let us take maritime law as just one subject. How much should the master know and to what level? Whole libraries have been written on maritime conventions, mandatory provisions, guidance notices, contract law, charter parties, bills of lading, insurance and now there is environmental legislation, health and safety, international law and the laws of coastal states. We have tried to provide some basic advice for the master.

The section on management has been expanded and the legal chapters have been redesigned to reflect the changing status of international conventions and the importance of customer satisfaction.

Captain Peter Boyle, my predecessor who put the original book together, asked past Command Diploma students to discuss the value of following a command development programme. Their comments make encouraging reading.

Captain Ian Mathison introduces the ISM Code which is, of course, new but it will soon become mandatory for all ships. For some, there is experience already of its implementation but for many this is not the case. Using the code to improve company and shipboard performance is such a sensible and positive response to this mandatory requirement.

New techniques and issues have been introduced where they are topical and The Nautical Institute can be helpful through the knowledge and experience of its members.

Captain Alan McDowall admirably covers the anchoring of large ships. Environmental issues like waste management are put into perspective by Captain Derek Yeomans and Mr. David Patraiko addresses ballast water safety issues. The demise of the radio officer has caused much controversy but GMDSS is covered by former radio officer Mr. Ian Waugh. Similarly, Captain Murdo McLeod brings the use of shipboard computers for maintenance much more up-to-date.

A number of chapters from the old book are reproduced because of their classic value and some are redeveloped. The chapter on navigation in pilotage waters by Captain Francois Baillod encourages good master/pilot relationships and describes practical safe management in passage planning.

To all the contributors who have helped to provide an answer to that difficult question "*What is the best advice that I can give shipmasters?*" – a very sincere and heartfelt "Thank you".

I would also like to express my sincere thanks and admiration to all the staff at The Nautical Institute headquarters for their unfailing support throughout the project.

THE NAUTICAL INSTITUTE COMMAND DIPLOMA
The road to promotion

by Captain P. Boyle MRIN FNI

It is twelve years since The Nautical Institute developed its Command Diploma scheme. There have been many changes since then and The Nautical Institute Command Working Group consider that the time has come for a new edition of the study guide and a reappraisal.

What does the international shipping industry require of its captains? They must be skilful at doing their job is the short answer but in order to achieve this a captain has just about to be all things to all men. Not only must he be very good at the quantifiable skills of navigation, stability, cargo care, ship handling, pollution prevention, safety, commercial awareness, etc. but he must also be very good in more fuzzy areas such as man management, relationships with owners, charterers, agents and with port and national authorities, stevedores and pilots.

In the previous paragraph I have deliberately stated that captains must be 'very good' at doing their tasks. Any lesser standard is not good enough for the industry. How can captains become 'very good' at what they do? In times gone by future captains learned much of their skills by watching and absorbing the style and ability of their superior officers. They usually did this under some form of apprenticeship scheme attached to one shipping company, slow promotion to senior officer level where the company could ascertain whether the chief officer was suitable command material and eventually promotion to command of his own ship. Surely one of the most satisfying events in any seaman's life. There was a mutual acceptance that the company and the new captain would be good for one another. Even when personnel moved between companies their training was similar and national characteristics and cultural styles determined the quality of training.

All has now changed. Systems of employment at sea today are very different to what they were twenty years ago. Standards of training are, in many cases, not good enough. It is no use absorbing the style or the ability of an inadequately trained senior officer. Owners, however, still require captains. It is expected that the Seafarers Training Certification and Watchkeeping requirements as amended in 1995 (STCW'95) will address the problem of inadequate training and ensure that there is an acceptable minimum standard for all seamen. Minimum standards are not good enough for captains however.

How can today's shipowner identify the right man to promote to captain? The system is such that he can no longer watch a potential captain, perhaps over a period of years, before giving him a command. What is more, many modern shipowners, not having knowledge of ships other than as cost centres, do not know what to look for in a future captain. The Nautical Institute Command Partnership Scheme will give the holder an edge when seeking promotion and it will indicate to owners that a person undertaking such a course of study is worthy of promotion.

Change is taking place throughout the world at an increasing rate. Aided by IT, the Internet, increasing use of computers, etc. the totality of knowledge is growing exponentially. Ship's captains can't afford to get left behind. The master of a ship is every bit the managing director of his enterprise as his colleague running a factory ashore. His financial responsibilities are huge and frequently in excess of 100 million dollars of ship and cargo. It requires an intelligent, numerate and literate person to run such an enterprise. Participating in the Command Partnership Scheme will enable the person of the right calibre to develop his potential to the full, a potential which may well carry him to the highest levels of ship operations.

Some twelve years ago, the first person to enrol in the Nautical Institute Command Diploma scheme was Captain Peter Roberts FNI. After being awarded his diploma he went on to achieve command, became Marine Superintendent of a shipping company, wrote a very successful book (*Ship Safety and Cargo Management in Port*, a Nautical Institute publication) and he is now a successful maritime consultant. Captain C.M. Mahidhara FNI says "the Command Diploma Course ...... brought new enthusiasm and zeal to my job ...... I think it will be useful for anyone aspiring to command, as it is a very practical guide". Captain Michael Fagan MNI says that he approached a number of prospective employers before agreeing to work for his present employer. "In every case the interviewer seemed to be more interested in the Command Diploma than in anything else ...... taking the Diploma made me think again about all manner of various issues and made me go back to the pen". Captain Fagan goes on to say that doing the Command Diploma Course has stimulated his intellectual curiosity.

Captain James T. Jamieson MNI found that the Diploma Course was mentally stimulating and he obtained the Luddeke prize for the highest overall score in 1997. He goes on to say "I would urge all senior chief officers and newly promoted masters to undertake the Diploma for their own benefit as it will make them better officers".

Captain John Dunne MNI obtained his Command Diploma in 1995 and was promoted to command in 1996. He states "I attribute my achieving command to two main factors – that I had worked at completing the company's own 'promotion checklist' and that I had completed the Nautical Institute Command Diploma Scheme and was able to send a copy of the diploma to my employers". Ian C. Biles Master Mariner, BEng (Hons) MA CEng MNI obtained his Command Diploma in 1990. In 1992 he started up his own very successful consultancy business. Ian says "the Command Diploma was to start my mind thinking again and to return to the routine of studying. Having been away from 'academia' for some time since passing my master's certificate I felt I could go further and the Command Diploma was my first step". Ian has fulfilled his ambition as the letters after his name indicate and he goes on to say that "Having now developed the study ethic I have continued with what I see as my 'Continual Professional Development'".

Captain Christopher J. Shill MNI obtained his Diploma in 1996. He says "I found the Command Diploma Scheme an extremely useful aid to furthering my career" ...... "undertaking the scheme helped my promotion prospects ...... seen by (my company) as positive and has been rewarded". Captain Martin Stott MNI obtained his Diploma in 1994 and achieved command in 1996. He subsequently changed employers and states "the Diploma stood me in good stead when applying for (my present) position". He goes on "The scheme was very rewarding in completing it". Captain Stott achieved the highest marks in the scheme in 1994. Captain R.S. Gilbert (the 1998 Command Diploma prizewinner) goes on to say that "the master was in no doubt as to what my aspirations were. I also had a break in command employment and being able to pick up the Command Diploma after a period was an advantage to me".

The foregoing gentlemen, being men of achievement, have suggested a number of areas where this second edition of The Nautical Institute on Command can be modified and updated. Their suggestions have been incorporated.

Today's favoured management style is that of the "network" rather than that of the "hierarchy". The manager in the network is needed for his expert knowledge and not solely for his ability to be a good subordinate. The good shipowner and manager will understand that and allow the captains in their organisational networks to contribute their unique expertise to the profitability of the company. Up to date expertise can only be achieved through continuous learning. The Nautical Institute Command Partnership Scheme and Diploma is a step in the right direction.

LETTER TO A NEWLY PROMOTED MASTER

by Captain A.C. Collop MNI

Dear Bill

Congratulations on your well-deserved promotion. On thinking back to my own first command and all its pitfalls, I thought maybe that you would appreciate a bit of advice. As far as discipline and your comportment as captain are concerned, you will have made up your own mind about these aspects long ago. The following are just a few bits of practical advice.

On taking over command, the outgoing captain may not know it is your first trip and will not have written his handover notes on that basis. Therefore, when talking things over with him, make sure he sticks to the subject. A master being relieved visibly drops quite a burden from his shoulders and is inclined to be talkative – especially to another master. He will talk about everything under the sun if you let him and it will often be difficult to keep him to the point.

After reading the handover notes your best bet is to read the incoming and outgoing e-mails, telexes and faxes at least for the current month. It is by far the best way to find out what has been going on and you often come across items not in the handover notes. Read them while the relieved master is still aboard and ask questions about things you are not sure about.

Make sure you know where everything is and who keeps what. There is nothing more embarrassing than having a superintendent or repair squad chief asking where such and such a document or plan is and you do not know. The mate and chief will probably be busy and there is no-one to ask. Most companies will have handover forms, usually requiring you to sight and sign for these, but not all items are always included. They are normally not important – except on that one vital occasion.

For instance, if you have to take over on the run, say by helicopter off Dubai a day before you go in to load, make sure you know where the last port clearance is kept. Failure to find it can land you in trouble with the next port authorities.

Port authorities, in some parts of the world, can be very unpleasant for the master. I don't mean surveyors, port state inspectors and such like – they usually do a reasonable job. It is the Customs, Immigration, Port Health and some Harbour Authorities who can cause problems. They often seem to have a power far out of proportion to their responsibilities or their capabilities. Sometimes even the Agent, usually the master's best friend, can be on their side in some ports. Generally you just have to grit your teeth and bear it.

Before arriving in port, read all the pertinent books carefully. Do not do what I did on my first trip in command. Before arrival at Rotterdam I had heard that it was a free port. "Oh, good" I said to myself, "no port papers to do". So I didn't do any, despite the doubts of the Chief Steward, who also happened to be new at the job. We sailed blithely in with absolutely nothing done. A good job we had an excellent agent there. We spent the next few hectic hours running round, getting the officers and crew to sign manifests, counting the cigarettes and bonded stores, typing crew lists – the lot. The port authorities were very good to me that time. In fact, they laughed their heads off!

Try to get on with the chief engineer, so there is no 'divide and conquer' syndrome on board. If you find yourself with a bad cook, get rid of him as soon as you can. If you have a good one, then spoil him. He'll help to make a happy, contented ship. We British tend to treat the catering staff with contempt. Try not to and you will have a happier ship.

You will have to look after some thousands of dollars and other currencies. Make certain you keep a note of every penny going in or out of the safe. I usually keep an 'In and Out' account on the computer and back it up with a ledger type book. If you don't do this or let it slide you can have problems at the end of the month or upon being relieved yourself. Also, do not let the outgoing captain short change you when he hands over the cash to you. Every last cent must be accounted for – or you could find yourself out of pocket. I have seen some relieved masters miss their flights home due to money they cannot trace.

Pilots can be a pain in the neck at times. There is usually no problem with them when entering port or manoeuvring. It's the tying up when the problems usually start. They think you have a large crew and you can see your three men on the foc's'le head, desperately trying to put out springs and headlines and let go the tug at the same time. If you get a pilot who gives loads of unnecessary orders when tying up, then I found it best to relay them all over the walkie-talkie – but omit sometimes to press the 'send' button. As you know, I was an offshore pilot myself at one stage of my career. Due to this I don't agree at all that pilots should interfere with the ropes and wires. I seldom did.

Finally, when you leave your first port as master, remember you have no 'L' plates on display. None of the other ships around you know it is your debut. Always ask the pilot to point out the next buoys or marks before leaving. Things are easier now, when you can mark them on your radar displays.

Anyway, Bill, all the very best of luck and love to Jenny and the girls.

Chapter 1

THE NAUTICAL INSTITUTE ON COMMAND

A Council report prepared by The Nautical Institute Command Working Group

Nature of command

COMMAND IS EXERCISED through the organisation on board a ship, which has been developed over a long time to minimise the risk of danger to the ship when at sea.

The characteristic of a command structure is that it is quick to respond; so enabling decisions to be taken to avoid accidents.

The master or commanding officer is ultimately responsible for ensuring that the command organisation is effective. He has to satisfy himself that the vessel can be run safely by day and night in all prevailing weather conditions and port situations. He delegates authority to his subordinates to operate the ship under his command.

A ship is also a commercial or fighting unit and has to be managed accordingly. This involves communications between departments on board and with the supporting organisation ashore. In addition to his other duties, the captain therefore has an important coordinating role. As titular head of the ship the captain must be a leader and a counsellor.

By law the shipmaster has to have a certificate of competency and has the authority to take decisions in the best interests of the ship, her cargo and all who sail in her. Where the safety of the ship is concerned he has the duty not to take his ship to sea if, in his opinion, the vessel is unseaworthy.

Advantages and limitations of the command structure

The supporting organisation on board, of which the captain is the head, derives its structure from the need for routines and a system of communication which feeds information to him quickly and accurately. It follows that the captain, with his experience and overall appreciation, is the best person to assess a situation and take the appropriate decisions, especially in an emergency.

Delegation

Delegation is necessary to maintain continuous operation of the ship. It is not an exact process and depends upon the relationship between people and the tasks to be undertaken. Successful delegation requires that a ship be operated on consistent policy lines so that particular phases of operation may be delegated without having to pass more instructions than the junior can assimilate at the time.

Management decisions relating to the best use of resources require a different supporting structure which must enable those concerned to acquire all relevant information and provide the opportunity for everybody involved with the use of' resources to understand their role in optimising results or minimising costs. Similarly, when running a meeting where conflicting demands on down time or resources are involved between departments, the captain is best placed to adopt the role of chairman to weigh up the arguments and assign priorities.

The level of involvement of the shipmaster in the management of' the ship depends upon company policy. Where all decisions are devolved to the ship, with management in support, the master becomes accountable for vessel performance, retaining maximum revenue, keeping stores, maintenance and labour costs within budget, and minimising losses.

Alternatively, some companies maintain a centralised control system so that the master is primarily concerned with navigational safety, ship handling and crew welfare.

In between there are a variety of different approaches which depend upon the type of ship being operated and the management style of the company. Whichever system is used it is the captain who must retain the coordinating role.

Where the Navy is concerned, the manning levels are such and the tactical demands so immediate that there is an established role for the commanding officer who is backed up by a specially trained ship's company. The complexity of modern warfare also dictates that a very responsive and dynamic approach is adopted towards the interpretation and use of tactical data and weapon systems. The concept of appointing a principal warfare officer to a ship relates more to the principles of management than to a traditional system of passing orders down the line.

Command decisions need systematic evaluation

When considering the basis upon which command decisions are made, the, Council of The Nautical Institute recommend that a careful analysis is undertaken of all those factors which can influence the way decisions are taken on board.

This is necessary whenever an incident is being investigated and a proper system of enquiry must be introduced. To this end The Nautical Institute has produced a check list which should be used by all parties involved as a way of establishing the underlying causes of the accident and the remedies to be implemented. The checklist is included at the end of this chapter.

Promotion from chief officer to captain is significant. Clearly, the human qualities (professional competence, ability to plan and carry through a programme of work, flexibility, stamina, integrity, the ability to make decisions, leadership and that sixth sense or shipboard awareness), which make for a good captain, cannot be tested by examination alone and the process of selection is crucial.

Notwithstanding, there are fewer traditional companies with a full programme of career development from cadet to master and, increasingly, the modern officer is having to go out and sell his services in a variety of companies overseas. It is unlikely that such an officer will have received any formal training after completing studies for his master's certificate of competency.

The Council of The Nautical Institute therefore believe it is desirable to have a voluntary scheme for those who want to follow a programme of study to prepare themselves for command.

The Nautical Institute therefore believe it is desirable to have a voluntary scheme for those who want to follow a programme of study to prepare themselves for command. To this end the Institute has prepared this self-development programme leading to a Command Diploma. Further details appear in chapter 58.

Need for properly defined terms

The concept of command is given two principal meanings in general English usage. In one sense it implies the subject or area under command: in an active way it means to order or demand with authority.

Command is expressed at three levels: in terms of society as a whole; in the context of an organisation and specifically on board.

Authority is a more ambiguous word since at one level it implies a legal power or right, but on the other hand it has an equally positive meaning as the influence exercised by virtue of character, office, mental or moral qualities.

A commanding officer is given one kind of authority by status but because he works within an organisation he needs a management authority to control resources to achieve objectives and personal qualities of competence and ability to obtain support.

Delegation is entrusting authority to a deputy, but the problem with this general idea is that there are certain obligations implicit in command which cannot

be delegated; equally important then is the industrial or military context in which the ship is operated.

In one sense the commanding officer is the head of a command tree, in another sense he is part of it. Certain decisions he can make concerning the use of people and resources; but he seldom decides which cargo will be carried, which weapon systems fitted, who will be appointed, promoted or trained. In this sense the organisation has to assume some responsibility for command, yet this may not be fully recognised in law.

Problems arise therefore when the same words are given different meanings in the varied contexts in which they are used. If steps are to be taken to improve the effectiveness of command then it is essential that definitions are provided which differentiate between the different aspects of command and the way it is exercised.

Definitions

Accountability:	The process by which control is exercised over decisions and actions which is implicit in the concept of responsibility.
Authority:	The power and the right to require obedience to instructions.
Authority, legal:	The authority given to an individual by society to fulfil specific obligations within the law.
Authority, organisational:	The authority given to an individual by military or commercial organisations to discharge the function of command in pursuit of military or commercial objectives.

Authority, personal:	The authority exercised by virtue of character, experience and officer-like qualities.	Liability, vicarious:	The civil liability attaching to an employer for the negligence of his employees.
Authority, shipboard:	The authority given to an individual derived from legal and organisational authority to meet the obligations of the commission or voyage.	Management:	The process of involving people and utilising other resources to achieve a given objective.
Chain of command:	The means by which orders are passed down devolving authority.	Responsibility:	The duty to meet obligations.
		Responsibility, legal:	The duty placed upon those concerned with the control of seagoing craft to ensure that the ship is operated within the law.
Charge of the ship:	Authority delegated to an officer for the safe conduct of a vessel in accordance with standing orders and captain's instructions.	Responsibility, organisational:	The obligation placed upon those in organisations owning the ship to ensure that it is provided with competent personnel, material and is in a fit state to fulfil the requirements of the commission or voyage.
Command, naval:	The authority vested in an individual to direct, coordinate and control naval forces.		
Command, ship:	The authority to direct and control a ship.	Responsibility, personal:	The moral/ethical and professional way through which command is exercised.
Commanding officer:	Captain of a naval ship commissioned by the appropriate national defence authority who has ultimate responsibility for the safe conduct and fighting efficiency of the ship and the wellbeing of the ship's company. In the event of death or incapacity command normally descends to the Executive Officer and then by seniority through those entitled to exercise ship command.	Responsibility, ultimate:	The responsibility which attaches to the captain of a ship for its overall safety and efficiency.
		Ship manager:	An individual or company contracted by the ship owner to carry out the operational management of the ship. Full management will comprise crewing, technical management, insurance, freight management, accounting, chartering, provisions, bunkering and operations. A ship management contract may include all or some of the above provisions and is usually negotiated in relation to a 12 monthly budget. Sometimes additional payment may be requested for training purposes.
Delegation:	Entrusting authority to a competent person and holding that person accountable to the level set.		
Designated person:	A suitably qualified and experienced shore based employee required under the ISM Code for monitoring the safety and pollution prevention aspects of the operation of each ship with the responsibility to ensure that adequate resources and shore-based support are applied when needed. The designated person should have both independence and authority to report deficiencies to the highest level of management and is responsible for ensuring that non-conformities derived as a result of the safety management system are rectified.	Ship master:	The captain of a merchant ship qualified by the appropriate certificate of competency who is appointed by the ship owner. He has the responsibility to efficiently prosecute the voyage and an overriding responsibility to ensure the safety of his passengers, crew, ship and cargo with the duty generally to save and preserve life at sea. In the event of his death or incapacity command descends to the second in command who is the senior deck officer and then through the other deck officers in order of rank.
Discipline:	The requirement for personnel to comply with regulations and respond to authority.		
Liability, civil:	The obligations to pay compensation for damage caused through negligence.		
Liability, criminal:	The liability to suffer a fine or penalty for breach of a Regulation.	Ship owner:	The person or persons whose names appear in the ship's register. They may be the managing owner, ship's husband or other person entrusted with management. The owner seeks to use his ship(s) for profitable enterprise but in so doing has to comply with national and international legislation. The shipowner has to ensure that the ship's safety certificates are in order, that the ship is seaworthy, properly manned and in a fit condition to meet the requirements of the intended voyage.
Liability, strict:	The criminal liability arising when specified regulations are unwittingly breached. It is often called 'absolute liability' though the regulation imposing it usually provides defences which can be pleaded on proof of certain circumstances.		

Status of the shipmaster in international law: Resolution A443 (XI) International Maritime Organisation 15 Nov 1979

'The IMO Assembly invites Governments to take necessary steps to safeguard the international shipmaster in the proper discharge of his responsibilities in regard to maritime safety and the protection of the marine environment by ensuring that:

(a) The shipmaster is not constrained by the shipowner, charterer or any other person from taking in this respect any decision which, in the professional judgement of the shipmaster, is necessary;

(b) The shipmaster is protected by appropriate provisions, including the right of appeal, contained in, inter alia, national legislation, collective agreements or contracts of employment, from unjustifiable dismissal or other unjustifiable action by the shipowner, charterer or any other person as a consequence of the proper exercise of his professional judgement.

The Council of The Nautical Institute concludes that the principles and practice of exercising effective command at sea is an essential part of the expertise of the nautical profession.

Annex – In the event of an incident

Any person investigating a marine incident should establish the basis upon which command decisions were taken.

1. The incident
   (a) Record what happened and all relevant times with supporting documentation.
   (b) Record all relevant communications.
   (c) Establish what steps were taken after the event to minimise the risk of danger to those on board the ship, the cargo, life, property and the marine environment.

2. Ultimate responsibility on board
   (a) What was the organisational structure on board and what normal or special operating precautions were established to minimise the risk of the incident occurring?
   (b) Had authority been delegated properly?
   (c) Did subordinates fully understand their obligations and duties?
   (d) Were there available enough competent personnel to carry out routine duties?
   (e) Were there available enough competent personnel to meet the contingency?
   (f) If not, what compensating measures were adopted?

3. Organisational responsibility ashore
   (a) Was the captain adequately prepared by training and experience to meet the contingency?
   (b) Did the captain have all the relevant information and equipment on board and know how to use it?
   (c) Was the ship adequately provided with trained personnel to carry out efficiently and safely the routine duties?
   (d) Was the ship adequately provided with trained personnel and material to meet the contingency?
   (e) What action was taken to support the captain at the scene of the accident?
   (f) What systems of accountability were in operation for the safe operation of the ship, her commercial performance and crew incentives?

4. Personal responsibility
   (a) Who was in charge at the time of the incident?
   (b) What steps were taken to avoid the incident?
   (c) Were the actions taken consistent with company instructions and the operating philosophy on board?
   (d) Were the actions taken consistent with good seaman-like practice?

General
What corrective measures *were taken*?

Note: These facts may also be used to determine legal liabilities but must first be subjected to legal tests of reasonableness and remoteness.

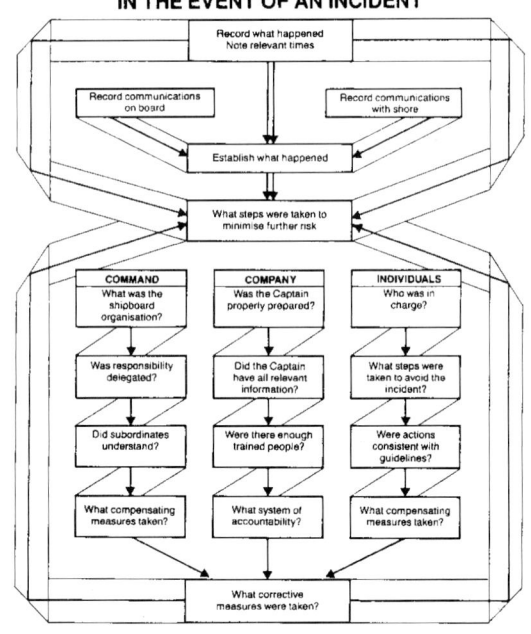

Figure 1.1 In the event of an incident

Chapter 2

WHAT A SHIP OWNER REQUIRES FROM A MASTER

by Captain P. Chawla FNI MICS
General Manager, Quality Assurance and Training, Anglo Eastern Ship Management Limited

Captain Chawla started his seagoing career in 1974 and was appointed master in 1986. In 1992 he was brought ashore to set up the quality management system throughout the Anglo Eastern Group. Captain Chawla has represented the Hong Kong Ship Owners Association and The International Ship Managers Association at the IMO.

Introduction

THE STRUCTURE OF SHIP OWNING companies has been changing continuously over the last couple of decades. A 'ship owner' today might be a large corporation, a company owned by doctors or lawyers, a trading house or a bank, etc. The traditional ship owning office has therefore given way to a number of different styles of management of ships. The expectations from a ship's master may therefore be quite different in different companies.

In order to put forward to you a wide range of views of what ship owners expect from their ship masters, a survey was carried out amongst senior executives of various ship owners and ship managers. The views of a few serving ship masters were also taken, to see whether there was any difference in the perceptions of the ship owners and presently serving senior ship masters. I am pleased to say that the good qualities listed by the shipowners as well as the serving ship masters were very similar.

This chapter is essentially a collection of the common requirements which were put forward by various people, mingled with my personal views. I take this opportunity to thank all those who were kind enough to assist in the writing of this chapter and hope that the students of the Nautical Institute Command course and newly promoted masters find it useful in their daily lives on board.

Let us consider a few situations you may find yourself in as a ship's master. You are sailing on a fully loaded VLCC, in the North Sea, through terrible weather. It is 0400 hours, and you are called up to the bridge by the chief officer. You rush to the wheelhouse and are told "the second engineer just called saying they have a problem with the fuel oil system and it may take some time to repair". You quickly look at the chart and realize you have just 2 hours before the ship drifts into shallow waters!

What will be your actions?

You are lucky. The engineers are able to run the engines and you arrive in port safely, after being awake on the bridge for twenty hours.

The immigration, customs, port health, agent and ship chandler are followed by two vetting inspectors, a port state control inspector, the terminal representative, a charterer's representative and the company's engineering superintendent.

The voyage orders have been changed and you are to go to an additional port. The original bills of lading are not available, and the charterer's representative would like you to accept a letter of indemnity and discharge the cargo.

What actions do you have to take?

You sort out the situation with the charterers, vetting inspectors, port state inspector and the superintendent and are about to get some rest when the second officer comes up to you. He has just spoken to his family and has been informed that his home was damaged by a typhoon. He would like to be relieved immediately, as he is extremely worried about the welfare of his family.

Handling all these situations require different types of skills and qualities. Handling emergencies, understanding the commercial business of the ship and motivating the ship crew are just a few of the abilities expected from a ship master.

Since the time man learnt the art of building a ship, the person in charge – the master – has been fully responsible for the **safety of people, ship and cargo** on board his ship and will continue to be so as long as people are required to operate ships. Hence some of the qualities expected by a ship owner from a master have not changed over the centuries. What is written in this paper will therefore, in some part, be a repetition of traditional advice available in many books.

At the same time, seafaring has changed significantly in the last couple of decades. Crew sizes have reduced from 30 to 40, to the present day norm of 12 to 22 people on most ships.

Global Positioning Systems (GPS), GMDSS, electronic navigation charts combined with the International Safety Management (ISM) Code and STCW 95 require learning of new skills and new ways of management on board.

The shipping industry is presently going through a phase of serious introspection and change. The ISM Code, STCW 95, Port State Control, Risk Assessment,

Quality Assurance ISO 9002, e-mail and a number of other developments are challenging traditional methods of work and management of ships. These changes will affect every crew member on board, but as master you will be affected the most.

Change is always difficult in any industry. As a master in today's world, you need to manage this change. Traditional values, which have served us well over the centuries, will need to be retained. New ideas will have to be tried out with an open mind and nurtured with care so that the next generation of seafarers is trained to cope with the new demands of the industry.

Managing this change is a responsible task and will require your devoted attention as a ship's master. The list of desirable qualities and advice collected together here will, we hope, assist you to appreciate the traditional values and at the same time manage this change . We hope they help you meet the various demands made on you while in command as a ship's master.

No individual is likely to possess all these qualities in a perfect balance, and different circumstances will require the use of different methods, so do not dissect your personality to shreds over it! Knowing your personal strengths and weaknesses is the first step in good management.

Before I list the qualities desired by shipowners, it is probably worth mentioning something that no master must ever forget. Ship owning is a commercial venture with the aim of earning profits for the ship owner or the shareholders of the ship. As a master you are the owner's representative and therefore every decision that you take must be in the interest of the owners. At the same time, you are also the crew's representative with the owners. This leads us to the first and the most important responsibility and desired quality of a master.

1. Safety of people, ship, cargo and environment

Under all legal systems, for centuries past, the master is fully responsible for the safety of the people on board, the ship, the cargo and the environment. By giving you command the ship owner entrusts you with his multi million-dollar asset – his ship. The cargo owners entrust you with their cargo, which may be worth millions of dollars, and above all the crew entrusts you with their lives. Society expects you to take care of the environment. The ship owner and others expect you to carry out your duties with the highest sense of responsibility at all times.

Recognizing the importance of your responsibilities the law gives you complete and 'overriding authority' in all matters of safety of the crew, ship, cargo and environment. In resolution A.443(XI), IMO urged governments to take steps to safeguard the ship master from being pressurised by anybody, in the proper discharge of his responsibilities in regard to maritime safety and the protection of the marine environment.

2. Thorough knowledge

If the company has decided to give you command, you have obviously been considered competent! The reason for making this point is that a master's responsibility includes certain new areas, for which nobody else on board may have adequate knowledge, for example, seaworthiness (legal and commercial implications). A good knowledge in such subjects is therefore essential. Maintaining a good reference library on board is helpful to refresh your knowledge.

In this changing world of new regulations, it is also important that you stay abreast of the changes in regulations. The ISM Code also implies that the industry codes and guidelines must be adhered to as applicable. A modern day master thus needs to read a lot and it is essential that the process of continuous learning is maintained even after attaining command of the vessel. Try to read as much as you can, about the developments in the industry. The Nautical Institute magazine *SEAWAYS* is a good one to start with! As a master, you need to know your ship thoroughly. You are expected to know the full details of whatever is happening on board your vessel. A first hand knowledge is especially important when you are reporting a problem of any kind to the ship owner or manager.

3. Personnel management skills / communication skills / leadership

The efficient running of a ship, similar to an office or any business unit, is dependent on the contribution of each individual on board. A master is the leader of this team. He is expected to be capable of motivating his team.

What do 'leadership' and 'motivation' mean? Every seafarer knows that the work people do, is sometimes done superbly and at other times it is done atrociously. The main reason for that difference is motivation or the lack of it. It is the difference between doing as little as one can get away with and doing everything one possibly can. Motivation is the art of helping people to focus their minds and energies on doing their work as effectively as possible. It is the art of creating conditions that allow everyone to give out their best.

Innumerable books and theories have been written on motivation. In the 'real world', even if you were to read all the theories, the facts do not always allow the direct application of the theories. There is no motivational technique which works with everyone. In fact it is unlikely that the same technique will work with the same individual all the time.

So what does work? How does a master motivate his crew? How does a master lead his team? I mention below some of the beliefs that have served me well in my experience of sailing with seafarers of eighteen different nationalities in a variety of companies.

All human beings, irrespective of colour, religion, nationality or cultural diversity like to be treated with respect, compassion and impartiality. Irrespective of any cultural differences, if you treat people as you would like to be treated, you will not go wrong. You should be able to understand the other persons viewpoint. You must treat others with respect, even if you disagree with their views. People like to be recognized for their efforts in public, but prefer to be reprimanded only in private. People like to participate in decisions affecting them and appreciate their views being listened to attentively. People like to be given responsibility and left alone to carry out the task in their own way.

Most people try to do a good job. If they are not performing to your satisfaction, other factors like their training level, working environment and relationships with their immediate supervisor may need to be investigated. To get the best out of people, you need to convince them why the job needs to be done well.

Motivating people requires strong communication skills. To be able to communicate well with people you need to relate well with people. Without going into any theories on interpersonal relationships, it is sufficient to remember that an important part of communicating is LISTENING. If you are having problems in motivating people, talk to them and you will find that by solving their problems, your problem of motivating them gets solved by itself. **You should be easily approachable at all times**.

In today's work environment, the traditional tasks of navigation and cargo work have been made easier by technology. Keeping a lookout with the help of a radar is far easier than sitting in a crow's nest, in freezing weather. Loading a tanker from a remote control room is certainly easier than opening valves with a long spanner. But the task of motivating the staff on board has not changed.

The autocratic ways of the past are no longer acceptable in shipping, or in society. Hence as a master, it will be necessary that you learn as much as you can on how modern day participative management can be carried out on board. Having said that, there should be no hesitation on the part of a master in being assertive and taking full control and responsibility, whenever required, especially during emergencies.

Safety meetings, quality circles, senior officers meeting, etc. whether done formally or informally over coffee time, are all designed to encourage participative management in day to day operation of the ship. Remember, you are only as good as your team. Lead by setting a good example in all the qualities that you want your team to have.

4 Commercial skills

Different trades and different owners have very different expectations from masters in terms of their commercial duties. On a container liner service public relations with agents and appreciation of keeping to schedules may be the most important commercial expectation. On a bulk carrier, loading the last possible tonne of cargo, or understanding the importance of hold cleanliness surveys may be more important than arriving at the pilot station on schedule.

An owner expects the master to make decisions keeping in mind the effect of the decision on the profits and reputation of the shipowner. A master must therefore try to learn the requirements of the trade and the owner's special requirements in detail. A master is expected to have a thorough knowledge of commercial matters. The syllabus covered for certificate of competency examinations is typically of an academic nature only. You need to supplement it by extensive reading in order to gain sufficient practical knowledge.

The legal interpretations of seaworthiness, safe port, arrived ship, deviation, delivery, notice of readiness, speed and consumption clauses in charter parties, are some of the topics on which you may need to supplement your knowledge. Legal responsibilities assumed by the master's signature must be clearly understood. Never sign a paper without reading it carefully and understanding the liabilities that you or the owner may be subjected to, by signing it.

The master must take a keen interest in reading the governing charter-parties, understanding the possible problems with bills of lading, and understanding the master's legal obligations under voyage and time charters. A good knowledge of P&I Club rules and marine insurance clauses, are some of the things that would help in becoming a commercially astute master.

There are a number of good books available on commercial knowledge for ship masters, including some published by The Nautical Institute. The Institute can help in directing you to the right ones.

5. Handling of emergencies

Every ship owner expects a master to be able to handle all shipboard emergencies with a good presence of mind and with rational, logical thinking. The ability of the master to handle emergencies effectively is one of the most important qualities required and perhaps the most difficult to predict.

How does one learn to handle this responsibility? The traditional advice is training, training and more training. In the past, one obtained the necessary skills by observation of seniors and through personal experience. Traditional ship owning companies were able to retain the same seafarers for many years. Promotions to senior ranks were slow and training was given a high priority.

Every senior master will agree that there is no substitute for hands-on, on the job training. A chief officer doing ship handling, or learning to direct an emergency drill under the watchful eye of a master is perhaps the best way to train for 'Command'. But today, with fast turnaround in ports and reduced manning levels, senior officers seem unable to devote adequate time for training their juniors. The traditional methods of training therefore need to be supplemented with modern aids like simulators.

Simulators provide the opportunity of practising response to all kinds of emergencies, which cannot be replicated in on-the-job training. Courses like bridge resource management, bridge team management, etc., may not get the adrenaline flowing fully, but they do help an aspiring master to gain some skills, which can prove useful in emergencies.

An important aspect of handling emergencies expected by shipowners from their masters is good ship-shore communications. A master must ensure that in any emergency the ship owner/managers are continuously updated on the evolving situation. In any emergency a number of stakeholders e.g., owners, charterers, shippers, consignees, underwriters, P &I Club, etc., need such information as fast as possible.

While the first priority must always be to handle the emergency situation itself, the master must try to send in reports on the progress of handling the emergency in the best way he can.

6 Analytical thinking

Today, thanks to satellite communications a master can contact the office at any time. The shipowner's office may be able to give decisions in an emergency, and may even like to do so, but it must be understood that their decisions are based on the information given by the master. The shipowner therefore relies heavily on the master for a correct analysis of the situation on board. A good analytical mind is essential. A master must investigate the situation carefully, objectively, and in depth, in order to provide the office with the best possible information.

You must therefore, try to develop the ability to stand back, and review a situation and consider the pros and cons of every action and its short term as well as long term effects.

7. Self-motivation

The ISM Code recognizes that a safety management system can only succeed with 'commitment from the top'. This includes the shore management as well, but in case of a ship, in most situations, it is the commitment of the master, which determines the success of the safety management system on board.

It is expected by the ship owner that the master does not need to be reminded to carry out his duties. It is expected that the master will be self-motivated, enthusiastic and committed about his job.

8. Honesty

A ship owner entrusts the master with his multi million-dollar asset. It is therefore a position of great responsibility. Even the slightest suspicion or doubt about the honesty or integrity of the master is likely to result in adverse consequences!

9. Public relations

A ship owner expects the master to present a good image of his company to all the people with whom he deals e.g. port state inspectors, charterers, shippers, surveyors, port authorities, etc. Tact, diplomacy and a pleasant manner go a long way in presenting a good image of the vessel and its owner.

In some ports, the number of visitors may well be overwhelming and consequently trying on the master's patience. Yet it is in the master's own interest that all shore authorities are treated with courtesy and respect. Mistreated shore personnel can create problems, when least expected! At the same time, there may be situations that require a master to be assertive, in order to protect the owner's interests. For example, getting stevedores to sign damage reports, or firmly telling the pilot that you do not consider it prudent to proceed at "full sea speed" in two mile visibility in heavy traffic!

A master is expected to be appropriately dressed and presentable at all times. This may require alternating between full uniform to attend to the owner's customers and dirty overalls to accompany the surveyor!

10. Administrative skills/reports writing

Managing a ship is like operating a small village. The large number of tasks, with a limited number of people, requires a lot of administrative skills. A methodical approach is essential. Not many seafarers like doing mundane jobs, such as filing and record keeping. For centuries seafarers have been proud of their hands-on approach to problems and have considered 'paperwork' to be a job beneath the level of 'practical people'. Unfortunately, over the years the laws in every country have increasingly relied on 'paper' evidence. Courts and lawyers cannot do without it.

Efficient record keeping is therefore an essential part of a master's responsibilities and must be carried out. The importance of keeping factual and precise logs must be fully understood. The ISM Code, in fact, has made the task of proper record keeping of all aspects of shipboard operations a regulatory obligation.

It is expected that a master can write reports in a clear, factual and concise manner. Writing accurate reports is especially important in case of emergencies/ accidents which may lead to claims or legal cases. A poorly written 'statement of facts' may cost your owners millions of dollars! The Nautical Institute book *The Mariners Role in Collecting Evidence* is an excellent guide to assist you.

11. Information technology

2000 is the decade of information technology (IT). Personal computers, e-mail, digital cameras, etc. are changing working practices in every office in the world. It is affecting work practices on board the ships too. It is very likely that within the next three to five years a number of work practices will change significantly due to rapidly declining ship-shore communication costs. It is quite possible that in case of a breakdown, you may be seeking advice of a shore based specialist by showing him the broken equipment via video-conferencing over satellite!

A modern day master is therefore expected to possess or acquire some computer skills to be able to handle the increasing expectations of shore personnel to exchange / receive information. Manning levels are unlikely to increase and paperwork is unlikely to reduce. Computers can help in a small way to manage documentation better.

12. Delegation

A master is expected to be in control of all that is happening on his/her ship. It is not humanly possible for the master to do everything by himself. Learning to delegate may be difficult in the first few days/months of getting command, but it is essential that a master learns to delegate. In the beginning when you try to delegate work, some of these thoughts may cross your mind:

If you want a job done properly, do it yourself.

True – but if you try to do every job yourself, you will not have the time to do your own job. What if he makes a mistake? But don't we all make mistakes sometimes. Mistakes can be corrected. But I'll lose control. You will actually increase your control. Junior officers will be more motivated on being given the responsibility, and you will have more time to get other jobs done. The important point to remember when delegating is that the person to whom the job is being given must understand it clearly and must be capable of doing it. The keywords to remember when delegating are well expressed in these verses of Rudyard Kipling:

"I kept six honest serving men.
They taught me all I knew.
Their names were What and When and Where,
Why and How and Who."

In practical terms, when delegating, you need to explain:

WHY – Why the job needs to be done?
WHAT – What needs to be done?
WHO – Who must do the job?
WHEN – When does the job have to be done?
HOW – How should the job be done?

13. Maintenance

Most companies expect extensive maintenance work to be carried out by the ship's crew because of the increasing pressure on repair costs.

A master is expected to be able to organise, plan and monitor such maintenance jobs. This may often involve organising a large number of "riding crew". Equipment and material required for the repairs or maintenance will need to be planned carefully.

You are also expected to be familiar with the various technical guidelines issued by classification societies and other bodies on methods of repair and maintenance.

Conclusion

The qualities desired by a ship owner can be remembered very easily. The word 'ship master' covers them all!

S – Safety of crew, ship and cargo
H – Honest/hard-working
I – Ingenious and adequate knowledge of IT
P – Personnel management
M – Money/commercial and maintenance skills
A – Analytical thinker
S – Self motivated
T – Thorough knowledge/training
E – Emergency handling skills
R – Relations with shore personnel

Getting your first command is a great occasion. Prepare yourself well for it with the 'Command Scheme' and then take up the job with confidence and maturity. Keep your common sense sharp at all times and you will make a success of it.

Getting 'command' is the first step. Building up a reputation 'as a good master' with the ship owner and gaining the respect of your crew are the goals that you must aim for. The job of a ship master may have its drawbacks, but it is still one of the finest jobs in the world!

Figure 2.1 All in a days work !

Chapter 3

TRAINING FOR COMMAND

by Captain P. Roberts BSc FNI

Captain Roberts served his apprenticeship with Elder Dempster Lines, remaining at sea with the Ocean Group for the next twenty-five years until they withdrew from ship owning. He commanded Panamax Bulk Carriers with the International United Shipping Agency of Hong Kong, and was appointed Marine Superintendent of Cathcart Shipping Ltd. in London. He now works as a consultant with London and Offshore Consultants Ltd.

He is the author of The Nautical Institute publication "Watchkeeping Safety and Cargo Management in Port", is a founder Member and Fellow of The Nautical Institute and presently serves on its Council, Education and Training Committee and the Bulk Carrier Working Group.

All views expressed in this chapter are entirely personal and do not reflect those of his present or previous employers.

Introduction

DOES A MASTER MARINER'S CERTIFICATE of Competency qualify its holder to command a ship? To the examining authority, the answer appears to be yes. To most informed observers in the marine industry, the answer must be no, or at best partially.

The statutory certificate, or licence, demonstrates that the holder has a proven level of knowledge of the theory of the operation of a ship, mainly from a safety and legal point of view. Important though these aspects may be, in order to effectively and efficiently command a ship a lot more skills are required.

Prominent amongst the skills which are usually omitted from most courses for statutory certificates are:

*   Commercial awareness.
*   General management abilities.
*   Personnel management and interpersonal skills.
*   Practical ship handling.

So just how does the aspiring master acquire the training necessary for successful command. Some of the required knowledge can be obtained by reading and studying the published works of experienced practitioners. Other skills can best be acquired by attending training courses, particularly those involving simulators. However, there will always remain those most desirable attributes which can only be assimilated by that great teaching method known as experience. I believe this covers both job experience and experience of life. Command is still one of the few remaining true crafts, in the traditional sense. No amount of formal qualifications can replace the breadth of knowledge that comes from doing the job for an extended period, preferably under the guidance of a variety of different experienced and professional teachers – the true original craft master and his apprentice.

Background

The industry has endured an extended period of low returns on capital employed. When economies were sought in order to improve profitability, one of the first casualties was the training budget. This has resulted in a manpower shortage both in terms of quantity and quality. Although there is still a reluctance on the part of many ship operators to invest in training, there are signs that resources are once again being made available. Without investment in all stages of training, covering initial (pre-sea), intermediate (pre-certification) and ongoing (updating), there will continue to be insufficient properly qualified personnel available to efficiently operate the world fleet.

In the past, those aspiring to command acquired the necessary skills from the traditional training schemes of established ship owners. Whilst the fine details of such systems changed over the years, the end product was of a uniformly accepted standard. As one rose through the ranks, often slowly, there was time for everyone to be exposed to a wide variety of events, and undertake a vast range of activities, which provided the experience necessary to make reasoned, informed decisions. Many of the newly emerging nations followed a system adopted by one of the traditional maritime powers.

Today there is a whole range of different training schemes in place, with widely varying standards. With increased mobility of labour, and the internationalising of shipboard staff, it is difficult to know what skills are possessed by today's seafarers. Despite the recent changes to the STCW convention, it will be a long time before the candidate for command can rely on an industry system to provide him with the education and training necessary for him to acquire all of the requisite skills.

So, except for the few lucky seafarers employed by first class operators, most have to rely on their own resources for their maritime training and education. In many ways command is an occupation which relies on personal initiative, the captain is frequently on his own in a hostile environment – be that physical or commercial. Hence perhaps it is a fitting introduction to this career that he has to organise his own training.

One must not think that the master's job is so different than many other occupations in other industries. Essentially, the master is the general manager of that small commercial unit of operation known as a ship. His only difference from others holding that title is that he is often acting completely alone, as he is usually physically separated from all other management assistance and backup.

The formal training for command as provided by the STCW certificate structure is well documented elsewhere, and the reader aspiring to command can readily obtain this information from statutory regulations and a whole range of other commercial publications. I limit the scope of this short chapter to those aspects of command for which I believe no formal training exists, and whilst I do not have the answer as to how the aspiring commander can acquire these skills, I hope I can provide some pointers, and a few points on which to ponder.

Shiphandling

There are a few books describing the principles of ship handling, and providing hints from experienced practitioners. The candidate for command should study these carefully, but there can be no substitute for learning by doing it yourself. One should not loose any opportunity to watch masters and pilots in action, try to relate their actions to principles discussed in the textbooks. It is especially useful to anticipate their actions, try to imagine what you would do in the circumstances, before action is taken.

As you gain more experience on the bridge, you should actively enquire from masters and pilots the reasons for their actions. Many of these professionals will be only too willing to teach a junior officer who shows an active interest, though usually few will offer advice if this is not requested.

Experience can best be gained by practice in non-critical situations. After demonstrating his interest, the officer should request that the master allow him to undertake some of the normal manoeuvres which are required during his watch. As he builds up confidence and experience, more complicated situations can be tackled, always under the supervision and guidance of the master.

A suggested work experience list (in progressive order):

1. Manoeuvres in open waters: simple alter courses.
2. Anti-collision manoeuvres deep sea.
3. Recovery of a dummy man overboard.
4. Obtain original data for turning circles (and crash stops).
5. Manoeuvres in sheltered waters: maintaining the desired track after an alter course, taking into account wind, tide, etc.
6. Anti-collision manoeuvres in areas of busy traffic.
7. Knowledge of variations in pivot points when moving ahead or astern, and the effects of draft and trim.
8. Anchor in an open roadstead.
9. Anchor in a specific location in a confined anchorage.
10. Manoeuvres in confined waters, sea lanes, narrow channels, etc.
11. The use of engines, thrusters, and tugs.
12. Manoeuvre to pick up a pilot in open waters.
13. Manoeuvre to pick up a pilot in confined waters, channels, rivers, etc.
14 Unberthing and proceeding to sea; plan passage with a pilot.
15. Plan the approach to a berth.
16. Manoeuvring in heavy weather. Heaving to.
17. Manoeuvring alongside another vessel.

Sometimes it is useful for the officer to present the master with a formal plan designed to assist with his ongoing training. The Command Diploma Scheme run by the Nautical Institute is very useful in this respect. It includes a log book, with a section on ship-handling. The presentation of such a log book may encourage an otherwise reluctant master to permit his junior the opportunities to practice and acquire ship handling skills.

One often hears the term ship handling being referred to as seamanship. But I prefer a much wider definition of that term. Seamanship is the application of common sense and experience to the marine environment.

Personnel management

I have always believed that a major part of the master's job is personnel management. For this he receives no formal training. Indeed, a lot of personnel skills are a reflection on his character. That is not to say that these skills cannot be improved by training and, of course, they certainly change with experience.

Many books are written on personnel management, although very few apply directly to the marine industry. Those aspiring to command would do well to study a selection of textbooks dealing with the various aspects of personnel management. Some training courses are also available, and the lessons learned from role-playing are especially useful. It is possible to organise role-playing situations onboard ship, so that the junior officers may learn valuable lessons on how to deal with others.

A good master is one who can inspire others, a leader who can bring out the best in his subordinates by encouraging their strengths and retraining their weaknesses.

A well run ship is achieved by the master taking a personal interest in his crew. It is by encouraging others to give of their best that the ship's crew perform in the best possible manner. Taking the time to talk to all the crew can pay huge dividends. Take an interest in their day-to-day jobs, encourage good performance and do not limit contact to reprimands. Present a human face, encourage frequent dialogue with all onboard, hold regular informal meetings, preferably in their own environment. The use of the crew bar with a can of beer can break the ice and much more will be revealed. Listen to their problems, both job related and personal. Ensure mail is regular and take an interest in their welfare and their families.

With multinational crews, there is sometimes a tendency for some people to misunderstand other cultures. This can lead to problems with work, and even to a breakdown of relationships, which ultimately results in a very inefficient and unproductive crew. One important part of experience is the ability to deal with the various nationalities found onboard most ships. As we have to deal with an increasingly wide and varied spectrum of cultural backgrounds onboard, so we must all learn to cope with their individual idiosyncrasies. There are vast differences in the best ways of dealing with various ethnic groups. If some people onboard have no experience of dealing, working, and living with some of the other ethnic groups onboard, then the master must be prepared to give them guidance with their approach.

One must be careful not to tar all members of one nationality or ethnic group with the same brush and to avoid the thoughts that all --- act like that. That is not to say that one should not be alive to national or ethnic characteristics.

The potential master must never allow himself to acquire prejudices, be these colour, race, religion, regional, educational, political, and so on. He must strongly discourage such prejudices in others onboard. Too often one sees an unproductive crew, whose poor work is really a result of the uncompromising attitudes of their senior officers.

A problem with some groups is the attitude to those more junior. Many nations have a strict social structure in which the elite members have a rather low regard for the lower classes. This can become an extremely thorny point when transcribed into onboard relationships in a multi-cultural crew. Clicking of the fingers to summon assistance may seem disgusting behaviour to the westerner in these days of equality. Indeed it is often viewed a such by some of the recipients. But the perpetrators of such actions may have been brought up in an environment where such behaviour is perfectly acceptable, and they need careful nurturing out of what others see as denigrating habits.

Similarly there is a problem of seemingly natural antagonism. Certain people just don't seem to be able to get along with certain others, and there are often problems when they sail together. This may sound like a sweeping generalisation, especially when applied to nationalities, but I found it to be true. It can manifest itself simply as a lack of cooperation, but in extreme cases can result in open hostility. There can be similar problems even between personnel from one country, where regional, tribal, political or religious differences can be a source of controversy.

There can be an unwillingness to become involved in the whole ship concept. We have all come across the 'not my job' syndrome. Some people are much more flexible than others, but it is the master's role to knit these various personalities into one viable shipboard working team. Another personnel problem is the inability to give or take orders.

Another trait to overcome is the preconception that certain tasks are beneath one's dignity. We have all come across the officer in a pristine sparkling white boiler suit and gloves who regards himself as a supervisor and that only the ratings actually do manual work. It is sometimes difficult to persuade such juniors that they are part of a working team.

I am not really too sure how any education or training can assist with problems of personalities, other than the overall education of character development that comes with exposure to having to deal with such problems. Perhaps recognising that they exist is the first lesson. In general, the master's ability to deal with these problems will depend upon his own strength of character, and personal characteristics. I believe that life is a great teacher in this respect, and that the experience that the passing years brings is invaluable in personnel work. Hence my strong belief that there is a definite minimum age before which no candidate should be considered for promotion to master.

Some people onboard may be unable to comprehend onboard training and guidance due to language difficulties, or due to a lack of basic education. There is only the reward of personal satisfaction for the master who is both willing and able to teach basic educational and personal skills to the underprivileged shipmate. Time should be taken to teach people about unfamiliar tasks and it is advantageous to have a briefing session before undertaking any non-routine job. The right person in the right place at the right time makes operations go much smoother.

Another aspect of the master's personnel work is assessment. The master must keep himself well informed on the abilities, attitudes, and character of everyone onboard. These must be monitored regularly to spot early signs of problems before they get out of hand. He should be able to present unbiased reports on each member of the crew to the owner at regular intervals, so that suitable candidates can be offered re-employment or promotion. Further, the master must be able to detect those who may have false qualifications.

The ship has a social infrastructure, and the master must be able to spot social problems before they effect the ship's operation. This includes alcohol or other drug problems, sexual problems, excessive gambling, and character defects which result in bullying, violence, thieving, bribery and extortion, etc. Although everyone onboard has their own characteristics, strongly antisocial behaviour of any form must be strongly discouraged. The saying that a happy crew is an efficient crew is still valid.

Above all, the master must exercise effective leadership. The master who fails to maintain standards, both professional and personal, cannot expect others to maintain them.

It has been suggested that all masters should undertake a course in psychology and psychiatry to enable them to deal with the numerous personnel problems which arise sometime on most voyages. Unfortunately, that is not a practical possibility for most, so that all the master has to draw upon is his own strength of character, his experience of life, and good old fashioned common sense.

Perhaps this is a good point at which to consider what characteristics make a good shipmaster. There will always be as many styles of command as there are styles of character. Some personal characteristics are genetic or acquired during early life. Those desirable in a master include loyalty, honesty, integrity, humaneness, a sense of fair play and the ability to command respect.

Other characteristics can be altered by education, and experience. In this group I would include leadership, perception, judgment, flexibility, communication, interpersonal skills, commercial awareness and the ability to assume responsibility.

The master needs to be a forward thinker and someone who can plan ahead and anticipate problems. An intelligent assessment of what might happen has avoided many a potential tragedy. He should be authoritative (not authoritarian), enthusiastic, positive in his approach to the inevitable problems which occur almost daily and not to be depressed by setbacks. He must be able to cope with stress, and have the physical and mental stamina necessary to withstand the pressures of a concentrated and/or extended workload.

General management skills

As the general manager of the ship, the master will have to compile the vessel's accounts. The degree of his involvement will vary with the practice of the owner, but increasingly, more financial accountability is being place upon the ship, and hence the master. Apart from improving his numeracy skills, the aspiring master is well advised to undertake some self education in general accountancy. This can be achieved by studying elementary textbooks, but it is preferable if he enrolled on a basic introductory distance learning course, to provide an understanding of the principles involved. The extra effort will be more than rewarded in the future when he becomes responsible for the vessel's accounts.

Today's master must also be computer literate. This does not mean he needs to be an expert programmer but he should have a working knowledge of the operation of a personal computer (PC), and be able to use a basic word processor and spreadsheet. The master needs to be a good organiser, and there are various standard management tools which can assist him with such tasks. Apart from reading through standard textbooks on management skills, a good appreciation of the systems involved can be obtained by enrolling on the Nautical Institute's management self-development programme. This covers setting objectives and planning, control, solving problems and making decisions, leadership and motivation, delegation, time management, running meetings, and training.

A knowledge of logistics and stock control will assist the master to control the stores in an economical manner and maintain a realistic level of stocks. This means there will be sufficient spares available for use on the current voyage, without too many items being held in the stores, which means tying up capital – an unnecessary financial burden on the ship owner.

Commercial awareness

Commercial awareness really means being alive to the financial consequences of one's actions and decisions.

Whilst the legislative and contractual obligations associated with the carriage of goods by sea is well covered by the syllabus for the master's licence, such teaching concentrates on knowledge of facts. Little is done to train the master for the commercial decisions he will have to make in running the ship, especially judgment skills.

The general lack of commercial awareness amongst mariners has been addressed recently by the P&I clubs, who ultimately pick up the bill for the mariner's errors. They all issue newsletters, and have various other programmes available to try to improve the mariners knowledge of the commercial implications of their actions, judgments and decisions.

The UK Club went further than most in sponsoring the Nautical Institute in the publication of two practical guides aimed at raising the level of commercial expertise amongst junior officers and ship masters. These textbooks can be wholeheartedly recommended to all seafarers, particularly those aspiring to command.

The subjects covered by *Commercial Management for Shipmasters* and *Watchkeeping Safety and Cargo Management in Port* for junior officers enable the mariner to make decisions and take actions onboard ship which will have a beneficial effect on the profitability of the voyage, and thus of the company employing him. Space does not permit here to go into much detail, but they give the reader a good background to the law and practice of contracts use in the maritime industry.

The master needs a good working knowledge of the documents used for the carriage of goods by sea. He will need to study the clauses of standards voyage and time charter parties, and bills of lading, and be aware of the responsibilities implied in each clause. He must know the exact division of responsibility between the ship owner and charterer, and fully understand such standard clauses as the Interclub agreement. He must appreciate what is involved in establishing cargo quantity and condition, and the use of a notice of readiness, statement of facts, letter of protest and letter of indemnity. He should understand delivery, lay time and weather working days. He must have a full working knowledge of the various surveys which are regularly undertaken onboard his ship – hold condition, on/off-hire, draft, cargo condition, flag and port state control, P&I condition, class and statutory surveys.

The master must ensure that full records are maintained onboard, and he should be aware of the documents required both for routine operations and following an incident. The Nautical Institute publication *The Mariner's role in Collecting Evidence* is highly recommended.

Also under this heading, the master must make himself aware of all local regulations whenever he enters a new port. Apart from not wanting to break local statutes, he must be alive to the implication of local labour rules, so that he does not inadvertently land the owner with a huge bill for infringing union agreements.

How does the potential master acquire commercial awareness? Partly by continually observing all that is happening around the ship and its operations, and thinking about the costs involved in each activity. No-one must forget that we are engaged in a competitive business, and for a commercial enterprise to succeed income must exceed expenditure to realise a profit. Despite all the efforts that can be put into running a good ship, these will be fruitless if the ship does not earn a profit for the owners, as ultimately it will be sold, and all the efforts will have been in vain.

The Marine Society's education officer can assist in identifying other courses which, although primarily designed for other industries, may be suitable for the mariner. This organisation also provides the encouragement which many mariners need to complete these schemes. The education provided by the Institute of Chartered Shipbrokers as part of their membership entrance examination system is highly recommended to potential masters.

The shipowner's view

What does the ship owner require from his master?

1. First and foremost, someone who will look after the owner's interests above all else. A person who is dedicated to the success of the business.
2. A person who is commercially aware:
   - Someone who has a full working knowledge of contracts of carriage, and their numerous implications.
   - Serve the charterer according to the contract and cooperate with their operations, but always remembering who pays his salary.
   - Minimise expenditure, control budgets, reduce delays.
   - Maximise income.
   - Keep tight control on information regarding the operation of the vessel. Do not reveal facts to others which may embarrass the owners financially, legally or morally.
3. A skilled negotiator. Someone who can deal with surveyors, inspectors, officials, and the crew, and the problems these create. The ability to deal with corruption in a sensible manner.
4. A decision maker. Someone who can weigh up the pros and cons of a situation, make a reasoned decision, and act upon it.
5. A good personnel manager. Maintain a happy, healthy, disciplined and efficient crew, who give a fair days work to the best of their ability. Deal with all shipboard problems without involving the office.
6. A good communicator. Know just how much to say, to whom, and when. Know what not to say and when! Understand all the implications of that famous expression "economical with the truth".
7. A good accountant. Maintain the vessel's accounts for wages, victualling, bond, cash, stores and general expenditures. Stock control. Do not order large quantities of items which will remain unused for some time, so that large quantities of capital are tied up in idle resources.
8. A good operations manager Someone who can exercise the correct balance between what should be done, what could be done, and what needs to be done.
9. A professional master mariner. A qualified and experienced seafarer who will conduct the voyage with due regard to the safety of the ship, her cargo and her crew and all relevant international regulations.

Conclusions

How does one train for command?

1. Undertake the N.I. command scheme.
2. Expand your knowledge by studying practical books written by other professionals who have different experience from you. The Nautical Institute has a range of valuable guides which are all up to date and highly relevant.

3. Watch the methods of all masters under whom you serve. Try to emulate those characteristics which you consider to be their strengths, and learn from their weaknesses. Would you act in the same way, or make the same decisions? What would be the implications?

4. Read, read, read: 'M' notices, IMO publications (new international regulations), Lloyds list, *SEAWAYS*, any other nautical magazines which come to hand and as many commercial and management textbooks as possible. Keep up to date.

5. Continually watch what is happening both onboard your own ship, onboard others you come across, and around all the ports you visit. Be aware of developments by personal observation.

6. Enrol on self-tuition courses. Interactive schemes using onboard PCs are especially useful.

7. Discuss experiences with contemporaries. Everyone has something to learn from other people's experiences and it is always best if someone else makes the error. Institute events are useful meeting points.

8. Read the instruction manuals of all new equipment fitted to your ship and ask the manufacturer for background literature.

9. Attend as many updating courses as possible.

10. Attend all seminars and industrial exhibitions you are able.

11. Try to gain as much practical experience as possible. Never miss an opportunity to participate in an unfamiliar activity.

12. Personnel skills are learned from your very first voyage. Getting on well with people means that you will be able to get the best out of people, which also helps you to do well. Treat others just as you would like to be treated yourself.

13. Try to appreciate the benefits of tact and diplomacy. Learn to engage brain before engaging mouth.

References
- Tallack, R.L., *Commercial Management for Shipmasters*, The Nautical Institute, 1998
- Roberts, P., *Watchkeeping Safety and Cargo Management in Port*, The Nautical Institute, 1997
- *The Mariner's Role in Collecting Evidence*, The Nautical Institute, 1998

Chapter 4

THE MASTER'S RESPONSIBILITIES IN LAW

by Captain M.S. Maclachlan MICS FNI

Malcolm Maclachlan trained on HMS Worcester in the early 1960s and served a deck apprenticeship with Alfred Holt & Company. He commanded seven Bell Lines' short-sea containerships in the 1980s and has taught Business and Law at Glasgow College of Nautical Studies since 1989. He is the author of The Shipmaster's Business Companion, published by The Nautical Institute, and The Business and Law Self-Examiner for Deck Officers, published by North Sea Books.

Introduction

IT IS DIFFICULT TO THINK OF ANY WORKER, in any industry, with so many legal responsibilities as a ship master, or with a liability to heavier criminal penalties than those of a ship master. Long books could be written on the master's legal responsibilities, but this volume allows one short chapter. Saying so much in so few words – for an international readership subject to the regulations of over 150 flag states (in addition to laws of port and coastal states) – calls for a good deal of licence and brevity; the following notes are therefore condensed mostly from *The Shipmaster's Business Companion*, which attempts to explain only United Kingdom law. Happily, many other maritime states have adopted the same international conventions as the UK and to give them legal effect have enacted broadly similar statutory regulations as the UK's, while in many countries the civil law applicable to ship masters is similar to English civil law.

Whose law?

The law governing any shipboard matter will depend chiefly on (1) whether any international convention deals with the matter, (2) whether the convention has any legal effect in the flag state, (3) where the flag state is not a party to the convention, any other law in the flag state and (4) the law of the coastal state or port state in which the vessel is. Not all maritime states have adopted the major maritime conventions, and it is unsafe to assume that the law applicable to your ship is the same as the law applicable to another.

In overseas ports it is essential, if you are to avoid fines and detention of your ship, to be aware of any quirks of local law. Your best sources of advice – apart from your owners or charterers or their agents – are, for customs, pilotage, health clearance and immigration requirements, corrected Sailing Directions and Lists of Radio Signals and for cargo, pollution and other matters involving liability to a third party, your P&I club's local correspondent. The consul for the flag state may be able to advise on local commercial law.

Common law responsibilities

In English common law, i.e. the law as interpreted for the most part by judges in English civil courts, your chief responsibilities as master can be summarised as follows:

- To preserve the safety of the crew, passengers, ship and cargo (acting as if ship and cargo were your own uninsured property).
- To safeguard the marine environment.
- To prosecute the voyage with the minimum of delay and expense.
- To act always in the best interests of the owners;
- To carry out all that is usual and necessary for the employment of the vessel.
- To obey the owner's lawful instructions (but without any requirement to obey unlawful instructions, e.g. where a breach of a statutory requirement or prohibition would result).
- To exercise care of the goods entrusted to you as bailee and to see that everything necessary is done to preserve them in good order and condition during the voyage.

Statutory duties

Acts and statutory instruments

Most of your detailed duties as master are defined by government and given Parliament's approval in acts and statutory instruments (SIs). Although these documents are not legally required to be carried on board, ignorance of their requirements through your company's failure to supply them will be no defence when charged with a breach. How, then, can you stay informed of the law? Merchant Shipping Notices (MSN), which must be carried, do not describe all statutory requirements. No current MSN, for example, informs you of the two '£250,000 offences', or the nine '£50,000 offences' which you might commit. You could request your company to keep you fully briefed on legal requirements, but unless they have a legal department it is doubtful whether they could. If they do place shipping legislation on board, it should be corrected up to date like a chart folio, which is no easy task. Not surprisingly, many masters sail in ignorance of some of their legal obligations.

The Merchant Shipping Act 1995 (MSA 1995) consolidated the shipping law of the previous 101 years and is now the 'principal act' that spawns most new UK merchant shipping regulations. Amendments to

MSA 1995 appear in newer acts, such as the Merchant Shipping and Maritime Security Act 1997 and in time much confusing cross-referencing will become necessary.

Several less prominent acts, such as the Carriage of Goods by Sea Act 1971 and the Marine Insurance Act 1906 also have a bearing on your legal duties, while roughly 200 SIs contain dozens of detailed obligations of masters. A list of your statutory duties in relation to lifting plant alone would run to half a page of this book! The vast majority of relevant SIs are listed in a useful Marine Information Note (MIN) published annually by the Maritime and Coastguard Agency, but the MIN does not include regulations concerning public health, customs or immigration matters, which also impose duties on masters of ships arriving at UK ports.

Penalties

For a breach of most statutory duties contained in acts and SIs there are two types of penalty. Most minor offences – but also some quite serious ones – are generally dealt with by UK criminal courts under 'summary procedure', which may result in 'summary conviction'. For numerous offences a magistrate or sheriff may fine you, like any ordinary citizen, up to £5,000 on summary conviction, but for two oil pollution offences they could fine you up to £250,000. Nine offences attract fines of up to £50,000, while three offences of pollution by garbage and noxious liquid substances carry maximum fines of £25,000.

Numerous breaches carry summary conviction penalties described as 'a fine of the statutory maximum' (which currently means £5,000), or a fine of a certain 'level' between 1 and 5 on the 'standard scale'. (Currently Level 1 equates to £200, Level 2 to £500, Level 3 to £1,000, Level 4 to £2,500 and Level 5 to £5,000, but these sums will eventually be raised by Parliament to reflect increased wealth.) 'Conviction on indictment' may follow a jury trial in a higher court and result in a penalty (at the judge's discretion) of an unlimited fine, a jail sentence of up to two years, or both!

Many merchant shipping offences are crimes of strict liability, meaning that, in order to secure a conviction, the prosecution will not have to prove that you had *mens rea* (literally, 'guilty mind'). Under the MSA 1995 there is strict liability to comply, for example, with a 'Section 137 direction' given by the MCA following a pollution incident. That the offence was committed will be enough, whether or not there was any intent or fault on your part. Set against this intimidating background, some – but by no means all – of your statutory responsibilities are outlined below in relation to the ship, the crew, the ship's employment, operations at sea, and operations in port.

The ship
Handing over

Your first statutory duty on joining as master is to take over all documents relating to the ship and her crew which, under MSA 1995, must be delivered by the off-going master when he ceases to be master. He having made an entry (jointly signed by both of you) in the narrative section of the Official Log Book confirming delivery of the items, you legally assume command and total responsibility – even for the appalling state of affairs he might leave behind!

Log books and records

You must keep an Official Log Book (OLB), an Oil Record Book, a Garbage Record Book and a Radio Log Book and make entries in accordance with relevant SIs. However, unless you have a copy of the Schedule to the Official Log Books Regulations you may be at a loss to remember the nineteen entries required in the blank 'narrative' pages of the OLB, since no instructions about them are given in the book! As far as the civil (i.e. non-criminal) law is concerned, judges and arbitrators prefer contemporaneous evidence recorded at or just after the event, not at a more convenient later time and you have a duty to keep even scribbled notes of cargo temperatures, damage, etc. on dirty scraps of paper. (See *The Mariner's Role in Collecting Evidence* for more on this topic.) Compliance with the ISM Code Regulations entails keeping a multitude of records confirming that you have adhered to your ship's Safety Management System and the recording of all non-conformities.

Ship's construction, equipment, certification and publications

It is the company's responsibility to have the ship constructed, equipped and surveyed under the Cargo Ship or Passenger Ship Construction Regulations, and the Fire Protection and Life-saving Appliances Regulations. However, these SIs also impose several personal duties on the master, such as that in the Passenger Ship Construction Regulations to ascertain and record draughts, trim and freeboard and to calculate stability before departure. Many such duties may be delegated to another officer, but if he fails to carry out the duty, you have breached the law. If in doubt as to who bears responsibility, check the regulation in the relevant SI headed 'Penalties' and look for wording such as '.....shall be an offence on the part of the owner or master' or 'the owner and master of the ship shall each be guilty of an offence punishable on summary conviction......'.

Proceeding, or attempting to proceed, to sea without SOLAS and Loadline Convention certificates renders you liable to prosecution. You must produce the certificates on demand to authorised officials and post up copies. To maintain validity of any SOLAS certificate, you (and the owner) must ensure, under the Survey and Certification Regulations, that:
- The ship and equipment are properly maintained in accordance with the applicable regulations.
- No material change is made to the ship after survey without approval of the certifying authority.

- Any accident or defect affecting safety or the efficiency or completeness of the ship is reported as soon as possible to the certifying authority, a proper officer and the appropriate authorities of the port state.

MSA 1995 requires you to keep the Certificate of Registry in your custody and produce it on every occasion when clearing outwards from a UK port. Other countries' laws may require you to produce it before clearing their ports.

Classification is not a statutory requirement and there are no criminal penalties for breaching class rules. If your ship falls out of class, however, the owners may lose their hull and machinery insurance and P&I cover, which could put them in breach of ISM Code requirements, with detention in port a likely consequence. Where a foreign ship is found deficient in condition or equipment, the Port State Control regimes will usually ensure that it is the owner who is penalised (by the ship's detention), but in some countries you will be made the scapegoat and fined.

Regulations require you to carry the necessary charts and publications for the intended voyage; lack of them will amount to unseaworthiness in carriage of goods and insurance law. You must also carry navigational equipment complying with regulations. Proceeding or attempting to proceed to sea without carrying some required installation, or if an installation fails to comply with regulations, makes you automatically guilty of an offence, i.e. strictly liable.

Ship operation and safety management

For ship operators, the International Safety Management (ISM) Code has spawned the most onerous and far-reaching regulations of the last decade, yet they impose only one brief and apparently innocuous obligation on the master. Regulation 7 provides: 'The master of every ship shall operate his ship in accordance with the safety management system on the basis of which the Safety Management Certificate was issued'. When one considers all that is involved in 'operating in accordance with the SMS' (a subject dealt with in depth in another chapter of this book) it is hard to think of a sentence more heavily loaded with obligations. Breach of Regulation 7 carries a fine on summary conviction of the statutory maximum, or on conviction on indictment imprisonment for up to two years, or an unlimited fine, or both, indicating its importance. The operation of some high-risk ship types, such as gas carriers, ro-ro ferries and high speed craft, is meanwhile subject to additional regulations, all of which impose further duties on the master.

Whether you need to be told your duties or not, 'the Company' must now tell you. Marine Guidance Note MGN40 reproduces the Annex to IMO Resolution A.741(18) containing the ISM Code, which states in paragraph 5 (Master's Responsibility and Authority) that the Company should clearly define and document the master's responsibility with regard to:

- Implementing the safety and environmental-protection policy of the Company;
- Motivating the crew in the observation of that policy;
- Issuing appropriate orders and instructions in a clear and simple manner;
- Verifying that specified requirements are observed; and
- Reviewing the Safety Management System and reporting its deficiencies to the shore-based management.

The Company (paragraph 5 continues) should ensure that the SMS operating on board the ship contains a clear statement emphasising the master's authority. Furthermore, the Company should establish in the SMS that the master has the overriding authority and the responsibility to make decisions with respect to safety and pollution and to request the Company's assistance as may be necessary. Annex 2 provides an appropriate statement of the master's authority, and reminds you that you have full operational responsibility on board, while the Company has overall responsibility for the safe operation of the ship. A scan through the remainder of Annex 2 reveals the vast number of obligations under the SMS and the mountain of checklists and other paperwork required as evidence of conformity with practices that – for many masters – have long been the rule, simply as matters of good seamanship and command practice.

Insurance

Until an international convention is adopted requiring all ships to be insured, statutory regulations demand only that cover is held in respect of oil pollution by ships carrying more than 2,000 tons of cargo oil. Entering or leaving any port on such a ship without an Oil Pollution Insurance Certificate (OPIC) makes you liable in a UK court to a maximum fine of £50,000 on summary conviction.

The crew

Safe manning, hours of work and watchkeeping

A 1997 SI gives effect in respect of these matters to STCW 95 and requires that you ensure that your ship does not proceed to sea unless there is on board a valid safe manning document and that the manning of the ship complies with that document. In other words, you are no longer allowed to sail short-handed. MSN1682(M) explains that 'the responsibility to ensure that ships are safely, sufficiently and efficiently manned rests with owners and managing operators', which appears to absolve you as master from responsibility. However, the SI provides that the master must ensure that the watchkeeping arrangements for the ship are at all times adequate for maintaining safe navigational and engineering watches, having regard to Chapter VIII of Section A of the STCW Code. You must also give directions to the deck watchkeeping officers responsible for navigating the ship safely during their periods of duty, in accordance with Part 3-1 of Section A VIII/2 of the STCW Code and any requirements specified by the Secretary of State (which in practice means the Maritime and Coastguard Agency). It may be a relief to know that responsibility for giving directions for engineering watchkeeping arrangements is the chief engineer's, and that he can be fined up to £5,000 for breach of that duty.

The Safe Manning Regulations further require you to ensure that all seamen who are newly employed in your ship are given a reasonable opportunity to become familiar with the ship's equipment, operating procedures and other arrangements needed for the proper performance of their duties, before being assigned to those duties. Hopefully you will have enough time in port!

It is the ship operator's duty to ensure that a schedule of duties is produced setting out hours of work and rest periods, but before this is done you must seek the views of your officers and of the ship's safety committee or the seamen or their representatives or a trade union, as appropriate. The final decision on the schedule rests with the operator, who has the responsibility to ensure that it is safe for the ship and the performance of duties, but you are required to ensure, as far as reasonably practicable, that the schedule is adhered to.

Documents

The Safe Manning Regulations also require you to ensure that there are on board at all times all original certificates and other documents issued pursuant to the STCW Convention (including the 1978 version) indicating the qualifications of any member of the crew to perform his or her professional functions.

Engagement and discharge

Regulations require you to maintain two Lists of Crew – one of seamen who are engaged on a crew agreement and one of those who are not, e.g. riding crew, supernumeraries and ship staff contracted to another employer. You usually have a duty to act as the employer's representative in signing the proper crew's agreement, but since you are not employed on the same terms, you are not required to 'sign on' with them and should instead put your details on the ALC1(b). (Your own contract may be contained in written or oral instructions from directors, superintendents or the superseded master, and in the custom and traditional practice of masters.)

Inspections

You must make weekly inspections of provisions, water and the crew accommodation and record the results in the Official Log Book. These, like inspections of LSA and fire appliances, may be delegated, but legally they remain your responsibility.

Musters and drills

You are personally responsible for compiling the muster list, keeping it up to date and ensuring that copies are displayed conspicuously throughout your ship. You must ensure that every crew member participates in at least one boat drill and one fire drill each month, and in a passenger ship must hold drills each week. Your duties are well-detailed in MGN17; if every SI was so comprehensively explained, the master's legal duties would be much easier to define, if no less difficult to carry out!

Health and safety law

The Health and Safety at Work Regulations 1997 consolidate the old SORADO Regulations and Health and Safety: General Duties Regulations and provide that the master must, with the Company and employer, provide the necessary facilities to enable the 'competent person', safety officer and safety representatives to carry out their statutory duties under the regulations. The general duty of ensuring the health and safety of workers and other persons on board is that of the employer, but you, as the employer's representative on board, are normally expected to carry the heavy practical burden.

Ancillary health and safety regulations cover protective clothing and equipment, means of access, entry into dangerous spaces, safe movement on board ship, guarding of machinery and safety of electrical equipment, and hatches and lifting plant; compliance with corresponding chapters of the Code of Safe Working Practices for Merchant Seamen will ensure that obligations under these SIs are met. The 1998 edition of the Code (which must be carried), also contains detailed advice on how to make risk assessments and carry out health surveillance; these onerous and time-consuming duties are imposed by the HSW Regulations on the employer, but their implementation on board will probably be devolved to you.

Accidents

You must make reports to the MAIB of specified accidents and dangerous occurrences, while other 'hazardous incidents' such as 'near misses' may be reported either to the MAIB or to The Nautical Institute's MARS scheme. Should any person die on board, or if a crew member dies ashore, you must make a Return of Death to the Registrar of Shipping and Seamen in Cardiff, inform the next-of-kin within three days, and make entries in the OLB, including a list of the deceased's property.

Discipline

If the UK's Merchant Navy Code of Conduct is written into the crew agreement (which will be the case where your crew is on a 'BSF' agreement), you must deal with breaches of discipline in strict accordance with the Code. Since the Code only documents the basic principles of natural justice (as interpreted in the UK), there is no reason why its procedures should not be followed in other cases, unless the crew agreement or the flag state's law dictates otherwise. Under the Code you act as judge and jury, but must hear evidence from both sides, and record it, and give the accused a copy of relevant log entries. You may no longer impose fines, but can give oral warnings, written reprimands or – your ultimate sanction – dismissal.

The ship's employment
Common law duties
Contractual disputes have yielded judges' interpretations of the master's responsibilities with respect to matters such as deviation, voyage speed, tendering of notice of readiness and use of unsafe berths. You may not enjoy reading a mass of small print, but charter party and bill of lading clauses are meant to be read and understood by masters as well as lawyers!

Bills of lading
Even where you do not personally sign Bills of Lading (B/Ls), you must, as the carrier's servant and agent, take proper care of the merchant's goods. Whenever a B/L or sea waybill has been issued, either the Hague Rules or Hague-Visby Rules will almost always be part of the contract (see the Clause Paramount) and will impose a duty to 'properly and carefully load, handle, stow, carry, keep, care for and discharge any goods carried'. If the shipper demands, either the carrier, or the master, or the carrier's agent must issue a B/L to him, but you need not insert any inaccurate statements or give any details which you cannot reasonably check, such as weights.

On time charter
You should pay special attention to the text in a time charter party, including all those confusing deletions, insertions, side clauses and rider clauses. You are obliged to carry out the charterer's orders as far as employment of the vessel is concerned and must normally give him 'customary and reasonable assistance'. Remember, however, the Master's Discretion Regulations which prohibit any interference with your decisions concerning safe navigation.

Cargo-related SIs
The Carriage of Cargoes Regulations impose several duties and prohibitions on you with regard to acceptance, documentation, loading, stowage and securing of cargo, while other SIs define your duties regarding the carriage (and disposal) of dangerous goods and marine pollutants, the carriage of dangerous or noxious liquid substances in bulk, and the weighing of goods vehicles and other cargo.

At sea
General; routeing
Statutory regulations create many obligations on you as master when at sea, for example with respect

to using automatic pilot, sending distress messages, complying with Collision Regulations, sending mandatory ship reports and navigational warnings and taking mandatory routes. The common law meanwhile requires that your vessel takes the shortest route consistent with safety and the law, which is normally the customary route for the trade. If she is not insured for going beyond Institute Warranty Limits, you must advise the owners when it becomes necessary to do so. Ordinarily, you are prohibited from taking your ship into offshore safety zones.

Master's discretion
A 1997 SI prohibits the owner, charterer or manager, or any other person, from preventing or restricting you from taking or executing any decision which, in your professional judgement, is necessary for the safe navigation of your ship – a useful tool against those who might seek to undermine your supreme authority on board.

Pollution prevention
In UK law you currently have duties under SIs dealing with prevention of pollution by oil, noxious liquid substances and garbage. Within a few years, SIs covering air pollution and sewage will also be in force. Discharging oil or a mixture containing oil into UK national waters, or breaching MARPOL's discharge criteria anywhere beyond them, will render you liable for a fine of up to £250,000, while pollution by other substances carries a maximum fine of £25,000. You have a duty to report any 'serious harm to the environment' to the MAIB and any oil or NLS pollution to the nearest coastal state in accordance with M1614. Growing concern for the marine environment has in recent years added 'custodian and protector' to your various roles.

Distress, rescue and salvage incidents
Under the Distress Messages Regulations you have a duty render assistance (if you can do so without serious danger to your vessel and the persons thereon) to any person in danger of being lost at sea – but not to maritime property, salvage being a commercial venture. If you go in for it, Article 8 of the Salvage Convention – as enshrined in the MSA 1995 – will impose several duties on you, whether you are salvor or master of the property in danger; in either case you must exercise due care to prevent or minimise damage to the environment.

In port
Arrival
The contract in a voyage charter imposes a clear duty on you to tender notice of readiness at the earliest opportunity on the owner's behalf; the charter party's wording should be carefully read, however, for detailed instructions. In most ports you will have statutory duties in connection with pilotage and to make declarations to customs, port health and immigration officials. There may be a local requirement for you to note protest, particularly if

landing damaged goods; your P&I club correspondent can advise on this.

Stowaways

IMO Resolution A.871 (Guidelines on the Allocation of Responsibilities to seek the Successful Resolution of Stowaway Cases) contains suggested responsibilities of masters in such cases, running to half a page of MGN70(M). Even so, if you are to avoid a fine, bringing stowaways to a foreign port will require special attention to local law.

Watchkeeping in port

Chapter VIII of the STCW Code provides clear guidelines on responsibilities for safe watchkeeping and pollution prevention in port, including when carrying hazardous cargo and the Safe Manning Regulations require you to follow them. Port State Control regimes will check your compliance with the Code.

Seaworthiness

Section 98 of MSA 1995 provides that if a ship in a UK port, or a UK ship in any other port is dangerously unsafe, then subject to certain provisos, the master and the owner of the ship shall each be guilty of an offence punishable on summary conviction by a fine of up to £50,000 or on conviction on indictment by imprisonment for up to two years, or an unlimited fine, or both. The penalty is aimed primarily at owners of substandard ships, but if the prosecutor cannot find the owner, the master makes a convenient alternative target. The common law requires your ship to be seaworthy before departure for each stage of her voyage in respect of (1) technical matters (e.g. structure and stability), (2) cargo care, and (3) 'fittedness for the voyage' (meaning manning, charts and publications, stores, bunkers, etc.). Where the owner has contracted only to exercise 'due diligence' to ensure that the vessel is seaworthy for the voyage, you have a duty to make (and record) every reasonably practicable check before departure.

Section 42 of MSA 1995 provides that in every contract of employment between the owner of a UK ship and its master or any seaman employed in it, there is an implied obligation on the owner that the owner, the master and every agent charged with loading the ship, preparing the ship for sea or sending the ship to sea shall use all reasonable means to ensure the seaworthiness of the ship for the voyage at the time when the voyage commences, and to keep the ship in a seaworthy condition for the voyage during the voyage. This obligation applies notwithstanding any agreement to the contrary (i.e. it cannot be contracted out of).

Load line

You will be guilty of an offence if your ship, not being exempted, proceeds or attempts to proceed to sea without being surveyed or marked with deck and load lines, or fails to comply with Conditions of Assignment or to carry statutory stability information. You commit a further offence if your ship is overloaded in port, and another if you attempt to take her to sea overloaded. Serious overloading could render your ship 'dangerously unsafe', as could undermanning and a range of other defects and deficiencies.

Passengers

SIs dealing with boarding cards, counting and recording systems, emergency information and musters and drills all impose further legal duties on you in connection with passengers, while carrying more passengers than is allowed by the Passenger Certificate is another £50,000 offence.

Conclusion

While a shipmaster's traditional authority has been reduced by modern communications, this brief outline shows that his legal responsibilities have grown enormously. Amendments to maritime conventions have brought new and onerous duties, the ISM Code alone generating what amounts to a wholesale change in the master's job description. In EC waters, meanwhile, a whole new branch of shipping legislation grows with each new Directive, while the mandatory status of new UK Merchant Shipping Notices means yet more documents to be read and filed away in the master's memory.

The weight of both the legal burden and the extra paperwork accompanying it has become intolerable for masters. Regulators ashore should not be surprised at the growing shortage of future masters, for what office worker would want to leave his family to become the legal scapegoat for the shortcomings of a shipowner, manager, charterer or classification society, while accepting the physical risks of seafaring?

References
* Maclachlan, M.S., *The Shipmaster's Business Companion*, The Nautical Institute, 1997.

Chapter 5

THE ISM CODE AND THE MASTER

by Captain I. Mathison FNI
Fleet Safety Manager, Bibby-Harrison Management Services Limited

Captain Mathison started his seagoing career in 1965 with Ellerman and Papayanni Line of Liverpool. On obtaining his first certificate of competency in 1969 he sailed with Palm Line for two voyages – deciding West Africa wasn't for him before moving to his present company, Thos. & Jas. Harrison Ltd., of Liverpool, in 1970. During his nearly 30 years of service with this traditional ship owner he has sailed in every rank, third mate to master and was seconded as Operations Manager ashore in Houston and London in the period he was classed as sea staff. He was appointed Chief Marine Superintendent in 1994, a position he retains with the parent company Charente Steam Ship to this day. In 1997, when the two oldest shipping companies in Liverpool formed a joint venture company, Bibby-Harrison Management Services Ltd., he was again seconded, this time as Fleet Safety Manager. His safety related responsibilities now encompass all class of vessels, managed by BHMS, the off shore and accommodation units.

Introduction

THE INTERNATIONAL SAFETY MANAGEMENT (ISM) Code or to give it its full title, the International Management Code for the Safe Operation of Ships and Pollution Prevention, was adopted by the International Maritime Organization (IMO) by resolution A.741(18) at the 1994 Safety of Life at Sea Convention. It is embodied with Chapter IX of the SOLAS convention and required that all passenger ships, oil tankers, chemical tankers, gas carriers, bulk carriers and high speed craft of 500 gross tonnage and above complied no later than 1st July 1998. All other ships and mobile offshore drilling units of again 500 gross tonnage and above will have to comply by no later than 1st July 2002.

Certain commentators have stated that the Code is the most radical shipping legislation to come before the international shipping community for many years. When the Code is studied in detail, which we will do later, it can be seen quite clearly how the IMO has tried to address under one chapter of SOLAS all the maritime disasters which have occurred over the last thirty-five years. The Torrey Canyon – Clauses 7 "Development of Plans for Shipboard Operations" and Clause 8 "Emergency Preparedness". The Amoco Cadiz – Clause 5 "Master's Responsibility and Authority", the Herald of Free Enterprise again Clause 7 "Development of Plans for Shipboard Operations" and Clause 4 "Designated Person(s) Ashore". The Scandinavian Star – Clause 3 "Companies Responsibilities" and the Grace Darling Clause 2 "Safety and Environmental Protection Policy" and Clause 10 "Maintenance of the Ship and Equipment".

The maritime industry has, up to this time, always been retroactive in its legislation but hopefully with the correct use of the Code and remembering the basis of good seamanship practice, this may be the first opportunity that the shipping industry can prove to the world at large that we are at last being pro-active towards legislation.

Before dissecting and, in certain cases, translating the elements of the Code, it must be said that for masters who have served on well run vessels during their seagoing careers and who now manage similar vessels there is absolutely nothing new in the Code. Because the Code was written by persons who were formerly involved with the quality assurance industry, key words and phrases have been adopted by the Code which have been transposed from that sphere. Once these are explained then I am certain the visibility, as far as the Code is concerned, improves dramatically.

The certificate relating to the Code is a trading certificate similar to the Load Line, Safety Equipment, Safety Radio etc., etc. and, as the name implies, without them your vessel will cease to trade. We can now see how important this legislation is, and how the master's responsibility is recognised and in fact is enhanced by implementation of the Code.

As I stated previously there is nothing new in the Code, but certain of the phrases have been transposed from the quality assurance world and to assist you here is a small glossary which should help you when we look at the elements of the Code in detail.

Brief glossary
Audit inspection
Object evidence
> Documented proof i.e., signed and completed checklists, passage plans, etc.

Non-conformance
> A part of the Safety Management system is not being complied with.

Major non-conformance
> An element of the Safe Management Code is not present or not being complied with e.g., no internal audit or no emergency preparedness.

Defect
> Part of the "hardware" is not working e.g., fire nozzle seized, fire extinguisher empty, etc.

Observation

An auditor's opinion as to how the Code should be interpreted.

Safety management system

The Company's interpretation of the ISM Code.

The Code

In formulating the elements of the Code, of which there are 13, the International Maritime Organization has recognised and highlighted in the preamble that no two ship owners or shipping companies are the same and the Code has been written in broad terms (some would say too broad, which is allowing for individuals to interpret it incorrectly). To ensure widespread application the foundation to good safety management is the absolute commitment for implementation of the Code from the top. The top in this instance is not only you on board but also the very highest levels of management within companies and we will see how this commitment can be shown graphically when companies' organograms are displayed.

The Code itself is divided into a preamble and 13 sections and I will attempt to expand on each section as follows:

Preamble

Recognises that no two ship owners or managers are the same and whilst each operate under a wide range of conditions, the Code is based on **general** principles and objectives.

The emphasis is that the foundation of good ship management is total commitment from the top in all matters of safety and pollution prevention is essential.

General

This is divided into four subsections entitled Definitions, Objectives, Application and Functional Requirements for a safety-management system.

The Definitions given are for the ISM Code itself, the Company and the Administration.

The Objectives of the Code are simply those which any well run company should try to achieve, namely that risks are assessed, a safe working environment is provided, standards will be continually improved and that all mandatory rules, regulations and industry recommendations are followed.

The Code is Applicable to all ships (after the year 2002).

The Functional requirements of the Code stipulate that the Company must develop and maintain such items as a safety and environmental protection policy and develop instructions and procedures for the safe operation of ships. (This heading, when the number of operations on board which relate to safety are considered, is all embracing). The Company must define levels of communication and authority i.e., it must produce an organogram for the management structure ashore and afloat. The Company must also develop procedures for reporting accidents and non-conformances (see definitions), to prepare for any emergency situations and carry out internal audits and reviews.

The points highlighted under the first sections are very broad based in their definitions. As we move through the following sections of the Code it will be seen how they are expanded but not to such an extent that it does not allow for a degree of interpretation.

Safety and environmental protection policy

The Company must establish a policy and then ensure it is implemented throughout the organisation, both ashore and afloat. How the policy is implemented and who implements it are described in other sections of the Code.

Company responsibilities and authority

The Code requires that within this heading the Company responsible for the management of the vessel provides the Administration with its full name and details and it must also define and document the levels of management and how the lines of responsibility are interlinked. This will normally take the form of an organogram and a typical simplistic Company organisation could be as follows:-

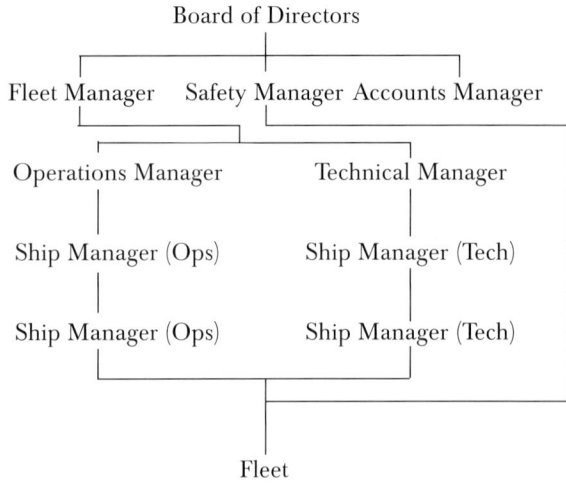

Figure 5.1 Typical simplistic company organisation

The Company must also provide adequate resources and support to ensure that the designated person ashore can fulfil his/her duties. It can be seen that the intention of this part of the Code is to ensure that corporate responsibility is totally transparent and those that are responsible for all operations are now easily identified.

Designated person(s) ashore (DPA)

This is one of the most important sections of the Code, both for the ship's master and the Company in general. Before discussing the implication of section 4 it is important that the text is known:

"To ensure the safe operation of each ship and to provide a link between the Company and those on board, every Company, as appropriate, should designate a person or persons ashore having direct access to the highest level of management. The responsibility and authority of the designated person or persons should include monitoring the safety and pollution prevention aspects of the operation of each ship and ensuring that adequate resources and shore-based support are applied, as required".

The key words in this text are "link", "monitoring" and "adequate resources". The DPA is the link between the master and the Company's Board. If possible, he or she should be removed from the day to day line management of the vessels and not have any budgetary responsibilities for the vessels' running costs.

The DPA must also monitor the safety and pollution prevention aspects of each ship. In practice he/she must be aware of most facets of the ship because the majority of operations on board vessels today have a safety or pollution aspect to them.

The DPA must also ensure adequate resources and shore based support are provided to the vessel, this can encompass the supply of equipment and stores to ensuring sufficient shore management time is allocated.

To illustrate the functions of a DPA the following organogram is shown:

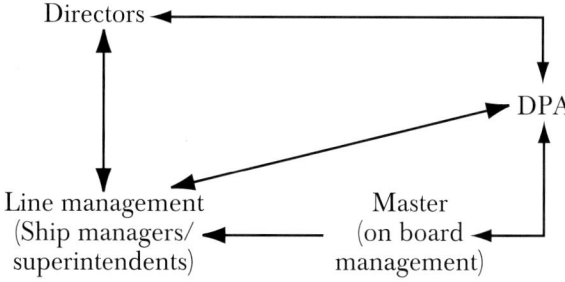

Figure 5.2 Functions of a DPA

In the "normal" course of managing a vessel the master, as chairman of the onboard management structure, communicates with the ship managers/superintendents ashore. They in turn are responsible to the Board of Directors for operating the ship in a safe condition and in line with Board approval concerning running costs.

If a condition arises on board which the master considers unsafe, for example the radar is giving persistent problems or the oily water separator has ceased to function correctly, he would in the first instant approach the respective manager or superintendent requesting action. If this action is not forthcoming and the master is still concerned he now has the option of approaching the DPA. It is then incumbent upon the DPA to investigate the situation

and bring it to the attention of the Board of Directors. If, in the examples given, additional monies above Board approved figures are required, the Board will then have to approve or otherwise any additional expenditure. If they make the decision to veto the masters/DPA's recommendations then, if an incident occurs in the future, it can now be proved the responsibility rested with the highest level of management within the Company.

The position of the DPA can now be seen to be extremely important within any Company, not only to protect the master's interests but also to ensure that the Board of Directors is kept fully aware. Make certain you know who the DPA is within your Company.

Master's responsibility and authority

Section 5 is divided into two parts. Part 1 requires the Company to "define and document" the master's responsibility regarding implementing the policy, motivating the crew to observing their policy, issuing orders and instructions, verifying that special requirements are observed and reviewing the Safety Management System (SMS) and reporting any deficiencies to the shore based management. Three of these five subsections are self-explanatory i.e., implementing the policy, issuing orders and verifying special requirements. The remaining two sections are worthy of an explanation.

Motivating the crew

How is this done? Remember, in the ISM regime, objective evidence is required. Safety and management meetings are held on a regular basis on well managed vessels. Each of these meetings will consist of representatives from the junior officers and the ratings and will be minuted. Members of the committee should be encouraged to pass on to their shipmates the dialogue of the meetings. Safety drills are held with post drill discussion afterwards, when all crew members should participate. Again, these discussions should be recorded by the safety officer. Safety videos are shown and their contents discussed. Heads of departments, when giving out work schedules, will discuss what personal protection equipment is required and presumably the safety implication involved when the work is being carried out. When crew members do not adhere to Company requirements regarding P.P.E. then disciplinary action is taken. All these factors can ably demonstrate to an auditor that you "motivate the crew".

Reviewing the safety management system

How this is achieved is entirely dependent upon the master and the Company. It can be as simple as a sentence in the Safety Minutes that the system has been reviewed or a checklist which shows clearly what sections have been scrutinised. The important point is that the system isn't "carved in stone". It is, in fact, or should be, a "living, breathing" set of documents and it is only by the input of both shore and ship based management will it really work.

The second part of section 5 requires the Company to ensure that a statement is embodied in the SMS giving the master clear and unambiguous authority to take whatever steps he deems necessary in respect of safety and pollution prevention. Be sure you are aware of this statement and where it is within your S.M.S.

Resources and personnel

This section is divided into seven subsections and defines what the Company should do. It must ensure that you are properly qualified for command, fully aware of the Safety Management system and are given the necessary support.

It must also ensure that the vessel is manned by qualified, certificated and medically fit seafarers. Today the majority of seafaring personnel are employed by manning agents and therefore the contractual obligations and verification procedures between ship owners or ship managers and these agencies are a critical part of ensuring the "letter" of the Code is observed. If you have any doubts regarding the qualifications or fitness of newly appointed crew members then this must be brought to the attention of the Company without delay.

The third subsection of section 6 requires that new personnel must be given familiarisation related to safety and environmental protection. Within the system there should be a familiarisation procedure which must be given to new joiners. My definition of a new joiner is anyone who stays on board the vessel overnight. This thereby ensures that everyone is aware of the location of fire fighting equipment, emergency signals and their survival craft location.

The Company must ensure that all personnel have an understanding of the "relevant rules, regulation codes and guidelines". How do you carry out the company's requirements for this? One of the simplest methods are signature pages attached to the company's SMS, Merchant Shipping Notice Files, Statutory Instrument Files, Technical Indices, etc. etc. I am aware of the old adage "you can take a horse to water but you cannot make it drink". But you, the master, must ensure that individuals have access to all the required information and once you prove that (objective evidence again) then it becomes that individual's responsibility.

The training needs of all personnel involved in the SMS must be identified. The Company should establish and maintain procedures for this. It must be remembered that the training required is to maintain the SMS and the ISM Code is part of the SOLAS convention.

The Company should stabilise procedures to ensure the ship's complement receive relevant SMS information in a working language(s) which is understood by them. The keyword here is relevant, and how that relevant information is passed down the line is a matter for individual companies, whether by translation or by ensuring that all officers and ratings have a common language and an understanding of English, or a combination of both.

The final sub section requires that the Company ensure that personnel on board can communicate between themselves. It should be noted that the word language is not used and how people communicate may in certain instances relate to onboard management.

Development of plans for shipboard operation

This is the smallest section of the Code, two sentences which make up three and a half lines, but the largest section within any Safety Management System.

It is easy to see why this section is so long when all the shipboard operations are considered, for example, arrival and departure from port, cargo operations, bunkering procedures, navigation, engineering practices and the host of other operations which ensure the vessel moves safely from port to port.

Emergency preparedness

The Company must establish procedures which identify potential emergency situations which could occur on board. Having identified these potential situations, a programme of exercises and drills must be drawn up to ensure all concerned are fully prepared to react to these situations.

This will predominantly be the crews on board the vessels, but the Code requires that the "Company's Organisation" can respond at any time to emergency situations. This means that the shore emergency organisation must be known to the ship and an emergency contact communication system should have been set up.

To ensure that the procedures are effective, regular drills must be held and the results documented, not only for those drills on board but for ship-to-shore drills. The period between drills will be specified within the SMS and you should be guided accordingly.

Reports and analysis of non-conformances, accidents and hazardous occurrences

The Code requires the SMS has provision for making certain that any non-conformances (a part of the system which is not being complied with) accidents, or near misses are reported, investigated and analysed. Having done that then the appropriate corrective action is applied.

This was the section of the Code which, on first reading, I thought needed translation but when related to good ship management practices it made sense. Safety Committees, both ashore and afloat, have encompassed the requirements of this section. Fleet circulars have advised of others misfortunes and statistics produced during the year have produced the analysis required. Once again there is nothing new in the Code.

Maintenance of the ship and equipment

This section requires the Company to establish procedures to ensure the ship is maintained to a minimum requirement by the relevant rules and regulations, specified by Flag Administration, Classification Society, Insurance Underwriters etc., but also any additional requirements it specifies.

The section itself is divided into four sections and in addition to stating that rules and regulations must be complied with, the Company must ensure inspection takes place, and defects are rectified and records are kept.

The Company must identify any equipment or system, the failure of which could result in a hazardous situation for example steering gears, electrical generators, anchor systems, etc. Having identified such systems then they should be tested regularly together with any backup equipment.

Documentation

All documentation and data used within the SMS must be controlled. The Company is required to ensure that documentation is available at relevant locations and that any changes are only made by authorised personnel and obsolete documents are removed. To facilitate this, documentation within the system is usually "controlled" or "uncontrolled".

There will be a procedure which should describe how sections within the SMS are numbered, collated and corrected.

The final sentence in this section states that "Each ship should carry on board all documentation relevant to that ship". This does not only apply to the obvious certification but also refers to plans, instruction books, navigational charts and publications and, of course, crew documentation.

An element of document control are those diagrams and instructions previous Masters, Chief Engineers and Heads of Departments have produced and posted on various notice boards and bulkheads throughout the ship. When you join the ship have a look around and if you agree with what has been posted up sign and date it. Similarly for the Chief Engineer, and heads of department. If you or they don't agree with the notices take them down. For such diagrams and drawing as the Safety and Fire Plans these should be signed and dated to indicate when and by whom they were last checked.

Company Verification, Review and Evaluation

Having established a Safety Management System the Code now requires the Company to carry out internal audits to verify the system is fully operational and section 12 and its 6 subsections deal with this. A procedure will have been established within the system which should dictate the minimum period between audits, phrases such as "at least once year" are used. This then allows Companies a degree of flexibility in scheduling visits. An audit schedule should be drawn up, which is normally only available ashore in the office. I firmly believe that your ship should be ready for an audit at any time without the necessity of pre-warning.

I have seen Flag State and on their behalf Classification Society auditors conduct audits and for your benefit here are examples of the type of questions asked of Masters during these periods.

For the Master:
- Show me all the certificates
- Show me in the SMC where it describes your duties and describe the familiarisation procedure in force on board your ship.
- Describe the format of the safety committee meeting
- How are the crew made aware of Merchant Shipping Notices (or their equivalents) and Statutory Instruments.
- What is and show me the Company's Drug and Alcohol Policy. How do you check and review individuals consumption on board?
- How are the hours of work and rest recorded on board? What actions do you take if they are exceeded?
- How do you know when tank and hold maintenance has been carried out?
- Show me your standing orders and the official logbook.
- Describe your handover procedures and show me any documentation relating to this.
- Show me the last internal safety audit report.
- Show me the Officers and ratings' certificates and any Flag State endorsements.
- Who is the designated person ashore?

Obviously other senior officers and certain ratings are questioned during the same audits so here are brief examples of the type of questions they are asked

Chief Engineer
- Explain your planned maintenance system and show me the history of a general service pump, lubricating oil pump, emergency fire pump and steering gears.
- The ISM Code Section 10.3 requires the company to establish procedures in its SMS to identify equipment and systems, the sudden operational failure of which may result in a hazardous

situation. Show me in your system what equipment has been identified.

- Describe the procedures that are in place for when the main engine fails.
- Describe your actions with regard to the generator failure, where are these procedures in your SMS.
- Describe your bunker procedures. Show me the checklist for the last occasion when you bunkered.
- How do you communicate with the bunker barge?
- How do you check the bunker receipt?
- Show me your standing orders and your night orders.
- Describe how your sewage system is chlorinated.
- Show me the permit to work records for hot work and entry into enclosed spaces.
- Show me the certificates for the engine room chain blocks.

Chief Officer
- How do you calibrate the gas monitor?
- What is the deck maintenance and greasing schedule?
- Explain the de-ballasting/ballasting operations.
- How do you exchange information with shore authorities?
- How often do you inspect the ballast tanks? Show me the records.
- How do you check the vessel's water tightness before proceeding to sea?
- How do you pass on information to the 2nd and 3rd Officers during your off duty time.
- How do you assign work to a first trip cadet to ensure he works in a safe manner.
- Checked the cargo gear register.
- Checked "Garbage" manual.

Second Officer
- Checked chart catalogue.
- Show me the charts for last voyage.
- Checked a number of chart corrections.
- Checked passage plan against charts.
- Checked arrival and departure checklists.
- Checked pilot card.
- Checked Ship/Shore checklists.
- Show me the compass error book.

Safety Officers
- Checked Safety Officers Record Book.
- Checked Safety Committee Minutes.
- Show me evidence that the Company provides the ship with safety information.
- Sighted records of drills.

Bosun
- What are the emergency signals on this ship?
- How do you receive your instructions regarding deck maintenance?
- Are you responsible for the paint locker?
- Show me how the paint locker sprinkler system works?
- When you grease wires, how do you dispose of the rags and residue?

Cook/Steward
- What do you do with the used oil from the deep fat fryer?
- What chemicals do you use in the galley for cleaning?
- How do you clean the galley filters?
- How do you activate the fire alarm?
- How many fire blankets do you have and who checks them?
- How often are the fire blankets checked?
- What do you do with the tins and bottles?
- Inspected domestic fridges and galley?
- How do you rotate the stock?

These are only examples of the type of questions asked but you can see the patterns emerging. You know your Safety Management System better than any external auditor, so carry out audits on your own vessel to ensure other members of the ship's complement are fully familiar with the aspects of the system which relate to them.

Certificates, Verification and Control

ISM documentation is divided into two parts, the Document of Compliance (DOC) and the Safety Management Certificate (SMC) each issued by the Flag State Administration or their authorised bodies. The Document of Compliance is issued to the Company and under the Code the Company can either be the owner of the ship or manager who has assumed the owners responsibilities in the operation of the ship. The D.O.C. must be issued prior to the ship's SMC.

To obtain a Document of Compliance the Company must demonstrate to Administration auditors that it has a structured and documented system in place ashore and afloat. The certificate is valid for five years and is subject to annual reviews and a copy must be carried on board your vessel. The SMC is issued to the ship when it has proved, following an audit on board, that it complies with the Company Safety Management System. The certificate is also valid for five years with an intermediate external review after $2\frac{1}{2}$ years. (As will be shown, the Code also requires the Company to carry out internal reviews, so don't be under the misapprehension that once the S.M.C. has been issued personnel on board are devoid of scrutiny for thirty months).

The two certificates now form the ISM certification and, as stated previously, they are trading certificates and therefore if withdrawn could result in the ship and Company being unable to trade. Therefore if the Company ceased trading then those on board and those ashore would not be required. It is imperative that all Masters and Managers play their full part in ensuring that the Code works, because in theory it could be possible for an SMC to be withdrawn on one of the company's vessels which would result in the DOC being withdrawn which would then in turn stop the rest of the fleet from trading.

Summary

Hopefully this has given you, the master, a flavour of what the Code is and how it is supposed to work and it will inevitably generate an amount of paperwork, if only to provide the objective evidence. There are various ways to reduce this paperwork or at least the archiving of it. It will depend upon whatever system your company has in place.

An example of how my company deals with such returns is as follows. The arrival and departure bridge checklists have been laminated and are completed when required. Then, instead of filing the checklist, an entry is made in the deck log confirming the fact it has been completed. The entry in the logbook then becomes the objective evidence that is required by auditors. This methodology can be used for numerous other checklists thereby reducing the amount of paper which is stored onboard.

The Code is here to stay and it must be used to its full advantage by those onboard. It is and will become more and more imperative that everyone is fully familiar with it and how it works. That having been said it is also imperative that the system is in place and working, your heads of department should not be so focused on ensuring that all the paper is in place, that the cargo compressors are not working, the hatches will not open, or the purifiers in the engine room are defunct. The right balance must be achieved between time in the ship's office and out on deck or in the engine room.

Finally whenever port state inspectors, classification society auditors or those from the office come aboard remember it is your system and you should know it better than anyone!!

Chapter 6

HEALTH MANAGEMENT ON BOARD

by Dr. A.C. Kulkarni
Consultant in Diving Medicine, India

Introduction

During the past decade or so the shipping industry has undergone vast change. New regulations about marine pollution, cargo carrying, safety management, etc., are strictly implemented by various authorities. Ships have become bigger and crew sizes smaller; documentation has increased but very little time is available to complete it. Contract periods have reduced but the time in port is almost nil. Signing off crew members have often complained of "difficult, trying times" on board.

It is not uncommon to find a 300,000 ton tanker fully loaded, cruising at 18 knots with a handful of fatigued crew. During the entire contract period they have seen only the shore terminals at loading and discharge ports! The same applies to bulk carriers or container vessels. Preserving the physical and psychological wellbeing of the crew, therefore, is another important responsibility of the master.

Although every crew member undergoes a periodic medical examination, one of the commonest health problems observed amongst seafarers is being overweight. A seafarer requires 2500 to 3500 calories per day, depending on the amount of physical work performed. Overindulgence in the wrong types of food is often the cause of being overweight. Isolation and boredom quite often lead to this over indulgence.

Exercise

Regular exercise is an absolute must. Exercises should be chosen so that they can also be done in the confines of a cabin. The exercises should increase the heart rate to a minimum level, called target heart rate (THR). Target heart rate can be calculated by deducting age from 180, i.e. for a 35 years old individual the target heart rate will be 145. Exercise should be sufficiently vigorous to increase the heart rate to 145 beats per minute, continuing the exercise and maintaining it for about eight to ten minutes. Jogging on the spot is the most convenient way of achieving this without any equipment.

Precautions should be taken to wear proper footwear, to avoid damage to knee joints by jogging on a hard deck surface. Another practical exercise regime used extensively is the "modified British Army Physical Fitness Test". This test involves stepping up and down on a stool 43 cms in height, 30 times a minute for five minutes. If you can complete the test you are fit! You need not count the pulse.

Weight control

Regular exercise also helps to keep weight under control. Being overweight makes an individual susceptible to many disorders. Calculating body mass index (BMI) is a simple method of determining "obesity level". BMI is a ratio of

$$\frac{\text{Weight in kilograms}}{\text{Height in metres}^2}$$

Ideally the ratio should be between 20 and 25. If it is above 30, the individual is definitely overweight. This should be investigated and remedial measures taken.

Weight control and regular exercise reduce cholesterol levels, which is the single most contributing factor in coronary artery disease (CAD).

Drugs and alcohol

A strict control on drug and alcohol indulgence is maintained by Port State Controls and many ship owners. Every endeavour must be made to enforce drugs and alcohol policies. Crew returning aboard after shore leave are likely to "smuggle" these on board. Additionally, the master should be vigilant about the innocuous looking new "intoxicants" which are available on board, e.g. cough syrup. Most cough syrups have an alcohol content of more than 15 to 20%. People are known to consume large quantities of cough syrup daily, which is equivalent to several whiskies.

"Sniffers"

Tanker crew will recall the sickening, sweet smell of naptha on board. These crew often complain of a 'heavy head' after working for a while. All volatile cargoes produce a similar effect. 'Heavy head' is due to intoxication. "Sniffing" is a fairly common mode of intoxication. Aromatic compounds like paint thinners, varnishes and dilutants give a "kick" when sniffed. Toners used in photocopying machines are another commonly available intoxicant, extensively used by "sniffers".

Smoking, tobacco and its derivatives

Cigarette smoking is a habit picked up very easily during youth. Quite often it starts with a supposed "macho" image and soon an individual is addicted to the nicotine. The nicotine content of cigarettes varies considerably from brand to brand and in the same brand, depending on the geographical location of distribution and sale.

Smoking affects respiratory and the cardiovascular system. The effects are observed as chronic bronchitis, emphysema and cancer of the lungs. It also affects heart rate, blood pressure, hardening of the blood vessels and is a major contributory factor in coronary artery disease. A heavy smoker, due to reduced physical fitness, would become a liability in case of an accident.

Chewing tobacco produces local effects in the mouth. Cancer of the tongue and mouth are commonly seen amongst those who chew tobacco. Recently a number of orally consumed tobacco derivatives have been introduced, mainly in the Indian subcontinent. In addition to tobacco these have a mixture of many ingredients. Some of these compounds have been found to be carcinogenic.

Strong willpower is required to quit smoking. There are many anti smoking programmes available to assist an individual. Nicotine skin patches are freely available as an "over the counter (OTC)" item. They have been found to be very effective amongst chronic heavy smokers. Consumption of tobacco derivatives should be discouraged in a manner similar to smoking in public places.

Medical emergencies

The Shipmaster's Medical Guide is an excellent reference book which is a mandatory publication to be held on board. It should be referred to while handling sicknesses and accidents on board. While obtaining radio medical advice, the instructions received could be read in conjunction with the guide. This will make implementation easier.

Radio medical advice

Inmarsat has improved communications on board. During medical emergencies the master must contact the company's medical adviser or the nearest coastal station for advice. These medical authorities are familiar with the facilities on board and the constraints under which the crew operate. Except to obtain relevant past medical information, the victim's GP should not be contacted.

History taking

History taking is an art. It provides a lot of information about an acute exacerbation of a chronic disease. For example, in the case of pain in the abdomen, a crew member on questioning might reply "I often get acidity. One to two tablets of an antacid normally give relief, but today I have not got any relief". Diagnosis of an acute peptic ulcer is more or less a certainty. The master should not impose his authority while history taking but should adopt the attitude of a concerned "next of kin". Relevant symptoms, the history and signs should be written down before asking for radio medical advice.

While obtaining radio medical advice, it is recommended that the conversation be taped, if such facilities exist on board. The tape can then be replayed to understand the instructions. Transcripts can be obtained when required, especially in case an enquiry is ordered afterwards.

The scale of medical equipment and medicines has increased considerably. A variety of modern diagnostic equipment is now available on board and the master must make himself familiar with its use. In case of an emergency he would be required to use them. "The buck stops at him!"

Medical inventory

Current medical scales provide an extensive medical inventory. Certain "controlled" drugs need to be kept in safe custody and their use accounted for. It is practicable to replenish the stock of medicines directly from ship owners/operators by having supplies hand carried aboard by crew when joining the vessel. These medicines will a need certificate from the company's medical advisor before transportation.

Whenever medicines are obtained directly from "non-English speaking" ports, the generic names of the medicines must be written on the packaging. Help from local medical authorities could be sought for this.

Disposal of hospital waste

Waste from a ship's hospital would not usually be contaminated like that from a regular surgery or hospital. However, the waste must be disposed of hygienically as per the "Waste Management Plan" of the vessel. Needles and sharps must be capped and syringes broken off before disposing of them. Out of date medicines should be destroyed in a similar manner. In the case of the disposal of "controlled" drugs, a destruction note (certificate) will need to be prepared.

Use of O_2 resuscitator

The current medical scale recommended by the International Maritime Organization (IMO) includes oxygen resuscitators. These resuscitators provide pure oxygen to the patient. Various flow rates can be regulated but four litres a minute is most commonly preferred. It is also possible to dilute the oxygen content. Positive pressure resuscitators, when fully charged, provide oxygen for over an hour. Some of the resuscitators have an additional air cylinder attached which can be used as a suction device to clear the throat of secretions, vomit, etc.

In spite of various training programmes and on board safety instructions, cases of "gassing" do occur. During "gassing" the victim is affected by the effects of hypoxia or toxic gases, or by both. Such victims should always be resuscitated by an O_2 resuscitator. Mouth to mouth respiration provides only about 18 to 19% of required oxygen and should continue only until an oxygen resuscitator can be brought to the site of the accident. With this the victim has a better chance of survival.

Every crew member should be thoroughly proficient in the use of an oxygen resuscitator. Regular drills must be carried out to demonstrate competence in use of the equipment. Periodic pressure records should be maintained. This is vital life saving equipment and should always be in a state of operational readiness.

Evacuation by stretcher

While evacuating an injured/sick seaman, adequate attention must be paid to strapping the casualty to the stretcher so that there is no possibility of the casualty slipping out. This is particularly important when the stretcher is manoeuvred vertically through manholes or from holds, etc. During a ship to ship transfer when the stretcher is required to be picked up by a crane, it is advisable that the stretcher is secured inside a rubber inflatable (Zodiac) if available on board. Slings should be attached to the inflatable. One crew member can also escort the casualty. This is a much safer way of casualty transfer, especially during heavy weather.

Psychological aspects of seafaring

The seaman lives and works in a peculiar environment, where he has constantly to adapt to changing conditions. He may join a vessel in a tropical port, pass through the Roaring Forties to a snow covered port and return to another tropical port – all within a month! Under these conditions, monotony of life becomes unbearable and added to this are the problems of continuous noise, vibration, fatigue, lack of sleep, an unsettled way of life and exposure to hazardous cargo. Reduced manning levels on board have enhanced the problem. He is exposed to these abnormal and hazardous factors for 24 hours a day and has no respite or period of recovery away from these conditions, as happens to an industrial worker ashore.

When combinations of these factors interplay along with worry, homesickness and other mental tensions continuously and constantly, a peculiar reaction is set in motion. The deleterious effect of these psychological reactions may prove to be much worse than a single psychological trauma. Hence the basic personality assets of a seafarer become an important factor. However, although unified and stringent medical standards for seafarers have been evolved worldwide, psychological selection is not yet obligatory nor is it widely applicable. Hence a background knowledge of the psychological aspects of seafaring will go a long way to understanding and capitalising on the innate strengths and weakness of the crew vis a vis the peculiar working conditions of seafarers.

Desirable psychological characteristics

a) Motivation
   Motivation influences the power of observation at sea, decision making and sustains hardship.
b) Emotions
   Emotions affect the capacity for work stability and well balanced emotions are necessary to withstand difficult stress situations.
c) Will power
d) Intelligence
   Intellectual factors such as quick appreciation of a situation, flexibility, concentration, imagination, faculty to abstract and a retentive memory are of basic importance. Officers, especially, must be able to recognise interrelationships in new situations, to find adequate solutions and to verbalise them. Actually, we do not yet know the effect of intelligence – whether a higher level produces fewer mistakes or an average one produces a better capacity for observation and better work output.
e) Perception
   Every individual has limits of perception under trying conditions.
f) The man-machine interface
   Advancement in the technical components of the ship demand special capabilities, technical knowledge and know how, control of operations and quick reactions, etc.

Factors in a ship's environment which may contribute to psychological malfunctioning

A new equilibrium in working and living conditions. For most careers ashore, working and living conditions can normally be separated into the working environment (when "on duty") and the social and family environment (when "off duty"). There are different functions and roles under the two environments.

On board, both the environments are inseparable and unchanging. In fact, both merge into one single environment where one aspect constantly influences the other aspect. There is a fixed working hierarchy and schedule, unvarying living conditions and quarters and the ever present and never changing company of the other crew members. This means that crew members cannot play different roles during working time and leisure time. However, psychological theories propose that for normal mental hygiene and development a change in roles is essential. If a person is denied such a change it may result in frustration, leading to aggression and indifference which may manifest itself as accidents, sickness, crime, quarrels, fights, alcoholism and so on.

Change from a natural to artificial environment

Under natural environmental conditions, people react as if by an innate instinct to avoid failure. However, modern day ships present an artificial environment, hence people can no longer rely on innate instincts – they have to adapt to specific laws and rules to master the technical world. If they continue with natural patterns of behaviour under the new artificial environment, this may result in more failures.

Communication on board

Multinational crews have become an accepted feature of seafaring, hence communication among crew members may not be possible on all vessels to any great extent. Although good communication is indispensable for the safety of the crew, the vessel and for smooth operations, it has added necessity from a psychological point of view. Communication with other people is necessary if individuals are to be balanced and efficient. Isolation results in changed mental attitudes and abnormal behaviour with resultant undesirable consequences. Linguistic competence is essential for achieving a versatile personality and development of a broader approach to life.

Body language

Certain body language may be considered offensive in some societies whereas it may be normal or accepted in others. Know your crew well!

Psychological consequences of separation from family and society

Separation from family not only influences the emotional relationships between partners, but also causes problems in family management and the upbringing of children. Mostly, this results in changing from a patriarchal form of management to a matriarchal system during the absence of the seaman father, since the mother has to solve all daily problems. This situation changes again during the long vacation stay of the male seaman.

On board he has to live with other seamen and he has no chance to select his co-workers. He has to come to terms with others, whether he likes them or not. His real friends are ashore and far away and he misses the privileges of good friendship, confidence, relaxation, empathy, common interests, etc. A few of the potential sources of dissatisfaction / conflict are:

1. Knowledge and skills deficiency.
2. Personal styles of interaction.
3. Breakdown of support system ashore.
4. Broken promises.
5. Inadequate/inappropriate induction or training.
6. Poorly designed equipment or technology.
7. Job/career dissatisfaction.
8. Alcoholic beverages and food.
9. Physical environment and amenities.
10. Personality clashes.
11. Insecurity of employment.
12. Class structures and attitudes.
13. Failures, sensitivity to appreciate interplay of work, social, personal and community relations.

"Man management" is the key to preventing these problems. The master cannot be indifferent and "mind his own business". The master must know his crew well. With a little effort he should be able to remember their names within a week. If an able seaman, oiler or cadet is called by his name and not by his position, there is an instant feeling of closeness or belonging. The master must keep his eyes and ears open to identify potential victims; for that, he should be accessible to all. He has to play the role of a counsellor. Knowledge, skill and experience of the "wise old man" will be on test.

Every endeavour must be made to break the monotony on board. There are numerous ways of doing it. The essential component of this stress relieving is group activity. Revival of some old seafaring traditions and customs is one such group activity. How many of us know of and have participated in a "crossing the line" ceremony? It is an age old custom!

If the crew are having a table tennis match, the master should preside over and give away the prizes. Ideally he should take part in the tournament. There is no harm (or insult) if a seaman or oiler defeats him!

A "happy ship" will sail for a long time – in spite of hard work.

Chapter 7

INTERNATIONAL OIL POLLUTION LEGISLATION AND CONVENTIONS – AN UPDATE

by Captain N.K. Gupta MICS(UK) MNI
Deputy Conservator, Jawarharlal Nehru Port Trust, Mumbai, India

Captain Neerav Kumar Gupta, as Deputy Conservator, is the head of the Marine Department of Jawaharlal Nehru Port Trust, Navi Mumbai. He is responsible for pilotage, fire and safety, marine conservancy, port crafts, etc. He has over 25 years of experience in the shipping industry. Earlier he was with Bombay Port Trust as Master Pilot and prior to that sailed as Master with The Shipping Corporation of India Ltd. He is a member of The Institute of Chartered Shipbrokers (UK), The Nautical Institute (UK), and the first Indian member of the International Harbour Masters' Association (UK).

Note

This chapter was originally presented as a paper at the First International Conference on Oil Spill Response, held in Mumbai on 19th and 20th April 1999.

Introduction

Most of the time, the world's 85,000 ships perform their business silently, out of sight and out of mind. Yet, whenever an oil pollution incident occurs which is caused by a ship, it attracts headlines world over, as we all know. Whether the shipping industry has been unfairly singled out is somewhat a debatable issue.

To my mind marine pollution will continue to occur, despite the best of efforts and measures. This is a fact of life. There have been incidents both minor and catastrophic, such as *Torrey Canyon* in 1967, *Amoco Cadiz* in 1978, and *Exxon Valdez* in 1989, each at intervals of 11 years. Judging by the time intervals is the year 2000, i.e. the new millennium, slated for another major pollution disaster? I sincerely hope not.

These and other incidents have had a profound effect on maritime transportation and regulations. There exists a very real relationship between major marine disasters and new international regimes. I have made an attempt in this paper to establish the fact that pollution incidents have led to more legislation, regulations, enforcement, inspections, etc. As a result, the amounts spilled over the years have dramatically reduced – from 301,000 tonnes in 1970 to 67,000 tonnes in 1997.

The world's merchant cargo fleet is approximately 45,000 ships of 700 million dwt and 500 million gt. According to Intertanko, the number of tankers operating worldwide is 3428, totalling 300 million dwt. Tankers comprise 40% of the total fleet in dwt terms. The Indian merchant fleet comprises 478 ships of 11 million dwt of which 93 are tankers, totalling 5 million dwt. The total annual cargo transported worldwide by sea is 4·22 billion tonnes. 45% of this i.e. 1·9 billion tonnes of oil, is moved in tankers. Of this amount 99.9995% is delivered safely, i.e. only about 0.0005% is lost.

I will now briefly outline the various legislation and conventions dealing with oil pollution only. Concern over oil pollution originated shortly after World War 1. The first international convention regarding oil pollution, 'The International Maritime Conference', was held in Washington in 1926. It was not ratified by any nation due to legal and technical problems and therefore failed. World War 2 caused considerable pollution, particularly on the shores of the Atlantic, as a result of torpedoing and sinking of ships. Consequently, concern about oil pollution began to grow again.

OILPOL 1954

The 'International Convention for Prevention of Pollution of the Sea by Oil, 1954', was held and adopted in London in 1954. It was the first international convention dealing exclusively with oil pollution. It prohibited the discharge of oil and oily mixtures from certain vessels in specified ocean areas. It came into force on 26th July 1958, after almost four years. IMO took over responsibility for this treaty in 1959. Although it contributed to cleaner seas, no enforcement system existed other than the flag state. India ratified OILPOL'54. It continues to be applicable in many countries, though it is superseded by MARPOL 73/78.

Torrey Canyon, a tanker, ran aground in March 1967 and spilled more than 120,000 tons of crude oil into the sea. It grounded 16 miles from the south west corner of England, beyond the three miles jurisdiction, as England then claimed a territorial sea of three miles. The concept of EEZ had not yet emerged. 80,000 tonnes of crude oil spread along the British and French coasts. Until then most people believed that the oceans and seas were big enough to cope with any pollution caused by human activity. Ultimately the ship had to be bombed by the Royal Navy as there was no better way to deal with the wreck and the oil. Damage claims in the UK amounted to £6 million and in France to FRF 40 million. It is interesting to note that this incident had the same impact in the USA as in Europe, since the US Congress realised that it had no law for compensation caused by marine oil pollution.

The direct result of the *Torrey Canyon* disaster was two international conventions, one private international agreement and the formation of the Marine Environment Protection Committee (MEPC) of IMO.

CLC 1969

The International Convention on Civil Liability for Oil Pollution Damage, 1969, (CLC'69) was held in Brussels in November 1969 and entered into force on June 19, 1975. As at the date of writing (1999) 75 countries are party to it. India ratified it on May 1, 1987 and it entered into force on July 30, 1987.

Until 1969 no liability was placed on polluting ships, though there were port rules and regulations, national laws, etc. The ship's total financial liability was restricted to the ship's liability tonnage as per the Limitation Convention 1957, i.e. about US$ 60–70 per ton.

The CLC establishes liability limits of ship owners for payment of damage caused by oil pollution. It provides a uniform set of international rules and procedures for determining liability and consequently provides compensation to those who suffer damage due to the escape or discharge of persistent oils from laden tankers. It is based on strict ship owner liability, compulsory insurance and limitation of liability.

CLC applies only to all tankers carrying oil in bulk but insurance is required only when a tanker is carrying 2000 tonnes or more oil in bulk as cargo. Oil should be "persistent oil", i.e. crude, fuel, heavy diesel, lubricating and whale oil. The owner is required to maintain an insurance or other financial security for an amount as required under CLC. In India the certificate for such financial security is issued by the Director General of Shipping. P&I Clubs usually stand guarantee for CLC liability. More importantly, P&I Clubs offer US$ 500m of cover for oil pollution claims.

The 1976 Protocol entered into force on April 8, 1981 and in India on July 30, 1987. It was not until 1992 that another Protocol was agreed. It came into effect on May 30, 1996. To date 39 countries have ratified it. In India it is under consideration by the government. Whereas the main purpose of this Protocol is to increase the shipowner's limit, it has become very difficult to break the right to limitation so as to protect the ship owner.

The main differences between the convention and its Protocol of 1992 are:
1. The amounts have more than doubled. From SDR 133 per limitation ton to a maximum of SDR 14 million, under the Protocol it is SDR 3 million for up to 5000 gt. For ships of more than 5000 gt and up to 140,000 gt it is SDR 3 million plus SDR 420 per gt beyond 5000 gt. For more than 140,000 gt it is SDR 59·7 million.
2. Persons who could not be prosecuted for claims were servants or agents of the ship owner, but now also include crew, pilots, charterers, salvors and their servants.
3. Right to break the shipowner's limitation of liability was "actual fault or privity" of the shipowner. This has now been made more difficult and changed to the concept of "wilful misconduct of the shipowner". This is done to reduce litigation in view of enhanced amounts.
4. The tonnage on which limitation is based is changed from Limitation ton which is the sum of Net Tons and the engine room space to Gross Tons.
5. Ballast passages including bunker spills of tankers are now covered in the Protocol provided some cargo residues remain on board, which is usually the case.
6. Grave or imminent threat is now covered even if it does not result in a spill, whereas previously actual pollution must have occurred to claim compensation.
7. Whereas earlier only Territorial sea was covered now the Exclusive Economic Zone is also covered.

FUND 1971

The International Convention on the Establishment of an International Fund for the Compensation for Oil Pollution Damage 1971. It entered into force on October 16, 1978. Today 52 countries are party to it. India ratified it on July 10, 1990 and entered into force on October 8, 1990.

It was considered necessary to shift some burden of compensation to the oil industry, the other main beneficiary of the carriage of oil by sea. Fund'71 creates an oil spill compensation fund, funded by oil companies in the member states to supplement compensation provided by the ship owners under CLC. These two conventions therefore form an integral part of the international oil pollution compensation regime.

The Fund pays compensation to claimants where the total claim exceeds the shipowner's limit or where compensation is not receivable from a shipowner or when full compensation is not available under CLC. The types of claim covered by both schemes include physical damage to property, cost of preventive measures when a spill actually occurs and reasonable costs of clean up.

The 1976 Protocol entered into force on November 22, 1994 but not many states have accepted it. The 1992 Protocol entered into force on May 30,1996. Today 39 countries are party to it. India has yet to ratify it as the matter is under consideration by the government. The main difference between the Fund and its Protocol of 1992 are:-
1. The maximum amount is more than doubled from SDR 60 million to SDR 135 million. In special circumstances it can be increased to SDR 200 million.

2. The other three differences are same as those stated in CLC under 4, 5, 6 and 7.

The advantage of the '92 Protocol is that much higher amounts are available for disbursement. Therefore if an incident occurs in our waters, be they territorial or EEZ, those who have suffered economic loss such as fishermen or seaside residents, etc. or even those involved in cleanup operations, etc., will have a much larger basket of money to claim from. It is therefore very much in the interest of potential Indian claimants to see India joining the 1992 liability and compensation schemes. Therefore it is clearly evident that India would benefit and should ratify the Protocols as early as possible.

Italy is the largest contributor to Fund'71, its contribution being 45·04%. India, with 13.6%, is the second largest contributor. If Italy also leaves and joins the Protocol of 1992 as many countries have done so then India will be the largest contributor to the Fund, exceeding 50% of the total contribution. It is hardly a desirable situation. It is also in the interest of Indian oil receivers to join the new regime because their obligation to contribute to the 1971 Fund will become heavier and heavier, as less and less countries remain in it.

Intervention Convention 1969

The International Convention Relating to Intervention on the High Seas in Cases of Oil Pollution, 1969. It was held in Brussels in 1969 and entered into force on May 6, 1975. It has been ratified by 72 countries comprising 67% of the world's tonnage. India has yet to ratify it.

It was adopted in the aftermath of the *Torrey Canyon* disaster. It provides coastal states with limited rights to take measures on the high seas to prevent, mitigate or eliminate danger which may pose a grave and imminent risk from pollution by oil to its coastline, as a result of a maritime casualty. The Protocol of 1973 entered into force on March 30, 1983. Today 41 countries have ratified it.

In the UK, for example, it permits the Secretary of State for Transport to intervene after an accident has occurred to a ship which will or may cause pollution to UK waters and or the coastline. The powers are exercisable when pre-defined conditions are met.

MARPOL 73/78

The International Convention for the Prevention of Pollution from Ships, 1973 (MARPOL). It was adopted in November 1973 but was not ratified due to its complexity. Between December 1976 and January 1977 a series of tanker disasters took place such as *Argo Merchant, Olympic Games, Daphne, Grand Zenith* and *Barcota*. Almost all were caused due to human error or failure. These disasters led to a conference which resulted in the MARPOL Protocol of 1978.

However, just a few weeks later the Titanic of the tanker disasters occurred. On March 16, VLCC *Amoco Cadiz* ran aground in rough weather off the north coast of France. She struck rocks twelve hours after a steering failure, despite the assistance of tug *Pacific*. She broke up quickly, spilling her entire cargo of 230,000 tonnes of crude oil, resulting in the single largest spill in history. It also resulted in France becoming a fierce regulatory state from a pragmatic maritime state. Final settlement amounted to US$ 32 million for the ship and cargo and over US$ 253 million for claims by French interests.

IMO was then asked to take immediate steps to prevent similar incidents. The *Amoco Cadiz* grounding led to the eventual acceptance of MARPOL. It was agreed to amalgamate the convention and Protocol '78 into one single instrument. Accordingly it is titled MARPOL 73/78. It eventually entered into force on October 2, 1983 after 10 years. This disaster also showed that CLC and the Fund were inadequate to meet claims and led to their revisions. It also led to the re-examination of the Law of Salvage, which was also found to be inadequate for serious oil spillages.

Today 106 states, comprising 94% of the world tonnage, have ratified the convention. India ratified it on September 24, 1986 and entered into force on December 24, 1986. Annex 1 deals with regulations for prevention of pollution by oil. Four of the five Annexes are in force. A new Annex VI, on Air Pollution has been accepted by only two states so far. Another Annex VII, on Ballast Water Management, is on the anvil. India has so far ratified only Annex 1 and 11, whilst the others are under consideration by the government.

OPRC 1990

The International Convention on Oil Pollution Preparedness, Response and Cooperation, 1990. It entered into force on May 13, 1995 and is ratified by 40 countries comprising 43·14% of the world's tonnage. India ratified it on November 17, 1997 and entered into force on February 17, 1998.

It was the direct result of the *Exxon Valdez* disaster in 1987. It is one of a number of measures adopted by IMO in response to the disaster. Although it did not enter into force, it received its first test when major oil spills occurred in the Persian Gulf due to military hostilities. IMO acted as if the convention was in force and set up a Disaster Fund and an Oil Spill Coordination Centre which provided valuable assistance in preventing major damage to the environment off the Saudi Arabian coast.

Under the convention the burden is on the government to prepare for response to spill emergencies. Its establishes a global system for responding to major oil spills. Parties are encouraged to develop contingency plans, establish stockpiles of equipment and develop expertise to be shared on request with others. Parties are required to take legal and administrative measures to facilitate arrival, utilisation and departure of ships, aircraft, equipment and personnel involved in dealing with an incident. Ships are required to have Shipboard Oil Pollution Emergency Plans (SOPEP) for dealing with spills. Ships are also required to report incidents of pollution to coastal authorities. A survey by ITOPF in 141 countries established that governments in over 100 countries have accepted the primary responsibility of dealing with ship-source oil pollution.

OPA 1990

Oil Pollution Act, 1990 of the USA. It was signed into law on August 18, 1990. It is a unilateral system of the USA.

It was drafted in the aftermath of the *Exxon Valdez* disaster of March 24, 1989. This tanker of 214,816 tonnes was under the command of Captain Hazelwood. After sailing from Valdez terminal, Alaska, she ran aground on Bligh Island Reef, 45 minutes after the pilot disembarked. She was loaded with 177,000 tonnes of crude. Eight of her eleven tanks suffered extensive damage resulting in a spill of 37, 000 tonnes of oil. To date it is the worst spill in the USA. Captain Hazelwood and Third Officer Gregory Cousins were found guilty of criminal negligence and had their licences suspended by the court of enquiry. The captain was fined a punitive US$ 5000.

A sum of US $3·5 billion has been paid so far to fishermen, property owners, municipalities, etc. for compensatory claims, fines, damages etc., though the total bill for the spill is reckoned to be US$ 18 billion. Only a company such as Exxon could have survived such a catastrophe. The vessel, now named *SeaRiver Mediterranean*, is barred from entering Prince William Sound, Alaska, under OPA'90. The only criminal charge that could be brought for the spill was for discharging oil in navigable waters without a permit, a misdemeanour. Available criminal penalties for such a discharge were viewed as insufficient for such a damaging spill. It thus gave impetus for OPA'90. Today violators can be prosecuted for a misdemeanour if the discharge is done negligently with penalties of imprisonment up to one year and or fines up to US$ 25,000 per day of violation. If done knowingly, imprisonment could be up to three years and or fines up to US$ 50,000 per day.

OPA'90 deals not only with pollution as a result of maritime transportation, but also pollution from oil facilities producing oil at sea. It encompasses prevention and response as well as liability and compensation. It sets new requirements for vessel construction, crew licensing and manning. It mandates contingency planning, enhanced federal response capability, enhanced enforcement authority and increased penalties and creates new research and development programs, increased potential liabilities and significantly increased financial responsibility requirements.

It covers all types of oils and all types of ships, whereas the Convention regime relates to persistent oil and tankers only. The empirical approach of the Convention regime was based on the circumstances surrounding the *Torrey Canyon* incident and the fact that only persistent oil was likely to cause significant pollution damage which required specific regimes to deal with it. It was felt that general liability law would suffice to cover pollution by nonpersistent oils or pollution from dry cargo ships.

One of the biggest differences between the OPA and the CLC is that the CLC channels as much liability as possible to the registered shipowner, whereas the US law seeks to impose liability on as many people as possible. Under OPA, the principle is "the polluter shall pay". In the USA, owners and operator's of pleasure boats have been fined to the tune of US$ 16 million to date.

Conclusion

There is no international regime for pollution damage caused by non-tankers carrying persistent oils. Owners may limit their liability as per the Limitation of Liability for Maritime Claims Convention, 1976 (LLMC'76). Owners are not required to maintain insurance as in the case of CLC. Many European countries, including the UK, have introduced national legislation making owners of non-tankers strictly liable for damage caused by persistent oils.

Also, there is no international regime covering nonpersistent oils. Compensation in these cases is governed by rules of the Admiralty or common civil law.

A cost analysis done by the International Oil Spill Database, USA indicates that spill cleanup costs vary considerably. A simple manual recovery can cost as little as US$ 0·37 per gallon or US$ 108·78 per tonne. Shore line cleanup, wild life rescue and rehabilitation, etc., add significantly to the cost, making it almost US$ 297 per gallon or US$ 87,111 per tonne. In the February 1996 spill of *Sea Empress* in which 72,361 tonnes were spilled in Milford Haven, UK, the cost came to US$ 18·32 million or about US$ 0·86 per gallon or US$ 253·23 per tonne.

In conclusion, I wish to say that 40 years after OILPOL'54 marine pollution has become a major cause for concern in the international community. A formidable and complex array of international, national and regional regulatory regimes have been put in place for ship operations, with serious fines, detentions, imprisonment and even vessel confiscation for pollution incidents. All this has had a profound and positive effect on the number and quantity of spills as well as in the way oil is now transported globally.

Chapter 8

MARINE INSURANCE AND THE MASTER

by Mr. P. Anderson BA(Hons) FNI

Philip Anderson is a master mariner and head of loss prevention at The North of England P&I Association. He is also Vice President of The Nautical Institute. He has written a number of books and guidance documents including "The Mariner's Guide to Marine Insurance" from which extracts are reproduced in this chapter.

The nature of marine insurance

INSURANCE EXISTS TO AVOID or minimise financial uncertainty. It provides individuals and organisations with financial protection against the outcome of events which involve monetary losses or liabilities which were not anticipated or predicted and over which they had no effective control. In return for this financial protection, the 'insured' individual or organisation pays money, usually by way of a 'premium', to another individual or company, the 'insurer', and a policy or contract of insurance is drawn up to formalise the legal relationship between those parties.

The Marine Insurance Act 1906 actually provides a definition of marine insurance at section 1:

A contract of marine insurance is a contract whereby the insurer undertakes to indemnify the assured, in manner and to the extent thereby agreed, against marine losses, that is to say, the losses incident to marine adventure.

Much of the language used in marine insurance, particularly where Lloyd's policies or institute clauses are concerned, is archaic. However, over many years, the courts and the industry have given very specific meanings to particular words and phrases, such that those involved in the marine insurance business know exactly what is meant and to change the wording would lead to confusion and uncertainty.

In the case of a shipowner or shipmanager, insurance is usually confined to the financial consequences of damage to its own ship, damage to other people's property or death or injury to people. A charterer's insurance requirements, particularly a time charterer's, are similar in many respects to those of the shipowner. A cargo owner's requirements are usually confined to loss or damage to its cargo.

Crew members, supernumeraries, passengers, pilots, stevedores, port officials and many other categories of individuals who may find themselves on board a vessel will usually require their own personal insurance for injury, illness or death. Some risks are virtually uninsurable such as freight, demurrage and a whole range of bad debts and disputes under charterparties, for example.

If there are any accidents or other incidents during the voyage involving any of the parties under any of their insurance policies or contracts, the master of the ship is very likely to become involved. Whether or not the master takes the correct action at the correct time in response to such an incident can often make the difference between the matter remaining a minor inconvenience which is kept under control or else a major disaster which quickly gets out of control, usually involving the shipowner in considerable expense.

In reality, for any one incident there may be a number of insurers involved. For example, if the cargo has been damaged this may involve not only the cargo insurer but also the shipowner's protection and indemnity (P&I) club and possibly the time charterer's P&I Club. A collision may involve these insurers as well as hull and machinery (H&M) underwriters, personal insurers of individuals, property underwriters and so on.

The master may find that in law he has obligations and duties to many of the insured parties and consequently to their underwriters – for example as an agent of necessity. But his principal and indeed employer – the shipowner – may find itself in conflict with these other parties. If they can prove a breach of contract or negligence against the shipowner, they may be able to pursue an indemnity claim against it. It is therefore crucial that the master has a clear understanding of the different types of insurances which may be involved in the many potential accidents, incidents and liabilities with which he may be confronted during his time in command.

To bring the whole issue of insurance into perspective and to consider its real implications for the ship master, it is important to appreciate the enormous financial implication of claims. H&M and cargo claims on the London insurance market alone amount to more than US$10,000,000,000 each year. Annual P&I claims cost a further US$2,000,000,000.

But what is the cost to the individual shipowner? The answer is not straightforward as it depends on the type, size and age of the vessel being considered, the trade in which the vessel is involved and a number of other relevant factors. However, the most significant factor influencing what any particular shipowner is paying for insurance is the past claims record. A shipowner with a bad claims record will be paying many times more for insurance than one with a good record.

Figure 8.1 shows the daily operating budget of a reefer vessel of 300,000 cu.ft. and figure 8.2 shows the percentage breakdown of claims by number derived from The North of England P&I Association. Where tankers are involved, with the attendant high risk of pollution claims, insurance can typically reach 40% of the operating budget. It is a major item and needs to be carefully managed accordingly.

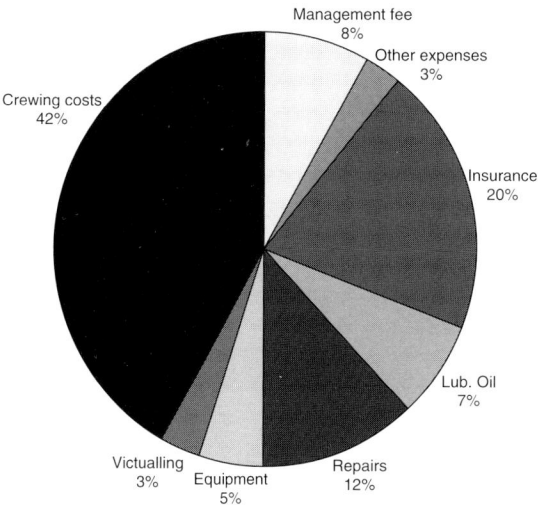

Figure 8.1 Daily operating budget – reefer vessel 300,000 cu.ft.

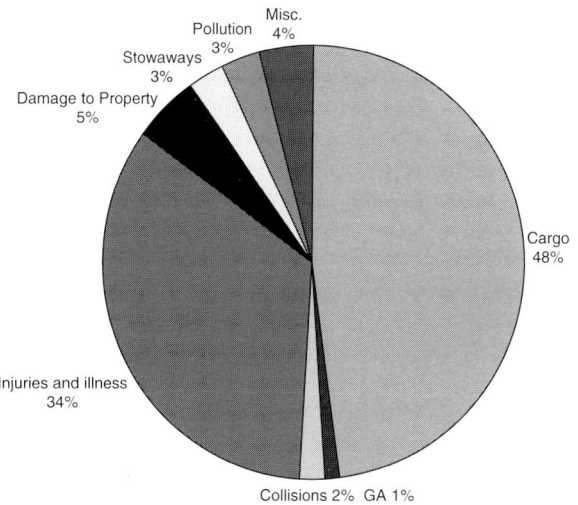

Figure 8.2 Percentage breakdown of claims by number – source North of England – Policy Year 1998

In order to keep insurance premiums as low as possible, shipowners usually take ever larger 'deductibles'. This is the part of any claim which the shipowner insures out of its own resources and may amount to many tens or even hundreds of thousands of dollars. In addition to any human suffering, inconvenience or annoyance an accident or claim may bring, it can also prove to be financially disastrous for the shipowner.

The master and his officers and crew can have a major effect on whether or not there are accidents and claims and also to protecting the shipowner's position by taking the correct action quickly if there is an incident. It is therefore crucial that the master has a good understanding of the various insurances involved in the commercial operation of the ship, of what he can do to minimise the risk of accidents occurring and of what to do in the event that problems do arise.

The shipowner's insurance requirements

The shipowner or ship manager has many different insurance requirements. Figure 8.3 identifies some of the more usual insurances.

The two most significant insurances for the shipowner are H&M and P&I. An approximate analogy could be drawn with the normal insurance which may be considered for a motor car. P&I insurance might equate to straight 'third party' cover and, with the addition of H&M, would constitute 'fully comprehensive' cover.

Hull and machinery (H&M)

Hull and machinery (H&M) insurance covers the ship itself and the equipment on board the ship including the propulsion and auxiliary machinery, cargo handling and navigation equipment, and similar items of plant. H&M may also cover the ship's contribution to general average and salvage as well as $^3/_4$ of the liability to the other vessel in a collision.

Protection and Indemnity (P&I)

During the course of operating ships, a shipowner can incur liabilities towards all manner of third parties. Protection and Indemnity (P&I) insurance provides this third party liability cover. P&I also covers a variety of other losses which a shipowner may suffer and which may not be insured elsewhere, although there are a number of specific exclusions from cover.

A shipowner may also have additional insurance requirements depending very much upon the type of vessels involved, and the trade or use to which the vessels are being put. For example, a shipowner operating a fleet of container ships may require insurance cover for the containers themselves. Some of the more usual additional insurance could include the following.

Freight, demurrage and defence (FD&D)

A shipowner is exposed to a number of liabilities or losses for which it does not have insurance cover. Examples include disputes under charterparties and sale and purchase of ship disputes. Freight, demurrage and defence (FD&D) cover does not provide insurance for these risks, but, rather, provides a legal costs insurance. It covers the cost of providing legal and technical support and assistance to defend or prosecute a wide range of uninsured claims and disputes. Many P&I Clubs offer FD&D as an additional class of insurance available to its members. There are also independent FD&D associations.

Strike insurance

Strikes by stevedore labour, ships' officers and crew or others who can disrupt the normal working of the ship can have devastating financial consequences. Strike insurance is available to alleviate the serious losses which may arise from strikes.

War risks

If a vessel finds itself in a war zone or other area of hostilities, the normal H&M and P&I insurances are likely to be suspended. War risks insurance provides the shipowner with continuity of cover as required.

The charterer's insurance requirements

Dependant upon the terms and conditions of the charterparty, a charterer may be exposed to many similar risks and liabilities as a shipowner. This is particularly the case with time charterers.

It is unlikely that the charterer will be exposed to liabilities with regards to collisions or pollution or damage to third party property or personal injuries to the crew, for example, but may very well find that it has an exposure to cargo claims.

A time charterer can in fact take out full 'P&I' cover with a P&I Club and be provided with the same cover as a shipowner member – although the method of underwriting will be different. An unusual situation arises with a time charterer's P&I cover in that the time charterer may include damage to the ship in its P&I cover. This is something which is specifically excluded as far as a shipowner member of a P&I Club is concerned. As far as the shipowner is concerned, then obviously damage to his own ship is covered under the H&M policy. The reason a time charterer may decide to take this cover through a P&I Club is that, as far as the charterer is concerned, the ship is another piece of third party property. If the ship is damaged as a result of some negligence on the part of the charterer – say because of some badly stowed cargo shifting – then the shipowner may have a valid claim for compensation against the charterer.

In a similar way, although it is not quite as common, a charterer may also require FD&D insurance, war risks insurance and strike insurance but not usually H&M.

Voyage charterers who own the cargo – which is often the case in trading bulk commodities such as oil – would also be interested in cargo insurance.

The cargo owner's insurance requirements

The cargo may be owned by the charterer or even the shipowner but, in the majority of cases, belongs to a third party. Whoever owns the cargo would usually arrange for insurance cover on the cargo to protect themselves against loss or damage as well as their contribution to general average and salvage. If the cargo sale contract was on cost, insurance and freight (CIF) terms, then the seller would usually arrange for the insurance. On free on board (FOB) terms, it is usually the buyer who insures.

The important point for masters to note is that, even though a cargo owner may have insured the cargo, it (or its insurer under subrogated rights) can pursue an indemnity claim against the carrier – usually the shipowner but possibly the time charterer – if the cargo is lost or damaged while in the carrier's custody. Under Hague or Hague-Visby Rules or similar carriage of goods by sea acts, carriers can raise various defences to such claims provided they can show they exercised due diligence to make the vessel seaworthy and that they properly cared for the cargo.

If the cargo owner or subrogated cargo underwriter is successful in its claim against the carrier then the shipowner/charterer should be covered for such liabilities through its P&I Club. It is important, however, to recognise the important distinction between what cargo underwriters cover and what P&I Clubs cover – P&I Clubs are liability underwriters, not cargo insurers.

The principles of marine insurance

Underpinning every contract of marine insurance that is written in England and/or is subject to English law is the Marine Insurance Act (MIA) of 1906. Specifically, this Act applies to H&M, P&I and cargo insurances and at section 3 it describes how every lawful marine adventure may be the subject of a contract of marine insurance. Selected sections are considered and they provide:

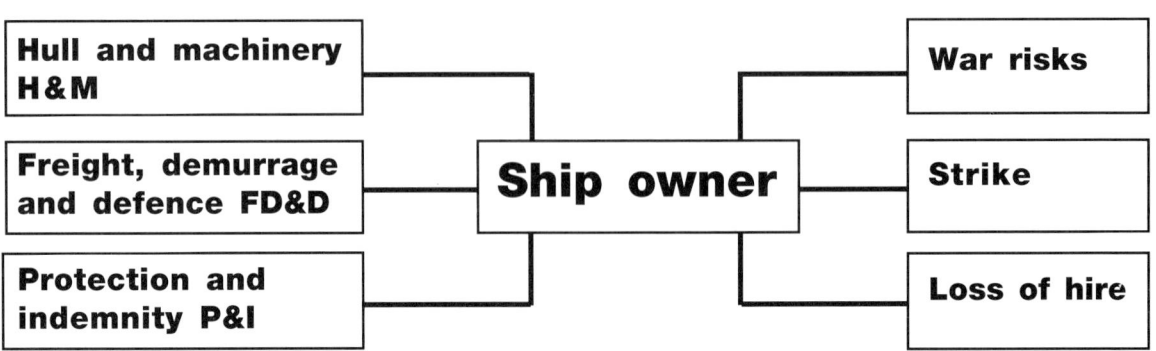

Figure 8.3 Typical insurances for a ship owner

3.   (1)   Subject to the provisions of this Act, every lawful marine adventure may be the subject of a contract of marine insurance.
     (2) (a)   Any ship, goods or other moveables are exposed to maritime perils. Such property is in the Act referred to as 'insurable property';
          (b)   The earning or acquisition of any freight, passage money, commission, profit, or other pecuniary benefit, or the security for any advances, loan or disbursements, is endangered by the exposure of insurable property to maritime perils;
          (c)   Any liability to a third party may be incurred by the owner of, or other person interested in or responsible for, insurable property, by reason of maritime perils.

'Maritime perils' means the perils consequent on, or incidental to, the navigation of the sea, that is to say, perils of the seas, fire, war perils, pirates, rovers, thieves, captures, seizures, restraints, and detainments of princes and people, jettisons, barratry, and any other peril, either of the like kind or which may be designated by the policy.

Section 39(5) on seaworthiness would usually apply to H&M and P&I insurance though the whole section is reproduced here since a number of the other policies, such as cargo insurance, may need to be considered under one of the other sub-sections:

39.   Warranty of Seaworthiness of Ship
     (1)   In a voyage policy there is an implied warranty that at the commencement of the voyage the ship shall be seaworthy for the purpose of the particular adventure insured.
     (2)   Where the policy attaches while the ship is in port, there is also an implied warranty that she shall, at the commencement of the risk, be reasonably fit to encounter the ordinary perils of the port.
     (3)   Where the policy relates to a voyage which is performed in different stages, during which the ship requires different kinds of or further preparation or equipment, there is an implied warranty that at the commencement of each stage the ship is seaworthy in respect of such preparation or equipment for the purpose of that stage.
     (4)   A ship is deemed to be seaworthy when she is reasonably fit in all respects to encounter the ordinary perils of the sea of the adventure insured.
     (5)   In a time policy there is no implied warranty that the ship shall be seaworthy at any stage of the adventure, but where, with the privity of the assured, the ship is sent to sea in an unseaworthy state, the insurer is not liable for any loss attributable to unseaworthiness.

Section 39(5) basically means that, if the insurer can demonstrate that the ship was unseaworthy when it put to sea and that the assured had positive knowledge or 'turned a blind eye' to facts which rendered the ship unseaworthy and the loss was attributable to that unseaworthiness, then the insurer may refuse to pay the claim. But exactly who is the 'assured'? Is the knowledge of the master, for example, sufficient to implicate the shipowner? The answer, under English law at least, is probably no. However, with the reporting requirements of the safety management systems of the ISM Code and the appointment of the designated person ashore, it may become increasingly difficult for a shipowner to argue that it did not know of the unseaworthiness and had no reasonable means of knowing. Of course, if there is a failure to make the necessary reports, then that is likely to constitute a serious breach of the ISM Code requirements.

If there was a breach of section 39(5) of the MIA, then not only would the shipowner run the risk of losing its P&I cover but it may seriously risk losing its right to limit its financial liability in certain circumstances.

There are a number of other underlying basic principles of most marine insurances of which the master should be aware. Firstly, it would usually be a strict condition that the vessel must be classed with an approved classification society and that class is maintained. This does not necessarily mean that the classification society actually has to cancel the classification – simply for a situation to exist which would have led to withdrawal of class would be sufficient.

It is also usual that insurance cover may cease if the shipowner does not comply with certain international conventions, in the form ratified by their flag state administration – for example the SOLAS convention. Indeed many insurers have made it a specific requirement that relevant vessels must have valid ISM safety management certificates (SMCs) and the operating company a valid document of compliance (DOC). This probably also extends to actual implementation and maintenance of the safety management system (SMS) of the ISM Code.

[see footnote]

The ISM Code will be the benchmark against which such things will be measured in the future and there may well be cases whereby shipowners are considered to have failed to act as a prudent insured if they have not been maintaining the recruitment/ employment procedures of their SMS.

Hull and machinery insurance

The standard perils covered by the ITC (Hulls) 1.10.83 policy are set out in clause 6 of the policy. It is worthwhile separating these risks into two categories:

[Footnote: For a detailed discussion of related issues see Anderson P. 'The ISM Code - A Practical Guide to the Legal and Insurance Implications' LLP Limited, 1998, ISBN 1 85978 621 9].

- Basic perils – set out in clauses 6.1.1 to 6.1.8 inclusive.
- 'Inchmaree' perils – set out in clauses 6.2.1 to 6.2.5.

Basic perils

6.1 *This insurance covers loss of or damage to the subject matter caused by:*

6.1.1 *Perils of the sea, rivers, lakes or other navigable waters.*

6.1.2 *Fire, explosion.*

6.1.3 *Violent theft by persons from outside the vessel.*

6.1.4 *Jettison.*

6.1.5 *Piracy.*

6.1.6 *Breaking of or accident to nuclear installation or reactors.*

6.1.7 *Contact with aircraft or similar objects, or objects falling therefrom, land conveyance, dock or harbour equipment or installation,*

6.1.8 *Earthquake, volcanic eruption or lightning.*

Inchmaree perils

6.2 *The insurance covers loss of or damage to the subject matter insured caused by:*

6.2.1 *Accidents in loading, discharging or shifting cargo or fuel.*

6.2.2 *Bursting of boilers, breakage of shafts or any latent defect in the machinery or hull.*

6.2.3 *Negligence of masters, officers, crew and pilots.*

6.2.4 *Negligence of repairers or charterers provided such repairers are not an assured hereunder.*

6.2.5 *Barratry of master, officers and crew, provided such loss or damage has not resulted from want of due diligence by the assured, owner or managers ......*

There is also an additional clause, which is included here for reasons of completeness:

6.3 *Master, officers, crew or pilots not to be considered owners within the meaning of this Clause 6 should they hold shares in the vessel.*

Other clauses cover accidents in loading, discharging or cargo handling.

Section 8 of the policy covers certain liabilities arising out of collisions – the relevant part reads as follows:

8.1 *The underwriters agree to indemnify the Assured for three-fourths of any sum or sums paid by the Assured to any other person or persons by reason of the Assured becoming legally liable by way of damages for:*

8.1.1 *loss of or damage to any other vessel or property on any other vessel.*

8.1.2 *delay to or loss of use of any such other vessel or property thereon.*

8.1.3 *general average of, salvage of, or salvage under contract of, any such other vessel or property thereon, ...*

An explanation as to why H&M only covers three-fourths in this so-called 'running down clause' (or RDC) is provided later dealing with P&I Club cover. The P&I Clubs tend to cover the remaining RDC and it was this unusual split of the collision liability, which partly led to the formation of the P&I Clubs.

Also of relevance to the P&I Clubs is section 8.4 of the ITC (Hulls) – 1.10.83 policy which sets out specific exclusions. Because they are excluded under the H&M policy, they are usually included under the P&I cover. Section 8.4 reads:

8.4 *Provided always that this Clause 8 shall in no case extend to any sum which the assured shall pay for or in respect of:*

8.4.1 *Removal or disposal of obstructions, wrecks, cargoes or any other thing whatsoever.*

8.4.2 *Any real or personal property or thing whatsoever except other vessels or property on other vessels.*

8.4.3 *The cargo or other property on, or the engagements of, the insured vessel.*

8.4.4 *Loss of life, personal injury or illness.*

8.4.5 *Pollution or contamination of any real or personal property or thing whatsoever (except other vessels with which the insured vessel is in collision or property on such other vessels).*

Another major cover provided under the H&M policy is the vessel's proportion of general average (GA) and salvage and there would usually be a requirement that the adjustment of general average would be in accordance with the York Antwerp Rules. The other contributing parties to general average and salvage would be the cargo owner/cargo underwriter and possibly time charterer's bunkers if their property was saved, and possibly freight.

If an accident or incident does occur which is likely to result in a claim being made under the H&M policy, it is very important – and probably a condition of cover – that the underwriter should be advised. It is quite normal still to see in the policy terms that, if the vessel is abroad, then the nearest Lloyd's agent should be contacted.

Insurances are usually warranted 'class maintained'. Also it is usually a condition of cover that the class does not change during the period of insurance. Similarly, the ownership of the vessel must not change during that period. Any of these events could mean that the insurance becomes void.

Of special relevance and interest to the master and those on board is a duty on the assured (i.e. the shipowner) to take such measures as may be reasonable for the purpose of averting or minimising a loss which would be recoverable under the H&M policy. This duty is usually referred to as 'sue and labour'. If steps to minimise, reduce or avoid the loss or further damage are not actually successful but are reasonable and taken in good faith, then the losses –

even though they may now exceed what they would have been if no steps had been taken – would still be covered under the policy.

Protection and Indemnity insurance

The scope of cover provided by any one P&I Club member of the International Group will be almost identical with the cover provided by any other member club, although the specific wording may vary slightly. The reason for this is that all the clubs are sharing in the larger claims through the pooling agreement and also in the cost of the reinsurance contract. It would therefore be unfair and unworkable if each club was covering different risks and liabilities.

In addition to the heads of risk specifically identified in the rule book, the club also covers the costs of correspondents, lawyers, surveyors and other experts who may be needed to investigate or otherwise handle and deal with a particular problem.

Set out below is a list of the heads of cover specifically identified by a typical P&I Club:

- Liabilities in respect of seamen.
- Liabilities in respect of supernumeraries.
- Liabilities in respect of passengers.
- Liabilities in respect of third parties.
- Stowaways.
- Diversion expenses.
- Life salvage.
- Person in distress.
- Quarantine.
- Liabilities arising from collisions.
- Non-contact damage to ships.
- Damage to property.
- Pollution.
- Wreck removal.
- Towage.
- Contracts, indemnities and guarantees.
- Liabilities in respect of cargo.
- General average.
- Fines.
- Legal costs, sue and labour.
- Risks incidental to ship owning.
- Special cover.
- Special cover for salvors.
- Special cover for containers.
- Special provisions for charterer's entry.

The percentage breakdown of claims under the different liability categories will vary from club to club and will be influenced by the membership profile of the particular club. For example, a club with a large tanker entry may show a relatively large proportion of pollution claims and a club with a large passenger ship entry may show a relatively large number of passenger injuries.

The above list of liabilities can be shortened since most of the liabilities covered by a P&I Club can probably be included under one of three general headings:

- Liabilities in respect of people.
- Liabilities in respect of cargo.
- Liabilities in respect of ships.

P&I insurance liabilities – people

A shipowner has a general duty of care towards anyone who comes on board its ship or even finds themselves in proximity of the ship. It must provide a safe access to and from the ship, it must not allow unauthorized people to wander around the ship, it must provide safe routes around the ship as well as a safe work place and generally a safe environment where all reasonable steps have been taken to prevent people being injured. If the owner fails in this duty of care and someone is injured as a consequence then, provided the claimant can demonstrate that the owner was in some way negligent, they will be entitled in many jurisdictions to bring a claim for damages against the owner.

Such people might include members of the crew, passengers, supernumeraries and third parties such as stevedores, pilots, port officials, P&I surveyors and even people who should not even be on board such as stowaways. In addition to this general obligation of a duty of care, a shipowner will also have specific contractual obligations to certain categories of people such as the crew under the relevant crew contract and passengers under the passenger ticket contract.

Crew contracts differ widely in the conditions of service offered and this includes compensation payments in respect of illness and injuries suffered. Passenger contracts may include the terms of an international convention such as The Athens Convention, which sets out the respective responsibilities and liabilities including financial limits of liability.

The P&I Club will cover the shipowner member for most liabilities to people in negligence and in contract, as well as under certain domestic laws and statutes such as health and safety at work acts, or the Jones Act in the US. It is essential that the P&I Club managers be given the opportunity of reviewing the respective contracts prior to agreeing financial terms for the insurance.

In addition to compensation to the injured individual or his or her family if deceased, along with all the hospital and other medical bills, the club will also reimburse the shipowner for the costs of any necessary repatriation expenses of the injured person and the costs of sending out a substitute. Neither the shipowner nor its P&I Club operate private health insurance although the extent of cover being provided in some crew contracts could be viewed by some as getting very close to that position.

There may also be other incidental expenses which the shipowner may have incurred such as the costs of fuel, wages and other expenses while diverting to land a sick or injured individual. In certain circumstances the club may also cover loss of or damage to the personal property of the crew if the shipowner has such a liability towards its crew.

Another important and significant head of claim which could fall into the category of liabilities in respect of people and which is becoming an increasingly difficult and expensive problem to deal with is that of stowaways. The P&I Club would usually expect to see evidence that the member has taken reasonable steps to prevent stowaways coming on board and to detect them prior to sailing.

Subject to that caveat the P&I Club will cover a member for the direct costs incurred in having the stowaways on board as well as the costs of supplying guards, when necessary, and the expenses involved in repatriating the stowaways back to their home countries. Sometimes this process of repatriation can not only be very expensive but also extremely frustrating when the stowaways have hidden or lost their identity papers, will not cooperate by declaring their true details such as name and nationality, and where ports and countries of call will not assist – which is becoming increasingly common. Sometimes the ship is even fined for having the stowaways on board, but usually the club would cover such a fine.

Liabilities with respect to cargo

The first important point to realise is that neither the shipowner nor the P&I Club is a cargo insurer, and nor is the club offering cargo insurance to the shipowner. The prudent owner of cargo will need to insure its cargo properly. However, if the cargo becomes lost or damaged while in the custody of the carrier, usually the shipowner, then the carrier may very well have to compensate the cargo owner unless it can bring itself within one of the exemptions of the Hague-Visby Rules, for example.

The cargo owner may not wish to have the trouble of pursuing a claim against the carrier in the name of the cargo owner. This right is known as subrogation.

The majority of cargo claims are brought against carriers by subrogated underwriters. These cargo claims are frequently dealt with by recovery agents acting on behalf of the cargo underwriter and the P&I Club claims handler on behalf of its members.

Under regimes which have incorporated the Hague or Hague-Visby Rules into their domestic legislation, often under a carriage of goods by sea act (COGSA) or as part of their national commercial code, there are a series of obligations imposed upon the carrier. Article III, rules 1 and 2 of the Hague-Visby Rules set out the most important obligations and it is a failure on the part of the carrier which leads to most of the cargo claims handled by P&I Clubs. If either of these rules are not complied with then it is very unlikely that the shipowner can rely upon the long list of defences which are set out in article IV, rule 2.

To understand exactly what sort of cargo liabilities the P&I Club will be covering it is worth looking at what article III, rules 1 and 2 actually say:

Article III

> *Rule 1. The carrier shall be bound before and at the beginning of the voyage to exercise due diligence to:*
> *(a)   Make the ship seaworthy.*
> *(b)   Properly man, equip and supply the ship.*
> *(c)   Make the holds, refrigerating and cool chambers, and all other parts of the ship on which goods are carried, fit and safe for their reception, carriage and preservation.*

> *Rule 2. Subject to the provisions of article IV, the carrier shall properly and carefully load, handle, stow, carry, keep, care for, and discharge the goods carried.*

The obligation in both these cases is one of 'reasonableness'. It is not a strict obligation of seaworthiness but the shipowner, usually through the activities of the master, officers and crew, must show that they did all that was reasonably and realistically possible to check and ensure that the ship was in all respects seaworthy and in a suitable condition to load the intended cargo.

The most common types of problem encountered which lead to cargo damage are:

- Leaking hatch covers and ventilators.
- Dirty or inadequately prepared carrying compartments.
- Inadequate ventilation.
- Cargo shortage.
- Cargo in "apparent good order and condition" which is not so.

Whereas there will be liabilities to be considered between the shipowner and the cargo owner under the terms of the contract of carriage evidenced by the bill of lading, there will also be various obligations between the shipowner and the charterer arising under the terms of the relevant charterparty. In many cases, if a shipowner is found to have a liability towards a cargo owner, or subrogated cargo underwriter, under the terms of the contract of carriage evidenced by the bill of lading the shipowner may very well have a legal indemnity claim against the charterer under the charterparty.

Consequently the shipowner would make a recovery from the charterer rather than from the P&I Club. Alternatively, a charterer may be considered to be the legal carrier under certain bills of lading and it may be the charterer which has to deal with cargo claims in the first instance. It may therefore be the charterer which brings the indemnity claim against the shipowner under the terms of the charterparty. Under normal circumstances the charterer cannot take advantage of the shipowner's P&I cover but rather would take out its own, independent, cover.

There are numerous charterparty forms but often there will be provision whereby the charterer has a responsibility with regard to the loading and stowing of the cargo. For example, in a GENCON Voyage charterparty form, there is a 'free in and out stowed and trimmed' (FIOST) clause, meaning that the charterer is undertaking these functions and not the shipowner. In time charters such as the NYPE form 'charterers are to load, stow, trim the cargo at their expense'. Again this is a charterer's operation and, as such, is likely ultimately to involve its liability if it does it wrongly or badly. Charterers can, and time charterers frequently do, take out their own P&I cover primarily to provide themselves with liability insurance cover for these risks.

One of the most frequent problems which arises with the carriage of cargo, giving rise to potential claims and the risk of a shipowner losing its P&I cover, is where cargo is loaded on board not in 'apparent good order and condition' but so-called 'clean' bills of lading are issued.

The bill of lading performs a number of different functions. A very important and fundamental function is as a receipt for the cargo. To comply with the requirements and obligations of the Hague-Visby Rules, or similar, it should describe the apparent order and condition of the cargo at the time of loading and also state the number of pieces or weight of the cargo.

As a receipt it will be given to the shipper of the cargo, which will then use the bill of lading in another way: as a document of title or negotiable instrument. Under the contract of sale which will have been negotiated between the buyer and the seller of the cargo, there will have been established, in most cases, an irrevocable letter of credit (LOC) within an international banking system. Under the LOC the seller will be paid for the goods provided it produces certain documentation in a particular form. This will inevitably require a bill of lading, which will confirm that:

- The goods have been shipped on board a particular ship at a particular port and bound for a particular port.
- The goods were loaded by a particular date.
- The goods were in apparent good order and condition, or in such a condition as allowed under the terms of the LOC.
- A particular quantity had been loaded.

The buyer of the cargo is thus relying on the statements in the bill of lading when handing over its money to the seller and, if these statements subsequently turn out to be inaccurate or untrue, then the shipowner will have to compensate the cargo receiver. If such a bill of lading was issued by the master or the shipowner (or with its knowledge) then the P&I cover may be prejudiced.

If the shipowner has accepted a so-called 'letter of indemnity' (LOI) to issue 'clean' bills of lading, then it could try and recover under that LOI. But if the shipper or charterer refused to honour their promise, there is little the shipowner can do. The courts will not recognise LOIs as having any validity since they came into existence to perpetrate a fraud and the shipowner is implicated in that fraud. It may therefore have to bear the loss out of its own resources and also lose its P&I cover.

In addition to describing the apparent order and condition of the cargo, the bill of lading will also state the date when the cargo was loaded. This date may be crucial under the terms of the sale contract. If the date has not been correctly stated and consequences arise, then the shipowner is likely to be liable to compensate the cargo owner and may also lose its P&I cover.

It is not possible to go into too much detail in this chapter, but more information is contained in the book *The Mariner's Guide to Marine Insurance*. For example, deviation can give rise to claims and there are different legal rules applying carriage requirements. General Average is usually covered by the H&M policy but can be a P&I concern if the ship was unseaworthy at the commencement of the voyage.

Also, if the cargo interests simply refuse to pay their contribution then that would be a bad debt – for which the shipowner would not have any insurance cover. However, if the shipowner did have FD&D cover then the FD&D lawyers may assist the shipowner with the debt recovery exercise.

Liabilities in respect of ships

It could be said that P&I insurance covers those risks which have not been covered under the H&M policy. To some extent this is true and particularly so when considering risks specifically relating to the ship itself in contrast to risks related to people and cargo.

Most P&I Clubs assume that their members will be contracting for their H&M cover on Lloyd's Marine Policy with Institute Time Clauses (Hulls) – 1.10.83 or similar. However, whereas these particular H&M policy terms are very popular, shipowners will make their own choice as to the terms and policy under which their hull and machinery risks are covered.

There are other popular H&M policy terms in place in other insurance markets around the world such as, but not limited to, Scandinavia, Germany and the US. These may differ significantly from the standard forms used on the Lloyd's market.

It is extremely important for the shipowner to know what is covered under its H&M policy for two related reasons. Firstly, if certain risks are covered under the H&M policy then those same risks do not need to be covered under the P&I insurance. This reduced risk should be brought to the attention of the P&I

underwriter, who should take it into account when calculating the call level for that particular member. Secondly, within the rules of the P&I Club, there will probably be a 'double insurance rule', which says that if a particular risk is covered under some other insurance policy, then it is not covered by P&I.

Of course the master also needs to know the terms of the H&M policy since, if there is an incident involving the ship, he needs to know whether to call in the P&I correspondent or the H&M representative.

The risks covered in this section include:

- Collisions.
- Non-contact damage to ships.
- Damage to property.
- Pollution.
- Wreck removal.
- Towage.

The extent to which a P&I Club will provide cover for liabilities arising out of a collision will depend very much upon the terms of the hull and machinery policy. Under the ITC (Hulls) – 1.10.83 H&M policy terms, three fourths of the collision liability (three quarters RDC) will be covered. The other quarter RDC would be covered by P&I. Damage to the shipowner's own ship falls under H&M insurance.

Another liability risk which is not usually covered under the H&M policy, although it may be under certain policies, is damage to third party property. Such damage can often arise when the ship comes into physical contact with the third party property. For example, the ship may run into a wharf, jetty or pier or hit the arm of a container gantry crane or a navigational marker buoy – plus an almost unlimited range of other so-called 'fixed and floating objects' (FFO) incidents.

Pollution is included here because many of the potential liabilities arising from a pollution incident are basically in respect of damage to third party property – except that in this case it is likely to involve cleaning the property rather than rebuilding a physical structure.

It is natural to think of thick black oil when the word pollution is mentioned, but there can be many other different types of pollution – from chemicals and garbage to smoke and hold sweepings. The P&I Club provides insurance cover for most types of pollution, including claims for damages, clean up and fines. However, the financial level of cover available within the P&I Club for oil pollution is limited at US$500,000,000.

During its employment a vessel or the people operating it may find themselves being fined for all manner of alleged or actual offences. These could include fines for failure to maintain safe working conditions, customs fines for short or over-landed cargo or for smuggling, for having illegal immigrants on board (e.g. an undeclared stowaway), as a punishment following a pollution incident and for many other violations and offences. All of these fines will be covered by P&I although the directors of the club may need to be satisfied that the members were not privy to the incidents for which the fines were being levied. It is possible under this particular head of risk that the P&I Club, rather than the H&M underwriters, may have to compensate the shipowner for the loss of its ship. This could arise if, for example, customs or police found a large consignment of drugs which were being smuggled on board the ship. As a consequence, and by way of a punishment, the local authorities or court confiscated the ship by way of the fine or penalty.

As stated, P&I cover is open-ended. Because of the unique way in which the clubs are structured they can, and do, respond to new risks and liabilities which arise or changes in the law which may occur. The aim is to provide the protection the shipowner members of the club require during the commercial operation of their ships. If a risk or liability arises and, provided it is not specifically excluded and it is of a P&I nature, then the claim can be referred to the board of directors of the club under the omnibus rule for approval.

Freight demurrage and defence (FD&D)

The purpose of FD&D insurance is to provide the member with cover for the enforcement of all proper claims and the defence of all claims improperly brought relating to:

- Freight, deadfreight and demurrage.
- General average, insurance monies and salvage.
- Breach of charter or contract of affreightment or hire.
- Detention through collision or any other cause.
- The negligent repair or alteration or the supply of short, defective or improper outfit, equipment, bunker fuel or other necessaries.
- Loading, stowing, trimming, or discharge of cargo.
- The building, purchase or sale of the ship.
- Disputes with mortgagees of the ship.
- Wrongful arrest.
- Improper action by national authorities or similar bodies.
- H&M claims below deductible.

FD&D also covers legal representation at coroner's inquests, formal investigations or other inquiries into casualties, or the conduct of servants of the member.

The actual cover provided by different FD&D insurers may vary slightly from the above list; there may be some additional areas specifically identified or some of the above may not be specifically mentioned. The various areas of cover identified may also have restrictions imposed before cover is provided – for example, if FD&D was assisting a member with a claim falling below the H&M deductible then the member would need to demonstrate that the H&M deductible was set at a realistic and reasonable level.

Responding to an incident – the crucial role of the master

Imagine a ship which has arrived at the discharge port, the hatch covers have been opened and discharge has commenced. Damaged cargo is then discovered. Often the master on board the ship will be amongst the first to be aware of the problem. Whereas the master may be in a position to render some 'first aid' measures to keep the situation under control, it is important that he recognises that he should advise his shipowners or shipmanagers as well as the P&I Club immediately in order that the necessary back up and support can be provided.

Figure 8.4 shows that there are a number of possible routes which the master may take. He may initially report the problem to the operations department at the shipowner's office. The shipowner or shipmanager may then establish contact with its P&I Club to advise the club of the problem. There is no reason why the master should not contact the P&I Club directly but this does not occur very often – it being more usual for the master to contact the local representative or correspondent of the P&I Club.

The master should have on board the list of correspondents of the particular P&I Club covering that particular vessel. He should therefore have available all the relevant details of the local correspondents. However, he may approach the local ship's agent, who will usually know who the local P&I correspondents are and how to communicate with them. The agent may also be used to relay advice of the incident to the shipowner or shipmanager.

However, some caution may need to be exercised because the agent may find itself in a slight conflict of interest situation. If, as is often the case, the vessel is operating under a charterparty then the ship's agent is likely to have been appointed by the charterer rather than the shipowner. If the incident has arisen from an alleged breach of the bill of lading contract by the shipowner, as carrier, this may also involve, for similar reasons, a breach of the charterparty contract. It may therefore be inappropriate for the charterer, via its agent, to become involved in the investigation on board until the facts have been clarified and the evidence collected.

Once the immediate problem has been resolved the extent of the damage has been minimised, the quantum of the damage has been established, security has been provided, if necessary, and the ship has sailed, then each of the interested parties will assess its respective position.

Prior to the vessel sailing the master should have been working closely with the surveyor, lawyer and possibly consultant who were attending on behalf of the shipowner and its P&I Club to ensure that all the relevant evidence has been collected together and that any statements that need to be taken have been taken. The role of the master and his officers in this activity is crucial.

The Mariner's Role in Collecting Evidence should be consulted for guidance on the types of evidence required for the particular incident under consideration.

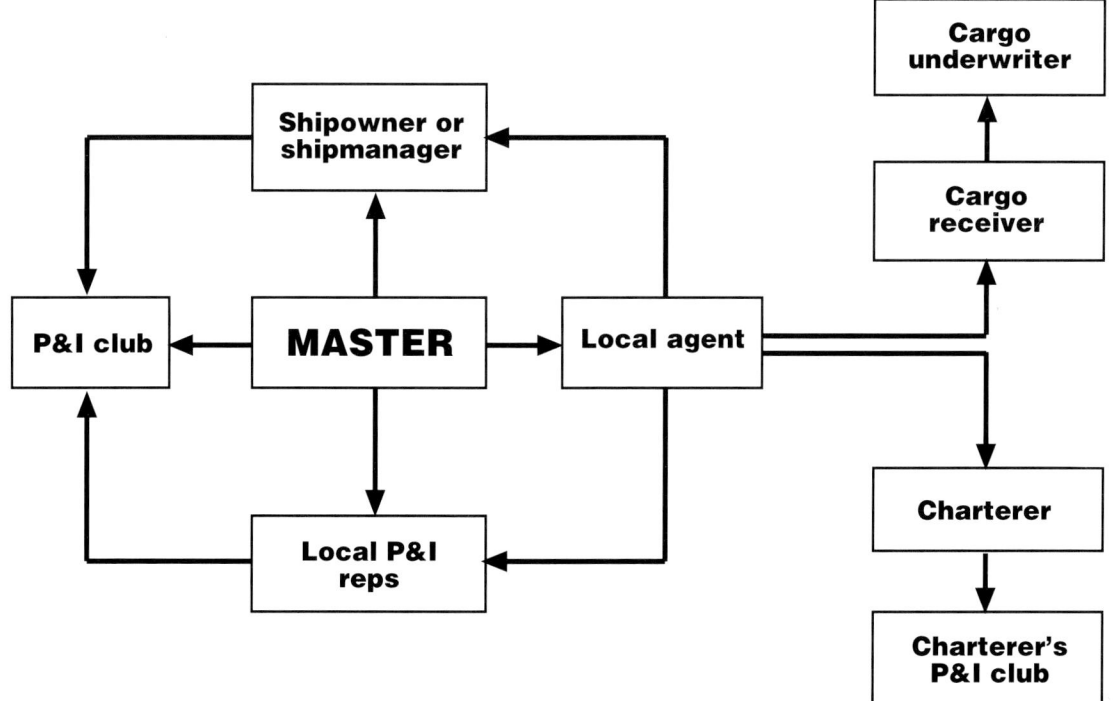

Figure 8.4 Initial reporting options

Conclusion

Whatever the type of incident might be, whether it is a P&I incident, FD&D or H&M, the matter will need to be investigated to try to establish the cause and the documentary evidence will need to be collected and reports will have to be prepared. The evidence and the reports prepared by the master and his team on board will be crucial if the shipowner and the P&I Club are to be protected.

If the claims cannot be resolved amicably then that documentation and the reports may have to be produced in a court or before an arbitration tribunal and the originator of that evidence, the master or officer may have to stand up and testify on oath that the information presented is accurate and correct.

The collection of evidence is not something which is done just following an accident or problem but rather it is an ongoing exercise as part of a well run ship. Log books should be properly maintained, records kept, reports made, and procedures followed both of the QA system and the safety management system of the ISM Code. Checks and inspection should be done to exercise due diligence to make the vessel seaworthy but records should also be kept of all those activities which can then be used to demonstrate, to a court of law if necessary, that the due diligence was indeed exercised.

Almost as a by-product, the activity of creating evidence as part of the running of a ship in this way will in fact make everyone more conscious of what they are doing which, in itself, is a most powerful loss prevention tool.

References

- *The Mariner's Role in Collecting Evidence*, The Nautical Institute, 1997.

- *The Mariner's Guide to Marine Insurance*, P. Anderson. The Nautical Institute, 1999.

- *Distance Learning Course in P&I Insurance*, The North of England P&I Association in conjunction with South Tyneside College UK.

Chapter 9

SURVEYS AND THE SHIPMASTER

a brief summary of a book by Captain W. Vervloesem AMNI
prepared by Lt Cdr J.A. Hepworth RN Ret'd MNI

Captain Walter Vervloesem was born and educated in Antwerp. After graduation from the Antwerp Maritime Academy, he was employed by different Belgian and Dutch shipping companies where he served on various types of ships (general cargo/multi purpose ships, reefer ships and gas carriers). After having gained sea experience as deck officer in both deep sea and coastal service, he left the sea in 1988 in the rank of chief officer on short-sea trade vessels.

He then decided to redirect his career and started as a marine surveyor in Antwerp where his activities subsequently comprised P&I work, surveys on behalf of cargo and hull & machinery underwriters. Shortly after coming ashore, he became actively involved in various types of ship inspection programmes and ship surveys, comprising condition surveys for several leading P&I clubs, H&M underwriters, pre-purchase inspections, flag state – and seaworthiness inspections.

He is presently a partner in IMCS, a well established survey company in Antwerp with seven branch offices throughout Europe, Russia and Ukraine, and co-manages the Antwerp based head office. His special interests include ship inspections, ISM consultancy, accident and damage investigation together with a wide range of transport and cargo problems.

Captain Vervloesem is founding chairman of the Belgian Branch of The Nautical Institute, which was established in April 1998.

Introduction

THE SHIP SURVEY AND AUDIT COMPANION, authored by Walter Vervloesem, was published in April 2000 by The Nautical Institute. It is a detailed and authoritative publication on the work of the ship surveyor and provides an enormous range of checklists for various situations.

Captain Vervloesem's book can be used as a guide not only for training institutes, students and cadets, but by ship's staff as a reference for cross-checking their own inspection programmes and in helping them to organise surveys and assisting inspectors in a proper way.

Masters will be aware of the demands on their time from surveyors. It is useful, therefore, to have an overview of what they are trying to achieve and how best to prepare for their work. As the author's foreword says:

'In the late nineteen eighties and partly as a result of a series of unexplainable bulk carrier losses, a wide variety of ship inspection programmes were worked out and existing programmes were expanded. The aim of these various types of ship inspection programmes was (and still is) to make an appraisal about the condition of a ship, to identify specific areas of concern and to provide those who initiated the inspection with information which will help them in a decision making process, in advising their customers and clients, or in determining strategies and the way forward.

'Every type of ship inspection consists of a very complex process whereby the ship inspector or auditor will need to focus on various shipboard procedures and evaluate the condition of shipboard equipment and material. This requires careful planning and experience and surveyors or auditors will have to use their organisational talents and flexibility throughout

the survey in order to achieve the intended result. This generally consists of a properly elaborated report, including the required information amplified by a number of useful comments and constructive remarks on the matters concerned.

'Normally, principals will provide their surveyors or inspectors with pro forma reports that cover the most important items likely to be found aboard ships. It will be appreciated that these checklists and formats have a general character and not all items can be covered. More specific inspection paths and criteria against which an item needs to be checked or tested are generally not mentioned and are left to the discretion and professional judgement of the surveyor in attendance.'

The book contains many samples of these checklists and a glance at them will help ship's staff to be aware of what the surveyor may be seeking during a visit. This should assist the master and officers to prepare for the survey and to ensure it is of least inconvenience and most benefit to all concerned.

Some examples of these checklists are shown:

- Master's responsibility and authority (checklist for ISM Section V) (figure 1.8.5 in the book)
- Example of a port state inspection report (figure 1.8.16 in the book)
- Ship certificate index (figure 2.3.2 in the book – first three pages only)
- Mooring and anchor equipment checklist (figure 2.6.1 in the book)
- Steering failure checklist (figure 2.11.2 in the book)
- Helicopter operations checklist (figure 2.11.17 in the book)
- Ship safety meeting minute format/guidelines (figure 2.12.16 in the book)

SECTION VIII
Guidelines for audits ashore and on board

ISM Section V – Master's responsibility and authority

Details	Available ? Acceptable? Satisfactory?		Comments / remarks
	Yes	No	
Shore items			
• Definitions of the master's duties, responsibilities and authority.	❏	❏	....
• Evidence that master is provided with and aware of details regarding his function, duties, responsibilities, authority.	❏	❏	....
• Statement of the overriding authority of the master re-decision making in ship/ crew safety and environmental protection related matters.	❏	❏	....
• Request to master to implement the S & E P policy of the company on board and motivating crew with respect to S & E P matters.	❏	❏	....
• Statement and details re-observation of SMS requirements re-shipboard operations, shipboard management and S & E P matters (ref. sections of book)	❏	❏	....
• Request/procedures for reviewing SMS (min. 1x/year) and reporting deficiencies.	❏	❏	....
• Records of shipboard reviews of the SMS.	❏	❏	....
• Evidence of immediate shipboard reporting of changed circumstances which might adversely affect the S & E P.	❏	❏	....
Ship items			
• Definitions of the master's duties, responsibilities and authority.	❏	❏	....
• Evidence that master is provided with and aware of details regarding his function, duties, responsibilities, authority. Documented procedures for specific duties delegated to officers under his command.	❏	❏	....
• Statement of the overriding authority of the master re-decision making in ship/ crew safety and environmental protection related matters.	❏	❏	....

Figure 1.8.5 Checklist for ISM Section V – Master's responsibility and authority

	Available ? Acceptable? Satisfactory?		Comments / remarks

<table>
<tr>
<td rowspan="2" align="center">Details</td>
<td colspan="2" align="center">Available ?
Acceptable?
Satisfactory?</td>
<td rowspan="2" align="center">Comments / remarks</td>
</tr>
<tr>
<td align="center">Yes</td>
<td align="center">No</td>
</tr>
<tr>
<td>• Request to master to implement the S & E P policy of the company on board and motivating crew with respect to S & E P matters (i.e. signature of crew confirming that company procedures manuals have been read/understood).</td>
<td align="center">❏</td>
<td align="center">❏</td>
<td>..</td>
</tr>
<tr>
<td>• Evidence re-specific measures to ensure that procedures and instructions are complied with during day to day shipboard operations, shipboard management and S & E P matters (checklists, job instructions, etc.)</td>
<td align="center">❏</td>
<td align="center">❏</td>
<td>..</td>
</tr>
<tr>
<td>• Evidence that SMS is reviewed (min. 1x/year) and deficiencies/ anomalies reported (Records of shipboard reviews of the SMS).</td>
<td align="center">❏</td>
<td align="center">❏</td>
<td>..</td>
</tr>
<tr>
<td>• Evidence of immediate shipboard reporting re-changed circumstances which might adversely affect the S & E P.</td>
<td align="center">❏</td>
<td align="center">❏</td>
<td>..</td>
</tr>
</table>

SECTION VIII
Guidelines for audits ashore and on board

ISM Section V – Master's responsibility and authority (continued)

Figure 1.8.5 Checklist for ISM Section V – Master's responsibility and authority (continued)

Using these checklists, and the many others in the book, masters can more easily prepare for the requests and requirements of surveyors. For example, if life saving equipment is to be inspected, it is quicker and more efficient if the gear is laid out beforehand. This saves time and also gives the ship's staff a good opportunity to practice with the equipment.

Usually, the time window for inspection will be limited and the surveyor will have to work under conditions of stress in order to complete his survey prior to departure of the ship. Planning, organisation and flexibility play a key role in the survey/audit process and the checklists mentioned in Walter Vervloesem's book should be of assistance in seeing how the surveyor will be working out inspection schedules by selecting from the required checklists or parts thereof. Furthermore the selected material might also serve as an "aide-memoire" during the execution of the survey or audit.

Masters have a huge amount on their plate already, so preparation for surveys, using Captain Vervloesem's book as a guide, could make life slightly easier. The book is a very worthwhile investment.

Concentrated Inspection Campaign on selected items in respect of ISM Implementation

---

Inspection Authority: *Port State Control*
Port of Inspection: ....
Date of Inspection: ....

Name of ship:	....	IMO number:	....
Ship type:	....	Name of Company:	....
Flag of ship:	....	Auditing body if not Flag state:	....
Call sign:	....		

		Yes	No
1.	Is the ISM Code applicable to ship as of 1/7/98?	○	❏
2.	ISM certification on board?	○	❏
3.	Are certificates and particulars in order?	○	❏
4.	Is Safety Management documentation (e.g. manual) readily available on board? Ref: Section 1.4 of the ISM Code	○	❏
5.	Is relevant documentation on the SMS in a working language or language understood by the ship's personnel? Ref: Section 6.6 of the ISM Code	○	❏
6.	Can senior officers identify the Company responsible for the operation of the ship and does this correspond with the entity on the ISM certificates? Ref: Section 3 of the ISM Code	○	❏
7.	Can senior officers identify the "designated person"? Ref: Section 4 of the ISM Code	○	❏
8.	Are procedures in place for establishing and maintaining contact with shore management in an emergency? Ref: Section 8.3 of the ISM Code	○	❏
9.	Are programmes for drills and exercises to prepare for emergency actions available on board? Ref: Section 8.2 of the ISM Code	○	❏
10.	Can the master provide documented proof of his responsibilities and authority, which must include his overriding authority? Ref: Section 5 of the ISM Code	○	❏
11.	Does the ship have a maintenance routine and are records available? Ref: Section 10.2 of the ISM Code	○	❏

	Yes	No
Ship detained	○	❏
Do detainable deficiencies, if found, indicate a failure of the Safety Management System? Ref: § 3.3.2 of Provisional Guidelines	○	❏

Paris Memorandum of Understanding on Port State Control
15 May 1998

Figure 1.8.16 Example of a Port State inspection report

SHIP CERTIFICATE INDEX

(Note: All certificates carried on board must be originals)

CERTIFICATE	ISSUED DATE PLACE	VALID/ * EXPIRY/DUE	REMARKS (INTERIM/ EXEMPTION)
1. REG — REGISTRY 1.01 Certificate of registry (FAL Convention)			indefinitely valid

2. STAT — STATUTORY
2.01 International loadline certificate
    (LL Convention article 16)
      Annual survey
      Exemption
		5 years	

2.02 I O P P certificate
      Intermediate survey
      Annual survey
      Form "A" (supplement)
      Form "B" (supplement)
    (MARPOL 73/78 Annex 1 Reg. 5)
		5 years	

2.03 Passenger ship safety certificate
    (SOLAS 74/78 Ch. I/12 as amended
      by GMDSS amendments)
      Exemption certificate
    (SOLAS 74/78 Ch. I/12)
      Safety certificate for special trade
        passenger ships
    (STP Agreement Reg. 6)
      Special trade passenger ships
        space certificate
    (SSTP 73 rule 5)
		1 year	

2.04 Safety construction certificate
      Intermediate survey
      Annual survey
      Record of construction and
      equipment for oil tankers (supp.)
    (SOLAS 74/78 Ch. I/12 as amended
    by the GMDSS amendments)
		5 years	

2.05 Safety equipment certificate
      Intermediate survey
      Annual survey
      Form "E"
      Exemption
    (SOLAS 74/78 Ch. I/12 as amended
    by the GMDSS amendments)
		2 years	

2.06 Safety radio certificate
      Form "R"
      Exemption
    (SOLAS 74/78 Ch. I/12 as amended
    by the GMDSS amendments)
		1 year	

Note: Validity and expiry dates may vary according to circumstances

Figure 2.3.2 Ship certificate index

SHIP CERTIFICATE INDEX (continued)
(Note: All certificates carried on board must be originals)

CERTIFICATE	ISSUED DATE PLACE	VALID/ * EXPIRY/DUE	REMARKS (INTERIM/ EXEMPTION)
2.07 Dangerous goods manifest or stowage plan (SOLAS 74/78 Ch. VII/5(5)) (MARPOL 73/78 Annex III Reg. 4-5 as amended)			for current voyage
2.08 Document of authorisation for the carriage of grain (SOLAS 74/78 Ch. VI/9)			indefinitely valid
2.09 Document of compliance with special requirements for ships carrying dangerous goods (SOLAS 74/78 Ch. II-2/54.3)		5 years	
2.10 Noxious Liquid Substances Certificate intermediate survey annual survey (MARPOL 73/78 – An II – R11.2)		5 years	
2.11 S O P E P manual (MARPOL 73/78 Annex I Reg. 26)			to be approved by administration
2.12 U S Coast Guard Letter of Compliance		2 years	yearly (mid-term) inspections
3. QA/ISM — QUALITY ASSURANCE/ISM 3.01 Document of compliance Initial survey Annual survey (SOLAS 74 Ch. IX Reg. 4.1-4.2)		5 years ± 3 months	specify type of ship copy on board
3.02 I S M: Marine management agreement			between owenrs and present managers
3.03 Safety management certificate Initial survey Intermediate survey (SOLAS 74 Ch. IX Reg. 4.3)		5 years 2-3 years	original to be on board
4. CLASS — CLASS RELATED CERTIFICATES / INSPECTION DATES 4.01 Cargo securing manual (SOLAS 74 Ch. VI Reg. 5.6)			to be class/administration approved
4.02 Class automation Annual class automation (SOLAS 74 Ch. II - 1 Reg. 46)		5 years	
4.03 Classification certificates A: Hull special survey continuous survey intermediate survey annual survey		5 years	

* Note: Validity and expiry dates may vary according to circumstances

Figure 2.3.2 Ship certificate index (continued)

SHIP CERTIFICATE INDEX (continued)
(Note: All certificates carried on board must be originals)

CERTIFICATE	ISSUED DATE	PLACE	VALID/ * EXPIRY/DUE	REMARKS (INTERIM/ EXEMPTION)
B: Machinery special survey continuous survey intermediate survey annual survey			5 years	
C: Refrigeration machinery special survey continuous survey intermediate survey annual survey			5 years	
4.04 Dry docking			every 2–5 years and 2x in 5 years	
4.05 Exhaust gas boiler			2·5 years	
4.06 In water survey				only for intermediate docking/mid-term/ class
4.07 Inert gas plant Annual survey (SOLAS 74 Ch. II - 1 Reg. 62)			5 years	
4.08 Oil fired boiler			2·5 years	
4.09 Tail shaft			5 years	
4.10 Thickness determination (hull)				every 5 years after first 5 years (first survey after 10 years)
5. LSA — LIFE SAVING EQUIPMENT 5.01 E P I R B Hydrostatic release Battery expiry (SOLAS 74 Ch. IV Reg. 4.1)			2 years	check MMSI no. or country code and callsign or country code and serial number
5.02 Immersion suit certificate (SOLAS 74 Ch. III Reg. 7-30-33)				(approved type)
5.03 Life jacket certificate (SOLAS 74 Ch. III Reg. 7-30-32)				(approved type)
5.04 T P A certificate (SOLAS 74 Ch. III Reg. 30-34)				(approved type)
5.05 Lifeboat certificate/rescue boat launching appliances			5 yearly test	
5.06 Lifeboat falls renewed Port and starboard side			5 years	

Note: Validity and expiry dates may vary according to circumstances

Figure 2.3.2 Ship certificate index (continued)

MOORING AND ANCHOR EQUIPMENT CHECKLIST

M.V: ....   *Date:* ....   *Port:* ....

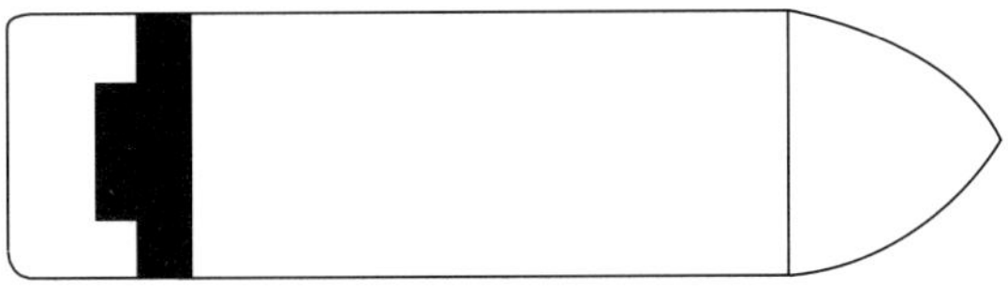

Key:
1. Windlass (electro-hydraulic/steam)
2. Winch (electro-hydraulic/steam)
3. Capstan (electro-hydraulic/steam)

Equipment	Fitted Provided	Condition				Remarks
		Operational	Good	Fair	Poor	
WINDLASS/WINCHES/CAPSTANS (ILO 134 Art. 4 §3g) Winch bed structure/structural integrity Self tensioning devices Wire/rope drums Drum ends and whelps Protection guards over moving parts Platforms/operator stand Platform/stand structure Brake linings Swivels Securing pins Adequate lighting (SOLAS '74 Ch. II-1 Reg. 40 / ILO 134 Art. 4 §3a) **For electro-hydraulic equipment** Piping arrangements Drip trays/save-alls Drip tray plugs **For steam driven equipment** Piping arrangements Pipe insulation						
MOORING ROPES/WIRES (ILO 134 Art. 4 §3g) Rope reels Ropes Wires Wire ropes/nylon tail Insurance wire Emergency towing wires Spare ropes Spare wires Fairleads Old man rollers Panama leads						
ANCHOR EQUIPMENT (ILO 134 Art. 4§3g) Bow anchors Stern anchor Spare anchor Anchor cables Shackle marks Securing chains Devil's claw Cable stoppers Smit type bracket and mooring chain Hawse pipe covers Bitter end release Bridge indication of shackles paid out						

State last date of testing   Windlass   Testing due:
    Winches   Testing due:
    Capstan   Testing due:
State date of turning anchor chains end for end
Means of communication (talkback – portable VHF)

Figure 2.6.1 Mooring and anchor equipment checklist

STEERING FAILURE CHECKLIST

A IMMEDIATE ACTION	B CONSIDER/ CARRY OUT	C REPORT TO OWNERS
01 Inform engine room ❏ 02 Inform master ❏ 03 NUC lights/shapes exhibited ❏ 04 Make appropriate sound signals ❏ 05 Keep VHF watch ❏ 06 Follow switch over procedures and engage manual/emergency steering as appropriate ❏ 07 Take way off ship if necessary (inform engine room) ❏ 08 Broadcast to other ships ❏ 09 Pass vessel's position to R/O-Radio Room ❏ 10 Use bowthruster for course corrections ❏ 11 Check vessel's position at regular intervals & keep R/O-R/R informed ❏	01 Steering gear room to be manned as per emergency procedures ❏ 02 Investigate situation ❏ 03 Record time, observations and damage ❏ 04 Establish type of damage (damage to steering gear or loss/damage to rudder) ❏ 05 Inspect damaged items in accordance with manufacturer's instructions ❏ 06 State type of damage ❏ 07 State extent of damage ❏ 08 Establish cause of damage ❏ 09 Check if damaged item can be repaired or is to be replaced ❏ 10 Check if permanent or temporary repairs can be carried out ❏ 11 Check if required spare parts are on board or fill out a store/spare part order form ❏ 12 Use correct and appropriate terminology in accordance with manufacturers instruction manual. Make reference to page, section, # ❏ 13 Ascertain whether repairs can be carried out by ships crew or if shore assistance is required ❏ 14 Check if other problems are to be expected ❏ 15 Consider all safety aspects prior to carrying out repairs ❏ 16 Keep damaged parts onboard for future reference ❏ 17 Take photographs ❏ 18 Make protest letter ❏	01 Time/date of incident (+ LT) ❏ 02 Exact position of ship ❏ 03 Current conditions ❏ 04 Weather conditions & forecast ❏ 05 Distance from coast/nearest land/ nearest port ❏ 06 Damaged machinery/equipment(use proper terminology) ❏ 07 State type of damage ❏ 08 State extent of damage ❏ 09 State cause of damage ❏ 10 State if onboard repairs can be carried out (makeshift or permanent) ❏ 11 State if shore advice/assistance is required ❏ 12 State if spares are to be delivered onboard ❏ 13 State if docking is required ❏ 14 State time necessary for onboard repair ❏ 15 Will vessel be able to proceed after repairs + ETA at port of refuge or destination) ❏ 16 Is vessel able to complete current voyage? ❏ 17 Is towage/salvage assistance required? ❏ 18 State actual condition and keep owner informed about progress ❏ 19 State if further problems are to be expected ❏ 20 List materials used for repairs ❏ 21 State coast station for radio contact or other means of communication ❏

Figure 2.11.2 Steering failure checklist

HELICOPTER OPERATIONS CHECKLIST

A — PREPARING FOR HELICOPTER ASSISTANCE/OPERATIONS	B — LANDING PROCEDURES	C — TAKE-OFF PROCEDURES	D — REPORT TO OWNERS
01 Define whether helicopter hook handling or landing operations will be involved ☐	01 Advise crew at landing area about time/moment of landing ☐	01 Agree take-off procedures with helicopter pilot ☐	01 Reason for helicopter assistance ☐
02 Select the most appropriate hook handling/landing area (keep deck strength in mind) ☐	02 Avoid shipping seas/sprays on deck during landing manoeuvre ☐	02 Tune radio equipment and establish radio contact deck-bridge and ship/helicopter ☐	02 Date and time of helicopter landing and take-off ☐
03 Remove obstructions/secure loose objects and equipment ☐	03 Inform deck crew to keep clear of rotors and exhausts ☐	03 Undo lashings and store them well away from the take-off area ☐	03 Any anomalies during helicopter operations, such as damage or injuries ☐
04 Hoist pennant/windsock in conspicuous position ☐	04 Give proper and clear signs to pilot during landing manoeuvre ☐	04 Observe same precautions/guidelines as during landing operations ☐	04 Whether operations was completed successfully ☐
05 Establish communication between landing area and bridge ☐	05 Ask pilot whether helicopter should be secured ☐	05 Record date and time of take-off and confirm operation successfully completed ☐	05 Delays encountered on account of helicopter operations ☐
06 Establish communication between ship and helicopter ☐	06 Keep detailed records of data time/course/speed/communications/landing time/reason for helicopter operations/any anomalies ☐		
07 Confirm when landing area is ready for landing ☐	18 Consider weather conditions ☐		
08 Ensure appropriate firefighting equipment is readily available ☐	19 Discuss most appropriate heading/speed with helicopter pilot ☐		
09 Keep firefighting squad ready for intervention ☐	20 Prepare rope messengers for helicopter securing ☐		
10 Pressurise fire main and keep fire pumps running ☐	21 Avoid intermittent discharge from pipelines/manifolds ☐		
11 Prepare medical assistance team and arrange hospital to receive injured persons ☐	22 (Gas tankers) Avoid emission of gas/vapours on deck (when no IGS is fitted) ☐		
12 Prepare a rescue room ☐	23 (Tankers) Release pressure from cargo tanks (30 minutes before helicopter operations) ☐		
13 Prepare rescue boat (ready for launching) ☐	24 (Tankers) Reduce IG pressure in cargo tanks ☐		
14 Ensure emergency equipment is readily available (crowbar, wire cutters, red emergency signal/torch, marshalling batons) ☐	25 (Tankers) Secure tank openings following venting operations ☐		
15 Arrange for proper illumination of deck area ☐	26 (Bulk carriers) Cease all surface ventilation to dry bulk cargoes and batten down hatch covers and access lids ☐		
16 Only allow necessary crew on deck/at landing area ☐			
17 Consider ship's course/speed ☐			

Stamp: USUALLY FOUND ON BOARD

Figure 2.11.17 Helicopter operations checklist

SHIP SAFETY MEETING MINUTE FORMAT / GUIDELINES

M.V: .... **Date:** .... **Port:** ....

Persons attending the meeting:		
Rank	Name	Signature
Master		
First Officer		
Chief Engineer		
Second Officer		
Other		
Other		

Safety meeting started at: .... hrs.   and was completed at: .... hrs.

Meeting Agenda

01. Review previous minutes.
02. Discussion of outstanding items.
03. Trading/current trade safety/health hazards. (cargo, ballast, bunker, stowage/lashing and securing operations) precautionary measures.
04. Deficiencies/damages to safety equipment and corrective action.
05. Discuss accident, hazardous occurrences, danger situations.
06. Safety information communicated to company.
07. Safety information received from company.
08. Planning of next drills and consideration of scenarios.
09. Discuss on board training issues.
10. Welfare and recreation items.
11. Safety related items proposed/introduced by non-team members.
12. Safety of riding crew, shore labourers, visitors.
13. Corrective actions to be taken.

Note:
File original minute as appropriate in ship's file   ❑
Send copy to office/company   ❑
Display copy on crew messroom notice board   ❑
Display copy on notice board in officer's messroom   ❑

Figure 2.12.16 Ship safety meeting minute format/guidelines

Chapter 10

FLAG STATES AND THE SHIPMASTER

by Captain D.J.F. Bruce FNI, Senior Vice President – Europe, International Registries Inc.

Captain David J.F. Bruce went to sea in 1956 and, after serving as master with Canadian Pacific Steamships, took up shore employment with the Milford Haven Port Authority. He has worked with marine administrations and shipping registries since 1972, first with Liberian Services Limited and then, after a period as Chief Marine Surveyor for the Isle of Man Government, he took up his present position as Senior Vice President – Europe with International Registries Inc., (IRI), in 1994.

IRI manages the maritime registries for Liberia and the Marshall Islands. In charge of the operation of IRI's four European offices, Captain Bruce is responsible for safety inspections within Europe, Africa and the Middle East, handling ship registrations and, as Senior Deputy Commissioner for the Marshall Islands Marine Administration, attends IMO meetings for them in that capacity.

Definition

The flag state is the country in which a vessel is registered and which has jurisdiction over that vessel and the certification of the crew, including the master. The master must ensure that he is aware of, and complies with, the requirements of the flag state relating to the operation of his vessel. He should cooperate with the flag state in any investigations and in the making of any necessary reports.

Flag states and the shipmaster

The relationship between shipmaster and a flag state is one which is dictated by law, developed over the ages according to changing needs and the position of the master. As all are aware, the master is the person in command of a ship – but such privilege also has its responsibilities, and these are well detailed by flag state administrations. In taking command of a ship, the master is the person appointed by the shipowner to take care of the owner's property and, as such, may be appointed and removed from office by the shipowner. His duties, responsibilities and authority are therefore governed firstly by his contract of employment with the shipowner, by the general employment law of the country of the contract, and by the maritime law of the country in which his vessel is registered.

Why flag state?

Vessels sailing on the high seas possess a national character usually granted by the registration of the vessel in the public records of a state. This then permits the vessel to fly the flag of and be subject to the laws of that state. International law protects principles such as that of the 'freedom of the high seas', but it also looks to individual flag states to enforce compliance with safety and environmental requirements over the national fleets under their jurisdiction. Hence the concept of flag state control has been, traditionally, the primary basis for the control of vessels.

The duties and responsibilities of the flag state are contained within a multiplicity of international conventions and regulations which set the parameters for the role of the flag state. One such convention is the United Nations Convention on the Law of the Sea which declares that each state may decide the conditions for entry onto its register. However, Article 94 of the convention delineates the jurisdiction and control the flag state may assert over the administrative, technical and social matters of vessels flying its flag as are necessary to ensure safety at sea. It establishes steps which may be taken by the flag state such as to ensure the utilisation of qualified surveyors and the provision of proper navigational equipment on board vessels. It also requires that appropriate manning be on board and crew appropriately qualified.

A flag state's national legislation has, as its basis, the provisions of international conventions – many of these having been adopted through the International Maritime Organization (IMO). These international conventions are adopted by the member countries of IMO, and each government then undertakes to give effect to their provisions – by including them within the government's national laws, and by implementing and enforcing the requirements of each such convention. However, whilst virtually all flag states are members of IMO, their acceptance and implementation of international conventions are by no means total. Complications arise where vessels of countries not party to a particular convention still have to comply with the provisions of that convention if they are to be able to trade internationally. And, in that case, the master may have to rely upon the national laws of the port state for guidance. However, international conventions are minimum standards, and many countries – or flag states – have additional requirements or higher standards in their national legislation. These higher standards apply to a vessel registered in that country.

Certification of the vessel

As proof that a vessel complies with the provisions of international conventions, certificates are, after survey, issued to a vessel, by or on behalf of the flag state. Although the surveys in this connection are frequently carried out by classification society surveyors, and the certificates issued by them, these certificates remain the responsibility of the flag state.

The number of these 'statutory' certificates required to be carried by a vessel is ever increasing, and it is wise for the master to maintain a file of certificates with a separate list detailing the expiry dates of the certificates and the dates when the next surveys or inspections are due.

On taking over command, the master should verify that the vessel's certificates are in order. These certificates are frequently the first items to be checked by port state control inspectors, so it is vital that a complete record is maintained.

Due to the large number of certificates issued under International Conventions, the permutations of vessels required to be so certificated and the gradual implementation of the Harmonised System of Survey and Certification, it is not possible to give here an accurate listing of required certificates. If in any doubt as to whether a vessel is required to be issued with a particular certificate, the master should refer to Annex 3 of the SOLAS Consolidated Edition 1997, published by IMO, which lists, in some detail, certificates and documents required to be carried on board and thereafter to refer to the applicable convention.

Certification of the master

Whilst the training of seafarers has been going on for hundreds of years, it was only in 1978 that the first comprehensive international conference on the training of seafarers was held. This gave rise to the International Convention on Standards of Training Certification and Watchkeeping of Seafarers (STCW) which came into force in 1984. An extensive revision of the convention in 1995 is still being progressively introduced.

The maritime law of the flag state will normally lay down the qualifications and certification (based upon the STCW Convention) required by the person permitted to be master of a vessel registered in that state. Also, as a result of these 1995 revisions to the STCW Convention, it is required that the master (and officers) of a vessel hold certification issued by the flag state administration. Accordingly, a master, in addition to probably holding certification issued by his own national government, is required to hold certification (known as an endorsement) issued by the flag state of the vessel on which he is master.

Traditionally, a ship's officer, and subsequently a master would have been certificated by his country of nationality. He would be trained in accordance with that country's laws, would have a knowledge of the maritime law of that country, and would have sailed on vessels registered in that country. He would no doubt also have been sailing to and from that same country, in which it might be said that the ship was based.

However, the last half century has seen a rise in the number of ship registers and in the popularity of open registers. It is now very likely that a shipmaster will be sailing on a vessel which is not registered in the country of his nationality. This has placed an additional burden upon the shipmaster, for no longer need he only be aware of the laws of his own country, the country which originally certificated him and found him competent to be master, but he must also be aware of the laws of the country of registry of the vessel – or flag state.

Whilst the basic responsibilities of the master and requirements under the convention remain the same, flag state administrations do have differing national legislation regarding the operation of a vessel, and of which the master must have knowledge. It is therefore incumbent upon the master to be aware of the particular National requirements of a particular flag state prior to joining a vessel otherwise he might not be able to operate the vessel to the requirements of that flag state. This requirement is also contained within the STCW Convention Regulation 1/10 which states:

Measures shall be established to ensure that seafarers who present, for recognition, certificates issued under the provisions of regulations II/2, III/2 or III/3, or issued under VII/1 at the management level, as defined in the STCW Code, have an appropriate knowledge of the maritime legislation of the administration relevant to the functions they are permitted to perform.

Accordingly, it would not be acceptable for a master or officer to state on some future occasion that he was not aware of the national legislation of the country of registry of his vessel. This is particularly important today with the implementation of the International Safety Management (ISM) Code, where maintenance of operational procedures is required for both the Document of Compliance (DOC) and the Safety Management Certificate (SMC) to remain valid.

For the master who did not study for, nor pass an examination held by the flag state, this knowledge is obtained from the regulatory publications supplied by the flag state. In some cases, applicants for officer certification based upon equivalency, are required to sign that they have received a copy of and are aware of the national legislation relating to their functions. Such a declaration, for instance, is included within the application forms for both Liberia and Marshall Islands certification. Therefore, on taking over command, the master must make sure that adequate information regarding flag state requirements, is available on board.

It is important to realise that, whilst a state may issue certification to a person certifying they are competent to be the master of a ship, it is the flag state administration which issues the certification, or license, for a person to be master of a vessel registered in that flag state. It has already been established that the jurisdiction of the flag state applies on board that vessel.

Therefore, in disciplinary matters, the state which has issued the master's certificate of competency or license shall alone be competent, after due legal process, to pronounce the withdrawal of such certificates, even if the holder is not a national of the state which issued them. (Law of the Sea Convention, Article 97). One anomaly to this is that, following such a hearing, a certificate holder may have the certificate issued by that flag state withdrawn, while still be able to retain certificates issued by other flag states.

What does the flag state require of a master?

Simply put, the master is responsible to the flag state administration for the safety of a vessel, and for operating the vessel in accordance with the provisions of all International Conventions to which the flag state is a party (such as SOLAS, COLREGS, MARPOL); other conventions, such as those developed through the International Labour Organization, to which the flag state is also a party; and to that flag state's national legislation. This national legislation is based upon the international conventions as indicated above. That is the 'catch all', but some specifics are:

1) To enter into shipping articles with seamen:
The master is responsible for the conduct and care of the crew – responsible that all crew sign the Articles of Agreement and that the terms of this agreement are maintained.

This places the master in the position of being both employer and employee. Whilst the master is employed by the owner, he employs the seafarers on board his vessel and, therefore, also has the right to discharge them. In this, he is no different from a plant manager ashore.

Flag states will normally have their own form of shipping articles – the need for which is provided in ILO Convention No 22. These Articles of Agreement constitute an employment contract and it is up to the master to ensure that their provisions are complied with by the crew members. It is of course a two way contract. It must also be ensured that the obligations to the seafarers are complied with by the company and by the master.

The master is permitted to make entries in the Seafarer's Official Discharge Book or Record Book issued by the flag state, or may issue Certificates of Service testifying to that seafarer's service on board a vessel. In the event of a dispute with the seafarer with regard to contractual obligations, the master must attempt to mediate before referring the matter to the flag state administration.

2) To maintain discipline on board the vessel and to take all such steps as are necessary and appropriate (bearing in mind that the law of the flag state applies)
Penalties which may be imposed for breaches of discipline will be given in the laws of the flag state.

3) To assume responsibility for the receipt of cargo by the vessel, stowage of cargo on board the vessel insofar as such stowage affects the safety or navigation of the vessel, and for the discharge of cargo from the vessel.

4) To assume full responsibility for the safety of the members of the crew and passengers, if any.

5) To render assistance in the saving of life and property at sea.

6) To assume full responsibility for the navigation of the vessel
This includes:

- The responsibility that the vessel will be fully and correctly manned with properly certificated seafarers in accordance with the provisions of a Minimum Safe Manning Certificate issued by the flag state.
- Compliance with the Regulations for the Prevention of Collisions at Sea.
- Compliance with the appropriate sections of the SOLAS Convention Chapter V (including the necessity to have on board up to date charts and nautical publications for the voyage; to maintain an efficient lookout whilst at sea and to report ice sighted at sea, etc.).

7) To see that the log books of the vessel are properly and accurately kept
Here, a master must be guided by the specific requirements of the flag state. Some states have their own Official Log Book which must be on board and utilised. Other states require that specific entries are made in the Bridge Log Book. Regardless, such entries will nearly always include:

- Change of command.
- A record of offences and penalties imposed (see para 2 above).
- Births, marriages or deaths. Note that under the laws of certain flag states, the master may also marry passengers or other persons on board; issue birth certificates for children born at sea; or bury persons who have died on board the vessel while at sea.
- A record of accidents or incidents affecting the vessel or persons on board. This includes major incidents such as collisions, groundings, fires, equipment failures, spills of hazardous and/or polluting substances, personal injuries or deaths on board.
- Load line and draft information prior to departure.

- Details of boat and fire drills, musters and emergency exercises, such as the lowering and taking away of boats, or instruction in the use of the line throwing apparatus. Note that different flag states stipulate different time intervals for conducting such drills, many of whose requirements are more frequent than the minimum stipulated in SOLAS.
- Closing and opening of watertight doors and other emergency drills such as the testing of emergency steering gear.
- Stowaway searches prior to leaving port.

The above is just a sample of the type of entries which should be made in the 'official' or Bridge Log Book and reference should be made to the requirements of individual flag states in this regard. There are numerous other log books and records that must also be maintained – Oil Record Book, Cargo Record Book, Medical Log Book, Engine Room and Deck Logbooks, Engine Order or Movement Books or Records – all of which should record the daily workings of the vessel together with details of any unusual occurrences.

The master should be aware that many flag states operate their own ship safety inspection regimes and the contents of log books will be checked during periodic inspections. Not only will failure to maintain log books correctly result in a report or letter from the flag state administration to the ship manager or owner, it may now be deemed to be a nonconformity with the provisions of the ISM Code. So the Safety Management Certificate for the vessel could be in jeopardy.

It is very wise for a master, if in doubt, to make an entry in the log book. One never knows when a contemporaneous record may be of use to the master or ship owner.

8) To keep in his custody all the vessels documents, the vessel's funds, and control the use and disbursement thereof

9) To make all reports as may be required by the flag state according to their laws and regulations

This is very important. Flag states do not like to be ignored. Failure to make required reports may be deemed to be a nonconformity within the ISM Code and so could result in the suspension of the Safety Management Certificate for the vessel. What should be reported?

- A change of command of the vessel.
- Changes of officers and crew on board.
- Accidents to the vessel or crew or persons on board. (The flag state may have minimum requirements before such reporting needs to be made.)
- Vessel detention by port state control authorities or other bodies.
- Any reports or pending prosecutions for alleged violations of regulations such as oil pollution allegations, allegations of pollution by garbage; allegations of violations of traffic separation schemes. The master should be aware that the flag state will be advised of those alleged violations by the port or coastal state involved, but would much prefer to have received a report from the master first. If the master does not report, then the flag state will be in contact with the ship owner, ship manager or even with the master directly.

10) To cooperate in flag state investigations

If a master is involved in a casualty or incident which results in an investigation by flag state authorities, it is expected that the master will cooperate with the flag state inspectors or investigating officers. If the master cooperates fully, he will usually find the flag state looking much more kindly upon any violations, than if they are forced to find out for themselves. Should the master be unlucky enough to be called to attend an investigation, he should cooperate fully. The master will not be able to avoid the consequences, bearing in mind that the flag state is the body which issued the certificate of competency to be master of that vessel and, as mentioned before, they have the right to withdraw that certificate.

Responsibilities of the shipmaster

A shipmaster has many responsibilities. He is responsible to the owner for the ship, the crew and the out-turn of the voyage. He is responsible to the cargo owner for the care of the cargo and he is responsible to the public through the flag state administration. Keeping all these demands in balance can be difficult at times but a good relationship with the flag state, complying in a timely manner with flag state requirements, will ensure that the ship is not held up or disadvantaged, particularly through port state control.

SOLAS Consolidated Edition 1997
Annex 3
Certificates and documents required
to be carried on board ships
(Note: All certificates to be carried on board must be originals)

	Reference
1 All ships	

International Tonnage Certificate (1969)

An International Tonnage Certificate (1969) shall be issued to every ship, the gross and net tonnage of which have been determined in accordance with the Convention.

Tonnage Convention, art. 7

International Load Line Certificate

An International Load Line Certificate shall be issued under the provisions of the International Convention on Load Lines, 1966, to every ship which has been surveyed and marked in accordance with the Convention.

LL Covention, art. 16

International Load Line Exemption Certificate

An International Load Line Exemption Certificate shall be issued to any ship to which an exemption has been granted under and in accordance with article 6 of the Load Line Convention.

LL Convention, art. 6

Intact Stability Booklet

All ships of 24 m and over shall be inclined on completion and the elements of their stability determined. The master shall be supplied with a Stability Booklet containing such information as is necessary to enable him, by rapid and simple procedures, to obtain accurate guidance as to the ship under varying conditions of loading.

SOLAS 1974, reg. II-1/22

Minimum safe manning document

Every ship to which chapter 1 of the Convention applies shall be provided with an appropriate safe manning document or equivalent issued by the Administration as evidence of the minimum safe manning.

SOLAS 1974 (1989 amdts.) reg. V/13(b)

Certificates for masters, officers or ratings

Certificates for masters, officers or ratings shall be issued to those candidates who, to the satisfaction of the Administration, meet the requirements for service, age, medical fitness, training, qualifications and examinations in accordance with the provisions of the annex to the Convention on Standards of Training, Certification and Watchkeeping for Seafarers, 1978. Certificates for masters and officers issued in compliance with this article shall be endorsed by the issuing Administration in the form prescribed in regulation I/2 of the annex.

STCW 1978, art. VI

International Oil Pollution Prevention Certificate

MARPOL 73/78, Annex 1, reg. 5

An International Oil Pollution Prevention Certificate shall be issued after survey in accordance with regulation 4 of Annex I of MARPOL 73/78, to any oil tanker of 150 gross tonnage and above and any other ship of 400 gross tonnage and above which are engaged in voyages to ports or offshore terminals under the jurisdiction of other Parties to MARPOL 73/78. The certificate is supplemented by a Record of Construction and Equipment for Ships Other Than Oil Tankers (Form A) or a Record of Construction and Equipment for Oil Tankers (Form B), as appropriate.

Oil Record Book
Every oil tanker of 150 gross tonnage and above and every ship of 400 gross tonnage and above other than an oil tanker shall be provided with an Oil Record Book, Part I (Machinery space operations). Every oil tanker of 150 gross tonnage and above shall also be provided with an Oil Record Book, Part II (Cargo/ballast operations).

MARPOL 73/78, Annex 1, reg. 20

Shipboard Oil Pollution Emergency Plan
Every oil tanker of 150 gross tonnage and above and every ship other than an oil tanker of 400 gross tonnage and above shall carry on board a Shipboard Oil Pollution Emergency Plan approved by the Administration. In the case of ships built before 4 April 1993 this requirement shall apply 24 months after that date.

MARPOL 73/78, Annex 1, reg. 26

2.   **In addition to the certificates listed in section 1 above, passenger ships must carry:**

Passenger Ship Safety Certificate[1]
A certificate called a Passenger Ship Safety Certificate shall be issued after inspection and survey to a passenger ship which complies with the requirements of chapters II-1, II-2, III and IV and any other relevant requirements of SOLAS. A record of equipment for the Passenger Ship Safety Certificate (Form P) shall be permanently attached.

SOLAS 1974, reg. 1/12, as amended by the GMDSS amdts.

Exemption Certificate[2]
When an exemption is granted to a ship under and in accordance with the provisions of SOLAS 1974, a certificate called an Exemption Certificate shall be issued in addition to the certificate listed above.

SOLAS 1974, reg. 1/12

Special trade passenger ships
A form of safety certificate for special trade passenger ships, issued under the provisions of the Special Trade Passenger Ships Agreement 1971.

STP Agreement reg. 6

Special Trade Passenger Ships Space Certificate
Issued under the provisions of the Protocol on Space Requirements for Special Trade Passenger Ships, 1973.

SSTP 73 rule 5

3.   **In addition to the certificates listed in section 1 above, cargo ships must carry:**

Cargo Ship Safety Construction Certificate[3]
A certificate called a Cargo Ship Safety Construction Certificate shall be issued after survey to a cargo ship of 500 gross tonnage and over which satisfies the requirements for cargo ships on survey, set out in regulation I/10 of SOLAS 1974, and complies with the applicable requirements of chapters II-1 and II-2, other than those relating to fire-extinguishing appliances and fire control plans.

SOLAS 1974, reg.I/12, as amended by the GMDSS amdts.

Cargo Ship Safety Equipment Certificate[4]
A certificate called a Cargo Ship Safety Equipment Certificate shall be issued after survey to a cargo ship of 500 gross tonnage and over which complies with the relevant requirements of chapters II-1, II-2 and III and any other relevant requirements of SOLAS 1974. A Record of

SOLAS 1974, reg. 1/12, as amended by the GMDSS amdts.

---

*   The form of the certificate and its record of equipment may be found in the DMDSS amendments to SOLAS 1874.

\+   SI.S 14/Circ. 115 refers to the issue of exemption certificates.

**   The form of the certificate may be found in the GMDSS amendments to SOLAS 1974.

Equipment for the Cargo Ship Safety Equipment Certificate (Form E) shall be permanently attached.

Cargo Ship Safety Radio Certificate[5]

A certificate called a Cargo Ship Safety Radio Certificate shall be issued after survey to a cargo ship of 300 gross tonnage and over, fitted with a radio installation, including those used in life-saving appliances which complies with the requirements of chapters III and IV and any other relevant requirements of SOLAS 1974. A Record of Equipment for the Cargo Ship Safety Radio Certificate (Form R) shall be permanently attached.

SOLAS 1974, reg. 1/12, as amended by the GMDSS amdts.

Exemption Certificate[6]

When an exemption is granted to a ship under and in accordance with the provisions of SOLAS 1974, a certificate called an Exemption Certificate shall be issued in addition to the certificates listed above.

SOLAS 1974, reg. 1/12

Document of compliance with the special requirements for ships carrying dangerous goods

An appropriate document as evidence of compliance with the construction and equipment requirements of that regulation.

SOLAS 1974, reg. 11-2/54.3

Dangerous goods manifest or stowage plan

Each ship carrying dangerous goods shall have a special list or manifest setting forth, in accordance with the classification set out in regulation VII/2, the dangerous goods on board and the location thereof. A detailed stowage plan which identifies by class, and sets out the location of all dangerous goods on board, may be used in place of such a special list or manifest. A copy of one of these documents shall be made available before departure to the person or organization designated by the port State authority.

SOLAS 1974, reg. VII/5(5); MARPOL 73/78, Annex III, reg. 4

---

* The form of the certificate and its record of equipment may be found in the GMDSS amendments to SOLAS 1974.

+ SLS. 14/Circ. 115 refers to the issue of exemption certificates.

Document of authorization for the carriage of grain

A document of authorization shall be issued for every ship loaded in accordance with the regulations of the International Code for the Safe Carriage of Grain in Bulk either by the Administration or an organization recognized by it or by a Contracting Government on behalf of the Administration. The document shall accompany or be incorporated into the grain loading manual provided to enable the master to meet the stability requirements of the Code.

SOLAS 1974, reg. VI/9; International Code for the Safe Carriage of Grain in Bulk, section 3

Certificate of insurance or other financial security in respect of civil liability for oil pollution damage

A certificate attesting that insurance or other financial security is in force shall be issued to each ship carrying more than 2,000 tons of oil in bulk as cargo. It shall be issued or certified by the appropriate authority of the State of the ship's registry after determining that the requirements of article VII, paragraph 1, of the CLC Convention have been complied with.

CI.C.69, art. VII

Enhanced survey report file[7]

A survey report file and supporting documents complying with paragraphs 6.2 and 6.3 of annex A and annex B of resolution A.744(18). Guidelines on the enhanced programme of inspections during surveys of bulk carriers and oil tankers.

MARPOL 73/78, Annex 1, reg. 13G; SOLAS 1974 reg. XI/2

4. **In addition to the certificates listed in sections 1 and 3 above, where appropriate, any ship carrying noxious liquid chemical substances in bulk shall carry:**

International Pollution Prevention Certificate for the Carriage of Noxious liquid Substances in Bulk (NLS Certificate)

An international pollution prevention certificate for the carriage of noxious liquid substances in bulk (NLS certificate) shall be issued, after survey in accordance with the provisions of regulation 10 of Annex II of MARPOL 73/78, to any ship carrying noxious liquid substances in bulk and which is engaged in voyages to ports or terminals under the jurisdiction of other Parties to MARPOL 73/78. In respect of chemical tankers, the Certificate of Fitness for the Carriage of Dangerous Chemicals in Bulk and the International Certificate of Fitness for the Carriage of Dangerous Chemicals in Bulk, issued under the provisions of the Bulk Chemical Code and the International Bulk Chemical Code, respectively, shall have the same force and receive the same recognition as the NLS Certificate.

MARPOL 73/78 Annex II, regs.12 and 12a

Cargo Record Book

Every ship to which Annex II of MARPOL 73/78 applies shall be provided with a Cargo Record Book, whether as port of the ship's official log-book or otherwise, in the form specified in appendix IV to the Annex.

MARPOL 73/78, Annex II, reg. 9

5. **In addition to the certificates listed in sections 1 and 3 above, where applicable, any chemical tanker shall carry:**

Certificate of Fitness of the Carriage of Dangerous Chemicals in Bulk

A certificate called a Certificate of Fitness for the Carriage of Dangerous Chemicals in Bulk, the model form of which is set out in the appendix to the Bulk Chemical Code, should be issued after an initial or periodical survey to a chemical tanker engaged in international voyages which complies with the relevant requirements of the Code.

Note: The Code is mandatory under Annex II of MARPOL 73/78 for chemical tankers constructed before 1 July 1986.

BCH Code, section 1.6

or

International Certificate of Fitness for the Carriage of Dangerous Chemicals in Bulk

A certificate called an International Certificate of Fitness for the Carriage of Dangerous Chemicals in Bulk, the model form of which is set out in the appendix to the International Bulk Chemical Code, should be issued after an initial or periodicl survey to a chemical tanker engaged in international voyages which complies with the relevant requirements of the Code.

Note: The Code is mandatory under both chapter VII of SOLAS 1974 and Annex II of MARPOL 73/78 for chemical tankers constructed on or after 1 July 1986.

IBC Code, section 1.5

6. **In addition to the certificates listed in sections 1 and 3 above, where applicable, any gas carrier shall carry:**

Certificate of Fitness for the Carriage of Liquefied Gases in Bulk

A certificate called a Certificate of Fitness for the Carriage of Liquefied Gases in Bulk, the model form of which is set out in the appendix to the Gas Carrier Code, should be issued after an initial or periodical survey to a gas carrier which complies with the relevant requirements of the Code.

GC Code, section 1.6

or

International Certificate of Fitness for the Carriage of Liquefied Gases in Bulk
A certificate called an International Certificate of Fitness for the Carriage of Liquefied Gases in Bulk, the model form of which is set out in the appendix to the International Gas Carrier Code, should be issued after an initial or periodical survey to a gas carrier which complies with the relevant requirements of the Code.
Note: The Code is mandatory under chapter VII of SOLAS 1974 for gas carriers constructed on or after 1 July 1986.

IGC Code, section 1.5

7.   In addition to the certificates listed in sections 1 and 3 above, where applicable, high-speed craft must carry:[8]

High-Speed Craft Safety Certificate
A certificate called a High-Speed Craft Safety Certificate should be issued after completion of an initial or renewal survey to a craft which complies with the requirements of the High-Speed Craft (HSC) Code in its entirety.

SOLAS 1974, reg. X/3; HSC Code, para. 1.8

---

[8] Subject to entry into force of the amendments adopted by the 1994 SOLAS Conference on 24 May 1884

Permit to Operate High-Speed Craft
A certificate called a Permit to Operate High-Speed Craft should be issued to a craft which complies with the requirements set out in paragraphs 1.2.2 to 1.2.7 and 1.8 of the HSC Code.

HSC Code, para. 1.9

Miscellaneous other certificates

Special purpose ships

Special Purpose Ship Safety Certificate
A certificate may be issued after survey in accordance with the provisions of paragraph 1.6 of the Code of Safety for Special Purpose Ships. The duration and validity of the certificate should be governed by the respective provisions for cargo ships in SOLAS 1974. If a certificate is issued for a special purpose ship of less than 500 gross tonnage, this certificate should indicate to what extent relaxations in accordance with 1.2 were accepted.

Resolution A.534(13)

Additional Certificate for Offshore Supply Vessels
When carrying such cargoes, offshore supply vessels should carry a Certificate of Fitness issued under "Guidelines for the transportation and handling of limited amounts of hazardous and noxious liquid substances in bulk on offshore support vessels".

Resolution   A.673(16); MARPOL 73/78, Annex II, reg. 13(4)

If an offshore supply vessel carries only noxious liquid substances, a suitably endorsed International Pollution Prevention Certificate for the Carriage of Noxious Liquid Substances in Bulk may be issued instead of the above Certificate of Fitness.

Diving Systems

Diving System Safety Certificate
A certificate should be issued either by the Administration or any person or organization duly authorized by it after survey or inspection to a diving system which complies with the requirements of the Code of Safety for Diving Systems. In every case, the Administration should assume full responsibility for the certificate.

Resolution A.536(13), section 1.6

Dynamically supported craft

Construction and Equipment Certificate
To be issued after survey carried out in accordance with paragraph 1.5.1(a) of the Code of Safety for Dynamically Supported Craft.

Resolution A.373(X), section 1.6

Permit to operate

Mobile Offshore Drilling Units

Safety Certificate

To be issued after survey carried out in accordance with the provisions of the Code for the Construction and Equipment of Mobile Offshore Drilling Units, 1979, or, for units constructed on or after 1 May 1991, the Code for the Construction and Equipment of Mobile Offshore Drilling Units, 1989.

Resolution A.414(XI) section 1.6; resolution A.649(16) section 1.6

Noise levels

Resolution A.468(XII), section 4.3

Noise Survey Report

A noise survey report should be made for each ship in accordance with the Code on Noise Levels on Board Ships.

Chapter 11

PORT STATE CONTROL AND THE U.S.A.

Principal Features at a glance – an extract from *Port State Control* published by The UK P&I Club

Agency

THE UNITED STATES COAST GUARD.

Jurisdiction

Foreign ships operating in US waters are subject to inspection under Title 46 United Stales Code (USC) Chapter 33. Reciprocity is accorded to ships of countries that are parties to the Convention for the Safety of Life at Sea (SOLAS) (46 USC 3303(a)). In addition, certain provisions of the pollution prevention and navigation safety regulations (33 Code of Federal Regulations (CFR) 154-156 and 164 respectively) apply to foreign ships operating in US waters.

Relevant instruments

Applicable domestic statutes

- 46 United States Code (USC) 5101-5116. Load line requirements for foreign ships.
- 46 USC 2101 (12) 3306(a)(5) and 49 USC 1801-1812. Safety requirements for carriage of dangerous articles and substances aboard foreign ships.
- 46 USC 2101 (12) (21) and (35), 3504 and 3505. Safety requirements for foreign ships carrying passengers from any US port to any other place or country.
- 46 USC 2101 (1 2), (21), (22) and (35), and Chapter 35. Inspection and certification requirements for all foreign passenger ships which embark passengers at and carry them from a US port. (These statutes are also relevant for ships having valid SOLAS 74/78 Certificates or Canadian Certificates of Inspection, that must be examined to verify compliance with the flag administration's safety verification requirement.)
- 46 USC 2101 (12) and (39), 3301 (10) and Chapter 37. Safety requirements that apply, with certain stipulations, to all foreign ships regardless of tonnage, size, or manner of propulsion, whether or not carrying freight or passengers for hire, that enter US navigable waters while carrying liquid bulk cargoes that are.
  a. Flammable or combustible
  b. Oil of any type or in any form, including petroleum, fuel oil, sludge, oil refuse and oil mixed with wastes, except dredged spoil.
  c. Designated as a hazardous substance under Section 311(b) of the Federal Water Pollution Control Act (FWPCA) (33 USC 1321) or . . .
  d. Designated as hazardous materials under Section 104 of the Hazardous Materials Transportation Act (HMTA) (49 USC 1803)
- 46 USC 2101 (21) and 3304. Permission for US

ships transporting cargo to carry a limited number of individuals without being considered a 'passenger ship' for most inspection purposes and extension of this privilege to cargo ships of those nations that accord reciprocal treatment.

- 46 USC 2101 (33) and 3301 (7). Directs that safety requirements of 46 USC Chapter 33 are applicable to seagoing motor ships of 300 or more gross tons.
- 46 USC 2101 (35) and 3301 (8). Safety requirements for foreign small passenger ships carrying more than six passengers from a US port.
- 50 USC 191. Requirements for security of ships, harbours and waterfront facilities, and provision for control of the movement of foreign ships in US waters by the local OCMI/COTP.
- 33 USC 1221-1232. Statutes for advance notice of arrival and navigation safety regulations.

Applicable Regulations

Most US regulations applicable to US and foreign ships, per Titles 33, 46 and 49 Code of Federal Regulations.

Applicable International Conventions

- International Convention on Load Lines 1966, as amended and its 1988 Protocol. (LOADLINES 66/88)
- International Convention for the Safety of Life at Sea (SOLAS), 1974, its Protocol of 1978, as amended, and the Protocol of 1988, (SOLAS 74 78/88).
- International Convention for the Prevention of Pollution from Ships, 1975, as modified by the Protocol of 1978, as amended (MARPOL 77/78).
- International Convention on Standards of Training, Certification and Watchkeeping for Seafarers 1978, as amended (STCW 95).
- Convention on the International Regulations for Preventing Collisions at Sea 1972, as amended (COLREG 72).
- Merchant Shipping (Minimum Standards) Convention, 1976 (ILO Convention 147).
- International Convention Relating to intervention on the High Seas in cases of Oil Pollution Casualties, 1975 and the Protocol relating to intervention on the High Seas in Cases of Marine Pollution by Substances other than Oil, 1983.

Ship Selection – The Boarding Priority Matrix

Until 1994, the US Coast Guard's ship boarding programme was largely ad hoc, but now they have developed a Boarding Priority Matrix to determine the probable risk posed by non-US ships calling at US ports. The Matrix is used to decide which ships Port State control inspectors should board on any given day, in any given port. Ships are assessed in various categories and then added together for a total point score This numerical score, along with other performance based factors, determines a ship's boarding priority from Priority I through IV.

In developing this points system, the US Coast Guard has identified five features which directly influence a ship's operational condition and compliance with international safety and environmental protection standards. These are:

1. Flag States
2. Classification societies
3. Owner and operators list
4. Ship type, and
5. History

The first three are particularly significant and are explained below.

Flag States

The flag list is composed of those flag states whose detention ratios exceed the average detention ratios for all flag states whose ships call at US ports.

A flag state's detention ratio is ascertained by dividing the number of its ships which have been detained in the last three years by the total number of its ships which have called at US ports within the same period. For example, if a flag has had three of its ships detained during the last three years, and a total of 60 of its ships have had US port calls in the same period, the detention ratio would be 360 x 100% = 5%. The average detention ratio is ascertained by dividing the total number of detentions by the total number of arrivals for all flag states.

The flag list is updated annually on 1 April and remains in effect for the ensuing twelve months. This information is sent to all Coast Guard Marine Safety Offices. A flag state is removed from the list when its detention average drops below the overall average flag state detention average or when it is associated with less than two detentions within a twelve month period.

Classification Societies

This consists of a two-stage process whereby any classification societies with less than ten arrivals to the US in the previous year are eliminated from the process.

Then, classification societies with more than ten distinct arrivals in the previous year are evaluated on their performance over the previous two years. Their performance is based on their detention ratio (number of detentions divided by number of distinct arrivals). This ratio is then compared to the average detention ratio (total number of detentions divided by the total number of distinct arrivals). Classification societies are then assigned points according to where their detention ratios fall in relation to the average detention ratio.

Below the Average Detention Ratio = 0 Points
Between the average and 2 times the average = 1 Point
Between 2 times and 3 times the average = 3 Points
Between 3 times and 4 times the average = 5 Points
More than 4 times the average = Priority 1

This list is sent to all Coast Guard Safety offices.

Owner/Operator List

The US Coast Guard Headquarters Ship Compliance Division (G-MOC-21) compiles a list of owners and operators associated with ships that have had more than one ship detained by the Coast Guard under the authority of an international convention within the last twelve month period. Any ship making a US port call that is owned or operated by a person or entity that has had that ship, or a different ship, subject to more than one intervention action within the last twelve months, is accorded high priority status.

The owners' list is updated monthly and is published on the USCG website and sent to all Coast Guard Marine Safety Offices. *see figure 11.1 – Point score summary.*

Boarding Priority Matrix – Priority I-IV and effects thereof

The points are added up for a total point score and the ship's boarding priority determined as follows:

Priority I ships:
- 17 or more points on the Matrix, or
- Ships involved in a marine casualty, or
- Where USCG Captain of the Port determines a ship to be a potential hazard to the port or the environment, or
- Ships whose classification society has ten or more arrivals the previous year and which a detention ratio more than four times the average, or
- Ships whose classification society has less than ten arrivals the previous year and which have been associated with at least one detention.

Port entry may be restricted until ship is examined by the Coast Guard. Priority I ships are targeted for examination prior to entry into US ports. Where feasible, these ships are boarded prior to port entry to ensure deficiencies are corrected. Otherwise, they are boarded upon entry and prior to commencement of cargo transfer operations or passenger embarkation.

Priority II ships:
- 7 to 16 points on the Matrix, or
- Outstanding requirements from a previous boarding in this or another US port, or
- The ship is overdue for an annual tank or passenger exam.

POINT SCORE SUMMARY		
Owner	Listed owner 5 pts	
Flag	Listed flag state 7 pts	
Class	Priority 1 OR	10 arrivals with detention ratio more than 4 times the average
		<10 arrivals, but involved in a detention in the previous 2 years
	5 points	10 arrivals with ratio between 3 & 4 times the average
	3 points	10 arrivals with ratio between 2 & 3 times the average
	1 point	10 arrivals with ratio between average and twice the average
	0 point	10 arrivals with ratio below average
	OR	<10 arrivals. 0 detentions in the previous 2 years
History	Intervention within 12 months 8 PtsEsa Other Oper. Control within 12 months 1PtEa Casualty within 12 months 1 PtEa Not boarded within 6 months 1 PtEa	
Ship Type	Oil or chemical tanker 1 Pt Gas carrier 1 Pts Bulk freighter > 10 years 2 Pts Passenger ship 1 Pts Carrying low value commodities in bulk 2 Pts	

Figure 11.1 Owner/Operator List – Point Score Summary

Cargo operations may be restricted until ship is examined by the Coast Guard. Priority II ships are targeted for boarding prior to commencement of cargo transfer operations or passenger embarkation. An exemption to the requirement for boarding prior to commencement of cargo transfer operations or passenger embarkation may be granted if there are clear indications that the ship is in substantial compliance with applicable standards.

Priority III ships:
*   4 to 6 points on the Matrix, or
*   Alleged deficiencies reported, or
*   The ship is overdue for an annual freight examination

Priority III ships may be targeted for boarding after entry into port, but no operational restrictions are imposed.

Priority IV ships:
*   3 or fewer points on the Matrix

Priority IV ships are not targeted for boarding, but may be boarded and examined by the US Coast Guard at the discretion of the local Captain of the Port or the Officer in Charge, Marine Inspection.

Ship Inspection Principles

In addition to the Boarding Priority Matrix the US Coast Guard has also published the 12 'principles' employed as guidance by its ship inspections. These are:

*   Detentions are conducted only when a ship is unfit to proceed to sea or poses a threat to the marine environment.

*   Voyage damage will not be associated with a classification society non-conformity unless other class-related deficiencies are noted during the course of the damage survey.

*   Class non-conformities will only be associated with equipment covered by a survey, conducted by class, or in which class issued the certificate on behalf of the flag state.

*   When multiple deficiencies are noted, only those deficiencies serious enough to justify detention will be evaluated to determine class non-conformities.

*   Outdated equipment, when the cause of an intervention, will not be associated with a class non-conformity unless the equipment was outdated at the time of the last survey conducted by the class society on behalf of the flag state.

*   The absence of easily stolen equipment, such as fire hose nozzles and extinguishers, will generally not be listed as a class society non-conformity unless a large number are missing and the inspection takes place within 90 days of the last survey by the class society for the flag state.

*   Expired certificates will not be associated with a class non-conformity unless the certificates were not endorsed or were improperly issued by the class society when it conducted the last survey for the flag state.

*   Interventions based on manning issues will not be issued as class non-conformities.

*   A time limit of 90 days will generally be placed on associating non-conformities with equipment

failures, such as non-operational fire pumps, and emergency generators, unless it is apparent that the deficiency is long standing.

- Failure of human-factor-related testing - such as fire drills and abandon-ship drills - will be associated with a classification society non-conformity only when the class society issued the relevant certificate on behalf of the flag state within 30 days on inspection.
- Serious wastage or other structural deficiencies not caused by voyage damage will be listed as a class society non-conformity.

Note: The class society will be notified in writing in all cases on society non-conformities.

Definition/Terms of Reference

The following are key definitions and terms of reference employed by the USCG as part of its Port State Control programme.

Contravention. An act, procedure, or occurrence that is not in accordance with a convention or other mandatory instrument, or its operational annex.

Deficiency. A condition found not to be in compliance with the conditions of the relevant convention, law and regulation.

Detention. A control action which restricts a ship's right of free movement. The imposition of a restriction on the movement of a ship constitutes a detention regardless of whether or not a delay from a ship's normal or expected itinerary occurs. Detentions may be carried out under the authority of SOLAS 1974 as amended. Regulation 19, ICLL Article 21; MARPOL Article 5; STCW Article X and Regulation 1/4; ILO 147 Article 4; the Ports and Waterways Safety Act, or a US Customs detention.

Examination. The process of assessing a ship's compliance with the relevant provisions of applicable international conventions, domestic laws and regulations. The scope of an examination shall be to the extent necessary to verify the validity of the relevant certificates and other documents, and to ensure no unsafe conditions exist. An examination may include, but is not limited to, checks of documents, certificates, manuals, the ship's structural integrity, machinery, navigation, pollution prevention, engineering and safety systems, maintenance programmes and crew proficiency.

Intervention. A control action taken by a port state in order to bring a foreign flag ship into compliance with applicable international convention standards. Interventions are undertaken by a port state when a ship's flag state has not, can not, or will not exercise its obligations under an international convention to which it is a party. This may include requesting appropriate information, requiring the immediate or future rectification of deficiencies, detaining the ship,

or allowing the ship to proceed to another port for repairs.

Nonconforming Ship. Any ship failing to comply with one or more applicable requirements of US law or international conventions is a nonconforming ship. A nonconforming ship is not necessarily a substandard ship unless the discrepancies endanger the ship, persons on board, or present an unreasonable risk to the marine environment.

Substandard Ship. In general, a ship is regarded as substandard if the hull, machinery, or equipment, such as lifesaving, firefighting and pollution prevention, are substantially below the standards required by US laws or international conventions, owing to:
a. The absence of required principal equipment or arrangement.
b. Gross noncompliance of equipment or arrangement with required specifications.
c. Substantial deterioration of the ship structure or its essential equipment.
d. Noncompliance with applicable operational and/or manning standards or
e. Clear lack of appropriate certification, or demonstrated lack of competence on the part of the crew.

If these evident factors as a whole or individually endanger the ship, persons on board, or present an unreasonable risk to the marine environment, the ship should be regarded as a substandard ship.

Valid Certificates. A certificate that has been issued directly by a contracting government or party to a convention, or on the behalf of the government or party by a recognised organisation, and contains accurate and effective dates, meets the provisions of the relevant convention, and corresponds to the particulars of the ship and its equipment.

Types of Examination

USCG Port State Control examinations consist of annual examinations and then re-examinations or deficiency follow-up examinations. These examinations may be broadened in scope or depth into an expanded examination if clear grounds exist that lead a boarding team to believe that the condition of the ship or its equipment does not correspond with the certificates or the ship does not comply with applicable laws or conventions.

Annual Examinations

An annual examination consists of the specific procedures outlined in the freight, tank, or passenger ship examination chapters of the Marine Safety Manual. It includes an examination of the ship's certificates, licences and documents followed by a general examination, i.e. "walk through" of the ship to develop an impression of shell maintenance and the general state of the deck and side shell of the ship to determine its seaworthiness. It will also include examination and testing of specific equipment, as well as the conduct of operational testing and emergency drills to ensure the crew's proficiency at carrying out critical tasks. As a minimum, the following items are part of each annual examination and are taken from the MSM Volume 1, Chapter 19, which sets out the requirements listed below in greater detail.

Certificates, Licences and Documents
1. International Tonnage Certificate (1969)
2. Passenger Ship Safety Certificate
3. Cargo Ship Safety Certificate
4. Cargo Ship Safety Equipment Certificate
5. Cargo Ship Safety Radiotelegraphy Certificate
6. Cargo Ship Safety Radiotelephony Certificate
7. Cargo Ship Safety Radio Certificate
8. Exemption Certificates
9. International Certificate of Fitness for Carriage of Liquefied Gases in Bulk
10. Certificate of Fitness for the Carriage of Liquefied Gases in Bulk
11. International Certificate of Fitness for the Carriage of Dangerous Chemicals in Bulk
12. Certificate of Fitness for the Carriage of Dangerous Chemicals in Bulk
13. International Oil Pollution Prevention Certificate
14. International Pollution Prevention Certificate for the Carriage of Noxious Liquid Substances in bulk
15. International Load Line Certificate (1966)
16. International Load Line Exemption Certificate
17. Oil Record Book part I and II
18. Cargo Record Book
19. Minimum Safe Manning Document
20. Crew Licences or Certificate of Competency, Medical Certificates, of ILO Convention No 73 concerning Medical Examination of Seafarers
21. Stability information

Areas/items/operations
1. Deck Portion
2. Hull Portion
3. Ballast Tank Entry
4. Load Lines
5. Seaworthiness
6. Voyage Damage
7. Machinery Spaces
8. Operation
9. Maintenance
10. Tests and Trials
11. Oil and Oil, Mixtures
12. Sufficient Power
13. Lifesaving Equipment
14. Fire Safety Equipment
15. Fire Doors
16. Ventilation Systems
17. Escape Routes
18. Navigation Safety
19. Cargo Ship Safety Construction Items
20. Cargo Ship Safety Radio Operation
21. Equipment in Excess of Convention or Flag State Requirements
22. Garbage
23. Manuals and Instructions
24. Items to be Examined or Tested
25. Operational Tests
26. Muster List
27. Communication
28. Fire and Abandon Ship Drills
29. Damage Control Plan
30. Bridge Operation
31. Cargo Operation
32. Loading, Unloading and Cleaning Procedures for Cargo Spaces of Tankers
33. Dangerous Goods and Harmful Substances in Packaged Form

Re-examinations
A re-examination is an examination to ensure that a ship remains in compliance with appropriate US laws or international conventions between annual examinations. As with the annual examination, it usually consists of an examination of the ship's certificates, licences and documents, and a general examination conducted by walking through the ship. Except aboard passenger ships, a re-examination will not normally include operational testing or drills, but, in the case of foreign passenger ship re-examinations, the re-examination should include the witnessing of fire and abandon-ship drills to ensure that the ship's crew can adequately ensure the safety of the passengers in any emergency.

Expanded Examinations
An expanded examination is a more detailed examination or testing conducted when an annual examination, re-examination, or deficiency follow-up establishes "clear grounds" for believing that the condition of a ship, its equipment or crew are not in compliance with applicable US laws or international conventions. Expanded examinations should focus on those areas where "clear grounds" have been established and should not include other areas or systems unless the general impressions or observations of the boarding team support such examination.

"Clear Grounds" for an Expanded Inspection
To assist the boarding team, a list of deficiencies that establish "clear grounds" to expand an examination has been developed. The following deficiencies, grouped under the relevant conventions and/or codes, are considered of such a serious nature that they may warrant the detention of the ship involved. This list is not exhaustive.

General
Absent or invalid certificates required under applicable   conventions.

SOLAS
• Failure of proper operation of propulsion and other essential machinery as well as electrical installations.

- Insufficient cleanliness of engine room, excess amount of oil-water mixture in the bilges; insulation of piping including exhaust pipes in engine room contaminated by oil; and improper operation of bilge pumping arrangements.
- Failure of the proper operation of emergency generator, lighting, batteries and switches.
- Failure of the proper operation of the main and auxiliary steering gear.
- Absence, insufficient capacity, or serious deterioration of personal lifesaving appliances, survival craft and launching arrangements.
- Absence, noncompliance, or substantial deterioration - to the extent that it can not comply with its intended use - of fire detection system, fire alarms, fire fighting equipment, fixed fire extinguishing installation, ventilation valves, fire dampers and quick-closing devices.
- Absence, substantial deterioration, or failure of proper operation of the cargo deck area fire protection on tankers.
- Absence, noncompliance, or serious deterioration of lights, shapes, or sound signals.
- Absence, or failure of the proper operation, of the radio equipment for distress and safety communication.
- Absence, or failure of the proper operation of navigation equipment, taking the relevant provisions of SOLAS Chapter V/12(0) into account.
- Absence of navigation charts and/or all other relevant nautical publications necessary for the intended voyage, taking into account that electronic charts may be used as a substitute for the charts.
- Absence of non-sparking exhaust ventilation for cargo pump rooms.
- Serious noncompliance with procedures stipulated under the Certified Safety Management System on ships required to comply with SOLAS Chapter IX.

Areas Under the IBC Code
- Transport of a substance not mentioned in the Certificate of Fitness or missing cargo information.
- Missing or damaged high pressure safety devices.
- Electrical installations not intrinsically safe or not corresponding to the code requirements.
- Sources of ignition in hazardous locations.
- Contravention of special requirements.
- Exceeding of maximum allowable cargo quantity per tank.

Areas Under the IGC Code
- Transport of a substance not mentioned in the Certificate of Fitness or missing cargo information.
- Missing closing devices for accommodations or service spaces.
- Bulkhead not gastight.
- Defective air locks.

- Missing or defective quick closing valves
- Electrical installations not intrinsically safe or not corresponding to the code requirements
- Ventilators in cargo area not operable
- Pressure alarms for cargo tanks not operable
- Gas detection plant and/or toxic gas detection plant defective
- Transport of substances to be inhibited without valid inhibitor certificate

Areas under ICLL
- Significant areas of damage or corrosion, or pitting of plating and associated stiffening, in decks and hull affecting seaworthiness or strength to take local loads. However, this is waived if authorised temporary repairs for a voyage to a port for permanent repairs have been carried out.
- A recognised case of insufficient stability
- The absence of sufficient and reliable information in an approved form which, by rapid and simple means, enables the master to arrange for the loading and ballasting of the ship in such a way that a safe margin of stability is maintained at all stages and at varying conditions of the voyage, and that the creation of any unacceptable stresses in the ship's structure is avoided.
- Absence, substantial deterioration, or defective closing devices, hatch closing arrangements and watertight/weathertight doors.
- Overloading
- Absent or improper draft and/or Load Line Marks

Areas Under Marpol Annex I
- Absence, serious deterioration, or failure of proper operation of the oily-water filtering equipment, the oil discharge monitoring and control system, or the 15 ppm alarm arrangements.
- Remaining capacity of slop and/or sludge tank insufficient for the intended voyage.
- Oil record book not available
- Unauthorised discharge bypass fitted

Areas Under Marpol Annex II
- Absence of Procedures and Arrangements Manual
- Cargo not categorised
- No cargo record book available
- Transport of oil-like substances without satisfying the requirements or without an appropriately amended certificate
- Unauthorised discharge bypass fitted

Areas Under STCW
- Number, composition, or certification of crew not corresponding with Safe Manning Document.

Areas Under ILO 147
- Insufficient food for voyage to next port
- Insufficient potable water for voyage to next port
- Excessively unsanitary conditions on board
- No heating in accommodation of a ship operating in areas where temperatures may be excessively low.

For further details on the above points, consult the MSM Volume 1, Chapter 19.

Intervention and Detention

Detention

Interventions of the USCG, may involve:

- allowing the ship to sail with the deficiency uncorrected (e.g. a warning).
- corrective action prior to returning to a US port.
- allowing the ship to proceed to a specific port for repairs.
- denying port entry.
- detaining the ship in port until the deficiencies are corrected.

If a USCG inspector takes an intervention action against a ship, the flag state must be notified of all the circumstances, in addition to the classification society as well as the International Maritime Organisation (IMO). If the ship is allowed to depart without all identified deficiencies being corrected, the USCG must also notify the authorities of the next port of call of the uncorrected deficiencies.

Appeals Procedure

A detention decision may be appealed under the provisions of Title 46, Code of Federal regulations (CFR), Part 1.03-20 of Title 33, CFR, Part 160.7. The appeal must be in writing within 30 days after the decision is made or action is taken, and should give reasons as to why the decision or action should be set aside or revised. It should be addressed to the Coast Guard officer in command where the decision was made or action was taken, generally the Officer in Charge, Marine Inspection (OCMI), Captain of the Port (COTP), or Commanding Officer, Marine Safety Office (CO.MSO).

If the initial appeal is unsuccessful, a formal appeal may be made to the District Commander. A further formal appeal may be made to Coast Guard Headquarters.

Note: While a request for reconsideration or a formal appeal is pending, the original decision or actions remains in effect, unless specifically stayed by the District Commander or Headquarters.

Dissemination of Detention Information

Blacklisting - Detention Information

The Ship Compliance Division produces a List of Ships Detained, under the authority of Titles 14, 33, and 46, United States Code.

This List of Ships Detained includes the ship name, IMO number, date of detention, ship type, port, flag, classification society and deficiency summary.

The list is subject to change without notice based on appeals made by the owner, operator, and/or classification society.

General Publicity Information

There is a lot of helpful information as to the criteria employed by the USCG published by the United States Coast Guard and available on the internet at http://www.dot.gov/dotinfo/uscg/hq/g-m/psc/psc.htm. See in particular the Marine Safety Manual, Volume 1, Chapter 19. The US Coast Guard Headquarters' Port State Control Branch may be reached at the following address:

Commandant (G-MOC-2)
US Coast Guard
2100 Second Street S.W.
Washington DC 20593-0001

Arrangements have also been made to exchange information with other port state authorities, international organisations, regional authorities, etc.

This chapter is provided by kind permission of the UK P&I Club.

Chapter 12

DISTRESS – THE MASTER'S RESPONSIBILITIES

extracts from Peril at Sea and Salvage – The International Chamber of Shipping

The need for assistance

WHEN A SHIP SUFFERS a casualty or is otherwise in a position of peril, the master must decide, as a matter of urgency, whether assistance, including salvage assistance, is needed or if the situation can be handled using the ship's own resources.

The master's responsibility

The master should be authorised to take whatever measures he considers necessary to protect life, his ship and the environment, without reference to a third party.

Authority of the master

The authority of the master is not altered by engaging salvors. He remains in command of the ship despite the presence of a salvage master and he should therefore ensure that he is fully aware of the action taken in the rendering of salvage services. Even though services have been accepted and assistance is being rendered, the salvor must cease his services in response to a reasonable request to do so by the master.

The master should cooperate fully with the salvors, who are experts in salvage operations and in so doing exercise due care to prevent or minimise damage to the environment. He should take account of any advice given by the salvage master or other person in charge of rendering or advising on salvage services. The salvors may not be experts in the safety and handling of cargo or familiar with the ship. If in doubt about the advisability of any action suggested by the salvors, the master should not hesitate to challenge the advice given, bearing in mind his overriding responsibility for the safety of those onboard, the ship and its cargo.

Legislation may exist in some countries requiring the master to accept services or instructions provided by the coastal state concerned. In such cases the coastal state to which the occurrence has been reported may be expected to inform the master of national requirements. However, the master should also consult documents on board which might contain guidance, e.g. sailing directions, notices to mariners, etc.

Assessment of urgency

The master should immediately assess the dangers to which the ship is exposed and the urgency with which assistance may be required from outside sources. It is better to overreact on the side of safety and pollution prevention than to delay action in the hope that the situation may improve. When making judgements, it should be assumed that the situation will not improve.

Account should be taken of all circumstances including the following:

- Safety of personnel.
- Proximity to shore or shoal water.
- Weather and sea conditions.
- Current and tide.
- Nature of sea bed and shoreline.
- Potential for safe anchoring.
- Availability of assistance.
- Damage already sustained by the ship.
- Risk of further damage to the ship.
- Prospect of maintaining communications.
- Threat of pollution.
- Manpower and material requirements.

In addition to any threat to life, ship and cargo, the necessity to avoid or reduce the risk of pollution cannot be emphasised too strongly.

Obtaining assistance

Once the master has decided that assistance is necessary, he should act promptly to request it from any available source using the most expeditious means at his disposal. When one or more suitable ships respond to the call for assistance, the master should immediately request such ship(s) to undertake whatever action is necessary.

Assistance should never be delayed merely to negotiate a particular form of agreement or contract terms.

Generally, those rendering beneficial assistance to a ship in peril are entitled to salvage. It is not essential to agree upon the contractual terms for the assistance required, since there is a right under maritime law to salvage which exists independently of contract.

If the assisting ship(s) request(s) the master to agree to a contract for the assistance, Lloyd's Standard Form of Salvage Agreement, known as Lloyd's Open Form (see Appendices C and D), is the form most usually offered and should be agreed upon to avoid any delay in assistance being rendered. The Lloyd's Form provides protection for both parties to the salvage agreement.

Lloyd's Open Form has been revised to coincide with the incorporation into English law (with effect from 1 January 1995) of the provisions of the International Convention of Salvage 1989 (the "Salvage Convention"). The revised Forms bears the reference LOF 1995.

LOF 1995 can be agreed orally or by radio by sending the following message:

"ACCEPT SALVAGE SERVICES ON BASIS LLOYD'S STANDARD FORM LOF 1995 NO CURE NO PAY. ACKNOWLEDGE REPEATING FOREGOING. MASTER".

If an earlier edition of Lloyd's Open Form is offered and accepted, the message should refer to that Form.

The engagement of one salvor under LOF 1995 does not preclude the master from engaging other salvors. Similarly, the salvors may engage other salvors as sub-contractors. If more than one salvor is involved, every effort should be made to obtain the agreement of the salvors to cooperate with each other and to appoint one leading salvor.

Other forms of contract

It is possible that the ship offering assistance may decline LOF 1995 and propose other terms or an earlier edition of Lloyd's Open Form e.g. LOF 1980. If the master considers that immediate assistance is essential, he should accept the terms offered, but if he feels that the terms offered are unreasonable or extortionate he should register a protest immediately or, if he thinks that this may delay the assistance, on completion of the service. If the master considers that immediate assistance is not essential it may be possible, where time allows, to have the assistance arranged on a contractual basis stipulating ordinary tariff fixed lump sum or daily rates. However, it is emphasised that where life, the ship, its cargo or the marine environment are in peril, such negotiations should not in any way delay the engagement of the salvors.

Masters of oil tankers should note that LOF 1980 is likely to remain the preferred salvage contract for salvors involved in mid-ocean laden tanker casualties. This is due to the 'safety net provision' contained in LOF 1980. This provision requires that salvors, while performing salvage services, also use best endeavours to prevent the escape of oil from the ship and entitles salvors, as against the vessel owner only, to recover their reasonable expenses and an increment thereon of up to 15%. The provision applies only in respect of a tanker laden or partly laden with a cargo of oil and to cases where a salvor is either unable to earn any salvage remuneration because the salvage efforts are unsuccessful or only able to earn salvage remuneration which is inadequate to cover the salvor's expenses. Although LOF1995 provides for a similar (but more enhanced safety net), it is geographically restricted in that it is only applicable if the salvage operations prevented or minimised damage to the environment in 'coastal or inland waters or areas adjacent thereto'.

This extract is taken from Peril at Sea and Salvage, a guide for masters by kind permission of The International Chamber of Shipping.

Chapter 13

SALVAGE – CONTRACTS AND THE MASTER

by Mr. C.P. Beesley, Ince & Co., London

Chris Beesley has worked with Ince & Co., Maritime Solicitors, since 1972 primarily dealing with all aspects of marine casualty law and in particular salvage claims for shipowners and salvors. In 1979 he set up the firm's Hong Kong office from where he handled marine casualties throughout Asia and the Pacific Rim before returning to Ince & Co. London in 1984. He is joint Chairman of the firm's Admiralty Group. He travels extensively and frequently addresses seminars on safety and navigation issues and has had numerous articles published in his specialist areas. He has also delivered papers on salvage at the ever popular Nautical Institute Master and Maritime Law Series of seminars in Newcastle and at the International Tug and Salvage Symposium.

Summary

This chapter deals with the infrequent occurrence where a master may be confronted with a number of different salvage problems and contract wordings and examines his options from a practical rather than strictly legal viewpoint. The authority of the master to engage help and his duties and obligations under the most commonly used salvage contract (Lloyd's Open Form) are also considered.

Introduction

A vessel in distress requires assistance and depending on her circumstances may be required to seek help (MARPOL). A claim for salvage can be pursued at common law by anyone who is a volunteer (i.e. not acting under the existing obligation – for example a statutory duty that may be the case of some port authorities) and who saves property in danger that has some value. This long established formula, which still holds good today, is the foundation on which many published and widely used salvage contracts are based – the 'No Cure – No Pay' principle. There is no payment where property is not saved except in certain pollution related cases.

Successful salvage claims have been pursued by individuals (pilots, tug crew members, firemen and lifeboatmen for example) as well as companies, owners and crews of merchant ships, tugs and of course professional salvage companies. It is the intervention of tugs and the confusion over their terms of engagement (on "contract" or "tariff" terms, etc.) which gives rise to most legal disputes concerning entitlement to claim salvage. Salvage services can be refused or prohibited by ship's masters but only if 'reasonable' to do so[1]. Under those same conventions, masters of ships are obliged to render assistance to persons in distress at sea. Responding to a distress message however does not deprive a salvor of reward if property is salved. English law does not recognise the concept of life salvage (where only lives are saved)

but an enhanced salvage award will be made where lives as well as property were at risk and saved.

Types of salvage contract

The most common dedicated salvage contract in worldwide use is the Lloyd's Open Form. In its various guises, this contract has been in common use since 1908 and there have been ten versions of the contract published by the Council of Lloyd's since then. In those early days, the 'open' part of the title referred to the amount of the salvage award: either the amount was agreed between salvor and the ship's representatives and inserted in the contract or it was left 'open' for determination by arbitration in London at a subsequent date. The latest variant of the form, LOF 95, (and most of its recent predecessors) provides for assessment of the award by arbitration in London and a ship's master should not be concerned that in signing LOF he is exposing his owners and underwriters to an open ended payment of money. If the ship, its crew, cargo or the environment is in any way threatened by a particular misfortune then engaging suitable salvage help on Lloyd's Form terms (if available) will invariably be the most sensible thing to do. The level of the award will be determined by amicable negotiation or by arbitration applying criteria embodied in English (and also International) Law. An award will only become payable when property is saved ('no cure – no pay') except in certain circumstances when anti pollution measures are undertaken. Salvage operations which predate the agreement to LOF can be included within the LOF (clause 1 (d)).

A specimen LOF 95 appears in the appendices. Other versions of the form are also in use and contain very different terms, particularly LOF 80 (LOF 90 is not materially different to LOF 95 and if a contract is offered on these terms this probably represents 'old stock'). Space here does not allow a detailed comparison between LOF 80 and LOF 95 but significant differences in the level of the salvage awards under each could arise in certain circumstances on identical facts and it is very unlikely that a professional

---

[1] The Brussels Convention on Salvage 1910 and the London Salvage Convention 1989.

salvor will be offering the old version of the form by mistake. As in any situation where salvage assistance is being negotiated, then owners or local representatives of insurers should be consulted where the circumstances allow. Agreeing LOF rarely if ever creates grounds for a salvage claim where these did not exist previously. In the legal systems of most countries each interest salved (ship, cargo, freight and bunkers) will be responsible for paying its share of the ultimate award or settlement in proportion to the value of the property salved.

Most of the terms of LOF 95 relate to procedures which will not concern masters of salved ships. However, some clauses are of a practical operational character and should be familiar to masters, preferably in advance and certainly after the contract has been agreed or signed. In particular, masters should be aware of the following:

1 (a) The Contractor shall use his best endeavours:-

   (i)   To salve the "[ship]" and/or her cargo freight bunkers stores and any other property thereon and take them to .... or to such other place as may hereafter be agreed either place to be deemed a place of safety or if no such place is named or agreed to a place of safety and

   (ii) while performing the salvage services to prevent or minimise damage to the environment.

1 (d) In the event of the services referred to in this Agreement or any part of such services having been already rendered at the date of this Agreement by the Contractor to the said vessel and/or her cargo freight bunkers stores and any other property thereon the provisions of this Agreement shall apply to such services.

3. *Owners cooperation*: The owners their servants and agents shall cooperate fully with the contractor in and about the salvage including obtaining entry to the place named or the place of safety as defined in clause 1. The contractor may make reasonable use of the vessel's machinery gear equipment anchors chains stores and other appurtenances during and for the purpose of the salvage services free of expense but shall not unnecessarily damage abandon or sacrifice the same or any property the subject of this agreement.

5 (d) The owners of the vessel their servants and agents shall use their best endeavours to ensure that the cargo owners provide their proportion of salvage security before the cargo is released.

19. *Inducements prohibited*: No person signing this Agreement or any party on whose behalf it is signed shall at any time or in any manner whatsoever offer provide make give or promise to provide demand or take any form of inducement for entering into this Agreement.

International Convention on Salvage 1989
As incorporated into LOF 95, English and many other countries' domestic laws).

Article 6
2. The master shall have the authority to conclude contracts for salvage operations on behalf of the owner of the vessel. The master or the owner of the vessel shall have the authority to conclude such contracts on behalf of the owner of the property on board the vessel.

Article 8
Duties of the salvor and of the owner and master
1. The salvor shall owe a duty to the owner of the vessel or other property in danger:

   (a) to carry out the salvage operations with due care;
   (b) in performing the duty specified in sub-paragraph (a), to exercise due care to prevent or minimize damage to the environment;
   (c) whenever circumstances reasonably require, to seek assistance from other salvors; and
   (d) to accept the intervention of other salvors when reasonably requested to do so by the owner or master of the vessel or other property in danger; provided however that the amount of his reward shall not be prejudiced should it be found that such a request was unreasonable.

2. The owner and master of the vessel or the owner of other property in danger shall owe a duty to the salvor:

   (a) to cooperate fully with him during the course of the salvage operations;
   (b) in so doing, to exercise due care to prevent or minimize damage to the environment; and
   (c) when the vessel or other property has been brought to a place of safety, to accept redelivery when reasonably requested by the salvor to do so.

Modern communications now make it possible for masters to be in contact with their owners/managers and thus often allow discussion to take place before salvage help is taken. Some hull insurance companies actually require prior consultation and masters should be familiar with an insurers' own wishes in this respect – often through claims handbooks or circulars. Whilst the master has actual authority to enter into salvage contracts on behalf of the ship, her cargo and bunkers (regardless of ownership), where circumstances allow, consultation is always preferable. Owners/managers/insurers will have access to a number of international salvage companies and tug brokers and may be able to secure more favourable commercial terms than perhaps a master left to his own devices. Consultation also prevents an unfortunate situation developing where more than one salvor is engaged to do the same job resulting in the possibility of double payment.

Salvors, by the nature of the agreement entered into, generally take a risk when salving a stricken vessel. On occasions, the best equipment for the job may not readily be available and a vessel inappropriate for the entire contract may initially be offered on the understanding that a more substantial unit will be substituted at a later date. It is not uncommon, for example, for a harbour tug to be despatched in an attempt to stabilise the position initially, on the understanding that a more powerful vessel will be provided subsequently. The master needs to assess the risks that such proposals involve and ensure that insofar as is possible the best salvage "service" is selected. The closest salvor is not necessarily the best nor is the cheapest offer necessarily the one that should be accepted. Obviously the urgency and severity of the situation need to be taken into account, looking particularly at danger to life, risk to the environment and the safety of ship and cargo.

LOF or any other salvage contract does not have to be physically signed for there to be a binding contract in existence. There have been cases where LOF has been agreed over the VHF, by fax, telephone or cable.

Other 'standard' printed forms of salvage agreement also exist and contracts from the following areas are occasionally seen: Turkey, The Peoples Republic of China, some FSU countries, some Scandinavian countries, Germany and Japan. Professional salvors tend to prefer the certainty of LOF however and this is also true of most underwriters and P&I Clubs where no fixed price agreement can be reached.

Most of the recent changes to LOF (and some of its overseas 'cousins') have been driven by changing world attitudes to the environment and the need to encourage salvors to be particularly careful to prevent or reduce environmental damage – even where little or no residual property value remains at the end of the job. To take account of ever changing global needs and problems, a new LOF is being discussed by the LOF Working Group and it is quite possible that we will see LOF 99 or 2000.

Fixed rate or lump sum contracts will invariably be entered into when there is no threat of imminent danger. Almost always in these circumstances, the contract will be negotiated and signed ashore.

In a salvage situation there is frequently danger and many worrying aspects for the master to consider. In most cases the last thing the master thinks of is keeping a running note of key facts, position lines, day's run, engine movements, availability of personnel, communications, details of the salvage agreement and so on. Because salvage awards are settled generally by arbitration the master will need to testify in court and contemporary records, if possible with photographs, will be invaluable when the case is heard, generally months and sometimes even years after the event.

Other forms of salvage contracts

A contract to perform assistance does not have to be in writing for a successful salvage claim to be made. A discussion over the VHF or an exchange of written messages constitutes a contract upon which the foundations for a salvage claim exist. The most common of such cases are the services "at request" or "engaged services". If a vessel in difficulties requests a passing vessel to stand by whilst repairs are made or weather abates then a successful salvage claim can be made. The ship standing by, does not have physically to make fast or board the casualty (unless requested to do so) for her owners, master and crew to recover an award. To be successful in this respect, the ship and/or cargo must be saved – nothing would be recoverable in the event that the ship was totally lost – whether or not her crew were successfully rescued. If a vessel is engaged to undertake a specific task (such as towage service) then merely standing by, having failed to connect or perform the towage requested will give rise to no award. The "comfort" created by a vessel standing by to enable a crew to work on a stricken vessel will however give rise to a claim as will the provision of spare parts to a vessel in difficulty or the supply of some additional technical expertise.

In the *UNDAUNTED*[2] a ship lost her anchors in heavy weather and a passing merchant vessel was requested to seek a replacement anchor and cable. The merchant vessel duly put into port in accordance with this request but in the meantime the *UNDAUNTED* reached port safely partly under her own power and partly under tow of another vessel. The requested services gave rise to a successful salvage claim.

The rationale behind engaged services is easy to understand. The mere presence of a vessel standing by (invariably a merchantman) whilst essential repairs are undertaken can very often provide the comforting difference between property (and lives) being saved or the ship and her cargo becoming totally lost. "Salvors" in these situations deserve encouragement by way of salvage award. The law of contract applies equally to salvage as it does in many other walks of life. If a request is made for a job to be performed and the job is successfully completed in accordance with the terms of the request then a reward is payable. Similarly, if an offer to perform a job is accepted and performed then again remuneration will be payable. This is the most basic form of salvage contract and masters should always take particular care in choosing words for discussions with third parties as misunderstandings can and do frequently occur.

---

[2]   (1928) 31 LLR 339

Photograph courtesy of Hong Kong Salvage & Towage Company Ltd.

*Figure 13.1 A routine berthing operation could give rise to a salvage
claim if something unexpected happens.*

Photograph by M.J. Gaston, courtesy of Howard Smith Towage & Salvage

Figure 13.2 A vessel in difficulty requires salvage assistance

Legal procedures

Lloyd's Form currently provides for determination of the salvors remuneration by way of arbitration in London. Much of the wording of the Lloyd's Form contract is taken up by the procedural methods by which the salvors claim will be brought before a single Arbitrator in London. There is a right of appeal from that Arbitrator and, in rare cases, awards can be heard by the Courts in England if any point of law is involved or the Arbitrator has perhaps mis-conducted himself in some way.

In a salvage situation, danger to life and property is often present and the master has many worrying matters to consider. In most cases the last thing the master will think of is to keep a running note of key facts, position of ship and tugs, deployment of lines and wires, engine movements and other details of the salvage operation. Masters should bear in mind that whether or not they are required to give evidence in person at any subsequent stage (and hearings can take place years after the event) detailed records of events should be maintained and that those records are likely to come under close scrutiny in the future. Tape recordings, photographs and videos of key events may prove valuable and put vital matters, which may become contentious, beyond dispute.

Following the successful termination of salvage services it is usual for shipowners or their insurers to appoint a third party to investigate the circumstances of the casualty and the facts surrounding the salvage services. Invariably the investigator will be a lawyer – perhaps with seagoing experience, but in smaller value cases, surveyors, local agents or even owners themselves have been known to undertake the on board investigation. Arbitrations in London under LOF are almost always conducted on documents alone. When LOF has been agreed there is no dispute that the services are salvage by nature giving rise to the entitlement to remuneration. There is accordingly very little issue relating to the underlying merits of the claim. Experienced Arbitrators appointed by Lloyd's are accustomed to dealing with issues of dispute on facts occurring during the salvage services. If a salvage claim is heard by the Court or by way of a submission to arbitration without salvage being admitted then the need for oral evidence becomes more relevant and, in certain cases, ship's masters have been called to give evidence before the Court or Arbitrator. This will take place after a passage of time and the need to record facts as early as possible after the events giving rise to the salvage claim cannot be stressed too highly as this will form the backbone of any evidence given subsequently. Lawyers will assist ships masters and senior officers in preparing to give their evidence in this way.

In certain jurisdictions outside England, it is possible that the master's evidence will be taken orally by way of deposition. This is very rare indeed in salvage cases but ships' masters should be aware that they can face Court procedures in this way at short notice and ensure that in conjunction with their owners and insurers they have arranged adequate preparation time before any evidence is given.

Salvage claims under common law – that is to say where no contract has been agreed or specific request for help made – are not uncommon and salvors may wish to begin legal proceedings before the courts of the location where the services are alleged to have taken place. Tug owners in Italy, for example, are keen to have matters determined before the courts of their own country although, in almost all cases, amicable negotiation between all parties generally leads to a conclusion of the case short of a Court or arbitration hearing. In some cases it is possible that local Court procedure will require the master to give oral evidence soon after the incident in question either before the Court or perhaps to a specially appointed Court Surveyor.

Salvage without contract

Whether seen by a ship's master or not, every ship arriving or leaving port with the assistance of tugs has (through her owners or agents) entered some form of contract. Frequently, the terms of that contract will be agreed in advance and be performed efficiently and without recourse to any claim. Tugs are engaged 'per movement' or 'per hour' and all parties to the transaction are usually happy – an invoice is rendered and paid.

Many masters are surprised to learn that without their having agreed (in writing or verbally) to any variation of that original contract, circumstances can arise where a salvage claim can be generated by the assisting tugs and/or their crews. The sudden onset of bad weather or an intervening casualty such as fire or grounding can turn a routine berthing operation on tariff terms into a salvage situation. The leading authority on the subject[3] summarised the test to be applied as follows:

"To constitute a salvage service by a tug under contract to tow two elements are necessary:

That the tow is in danger by reason of circumstances which could not reasonably have been contemplated by the parties;

That risks are incurred or duties performed by the tug which could not reasonably be held to be within the scope of the contract."

There is little a ship's master can do in these circumstances and he may sometimes be more than happy that 'salvors' are on hand to help (even at an enhanced rate of pay). Masters should, however, be aware that where circumstances arise which were not envisaged at the time the original contract for

---

[3]   (1860) Lush 90 @ 92

assistance was entered into then a separate salvage claim may be pursued.

Masters are often surprised to find themselves involved in a salvage claim long after they have left the port in question. It is by no means unheard of for masters to first hear of a claim from the lawyer boarding his ship to collect evidence relating to the incident! An agreement for a tug to assist heave an anchor or turn a ship through the wind without clearly agreeing terms will almost certainly provide the necessary ingredients for a successful salvage claim. If an agreement to tug assistance on "tariff" terms is made then those terms should be clearly spelled out and recorded – preferably in writing or if necessary on tape (audio or video). Masters and senior officers should have in mind the useful guidelines and suggestions in the Nautical Institute publication, *The Masters Role in Collecting Evidence*. Additional helpful material is contained in *Peril at Sea and Salvage — A guide for Masters*, jointly published by the International Chamber of Shipping and the Oil Companies International Marine Forum.

Conclusion

In summary, masters should be aware that they have authority to engage salvage assistance appropriate in extent and form to the circumstances they face and consistent with ISM on board procedures and SOPEP plans. LOF is the most commonly used and accepted salvage contract but some insurers/owners/managers are more keen than others to explore alternatives and masters should be aware of any specific instructions in this respect. Extreme care should be taken when engaging assistance from harbour tugs to ensure terms of engagement are clearly understood by all parties.

LOF 1995

LLOYD'S

STANDARD FORM OF

NOTES

1.   Insert name of person signing on behalf of Owners of property to be salved. The Master should sign wherever possible.

2.   The Contractor's name should always be inserted in line 4 and whenever the Agreement is signed by the Master of the Salving vessel or other person on behalf of the Contractor the name of the Master or other person must also be inserted in line 4 before the words "for and on behalf of". The words "for and on behalf of" should be deleted where a Contractor signs personally.

3.   Insert place if agreed in clause 1(a)(i) and currency if agreed in clause 1(e).

SALVAGE AGREEMENT

(APPROVED AND PUBLISHED BY THE COUNCIL OF LLOYD'S)

NO CURE - NO PAY

On board the..

Dated.................................

+ See Note 1 above

IT IS HEREBY AGREED between Captain+..
for and on behalf of the Owners of the "..." her
cargo freight bunkers stores and any other property thereon (hereinafter collectively called "the Owners")
and..for and on behalf of ....

* See Note 2 above

....(hereinafter called "the Contractor"*) that:-

1.   (a)   The Contractor shall use his best endeavours:-

 # See Note 3 above

(i)   to salve the ".."and/or her cargo freight bunkers
stores and any other property thereon and take them to #... or
to such other place as may hereafter be agreed either place to be deemed a place of safety or if no such
place is named or agreed to a place of safety and
(ii)   while performing the salvage services to prevent or minimize damage to the environment.

(b)   Subject to the statutory provisions relating to special compensation the services shall be rendered and accepted as salvage services upon the principle of "no cure - no pay."

(c)   The Contractor's remuneration shall be fixed by Arbitration in London in the manner hereinafter prescribed and any other difference arising out of this Agreement or the operations thereunder shall be referred to Arbitration in the same way.

(d)   In the event of the services referred to in this Agreement or any part of such services having been already rendered at the date of this Agreement by the Contractor to the said vessel and/or her cargo freight bunkers stores and any other property thereon the provisions of this Agreement shall apply to such services.

(e)   The security to be provided to the Council of Lloyd's (hereinafter called "the Council") the Salved Value(s) the Award and/or any Interim Award(s) and/or any Award on Appeal shall be in

 # See Note 3 above

.... currency.

(f)   If clause 1(e) is not completed then the security to be provided and the Salved Value(s) the Award and/or Interim Award(s) and/or Award on Appeal shall be in Pounds Sterling.

(g)   This Agreement and Arbitration thereunder shall except as otherwise expressly provided be governed by the law of England, including the English law of salvage.

15.1.08
3.12.24
13.10.26
12.4.50
10.6.53
20.12.67
23.2.72
21.5.80
5.9.90
1.1.95

PROVISIONS AS TO THE SERVICES

2. *Definitions*: In this Agreement any reference to "Convention" is a reference to the International Convention on Salvage 1989 as incorporated in the Merchant Shipping (Salvage and Pollution) Act 1994 (and any amendment thereto). The terms "Contractor" and "services"/"salvage services" in this Agreement shall have the same meanings as the terms "salvor(s)" and "salvage operation(s)" in the Convention.

3. *Owners Cooperation*: The Owners their Servants and Agents shall co-operate fully with the Contractor in and about the salvage including obtaining entry to the place named or the place of safety as defined in clause 1. The Contractor may make reasonable use of the vessel's machinery gear equipment anchors chains stores and other appurtenances during and for the purpose of the salvage services free of expense but shall not unnecessarily damage abandon or sacrifice the same or any property the subject of this Agreement.

4. *Vessel Owners Right to Terminate*: When there is no longer any reasonable prospect of a useful result leading to a salvage reward in accordance with Convention Article 13 the owners of the vessel shall be entitled to terminate the services of the Contractor by giving reasonable notice to the Contractor in writing.

PROVISIONS AS TO SECURITY

5. (a) The Contractor shall immediately after the termination of the services or sooner notify the Council and where practicable the Owners of the amount for which he demands salvage security (inclusive of costs expenses and interest) from each of the respective Owners.

(b) Where a claim is made or may be made for special compensation, the owners of the vessel shall on the demand of the Contractor whenever made provide security for the Contractor's claim for special compensation provided always that such demand is made within two years of the date of termination of the services.

(c) The amount of any such security shall be reasonable in the light of the knowledge available to the Contractor at the time when the demand is made. Unless otherwise agreed such security shall be provided (i) to the Council (ii) in a form approved by the Council and (iii) by persons firms or corporations either acceptable to the Contractor or resident in the United Kingdom and acceptable to the Council. The Council shall not be responsible for the sufficiency (whether in amount or otherwise) of any security which shall be provided nor the default or insolvency of any person firm or corporation providing the same.

(d) The owners of the vessel their Servants and Agents shall use their best endeavours to ensure that the cargo owners provide their proportion of salvage security before the cargo is released.

6. (a) Until security has been provided as aforesaid the Contractor shall have a maritime lien on the property salved for his remuneration.

(b) The property salved shall not without the consent in writing of the Contractor (which shall not be unreasonably withheld) be removed from the place to which it has been taken by the Contractor under clause 1(a). Where such consent is given by the Contractor on condition that the Contractor is provided with temporary security pending completion of the voyage the Contractor's maritime lien on the property salved shall remain in force to the extent necessary to enable the Contractor to compel the provision of security in accordance with clause 5(c).

(c) The Contractor shall not arrest or detain the property salved unless:-

    (i) security is not provided within 14 days (exclusive of Saturdays and Sundays or other days observed as general holidays at Lloyd's) after the date of the termination of the services or

    (ii) he has reason to believe that the removal of the property salved is contemplated contrary to clause 6(b) or

    (iii) any attempt is made to remove the property salved contrary to clause 6(b).

(d) The Arbitrator appointed under clause 7 or the Appeal Arbitrator(s) appointed under clause 13(d) shall have power in their absolute discretion to include in the amount awarded to the Contractor the whole or part of any expenses reasonably incurred by the Contractor in:-

    (i) ascertaining demanding and obtaining the amount of security reasonably required in accordance with clause 5.

    (ii) enforcing and/or protecting by insurance or otherwise or taking reasonable steps to enforce and/or protect his lien.

PROVISIONS AS TO ARBITRATION

7. (a) Whether security has been provided or not the Council shall appoint an Arbitrator upon receipt of a written request made by letter telex facsimile or in any other permanent form provided that any party requesting such appointment shall if required by the Council undertake to pay the reasonable fees and expenses of the Council and/or any Arbitrator or Appeal Arbitrator(s).

(b) Where an Arbitrator has been appointed and the parties do not proceed to arbitration the Council may recover any fees costs and/or expenses which are outstanding.

8. The Contractor's remuneration and/or special compensation shall be fixed by the Arbitrator appointed under clause 7. Such remuneration shall not be diminished by reason of the exception to the principle of "no cure - no pay" in the form of special compensation.

REPRESENTATION

9. Any party to this Agreement who wishes to be heard or to adduce evidence shall nominate a person in the United Kingdom to represent him failing which the Arbitrator or Appeal Arbitrator(s) may proceed as if such party had renounced his right to be heard or adduce evidence.

CONDUCT OF THE ARBITRATION

10. (a) The Arbitrator shall have power to:-

(i) admit such oral or documentary evidence or information as he may think fit

(ii) conduct the Arbitration in such manner in all respects as he may think fit subject to such procedural rules as the Council may approve

(iii) order the Contractor in his absolute discretion to pay the whole or part of the expense of providing excessive security or security which has been unreasonably demanded under Clause 5(b) and to deduct such sum from the remuneration and/or special compensation

(iv) make Interim Award(s) including payment(s) on account on such terms as may be fair and just

(v) make such orders as to costs fees and expenses including those of the Council charged under clauses 10(b) and 14(b) as may be fair and just.

(b) The Arbitrator and the Council may charge reasonable fees and expenses for their services whether the Arbitration proceeds to a hearing or not and all such fees and expenses shall be treated as part of the costs of the Arbitration.

(c) Any Award shall (subject to Appeal as provided in this Agreement) be final and binding on all the parties concerned whether they were represented at the Arbitration or not.

INTEREST & RATES OF EXCHANGE

11. *Interest:* Interest at rates per annum to be fixed by the Arbitrator shall (subject to Appeal as provided in this Agreement) be payable on any sum awarded taking into account any sums already paid:-

(i) from the date of termination of the services unless the Arbitrator shall in his absolute discretion otherwise decide until the date of publication by the Council of the Award and/or Interim Award(s) and

(ii) from the expiration of 21 days (exclusive of Saturdays and Sundays or other days observed as general holidays at Lloyd's) after the date of publication by the Council of the Award and/or Interim Award(s) until the date payment is received by the Contractor or the Council both dates inclusive.

For the purpose of sub-clause (ii) the expression "sum awarded" shall include the fees and expenses referred to in clause 10(b).

12. *Currency Correction:* In considering what sums of money have been expended by the Contractor in rendering the services and/or in fixing the amount of the Award and/or Interim Award(s) and/or Award on Appeal the Arbitrator or Appeal Arbitrator(s) shall to such an extent and in so far as it may be fair and just in all the circumstances give effect to the consequences of any change or changes in the relevant rates of exchange which may have occurred between the date of termination of the services and the date on which the Award and/or Interim Award(s) and/or Award on Appeal is made.

PROVISIONS AS TO APPEAL

13. (a) Notice of Appeal if any shall be given to the Council within 14 days (exclusive of Saturdays and Sundays or other days observed as general holidays at Lloyd's) after the date of the publication by the Council of the Award and/or Interim Award(s).

(b) Notice of Cross-Appeal if any shall be given to the Council within 14 days (exclusive of Saturdays and Sundays or other days observed as general holidays at Lloyd's) after notification by the Council to the parties of any Notice of Appeal. Such notification if sent by post shall be deemed received on the working day following the day of posting.

(c) Notice of Appeal or Cross-Appeal shall be given to the Council by letter telex facsimile or in any other permanent form.

(d) Upon receipt of Notice of Appeal the Council shall refer the Appeal to the hearing and determination of the Appeal Arbitrator(s) selected by it.

(e) If any Notice of Appeal or Cross-Appeal is withdrawn the Appeal hearing shall nevertheless proceed in respect of such Notice of Appeal or Cross-Appeal as may remain.

(f) Any Award on Appeal shall be final and binding on all the parties to that Appeal Arbitration whether they were represented either at the Arbitration or at the Appeal Arbitration or not.

CONDUCT OF THE APPEAL

14. (a) The Appeal Arbitrator(s) in addition to the powers of the Arbitrator under clauses 10(a) and 11 shall have power to:-

   (i) admit the evidence which was before the Arbitrator together with the Arbitrator's notes and reasons for his Award and/or Interim Award(s) and any transcript of evidence and such additional evidence as he or they may think fit.
   (ii) confirm increase or reduce the sum awarded by the Arbitrator and to make such order as to the payment of interest on such sum as he or they may think fit.
   (iii) confirm revoke or vary any order and/or Declaratory Award made by the Arbitrator.
   (iv) award interest on any fees and expenses charged under paragraph (b) of this clause from the expiration of 21 days (exclusive of Saturdays and Sundays or other days observed as general holidays at Lloyd's) after the date of publication by the Council of the Award on Appeal and/or Interim Award(s) on Appeal until the date payment is received by the Council both dates inclusive.

(b) The Appeal Arbitrator(s) and the Council may charge reasonable fees and expenses for their services in connection with the Appeal Arbitration whether it proceeds to a hearing or not and all such fees and expenses shall be treated as part of the costs of the Appeal Arbitration.

PROVISIONS AS TO PAYMENT

15. (a) In case of Arbitration if no Notice of Appeal be received by the Council in accordance with clause 13(a) the Council shall call upon the party or parties concerned to pay the amount awarded and in the event of non-payment shall subject to the Contractor first providing to the Council a satisfactory Undertaking to pay all the costs thereof realize or enforce the security and pay therefrom to the Contractor (whose receipt shall be a good discharge to it) the amount awarded to him together with interest if any. The Contractor shall reimburse the parties concerned to such extent as the Award is less than any sums paid on account or in respect of Interim Award(s).

(b) If Notice of Appeal be received by the Council in accordance with clause 13 it shall as soon as the Award on Appeal has been published by it call upon the party or parties concerned to pay the amount awarded and in the event of non-payment shall subject to the Contractor first providing to the Council a satisfactory Undertaking to pay all the costs thereof realize or enforce the security and pay therefrom to the Contractor (whose receipt shall be a good discharge to it) the amount awarded to him together with interest if any. The Contractor shall reimburse the parties concerned to such extent as the Award on Appeal is less than any sums paid on account or in respect of the Award or Interim Award(s).

(c) If any sum shall become payable to the Contractor as remuneration for his services and/or interest and/or costs as the result of an agreement made between the Contractor and the Owners or any of them the Council in the event of non-payment shall subject to the Contractor first providing to the Council a satisfactory Undertaking to pay all the costs thereof realize or enforce the security and pay therefrom to the Contractor (whose receipt shall be a good discharge to it) the said sum.

(d) If the Award and/or Interim Award(s) and/or Award on Appeal provides or provide that the costs of the Arbitration and/or of the Appeal Arbitration or any part of such costs shall be borne by the Contractor such costs may be deducted from the amount awarded or agreed before payment is made to the Contractor unless satisfactory security is provided by the Contractor for the payment of such costs.

(e) Without prejudice to the provisions of clause 5(c) the liability of the Council shall be limited in any event to the amount of security provided to it.

GENERAL PROVISIONS

16. *Scope of Authority*: The Master or other person signing this Agreement on behalf of the property to be salved enters into this Agreement as agent for the vessel her cargo freight bunkers stores and any other property thereon and the respective Owners thereof and binds each (but not the one for the other or himself personally) to the due performance thereof.

17. *Notices*: Any Award notice authority order or other document signed by the Chairman of Lloyd's or any person authorised by the Council for the purpose shall be deemed to have been duly made or given by the Council and shall have the same force and effect in all respects as if it had been signed by every member of the Council.

18. *Sub-Contractor(s)*: The Contractor may claim salvage and enforce any Award or agreement made between the Contractor and the Owners against security provided under clause 5 or otherwise if any on behalf of any Sub-Contractors his or their Servants or Agents including Masters and members of the crews of vessels employed by him or by any Sub-Contractors in the services provided that he first provides a reasonably satisfactory indemnity to the Owners against all claims by or liabilities to the said persons.

19. *Inducements prohibited*: No person signing this Agreement or any party on whose behalf it is signed shall at any time or in any manner whatsoever offer provide make give or promise to provide demand or take any form of inducement for entering into this Agreement.

For and on behalf of the Contractor	**For and on behalf of the Owners of property to be salved.**
.... (To be signed by the Contractor personally or by the Master of the salving vessel or other person whose name is inserted in line 4 of this Agreement)	.... (To be signed by the Master or other person whose name is inserted in line 1 of this Agreement)

INTERNATIONAL CONVENTION ON SALVAGE 1989

The following provisions of the Convention are set out below for information only.

Article 1

Definitions

(a) *Salvage operation* means any act or activity undertaken to assist a vessel or any other property in danger in navigable waters or in any other waters whatsoever

(b) *Vessel* means any ship or craft, or any structure capable of navigation

(c) *Property* means any property not permanently and intentionally attached to the shoreline and includes freight at risk

(d) *Damage to the environment* means substantial physical damage to human health or to marine life or resources in coastal or inland waters or areas adjacent thereto, caused by pollution, contamination, fire, explosion or similar major incidents

(e) *Payment* means any reward, remuneration or compensation due under this Convention

Article 6

Salvage Contracts

1.   This Convention shall apply to any salvage operations save to the extent that a contract otherwise provides expressly or by implication

2.   The master shall have the authority to conclude contracts for salvage operations on behalf of the owner of the vessel. The master or the owner of the vessel shall have the authority to conclude such contracts on behalf of the owner of the property on board the vessel

Article 8

Duties of the Salvor and of the Owner and Master

1. The salvor shall owe a duty to the owner of the vessel or other property in danger:

    (a) to carry out the salvage operations with due care;

    (b) in performing the duty specified in subparagraph (a), to exercise due care to prevent or minimize damage to the environment;

    (c) whenever circumstances reasonably require, to seek assistance from other salvors; and

    (d) to accept the intervention of other salvors when reasonably requested to do so by the owner or master of the vessel or other property in danger; provided however that the amount of his reward shall not be prejudiced should it be found that such a request was unreasonable

2. The owner and master of the vessel or the owner of other property in danger shall owe a duty to the salvor:

    (a) to co-operate fully with him during the course of the salvage operations;

    (b) in so doing, to exercise due care to prevent or minimize damage to the environment; and

    (c) when the vessel or other property has been brought to a place of safety, to accept redelivery when reasonably requested by the salvor to do so

Article 13

Criteria for fixing the reward

1. The reward shall be fixed with a view to encouraging salvage operations, taking into account the following criteria without regard to the order in which they are presented below:

    (a) the salved value of the vessel and other property;

    (b) the skill and efforts of the salvors in preventing or minimizing damage to the environment;

    (c) the measure of success obtained by the salvor;

    (d) the nature and degree of the danger;

    (e) the skill and efforts of the salvors in salving the vessel, other property and life;

    (f) the time used and expenses and losses incurred by the salvors;

    (g) the risk of liability and other risks run by the salvors or their equipment;

    (h) the promptness of the services rendered;

    (i) the availability and use of vessels or other equipment intended for salvage operations;

    (j) the state of readiness and efficiency of the salvor's equipment and the value thereof

2. Payment of a reward fixed according to paragraph 1 shall be made by all of the vessel and other property interests in proportion to their respective salved values

3. The rewards, exclusive of any interest and recoverable legal costs that may be payable thereon, shall not exceed the salved value of the vessel and other property

Article 14

Special Compensation

1. If the salvor has carried out salvage operations in respect of a vessel which by itself or its cargo threatened damage to the environment and has failed to earn a reward under Article 13 at least equivalent to the special compensation assessable in accordance with this Article, he shall be entitled to special compensation from the owner of that vessel equivalent to his expenses as herein defined

2. If, in the circumstances set out in paragraph 1, the salvor by his salvage operations has prevented or minimized damage to the environment, the special compensation payable by the owner to the salvor under paragraph 1 may be increased up to a maximum of 30% of the expenses incurred by the salvor. However, the Tribunal, if it deems it fair and just to do so and bearing in mind the relevant criteria set out in Article 13, paragraph 1, may increase such special compensation further, but in no event shall the total increase be more than 100% of the expenses incurred by the salvor

3. Salvor's expenses for the purpose of paragraphs 1 and 2 means the out-of-pocket expenses reasonably incurred by the salvor in the salvage operation and a fair rate for equipment and personnel actually and reasonably used in the salvage operation, taking into consideration the criteria set out in Article 13, paragraph 1(h), (i) and (j)

4. The total special compensation under this Article shall be paid only if and to the extent that such compensation is greater than any reward recoverable by the salvor under Article 13

5. If the salvor has been negligent and has thereby failed to prevent or minimize damage to the environment, he may be deprived of the whole or part of any special compensation due under this Article

6. Nothing in this Article shall affect any right of recourse on the part of the owner of the vessel

Chapter 14

COMMERCIAL MANAGEMENT AND THE SHIPMASTER

by Cdr R.L. Tallack RNR RD* BSc FNI, Northstar Maritime and Environmental Consultancy

Robert Tallack is a master mariner who followed service on a variety of general cargo, passenger and refrigerated vessels with wide experience of commercial and technical management within the shipping industry. He graduated in maritime studies following a course in commercial shipping at Cardiff University after which he joined Lambert Brothers as a Sale and Purchase broker.

He was then appointed a general manager for the Maersk Company and subsequently as managing director of a short-sea ferry operation. Two years establishing a joint venture in Romania and subsequently acting as advisor to the Minister of Shipping brought an understanding of both the problems and the potential of working within centralised economies.

Robert Tallack now runs Northstar Maritime and Environmental Consultancy. He is both a vocational assessor and ISM/ISO auditor.

Introduction

ALTHOUGH THE OVERRIDING commercial objective of the shipping industry is, quite reasonably, to make a profit; for many at sea it may well feel that owners and managers concentrate more on reducing daily operating costs than in striving to deliver a better and more efficient service. This cost cutting approach finds expression in many ways, from a creeping reduction in the maintenance resource to the provision of mixed crews of limited cohesion and an uncertain competency – far too frequently followed by that early casualty of belt-tightening; cuts in the training budget. All this provides an increasing challenge for the professional master.

Changing rules and regulations

The rewards of command have also been constrained by a seemingly never ending flow of rules and regulations, policies and procedures and surveys and inspections which fill the modern master's horizon. Like a small light at the end of the tunnel, there do now seem to be the signs of a change. On the legislative side, the ISM Code has redefined the crucially important relationship between the shore management team (now legally identified through the 'designated person') and the master and his team on board. At the same time, the master's authority, as well as his responsibilities, have been underwritten and a recognition of the need for adequate resources also forms part of the Code.

These developments, it is suggested, open a window of opportunity, perhaps more in some trades than others, for the master to play a more active role in the commercial as well as the technical operation of his vessel and consequently in the overall activities of the company. This window of opportunity is opened further in many cases, by the fact that recent reductions in manning have extended beyond the vessel and cut into the shore management organisation, leaving a reduced resource there as well. These reductions are only partially offset by the expansion of information technology and communications and this has resulted

in a consequential shift of large parts of the managerial – and administrative – workload from the office to the vessel. Whether this is seen as problem or potential by those at sea is a matter of circumstance and temperament.

Potential

For it to be seen as potential and for this potential to be realised, the master must understand the commercial dynamics of ship operations and, to a certain extent, international trade. He, or she, will need to develop a wider perspective, learn to apply existing – and some new – knowledge in different ways and to forge new relationships and lines of communication. This can be difficult, for the usual lines of communications run to those ashore whose remit is predominantly technical and whose own horizons are bounded by the need to keep within budget and meet all regulatory criteria. Indeed, even when one penetrates beyond the technical operating area to that commercial 'cutting edge' of the chartering department, one may find that five cents on the charter rate frequently outweighs the profit potential of optimum performance and good customer service, generated through effective cooperation.

Masters, depending upon their early maritime education, their temperament and experience and their current employment may well see their professional role on a scale which runs roughly and not in a particularly straight course, from 'high grade technical bus driver' to, if not 'Master under God', at least a manager who shapes his professional destiny. This chapter is designed to provide a brief overview of those areas, some familiar some possibly less so, where the professional mariner may need to re-focus his (and her) knowledge and develop new ways of applying their skills. Some of these will be in the technical 'ship driving', predominantly cost dominated areas and some in the commercial 'ship trading' and predominantly income earning areas. The contention is that key to success is the effectiveness of the bridge between these two areas of activity and their counterparts ashore. This chapter also argues, that the master's role requires his active participation in making and managing these links and that , except in moments of dire emergency, every technical operation has a commercial perspective.

The alpha and the omega

The life of every ship starts in the shipyard, either as a design crafted to a particular owner's requirements or as a standard shipyard design and almost inevitably ends in demolition – the alpha and the omega. Along the way, its life will frequently be marked by a number of changes of ownership, bringing with them different maintenance and manning regimes and different operating standards and procedures. Each change of ownership will also bring the sadness of parting – and possibly the depressing prospect of redundancy – to one crew and new challenges and possibilities to another. Despite the strong feeling of continuity enjoyed by many, mainly northern European, liner companies over the period 1945–1970, this is the natural background to seafaring. For many ship owners, selling vessels on a high market and buying on a low is an important, if not the most important, source of ship related revenue and has ensured that a number of companies have survived difficult times when others have gone to the wall. There are three points at which the master can have an impact on the successful outcome of the sale process.

The first is the arrival on board of a potential buyer's inspector. The master, by this time, should have received instructions as to the level of the inspector's rights of inspection. Certainly, he will be able to inspect and take photocopies of log books and certificates. The extent to which he may require ballast tanks, cargo spaces, or, indeed parts of the machinery to be opened up, should be clearly defined in the owner's letter of instruction. Frequently, this permission will be given on the basis of 'no delay or expense to the vessel'.

Inevitably, before the inspector arrives, an inspection of the vessel's classification records will have been undertaken. The inspector can be expected to focus on potential problem areas that have been identified from the inspection of records. The master should neither conceal nor volunteer information but present the vessel in the best possible light. This will inevitably require planning with the other involved heads of departments on board and members of the crew will need to be briefed not to 'volunteer' detrimental information about the vessel and its equipment.

The next stage comes as the vessel is prepared for delivery. Usually, though not always, a vessel will be delivered in port and the terms of the sale contract (the Memorandum of Understanding or MoU) will determine if and how dry docking is handled. Generally the sellers will be required to put the vessel in dry-dock at their expense for an underwater inspection by a classification society surveyor, surveying strictly in accordance with class rules.

There is a delicate relationship here between seller, class surveyor and buyer. The buyer's representative will naturally be interested in any borderline decision on whether an item, rudder, propeller, etc., needs repair falling in their favour, and influence on the classification society about the future class of the vessel is not unknown. At this stage, the surveyor is still technically a servant of the seller, tasked to act (as they always should) as an independent arbiter. Both the master and chief engineer will need to monitor and perhaps manage this aspect of the delivery process closely; substantial costs can be incurred or avoided depending upon the surveyor's decision.

By delivery, the master will need to have ensured that all owner and leased items, not staying with the vessel, are packed and landed. Professional courtesy requires that he should also endeavour to prepare a comprehensive handover to his successor. The actual handover and delivery frequently happens at difficult times of the day, which means that communications can be a problem and attention needs to be given to establishing good communications, with backup, to wherever the documentary, as opposed to physical, delivery of the ship will take place. Since the transfer of US dollars is usually cleared through the New York banking system, delivery will probably take place during American (east coast) banking hours.

At the documentary delivery, representatives of buyer and seller will meet, probably for the first time and quite probably in an anonymous meeting room in an international bank. Sellers will have a Bill of Sale, duly notarised and perhaps attested by the flag state. Buyers will have a draft for the balance of the purchase money and a letter releasing the (usually 10 per cent) deposit from a joint escrow account to the sellers. The sellers will be anxious for proof that the buyer's draft is 'good for value' and the buyers will be nervous about releasing large amounts of money for, for them, a relatively unknown asset. There are two areas which cause concern. The first is that the sellers, if they had a loan secured against the vessel, would have wanted to raise the loan and release the mortgage as late as possible although the Bill of Sale and a transcript of the vessel's registry entry should prove this. At the same time, the buyers (and their lending bank) will want to attach a mortgage to the vessel as quickly as possible. Both buyers and their bank will be very keen to ensure that there are no lingering claims or liens attaching to the vessel.

The other area of possible conflict is payment for bunkers remaining on board at delivery. During the sale negotiation, the cost per tonne of the bunkers will have been argued, and not always amicably, agreed. During the lead up to delivery, estimated bunkers on delivery will have been requested from the vessel and advised by the seller to the buyer. The buyer has the responsibility of organising payment, on the day of delivery, of the exact amount. The fact that after the vessel has settled on the blocks in dry dock and a new round of soundings (plus the last 24 hours' consumption and the final revaluation of what the chief engineer had up his sleeve), has changed the estimated RoB by 3·7 tonnes according to the sellers and 5·3 tonnes according to the buyer's representative can cause inordinate delays and tension. The master and chief engineer(s) should arrive at a firm and fair compromise as soon as possible.

As soon as agreement is reached, both on board and at the location of the documentary delivery that all is in order, Protocols of Delivery will be signed at both locations, stating the exact time of delivery. This time is important to both parties as the final act is to lift the seller's insurance and attach the buyer's cover, although this is usually done on a 'held covered' basis, with the exact time to be confirmed.

Management and managing people

The sale or purchase of a vessel represents more than just an ending or a beginning. It represents a major event which needs to be properly project managed. In fact, the operation of a vessel throughout its life is a succession of events, large or small, frequently repetitive but each unique in time and circumstance, which require proper management. As such, they all need to be properly planned and each plan, whether it be large or small, unique or routine, warrants a careful and structured approach.

The first and critical step in planning is the collection, collation and assessment of information. One of the major reasons why plans fail is because insufficient time is allowed for planning and in the busy, time pressured life of a ship's master, this is easy to understand. Another, important reason why planning fails is because it is given a low priority because the task is 'just routine', just another passage, just another port. It is essential to remind oneself that nothing is ever quite the same – it may be the weather or it may be the composition of the bridge management team, or it might be a small equipment fault. Any one of these may trigger a sequence of events which lead to a critical situation or even a major accident. How many times has a major incident appeared to be the result of an apparently coincidental sequence of minor events?

Identifying and guarding against these incidents is where risk management should be woven into the planning process. The first steps of hazard identification – 'This is a new third mate' – and risk assessment – 'How competently can he or she fit into my team?' may be time consuming, but they are essential for good management. The process of hazard identification is based upon the principle of gathering as much of the relevant information as possible. In other words it is a team task in which the master should involve his shipboard management team.

If the team is going to participate in a practical and meaningful way, they will need to be properly briefed. In other words, a prerequisite of proper planning is good communication. In many management systems, information equates to power and influence, so disseminating information can be a difficult process. It also means that the decision making process is much more open and potentially subject to criticism – no longer is it the unchallenged word emanating from the ivory tower of seniority.

This shift in the process of decision-making from a closed to an open forum can be difficult. Initially, for many, it may feel like abdicating the responsibility of leadership but, in effect, it is only moving it into public view. When all the information is gathered and all the advice and opinions assessed, it remains the master who has to draw it all together and select the correct course of action. Doing this in a forum where a decision can be judged and even criticised takes both courage and professional competence.

These skills really need to be learned as the young officer is promoted to the managerial role of chief officer. The good master, therefore, is not just a practitioner of these skills, he is also a teacher. In order to achieve this, he needs to develop a range of attributes starting with not just a good command of basic facts but also the relevant professional understanding to display them effectively. The master also needs to be sensitive to changing events, including developing technology, knowing when to set aside the old and familiar as well as when not to be seduced by the new but unproved. This requires good analytical skills.

The open forum of team based management mentioned earlier, as well as the master's unique command role in emergency situations, will demand highly developed problem-solving, judgement and decision making skills. The master's role and the fact that however he manages, he is in command, demands both emotional resilience and social skills. The need to plan and initiate will require proactivity and the inclination to respond purposefully to events. Creativity and mental agility together with the discipline to continue learning and developing skills, are the hallmark of the good manager as is the critical assessment of oneself as a manager and a person – self-knowledge or 'knowing thyself'.

Knowing thyself, understanding one's own strengths and weaknesses, demands a high level of both honesty and commitment. The analytical techniques which can help in this process are similar to those that can help the master understand the strengths and weaknesses of the officers and ratings who make up his management team and work force.

A number of the most commonly used methods of analysis divide people's characteristics between four areas of attributes, with one usually dominant but not, generally, totally so. A master might consider whether his officers, his managers, are predominantly:

- **Thinkers**
  who are good at facts and figures, researching, systems analysis, and will probably be good at setting up the on board computers. 'How?' questioners.
- **Sensors**
  who are good at initiating projects, setting up deals, troubleshooting and converting ideas into action. 'What?' questions.
- **Intuitors**
  who are good at long term planning, creative writing, lateral thinking and brainstorming – and who are probably well able to manage change. 'Why?' questioners.
- **Feelers**
  who are good at developing and cementing relationships, counselling, arbitrating – and will converse as happily with a stevedore as with a ship owner. 'Who?' questioners.

Useful as these aids may be, people are complex and there is a real danger in labelling people inaccurately. These techniques are an aid to understanding and managing people, as with aids to navigation, they can be invaluable but need to be checked by visual observation at frequent intervals.

The better the master understands the characteristics of his officers, the better able he is to build an effective and efficient management team on board. With reduced – and mixed – manning, a properly managed team approach is arguably the best, if not the only way in which to make best use the human resource at the vessel's disposal. Communication is a key element in achieving this.

The greatest mistake made about communicating in a business environment is in considering it as a one way flow – down the chain of command. Communication is the way in which management makes its needs and requirements known. It is also the way in which other employees make their needs and desires known too. It is important to them that their voices are heard in a considerate way. At the very least, their message might contain information which will improve the master's decision making.

In a multi-cultural environment such as a ship, the proper use of two way communication becomes even more important, for the meaning contained within the communication has to survive, not only translation but also cultural differences. Whatever the culture, a golden rule of communication is to take the time and trouble to work out what information the other person needs to know in order to enable them to carry out the required task efficiently.

There are a number of other aspects of communicating and of managing people in teams which a good manager needs to know, covering such diverse aspects as communicating effectively on paper, managing meetings and negotiating. A manager today needs new interpersonal skills just as he or she needs new technical skills. If there are doubts about this consider how both parent-child and employer-employee relationships have changed over the past half century.

Management information systems

One of the skills which today's manager needs is the ability to manage the vast amounts of information which the electronic age has spawned. In many ways, this consists of sifting the wheat from the chaff. One of the areas in which management information can be more readily and more rapidly managed by computer power, is an organisation's financial performance. There are a number of problems associated with this as well as obvious benefits.

It might be argued that computer based accounting has given 'the accountant' undue influence within shipping companies and focused decision making too far towards the cost side of the equation rather than on the income or commercial side. It is dangerous to generalise but part of the reason for this is that accountancy feels happier working with cost figures. They are in general terms both 'dead' figures and factual – they represent what has happened and stay where they are put (figuratively speaking). The technical database of historical fact makes an excellent platform for future projection.

Income figures, however, are alive and can be more problematical. They carry an aura of commercial confidentiality, defy easy prediction, are cyclical and not under the owner's control and are associated with difficult concepts like quality of service. For this reason, management information systems in the shipping industry and consequently the managerial ethos frequently concentrates on cost based accounting.

Conversely, one of the benefits of computer power is the ease with which electronic data can be transferred from place to place. This, coupled with the reduction in shore-based management staff has seen the ship's staff becoming increasingly involved in and aware of the cost side of vessel operations. For this involvement to be effective and professionally satisfying, authority needs to pass together with responsibility.

One of the skills which the master and his team need in order to assimilate this extension of managerial responsibility is the management of budgets. This has two major aspects:

- Building the budget and monitoring.
- Managing expenditure.

Here might be mentioned one of the potential problems of budgets and the associated information system. A budget, like a passage plan, is there for guidance. They can indicate whether a vessel is off course (or budget) but not necessarily whether this is good or bad. One does not sail through a major storm just because a line drawn on a chart five days previously takes the vessel through the storm's current location. In a similar way, safety requirements, as opposed to routine maintenance, can defy budget constraints but, just as a vessel cannot steam if she has no bunkers, so she cannot be technically operated if there are no funds.

The analogy can be developed further. A master will endeavour to use his navigational skills to achieve the best set of speed and consumption figures for a voyage, with the least possible use of that cost item, bunkers. In a similar way, the master needs to use his managerial skills in order to deliver the best possible technical operation of his vessel within budget constraints. The effective budget manager should know where he has some flexibility to adjust budgeted expenditure and must bear in mind that if economic conditions change, so might the vessel's economic course. Unfortunately, the 'accountancy approach' to budgeting means that adjustments are all too frequently on the cost reduction side and good commercial, or trading results are far too infrequently fed back into the equation.

Vessel costs, or the costs which must be covered by the income which the vessel must earn, can be logically divided into three areas. The first and perhaps the most remote from the seafarer's point of view, are the finance costs which relate to the cost of having purchased the vessel.

This budget area would typically include the interest due for payment during a given budget period, on any bank or other loan that had been used to support the purchase the vessel. On a statutory accounting basis, it would also include an allocation of the vessel's depreciation over whatever realistic life the vessel is allocated (typically 15–20 years) reducing to a residual value of, perhaps, ten percent of the vessel's original cost. Perhaps more useful from a management accounting point of view is the true cash-flow picture achieved by replacing the depreciation by loan instalment repayments falling due during the budget period in question.

In many cases, the financial aspects of the vessel's budget will be dealt with, corporately within the organisation. Nevertheless it is important to remember that the vessel carries these costs every minute of every day, whether on hire or idle, laid up or operating.

The next budget area covers the operating or technical costs – typically the block of costs which would be covered by a ship manager. Again these costs must be borne before the vessel has earned a cent, although they can be trimmed. This might be by laying the vessel up or, too many seafarers will be aware, by cutting maintenance, personnel, training or other similar costs.

There are many different ways of marshalling operating (or technical) costs but whatever way they are arranged, they should include:

- Personnel costs: the salary cost of sea-staff, the cost of filling the berths on board 365 days a year, thereby taking into account overlap and leave pay as well as the associated social costs of pensions, health insurance and employment taxes.
- Shifting costs: or the costs of travel to and from a crew change. The size of this can be affected by changes in the vessel's trading patterns and reduces the longer crew members say on board.
- Repair and maintenance costs: a large budget area which subdivides logically into a range of sub-areas and responsibilities. Budgeting in this area has a strong historical/statistical basis and relates to assumptions on trading patterns and machinery running hours. This is a cost area which will be affected by the corporate philosophy of the company ranging from 'repair when essential and keep the maintenance costs down' to a 'maintain properly and reduce the need for repair' approach.
- Stores and spares: an area where careful thought and analysis can save money by differentiation between high and low cost components and those that are essential (ship stoppers) and less essential spares. Put another way, thoughtful stock keeping. The overstocked vessel is effectively carrying 'dead' resources – ineffectively tied up funds which should be working for the vessel and for the company.
- Lubricating oils: an element usually borne in this sector of the budget and directly related to the expected use of individual machinery items and to the vessel's anticipated trading pattern. This is an area where a good link between commercial planning and technical operation can make effective savings by increasing or reducing the lubricating oil stock depending upon the expected trading pattern.
- Victualling and Pantry Stores: usually handled separately from the general stores and again an area where advance notice of anticipated trading patterns can contribute to cost savings.
- Insurance: covering hull insurance, the vessel's entry into a P & I Club (liability insurance), war risk insurance, etc., either as a direct cost or an allocation from a fleet policy. It is always essential to remember that insurance, which imposes a high cost item on the operational budget, never does more than recompense the owner for part of the true cost of an accident – the inevitable 'perils of the sea' or the less inevitable negligence of master or crew. The true cost of an accident is invariably

higher than the claim, especially when the loss of (potential earning) time and the call of managerial resources is taken into account.

- Franchise: this is an allocation in the budget to account for the insurance deductible or excess, the most obvious part of an insurance claim not refunded or indemnified by the insurer but not, as indicated, the only uncovered cost arising from an accident.

Over and above this range of direct costs will be another block, sometimes referred to as overheads, which relates to costs which might be spread over the fleet or a particular class of vessel or which might have implications going beyond that budget period. Costs of training may appear here together with the costs of modifying or upgrading the vessel to ensure continued compliance with national and international rules and regulations. There may also be an allocation of time and travel costs for superintendents or other shore staff visiting the vessel.

Finally, the shore establishment costs need to be apportioned and allocated across the vessels in the fleet or, in the case of management, this may be replaced by a ship management fee.

The third area of the vessel's budget covers the operation of trading the vessel and is of critical importance, since it is the only sector of the whole budget which includes an income. This income may come from charter hire (voyage or time) or from direct freight income (container rates etc.) or from passenger fares. The costs associated with a vessel's trading budget cover such items as bunkers, port costs and cargo-handling costs (except of course when on time charter). Unfortunately, and not always necessarily, little of the information about a vessel's trading performance reaches the master and his officers. The pretext is generally 'commercially confidential information' although charter rates, to within a few cents, are generally well known to those competing in similar markets.

This lack of information is a pity because the master and his team can make a very real contribution to the trading performance of the vessel in one of the key areas where customer service is, or should be, delivered. It is also the area in which the time pressures imposed by commercial trading requirements translate into a heightened risk profile which can flow through the technical operation of the vessel. It is The Nautical Institute's contention that this is an area where a much greater involvement of the sea staff, coupled with a wider understanding of the commercial aspects of the ship operation, would be beneficial.

Trading and contracts of affreightment

The first part of commercial understanding comes from the recognition of what drives international trade and shipping's role as an, albeit critical, service provider. The globalisation of industry and its manufacturing and processing facilities both drives and is driven by shipping's ability to deliver a fast and efficient maritime link in an increasingly complex logistical network. The first major contribution to industrial globalisation was in the form of the economies of scale provided by the introduction of the very large raw material carriers in the late sixties (both VLCC and Panamax and Capesize dry bulk carrier). This, despite frequent and often quite violent freight rate fluctuations, effectively pegged the cost of transporting low value raw materials, particularly crude oil, iron ore and steam coal at a level which allowed other factors to determine where primary processing, heavy industrial manufacturing and energy generation would take place.

This was followed by containerisation and other forms of specialised carrier (such as the pure car carrier) which, in a similar way, enabled other factors than transportation cost and time to play a greater role in the location of the lighter end of both manufacturing and processing industry. These other determinants include the cost and availability of an efficient work force and a national governments' willingness to support the financing of the necessary means of production (or factories to use a slightly outmoded term). These decisions were overlaid in certain cases by the need to locate final manufacture within regional trade barriers in order to ensure tariff free access to markets. As a result, the components in a manufactured item may have made a number of substantial maritime journeys from raw material through semi-finished components to final product before that product finally reaches its market place. To a large extent, the cost of multiple maritime transportation is offset by an endeavour to keep stockpiles as low as possible and the means of delivery as fast and flexible as possible – the basis of 'just in time' delivery systems.

Over this pattern must be laid the major uncertainties which disturb, to a greater or lesser extent, the logistics manager's endeavours to establish a steady supply train. Climate is one major factor, which has its impact in two areas. Warm or cold (mainly northern hemisphere) winters have a direct effect on the demand for (liquid) bulk transportation which ripples through into the dry bulk sectors as combination carriers are drawn in or released. On the dry bulk side, it is the agricultural production of staple food crops – the rice and grain harvests – which directly affect vessel demand and freight rates. International and regional conflicts, trade barriers and tariff disputes as well as regional fluctuations in demand all impact back on the demand for shipping services. Crucially, too, against this picture of a monolithic, global trading system, there are new markets emerging and ever changing opportunities for traders to take advantage of inequalities in the market.

The first concrete stage in the process which leads to the movement of goods and thus directly to the employment of shipping is the negotiation of the sale contract. It is at this level that the division of risks between buyer and seller is negotiated and the result of this negotiation of the terms of trade flows right through the twin aspects of the logistical chain; the physical movement of the goods and the financing of and payment for the goods (and their transportation). Central to the buyer-seller negotiation is the decision of when risk in and title to the goods will change hands and how this relates to the payment for the goods (and their transportation). The outcome of this negotiation decides who will contract the shipping services (either through chartering-in tonnage or through the use of a 'common carrier' or liner service) and also indirectly affects that other 'evidence of a contract of affreightment' the bill of lading.

The terms of trade range from 'Come and collect from my factory gates' to 'I will deliver it to you.' The International Chamber of Commerce has codified the scale of variations into thirteen 'Incoterms' (from Ex Works to Delivery Duty Paid) and into four main groups (see figure 14.1).

Running parallel with this negotiation is the decision of how and when the buyer will pay for the goods – again a decision linked directly to the transfer of title and risk and through this directly to the bill of lading and the actions of the master – even though no vessel may yet have been contracted for the eventual carriage of the goods. Probably the most common method of financing international trade is the deferred credit[1]. The key and critical point to comprehend is that this financial transaction is only linked to the physical activity of transporting and delivering the goods by paper – or more accurately, on what appears on a set of specified documents, of which the bill of lading is central, and whether the wording on these documents agrees with what was agreed both in the sale contract and when the deferred credit facility was put in place.

Not surprisingly, the seller agreed to provide a certain quality and quantity of goods, in (apparent) good order and condition. The buyer and seller may well have established a date by when the goods should be shipped on whatever vessel is eventually contracted to transport the goods and frequently this date is used

Guide to Documentary Credit Operation: International Chamber of Commerce

Group B:	Departure	
EXW	Ex Works	(named place)
Group F:	**Main carriage unpaid**: F signifies that the seller must hand over the goods to the nominated carrier free of risk and expense to the buyer.	
FAC	Free Carrier	(named place)
FAS	Free Alongside Ship	(named port of shipment)
FOB	Free on Board	(named port of shipment)
Group C:	**Main carriage paid**: C signifies that the seller must bear certain costs even after the critical point for the division of risk for loss or damage has been reached.	
CFR	Cost and Freight (C&F)	(named port of destination)
CIT	Cost Insurance and Freight	(named port of destination)
CPT	Carriage Paid to	(named port of destination)
CIP	Carriage and Insurance Paid to	(named port of destination)
Group D:	**Arrival**: D signifies that it is seller's responsibility that the goods arrive at the stated destination.	
DAF	Delivery at Frontier	(named place)
DES	Delivery ex Ship	(named port of destination)
DEQ	Delivery ex Quay (Duty Paid)	(named port of destination)
DDU	Delivery Duty Unpaid	(named port of destination)
DDP	Delivery Duty Paid	(named port of destination)

Figure 14.1 Four main groups of Incoterms

to set a price against an international index or to meet contractual obligations to ship so many tonnes per month. The bank, which may be but one in a chain involving confirming banks as well as the buyer's and the seller's (different) banks has only one criterion against which to release what may be many millions of dollars in payment for goods it has never, and will never see.

This single criterion is 'Do the documents presented to me exactly match, word for word, the documents specified by the buyer when the credit was raised?' To add another layer of risk, since the goods may have been sold and resold, the person presenting the documents necessary to trigger payment and release the cargo, including one (only) of probably three original bills of lading, may well not be the original buyer.

It can immediately be seen that this transaction can be very different from the problems facing a master and his chief officer as they contemplate rain wetted and rusting steel or torn bags of infested rice. Since shipping is a service industry, the answer is not to clause the bill of lading but to take early and pro-active action to enable the buyer and the seller to solve the problem, and preferably this action needs to be put in motion before the cargo has been loaded.

The often quoted '*carefully to load, stow, carry and deliver*' the cargo really needs extending to include '*carefully to take receipt of, load, stow, etc.*' the cargo. In doing this the master assumes responsibilities to a number of different parties on behalf of the ship owner, and with some of them, notably the receiver, neither the owner nor the master will necessarily have a direct contractual relationship. Nevertheless, the receiver will be able to claim against the ship owner for the actions of the master.

The contractual arrangements which facilitate the physical movement of the goods and the transfer of title (ownership) in them can be complex, especially since they will frequently involve two related but separate contracts. One of these contract will relate primarily to the goods and to the shipper and receiver while the other will relate primarily to the provision of the method of transportation, the ship. In other words, the master will need to manage and coordinate the responsibilities and obligations surrounding both the bill of lading and the charter party (or, in the case of a vessel operating a liner service, the responsibilities and obligations which flow from being a common carrier).

In managing the contractual obligations which relate to the bill of lading, the master must take into account its three distinct but closely interrelated functions. Centrally, it is the title document to ownership of the goods. In addition it is the receipt for the goods issued on shipment and, so far as the financial side of the contractual arrangements are concerned, it needs to confirm that the quality, quantity and condition of the goods are as described under the original sale contract. At the operational level it is also evidence of the contractual responsibilities of the ship owner for the 'safe carriage and delivery of the goods' towards whoever might be the legal owner of those goods. As has already been mentioned, the person or persons to whom the master and ship owner hold this responsibility may change as title in the goods is sold and resold and may well be unknown, in direct contractual terms, to the carrier.

The master's management of his vessel may also be determined by one, if not two, charter parties, each of which, time and voyage, may have a different impact and require different decisions. At one level, the vessel may be taken on time charter and, while this relieves the owner of a number of responsibilities, of which a central one is the need to seek further employment, it also makes the master a servant of the time charterer in respect of the contractual carriage of cargo. Unfortunately, claims from unsatisfied receivers of cargo tend to find a way through to the ship owner despite the lack of a direct contractual agreement between them.

In the case of a voyage charter, the owner and master have a much more direct relationship with both the shipper and the receiver. Yet, even so, the owner of the cargo – the holder of the bill of lading – may be a third party who has no direct connection with these (charter party based) contractual arrangements but is (and justifiably so, according to the Courts) relying on the master's signature to ensure that the bill of lading accurately describes the goods he has contracted to buy (and for which he has possibly already paid) and that they will be delivered to the agreed port of discharge with due despatch and in good condition.

Around these contractual agreements, or the strict duties of a common carrier is the liner trades, have grown, over the years, a web of what can be fairly described as risk control and risk offset facilities. Some are legal and some are insurance based and they can illustrated in the form of protective circles around the core master/ship owner relationship.

Risk and insurance

Two insurance facilities offer the ship owner and thus the ship master, protection in two different areas of risk. The main role of what is generally termed Hull (or Hull and Machinery) cover is to indemnify the owner against damage to his vessel. As such it relates mainly to the risks associated with the technical operation of maintaining and operating the vessel and of its navigation from port to port, including those risks generally described as perils of the sea. It also, subject to certain constraints, provides recompense to the owner in the event 'of negligence or mistakes by the master, officers and crew, the shipboard management team'.

It is the liability cover provided by the mutual protection and indemnity associations (the P&I clubs) which is most relevant to the commercial operation of the vessel under discussion in this chapter. Here the cover reaches out into the area of charter party and bill of lading, but, in strict terms, stops short of providing protection if the master incorrectly signs or clauses a bill of lading, delivers the cargo to the wrong port or delivers the cargo without the correct presentation of a bill of lading. Having said that, the P&I Clubs are owned, mutually, by the ship owners they serve and they are well aware of the pressures and practices of international trade – and of the frequent non-availability of bills of lading at a discharge port.

The P&I Club, as well as the ship owner, will want to ensure that as much protection as possible is given to the commercial operation of the vessel from various legal conventions. This means that the protection offered by the Hague or The Hague-Visby (or the Hague-Visby with Protocol, or the Hamburg) Rules, which relate to the Bill of Lading (the contract of carriage of main interest to the eventual owner of the cargo) needs to be linked to the voyage charter (the contract of carriage between ship owner and shipper). This is, or should be, effected by a Paramount Clause in the charter party. In a similar way, the holder of the bill of lading needs to be aware of the existence of the voyage charter and an Incorporation Clause brings the existence of the charter party to the bill of lading (and this complexity is why one of the roles of a bill of lading is described as 'evidence of', rather than 'the' contract of carriage).

One of the most significant areas of protection offered by the Hague Rules (and its derivatives) is that it provides the ship owner with the ability to limit his liability, in monetary terms, against third party claims, including claims brought under the complex web of contracts described above. Part of a master's responsibility is to manage the operation of the vessel in both commercial and technical terms, so that the protection offered by these conventions remains intact and one of his foremost duties in this respect is to ensure that the vessel is seaworthy (and cargoworthy) at the commencement of (each stage) of a voyage.

The ship owner's ability to limit his liability (again in monetary terms) provided by the Limitation of Liability Convention, relates more closely to the technical operation of navigating the vessels safely through the perils of the seas rather than the perils of the contracts. In the event of an incident – or a mistake – occurring which brings the ship owner into a position in which he will be relying on the protection offered by either of the liability conventions or of his two complementary insurance covers, it is essential that the master, and his team on board, actively manage the situation. They must do this in a way which will mitigate (minimise) any loss whilst ensuring that the

owner and the vessel remain within the protection of the conventions and do not breach any of the warranties contained within the insurance cover.

This means that the master and his officers should understand the overall contractual relationships relating to the employment and risk protection of the vessel and its owner and be able to act in a way which takes into account the possibly conflicting priorities of the various interested parties. This does not mean, painstaking actions taking into account clause and sub-clause; nor does it mean waiting until a lawyer or owner's representative arrives to advise on a deteriorating situation. It means taking, and taking early, 'the reasonable actions of a prudent seafarer', both technically and commercially. Even more, it means planning and thinking ahead in order to prevent such situations arising. As stated earlier, the time to negotiate the clausing of a bill of lading is when the rust stained steel is on the quay, not when it is in the hold with the hatches closed.

The key relationship is between owner and master and the shore based and ship based management teams. A good relationship at this level is, perhaps, a shipping company's best way of managing risk and one which has been squandered in recent years, mainly, it must be said, by the actions of the ship owners. It can be hoped that the International Safety Management (ISM) Code will help to rebuild this relationship both for the technical and the commercial operation of the vessel. Neither side works in isolation and on the commercial side, the master is the person who has to manage the contractual arrangements and make them work.

The next layer of risk management is education, understanding, knowledge and the training to put the knowledge into effective action. It can be argued that education has more than ever been replaced by the expedience of 'training against regulations' in recent years – and even then, the training budget has been one of the first to suffer from 'the need to reduce daily running costs'.

There are encouraging signs that this is changing, but knowledge and understanding do need to be encouraged amongst the younger generation of officers.

Considerations relating to bills of lading

Although a bill of lading can appear for signature on the master's desk with little more ceremony than the many documents which he has to sign every port call, its role and the potential liabilities which it carries demand careful management and forethought. Some of the considerations which the master should bear in mind are:

1. Is it possible early during the port stay to sight, from the agent or shipper, a proforma bill and

establish whether there are any special terms and/or conditions or conflicts with any charter party?

2. Are the cargo officers briefed to bring promptly to the master's attention any potential problem of marks, quantity, quality or condition. These problems might then be resolved without giving rise to delay or a dispute about clausing the bill of lading.

3. Both when receiving and releasing cargo, it is important to know whether the bill of lading is:

   3.1 A straight bill, whereby the goods can only be released to the named consignee, or
   3.2 An open bill which may be made out:
      3.2.1 'To bearer' and thus the first person to present an original bill of lading
      3.2.2 'Named consignee or order' in which case the named consignee can receive the cargo or endorse on the back the name of another 'named consignee or order', or
      3.2.3 Endorse just the name of a consignee making it a non-negotiable 'straight' bill.

4. On releasing cargo, endorse the bill 'Accomplished' and date, stamp and sign this endorsement.

5. Establish whether the bill of lading:

   5.1 Is a 'Marine or ocean bill of lading' (sometimes called port-to-port) which should contain no indication that the bill is subject to a charterparty, or
   5.2 Whether the bill specifies that it is subject to a charterparty, in which case the Incorporation Clause in the bill of lading should be analysed to identify what terms and conditions from the charterparty are being incorporated.

6. Remember that a bill of lading is prima facie evidence that the goods are loaded as described therein and can be absolute proof when the bill is endorsed to a third party.

7. Be careful that the date on a bill of lading records the date on which the goods are actually shipped.

8. Never sign a blank bill of lading.

9. Never accept a letter of indemnity (unless clearly instructed and authorised by the owner – not the charterer – and even then preferably in conjunction with the advice of the P&I Club and backed by a bank guarantee).

10. Signing the bill of lading as a receipt for cargo, the master addresses:

    • The weight and quantity – here the addition of the word 'unknown' shifts the burden of proof on to the shipper but the master will have to provide a compelling reason why he was not able to conduct a tally or assess the weight through a draft survey or similar means.

    • The condition of the cargo – if there is no statement as to condition, one should not be added, although there is generally the statement 'shipped in good order and condition' printed on the face of the bill, or better still 'shipped in apparent good order and condition'. The master is not expected to see inside a crate but he is expected to react to such obvious signs as stained bags – and to be particularly vigilant if foodstuffs are being shipped.

    • The quality of a cargo – this, reasonably enough, is not an area in which the master is expected to show a high degree of expertise. Quality can be high and condition low and vice versa. Technically it is possible to add the wording (if not already in the printed wording) 'Quality and condition unknown' and the bill will still be a clean bill of lading.

    • The leading marks – the cargo should be clearly marked with the leading marks necessary for the identification of the cargo and the master is recommended to ask himself 'Are the goods marked in such a manner as should ordinarily remain legible at the end of the voyage?' and 'Are there reasonable grounds for suspecting that the information is not accurate?' The vessel may well be held responsible for delay and expense if, at the discharge port(s), there are delays because of poorly or improperly marked cargo.

11. If the cargo does not fit with the shipper's description on the bill of lading, then the overall guiding principle is:

    • Inform the shipper that if the matter is not resolved, then it will be necessary to clause the bill of lading, advising the shipper of the reasons.

    • If the shipper refuses to address the problem and refuses the master's right to clause the bill, he should be advised that sailing may be delayed until the matter is resolved, and the shipper held responsible for the cost of any delay;

    • Ensure that this stance on behalf of the owner's interests is backed up by firm and comprehensive evidence recorded at the time.

12. Remember the shipper is the customer – early action by a vigilant ship's staff can frequently enable a solution to be found which is acceptable to both shipper and carrier (charterer as well as owner) without the need to delay the vessel.

Managing charter parties

For many masters, much of his or her working life may be directed by one or more charter parties and their management approach can either be reactive or positive and pro-active.

The contractual web

The first and critical point always to bear in mind is that the charterparty expresses the requirements of that essential component of every business, the customer and the matrix of customers to whom the master may be responsible can be complex. Bearing in mind that a time charter is a contract for the use of a particular ship while a voyage charter is a contract for the hire of cargo space or capacity within the vessel, it is important to understand how:

- Both charter parties can coexist (and the chain can be lengthened if sub-charters exist), and why.
- Both charter parties impose different requirements and duties upon the vessel and her master.

For the master and his team, the management responsibilities can be complex and multilayered in that he may well have responsibilities to, and to a greater or lesser extent, be under the direction of:

- A time-charterer, who will issue sailing orders, is interested in such matters as speed and consumption and can instruct the master as to the signing of bills of lading,
- A voyage charterer, who is primarily concerned about a vessel's timely arrival at load or discharge ports with holds or tanks in an appropriate condition and cargo gear in good working order,
- The holder of a bill of lading, that evidence of a contract to carriage and who, when risk and title pass, to the receiver may be a third party to whom the vessel and the owner assume responsibilities and duties, while at the same time
- Managing the vessel on behalf of the owner with regard to such critical matters as personnel, the safe prosecution of the voyage and the routine maintenance of the vessel; and
- Ensuring that the business and customers receive a satisfactory service without exposing the owner or vessel to avoidable contractual liabilities.

Seaworthiness

Throughout all of this contractual web, one common obligation can be identified, and one which also relates to the vessel's insurance. The master has a prime, and in some cases absolute responsibility that the vessel should be seaworthy. The requirements of the obligations of seaworthiness and for a voyage charter, cargoworthiness, can be found in '*Commercial Management for Shipmasters*' and other Nautical Institute publications. Suffice it to say that the legal obligation is greatest at the commencement of each voyage or stage of a voyage – and that a disgruntled cargo owner or voyage charterer will endeavour to remove the owner's ability to limit his liability (as under the Hague Rules etc.) by challenging the seaworthiness of the vessel.

Planning and preparation

Masters should receive voyage orders from charterers and, hopefully and especially in the case of a time charter, from owners, highlighting the main points of the charterparty. These vary enormously in quality and are frequently written from the point of view of a charterer wanting a job done rather than the master addressing his complex matrix of responsibilities. Sadly, too, charter parties often arrive late, if at all. A first task, therefore, is to build up a library of frequently used charter parties and to ensure that the officers forming the management team are aware of their major requirements, their special peculiarities, and the obligations which they place on the vessel.

Charter parties can make dry reading so a little inventiveness is required. One approach is to make a chronological list of those aspects of a charterparty that affect the conduct of the vessel as she executes the charter voyage and correlate this with the relevant charterparty clauses, scattered as they will be in different places in different charter parties.

Voyage charters

For a voyage charter, some of the headings may be:

Charterer, shipper and freight

This identifies the customer and, crucially, how freight is paid. Charterparty and bill of lading fraud is not unknown – if a strange and new name appears as charterer or shipper, it might, especially in new trading areas, be sensible to make discreet enquiries as to the shipper's reputation.

Arrival

This establishes the immediate navigational requirement and, together with the discharge port, the bunker requirement (bearing in mind that to deviate to bunker once cargo is on board should have the agreement of the shipper or, perhaps more accurately, the person who has (insurance) risk in the cargo at the time of deviation.

Cargo to be loaded

This will establish, together with the required time to arrival, any cleaning required which might be needed for holds or tanks. If there is doubt about the exact level of cleanliness or preparation, the appropriate time to ask is when there is time left to take action.

Laycan and NOR

The method and time of tendering notice of readiness is an area where a pro-active approach can sometimes be advantageous for vessel and owner. There is, for example, little to be gained by burning bunkers to arrive just too late to tender NOR before a weekend or local holiday and when (according to a careful reading of the charterparty) it might not be possible to tender NOR.

Conversely, it may well be worth burning extra bunkers in order to tender NOR just before a weekend of no cargo work, giving the vessel a maintenance weekend in port 'on demurrage'. The requirements for a valid tender of NOR warrant careful reading, especially with regard to the place and method of tendering as well as the vessel's preparedness to accept cargo and ballast condition.

Bear in mind that the shipper must make a number of important decisions based on the ETA given by the master, decisions relating to moving the cargo into the port, ordering berths, labour and equipment which, if badly timed can waste money. Bear in mind too that if a vessel misses her Cancelling Date, the charter can be terminated and the owner find himself with an unemployed vessel and probably a very weak negotiating position.

Safe port, safe berth

An important and sometimes complex consideration, especially when trading to new areas. In assessing whether a port is safe or unsafe, the master needs to consider three factors:

- Is the port physically safe? E.g., is there sufficient water depth? What are the anticipated (seasonal / unseasonable) weather conditions? Has war or other internal hostilities broken out? etc.
- Is the basic port infrastructure safe? In other words are the systems such as pilotage, aids to navigation, tugs, etc., adequate?
- Can the event or occurrence which makes him consider that the port might not be safe, be described as abnormal or could it reasonably be foreseen?

Laytime and demurrage

Although 'once on demurrage, always on demurrage' slips easily off the tongue, before a vessel can earn demurrage, NOR must be correctly tendered and accepted. The owner needs careful and timely information to support his demurrage claim which, all too often, has to be negotiated and chased after the cargo is discharged and the voyage is ostensibly complete.

Cargo and bills of lading

The core reason for the charter and linked closely to the notes on bills of lading. The master should ensure as early as possible that he is satisfied with the obligations placed on him with respect to receiving cargo and signing for it and the liabilities to which he can expose the owner, especially with regard to third party receivers holding an endorsed bill of lading.

It is important to note if a Clause Paramount stipulates the inclusion of clauses relating to the Hague (or other) Rules into the bills of lading thus enabling the owner the ability to limit his liability. Consultation with a (husbanding) agent or the local P & I Club Correspondent may be advisable and the master should be ever watchful for attempts at the fraudulent use of bills of lading.

Additional clauses

Careful attention should be given to any additional, typed clauses which may extend the obligations and responsibilities of vessel and master.

Time charters

Time charters, as already mentioned, perform a different task and generate different requirements and responsibilities such as:

Description of vessel

It is important that this is correct, for if not, the charterer is sure to discover the discrepancy and, if possible, turn it to his commercial advantage. It is surprising how many discrepancies there can be between two descriptions of the same vessel.

Delivery, redelivery, hire payment and cancellation

Diverse but related clauses all with a common thread. It is not unknown for certain time charterers to load a vessel, pay the first time charter payment, sell the cargo and then to disappear with the proceeds. This leaves the owner and the vessel with a direct obligation to the 'innocent' holder of the bill of lading to deliver the cargo to the named port of discharge, without any further payment.

On and off-hire surveys

Be aware that the off hire survey may be conducted by different people at some future time, but it will be compared against the description of the vessel contained in on-hire survey (and charterparty). A wise master approaching the end of a charter, reads the original off-hire survey with care.

Owners/charterers to provide

An obvious clause for careful reading, but it is particularly important as it helps to define the responsibility and authority interface between charterer and master.

Safe berths, trading limits, sailing orders and liberty clauses

All fairly straightforward clauses but once again they define the master's responsibilities and his particular responsibility for the safety of the vessel and her navigation.

Cargo and cargo work

This helps to define the vessel's responsibilities and the charterer's responsibilities in respect of all cargo related aspects. It is important to establish a good line of communication with the time charterer's manager or representative responsible for the operation of the charter. This is an area where the need to protect the owner's interests can conflict with what is operationally the most expedient solution – it is an area where the master's experience and forethought can be invaluable.

Speed and consumption and bunkers

An area ripe for dispute which requires a sensible and pragmatic approach, especially if the chartering department have been over enthusiastic about the vessel's performance. Masters – and the chartering department should be aware that it is becoming increasingly easy to retrospectively check satellite records of meteorological condition.

Off-hire

Another area where careful planning and forethought can help to avoid or minimise loss of hire.

Passage and deviation

The cargo owner has the right to expect that the laden voyage is undertaken with due dispatch and, in general terms, without deviation. Unwarranted or unagreed deviation can prejudice the owner's right to limit his liability (with respect to claims from the charterer or cargo owner) under such conventions as the Hague or Hague-Visby Rules.

Cargo claims for damage or deterioration of goods on passage are often made and as well as attending to such matters as ventilation (if required) a careful record of the actions taken to care for the cargo during the passage is important. Sea water damage due to exceptional weather – or due to ill fitting hatch seals or the vessel being driven too hard? Retrospective satellite imagery can often establish how exceptional the weather was!

Delivery

The master has two overriding objectives at the discharge port(s).

- To ensure that the cargo is delivered to the rightful receiver, and
- To protect the owner's position if necessary with regard to the payment of freight and demurrage.

This accomplished it is time to plan and prepare for the next voyage.

Summary

Charter parties, whether voyage or time – or a combination of both, play a vital and central role for a large sector of the shipping industry. Professionally, a master needs to approach the challenges they pose in a knowledgeable and pro-active manner and ensure that his or her management team grows in their understanding of their commercial as well as their technical responsibilities.

References

- *R L Tallack Commercial Management for Shipmasters* The Nautical Institute 1996.
- *Managing Risk in Shipping* The Nautical Institute 1999

Chapter 15

MANAGING SAFETY ON BOARD

by Captain C.M. Mahidhara FNI

Captain Mahidhara trained on the T.S. Dufferin and T.S. Rajendra from 1971 to 72. He joined the Shipping Corporation of India (SCI) as an apprentice in 1973 and served in various capacities, obtaining command in 1981 and leaving SCI in 1982. In SCI he served on a variety of vessels – cargo ships, tankers, bulk carriers, product carriers and OBOs.

He joined Farsund Shipping A/S (part of Mosvold Farsund) as a chief officer and obtained command again in 1985. He has been with Farsund Shipping since then, serving mostly on Suezmax and Aframax tankers, and Capesize bulk carriers. For the last two years he has served on a 12000 ton multipurpose ship carrying project cargoes and operating container feeder services. Captain Mahidhara is due to join the tanker fleet again soon.

Introduction

Safety is an important and integral part of every aspect of running a ship. For managing safety on board the master must coordinate all activities contributing to safety. The key to this is providing good leadership, through personal commitment, personal example and a positive attitude to safety so that he can motivate and stimulate people. Unlike any other environment the shipmaster's example and attitude make a great impression on the ship's crew. Nearly every ship reflects the capability and personality of the master. The master must use this power of persuasion effectively and to advantage, to convince everybody of the value of safety through good communication, training and leadership.

The checks and balances provided with the implementation of the ISM code makes the task of managing safety on board all the more effective. The highest standards of safety can be achieved by instilling a sense of personal responsibility for the safety of both themselves and others into all persons on board. The shipmaster should approach the management of safety, so that it is introduced into every aspect of running and operating a ship. Personal safety is a very good starting point, and it should pervade the daily routines of the ship, maintenance, operations at sea in port, navigation, manoeuvring, safety of shore personnel, training, delegation, the formation of safety committees, good communication with the company and other shore establishments.

Master must set an example and lead

Firstly the crew must be convinced of the master's sincerity regarding safety on board. The shipmaster must be at the forefront in setting examples and must observe all the safety routines he and the company have established for the ship. The safety standards on board should not appear to be overly cosmetic and should pervade all aspects of running the ship. Applying safety only to specific areas serves no purpose and is not effective in achieving overall safety on the ship. The safety standards and atmosphere should be such that anyone observing the ship's operations should be able to immediately sense it. This sort of a safety culture has to be steeped on board by constant attention to detail, by training and repetition.

Personal safety

A very good starting point for safety on board is personal safety. It must be realised that without all on board having an awareness of their own personal safety and that of their mates, no vessel can be operated safely. Safe operating practices cannot be divorced from safe working practices. When a person joins a ship, he should be familiarised with the company's safety policies and indoctrinated on personal safety through a personal safety handbook. He should also be taken on a familiarisation tour of the vessel by one of the officers so that he can be brought into tune very quickly with the ship's operations and any potential hazards.

The master should, at the earliest opportunity, make personal acquaintance and appraise him of the company's safety policy, their drug and alcohol policy, his own commitment to it and his receptiveness to suggestions and discussions. He should try to inculcate a sense of responsibility for their personal safety, the safety of the fellow men and the ship. He must convince them that it is important to work safely rather than control their every move. They must also be made to feel that they are free to put forward their own points on any aspect of safety in the ship's running.

A lot of the safety training and indoctrination of company policies is usually done ashore today but it is always good to reinforce your own personal commitment to all these policies. While on the subject of personal safety it would be wise to guard against carelessness and complacency and regular checks and re-checks should be made of personal safe working practices. One should go back to the absolute basics often and reinforce the importance of safe habits and practices to minimise errors.

All safe working practices have evolved through experience, so it would be unwise to bypass them "just one time" because you are in a hurry. There is absolutely no reason that the unsafe practice will not harm you "just that once". It must be ingrained in everyone that they must think very hard before they try to overrule a safe working habit.

Delegation

Without the right amount of delegation, the master will be bogged down and fatigued by too many details and will not be able to function effectively and safely. He should be aware of the potential and shortcomings of his officers and crew and delegate responsibilities accordingly. Wherever there are shortcomings an attempt should be made to train and remedy the shortcomings, or give staff responsibility where they are capable.

Too much or too little delegation is unsafe and dangerous. Delegation of responsibility is good for the persons on board. It builds up their confidence and skills, they feel involved and needed on the ship and the feeling that they matter in the ship. It also assists in their training for taking on more responsibilities as they progress in their career. For the master it releases his time for further training and being available reasonably refreshed to tackle an emergency. It helps the master to monitor, oversee and analyse the safety of various operations and activities on board with a clear mind.

An important aspect of delegation is that, when the need arises, it is much easier for the master to advise and help in the work delegated, whereas when the master himself does the work, it is less likely to be inspected critically for any errors. For instance, if the shipmaster were to do the passage planning himself, then an error would be less likely to be detected by the navigating officer, or he may not have the temerity to point it out. However when it is delegated you can check and monitor the work and point out errors, inaccuracies or shortcomings.

Confidence in the master

The shipmaster should have an open management style and communicate well with all on board and be accessible. A good personal acquaintance with the sea staff and a good professional and personal relationship with senior staff are essential. There must be confidence on board that the master has an open mind to suggestions for improvement of safety or any other aspect of the ship's running. Everyone should always feel free to put forward their suggestions and these should be considered carefully and implemented if practical and feasible. If the suggestions require assistance and concurrence of the company they should be presented to the company as required. The confidence and accessibility that a shipmaster exudes is important in reducing the possibility of a one-man error. The ISM code will already have a system of checklists and double checks to avoid a one man error, however the master communicating well and creating

confidence can take the system of double checks further. The master and senior officers should be approachable, so that no one hesitates to report any damage or untoward incident or potential hazard he may have observed, or to point out an inadvertent error by any person on board which could jeopardise any aspect of safety on the ship.

People should be made to understand that no one is infallible and that mistakes can be made by anyone. When they feel a mistaken order has been given or an erroneous operation is being conducted they should not hesitate to point it out. They may be mistaken at times; they should not be ridiculed, but given an explanation and praised for their diligence.

Navigational safety

There have been numerous instances of minor navigational errors leading to major causalities like stranding, collisions, etc., leading in turn to loss of life, property and environmental damage. The shipmaster must lay down guidelines for safe navigational practices which are in compliance with various international, national and local laws. The Bridge Procedures Guide provides a good guideline and the watchkeepers should be made familiar with its contents. The master should discuss it with them so that they understand it fully. Standing orders should also be promulgated taking into account company policies, the experience and capability of the watchkeepers and the limitations of the equipment and the ship. Night orders should also be issued every night with pertinent instructions for the night watch and should indicate more specifically when definitely to call the master and any other specific instructions regarding position fixing, traffic, weather and so on.

Guidelines should be laid down for passage planning from berth to berth in accordance with established procedures. They should be detailed, easy to refer to and should also have contingency plans in the event of aborting the plan especially in congested waters, pilotage waters, heavy weather, etc. Weather routeing is very good today, however it would be prudent to check regularly local or heavy weather reports so as to take corrective and early action to avoid storms and disturbances. All phases of the passage plan should be discussed with the watchkeepers and the relevant details with the chief engineer and the pilots.

Just as the watchkeepers are taught the importance of not relying on only one method of position fixing, the master should also double check on his watchkeepers. Navigational safety also involves chart corrections. This is an important area and random checks on the corrections should be made so that they are not missed out inadvertently. Ultimately it is wise to remember that no single cause of ship collisions and grounding exceeds in frequency that of failing to maintain a proper all round lookout.

The limitation of navigational aids should be fully understood and exclusive reliance on any one aid should be avoided. In recent years there have been instances of radar-assisted collisions and GPS assisted grounding.

Watchkeepers and engineers must be encouraged to familiarise themselves with the emergency steering gear, and procedures for auto/hand changeover should be ensured.

Maintenance and proper use of equipment

Regular and good maintenance procedures are an integral part of safety management on board. Without this, equipment may not be reliable or perform within its specifications. Today there are very good maintenance programs which, if followed sincerely, should minimise the possibility of breakdown or malfunction.

Equipment should be used according to the maker's instructions and its operation should be within the parameters it was designed for. Abuse of equipment will only lead to breakdowns and could possibly put the vessel in an unsafe position. Misuse and abuse could also cause personal injuries. Training is very important for the proper use and maintenance of equipment and it should be repeated and reinforced regularly.

Inspections

The master should, along with his senior officers, regularly inspect the vessel and should discuss with them any shortcomings, defects and deficiencies which could lead to operational problems and hazardous and unsafe conditions. The inspections should not just be for the machinery and equipment but for the ship as a whole – the hull, cargo tanks and other structures – as they become available for inspection. The inspections should review operating procedures and modify them as experience dictates. A good inspection of various logs and routines will be very beneficial in getting a good picture of the effectiveness of all procedures and routines on board so that corrective measures can be taken if necessary. In accordance with the ISM code a lot of auditing tools have been provided to the ship which regularly highlight problem areas and allows for reporting procedures so that effective measures can be taken on board or ashore. Inspections from shore especially in the form of ISM audits, port state inspections, oil company inspections, etc. have provided a good tool for safety management in that the regular interaction brings about more awareness of faults and defects before they can become a liability. They provide more inputs than the ship alone can provide. The master should always take the suggestions given in the right spirit and should similarly motivate the crew. A positive assessment indicates that all on board have managed safety on board effectively and should greatly increase their confidence.

Good communication

Good communication with all on board and likewise with the shore management is essential. The better the communication, the better is the understanding of safety objectives on board. Similarly, good understanding and communication with the company is important. However good the communication and training on board, the ship does not have adequate resources to rectify and remedy every defect. It requires the advice, resources and authority of the company. Effective communication and understanding will always bring an early and appropriate response from the company. The care and consideration given to suggestions from the ship will definitely motivate the staff on board to more effectual safety management.

Safety committees, safety meetings, training

Safety committees and safety meetings are an effective forum for discussing and communicating. They can be used to investigate and report accidents and incidents, with the objective of determining cause (not blame) and preventing re-occurrence. It must be emphasised that discussions regarding accidents or hazardous situations on the ship should not be used to find fault with an individual. The lessons learnt should be used to improve safety conditions on board, tighten loose maintenance and operational procedures and implement new safety procedures as required. It is not enough simply to discuss accidents and incidents.

Near misses should also be investigated and appropriate precautions taken so they do not become an accident at a later date. Minutes of safety committee meetings should be communicated to the company so that they can provide their own input. There will be several instances when remedies may not be found on the ship and the company should be asked to provide the expertise or new equipment.

The meetings provide a good forum for discussing casualty reports received from the company. Similar situations can be recognised on board, parallels can be drawn and lessons learnt. The meetings will also schedule training and safety drills and discuss drills already concluded. Safety drills should be well thought out and imaginative. Drills are basically rehearsals for disasters and the object is readiness. The vessel's readiness to deal with an emergency depends on the level of training imparted. Drills should be well planned and varied to keep interest alive. It is a good idea to involve everyone on board in turn to plan the drills. Some very sound and innovative ideas are bound to surface and it keeps everyone involved.

Discussion, planning and implementation of various emergencies and contingency plans help bring about knowledge of the reliability and efficiency of equipment and plans. It also brings home the realisation of the difficulties faced in emergencies and more than anything else convinces people that prevention is better than the cure.

Safety involves a lot of repetition and back to basics most of the time. To keep people interested one has to find different ways of saying the same things. Discussing snippets from The Nautical Institute's *SEAWAYS*, MARS reports, casualty reports, etc. would go a long way in alleviating this problem. Videos and several good computer training programs are available to the ship and should be used for training and reinforcing safety habits. To keep things interesting, watchkeepers should be trained by their seniors, discussing various situations they may encounter and their response to it.

Planning

Planning of all operations on the ship is essential. A lot of accidents occur due to poor planning, where people are not clear about their part in an operation. This creates unsafe conditions and a breakdown of operations. With good planning, and discussion, potential hazards of a situation can be envisaged and guarded against. The company promulgates guidelines and procedures for routines and operations and these should be supplemented and modified for each ship and monitored regularly. As far as possible, operations should be planned afresh each time rather than modifying an old one, so that new inputs learnt from experience can be incorporated. Once a plan or procedure has been agreed, individuals must not try to take short-cuts, because it appears to be the easy thing at that time. Planning is done after a lot of thought and care and it coordinates various activities, so an impromptu short-cut could very well create more hazards.

Safety in port

When the ship is coming into port, the agents, pilots, surveyors, etc. will be able to provide local information, any special precautions to be taken and details of any dangers and the various facilities available in the port. Safety of shore personnel on board is the ship's responsibility. Proper warnings and notices should be posted, so that the crew are aware of unsafe areas. Gangways should be made safe and should always be manned so that unauthorised people do not enter the ship. Untrained persons on the ship pose a safety hazard to themselves and the ship.

Unfortunately lot of injuries to ship's personnel take place when they are embarking or disembarking from the ship. People boarding the vessel in an inebriated condition probably suffer the worst injuries. Special attention should be paid to the safety of gangways and drunken persons should be prohibited from using them.

Drug and alcohol abuse

Drug and alcohol abuse poses a severe safety problem and has a potential for jeopardising operations and safety of life. A drunken person must not be allowed on duty, even though there may be a shortage of people. It is far safer to do a job more slowly with less people.

Drug and alcohol abuse warrants swift action and one must not hesitate, however unpleasant it may be. The crew must be made aware of the company's drug and alcohol policy and the severe penalties that go with their abuse. Usually, in a well run company with regular screening prior to recruitment and a policy of unannounced screening, this problem is not common. However, one should be aware of the problem, be on guard and educate and re-educate people as often as required.

Conclusion

Ultimately, the management of safety on board is a lot of little things. Is the watchkeeper sufficiently rested, are we sailing out with sufficient bunkers, are we proceeding at a safe speed and so on. We should take care and manage the little things like good housekeeping, good seamanship, common sense, good communication and a fair degree of planning. Cleanliness and tidiness reduces fire hazards, slips and falls and equipment is found quickly when it matters. Good seamanship makes for safe working practices. Common sense is communication and leadership where the crew develops trust and confidence and it helps individuals develop to their full potential. Planning and discussion is essential, especially in recognising potential hazards.

Major accidents and causalities will always get publicity. However, it is important to remember that it is the little things, the safe management of daily work and practices, that go a long way in avoiding major accidents.

Chapter 16

MEASURES OF ECONOMIC EFFICIENCY IN SHIPPING

by Professor R.O. Goss MA PhD FNI, Department of Maritime Studies, Cardiff University

Richard Goss went to sea 1947–1955. After taking an economics degree at Cambridge he joined the head office of NZS. He spent 1963–1980 as an economist specialising in maritime matters for the UK government, rising to Under-Secretary. Since 1980 he has been Professor of Maritime Economics and Administration at UWIST.

EVERY SHIP'S CAPTAIN should be concerned with the *efficiency* with which his ship operates. It is his duty to his employer – whether owner or charterer; it is his duty to the shippers who use his ship's services; it is his duty to his crew, who may well wish to be employed there again and, for the same reason, it is his duty to himself. Because a shipping industry may also be of national value, it is also his duty to his country. Most shipping operates in competition; with this safeguard, the greatest *profit* is likely to be a measure of the greatest economic success in operating a ship; though of course no one would deny that there are some bad ways of making profits.

Much shipboard efficiency consists of maintaining well-established and effective routines like checking moorings in port, using parallel indexing in coastal navigation and keeping a good lookout. With safety there are absolute professional standards which should be maintained. Elsewhere, however, and particularly with economic or financial matters there are no such absolute standards: you have to do the best you can with what you have and in conditions some parts of which may be outside your control. But it is easy to exaggerate this and, as always, a systematic approach to measurement is helpful. Given a microcomputer (or even a simple hand calculator) the calculations are not tiresome. Indeed the arrival of these has made it possible to perform many kinds of calculation rapidly and with ease.

These measurements, often in the form of ratios, generally appear in two ways: the physical and the financial. Examples of the first might be the fuel consumption in tonnes per day at sea or of the amount of cargo worked per day in port. Examples of the second might be the fuel cost per day (or shp/hour), the daily cost of feeding the crew (per man/day), or of the stevedoring cost per tonne of cargo handled. As will be shown below, these two are at their most helpful when they are linked.

All trades – and all shipping companies – have their own characteristics. In this, as in so many other aspects of command, the shipmaster must adapt his training and ideas to circumstances. The object of this chapter, therefore, is to provide a general account, with practical examples, of what a master may do, or be expected to do, in a variety of circumstances. The greatest variety is likely to be found in the extent to which shipping companies seek to involve masters in economic matters, e.g. by delegation: but there are few today who do not welcome their masters taking an interest. Even, therefore, where company practice involves the master having a minimum of financial responsibility it is helpful for him to know how economic efficiency is likely to be measured.

This chapter is laid out in four sections. The second (next) concerns the development of *cost centres*, the third outlines *budgetary control* and the fourth concerns the economic or financial measures which may be derived from these – i.e. *profits*. The chapter as a whole thus concentrates on the economics of operating an existing ship: not on those of designing, choosing or buying a new one. Whilst there is nothing essentially new in much of this, it is believed to be the first time that such material has been addressed specifically to the potential shipmaster.

Accounts, like any other written record, have two purposes: to render an accurate account of what happened; and to enable better decisions to be made in the future. Whilst much the same accounts may be used for each purpose this chapter is concerned only with the second of these.

Cost centres

A cost centre is a specific area, output or activity, whose costs can be identified, and thus measured, with reasonable case. It is not necessarily an input, such as crew wages, since these will contribute to a number of activities. Cost centres can be divided or combined as required. Modern calculation facilities make this very easy.

Thus, it is common for each ship to be regarded as a 'cost centre in itself' and, within it, to have such activities as cargo-handling and fuel consumption separately identified. When listed these are usually arranged in order of *escapability*. Thus, at the simplest level, if the ship sailed without cargo there would be no costs of loading and discharging it, but the other costs would be much the same. At the next level, if the ship stayed 'In port the port charges would continue but the main engine would use no fuel or lubricating oil and need less maintenance, though most other costs (crew wages, for example) would continue.

Ultimately, however, the crew could be paid off and the ship laid up. Then only the capital charges of depreciation and any relevant loan payments would continue.

Individual cost centres may thus cover one or a variety of activities, provided these are related in practical terms. Thus, it may be useful, for some purposes, to consider the whole of the costs associated with maintenance, or with the operation of the engine room, or with catering. They may be divided, so that electricity generation is separated for examination: they may be combined – e.g. the crew costs for a whole fleet of ships. In constructing such a system of cost centres for the first time the emphasis should be on *activities* or *outputs* rather than on inputs. Thus, for example, 'crew wages' is an input: it is what they do that constitutes an activity or output, and that will usually involve other costs like paint or other stores.

Within each cost centre there will therefore be a number of items which, though possibly different in nature, are linked by being parts of the same activity. Catering crew costs, food and fuel for cooking it are examples. These will generally have both physical units, (numbers of people, Kwh of energy, say) and, for each of these, a unit price, cost or value paid. The sum for that item in that cost centre is the physical quantity multiplied by the price per unit.

The control of efficiency through the control of costs lies in appreciating that both of these can be identified and measured. One or the other – frequently both – can then be controlled.

Wherever the master is given the necessary data and control (but in some shipping companies this is not done) a system of cost centres should be constructed. Usually, they will be specified in some detail by the head office; the task is then to measure the physical inputs (per cargo, or per day as appropriate) and the unit values, to multiply one by the other and then to add up the results.

Budgetary control

A system of budgetary control uses the cost centres so as to *compare the expected results with the actual ones*.

Thus, budgetary control involves *forecasting* for each cost centre the physical units (e.g. tonnes of oil, tonnes of cargo loaded), the unit costs, the result of multiplying the two together and then comparing this expected result with the actual one. The object is to show just where and how the differences arose.

These differences are often termed *variances*. All of them should be examined, whether they showed results that were better or worse. It may then be possible to identify practices that save money (and should be extended or adopted more widely); or those which turned out to be unfortunate and should be avoided. Even if no practical lessons can be learnt it

will often be possible to improve the forecasting. Without such a systematic approach it is likely that good ideas will be missed, bad ones continued and, in any case, that the uncertainty of ship finances will be greater.

Obviously, many variances will be found to be beyond the control or responsibility of the ship or those aboard. They are not, for example, responsible for negotiating the price paid for the bunkers: usually that rests with the operator's head office and sometimes there are general price changes they are unable to affect. When these outside effects have been identified, therefore, attention can be concentrated on the others. By identifying what the results were, how they differed from what was expected and where the responsibility lies, the ship's overall efficiency can be improved.

An earlier method of financial control consisted of preparing 'voyage estimates' before a voyage took place and a 'voyage account' afterwards. Comparisons then concentrated on the final outcome or profit. This method is useful for chartering and some other management decisions – and therefore still used for some purposes. But the variances were not usually shown as such and the (usual) omission of the physical units and prices from the presentations made an item-by-item examination difficult.

Thus attention was inevitably concentrated on comparing the two figures for profit rather than on the details of how and why they differed. When all this was fed back to the people responsible for the estimates, they might well have had the chance to improve their forecasting methods: but the opportunity for a systematic, detailed and continuous examination of the financial results of the ship's operation was missed. Moreover, those responsible for the operation of particular areas of the ship had no chance of assessing their own performance in managing their cost centres.

Profit and economic efficiency

So far this chapter has concentrated on costs, largely because they represent those aspects of his ship's operations over which the master may expect to have most influence. Nevertheless, most ships exist to earn money and thus profits for their owners. (There is little sense in simply trying to minimise total costs: to do that you would send the ship to lay-up).

Profits, of which there are several definitions, are obtained by earning revenues and then deducting the relevant costs. In some industries, where many revenue-earning activities can go on together but with separately identifiable costs (a hotel, say, with restaurant, bars and bedrooms) there can be a number of separate *profit centres*. This is rare in shipping, since the whole ship may reasonably be said to earn the whole of the revenue and to incur the whole of the costs in doing so. (You could calculate a container ship's freight earnings for each hold, but it would not be useful since it would not be independent of the others; and it would be difficult to identify the related costs.)

Generally, therefore, *the ship forms a profit centre on its own* and is not subdivided as such. Indeed, in some trades where there is a high service frequency (e.g. ferries or container ships) it is further added with other ships to form a monthly *revenue centre* for each trade covered (e.g. southbound and northbound).

Just as with cost centres, so profit centres should show, in as much detail as is appropriate for the case in question, the physical units and the unit price. For a container ship the former is probably boxes (though possibly tonnes of cargo may be better for some trades). For a ship on voyage charter it is again tonnes of cargo. For a ship on time charter it is the number of days or months on charter.

Correspondingly, the unit prices are the box rates, freight rates or time-charter rates and so on. (On a voyage charter it may be necessary to allow for demurrage and despatch money). Multiplying the physical units by the unit prices provides the gross revenue. Deducting the cost centres in turn (in order of escapability, as noted previously, leaves the *gross profit* for the voyage, voyage leg, charter or period in question. The gross profits of several ships may be added to see the overall results for a company's fleet or for any particular service. Where ships are switched between one service and another it may be necessary to divide and recombine the profits accordingly.

The results of the profit centres described so far represent the financial surplus earned: no allowance has been made either for the head office costs or for the capital cost of the ship. For the first of these, company practices vary, with some 'allocating' such shore costs to the ship by some method as pence per deadweight tonne per voyage day. All such methods are, however, arbitrary and a more realistic approach is to treat the shore costs as a cost centre of their own, financed wholly out of the profits of the ships.

This, however, is not necessarily appropriate when it comes to dealing with the capital costs of the ships. Obviously, these occur at the start of their lives; moreover, once incurred, they are outside management controls – save by the drastic step of selling the ship secondhand. Some firms will thus ignore the capital cost for these purposes and leave matters as described above.

Others, however, will consider it reasonable to go a stage further and to *deduct depreciation from the gross profit to obtain the net profit*. Depreciation is a method of allocating the ship's capital cost over its life and there are various methods. The simplest, often used in shipping, is to divide the capital cost of the ship by its estimated life and then by 365 to obtain a daily rate; this is then multiplied by the number of days on the voyage or charter and deducted. Thus, if a ship costing £10 million is supposed to have a 15 year life the daily depreciation rate will be £ 1, 826. There are a number of other depreciation methods (reducing balance, sum of the years digits) but this, the *straight line depreciation* method, is the commonest in shipping. Were any allowance to be made for the increased cost of replacing the ship – i.e. for inflation – then the figure would be greater. Such adjustments are, however, controversial in all industries.. They are rare in shipping if only because of the sharp fluctuations which often take place in shipping markets and, therefore, in ship values.

It is also common for a large part of a ship's capital cost to be financed by borrowing. Again, there is much variation, but shipbuilding loans commonly extend over 8 years, cover 80 per cent of the ship's capital cost and carry an interest rate of 8 per cent per year. (Their cheapness comes largely from the desire of government to assist their shipbuilding industries.) As the loan is gradually repaid the outstanding balance falls and so, therefore, does the size of the interest payment.

As with depreciation, however, this is a cost which the ship's master cannot control or affect. If it appears at all in the structure of profit centres available to him, therefore, it will be because the same forms and figures are being used at the head office, or to show the master just how expensive his ship really is.

Further reading

- Downard, J.M., *Running Costs*, Fairplay Publications, 1981. (A comprehensive and practical account, though addressed primarily to the shore-based manager.)

- *Managing Ships*, Fairplay Publications, 1984. (A more advanced text, covering largely non-financial management topics.)

- Laurence, C.A., *Vessel Operating Economics*, Fairplay Publications, 1984. (Despite its general sounding title this book largely concerns ways of economising on fuel – e.g., by optimising routeing, speed, hull and engine maintenance)

- Chrzanowski, I., *An Introduction to Shipping Economics*, Fairplay Publications 1985. (A more academic and advanced text than those recommended above, it provides an insight into much of the underlying economic theory and many of the controversies involved in shipping today.)

Chapter 17

RUNNING COSTS *

by Mr. John M. Downard

The author began his career with P&O in 1944. His sea service was spent in tramp ships and bulk carriers and included a period as a hull inspector and eight years in command. He came ashore in 1968 and held positions as assistant marine superintendent, fleet personnel manager and assistant fleet manager. After service at director level with ship management, broking and agency companies, in 1981 he was appointed a regional director for Reefer Express Lines Pty. Ltd.

Budgets

Whereas a time scale puts substance to a plan, money gives it uniformity, bringing all the parts to a common denominator. There are very few plans which do not involve money and plans in money terms are known in organisations as Budgets.

Business budgets are based upon the plans and policy's of the company and, when completed, should be the best possible estimates of the costs of implementing those plans. As with all estimates, their accuracy depends upon the quality of the information and other factors used in their preparation. Poor information will result in poor budgets and *vice versa*. Budgets usually fall into two broad time categories, short-term and long-term, in the same way *as* long- and short term plans. The short-term budget usually covers a year while long-term budgets can be anything up to ten or more years.

The budgets are also named to indicate the area they cover such as unit or ship budgets, departmental budgets, divisional and corporate budgets. Thus one can have a long- or short-term corporate budget or ship budget. Each unit budget is made up of many parts like the bricks of a house and these 'bricks' are known as cost centres. To follow this analogy for a moment; the bricks are brought together to form walls, or departments and these in turn form the house, unit or ship budget. The bricks can be large or small as required but ideally they should all be the same size in financial terms.

In shipping, as in a number of other industries, the size of the cost centre 'bricks' can vary due to three factors.
(a) Convention: the traditional way of grouping certain items together.
(b) Convenience: certain items fall naturally into groups.
(c) High cost items: some items are of such high cost they can only be considered separately.

* These extracts are reproduced by permission of Fairplay Publications Ltd from the book of the same name in their Ship Management Series.

Figure 17.1 shows how the cost centres of one department relate to the unit or ship and the corporation as a whole, in a fairly typical shipping group. These terms will be used throughout, but it is important to note that the arrangements of particular cost centres into departments is not rigid and in some shipping companies they are arranged differently to suit new ship management concepts. Nevertheless, the cost centre components themselves are still required if the budget is to be constructed properly on the foundations of management knowledge and experience.

The diagram shows how the cost centre of 'crew wages' forms part of the crew 'department' budget which in turn forms part of the unit or ship budget and so on, eventually forming part of the large corporate budget.

Budget Organisation

	XYZ CORPORATION
	* Z Shipping Co. Ltd.
Corporate	YZ Freight Forwarders Ltd.
Budget	ADE Tankers Ltd.
	WEP Haulage Ltd.

	Z SHIPPING CO. LTD
	M. V. Red Line
Divisional	* M. V. Blue Line
or Company	M. V. Green Line
Budget	M. V. Yellow Line
	M. V. Brown Line

	M. V. BLUE LINE
	Technical Department
Unit or Ship	* Crew Department
Budget	Supplies Department
	Insurance Department
	Administration Department

	CREW DEPARTMENT
Department	* Crew Wages
Budget	Crew Travel
	Crew Training

Figure 17.1

Thus it can be seen that in the Z Shipping Company, for example, there will be many cost centres and a number of 'crew wages', each identified by the particular ship name. As this section is about the costs of a ship, the factors concerned in producing a short-term budget for such a unit will now be considered. However, it should not be forgotten that the unit plan is in itself dependent upon the corporation short- and long-term plans.

Budget responsibility

Because managers have to work within budgets they are more likely to achieve their objectives if they produce the budget themselves or are involved in its production. Modern management follows this philosophy and in most companies it is the managers who make the plans, estimate the costs of such planning and who carry the responsibilities for implementing and achieving the plans within the budgets. The number and levels of managers involved will vary considerably with the size of the organisation.

A one-ship company may only have one manager, whereas a ten-ship company may have an overall manager for a number of ships and managers for each department. Regardless of numbers involved, responsibility should lie with the person who produces the budget or portion of a budget – i.e. the manager. Of course, he must obtain approval before he can proceed with the implementation of his budget, but once this is received he should be allowed to carry it out with minimum interference.

Budget approval

Great care needs to be taken in approving or amending budgets. If the guidelines given are followed, i.e. that the budget should be realistic, capable of fulfilment but challenging; and providing it conforms to the overall plan, there should be little to amend. It is the manager's own plan and because he and his team have constructed it, within the parameters laid down, they will do their best to see it through.

Unfortunately, there is a tendency for top management to insist on a reduction in the budget as a matter of form, often in the belief that the manager has probably set his figure too high and will spend to the limit. This can have a detrimental effect upon the relationship between top management and the manager concerned as, having carefully prepared the budget in the first place, he will know it is impossible to achieve at the reduced level without some amendments to the plan itself.

Thus top managers should take care in pressing a manager to reduce his budget. Of course they should challenge the budget and satisfy themselves that the manager is not 'playing safe' by overestimating. But providing they are satisfied on these points, they should leave it alone and if it is too high for the overall plan, seek a solution elsewhere.

Procedure and timetables

The annual budget usually aligns itself with the financial year. Budget preparation at the cost centre level usually commences about five months before the commencement of the new financial year. This allows consideration of the actual running costs of the first half of the current year and gives sufficient time for completion and presentation of the draft budget for approval. Provided all goes according to schedule, the approved budget should be ready for presentation to the corporate planners three months before the new year commences, so allowing them time to include the data in their budgets.

The timetable should be agreed as company policy well in advance so that all involved can be properly prepared and can plan their work accordingly. An example of a typical timetable for work prior to a budget year commencing on 1 January, follows.

The XYZ Shipping Company budget timetable:

15th July	Department managers receive first half year results – commence preparatory work on cost centre estimates.
15th August	Department managers coordinate cost centre estimates and present draft budgets to ship manager for consideration.
1st September	Ship manager discusses budgets with department managers and on agreement coordinates into ship budgets.
15th September	Draft ship budgets presented to divisional manager for approval.
1st October	Approved/amended budgets finalised and passed to budgetary controller.

As one would expect, the more complex the budget the more time will be required to gather the information, calculate and estimate, particularly in the first stages of preparation – i.e. the cost centre level.

Budget preparation

Accuracy, attention to detail and method are essential factors in the preparation of a budget. The manager himself should decide the degree of detail required. It should be sufficient to give him the answers he requires, but no more, as too much information can create unnecessary work and confuse matters. Essentially budget preparation depends upon: assumptions, past records, current information, and detail.

Assumptions: Many of these should be provided by top management in order to ensure consistency with other budgets, particularly in such matters as currency exchange and inflation rates. Other assumptions should relate to corporate plans and policies – e.g. that the ship will remain in service, but will be sold for scrapping in two years' time and thus will not be dry-docked during the budget year being planned. Whatever the assumptions and plans, they must be known before budget preparation can begin.

Past Records: Examination and consideration of the previous years' costs and those of the first half of the current year can be of great assistance in some areas particularly of consumable commodities where it may be sufficient to apply an inflation factor, or currency factor, to obtain an estimate for the next year. Past records are also helpful in checking against estimates to ensure that the new calculations are reasonably accurate compared with past results.

Current information: The quality of estimating depends very much on the information available to the manager. If a manager knows that crew wage negotiations take place each June, with any increases to commence the following July, he can allow for an increase but can only guess the amount. However, if the previous year's negotiations allowed for wage changes in two stages over a two-year period he will know exactly the amount of increase and his budget will be that much more accurate. This applies to many areas in budget preparation and even the knowledge that a strategically-placed dry-dock may be closed may have an effect on repair costs.

Detail: When preparing a budget every item which will have a significant effect must be considered. In some departments the number of items may be so numerous that they have to be grouped under one cost centre; nevertheless, the manager must know within which centre items are grouped. Fortunately, in many cases the association of items is so close that grouping is almost automatic.

Budget setting forms and their arrangement

There is a good maxim that every form should be as much use to the person completing it as the person who gets it. Good forms are the keystone of any system and one can never spend too much time on their design in order to get the most effective result.

The form used to set the budget is called a 'budget setting form'. It should be arranged so that it helps the manager to prepare the budget and be useful for reference later. Although he can group items into cost centres as he wishes, in most industries there are some fairly conventional ways of grouping costs and it is perhaps best to adhere to these conventions whenever possible. It is particularly important to try to be consistent and keep the same groups and cost centres from year to year in order that useful comparisons can be made. With this in mind, budget setting forms should be pre-printed to ensure standardisation, not only of groups and cost centres but also of layout.

To avoid excessive detail on the budget setting forms it is preferable if small items grouped into cost centres are listed in a separate manual for easy reference. Thus the form should be as uncluttered as possible and only contain relevant detail.

On examining the cost centres of each department it will be found that some departments e.g. Supplies, have many while others e.g. Insurance, have few. In order to be able to summarise the costs easily on the form, they are grouped together as follows:

Cost centres are designated *3rd category costs.*
Groups of 3rd category costs are designated *2nd category costs.*
The sum of all the 2nd category costs is the *1st category or department cost.*

As stated earlier, if the cost centres, or 3rd category costs, are composed of a number of items, these are not shown on the budget setting form but are listed in a manual. In departments where there are very few cost centres, they will be designated 2nd category costs.

It should be noted that in addition to the need to group large numbers of cost items, there are requirements for different levels of information. Whereas top management may only want to know the total ship costs, or the ship costs broken down into departmental totals, the ship manager will want more detail and the departmental manager will want even more, to be able to highlight fluctuations in the cost centres. The significance of this will be seen when the aspects of control are considered.

One cost centre which should be carefully avoided is that of miscellaneous, a convenient dustbin into which staff can place costs rather than take the trouble to seek the appropriate allocation. There should never be a miscellaneous section in any budget as every item of any significance should be accounted for.

Each cost centre is usually given a code number which forms part of the overall coded company accounting system and these are printed on the budget setting form. Codes simplify the allocation of costs, and adapt well to computer and other accounting equipment. It is usual to arrange the codes into numbered groups and sub groups for easy identification of departments and categories; for example, crew costs may be arranged into a 3000 series, technical costs into a 4000 series and supplies costs into a 5000 series. Taking this one step further, 2nd category 'crew wages' may be arranged in the 100 group of the 3000 series (3100), 'crew travel' may be arranged in the 200 group (3200) and 'crew other costs' into the 300 group (3300). 'Ten' groups are arranged for 3rd category costs. These groups are usually preceded by a code to identify the ship and followed by other code groups used by the accounts department to identify suppliers, items to be recharged, etc.

Although the budget is for a whole year, it is usual to show costs for each quarter year on the budget setting form, in order to highlight exceptional changes compared with other quarters. To provide for this the budget setting form is usually arranged with columns

Ship Code: Refer to Ship Code List
Head Code: 5. Series 5000

2nd Category		3rd Category		Items
Item	Code	Item	Code	Uncoded items included
		Safety	5110	Safety equipment, Lifeboat stores, Lifesaving equipment, firefighting equipment pyrotechnics
		Paints	5120	Drydocking paints, other paints, primers, paint solvents.
		Cargo equipment	5130	Blocks, shackles, pulleys, chains
Marine Stores	5100	Ropes and wires	5140	Ropes, cordages, wires, mooring ropes, mooring wires, canvas.
		Deck stores	5150	Tools, painting equipment, flags.
		Fresh water	5160	Dry dock requirements
		Chemicals	5210	Refrigeration, tank cleaning, degreasing.
Engine Stores	5200	Gases	5220	C02, Frecon, Acetylene.
		Electrical	5230	Bulbs, tubes, shades, fittings, wire.

Figure 17.2

for costs for the four quarters and a total column for the year. Finally, each budget form should have space to show in writing all assumptions used and estimates of out-of-service time for dry-docking, crew changes and any other items of importance.

During the preparation of the budget a number of notes and calculations will be made in order to arrive at the figures and data entered on the budget setting forms. These should be kept carefully on file for reference and future use. The importance of these notes should not be underestimated.

There should be only one budget. The draft or proposed budget being only a draft is not a budget until properly approved. Once approved it should remain unchanged. If this rule is ignored, terms such as revised budget, first budget and second budget arise and staff become confused as to which budget people are actually referring. This causes considerable difficulties when explanations of differences between the budget and actual figures are required. Adherence to the 'one budget' rule will ensure that the yardstick against which results are measured remains the same.

Budgets have an additional use in that the information contained in them can be of considerable use in research and development projects. The data can save considerable time when a quick idea of costs is required and can be adapted to suit a particular project.

Once the background notes and calculations are finished the next step is to transfer the data and fill in the budget setting forms. Providing one's writing and figures are reasonably neat and legible it is preferable for the forms to be handwritten for the following reasons: if copied by a typist errors may occur; and the figures will be transferred to a computer or other

business system and thus it does not matter whether they are typed or handwritten. In other words, the less the figures are copied the better.

To summarise

- A budget is a plan in financial terms.
- It is based on the plans and policies of the company or organisation and on good information.
- Its creation and implementation is the responsibility of management with the approval of senior or top management.
- It must be both realistic and challenging.
- It must be meticulously prepared and produced in accordance with an agreed time table.
- It should consider every factor and each factor or group of factors should be given a cost centre label.
- It should never have a miscellaneous cost centre.
- It should be prepared on a standard form which should aid managers before and after the budget is approved.
- There should only be one budget.

Accounting practices

One of the difficulties experienced by ship managers when dealing with accounts and accountants lies in reconciling the financial data presented to them to events which they know have occurred. This is largely because accountancy is based on a number of philosophies regarding the arrangement of business accounts which appear strange to those not initiated into the mysteries of their conventions and practices.

Fortunately the development of management accounting has resulted in data which is much easier for non-accountants to comprehend, but there is, like many professions, a certain amount of professional jargon which needs to be understood. For example certain computer output sheets may be referred to as 'journals' or 'ledgers' which they are not, in the sense of bound books, but are so called because they contain the information which used to be contained in ledgers and journals when information was recorded by hand.

Accounts are prepared for three reasons: to show the financial position of the business; to allow tax calculations to be made; and to provide management with the information it needs to exercise proper control.

Accounting is the method of recording the money value of business transactions, sales, purchases, receipts and payments.

Financial accounting or reporting analyses the income and expenses (costs), by the type of transaction – e.g. cash, stock, creditors, debtors, assets, liabilities etc.

Cost accounting provides analyses of the costs of a business by function or activity. It is most effective in manufacturing and similar industries.

Management accounting or reporting presents relevant, up to date and accurate information to management to assist in the operation and control of the business. Like cost accounting the information provided is based on functions and activities – e.g. crew, technical supplies, etc. just as a manager's plans form part of the larger unit or corporate plan, so the budget he prepares and the costs he incurs form part of the overall corporate accounts and management information data of the business. These are recorded and presented in a number of different ways in the following accounts, statements and plans:

Balance sheet: Is a statement of the assets, share holders equity and liabilities of a company at a given moment in time. They are defined as long and short term as appropriate. For the purpose of these extracts it is sufficient to say that the effects of costs eventually find their way through to the balance sheet, shown under the heading of the 'profit and loss account'.

Profit and loss account or revenue account: Is a financial accounting statement which shows the earnings and expenses (costs) of the company for a given period. Running costs are seen more clearly in this account although the amounts need not relate directly to money spent during the period due to the accounting 'treatment' of certain expenses – i.e. when the money is considered to have been spent.

Management accounts or reports: Show the manager the detail he requires to control the department for which he is responsible. They show the total costs of each cost centre for the period and the year to date although, as in other accounts, the amounts accounted for will not necessarily relate to money actually spent. For comparison purposes the management accounts or reports will also show the budget for the period and year to date and any variances between the two sets of figures. The costs themselves can also be broken down into various components showing sums actually paid, assumed to have been paid or apportioned as will be described later.

Cash flow statement: Is a month by month statement of anticipated actual earnings and expenditure over a given period, summarised each month to show the high and low points of the actual cash situation. It highlights irregularities in the flow of cash and gives warnings of when there may be a shortage of cash, despite the fact that over the total period earnings may exceed expenditure. Managers may be required to supply data for these statements and in such cases the budget notes will be of considerable value.

Budgets: These have been described in some detail earlier. However, it is important to draw a distinction between the estimated expenditure shown on a budget setting form and the cash flow statement, with which it is sometimes mistaken. The budget shows costs expected to be incurred but which may not in fact be paid in the period, while the cash flow statement shows the actual movement of cash. For example, the cash flow statement would show the cost of an insurance premium when it is paid, whereas the budget would show the cost to the ship per month or quarter – i.e. spread over the period of the insurance cover. Because budgets form part of the total accounting system it is important that their format aligns itself with the format of other accounts.

Treatment of costs: It is most important that the accounting treatment of costs referred to earlier is consistent. Ship managers must have an understanding of the way the costs are 'treated' or dealt with, if they are to relate the facts presented in management accounts to what they know has actually happened The treatment with which ship managers are most likely to be associated are as follows:

The prudence concept: This is an accepted accountancy practice which indicates how a prudent businessman would 'treat' earnings and expenditure. In essence the philosophy is that exceptional or uncertain earnings should not be accounted for – i.e. considered as being earned – until they have actually been received, but once defined costs are incurred they should be accounted for even though not actually paid. It is important to note that although the emphasis is on 'prudence', much depends upon the type of transaction or business and the policy of the company.

Accrued and prepaid expenses: While the prudence concept endeavours to ensure that once costs are incurred they are included in the accounts, even if not paid, another concept ensures that only those costs which refer to the accounting period are included in the accounts. The resultant allocations and apportionments are known as accrued and prepaid expenses.

Accrued expenses: These are costs which have been incurred in the period but for which payment has not been made. Although there may be some flexibility, in the main any such sums 'accrued' would be known fairly accurately, such as a bill agreed with a repair yard but only part paid, the balance being due after the end of the accounting period. As the outstanding amount is known accurately it would be accrued accordingly.

Example: Ship repaired during the 4th quarter of the year.

	$
On completion of repair costs agreed as	520,000
Agreed sum paid on leaving repair yard	120,000
Balance due in 3 months i.e. in next financial year	400,000
But 4th quarter accounts show total repair costs	520,000

Prepayments: These are items such as rentals, property taxes and insurance premiums which are paid in advance for a period which does not align itself with the current accounting period. The total sum has been paid but only part applies to the accounting period; therefore only the appropriate proportion is shown in the accounts and the balance is carried forward to other accounting periods.

Example: Insurance premiums paid on 1st April for one year

	$	
Actual Cost	10,000	
2nd Qtr accounts show	2,500	cost
3rd Qtr accounts show	2,500	cost
4th Qtr accounts show	2,500	cost
Total for year	7,500	

Balance of the premium of $2,500 is carried forward and shown in 1st Qtr of next year's accounts.

Provisions: are sums of money accounted for as costs in two principal categories.

Depreciation: this is a charge to the accounts to reflect the use of an asset and its reduction in value over its useful life. As the depreciation period is usually longer than the accounting period a charge is made in each accounting period equal to the proportionate reduction in value of an asset. The treatment of this is very much a bookkeeping exercise as the depreciation will, in time, reduce the value to nil although the asset will still have a real value which in the case of a ship is its scrap value. Depreciation is a somewhat complex subject entering into the area of financial accounting and is often associated with tax allowances. From the point of view of the ship manager it is sufficient to have a general idea of what it means when seen on a management accounting report. The major asset treated in this way is the ship.

Amortisation: is similar to depreciation and is applied in the same way. It only applies to a loss of value of an asset through time, as distinct from use, as in depreciation. It is used in accounting for leasehold improvement charges in administration costs. Allowance for a liability, the cost of which cannot be determined with any accuracy is thus a sum which cannot be treated as an accrual.

Reserve: Is a charge which cannot be classed as a provision. It is a sum of money put aside for an anticipated purpose in the future. The action of putting the sum aside in the financial accounts prevents its allocation for other purposes (such as tax, profits, etc.) and ensures its availability in the future. However, it should be noted that shipping accountancy practice today does not make so much use of reserves as in the past.

To give an example: ships used to be taken out of service for a special hull and engine survey every four to five years. The cost of the work was high compared with the other years and the time out of service long. Because of the high cost of the survey a sum of money was placed in 'reserve' each year in readiness for the next special survey. Two things have changed this:

The time out of service necessary to carry out special surveys has been reduced considerably by the introduction of staged or continuous running surveys to spread the survey of individual items of hull and machinery over the period between the special surveys. Today, when a special survey takes place, it is only necessary to complete outstanding items which, for various reasons, have not been surveyed earlier. This has resulted in spreading the costs over the period and reducing the time out of service.

The uncertainty of shipping has resulted in a practice of letting costs lie where they fall – i.e. to face each year as it comes and budget and pay for costs for that particular year. It is argued that it is pointless to put money into reserve for a survey, or other purpose, in four years' time when the ship may have been sold by then.

Stock concept: Is similar to that used for accrued and prepaid expenses in that unused stock in hand is like a prepaid expense. Whereas once the costs of crew and repairs are incurred, money is spent in the sense that it has or must be paid out and cannot be retrieved, stocks of unused consumable stores can be considered as a credit – i.e. they are in place and unused at the end of the accounting period and, therefore, ready for use at the beginning of the next. To include them in the current accounting period may give the appearance of very high consumption and cost, particularly if the ship has only just taken on supplies before the accounting period ends.

In theory the detail of all the unused stocks in ships should be reported regularly and the value carried forward to the next period. In practice this may create work which is disproportionate to the sums involved and thus there should be a policy decision on stock to be treated in this way. This should reflect the magnitude of the costs.

In businesses which have large stocks of materials, stock accounting can be very complex due to the change in value of the stock which can occur while the materials lie in storage. Applied to a ship this means that a large quantity of lubricating oil bought near the end of one year and carried forward to the next could increase in value due to a worldwide increase in oil prices.

Shipping companies with a number of sister ships often keep stocks of common items, particularly spare gear, in storage ashore and such stock should also be treated in this way. Victualling stocks should always be reported regularly as, apart from their value, the information is required in order to calculate the daily costs of feeding the crew.

Capitalisation and capital costs: The ship and items bought for its future operations are generally 'capitalised' i.e. they are considered to be a long-term acquisition and therefore not something consumable. The initial outfit of a new ship may include some items which are normally considered to be consumables but are, by convention, included initially as capital costs. These are such items as the chart outfit, the original lubricating oil 'charge' and items of spare gear not included in the price of the ship. Modifications to the ship and its equipment at a later date are also capitalised.

Capital items are shown as assets in the balance sheet; they are reduced by the 'cost' of depreciation at each accounting period until 'paid for' and considered fully used, but will still be shown as an asset at a nominal or resale value. Most capital cost items are easily identifiable and their treatment follows the general accountancy conventions. However some items, such as training and management development, may or may not be treated as a capital 'investment' by companies arguing that such expenditure has long-term value. It is not usual to capitalise the cost of sea staff training.

Here are a few more terms, and their alternatives, which the ship manager may encounter:

Bought ledger: – alternatively **accounts payable ledger**, a record of all items and services purchased by the company.

Sales ledger: – alternatively **accounts receivable ledger**, a record of all 'sales' by the company.

Nominal or private ledger: – alternatively **general ledger**, (there are other terms), a record of all assets, liabilities, shareholders (or stockholders), equity accounts.

General: It must be stressed again that the foregoing are only very broad descriptions of accountancy practices and terms with which the ship manager will come into contact. Those seeking further information should read the many books on the subject. Accountancy is a very complex subject and oversimplification can be misleading.

Anything as complex as accounts needs systems, and management accounting is no exception. Reference was made earlier to lists of cost centres and codes being kept in a manual. Similar lists and codes for all management transactions – accruals, provisions, supplies, etc. are also kept in a manual and it is usual for the budget data, being part of the system, to be kept in the same manual, usually known as the management accounting system manual (MAS).

In general, management accounts cover and are contained in a financial year, even though costs incurred may not be paid for until the next year and, in the case of insurance claims, even later. This is dealt with by the use of accruals and provisions – i.e. the costs having been incurred they are accounted for in the books. When the accounts are finally settled any differences between the actual cost and the accrued or provided amount is borne by the current year. If the accounts department has been told of all costs incurred by means of invoices, order forms, etc., then the amount of any adjustments should be small in most cases. Sums reclaimable from insurance can usually be estimated with some accuracy, particularly if specific sums have been spent, but in some cases, such as crew and supplies costs reclaimable as a result of a deviation, the amounts are often the subject of negotiations and thus cannot be estimated with any accuracy.

The accounts should provide a complete record of all financial transactions which have taken place during the accounting period. They can only be as good as the people who put the information into the system – i.e. the managers and their staff. To ensure this yet another system is required. In essence this demands that every time anyone orders anything e.g. spare gear, paint, a surveyor, or a repair – it should be recorded on a sequentially numbered form in quadruplicate, preferably in different colours.

The top copy should go to the supplier as a request for the service. The next copy should go to the accounts department to indicate that a cost is being incurred. The next two copies should be retained by the person ordering the service, one of which he should send to the accounts department, preferably with the invoice or bill, once the service or supply has been received. He should retain one copy for his records. This can be made more sophisticated with an additional copy to the supplier, and so forth. However, the principal objective is that the accounts department should know as soon as a cost has been, or is about to be incurred. There are difficulties in that sometimes, in emergency, a request for services such as a survey or a repair are made by telephone, telex or cable, but this can be covered by attaching a note or copy of the telex to an order form and distributing it in the usual way.

The importance of sequential numbering lies in ensuring that no order and expense is missed and that everything is put into the accounts system. If an order is cancelled for some reason it should still be put into the system but as a cancellation. All this may seem a lot of paper work, but if managers and accountants are to know everything that is happening, (as they should), such procedures must be established and adhered to.

The prime purpose of a ship manager is to manage and the prime purpose of the accountant is to provide him with a service to assist him in his management. However, it must be remembered that the accountant provides a similar service to all managers and to the company as a whole. He also provides an advisory and counselling service and because of his training ensures that all the financial transactions are dealt with correctly.

The manager should be given the financial information he needs to control the department for which he is responsible, but his requirements must relate to the constraints of financial conventions placed upon the accountant and the requirements of the company as a whole. There is no reason why these requirements cannot be reconciled providing a spirit of mutual understanding, respect and cooperation exists between managers and accountants. Each should have a broad understanding of the others job. A point often forgotten is that the accountant with a staff is also a manager with managerial responsibilities like other managers.

To summarise

- The accounts with which ship managers are most closely associated are management accounts embodied in a management accounting system (MAS).
- Budgets form part of the MAS as a base against which actual costs are compared and these are shown in management reports.
- Once a cost is incurred it enters the system, whether paid for or not, and eventually finds its way through to the balance sheet via the profit and loss account.
- The 'treatment' of costs through accruals, prepayments, provisions and reserves can cause statements of accounts or reports to appear to be different to the payments that have actually been made.
- Cooperation between managers and accountants is essential and to this end ship managers should have an understanding of the conventions and jargon of accountancy.
- The accounts of a business should be a complete record of all financial transactions. For this objective to be fulfilled meticulous record keeping is required by all involved in costs.

Chapter 18

MANAGING PEOPLE ON BOARD

by Captain E.M. Scott RNR RD** FNI

Martin Scott has had a long and varied career at sea spanning some 38 years, the last 23 years in command of a variety of ships including passenger roro ferries, an Arctic research vessel, container ships and cruise liners.

He presently commands within the Holland-America Line/Windstar cruise fleet and retired as a captain in the Royal Naval Reserve last year, having served in a variety of naval units including frigates, minelayers and three of the UK's aircraft carriers. For the last 15 years of his career he was involved in Amphibious Operations, latterly as the Staff Officer, STUFT to the Commodore, Amphibious Warfare.

Introduction

Managing people on board any ship requires some very special skills and strengths to be successful. However, there are a number of areas in this complex subject that really are common to any management situation.

In the style of management required for the merchant navies of the world, some leanings towards the military were required. This leant towards the theory that "leadership" was a better title. Nowadays even I have to agree that the overall picture of the captain or senior officer's position on board is better described as management. This is really due to much greater involvement in the complex technical, budgeting and planning requirements, mostly brought about by computer generated communication with one's principals.

However, leadership remains one of the most significant skills that can affect the efficiency of any ship.

Managing, especially for the captain, means being seen to involve all concerned in any decision-making process. This not only allows you to use your senior officers' or crew members' knowledge or ideas to enable you to reach the best decision, but also makes them feel their professionalism is respected, their knowledge is useful and they are in your confidence.

For a captain or senior officer it is sometimes quite a surprise to realise how much your crew "look up" to you for guidance, advice and decision making. Whether they are looking up... or down... depends to some degree on the example you set, both privately and professionally, in your life on board. This, quite often, can be the hardest part of a successful senior officer's job as you are really on duty 24 hours a day, seven days a week while you are on board or in the vicinity of your ship and your actions and personal habits can be noted by members of the ship's company.

It is crucial that the captain is always in a position to be able to expect obedience to his orders and instructions. This requires motivation and, to some degree, agreement with the order or instruction given.

It is not unusual on any ship that you require that extra bit of effort, those extra hours of overtime, the quick response to an emergency and one cannot reasonably expect this to happen unquestionably without some sort of "reward".

The best sort of reward is one that you already have in the bank. For instance, during a quiet period of a voyage, you have been able to give some extra time off for shore leave – or maybe allow a special party or anniversary celebration on board.

The other must is that the crew are fairly treated regarding their living accommodation and personal entitlements. Make sure their cabins are properly appointed – clean, usable mattresses, light fittings and furnishings in good order, the bathroom properly maintained and a clean water supply.

To be seen to be fair is also a good morale booster. Any disciplinary action, decision or style must be seen both by officers and by crew members to be evenly applied – for example, should a senior officer miss the ship's sailing time his investigation should be as thorough as that applied to the most junior rating.

There has, of course, to be some reward for senior staff on board in recognition of their status and additional responsibilities. However, these privileges must be clearly seen to be appropriate and not against the code of conduct applied to all on board.

Most people at sea of any rank or discipline are usually reasonable decent human beings, willing to do an acceptable job if asked to. You should approach them with this as your main feeling. When a problem, requirement or disciplinary action has been explained to a crew member, even when he has been involved in the most basic tasks on board, you will receive an intelligent response almost without fail.

The few individuals who cannot respond to normal social or professional requirements are quickly identified within the majority and "moved on".

More than in any other industry does the variety of nationalities employed become evident. Shipping companies are able to take advantage of world conditions to employ the most suitable personnel in any position on board ship. More often than not this is based on cost effectiveness and invariably leans toward the cheaper end of the market.

You must not make the mistake of concluding that cheap automatically means poor quality and badly educated.

A significant number of people from the so called 'Third World' countries are intelligent, well educated and have been required by market forces in their own countries to seek acceptably paid jobs elsewhere. It is very much to your advantage to treat such people accordingly. Give them respect in your dealings with them and you will be repaid many times over. You will find that they are quite able to learn their jobs and skills quickly, which is especially valued on passenger vessels.

Each nationality on board, although they may work well together, usually enjoy having their own space and will congregate together for eating and socialising. Where possible, cabins should be shared by the same nationality. It is very much to your advantage as a captain or senior officer to study the customs and personal habits of the nationalities you are responsible for – respect for those is, on occasion, vital to good relations. "Culturegrams" are available from consulates for most nationalities and are an excellent resume of personal customs in their respective countries.

There is, of course, a world of difference in the make-up of the officers and ship's company of, say, an 80,000 ton passenger ship and a similar sized OBO or container ship. Whilst the cargo related unit has a much smaller crew, individually they are equally if not more responsible for the safe and efficient operation of the ship and her cargo.

The captain needs successfully to encourage each member of his small group, getting to know their individual characters and monitoring their performance to ensure each continue their varied tasks in a responsible manner as each crew member is especially valuable on such a large unit.

Due to the increasing popularity of cruising, the world's passenger cruise fleet continues to grow. We now have ships of over 100,000 tons capable of carrying up to 3,000 passengers with a crew size to match.

To be the captain of any significant sized passenger vessel requires particularly well developed management skills and personal ability. Here the captain must rely on his heads of department, the chief engineer, the hotel manager and the chief officer or staff captain, to run their departments effectively. It is obviously to your advantage that each of your heads of department understand your style and

requirements. This is best achieved by discussion and encouragement from yourself. In addition to the number of formal meetings invariably necessary for the efficient running of such a large undertaking, it is a good idea to meet with your senior officers on a daily basis semi-informally in your cabin or office.

It is in the captain's best interest, if he is to have a real grasp of his command, to get around all areas informally, talking to passengers and crew on a regular basis, monitoring people's attitudes and listening to their praise or complaints. Always involve the head of the appropriate department in any area you may be concerned with or requiring further investigation. You should, however, endeavour to obtain the facts from as many sources as possible before making your best judgement or decision – the facts are not always as first presented!

It is inevitable that some tasks on board have to be completed by reaction to circumstances and events as they occur. However, with advance planning and anticipation of tasks, the resulting organisation can improve results considerably. All concerned then have at least a general idea of how the task is to be performed and who is responsible for what. You have also had the opportunity to clear up any misconceptions early, preventing unnecessary discussion or confusion during the event.

A pre-docking or undocking discussion with your officers is a good example of short term planning. Long term would be preparing the ship for a scheduled dry-dock.

It is impossible for the captain of a ship physically to activate every manoeuvre and make every decision, oversee every action by every person on board. He is, however, responsible and accountable for every action of any significance on board his ship.

There has to be delegation. One of the most important that comes to mind is the navigational watch. During the night hours especially, your ship's immediate safety is in the hands of someone else. You have to judge, in advance, that person's ability to discharge this task competently. It is easier to make that decision if your watchkeepers are in possession of certificates of competency issued by a well established, acceptable body. After that it is your call and must be based on your own observations. Your own experience usually helps you decide to what level each officer can be left without your supervision or control. You should also make your wishes or intentions clear, allowing for the individual ability of your officers.

I have generally observed that your senior staff will tend to emulate your style when delegating to their staff. When appropriate, it is better to offer clear suggestions rather than give direct orders. As mentioned before – we are generally dealing with sensible people. Having delegated, always ensure your officers are comfortable in approaching you at any time should they be unsure in the responsibilities you have given them.

The ISM Code requires the master to motivate his crew. Be seen to be interested in their welfare. Talk to them – ask about their families – learn their names – there is nothing like addressing a crew member by name to make him feel wanted and noticed. Praise and thanks for a job well done, or a task completed. Encouragement to learn through on board training for those wishing to understand the job better and for those preparing themselves for promotion, is vital – where else will the future staff come from? A great motivator is to assist someone who wants to improve.

I cannot overemphasise how much the whole ship's company can react to your style and example – if you are seen to encourage and take an interest – follow through problems – use your influence as captain to assist others in achieving their goals, you will have done much to keep your crew focused on their work and motivated towards the ship's best interests, both environmentally and towards safe working practices.

To be responsible, ultimately, for the welfare, safety and lives of any number of people is a great responsibility. At sea this trust is absolute. Whilst with modern communication you are able to seek and use advice and assistance more easily, inevitably there are still many occasions where your immediate and ongoing judgement is required in areas which have a direct effect on the personnel on board your ship.

It is a significant compliment that the majority of good shipowners respect your unique position and bow to your judgement on shipboard matters.

This is, to a large degree, due to the many generations of captains, stretching back hundreds of years, who spent their careers at sea, many giving their lives to maintain a high standard of management and good judgement.

This is unique in industry management and we present captains must always acknowledge the tremendous debt we owe to our forefathers and be aware that the authority and respect we enjoy are based on the high standards of those who went before.

Managing people on board ship is a very special trust. Those of us who have the privilege of such trust must view themselves most fortunate in their task. I suggest they enjoy the opportunity and – if circumstances allow – keep a sense of humour!

Chapter 19

MANAGING SHIPBOARD MAINTENANCE

by Captain U. Zuber, Österreichischer Lloyd Shipmanagement, Austria

> *Captain Ulrich Zuber is the Quality Manager and Designated Person in Österreichischer Lloyd Ship Management, a company managing 50 ships in the dry cargo sector. Captain Zuber commenced sailing as a deck boy 36 years ago, successfully aiming at getting to know a wide variety of vessels and trades. After obtaining his mate's license he experienced several of his companies shutting down. He gained his first command as a master at the age of 32, which was early enough to be satisfying but also late enough to have collected a lot of experience.*
>
> *Seven years later Captain Zuber took over a superintendent's position in his company which he maintained for six years. He then worked independently as a nautical surveyor which finally led him to the area of Quality Assurance which he has found most satisfactory to work in until the present.*

Introduction

Ships are not forever. Each part of them is subjected to continuous wear and tear by adverse elements and working people. Deterioration can occur quickly if countermeasures are not practised in time, i.e. from the new building date. Therefore maintenance is, besides the mere running of a ship, the second largest task of shipboard personnel. Neglected maintenance accounts for many lost lives and billions of dollars worth of damage annually, worldwide. Wasted maintenance work and material also adds up to at least millions. Limited resources need careful management in order to obtain the most benefit from the costs incurred.

Defining standards ashore

The basic steps of optimising all efforts must be taken ashore.

1 The owners have to be sure about their strategy ("own & sell" or "own till scrapyard") and decide accordingly on the desired remaining lifetime/ operation time of the vessel as the basis for all planning. Furthermore, they have to decide on the standard of maintenance which they wish to be kept. In commercial shipping these two parameters are never infinite, so they should better be defined and the managers (in-house management or foreign) instructed accordingly.

2 Then the technical department has to draw up reasonable budgets which permit keeping to the desired standard, in close cooperation with the shore-based organisation which has to support the ship's management.

Only under these prerequisites can shipboard personnel be expected to maintain the ship safely and economically in accordance with the owner's instructions.

In lots of companies chaotic endless discussions are programmed by not defining any standards as outlined above, in that the budgets have to be at minimum and money is spent alternating between sometimes being too generous and then being too tight fisted. The latter usually causes further and greater expenditures than originally necessary.

The cost-benefit relationship of each major maintenance action must be justifiable. Often decisions must be made between renewal and repair. There must be a healthy relationship between the value of equipment and the costs for its maintenance. However, no universal advice can be given to determine an optimum. Too many parameters are involved and must be perused for each single case. For example, the commercial benefits of a well maintained ship on the freight market have to be weighed against higher maintenance costs. Such considerations are neglected in many companies (possibly as a result of separating the technical from the commercial management).

On board planning and documentation

> Just do what comes to mind?
> Better plan first!
> Just plan what comes to mind?
> Better use a system for planning!
> Just any planned maintenance system?
> Better subject your system to Quality Assurance!

In a small ship you may well be able to execute all maintenance works completely without making big plans; still, the few works which are not obvious should be documented for your relief. However, where complex maintenance works have to be planned and coordinated, you cannot keep all facts in mind and you cannot turn over all data to your successor if you haven't documented it all in a systematic way.

Why a system?

A system is a defined structure of regulations. 'Defined' means that the rules are written down, compliance is verified and the procedures are monitored for effectiveness. The employees concerned need not continuously think about or negotiate with each other as to what to do next. The system tells them the next steps. Instruments are provided to ease the flow of work. Formerly this planning work was done on paper forms, on card-indexes or on big tables on the wall. In modern environments a good computer program will guide the user along the right steps. However, this is a question of convenience. The principles of systematic planning can be realised by any of these means.

What makes a good system?

A good maintenance (planning and follow-up) system:

- Is consistent with the Safety Management System of the company.
  The ISM Code requires systematic maintenance of all safety-relevant equipment. However it would be narrow-minded to restrict a maintenance system to only these subjects. It should be capable to be applied to any kind of actual work, control job or training.
- Is thoroughly designed and well structured.
  Another day of system design can easily save many days of work. The more ships the company is managing, the more efforts must be made to perfect the system.
- Is easy to understand because of its logical arrangement.
  It takes more time to design a self-explaining system because the possibilities of wrong understanding are enormous. However the additional work pays for itself.
- Is known to all persons concerned.
  Persons assigned to work with the system have to get a thorough introduction. In a QA system procedures will be provided to safeguard that all necessary training is carried out.
- Provides for equal handling throughout the company.
  Allowing personnel having changed ship to take up their work instantly.
- Makes the planning and documentation work easier.
  Under the bottom line the system must constitute a considerable help. If it doesn't, then redesign it or go back to former methods!
- Is based on solid information about machinery, materials, etc.
  The person designing the system must be experienced in the subject and must thoroughly research the available sources like shipyard's and manufacturer's advice, former work reports and repair protocols. It is a good opportunity to think about and note down where the data (works and their intervals) come from (maker's instructions? Other tutorial material? Superintendent's decision? Own estimate? Source unknown?)
- Is continuously updated
  The best system becomes useless if it is neglected. It needs a good discipline to enter promptly all job executions, sufficiently comprehensive descriptions and spare part consumption.

- Provides for continuous improvement.
  During the practical work with any system you will find possibilities of improvement every day e.g. a misunderstood sentence, an incomplete description or a regular work missing. The system must allow continuous improvement of its structure and its descriptive data.
- Provides for completeness of maintenance job descriptions.
  Where enough efforts have been made in building up and improving the stock of data the system fairly warrants for completeness. The user must not permanently fear to have forgotten any important matter.
- Allows planning and documenting any extraordinary work.
  Most of the maintenance works on board have to be carried out regularly, but the lesser part of occasionally appearing work must be covered as well.
- Shows always the latest state of affairs.
  Important for relieving personnel to get quickly an overview of all due works as well as the executed ones, be it by an assorted card index or by computer listings.
- Shows the history of each item.
  Interesting to see where the problems have been in the past. The system must provide for sufficient space for documentation of all formerly done regular and irregular maintenance works including those done by shipyards and service companies. Where the information becomes too plentiful and difficult to overlook, authorized persons must have the option to delete part of it.
- Makes its documentation traceable.
  Whether the system is on paper or on a hard disk, it should provide space for documenting time and person with each important entry.
- Provides its own procedures of control.
  The procedures of regular as well as unannounced controls have to be laid down in writing naming the intervals and the responsible persons. Furthermore, there should be a specified person to safeguard that these controls are carried out. Such controls are not popular among the executives but the risk of having a neglected system, which can be worse than no system, makes them necessary.
- Ideally would be manipulation-proof.
  It is natural that people who have to document their own work are inclined to brighten the results. Specially when they are burdened with more than can be thoroughly done they are seeking for short cut possibilities. Partly the system can have procedures preventing this, but the system can never 'see' whether a work was really executed as described. There is no other way to avoid such wrong documentation except frequent follow-up from the top.
- Provides for identical information on board and ashore.
  This means that comprehensive information must be transferred from the ship to the technical management ashore at defined intervals, which the shorter the better.

Here again an EDP system is surpassing any paper system.

Please note that a structured maintenance system is not restricted to be used for maintenance works only. Once it is in place it can be used for any other work which must be planned and monitored e.g. any kind of controls or the regular on-board safety training which comprises many subjects to keep track of.

The benefits of a planned maintenance system can easily turn into chaotic conditions if it is not continuously taken care of. Sufficient working time must be available for training, for data maintenance and for controls.

What can go wrong in a planned maintenance system?

Works not existing in the system

Especially at the beginning it may easily happen that a few jobs are just forgotten and not entered. Experienced officers can find these and complete the system by and by. For each irregular job which they enter additionally they should think whether this one could be necessary regularly. For example, the repair of a damaged item may be a singular event, but possibly checking this item at regular intervals could have avoided the damage. So, you should add a periodical control job to the system. Works which cannot be assigned a certain interval because their necessity depends too much on external circumstances, can be entered as a 'reminder' which appears at regular intervals on the work list in order to ensure regular attention.

Another cause of a missing maintenance job can be that somebody has deleted it, either by ignorance or negligence or with ill will. A good system will be manipulation-proof in such a way, for example, that the persons concerned with the execution of the works have limited access rights in as much as they cannot delete a job. It would mean that the concerned crew members have to wait for the authorisation of a superintendent if they want to have a useless job description deleted. Alternatively, the system could provide for deactivating a job which, however, has to be logged in order to maintain traceability.

Job descriptions too complex

The maintenance staff spend more time on reading instructions than on actual work. Those involved feel treated in a patronising manner and missing the opportunity for making their own decisions. All job descriptions, therefore, must be consistent with the level of understanding that can be expected from the persons carrying out the work.

Job descriptions too short

If there is a gap between the job description and the knowledge of the executing staff the latter will seldom claim or ask because they fear they might be regarded as under-qualified. The deficiency will possibly only become detected when bad execution becomes obvious. This gap may be bridged by briefing the staff and by close supervision and communication during the work and, of course, by improving the descriptions.

Job descriptions not fitting exactly to the ship

This may occur particularly if the descriptions are copied from an external source. At least on starting work, the job description should be rewritten in accordance with the fresh experiences.

System not accepted by the executing staff

If a system is too far away from being practical, if it does not meet the expectations of the concerned, if they cannot recognize any advantage, it will be a dead-born child. Reluctant users have no interest in updating or improving such a system. However, the cause of such attitude will not necessarily be found in the quality of the given system or program. The cause can be poor motivation generally, due to other circumstances in the company. For example, job seekers will hardly be inclined to do something for a long-term matter on board.

Missing backup – data lost

A 'grown up' maintenance planning system contains a large amount of data which constitutes a valuable asset (possibly in the range of some hundreds of thousands of Euros) and must be protected appropriately. If you work on paper or with a card index, you should at least have photocopied the job descriptions and keep them apart from the working material. For users of computer programs there should be a strict procedure, ensuring that the data are regularly saved and kept away from the computer. Preferably the program should keep control and demand the production of external backups at regular intervals.

Data which are regularly sent to the shore-based technical department, can also be regarded as an emergency backup.

Defining standards of methods and materials ashore

So far the system provides for timely execution but not necessarily for good quality maintenance. In this respect the shore-based organisation is required to act again. While the executing persons on board have more or less random experiences with a number of methods and materials, the technical department ashore should be able to scan the market for the most suitable (and economic) products, tools and methods, provided they are granted the time and the means for appropriate research.

Examples:
- Determine the best kind of underwater coating according to guarantees of the producer.
- Find out the most effective and economic kind of inscriptions for the wet and salty areas on deck or

for the sometimes oily environment in the engine department.

- Find the best temporary repair material for cracks in fuel tanks or for other special tasks.

Whenever such investigations have a clear result, then these best materials and methods should be used on all ships of the company. This again necessitates making such decision known to all persons concerned, which can be done by circular letters or in briefing sessions, by providing tutorial material or even by sending some of the personnel to attend special courses. When this is done properly it would mean that a new company standard is set; but note well that such standards have a limited lifetime. They must be checked at regular intervals.

On board: execution of maintenance work

If you have well qualified personnel familiar with work throughout the ship, there will hardly be any problems in the proper execution of the work ordered. However the reality usually differs considerably from this ideal. You may have to cope with poorly trained personnel, lacking knowledge of the designated common working language or just having poor motivation; and possibly you have no effective way of changing this situation.

As an officer you should first of all think about measures to improve the climate on board. The more attention you pay to each single man and to particular jobs, the more you raise the attention of your crew. The more your crew is willing (motivated) to do their work satisfactorily the more they will listen to your explanations. You can only be a good leader if your commitments are continuous and not just single actions.

Even if you have a good crew, you have to execute control to a certain extent in order to be sure about your department. For example, when you send someone to grease the hinges of hatch covers you must at least spot check that the man knows what he is doing, in other words that grease really has passed through the hinges. When you send your crew to clean a tank bottom you may have to do at least the final check before the manholes are closed again. Remember, it is you who signs for the proper execution. It is not the poor execution of maintenance work but the negligent supervision that is the primary cause of damage.

While your long term planning is done by means of your system, you still have to decide daily which of the work due is to be done. Regular maintenance work has to fit between cleaning work and watch duties and have to be consistent with the weather expected. Some work needs a particular time span guaranteed available in order to get them completed. For example, if you intend to overhaul the tackle of a crane, you should be very sure to have it reassembled before it is needed in port or before bad weather makes further work impossible.

In your daily planning you must always have a number of alternatives available in order to cope with any changes of the prevailing circumstances. If the weather changes or if your stay in port is shorter than anticipated, if you have to use your crew for unexpected works or work that takes longer than expected, you should always be able to react and get things in line again. Therefore do not make your planning too tight. Leave yourself enough reserve of resources.

Hopefully you know your crew well enough to assign the jobs to the right persons. Especially at the beginning of the relationship you have to keep close contact during the works until you are sure about the abilities and skills of your men. Then you will know how much supervision is needed.

Chapter 20

MANAGING INFORMATION TECHNOLOGY AT SEA
Strengths, weaknesses, opportunities and threats

by Mr. D.J. Patraiko BSc MBA MNI, Project Manager for The Nautical Institute

David J. Patraiko graduated from the Massachusetts Maritime Academy (US) and sailed on a variety of international vessels in his twelve years in the Merchant Navy. He holds a Unlimited Master Mariner's licence and was awarded an MBA degree from Henley Management College (UK). After a brief period as an independent consultant.

Introduction

The use of Information Technology (IT) at sea, on board ships, is a very wide and complex topic. To begin with you might ask which information with what technology and for that matter, which ships. In the shipping industry today the full spectrum of IT usage can be found. If we take the world merchant fleet as a parameter, we can find very low-tech cargo ships with no computers or electronics what so ever. We can also find vessels with multiple computer networks, hundreds of micro-chips, and full 24 hour a day satellite communication links to wide area networks. In fact, in a recent survey conducted by The Nautical Institute on the use of IT at sea, one of the most sophisticated vessels was a small fisheries protection craft.

Scope

In order to limit the range of this topic, for the purpose of this chapter I will define the scope of my comments to the use of PC type computers aboard merchant vessels. In a wider context however, most on board computers are not placed on merchant ships in isolation, either in physical or management terms. Computers on board, are usually able to share files with other computers, either by disk, over networks (physical or virtual), but most often placed on board as the result of a management decision for a specific task or tasks. Therefore, the term IT at Sea encompasses IT for ship management.

Background

In 1988 The Nautical Institute first published 'Computers at Sea'[1]. This monograph dealt with such cutting edge technology as word processors, and the ability to program an IBM for stability calculations. No mention though of e-mails or gigabytes! How things change in ten short years.

As technology has developed (exploded?) over the years the Institute has tried to keep abreast of both the levels of technology and their strategic use for the industry. Our members keep us informed of certain developments. Some are exciting and, frankly, some are pretty frightening. In many cases computer systems have been placed on board in very ad-hoc fashion, with little or no thought to usability, training or even maintainability. Conversely, some shipping companies have shot well ahead of competition by developing successful systems that offer real commercial advantage.

To gain further insight into the use of IT at sea, the Institute has embarked on a project (aptly named IT@Sea) to investigate how IT is being used in the industry and how it can be used to best advantage. The project has included a survey of members, an international conference and a lot of research. So, how can computers best be used to advance the business of managing ships? As you can guess, there are no simple answers, but in order to look at the situation in a logical manner, I will use the familiar model of Strengths, Weaknesses, Opportunities and Threats (SWOT) analysis.

Strengths

Before one can think about computerising one has to identify what a computer is going to do. In the 1980s when personal computers started to become increasingly cheaper, more powerful and more user friendly, the mantra was raised to 'computerise'. Businesses rushed to take advantage of word processors and countless hours were needlessly wasted as untrained (or ill-trained) staff tried to use computers as fancy electric typewriters, without realising their real potential (and some still do).

So, what's so good about computers? Where do their strengths lie? Principally, computers are great at processing repetitive tasks and when linked to a memory device, they can store vast amounts of information. And if, a big if, things have been properly thought out, computers can retrieve this information and communicate it efficiently. In all seriousness, one of the great strengths of computers is that they are too dumb to make a mistake – they do exactly what you tell them to (their language, of course).

Processing

It is not surprising that some of the first ship management applications were for accountancy and stability and cargo calculations. In fact, according to the recent Institute survey[2], the areas of management and stability calculations are still the only two categories of software used by over 50% of respondents.

Some of the most impressive computer applications available today, that fully utilise the computer's ability to carry out sophisticated calculations, are 3D ship models that are used in live damage stability information. These programs calculate, in real time, with input from sensors, any ingress from water, whether from flooding or fire fighting (or even ice accumulation) the stability of a vessel. They can take into account effects from variable seas and wind, predict rates of lost stability, can develop scenarios and even transmit this same information via satellite to other computers. Other examples include the ability to calculate specific vessel trim to maximise fuel efficiency for any given sea condition, and extrapolating differentials in engine performance to give early indications of developing problems. High processing capacity in affordable PC's has also spawned an emerging market in the use of complex graphics for simulation programs.

Task repetition

The ability of computers to complete sequential tasks, precisely, efficiently and indefinitely is highlighted by tasks such as producing form letters, forms, payroll and communication functions. These advantages are also used to best effect through the use of monitoring, such as monitoring engine functions, cargo conditions, navigation and even hull stresses.

Record keeping and audit trail

The facilities for storing and retrieving large amounts of information for the purpose of record keeping and creating audit trails has really come into its own recently for the shipping industry. The reasons: ISM, STCW and even ISO and TQM for those that follow that route. If designed and operated properly, the average PC can store an amount of records, data, and information that would clog any chief engineer or master's office (even an entire cargo ship) beyond belief. Superintendents who could only look after a few ships a decade ago, can now (at least technically) maintain records of repairs, certificates status, and performance data for a much larger fleet.

In addition to satisfying the occasional auditors, benefits from this facet of technology include the ability to access historical records of maintenance, equipment inventories, reference manuals and vast amounts of operational data for managing a vessel.

One of the most powerful computer applications to be designed and used by ship managers is, of course, the database. Databases by definition are software applications designed to save information as structured sets of data that are accessible in various ways. As a stand-alone feature, databases are an extremely efficient method of saving information such as crew records, inventoried equipment, or even procedures.

Shared through communication, however, they become a phenomenal management tool.

Shared databases allow a wide group (as wide as a network enables) to access the same information. Following on from the examples give above, a single personnel database can be shared by the personnel department as well as a ship captain. Thus as training takes place aboard ship, a seaman's record is updated once for the entire fleet. A superintendent in Singapore as well as a purchasing agent in Piraeus can view equipment and spare parts for an entire fleet in real time. Given that personnel are disciplined in the maintenance of such systems, the potential for cost savings is tremendous.

Communication

The ability for computers to share information via communication may be the greatest strength of IT yet. At a basic level computer files can be transferred between one computer and another by using floppy disks or CDs. Gains in efficiency can be had by linking individual computers by wire (or fibre optics) into a Local Area Network (LAN). Many ships now have LANs aboard that enable, for example, the sharing of peripherals such as printers, drives and modems as well as files. For example, a chief engineer can monitor engine performance from his office, a third mate can update the ship's medical inventory, or a navigation officer can e-mail a noon report to the company through the master's computer

Further communication can see the development of a Wide Area Network (WAN), where the shipboard's LAN is linked via satellite, cellular or land line to the office LAN. This permits shared databases and direct e-mail communication at a fraction of the cost of voice communication. Communication technology is advancing by leaps and bounds. Costs are plummeting, bandwidth is increasing and compression technology is enabling larger and larger file sizes to be transferred economically. The growth in communications will fuel future opportunities more than any other aspect of IT for the ship manager.

Costs and experience

When looking at information technology for today's ship managers, it must be noted that, in contrast with past years, hardware and software solutions have never been as inexpensive. Modern computers with more speed and capacity than could have been imagined just a few years ago can be bought for less than $1000 (USD), and come equipped with CD drives and multimedia facilities. Off the shelf software for basic applications are powerful and reasonably intuitive and, again affordable. Customised ship management software that has been developed and improved over the years is also showing the benefits of economies of scale.

Experience is far easier to come by than ever before. For routine general and ship management applications, experienced technicians abound. Advances and developments in other areas of business are offering cross fertilisation for the ship management industry as well.

Weaknesses

With all the strengths outlined, one could be forgiven for thinking that computers on board must be a panacea. They're not. For many, IT at sea is a nightmare. Worse, for a few, it can lead to financial ruin.

As mentioned earlier, computers are too dumb to make a mistake. When things go wrong management is usually to blame.

Strategic planning

Successful computer systems don't just happen. They are planned, and planned from the top. The most common factor for failed or ineffective IT systems is reported to be lack of management support. Placing a single stand-alone PC aboard a ship to run a simple payroll programme might have succeeded in the past without much intervention from senior management, but networks and shared systems throughout a fleet will never work properly if not aligned with a company's business strategy and supported from board level.

Successful IT strategies are developed in harmony with a general business strategy. The most sophisticated inventory database will not succeed if the company is not committed to managing its inventory. If the employees do not recognise its value, if the superintendents and purchasing people do not embrace the philosophy, the hardware and software will be wasted. For an IT system to operate efficiently the senior management must incorporate it into their business plan, appoint properly skilled and educated people to implement it and be willing to commit the necessary resources. Advice from a prominent ship manager[3] also states that if a system that has been committed to looks like it will fail, it is far better to cut the project and lose the investment than to be lumbered with a poor system for years and lose continually.

Implementation

Implementation, if not properly managed, can be the next greatest weakness in developing an IT system. After a strategic decision has been made, resources budgeted for, and a project manager selected. A typical implementation plan might include[4]:

- Carry out detailed project planning; too many projects fail because of poor, or non-existent, planning.
- Involve key users throughout the project.
- Expend sufficient effort in identifying training needs; this includes sea staff, shore staff and those driving the project.
- Complete all preparatory work before commissioning the software.

- Have all key users test the system.
- Properly plan and manage the data conversion and loading process.
- Document the system.

During the planning stage, ship managers should also take advantage of the excellent guidance offered by the IMO[5] (MSC/Circ.891) 'Guidelines for the On-board use and Application of Computers' with an annex for 'Guidelines for Shipboard Loading and Stability Computer Programs'.

Once in use

Once a computer system has been properly designed and implemented, continued success relies on the monitoring of its use and efficiency, feedback from the users, the training of subsequent users (i.e. relief crews) and well managed upgrades as are appropriate for the commercial and regulatory environment. Many companies who have been praised for their design and implementation of IT systems, later suffer because the system they developed no longer meets the operational needs, or cannot function efficiently with hardware and operating systems not even imagined at the time of development. IT is changing rapidly and life cycles need to be addressed as part of strategic development.

Opportunities

Opportunities for improving ship management operations through the use of computers are limited only by the capacity of the computer and communication systems and human ingenuity. Some of the computer based ship management tools existing today could hardly have been imagined ten years ago. I will look briefly at what is available today, and then extrapolate as to what some future opportunities might be.

Here and now

Entire books have been published[6], and magazines[7] are dedicated to examining the vast range of maritime related software. In this chapter I will only just touch on some of the broad categories. The use of computers for payroll and accounting is well established and at a mature stage in its development. However, the use of computers for fleet and vessel management is a booming trade.

Opportunities for improving fleet and vessel management abound. Systems can range from simple single user programs on stand alone PCs that assist the master or operations manager to keep track of certificate status and maintenance logs, to large networked systems that link a whole fleet to head office, class society and suppliers and even agents. Such systems take advantage of the most modern communication systems and cover almost all aspects of fleet management including personnel, purchasing, maintenance, performance monitoring, messaging. Of particular interest in today's environment, they can document operational procedures, maintain records and create an audit trail as required for STCW and

ISM. These systems can be created as custom applications specifically designed for an operator, or can be purchased 'off the shelf' and adapted for use as required. There are a number of suppliers of such systems that cater for the ship management market and, increasingly, classification societies are offering ship management software. Fleet management software now makes it possible for fewer and fewer staff to manage greater and greater fleets, complying with ever more regulatory documentation.

Opportunities for streamlining stores and purchasing operations are also being created by the use of IT. This has always been a capital intensive area of ship management. Excessive stores and spare parts carried aboard vessels tie up valuable capital, but penalties for lack of spares can be prohibitive. As fleet sizes grow, savings of even a few per cent are worth pursuing. Purchasing and inventory software can improve efficiency by streamlining the purchasing of consumables and by coordinating stocks of valuable spare parts within a fleet. The advent of online ordering is also coming into it's own. At the most sophisticated level, stores can be barcoded and after reference to a stores database can automatically generate purchase orders. As suppliers are now establishing an Electronic Trading Standard Format (ETSF)[8], the process of submitting orders for tender electronically will save additional time and personnel intervention.

The use of computers for training is yet another area where opportunities are proving beneficial. Seafarer training is essential on ships growing in sophistication and is required by STCW95. A well balanced training programme using a variety of methods for different tasks and environments is always best, but the use of Computer Based Training (CBT) and even Internet Based Training (IBT) have valuable roles to play. Two of the major benefits of CBT are that modern processing power has enabled the development of very realistic simulation programs and properly designed CBT programs provide a unique environment for one-to-one interactive training that can concentrate on a student's areas of weakness and document successful (or unsuccessful) results.

Communication

Communications may be the fastest developing sector of the whole marine IT spectrum. Satellite systems, including Medium Earth Orbit (MEO), Low Earth Orbit (LEO) and even cellular are improving their range and fidelity, reducing the cost of air time and increasing their bandwidth. This in conjunction with compression technology, packet switching technology and scheduled data-bursts for off peak times is continually driving down the cost of ship-to-shore communication. Communication is a big deal! Businesses thrive, safety is increased and people exist through the use of communication.

Now, admittedly, this assumes increased quality rather than just quantity of communication, but none the less by having the option for low cost communication, the potential for improvement is vast. Already the use of e-mail has improved inter-fleet communication over the use of telex or fax and the ability of fleet management software to auto-generate messages from operational procedures such as position reports, maintenance scheduling, training and stores, just to name a few, saves time and improves communication flow.

The future

Unfortunately my laptop is not programmed with a virtual crystal ball, but I can predict that opportunities for the future will follow on from the themes discussed by taking advantage of greater computing and communication power.

As communication becomes less expensive, its use will expand. It is interesting to note that as the cost of communication has come down over the past decades, many operators report that their communication bill has remained steady, but the volume has increased many times over. This trend will likely advance to the point where vessels are on-line at all times, and ship managers will just pay a fixed fee. This will allow shore staff to monitor ship functions in real time and the vessel staff will be as incorporated in the operations of the company as any shore-side department might be. This facility will also permit unrestricted use of video conferencing for routine management as well as for diagnostics and maintenance purposes.

Fixed communication costs will also herald the use of the Internet. Use of the Internet will permit vessels to access wide ranges of current information and services. For example, maintenance and trouble shooting databases for engineering equipment might be available from manufactures, weather observation and forecasting will be a mouse click away and the cook might even find a new recipe – the mind boggles.

Ramifications for the quality of life on board also exist. Diminishing quality of life on board is often cited by seafarers as the primary reason for leaving the sea. As the industry changes the traditional rewards of a career at sea are disappearing. Poor retention of sea staff is an expensive problem. The ability to talk, or even video conference with family members, maintain hobbies, or even plan a holiday could make all the difference to the young engineer who can't even get ashore (further information on the uses and application of the Internet for seafarers can be found in The Nautical Institute's briefing paper on the subject)[9].

Opportunities for future benefits from Information Technology at sea are endless. The use of voice recognition and virtual reality will be affordable soon, and the use of Knowledge Based Decision Support Systems (KBDSS) are also available and increasing in popularity. One area of opportunity not yet discussed, however, is that of using IT to enhance the potential of on board skills. Skills of on board personnel are often not fully utilised for the benefit of the company. In most cases this is due to lack of communication or lack of realisation. Shipboard officers trained in the use of IT, whether word processors and spreadsheets, or more specialised programs like CAD or engineering programs and benefiting from good fleet communications can be a valuable company asset. As competition gets fiercer, such assets should not be ignored. For example, deck officers trained in specialised cargo operations could become a readily available fleet-wide consultant, as could engineers with specialist knowledge or experience. Other advantages can be had by masters and chief engineers participating in such things as shipyard preparation that takes advantage of their skills while some of their more mundane tasks are outsourced to others over the same network. This not only takes best advantage of fleet resources, but provides often needed career expansion opportunities for seafarers.

Threats

The primary threat to most businesses in terms of Information Technology is that of being lumbered with a poor system. There are a number of causes for poor operating systems, most of which are mentioned in the weaknesses section, most due to poor management at some point and most should have at least been caught in the testing phase of implementation. At best, a poor system reduces commercial efficiency, and at worst can cause the financial collapse of a company.

Good systems that have been well conceived, managed, tested and installed, can still suffer from inefficiency if staff are not properly trained and confident in their use. This is an important step and will be expanded upon later.

Communication between computers over a network and between programs operating on a single PC is entirely reliant on compatibility. Compatibility is a major threat to Information Technology. A well designed system should not suffer incompatibility problems and any new applications for that system should be checked for compatibility, but compatibility needs to be thought of at the strategic level if communication with outside sources is going to be achieved. This includes links made to other businesses, financial institutions, common networks, suppliers or customers.

Security is another major threat, not just physical security, but security of data as well. The loss of a physical unit can be accidental or malicious, but must be anticipated. The IMO (MSC Circ.891) offers good advice for planning redundancy for critical systems, but it cannot be stressed enough how awkward a computer crash can be to a crew, possibly on the verge of fatigue. Spare units with the ability to load from backups (especially servers) should be carried on

board. Threats to data security can come from accidental loss, malicious destruction or violation of privacy. Companies should have a security procedure that incorporates the use of backups, virus protection, security devices (hardware and software) and the use of passwords.

Opportunities for improving commercial performance include the ability to increase the number of management tasks that could be handled by a limited number of staff. Whereas this is truly an opportunity of which to take advantage, a company must always be aware of how dependent they are on IT systems and assess the risk accordingly. Alternative systems for important functions can come from manual paper based systems, or from other IT systems. In either case ship managers need to examine their use of, and reliance on computer systems.

The seafarer's role

Most IT systems for on board use are conceived, at least strategically, by the managers ashore. Seafarers, however, have a crucial role to play in insuring the maximum efficiency and effectiveness of any on board IT system.

Implementation

The most important contribution seafarers can make is by providing user feedback. User feedback is most helpful at the implementation stage when the involvement of key users is sought. Any opportunity to work with shoreside management should be taken. All on board users of the system, senior and junior officers and crew if applicable, should take every opportunity to inform the project leader of their requirements and carefully to test all trial or beta versions sent to the vessel, fully and for all conceivable circumstances or scenarios. Lists of testing procedures might be drawn up to ensure a thorough and methodical examination and documentation of the results, both positive and negative, is a necessity. Ship's staff are the only people who can truly represent their own best interests. The testing stage is the final stage before committing to a system and most ship managers will be eager to hear of any anomalies at this stage of design, where the cost of change is relatively inexpensive and consultants would not have been fully paid.

Security

Shipboard personnel have a responsibility, as operators and local administrators, to take all reasonable precautions to ensure the security of on board IT systems. This includes the proper securing of all hardware and adhering to company procedures for data protection, including the use of security passwords, virus protection and backups.

Data within an IT system is highly valuable, both in terms of cost to replace the information and the costs associated with any misinformation due to corrupted data, such as errors in financial data. Data corruption can be caused by many means. Power loss due to blackouts and greyouts (if the system is not connected through a proper uninterrupted power supply (UPS)), system failures, viruses and malicious damage are some of the most common. It has also been reported that crew and/or visiting personnel have attempted to obtain confidential documents held on shipboard computers.

Training

Competent operation of on board computer systems is absolutely necessary to ensure that they perform to maximum efficiency. Unfortunately, as revealed by The Nautical Institute, as well as other industry sources, training for seafarers in the use of computer systems is a great weakness. The root cause for this is that while IT solution providers are constantly driving the state of the art in computer programs, the associated training is less well thought out and often suffers from lack of budget when IT projects reach their final stages. Training needs must be examined early in the implementation stage and adhered to strictly. One of the most serious faults in training programmes for seafarers is that they only address the current staff on board at the time of installation, with little or no thought to training the relief crews. It is often assumed that the current staff will carry out the training of relief staff in the use of IT at the time of relief. This is a poor assumption due to the possibility that the current staff don't fully understand the system themselves, that they may not be qualified to train, and that in today's climate of shipboard operations in port, there is not time to give IT training as well as all other duties involved in the relief process. Some advice to seafarers in this predicament is as follows:

- Take advantage of any less demanding time, such as during ocean voyages, to study the operation of computer programs, with the emphasis on infrequently used aspects that could cause a problem at more critical times.

- Learn what the inherent limitations of the program are, with particular respect to inputs, calculations, and critical indicators such as in stability and stress programs.
- Enhance any existing documentation, such as manuals with marked tabs and clearly written notes that will assist any on board users to make better use of such reference material.

Conclusion

The use of computers and computer systems for improving operational performance in the shipping industry has been tried, tested and proved effective as well as ineffective. Computerisation is no panacea, yet few modern fleets can compete and survive without it. The difference is in their strategic use, the allocation of proper resources, and the management of implementation and training. Information Technology is a sophisticated tool, and as is true of any tool it has strengths, weaknesses, opportunities and threats. Understanding these parameters and the relationship they have on shipboard management is the key to successful exploitation of this exciting and dynamic technology.

1 Cole, Captain J.W., *Computers at Sea*, The Nautical Institute, 1988, ISBN 0 906835 26 7.
2 *IT@Sea — Survey Data*, The Nautical Institute, 1998.
3 Slesinger, P., IS Manager, Wallem Group, *Managing a Large Fleet*, Lloyd's Ship Manager IT Strategies in Shipping Conference, 1988
4 Jones, G., Managing Consultant, Horwath Consulting Ltd.
5 International Maritime Organization (IMO), 4 Albert Embankment, London, UK, www.imo.org.
6 *Marine Computing & Internet Guide*, Fairplay Publications Ltd., ISBN 1 901290 09 3, www.fairplay.co.uk.
7 Compuship Magazine, TLA Publishing Ltd., London, UK.
8 International Marine Purchasing Association (IMPA).
9 Nautical Briefing, The Internet for Seafarers, The Nautical Institute, 1999.

Chapter 21

MANAGING RISK ON BOARD

by Captain T.J. Bailey FNI

Captain Bailey started his career at sea with BP Tanker Co. Ltd. in September 1971 and stayed with them until gaining his Mate's Certificate. During this time he served on all classes of vessel within the BP fleet, ranging from oil tankers of 16,000 dwt to VLCCs of 215,000 dwt. In the heady days of the late 1970s, when jobs were easier to find, he joined Sea Containers on their fleet of innovative self-sustaining ro-ro/container ships. This represented a very significant change from oil tankers. With all ships chartered to a variety of operators, he found it most interesting to work in a very different commercial environment. He studied for his Master's Certificate at Plymouth in 1982 and gained his first command in 1983.

After a period with the National Shipping Company of Saudi Arabia as chief officer on their ro-ro/container vessels and a period ashore as a marine and cargo surveyor covering South Wales ports he joined Sealink British Ferries in 1988. Since then he has worked at every Stena Line UK port – probably the only person in their current fleet to have done so. In 1990 the company introduced their own guidelines on working hours and fatigue and, as one of the first mate/masters appointed in the company, he took command of the ship while the day master took his eight hour break. Captain Bailey was promoted to full master in 1992.

He gained fast craft experience with Hoverspeed on the introduction of the Hoverspeed Great Britain at Portsmouth in 1990 and with Stena Line when the Sea Lynx was introduced to Holyhead in the summer of 1993. Before transferring to the HSS he was senior master on the Stena Cambria – one of the multi-purpose ferries operating from Holyhead to Dun Laoghaire.

Captain Bailey is chairman of The Nautical Institute Command Working Group and now works ashore independently as a consultant, specialising mostly in training.

Introduction

THE SHIPPING INDUSTRY, by its very nature, is a highly risky business and is not 100% accident or incident free. To reduce accidents, incidents and claims, the shipping industry needs to move forward utilising risk-based management techniques.

The majority of prudent and 'professional' seafarers seem to have an inherent, innate ability to understand and assess the risks that the job places before them. The fact that they undertake this 'intuitive risk analysis' without formal guidance or training is a credit to these seafarers and to their professionalism. They are highly competent personnel who take their ships to sea and deliver their cargoes without accident or incident.

There is a need for improvement in day-to-day operational techniques on board ship. In the extremely efficiency-conscious and cost-conscious commercial climate of the late 1990s there is a need to reduce accidents, incidents and claims, both by their number and by their monetary value.

It is the aim of this chapter to look at how risk management techniques can best be implemented aboard the ship. In doing so, consideration will be given to all aspects of day-to-day shipboard operations.

Risk, risk management and risk assessment

What, then, is risk management? It has been defined as "the systematic application of management policies, procedures and practices to the tasks of identifying, analysing, assessing, treating and monitoring risk" where risk has been defined as "the chance of something happening that will have an impact upon objectives". It is measured in terms of consequence and likelihood.

If we take adequate steps to eliminate or minimise any risks that may be involved, the objective will effectively be achieved.

Risk assessment is defined as "the process used to determine risk management priorities by evaluating and comparing the level of risk against predetermined standards, target risk levels or other criteria".

Our primary aim is to avoid risk: where this cannot be avoided, we must evaluate the unavoidable risks and take action to reduce their effect. It is desirable to develop a strategy whereby day-to-day operations are considered from a 'risk' point of view – if they can go wrong, what effect will this have? If an operation or procedure has the potential for significant consequences, it must be given a higher level of priority than one that is unlikely to happen and, even if and when it does, it will not have an adverse impact on the voyage.

A risk assessment is intended to be a simple but meaningful exercise to determine, after careful examination of an operation, what processes may cause harm, what precautions can be taken and whether more could be done to prevent harm. The process need not be over-complicated and it may be appropriate to use a simple proforma to record the findings of the assessment.

The assessment of risks must be 'suitable and sufficient'. The degree of effort required by the risk assessment should depend on the degree of harm that may occur and whether there are current control procedures to ensure that the risk is as low as reasonably practicable.

In carrying out a risk assessment it is necessary to identify whether a hazard exists in the first place. The hazard then needs to be categorised according to its potential consequence and according to its likelihood of occurrence. Is it already covered by procedures and satisfactory precautions to control the risk? If so, what are those procedures? If it is not, what procedures and precautions need to be put into place?

There are no fixed rules about who should carry out the risk assessment but it is recommended that suitably experienced personnel, using specialist advice if appropriate, should carry it out.

Once a risk assessment has been carried out, it should be monitored when the work is taking place. Have the procedures and precautions put into place been adequate? If not, a further risk assessment should be carried out to review the original assessment and to make further recommendations.

All risk assessments should be held on file. When the task has been completed it may be possible to 'close out' the risk assessment but, if the task is regular or routine, the risk assessment should be kept 'live'. It should be reviewed at periodic intervals to ensure that it remains relevant and that the recommended procedures continue to apply.

To be effective, risk management must combine knowledge, experience and lateral thinking. One man alone cannot achieve all this and it is desirable that there is a workable framework in place that encourages teamwork and interaction between the members of the team and the ship's managers.

On board risk management
In port
Where, then, does the management of risk begin? It is difficult to appreciate a finite starting point but, for the purpose of this chapter, we shall assume that it starts when the Notice of Readiness (NOR) is tendered. The NOR may be considered to reflect the commitment of the ship to the 'risk' of the voyage.

The NOR may be tendered at the same time that the pilot boards on arrival in the loading port or when the first rope is landed ashore. These times are as good as any but there may be a number of procedures that still have to be completed before the vessel can load cargo. In other words, the vessel may not be 'ready in all respects': if the NOR has been tendered and the vessel is not ready, there may be financial penalties. Whether these penalties will have a significant outcome on the success of the voyage can only be realised at the end of the voyage.

The Charter Party (C/P) will specify criteria that will determine the commercial success of the voyage. To ensure the best possible management of the risk of the voyage, the master must be given adequate information regarding the terms of the C/P. He cannot be expected to fulfil his obligations in ignorance of the terms and conditions of the C/P.

Cargo operations need to be considered in the light of the 'risk'. The prudent risk manager should be aware of the intended procedures. He should discuss these with the terminal superintendent/stevedore and the ship's staff in order to minimise the risk to the overall operation. In the meantime, what else is happening on board the ship?

The navigating officer will prepare the passage plan for the intended voyage. If properly carried out, this passage plan is a formal risk assessment procedure. It should allow the vessel to be safely navigated at all times throughout the voyage, highlighting areas where there are levels of greater risks. The prudent master will ensure that his intentions and requirements have been followed through before committing his vessel to the voyage.

While preparing the passage plan, has the navigating officer ensured that the charts and publications to be used are fully up-to-date? There is still an unacceptably high incidence of reports of ships with out of date nautical charts and publications. This may lead, in many ports, to detention of the vessel or heavy financial penalties until the matter is rectified.

During the port stay the ship will require to take bunkers. Accidents occur during bunkering operations and the obvious consequence of these accidents is pollution. Any pollution incident will attract a financial consequence. The prudent risk manager will ensure that procedures for bunkering operations are in place and that they are strictly followed. He will also ensure that personnel designated to carry out this task have a complete understanding of the procedures and of their responsibilities.

Maintenance of key plant and machinery may also take place while the ship is in port. Do the port regulations allow for the ship to be immobilised? Will the work be completed in time for the ship to sail when expected? If it cannot, can the ship stay at the current berth or will it be necessary to be towed to another berth or to an anchorage? Will there be a long-term effect on the ability of the ship to complete the intended voyage?

This evaluation should not be done only by the chief engineer but he must consult with the master, the ship's agent in the port and, probably, with his principals. This consultation must be open, honest and realistic in its assessment if it is to have the desired effect of minimising the impact of any failures to complete the work.

Preparations for departure
The prudent master will have a good appreciation of the risks associated with port departure and he will have taken the opportunity to check with his heads of departments that they, too, are ready for sea. As we have already seen, risk management is a team effort and this concept should be brought into use at every possible opportunity.

Preparations for taking the ship to sea should follow a structured procedure. In many ships, check lists are used extensively for many operations and the checklist can play a significant part. When the checks provide an answer that is not expected, there must be the opportunity to report the 'wrong answer' to an appropriate person who can take responsibility for correcting the fault.

Much has been written in recent times of the importance of the master/pilot relationship – it is equally important when considering the management of risk on board a ship. Shiphandling in confined waters with the assistance of tugs is a time of high risk and the operation must be carefully thought out and discussed by the master and the pilot. The risk of the operation cannot be minimised without the fullest exchange of information and ideas from both the master and the pilot. This exchange must clarify exactly where responsibility lies at every stage.

Before leaving port, the master must be aware of the hours that have been worked by his watchkeeping officers and ratings immediately prior to taking the ship to sea. This does not only apply to the navigation watch – it has equal relevance to the engineering department and the master should ensure that all watchkeepers are suitably rested.

The effects of fatigue have the potential to create significant effects on the overall success of the voyage. It is particularly so at the beginning of the voyage and, in many instances, it is not unknown that the master will take the first sea watch to allow the appropriate OOW to gain sufficient rest after particularly long hours during a port stay.

And so to sea . . .

It may be considered that the safe navigation of the ship has the highest risk potential in terms of its effect on the outcome of the voyage. Collisions give rise to 17% of P&I claims. The old adage that 'a collision at sea can ruin your whole day' is undeniably true and a collision will certainly have an impact upon our objective of completing the voyage safely and satisfactorily.

In the event of a collision, there are many procedures that will come into play, not least of which will be the ship's emergency procedures. These are intended to provide an effective method of minimising loss or damage to the ship and the cargo, to the persons on board and to the environment in the event of an emergency.

The SOLAS requirement for regular exercises and drills is a risk management process. The prudent risk manager will ensure that the nature and content of these exercises and drills is varied so that he will have the opportunity to assess the capabilities of his crew, as well as the procedures. He will also ensure that there is a formal review process for each drill and exercise

by 'debriefing'. This will provide the opportunity to discuss any mistakes that may have been made and how to learn from those mistakes or to improve the management of an emergency.

Personal safety on board the ship is an individual as well as a collective responsibility. Every person on board the ship has a responsibility to ensure that they carry out their duties safely. They must not knowingly put themselves or anybody else into an unsafe situation. Although this responsibility may be considered to be common sense, it can be reinforced by good shipboard practices and training.

It can also be reinforced through consultation. The shipboard safety committee provides a forum where safety-related issues are raised for discussion by all departments. This frequently provides an element of lateral thinking that may not otherwise have occurred. Careful management of safety related issues will reap significant benefits. An increase in personal safety awareness should lead to a reduction in on board accidents and injuries. This in turn will lead to improved efficiency on board.

It is probably fair to say that the majority of ships will record, in some form or another, major incidents that occur on board the ship – for example, heavy weather damage to the ship or cargo or serious personal accident. Within the requirements of the ISM Code we also have the duty to ensure that appropriate corrective action is taken. This should also be viewed as a requirement to take preventative action to reduce the likelihood that the nonconformity will recur.

It is probable that the reporting of lesser incidents and, almost certainly, 'near misses' does not occur. A 'near miss' (in 'risk management speak') is defined as 'an unplanned event which does not cause injury or damage but could do so.' Examples of near misses include items falling from a height near to a worker or a short circuit in a piece of electrical equipment.

In an analysis of reported incidents carried out in the United States, the following were recorded. In the right hand column, they have been assessed on their approximate probability on an annual basis:

Serious injury	1	Once
Minor injury	10	Monthly
Property damage	30	Weekly
'Near misses'	600	Twice daily

Figure 21.1 Analysis of reported incidents

We are probably all well aware of the first three groups of incidents and we can readily appreciate their significance and occurrence. The 'near miss' is a concept that is much harder to appreciate. It may also come as something of a shock to realise the frequency with which they are considered to occur. For effective risk (and safety) management we must attempt to identify the near misses, record them and analyse them. We can then take positive steps to reducing or removing them from day-to-day shipboard operations. In doing so we make a positive contribution to reducing risk and improving safety on board the ship.

Before we arrive at the port of discharge, let us return briefly to the people on board. How have they spent their off-duty time while the ship has been at sea. What provisions have been made for them to be able to relax and to 'switch off'? Good welfare management is an integral part of good safety and risk management. A common feature in all aspects of the risks of day-to-day shipboard operations is the 'human factor'. We are all human and all prone to the frailties that go with it! 64% of claims can be attributed to 'human factors'.

Personal injury

It is perhaps worth considering, at this point, the effects of personal injury on the overall operation of the vessel, as well as its implication on the effectiveness of our risk management.

From my own experience, I know that the immediate costs can be significant but there are other effects on the ship's operation that may not be immediately apparent. On passage from Fremantle to Singapore, the chief officer was washed overboard. In the successful recovery of the chief officer, I was severely injured and it was necessary to divert the ship to land me ashore for hospital treatment. After several days in hospital, I was then repatriated to the UK – First Class (thank you, P&I Club!) – and was off work for a further three months.

The ship had to sail short handed for a further four days, someone had to be called back off leave early to take my place, additional air fares and hotel bills were incurred, damages had to be made good, the ship's schedule was interrupted, cargo was delayed, . . . and so it goes on. At the time, we might have considered that this was an unfortunate incident – with a good outcome – but I do not suppose that we thought of it as a major incident.

No doubt, we can all relate to some incident that has led to personal injury of some form or another. How could we have avoided those situations? What did we learn from those situations? What did we do afterwards? I suggest that better risk management may have minimised the chance of the incident in the first place. If we accept that, are we now assessing working practices more effectively? Have we ensured that there is a good 'safety culture' in place on board our own ship? If not, we should do so very quickly.

Our experiences should be utilised as learning tools and we should react accordingly to prevent a recurrence of that situation. In many cases, personal injury will lead to claims against the owner or operator.

To defend the claim, or to minimise his liability, the shipowner relies on the ship's staff to provide him with the evidence surrounding the incident. It is essential that witness statements are taken, photographs (or video film) are taken where appropriate and a thorough investigation by the safety officer is carried out as early as possible after the incident. The ensuing report should be as thorough as possible and, if any doubts exist, these should be carefully investigated until the report reflects the fullest possible picture of the incident.

In all ships, injuries to 'our own people' can be upsetting and disruptive. It is important to remember, however, that the truth must prevail. We must not be tempted to 'cover up' any relevant information – e.g. the injured man was only wearing flip flops when he slipped and broke his arm is as relevant as the fact that the deck was greasy and that no warning signs were posted.

It would be possible to expand on this subject at great length but it is perhaps better to refer you to other publications. In particular, I would recommend '*The Mariner's Role in Collecting Evidence*' published by The Nautical Institute.

Personal safety and accident prevention are very important to the P&I Clubs – almost all of them will publish guidance notes, videos, posters and the like to assist this process. If they are not on board your ship, you can always ask for them.

Welfare issues

STCW95 provides guidance on prevention of drug and alcohol abuse. This is not a requirement but it may assist companies in the development of their own policies. There are no easy answers and the prudent risk manager must ensure that he is aware of what is happening on board his own ship. He should be aware of the symptoms to be recognised in cases of both alcohol and drug abuse. He should also be aware of any national administration policies which may affect his ship and its crew when entering port or in territorial waters.

It is an essential part of prudent risk management that the manager is well acquainted with his staff. By taking an interest in people, the manager can significantly increase his response from those people. The prudent risk manager will encourage his staff to gain a better understanding of the day-to-day shipboard operations. By providing the team with the knowledge and skills required, the individual load becomes lighter but the group result should become greater.

Well trained and recently trained staff are a great asset and they should be valued and treated as such. When capable and competent staff are employed, the potential for good risk management of the ship and its cargo is high: when standards start to fall, there is the potential for the quality of risk management to fall also.

Port of discharge

Our time at sea should have been relatively routine but now, approaching the port of discharge, that routine is about to be broken. Shipping traffic may well increase as we approach the coast, our navigation skills must become better and more frequently applied. The regularity of watchkeeping is about to change – for some, it will mean 'go on, stop on' with the inherent dangers of fatigue.

It may also be that a number of the ship's company are about to leave the ship and to go home – their concentration and attention to their duties may not be at the high levels required. The prudent risk manager will be aware of these constraints and he should be able to recognise these 'symptoms' in his crew.

Have all the necessary preparations for arrival been made? Have all the conditions of the C/P been fulfilled? How good have we been at the management of the cargo on passage? Cargo records will need to be kept and may need to be inspected at a later date.

And finally . . .

We have already considered that 'jolly jack' has an intuitive approach to risk management. This is compounded in many cases by experience – it plays a major part in producing his 'feel' for the situations where hazardous occurrences might take place, e.g. the Malacca Strait for navigation and collision avoidance problems, the Bay of Biscay for rough weather and so on.

As every seafarer knows, before going to sea all loose items must be fastened down and the cargo properly secured for the voyage. Inexperienced mariners do not always appreciate the effect of the ship's movement and there are few old hands who have not suffered a loss of deck containers or drums or heavy items of cargo breaking free in a storm. In this context, no amount of risk management theory will convince the uninitiated about the perils of the sea.

As mariners we take pride in our seamanship – it is the skill applied to keep the ship safe in all the various conditions of the voyage. It is important to recognise that risk management as a technique cannot replace that feel for the sea that seamen acquire, but it can enhance our sensitivity to potential problems and assist us with assigning priorities.

Frequently, the master will face conflicting demands and difficult decisions in which the application of risk management alone will not provide all the answers. In this respect the advice given in The Nautical Institute's '*Code of Conduct*' is much more valuable:

"Where choices have to be made about protecting the ship, cargo, property and the marine environment, the preservation of human life must take precedence."

We have already considered the difference between hazard and risk. A further example is a smooth deck plate outside the galley door. In dry weather it is not slippery, in rough weather everybody knows it is necessary to take precautions but, on a damp morning with a gentle swell, the cook slips and falls. The problem can easily be overcome by painting the deck with non slip paint, but other problems caused by basic design faults like untrue fairleads present a danger throughout the life of the ship.

Experience is not always a good enough guide to risk. People easily forget the slips and lapses that are corrected without further thought – the so-called 'near misses' – so that the objective assessment of frequency is lost and the hazard may be missed. It pays to be attentive to comments like "I nearly fell down the stairs". It could mean that there was only one handrail or that it was broken. It will also pay to warn new crew members joining the ship that the fairlead is untrue and mooring ropes can get snagged.

Similarly, with passage planning for example, it helps to realise that risk of collision increases with the number of encounters and that extra watchkeeping assistance may be necessary in certain areas. Not only is the risk of collision higher but the workload in assessing risk and taking avoiding action is also higher.

So to the foundation of risk management. It depends upon an accurate assessment of the frequency and severity of events. On the ship it is useful to discuss with as many of the crew as possible the number of occasions when things nearly went wrong. That then becomes the ship's database for assessing risk on board. Good risk management implies that the master will encourage crew members to be aware of potential hazards and to make sure that they are brought up and recorded at meetings. Good risk management techniques help us to assess the risks more objectively.

As mariners we may choose to ignore the outcome. On the other hand, if we have planned carefully, considered the risks involved and thought about contingencies, then it should be possible to operate the ship within a reasonable envelope of safety to ensure that limits are not exceeded except in extreme conditions. In doing so the master discharges his primary obligation which is "to take all reasonable steps to ensure the cargo is loaded, transported and delivered in good condition".

It is well known and even more readily appreciated that paperwork is a time consuming task that seems to bear no relationship to the real job of the seafarer. For the prudent risk manager, paperwork becomes a necessity: he must consider the need to be able to prove that what he has done was done with the best intentions and within the letter of appropriate legislation. To be able to justify his decision at a later date may have profound repercussions in the event of a claim.

In his foreword to '*The Shipmaster's Business Companion*', Captain Eric Beetham, a Past President of The Nautical Institute, wrote the following:

'Compared with many other occupations, the level of knowledge and expertise required of a shipmaster is unique, extensive and at the highest level of professional competence. When the chief officer brings the supercargo and stevedore to the master's cabin, a decision is invariably required before they leave and there may be expensive implications in that almost instant decision. Two years later after many hours of work by lawyers, three arbitrators may take two weeks to consider whether that decision was right or wrong.'

When starting our 'voyage', the tendering of the Notice of Readiness was taken as the reference point. There is, of course, no finite beginning to the voyage and there is no finite end: shipping is a 24 hours a day, seven days a week, 365 days a year operation that demands the highest skills and competencies of its operators.

'Prudence' may be considered an old fashioned word but it should be the watchword of every professional seafarer – it is inherent in effective risk management.

It was not the intention to say 'you should do the job this way'.

We have asked many questions but not provided all the answers . . . the prudent risk manager must provide them for himself!

Note: This chapter is condensed from a chapter of the same title in the book *Managing Risk in Shipping,* also published by The Nautical Institute.

Chapter 22

PLANNING A DRY-DOCK

by Mr. J.L. Hutchinson CEng MIMarE

The author of the original complete paper thanked Exxon International Company and Esso Petroleum Company Ltd. for permission to use the information and also thanked his colleagues for their advice and comments during the preparation of this paper. These extracts are reproduced with kind permission of The Institute of Marine Engineers.

Introduction

THE AUTHOR'S COMPANY, in line with most of the major tanker operators, plan vessel shipyard repair periods around the 15 year dry-dock cycle which results in a substantial number of scheduled repairs having to take place each year. For tankers voyaging worldwide, a ship manager has a wide selection of shipyards from which to choose. Various methods of selection can be used, but usually it is a relatively simple choice based on an economic assessment of total repair costs, summating the best estimates for:

- Overall cost of repairs (yard quote against specification).
- Forecast of exchange rate.
- Owner supply items: cost of parts and spares, including freight costs.
- Diversion costs, including bunker costs.
- Agency and port costs, including tugs and shipyard services.
- Specialist expertise to be paid by shipowner, including coating and supervision.
- Tank cleaning and gas freeing costs.

In addition to the above costs, the cost of out-of-service repair time has to be included in the calculation covering the estimated calendar repair days (at vessel's daily rate at forecast Worldscale) plus days spent gas freeing and diverting to the repair port.

Most of the above information can be estimated by the tanker operator for budgetary purposes. However, the two most important pieces of data, the cost, and duration of repairs, have to be obtained from the shipyards. To do this one of the following three ways is used:

(i) Competitive bidding, based on a standard specification.
(ii) Competitive tenders based on actual ship's specification.
(iii) Cost-plus arrangements taking into consideration the owner's past experiences with the yard and the confidence the owner has in the ability of his repair superintendent to monitor and control the costs.

Competitive bidding

In an effort to overcome the sources of error in yard selection, the author's company has evolved a standard specification which is intended to represent the approximate volume of work which the yard will eventually execute, although in practice the standard specification items will normally cover only 70-80 per cent of items actually carried out. The missing 20-30 per cent is made up by new items in the final working specification which compensates for items deleted from the standard specification.

The standard specification approach permits each repair yard to be cost evaluated on an equal basis, permitting a ship to be allocated to the successful yard well in advance of the actual docking date, which enables the yard to plan its base load programme, takes the element of yard selection out of the communication and allows time for better preparation of the working specification. Where a number of ships of the different classes are to be dry docked, shipyards are screened so that only the bid invitations are sent to yards equipped with facilities appropriate to the vessel size.

The standard specification for each class of tanker will contain a detailed description of each item of the work which is normally carried out in dry dock – for example, normal survey work such as checking sea valves, and hull inspection, cleaning and painting. The specification also includes details of special projects planned for many or all vessels in a particular class – for example, crude oil wash (COW) modifications and inert gas installations. Yards are also asked to provide prices for certain unit items, such as cost of erected steel per kilogram, or cost of hull blasting and painting per square metre.

Since it is important that a competitive bidding analysis treats each yard on an equivalent basis, where a yard has not costed a particular item an appropriate figure has to be applied. A relatively simple way of dealing with 'excluded' items is to apply the highest bids received from yards in the same geographical area for the same items. This will penalise those yards with the highest number of excluded items.

Before the ship arrives at the repair yard, the yard should receive the working specification similar to that described in competitive tender, which will include items directly transferred from the standard specification plus a number of newly-identified items for which the yard will be asked to quote. The superintendent will compare the quotations against unit prices from the standard specification to check that they are consistent and any unexpected divergence should be resolved before the ship docks. The advantages of the standard specification method for selecting a repair yard are:

(i) Each repair yard receives the same specification well in advance of the docking.

(ii) The successful repair yard establishes a better comprehension of the repair work before the ship arrives, by communicating and planning with the owner's representatives. For example, the method of dealing with any outstanding 'unbid' items can be resolved in advance.

(iii) An owner operating a large fleet can select a yard on a fair and equitable basis, so providing a further incentive for yards to prepare competitive bids.

(iv) Both the shipowner and the selected shipyard gain through the learning curve of their employees when a number of similar ships with almost the same repair specification are overhauled in the same yard.

(v) Due to the 'standard' nature of most of the information required, after the first pass, very little effort is required by the repair facility to update the bid information each year.

(vi) Due to the 'standard' nature of most of the information supplied, comparisons on the competitiveness of the bid and settlements on completion of repairs are greatly simplified.

(vii) Where an owner has a large number of vessels, the system lends itself to improved competitiveness by the repair facilities offering additional incentives in the form of volume discounts, either for a number of vessels, or on the volume of cash flow, or both. It should be noted that this volume discount is discretionary: in the author's company it is not negotiated or used in order to give one facility an unfair advantage over another, nor is it used to induce shipyards into making non-commercially viable bids. The competitive bid in formation is strictly controlled to ensure that all of the bids received are held and opened at the same time, before being registered as official bids.

(viii) The system updates the information the shipowner has of the worldwide repair facility trends in prices, which can be used for unscheduled repair reviews.

(ix) Due to awards taking place well ahead of time of repair it enables a planned approach to 'positioning' the vessels in order to minimise any deviation debits.

(x) Lead time assists repair facilities in their future planning.

(xi) The lead time between the awards being made and the start of the vessel repair period also allows planned manpower deployment.

(xii) Information on repair costs is available in time to be included in the next year's budget forecasting.

(xiii) The single effort awards lends itself to being more

readily controlled and reviewed by in-house auditors.

The disadvantages of the standard specification are:

(i) When the standard specification does not represent a major part of the value of the final working specification the yard's expectation of work and advance planning will suffer.

(ii) If the ship repair yard employees do not appreciate the relationship between the standard specification and the working specification confusion will occur.

(iii) If the final invoice contains a small number of items of significant value which are not common to all vessels – e.g. installing an inert gas system, fitting a crude oil washing installation, installing bilge separators and sewage plants. In this case each item should be considered as a special project at the time of the bid inquiry with a separate specification. The quotation would then be considered at the bid analysis stage since these costs might have influenced the allocation of ships to repair yards.

Competitive tenders

With this system of yard selection the quality of the actual specification is all important. This is the most common method of yard selection, particularly with operators of smaller ships, such as coasters and the like where the opportunity for worldwide tenders does not exist, since the cost of diverting the ship outweighs the differential in yard costs. The specification in this case serves two purposes:

(i) to enable the shipyard estimator and buyer to assess time and material costs;

(ii) to inform the shipyard and the shipping company staff of the work required to be done.

The specification should describe and define the work so accurately that it can be costed and executed without the need to refer back to the ship, or to the superintendent and incurring additional expense and delay.

To meet this objective, the information required will vary according into which category it falls: standard item, repair item or modification.

Standard items

These items from the normal routine dry dock work are usually similar in content every docking, including for example:

- Anchors and chain; inspection and overhauls.
- Sea valves and sea chests; inspection and overhaul.
- Propeller and rudder; inspection and overhaul.
- Lifting equipment; inspection, overhaul and load test.
- Anodes; list of numbers, location and weights.
- Hull painting; description of surface preparation,

areas and film thickness required, including special hull markings.

Any special requirements known beforehand should be described and included in the appropriate specification item, especially with respect to the surface preparation for hull painting.

Repair items

Problems with extras usually occur with these items, which include: hull structure repairs, pipe renewals, machinery overhaul/reconditioning, boiler repairs, instrumentation and control refurbishing, and electrical repairs.

The repair specification of items in this category often fall short of the above objective and sometimes even seem to be an obstacle to good communication. A common example is an item such as 'open up for survey 2 in no. bilge pumps', to which the yard may respond 'to open up bilge pump for inspection £x (overhaul, reconditioning, replacing piston rings, grinding in valves, etc., extra). In such a case the shipyard may be faced at short notice with the need to supply new shaft sleeves, replacement impeller and casing rings, rebuild eroded casings or division plates, make and supply new couplings and coupling bolts.

Whereas, if this amount of work is expected the working specification for this item should list any owner's spares available, with sketches and descriptions of any new parts known to be needed, so that they can be made, rough machined, or obtained prior to the ship's arrival. In the case of piping renewals, a simple dimensioned sketch incorporated in the working specification aids identification and costing. The specification should also identify any equipment renewals in the way of the overhaul and the approximate dimensions of any access staging required.

The author has yet to know of a shipyard which issues guidelines on the preparation of specifications setting out how the specification is to be presented.

In some shipping companies the repair items are extracted from a defect list sent into head office by the ship's chief engineer. This defect list is seldom adequately dimensioned, may lack important descriptive detail and is usually assumed to be a communication between one expert and another. If such items are transferred directly to a dry-dock specification against which an estimator is expected to quote, it is no wonder that such important details as removals for access, staging and specific repair requirements are omitted. But the owner still insists on a firm price for the job.

Modification items

These items embody changes to the ship such as installation of: inert gas systems, major engine room or cargo system conversions, sewage plants and other mandatory equipment, and new automation and control equipment.

In these cases the specifications may include the equipment manufacturer's general arrangement drawings, but the ship repair yard is faced with siting and connecting up services. The shipowner may need to consider sending the superintendent with the ship repair yard's own drawing office people to visit both the ship and the manufacturer to ensure that all the relevant detail will be included in the drawings attached to the specification.

The advantages of using the actual specification are:

(i) The time scale for yard selection can be much shorter.
(ii) By working from the actual specification the yard can review the specification with departmental managers and plan the workload ahead in more detail.

The disadvantages are:

(i) If the specification is inaccurate, or lacks detail, the opportunity for excessive extra charges exist.
(ii) Yard selection is carried out ship by ship during the year and ties up shipowner's manpower analysing each bid.
(iii) The large shipowner does not have the same opportunity to use his purchasing power to obtain volume discounts.
(iv) The yard is prevented from planning its 'bread and butter' base workload throughout the yard.
(v) The yard cannot benefit from its employees' learning curve since it may only receive one ship and not a series of similar ships.

Cost plus

The 'cost plus' approach has often to be adopted with damage repairs or when the condition of the ship is more or less unknown. The relationship between the owner's representative and the repair yard management can be fraught with problems, since the approach enjoins the owner's representative to monitor, to the best of his ability, the manhours and materials used by the yard.

The yard has to plan the work and allocate its resources so that minimum time and material are wasted by its employees. This responsibility also extends to each supervisor, which includes chargehands and the willingness of employees on the job. To be successful it requires good relationships and communication throughout the yard.

Services by all repair yards

Any repair yard should be capable of supplying the following services:
- Liability insurance.
- Fire watchmen, normally two watchmen 24 hours a day, including connection and disconnection of

fire hoses from dock to ship's fire main.

- Electricity for power and lighting.
- Tugs for shifting vessel.
- Daily garbage removal.
- Shore steam, including connecting and disconnecting steam hoses.
- Supplying circulating water to the vessel's refrigerating plant, including connecting and disconnecting hoses.
- Supply of compressed air and/or steam or electrical power as required for docking and undocking the vessel and to weigh anchor.
- Supplying riggers and mooring men to assist vessel's crew in handling lines when shifting and securing vessel.
- Installation of telephone on board and removal after repairs.
- Wharfage.
- Skilled support for sea trials; say, five fitters and two riggers.
- Protective covering for accommodation alleyway floors.
- Facilities for slop disposal.

Repair yard skills

Fuel costs forced ship operators to consider means of improving overall fuel consumption. Such means include improving hull performance by surface treatment by grit blasting to remove accumulated paint and rust to restore so far as possible the original surface smoothness of the hull; by applying sophisticated anti-fouling paint systems which also polish the hull surface through the action of the sea water; and by improving propeller performance by polishing/refinishing.

These items are labour intensive, requiring responsible supervision and carefully conducted work to ensure good long-term performance from the expensive surface coatings. For this reason specialist subcontractors are often employed.

Investing in new equipment such as improved steering gear control systems, heat exchanger anti-fouling systems, conversions to enable cheaper fuels and fuel blending to be used, new automation systems, ship conversions to permit more cargo carried per tonne of fuel consumed, require drawing office staff and skilled craftsmen which are more likely to be found in a shipbuilding rather than a conventional ship repair yard. Also the coming into force of SOLAS and MARPOL conventions requires repair yards to be familiar with the installation of inert gas systems, crude oil washing systems, oily water separators, and steering gear modifications.

Shipboard planning for dry dock

Prior to arrival at the yard, the responsibilities and tasks of the ship's officers and crew should be discussed and agreed with the repair superintendent, ship's master and chief engineer, including any administrative details for travel, accommodation, feeding, etc. The main supervisory objectives delegated to the ship's officers and crew cover quality assurance, monitoring time and cost control, and ensuring the safety and security of the vessel, her people and equipment.

The ship's officers should clearly identify each repair item with the item number from the working specification and should also familiarise themselves with the specified work to be done in each case. It might also help if the appropriate ship's officers were also identified to the yard's supervisory personnel. Where necessary the owner will supply additional expertise for supervision of steelwork repairs, corrosion surveys, application of special coatings, and for repair and servicing of specific items of equipment, such as electronic navigation equipment. The repair superintendent will normally delegate the responsibility for quality assurance and monitoring time and cost control to the chief engineer, whose department traditionally reports item by item on job progress, materials consumed and even approximate manhours observed (by trade).

Other tasks include witnessing tests and keeping track of spares and special ship's tools used by the yard. The deck department generally monitor paint and special coating applications, paying particular attention to surface preparation condition, material preparation and consumption, spraying pattern, degree of overspray and film thickness. In addition, the owner will require the repair manager to maintain a running check of additional expenditure incurred.

While the repair superintendent retains the ultimate responsibility to the owner for security and safety in dock, the ship's master is responsible for ensuring that the ship is safely moored when afloat, and that safety and fire precautions are maintained.

The master is advised to prepare a safety check list in accordance with the Health & Safety Acts.

Role of the repair superintendent

The role of the owner's representative (repair superintendent) is to coordinate these activities and closely to monitor costs and time out of service. For this purpose he will generally use a daily report meeting of the ship's staff to monitor progress and quality of the specified work, to identify where additional work has to be specified by a field work order (FWO) or where work is deviating from the original specification and why. He will normally arrive at the yard a day or two prior to the ship's arrival to get to know the yard's organisation and to review the work schedule.

In the author's company the repair superintendent is the only person authorised to issue field work orders, and before committing the additional work to the yard he must obtain and accept or negotiate a price for the work. Unfortunately this requirement can result in delays if the yard cannot or will not respond quickly with prices which are consistent with those quoted at the block bid or contract negotiation stage.

Normally the owner will have established budgeting cash limits for the repair superintendent's authority and will require frequent financial reports to ensure no surprises. Generally, owners require managers to control the additional expenditure by having the repair superintendent sail with the vessel during the preparation of the final working specification, so that the repair superintendent can:

- Decide whether the work can best be done in service as voyage repairs, or in dock.
- Compile an accurate working specification for each item of work which is either not covered by the standard specification or inadequately described in the defect list.
- Brief the master and ship's officers on the preparation of the ship's organisation.
- Get to know who will be on board during the docking, and to delegate their responsibilities and tasks.

Once the ship is in dock the shipboard organisation will be centred upon the daily meeting at which the information needed by the repair superintendent will be exchanged and the ship's crew work progress objectives set. Properly organised, the repair superintendent should be at least as well informed as the yard management. After the ship arrives at the repair yard the owner's other priorities are: safety of the ship and her personnel, health and welfare of his employees, and avoidance of incidents.

Safety of the ship

The aim must be to make shipyards a safer place in which to work and increased attention must be paid to safety precautions and practices by increased cooperation between ship and repair yard personnel. For repairs undertaken in port the matter of safety is the responsibility of the shipyard. Safety regulations exist and equipment for tank cleaning, fire-fighting, rescue, first aid and monitoring tank atmosphere is supplied by the shipyard.

Failure to observe safety regulations, or inadequate safety practices have contributed to fires occurring on board ships resulting in loss of life, personal injury and damage to the ship's structure. Subsequent investigations showed that the safety aspects and the working conditions could have been improved. Two important requirements are to have the ship moored safely and to avoid fire.

The safe mooring of the vessel at the repair yard is a cooperative arrangement between ship's and yard's staff involving designers of ships and berths.

When a ship is in commission alongside an oil terminal pier or sea island, the responsibilities and capabilities of ship and shore staff and mooring equipment are well known, but once the ship is shut down and immobilised at a repair yard the capacity of the ship's crew and equipment to adjust the mooring in response to environmental changes is limited. Therefore the repair yard must anticipate the mooring requirements and the limitations of the vessel's equipment and when necessary augment the ship's facilities with shore-based mooring equipment.

Tank cleaning, gas freeing and ventilation of compartments in preparation for hot work is a major problem for shipowners and repair yards. Almost one third of all tanker fires and explosions involving the cargo areas and pump rooms are attributed to welding repairs and about 70 per cent happen during repair periods. The author's company has laid down procedures for issuing permits for entry into enclosed spaces and for carrying out hot work.

Nowadays, the tanker operator will endeavour to carry out a full crude oil wash at the last discharge port before the dry dock which will considerably reduce the oil soluble sediments in the cargo tanks. The cargo tanks are then water washed, gas freed and demucked as far as possible. It is the repair yard's responsibility to maintain the gas free certificate. The certificate is only a piece of paper and the delivery and posting of it in a prominent place is no guarantee that the ship will be safe without further effort. In this respect chapter 10 of the *International Safety Guide for Oil Tankers and Terminals* specifies the requirements. It is necessary to make periodic gas tests while hot work is in progress and before restarting after work has been stopped. The yard fire watchers should be trained in the use of combustible gas indicators, and in rescue from enclosed spaces.

In addition to the comprehensive safety requirements touched upon above, the shipowner has a responsibility for the welfare of his employees, who these days often live on board during the repair period. This calls for the repair yard to coordinate with the owner's representative to arrange either for the ship's sewage facilities to be retained in service or for suitable provision to be made adjacent to the ship. In addition, heating, lighting, cleaning and feeding services should be maintained so far as is practicable to a similar standard to those maintained when the ship is at sea.

On completion of the actual repairs, the ship's equipment has to be re-commissioned and tested, and it is during the closing stages when accidents often happen. The repair superintendent should coordinate and plan the closing stages of a repair period with the owner's representative and ship's officers so that equipment and systems become available for testing in the correct sequence and so that non-essential yard labour can be withdrawn during high risk periods – for example, when boilers are being flashed or safety valves tested. Adequate time must be provided to permit the ship to be prepared for departure in good order. More often than not the job seems to be dragged out to fill the time available and this has to be resisted, so that the ship is handed back to the owner and master in good order, tested and ready in all respects for sea.

Chapter 23

MANAGING DRY DOCK MAINTENANCE

by Captain S. Chandorkar MNI

Captain Chandorkar received his formal sea training at the training ship T.S. Rajendra, Bombay in 1981/82 and completed the training with the then Scindia Steam Navigation Company, Bombay. Since then he has served in varying ascending capacities on general cargo vessels, container vessels, bulk carriers, product tankers, crude oil tankers, chemical tankers and VLCCs.

He passed his Class 1 (Deck) certificate course at the Southampton Institute of Higher Education, College of Maritime Studies, Warsash. Later he completed a two year full time course, acquiring a Master's Degree in Business Administration (MBA) from the Institute of Management Education, Pune (India), specialising in "Production and Operations Management". There he got an insight into some valuable management tools and techniques and the wish to apply those to shipboard operations.

Captain Chandorkar joined his present company – Bergshav A/S Norway – in 1988 (it was then the Uglands Rederi A/S). He took his first command in January 1995 and has been commanding their large crude oil tankers since, presently being in command of a 276,000 dwt VLCC.

He has been a member of The Nautical Institute since 1990 and had a paper on "The practice of Ice Management" published in October 1994.

Introduction

PREPARATION FOR DRY DOCK, ironically, starts at the end of the previous dry dock itself. By regulation every ship is required to dry dock twice every five years with an interval of not more than three years between subsequent dry docks. Dry docking of an oil tanker poses peculiar problems. It involves 'planned execution' of a series of interrelated activities involving complete washing, purging, gas freeing and de-mucking of cargo systems to be safe for man entry and hot work.

Although preparation for tanker dry dock may be considered a routine operation it assumes critical proportions when operating against strict time benchmarks. This may be due to economic constraints imposed to reduce idle or off-hire time for the vessel.

Planning and control are the essential infrastructure of any project. Planning is a centralised activity and includes such functions as materials control, tools control, process planning and scheduling. Control is a diffused activity (in the field) and includes activities such as dispatching, progressing and expediting. A number of operational management tools are available, like Critical Path Analysis (CPA), Resource Smoothing, Resource Levelling, Job Scheduling and so on. However, there is little evidence of these being utilised on board ships, which by any stretch of imagination are a major production unit – the production of services. In this chapter I highlight one of the above techniques, namely CPA, as applied to tanker dry dock preparation. The given scenario is not just empirical but is actually used, with remarkable results.

Dry dock specifications

One of the major planning jobs is to draw up the dry dock specification. A typical dry dock specification file should, ideally, contain the following subsections:

1. The vessel's principal dimensions.
2. Condition of tenders – owner's requirements regarding the quality of material, quality of workmanship desired, staging, lighting, ventilation, tugs, pilotage, craneage, etc. Time frame allotted to the yard including penalty for delayed delivery. Details of bidding, detailed formats for billing and accounting. Sometimes, the applicable arbitration act to be referred to in case of disputes may be included.
3. General service specifications – the dry docking, number, location and spacing of keel blocks including the material of the top of the blocks (e.g. blocks with soft wood caps).
4. Wharfage.
5. Pilotage, tugs, line handling.
6. Gangways and safe access arrangements.
7. Draining and filling of ballast water.
8. Bottom drain plugs.
9. Disposal of water and oily water in bilges and tanks.
10. Electric power afloat and in dry dock.
11. Heating lamps and temporary lighting.
12. Telephone and other services.
13. Fire and security watch service.
14. Fire line.
15. Air conditioning plant and provision refrigeration plant.
16. Fresh water supply.
17. Compressed air.
18. Craneage for ship's provisions and owner's spares.
19. Garbage removal.
20. General cleaning.
21. Assistance for dock and sea trials, if any, including crew and launch service.
22. Ventilation, gas freeing and certification.
23. General steel renewal and quotes per unit.
24. Miscellaneous – working hours, meal hours, overtime and double overtime hours. The labour cost/man/hour, both skilled and unskilled.

25. Hull cleaning, blasting and painting – general specifications and specific requirements.

Jobs

Each job should have a unique identity code. For example H xx (hull jobs), D xx (deck jobs) and E xx (engine jobs). All possible jobs should be identified by the ship's staff through their running defect lists and Planned Maintenance System (PMS) routines. Jobs may be segregated into two basic categories – dry dock and ship's staff. Each job must have essential specifications like dimensions, material, pressure ratings, current ratings, initial preparation and disassembly and assembly procedures and be supported by drawings, plans and sketches. Each job must have an appraisal of spares/stores requirements that should be checked against the current inventories and orders (allowing for the 'lead time' for delivery prior to arrival at dry dock). An assessment of man hour requirements for each job should be made (see figure 23.4 for a useful format). Each job detail is kept in a separate soft folder along with the necessary supporting documents. A master index is then prepared, complete with job identification numbers and job titles. Responsible officers are then assigned to supervision, progress monitoring and reporting of specific jobs. A simple format could be:

- Job number.
- Job title.
- Officer-in-charge.
- Report to:
  – Master / Chief Engineer / Chief Officer.

The responsibilities and jobs of the ship's officers should be discussed and agreed with the repair superintendent, master and chief engineer. The main supervisory objectives delegated to the ship's officers and crew cover quality assurance, monitoring time and cost control and ensuring the safety and security of the vessel, her crew and equipment (see figure 23.2 for a list of major dry dock jobs).

The master's role in dry docking

A sea-change in the traditional role of a shipmaster is evident. He is now seen as the 'central hub' of most activities. Rather than being merely a liaison man he is now seen as a manager. The management process is replete with references to planning and the shipmaster is the distinctive key in the planning of dry dockings. He can contribute by applying the following principles:

Operational planning

Guided by a set of policies, procedures, rules, forecasts and budgets, the shipmaster is responsible for the formulation of management strategies for day-to-day affairs. With particular reference to dry dockings, he must bear in mind the time schedule and the need for compliance with local rules, international rules and company policies. His role, therefore, is to amalgamate the operational plans of all departments within the overall organisational plan so that they work in tandem with each other.

Project planning

This involves the planning of a clearly identifiable programme of work within the set time (dry dock time) and resource constraints (manpower and materials).

Management by objectives (MBO)

The main dry dock objectives (jobs) are divided into divisional or departmental objectives, further subdivided into individual objectives. The master must then monitor the activities of this interlocking system to serve as the basis for managing, evaluation and control of performance.

Contingency planning

Contingency planning rests on the premise that there is no one best way to do a job. The right approach depends on the situation. Moreover, one has very little control on the 'external-environment' (areas beyond direct control). Conditions in the external environment change so rapidly that often there are constraints in making tenable assumptions regarding further developments. A realistic approach to containing these problems is to adopt contingency planning. This involves taking incremental steps, reassessing strategies at each stage (daily) and reformulating plans in order to fulfil the dry dock objectives.

Feedback and control

A daily meeting is more than a necessity. The master can be instrumental in motivating the yard manager, superintendent, chief engineer, chief officer, paint supervisor and class surveyor. This closes the loop for operational control, status monitoring, variance evaluation, problem solving and decision making. Armed with his 'sixth-sense' the master must coordinate the activities of all these heads, supplementing resources where necessary and applying leverage where required. This daily meeting imparts that essential operational control. The author's company, in fact, once arranged for the superintendent, the class surveyor and two yard managers to board the vessel two days prior to dry dock, whilst the vessel was en route to the dry dock port. The advantages of daily meetings were being felt even before the vessel entered the dry dock.

Job decisions

Essential factors that contribute to assigning jobs as 'dry dock' items include:

i)   Jobs that cannot be done whilst afloat.
ii) Jobs that require shutdown.
iii) Jobs that require external assistance by way of manpower or specialised equipment.
iv) Special survey items and steel renewals.
v)   Major structural modifications.
vi) Looking to continuous improvement in performance

SPECIFICATION OF REPAIRS – Job No: D ....

SHIP: DATE:		TO BE INCLUDED
JOB DESCRIPTION:		Gas free certificate
		Light
ACCOUNT NO:		Ventilation
Make, type, rating, weight, volume, RPM, voltage. etc.		Cleaning before
		Cleaning after
		Staging
LOCATION:		Crane
Detailed specification, inc. size, amount, dimensions, materials, etc.		Internal transportation
		Transportation outside yard
		Access work
		Corrosion protection
		Paintwork
		Pressure testing
		Function testing
		Corrections drawings
		MATERIALS
		Yards supply
		Owners supply
		THE WORK TO BE SURVEYED ALSO BY:
		Class representative
		Maritime authorities
		Manufacturers representative
		Owners representative
		ENCLOSED:
		Photo
		Drawing
		Sketch
		Sample

Figure 23.1 Specification of repairs

MAJOR DRY DOCK JOBS

HULL
- Ship side and bottom cleaning and painting.
- Painting of vessel's topsides.
- Maintenance of sea chests.
- Renewal of external anodes.
- Ship side valves.
- Impressed current (ICCP) system.
- Draft gauges.
- Steel renewal, buckling, panting / grounding damage (if any).

DECK
- Deck equipment and machinery – repairs / overhauls / tests.
- Anchors and cables – ranging, blasting, painting, marking.
- Chain lockers – cleaning, coating.
- Load tests of lifting gear, including elevator and engine room gantries
- Steel renewals.
- Pipelines / valves – renewal / (rotate through 180°).
- Inert gas system – deck seal (inspection and coating), IG lines on deck.
- Deck fittings – rollers, fairleads, pipe supports, manifold drip trays.
- Cargo / ballast tanks – steel renewal / control of coating.
- Heating coils pressure test.
- In tank jobs – steel renewal – hydrostatic pressure test of cargo tanks.
- Deck winches – brake tests.
- Survey items.

NAVIGATION
- Radar scanners overhaul.
- Gyro servicing.
- Echo sounder and log servicing.

ENGINE
- Propellor – measure drop, nut to be retightened, travel to be measured, blades examined, polished and coated with approved protective coating.
- Stern tube – measure wear down, change seals.
- Rudder – remove plug, air test for leakages, change neoprene packing at plugs, hammer test palm bolts, measure clearances at upper pintle, lower pintle, rudder carrier, jump clearances.
- Ship side valves – all ship side valves opened, overhauled / changed and surveyed by classification.
- Steering gear – classification survey. Reliefs set, pumps, pipes, controls test.
- Main engine and auxiliaries – air coolers, turbochargers, main bearings, etc.
- Shutdown jobs – main switchboard – clean breakers, busbar and terminals. Record insulation readings, test on load. Surveys. Reverse power and overload trips.
- Fire and emergency fire pumps.
- Fuel oil transfer pumps.
- Cargo oil and ballast pump turbines.
- Sea water cooling pipes.
- IG system – scrubber cooling water overboard discharge pipes.
- Soil overboard pipes and storm valves.
- Boiler blowdown overboard pipe.
- Automation.
- Various motors – insulation and overhaul.
- Pump room fans, IG blowers, exhaust blowers – electrical overhaul and balancing.
- Control air and service air compressors.

CLASSIFICATION SURVEYS
- Docking survey.
- Special survey / intermediate survey.
- Load line / safety construction / IOPP surveys.
- Annual class survey.
- Continuous survey of machinery (CSM) items.

PENDING MAJOR PMS ROUTINES

Figure 23.2 Major dry dock jobs

and/or containing the rate of overall degradation. For example, cargo pipelines internal inspection and rotation by 180°. The jobs, once presented, must then be evaluated and ironed out by:

- The yard for feasibility.
- The class for acceptability.
- The owner's representative for financial viability.
- The ship for essential spares / stores availability.

Need for a systematic approach

A number of scientific tools are available for planning, but planning of projects such as 'tanker dry dock preparation' is best performed through a well known technique called Critical Path Analysis (CPA). In the light of tight time constraints, improper scheduling of activities would lead to delays, increased expenses, inability to meet delivery commitment and attract unwelcome penalties. CPA, as a planning tool, offers several advantages in that it:

a) Forces thorough pre-planning.
b) Increases coordination by establishing technological relationships between activities.
c) Helps computation of total duration and indicates the start and finish times of each activity.
d) Defines areas of responsibility of different department heads.
e) Facilitates progress monitoring.
f) Identifies trouble spots.
g) Helps to exercise 'control by exception' and prevent cost over-runs.

The test here is to fit all activities into a tight time frame, with adequate leverage available on operational controls. Most tankermen feel they are blessed with the art of "savoir-faire", relying primarily on their memory, but will find the usefulness of this technique combats mayhem, by proper forward planning and the efficient use of time, manpower and resources.

What is CPA?

CPA is an important aid to planning, scheduling and coordinating activities. It is a synthesis of two independent techniques – Project Evaluation Review Technique (PERT) and Critical Path Method (CPM). PERT was developed by engineers of the US Navy in charge of the Polaris Submarine Missile Project in 1958. CPM was developed by Morgan Walker of Du Pont and James Kelly of Remington Rand (USA) in 1957. Although both techniques were developed independently they are only superficially different. A brief theoretical background follows.

An entire project is broken down into activities. A practical assessment of the time required for each activity is made. The technological correlation of activities is established and identified by a precedence table, highlighting the sequence of activities and whether or not more than one activity can run concurrently. The CPA diagram is then drawn up as a master plan of all activities in their correct order. Dummy activities may be incorporated, either to signify a constraint or to avoid ambiguities or illogicalities. The completion of an activity is called an event. The flow chart is then annotated with activity times. The next step is to identify activity chains from the chart. The total time for each activity chain is then calculated and the maximum time chain becomes the 'critical path', with the total project duration being the time required for the completion of the critical path. The critical path is so named because a delay in any activity along this path will lead to an increase in total project duration. Should such a condition be foreseeable it may be possible to divert resources from a non-critical path and still be able to complete the project within the stipulated duration. Consider a simple illustration (see figure 23.3). Activities a, b, c, d, e, f and g are drawn up in the order of their interdependence, with activity times written below each. Three activity chains are established.

Activity chain	Duration
a–b–e–g	17 *
a–d–g	11
a–c–f–g	14

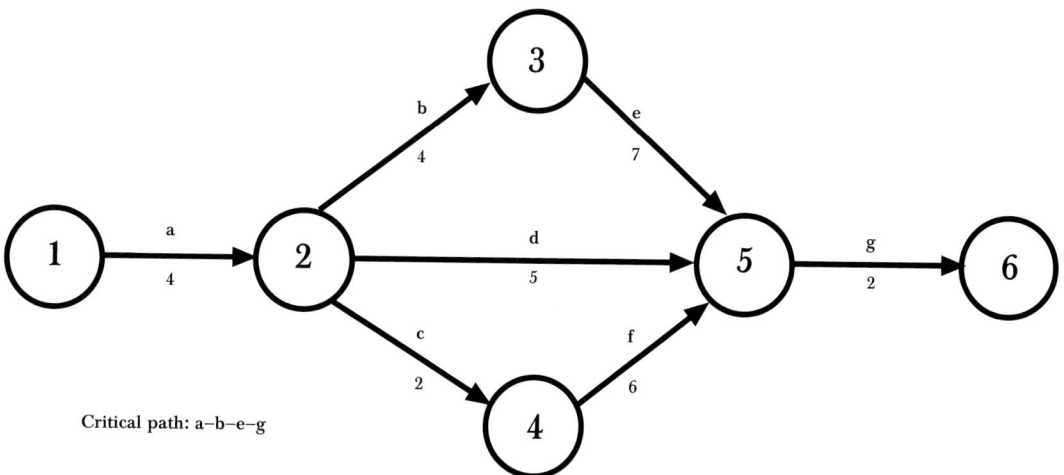

Critical path: a–b–e–g

Figure 23.3 Example of a critical path

The activity chain a–b–e–g has a total duration of 17 hours and is obviously the 'critical path'. The project duration, therefore, is 17 hours. The earliest and latest event occurrence times are then calculated for each event.

T_{e2} = earliest time for event 2 = T_{e1} (earliest time for event 1) + duration of activity 'a'. T_{j2} = latest time for an event = T_{j3} – a.

For a 'burst event' (event 2 in figure 23.3) the latest time is the minimum $(T_j$-a) of all activities diverging from it and for a 'merge event' (event 5 in figure 23.3) it is the maxima of $(T_i + a)$ of all activities converging on it. A useful concept now evolves which is called activity float analysis. The float of an activity is the excess of available time over its duration. It is the leeway available to the project planner for scheduling of the activity. It allows the planner to decide priorities in the allocation of resources, to transfer resources from less pressing areas to more demanding areas and to prevent peaks and valleys in the requirements of a resource.

Total float (of an activity) = latest occurrence
time of the succeeding event
minus
earliest occurrence time of the preceding event
minus
duration of the activity

In effect, therefore, the following procedural steps are required for a CPA:

1. Break down the project into a set of identifiable activities (***activity identification)***.
2. Establish technological relationships between activities (***activity relationships***).
3. Construct the network diagram (***network construction***).
4. Number the events (***node labelling***).
5. Estimate the time duration of each activity (***activity time estimation***).
6. Identify the critical path, critical activities and slack of non-critical activities (***network time analysis and activity float analysis***).
7. Establish the probability aspects of each activity (***probability determination***).
8. If possible, crash the project to its minimum duration (***project crashing***).
9. Allocate resources and ensure that resource requirements do not exceed the resource allocation (***resource allocation and resource levelling***).
10. Prepare a time schedule for the activities of the project (***project scheduling***, e.g. gantt charts).
11. Review progress periodically and expedite if required (***project monitoring***).

Armed with this valuable knowledge let us now formulate a strategy for 'tanker dry dock preparation'. I quote in this chapter a scenario of preparing a tanker for dry dock and the application of CPA techniques. In most cases, especially when a vessel on time charter off-hires herself for a routine dry dock, every moment off-hire is probably seen as a colossal loss by the owner.

The scenario: M T analysis – dry dock preparation

In any project one must first identify the project objectives and constraints.

Project objectives
1. M T analysis preparing for dry dock and special survey.
2. Dry dock readiness time 6 days.
3. Vessel to pick up class surveyor at intermediate point (IP) 4·5 days from start for close up survey of one pair of cargo tanks and thickness measurements. This involves ballasting No. 4 wings for close up survey and de-ballasting prior to arrival at dry dock.
4. Vessel to revert to estimated fuel oil consumption for the entire operation and stem bunker requirements for bunkering at last departure port prior to dry dock. Bunkering en route or at dry dock is not possible.
5. For safety reasons, de-mucking of cargo tanks is to be done during daytime only.

Project available resources
1. A conventional 150,000 dwt crude oil tanker, SBT, double skin/double hull. Three line arrangement, 12 cargo tanks, two slop tanks and 12 SBTs.
2. Three cargo pumps, one stripper pump, one cargo eductor and two ballast pumps for SBT.
3. Slop (P) is the primary slop tank with a balancing line from Slop (P) to Slop (S).
4. Four in number hydro blowers and the ability to gas free using inert gas blowers.
5. Maximum manpower available is 20. Optimum manpower for the bulk of the washing operation is four.

Activity time analysis
An evaluation of specific activity times based on past experience:

1. Washing time six hours per tank. A pair of tanks can effectively be washed and stripped concurrently.
2. Purging time to reduce hydrocarbon below 1·5% is eight hours. Two tanks can be purged concurrently.
3. Gas freeing time – eight hours per tank. Can only use two hydro-blowers per tank.
4. De-sludging time is not included in the original calculations, as it depends primarily on post inspection findings and it is otherwise very difficult to estimate the quantity of sludge.

Activity appraisal
Based on the primary data above, a sequential order is formulated (see figure 23.4). At this stage it

M.T. ANALYSIS – DRYDOCK – DETAILED ACTIVITY APPRAISAL

Activity	Details	Pumps	Manpower	Time
A	FLUSHING SEQUENCE			
	a) 591-592-594-595-COP1-570-549-517-585-slop(p) (open no. 1 manifold drain valves to 4ws)	COP 1	4	20 mins
	b) COP1-570-549-523-530-518-586-slop(p)	COP1	4	20 mins
	c) COP1-570-549-523-537-519-587-slop(p)	COP1	4	20 mins
	d) COP1-570-549-523-537-519-(3-1XO)-585-slop(p)	COP1	4	20 mins
	e) COP1-570-549-517-(1-2X0)-(2-3X0)-587-slop(p)	COP 1	4	20 mins
	f) 591-592-594-596-COP2-571-550-518-586-slop(p) (open no.2 manifold drains valves to 4ws)	COP 2	4	20 mins
	g) 591-592 594-597-COP3-572-551-519-587-slop(p) (open no.3 manifold drain valves to 4ws)	COP 3	4	20 mins
	h) sslop-600-567-541/542-no.3 manifold drain valves to 4ws (flushing marpol line)	STRIPPER	4	20 mins
B	P SLOP-EDUCTOR-P SLOP/STRIPPING 4WS INTERNALLY	COP 1	2	6 hours
C	PURGING 4WS		2	8 hours
D	2 DASIC BLOWERS EACH ON 4 P N S		4	12 hours
E	P-SLOP-EDUCTOR-PSLOP/STRIPPING 1WS INTERNALLY	COP1	2	6 hours
F	PURGING 1WS.		2	8 hours
G	2 DASIC BLOWERS EACH ON 1P N S		4	12 hours
H	P SLOP-EDUCTOR-P SLOP/STRIPPING 2WS INTERNALLY	COP 1	2	6 hours
I	PURGING 2WS.		2	8 hours
J	2 DASIC BLOWERS EACH ON 2P N S		4	12 hours
K	P-SLOP-EDUCTOR-PSLOP/STRIPPING 5WS INTERNALLY	COP1	2	6 hours
L	PURGING 5WS.		2	8 hours
M	2 DASIC BLOWERS EACH ON 5P N S		4	12 hours
N	P SLOP-EDUCTOR-P SLOP/STRIPPING 3WS INTERNALLY	COP1	2	6 hours
O	PURGING 3WS		2	8 hours
P	2 DASIC BLOWERS EACH ON 3P N S		4	12 hours
Q	P SLOP-EDUCTOR-P SLOP/STRIPPING 6WS INTERNALLY	COP1	2	6 hours
R	PURGING 6WS		2	8 hours
S	2 DASIC BLOWERS EACH ON 6P N S		4	12 hours
T	TRANSFER SLOP S TO SLOP P	COP1	4	1 hour
U	P SLOP-EDUCTOR-P SLOP/STRIPPING SLOP S	COP1	2	4 hours
V	PURGING SLOP S (SLOP P-SLOP P FOR BLR LOAD)	COP1	2	4 hours
W	2 DASIC BLOWERS ON SLOP S		2	8 hours
X	DECANT SLOP P TO SEA (24 hours settling, ODM RUNNING)	COP1	4	2 hours
Y	FLUSH BOTTOM LINES AND PUMPROOM	COP1	4	1 hour
	SEA TO SLOP PORT	COP2	4	1 hour
		COP3	4	1 hour

SECOND STAGE (Prep for close-up survey)

II-1	BALLASTING 4WS C.O.TS	COP1	4	8 hours
II-2	DEBALLASTING 4WS SBT(SIMULTANEOUS OPERATION)	BALL P/P	1	

THIRD STAGE (intermediate point to dry dock)

III-1	DEBALLASTING 4WS COT WITH SURVEY	COP1	4	8 hours
III-2	TRANSFER STRIPPINGS OF COT N LINES TO SLOPS	STRIPPER	4	3 hours
III-3	DEBALLASTING 1WS,3WS,5WS SBT FOR INTERNAL INSP (Staggered operation)	BALL P/PS	4	16 hours

FOURTH STAGE (arrival dry dock preparation)

IV	ARR DRAFTS FOR DOCK- POSSIBLY ALL BY GRAVITY (Only SBTS 2WS,4WS,6WS need to be dropped)	BALL P/PS (MAY AVOID)		6 hours

FIFTH STAGE (washing & discharge)

V-1	WASHING SLOP PORT AT SLOP BERTH	TC P/P	4	4 hours
V-2	DISCHARGE ASHORE	STRIPPER	4	6 hours

SIXTH STAGE (arr loading prep inerting all cots)

VI	ARR LOADING PREP INERTING ALL COTS	COP1	2	60 hours
	EXPECTED BOILER OPERATION TIMES			200 hours
	PLUS 10% CONTINGENCY OPERATION			20 hours

Figure 23.4 M T analysis – dry dock

may be prudent to highlight the manpower requirements for each activity, in order to facilitate manpower planning and to modify work schedules to suit activity requirements. The times quoted in the table have a safety buffer and are reasonably evaluated maxima. The line flushing sequence is elaborated with valve numbers specific to this ship. We are all aware that the most important activity in preparing a tanker is, in fact, line flushing. This can be done quite simply by tracing the path on a mimic or a lines plan and drawing up an elaborate flow sequence in order to avoid oversight and overlap of flushing lines. It is prudent to bear in mind the actual layout of lines in order to identify standing sections.

Precedence table

The next step is to draw a precedence table (see figure 23.5). This is where the interdependence of activities is established and care is taken to maintain ease of flow without time lost in changeovers. Quite simply, as in this illustration, it is a logical flow of operations, i.e. tank cleaning, followed by purging, followed by gas freeing.

The CPA diagram (figure 23.6)

Using the precedence table, a CPA flow diagram is drawn. A 'mega' event represents the end of a chain of activities, in this case a tank being ready for inspection. While drawing up a CPA diagram take care to maintain flow in the forward direction. You may need to insert dummy activities (with zero activity times) to maintain a logical flow. The dummy activities are used to simplify understanding and, since they have no activity times, have little or no implications for the total duration. It is assumed that the project has been crashed to its minimum duration.

Activity chains

As shown in the CPA diagram, four activity chains can be identified, namely a washing chain, a purging

---

M.T. ANALYSIS

ACTIVITY PRECENDENCE TABLE

ACTIVITY	DETAILS	PRECEEDING ACTIVITIES
A	FLUSHING SEQUENCE	NONE
B	WASHING/STRIPPING 4WS	A
C	PURGING 4WS	B
D	GAS FREEING 4WS	B, C
E	WASHING/STRIPPING 1WS	B
F	PURGING	E
G	GAS FREEING	E, F
H	WASHING/STRIPPING 2WS	E
I	PURGING 2WS	H
J	GASFREEING 2WS	H, I
K	WASHING/STRIPPING 5WS	H
L	PURGING 5WS	K
M	GASFREEING 5WS	K, L
N	WASHING/STRIPPING 3WS	K
O	PURGING 3WS	N
P	GASFREEING 3WS	N, O
Q	WASHING/STRIPPING 6WS	N
R	PURGING 6WS	Q
S	GASFREEING 6WS	Q, R
T	TRANSFER SLOPS TO SLOP P	Q
U	WASHING/STRIPPING SLOP S	T
V	PURGING SLOP S	U
W	GASFREEING SLOP S	U, V
X	DECANT SLOP P	U
Y	FLUSHING LINES AND PUMPROOM	X

Notes: a) Washing is carried out internally, drive water from slop starboard and tank educted back to slop port.

b) Slop port and starboard balancing line left open.

c) Purging – reducing hydrocarbon content of the tank to less than 1·5% by volume, by the introduction of inert gas. The tank atmosphere should be below the critical dilution line.

Figure 23.5 Activity precedence table

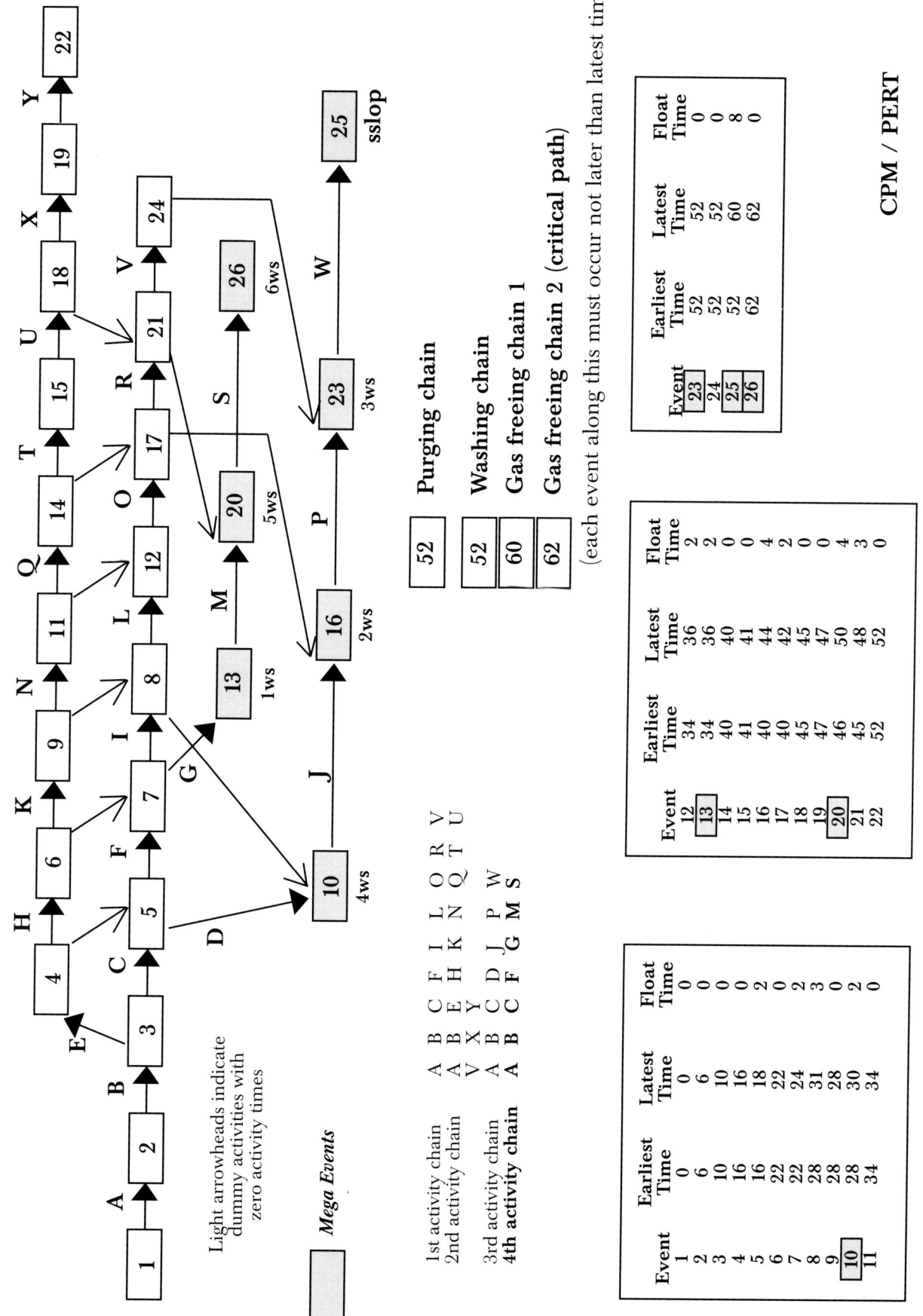

Figure 23.6 Critical path analysis / float analysis for tank washing and gas freeing prior to dry docking

chain, and two gas freeing chains. Adding up the activity times along each chain we get the following results:

Washing chain	52 hours
Purging chain	52 hours
Gas freeing chain 1	60 hours
Gas freeing chain 2	62 hours

Gas freeing chain 2, therefore, becomes the critical path with each activity along this chain being a critical activity. It should be re-emphasised at this stage that any delay along the critical path will lead to an increase in the overall project duration. The project duration for this example, being the duration along the critical path, is 62 hours.

Time and float analysis

A simple earliest and latest event time chart is then drawn up. Technically of course, as noted above, a float analysis involves working both forward and backwards between the first and the last events. However, in this case, a simple slack time assessment would suffice. For example, event 7 can be reached via activities a–b–c–f or via a–b–e–h. The times along each path, being 22 and 24 hours respectively, give two hours slack time for event 7.

Project monitoring

Monitor activities and event occurrence times as actually observed during project execution. Should a predictable delay be identified it may be possible to divert resources from another non-critical concurrent activity so as not to affect the critical activities.

Results

Having applied the above principles and with careful monitoring, the M T Analysis completed all operations in 56 hours. The valuable use of CPA techniques was obvious during its actual use. It should be noted that although the illustration given here is for a typical tank washing prior to dry docking, the author has successfully applied CPA to projects like voyage maintenance and monthly planned maintenance for routine ship operations.

Safety of the ship

Dry dock safety is a collective effort by both yard and ship personnel. On a 'partly' immobilised ship with 'disabled' safety systems it is absolutely essential that backup systems are readily available and understood and that the capabilities of both the yard's and the ship's systems are clearly defined and understood. Man entry and hot work are of primary concern. Guidelines given in *The International Safety Guide for Oil Tankers and Terminals* (ISGOTT) and the company's standing instructions should be strictly followed, with a 'permit to work' system enforced. Safety and management committee meetings prior to dry dock should include the ship's safety organisation during the repair period. Positive reporting to a central authority (master, chief officer or chief engineer) should be established, with clearly defined channels of upward and downward communication.

Re-commissioning after repairs is another crucial stage. A plan should be formulated to include:

- Testing of machinery, equipment, systems and appliances.
- Re-floating trim and stability requirements.
- Bottom plugs, manholes and restoration and checking of the watertight integrity.
- Removal of staging and temporary structures.
- Confirmation of restoration of vessel's safety and fire protection systems.

Sufficient time must be allowed for the vessel to confirm all above and to prepare for departure.

Footnote

More often than not, seafarers like to 'play it by ear'. It would greatly help to know how to play, how much to play, when to play and when to allow the brain, rather than the ear, to take operational management decisions.

The order of the day, then, is immense forethought, careful strategic planning, watchful progress monitoring and effective coordination and controls.

The result – apart from the project commitment – is a complete sense of command throughout the project, with the ability to cope with contingencies.

Chapter 24

A GUIDE TO THE 'CREWMAN' STANDARD SHIP MANAGEMENT AGREEMENT

by Photis M. Panayides BSc, University of Plymouth

reproduced from SEAWAYS, the journal of The Nautical Institute

Introduction

WITH THE INCREASING NUMBER of the world's fleet placed under third party ship management, the maritime world has seen the need for standard agreements which aim to regulate the manager-owner relationship. One such agreement is the *Crewman*, drafted by the Documentary Committee of BIMCO, and dealing specifically with the employment of crew on board vessels placed under independent management responsible solely for crewing purposes.

It is important for the seafarer to be aware of the provisions of such an agreement, especially the provisions which relate to employment on a vessel, safety, health, rights, liabilities and responsibilities.

Who is the employer?

First, it must be pointed out that, unlike the 'sister-agreement' *Shipman*, which deals with the provision of a number of ship management services, the *Crewman* agreement provides that the manager and not the owner is the legal and sole employer of the crew. This means that in case of dispute due to, for example, non-payment of wages or their late payment, the responsibility will lie solely with the third party managing the ship and not the owner.

The seafarers must check that their individual contracts clearly specify who their employers are. Despite this, crew members are obliged to obey all reasonable instructions given by the legal owners of the vessels. These instructions include orders relating to safety, navigation, pollution prevention and protection of the environment.

Further, the owners of the vessel have the right to demand the replacement of any crew member found on reasonable grounds to be unsuitable for service. Unsuitability for service must be deemed to include not 'qualified' or 'competent' for the standard of work required of him. It may also extend to cases where continuous misbehaviour of an otherwise qualified crew member has prompted the owners to order his replacement at the next reasonable opportunity.

Safety and communications

It is worth noting that all crew members must have sufficient knowledge of the English language in order to be capable of performing their duties in a safe manner. It is the responsibility of the crew managers to oversee this. The fact that the standard of English required has to be sufficient only for the performance of the crew members' duties is important because it raises the question of what will happen in emergency situations where the crew have to act in ways other than those of their customary duties.

All members of the crew must have undergone certain training relating to emergency situations before they go on board, but the dangers arising on board may not always be the same. Many dangerous situations may arise, especially where foreign crew members have just joined the vessel, and are faced with an emergency before even adapting to their new environment. A lack of communication is critical and all seafarers must become aware of it because the adverse situation may affect all of them, not just those incapable of communicating in English.

Connected persons

All crew members have a right, under the agreement, to invite on board any person or persons connected with them. Connected persons would reasonably include relatives of crew members. These persons may even stay on board during the voyage, as long as there are reasonable circumstances requiring their presence there. In some instances there is an express provision to this in the individual contract of employment. The prior consent of the owners of the vessel is required, but the owners are obliged not to unreasonably withhold such permission.

Crew managers are obliged to provide adequate insurance cover for connected persons. If they refrain from doing so the owners will be liable if anything happens to any connected person during their visit or stay on board.

Insurance

It is the obligation of the crew managers adequately to insure the crew members (as well as any connected persons sailing with them) with a first class insurance company, underwriter or protection and indemnity association (P&I Club). The agreement mentions the risks for which the crew must be fully covered. These include:

- Death
- Sickness
- Repatriation
- Injury

- Shipwreck unemployment indemnity, and
- Loss of personal effects

The agreement does not limit the risks for which the crew must be insured only to those mentioned above. It is up to the managers to insure the crew for other risks as well.

War risks trading limits

It is at the owner's discretion to decide whether or not to send the vessel to any area excluded by war risks underwriters by virtue of the current London market war risks trading warranties. The owners must, however, inform the crew managers prior to giving such orders; and crew managers must themselves in turn inform the crew. The crew members are not obliged to accept such orders and may demand extra war risks bonuses, or even refuse to embark on such voyage and demand repatriation. Crew managers are obliged to replace those crew members and pay all expenses in connection with their replacement which will ultimately be covered by the owners.

Provisions

The owners of the vessel are required under the agreement to provide all normal provisions and facilities for maintaining the standard of living of the crew on board and pay all the costs thereof.

The provisions and facilities include not only victuals, fresh water, linen, blankets, towels, soap, washing powder, laundry facilities, adequate accommodation and storage facilities but also entertainment and recreational facilities.

It seems that the people responsible for drafting the *Crewman* agreement recognised the need for avoiding boredom and fatigue on board and specifically introduced the requirement for leisure facilities.

Financial obligations

Normally, the contract of employment of the crew members will state that costs incurred in relation to obtaining various certificates with respect to the crew's service, transportation and accommodation costs as well as a series of related costs will not be borne by the crew members.

However, it is beneficial to seafarers to review the costs for which, under the *Crewman* agreement, they will not be responsible. These costs can be derived from the clause dealing with the fee of the crew managers and listing the various costs for which the managers will be entitled to charge on the lump sum fee due to them.

The crew is to be compensated for working overtime hours. The sum due in respect of overtime is payable by the managers to the crew, unless it exceeds a specific amount agreed by the owner and manager and which sum is expressly stated in a box

in the *Crewman* contract. If it is exceeded, it is the owners' responsibility to oversee that the excess is promptly despatched to the crew members concerned.

The seafarers will have no financial obligation as regards the costs of obtaining documentation necessary for their employment. Crewman refers to documentation such as medical and vaccination certificates, passports and visas and licenses; however, any costs incurred in relation to obtaining documentation with respect to the crew's employment is covered by the provision.

The costs of transportation of the crew to and from the vessel will be borne by the managers, but of course it will be charged to the owners. However, the owners are themselves responsible for the initial cost of transportation from the seafarer's country of domicile to the ship.

Costs for hotel accommodation, food, all types of crew communications from the vessel, working clothes and port disbursements and fees in respect of crew matters are for the managers' account, initially.

Indemnity

The agreement contains an indemnity clause which defines the responsibility of the owner of the vessel in case of legal proceedings or claims against the vessel, affecting the crew members or their employment agreement.

In the event of any legal proceedings, legal actions, claims and demands against the crew members arising out of, or in connection with the terms of the agreement, the crew members will incur no liability whatsoever. In the event that the crew member incurs loss or damage or expenses due to such actions, it is the responsibility of the shipowner to render the crew member fully indemnified.

The extent of the indemnity set out by the relevant clause does not include claims for which the crew managers themselves would be liable to the owners. It follows that the owners will be obliged to indemnify the crew members unless they can prove that the loss, damage or expense the crew members incurred resulted from their own negligence, gross negligence, wilful default or an act or omission done with the intent to cause the damage or recklessly and with knowledge that damage or loss would probably result.

Liability to owners

In order to protect the interests of crew members, a so called *Himalaya* Clause has been incorporated in the agreement.

Under this, crew members will incur no liability whatsoever to the owners of the vessel, for any loss, damage or delay of whatsoever kind arising or resulting directly or indirectly from any act, omission or default of the crew member while acting in the course of or in connection with his employment duties.

The latter expression is important, as it limits the exclusion of liability to the owners only to those cases where the problems occurred while the crew member was carrying out his duties as specified in the contract of employment. It follows that where such loss, damage or delay arose by the act, neglect or default of the crew member who was acting outside the scope of his employment, then that crew member will be liable to the owners.

In short this is usually expressed by the phrase: 'the employee embarked on a frolic of his own'.

It is, therefore, very important for the members of the crew not to engage in any duties which are outside those legally delegated to them. They must be well aware that the duties they perform are within the course of or in connection with their employment duties.

Termination of the contract

As has been stated, the employer of the crew is the manager and not the owner of the ship. The manager agrees with the owner merely to supply the crew for the particular ship. Sometimes, however, the agreement may come to an end, i.e. terminated prior to the date that has been specified and agreed under the terms of the contract. Hence, it is important for seafarers to know and understand their rights since their legal employer will no longer be able to keep them employed on board the particular vessel.

The *Crewman* contract specifies three types of termination that may arise during the period of the agreement. These include termination because of the owners 'default', termination because of the crew managers' default; and extraordinary termination through no default of either party but due to unexpected and unforeseen circumstances.

In case of termination of the agreement due to any of the above reasons, the crew managers are obliged to pay the crew what they are legally entitled to under their individual contracts of employment. These costs are termed in the agreement as 'severance costs' and the owners themselves are obliged to contribute up to a limit agreed by the parties and as long as the managers can prove that those costs were incurred because of the early termination.

It must be noted that crew members employed by crew managers who are responsible for crewing a large fleet of vessels will normally face no problem in finding alternative employment as it will be within the interests of the crew managers themselves to redeploy them.

Conclusion

The *Crewman* is a contract between the owner and the manager of the vessel and, therefore, the crew members will not have a say in the drafting of its terms under any circumstances whatsoever. From a practical point of view, however, it is important for the seafarers to know about its provisions which do affect indirectly their own contracts of employment.

My view is that the contract contains fair and reasonable terms as far as the crew members are concerned. The fact that the contract excludes the liability of the crew (unless they act outside the scope of their employment) and provides an indemnity clause protecting the crew members, is of immense importance in the crucial issue of liabilities. Furthermore, even if the agreement terminates, a special clause provides that the crew will be compensated for any consequential losses they might incur.

It must be noted however that this standard form is susceptible to alterations in accordance with the wills of the contractors who may wish to log in their own terms and conditions. Despite this, it is common practice for the parties to retain most, if not all, of the original clauses.

Knowledge of *Crewman*'s basic terms will prompt crew members to stand up for their rights in case there is a need. I hope I have contributed towards the achievement of the former through this article.

Acknowledgments
The author wishes to express his gratitude to Dr. Richard Gray – Head of the Centre for International Shipping and Transport – and Messrs. Sydney T. Harley and Paul G. Wright – lecturers – for their valuable suggestions in the writing of this article.

Chapter 25

MANAGING SOCIAL RELATIONSHIPS WITH MULTI-CULTURAL CREWS

by Captain A. Achuthan ExC MICS MNI

Captain Achuthan completed his pre-sea training from the T.S. Rajendra in 1976 and joined the Shipping Corporation of India, obtaining command in December 1986. From 1989-1991 he commanded various foreign flag vessels, after which he joined the LBS Nautical College (now named LBS College of Advanced Maritime Studies and Research).

He obtained his Extra Masters in 1993 and has taught various grades from 2nd Mates to Extra Masters. He has also been external faculty at T.S. Chanakya (a BSc nautical science course), T.S. Jawhar (3 month pre sea training), MTI Powaii (chemical tanker and LPG familiarisation), College of Insurance (marine pollution regulations), and at the Master Revalidation Course (oil major vetting and modern meteorology). He was also involved with the design stage of the liquid cargo handling simulator at LBS CAMSAR and was given the honour of starting the first course in July 1995.

He sailed for a short stint with Dynacom tankers in 1994-1995 and this enabled him to complete and present his dissertation on "Oil Major Inspections and Vetting – a study of non conformance's" and two papers: 1. Grey areas in operational pollution (understanding and rectifying oil content meters) and 2. Loss prevention through training on the liquid cargo handling simulator. Besides this he has presented various technical and non technical papers at seminars. Captain Achuthan is a lead auditor of ISO 9000 systems and strongly believes that quality, safety and loss prevention begins through education.

He was, for a brief period, Fleet Manager with IMS Ship Management, manning for V-Ships, after which he returned to his first love – empowering the mariner, with relevant maritime and self development studies. He is now the proprietor of the School of Synergic Studies, which conducts various courses for shipboard and shore personnel on human potential development, safety culture and pollution prevention.

Besides being the joint secretary of The Nautical Institute, Bombay branch, he is also a Member of the Loss Prevention Association, the Meteorological Society of India and Marine Technologists.

Preface

GLOBALISATION IS THE ORDER OF THE DAY. It is here to stay. It's not something we can wish away. In the present scenario of globalisation it means that the shipping industry needs personnel from all over the globe to work as a team on board ships and ashore, towards achieving organisational goals and meeting the challenges of the profession. Those challenges revolve around optimum profitability (i.e. safety of life, property, environment and material values).

Thus the multi-cultural dimension of shipping is brought to the forefront. Culture influences all aspects of management. With respect to shipboard management, managing social relationships has been the prime requirement on board for maintaining safety of the vessel's trade in all respects.

Human beings are diverse in nature and behaviour. One of the intellectual blunders we may make is to maximise differences between members of a diverse multi-cultural crew. It is imperative that we consider their strengths and value differences, for after all "the functions of shipboard management supersede the person who performs them – this forms the foundation of shipboard culture".

In this chapter an attempt has been made to dispel apprehensions towards working in a multi-cultural environment, clarifying social responsibilities and concepts of competence. This is an egalitarian approach – a way through which we can manage social relationships efficiently within a multi-cultural crew. The theme of this chapter will be discussed under the following headings:

1. Clarifying the topic.
2. Concepts of management, functions and organisation.
3. Genesis of personnel management on board.
4. Social responsibilities of the seafarer.
5. National differences.
6. Problems in multi-culture – myth or reality (a case study).
   - The meaning of the term exposed.
   - Human behaviour traits for social relationships.
   - How competence affects social relationships.
   - Relations between technical, managerial and social skills (T:M:S).
   - Solution.
7. Shipboard culture.
8. Communications within a shipboard culture.
9. Paving the path towards managing social relationships.
10. Conclusion.
11. Acknowledgements.

Clarifying the topic

To establish a common understanding of terms used in this paper it is prudent to define managing and management. From many definitions available the author has:

- The art of "Knowing what you want to do and then seeing that it is done in the best and cheapest way". – F.W. Taylor.
- "Management is work and as such it has its own skills, its own tools, its own techniques.

Management is practice. Its essence is not knowing but doing", – Peter Drucker.

As the name sounds, manage-men-t, could be expanded to

manage **m**en **t**actfully.

It is the art of managing an organisation or an individual, or even a country, towards a vision, goal or objective, with the efficient and effective use of resources to achieve objectives.

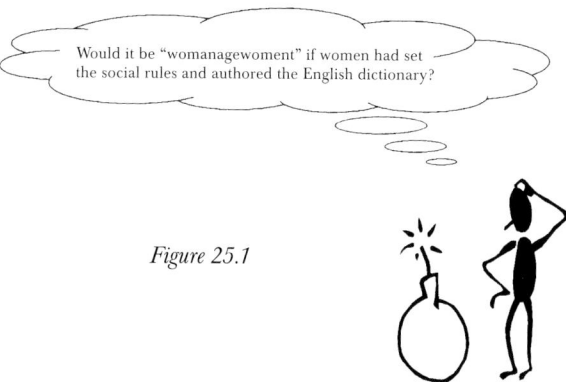

Figure 25.1

Social: The word social here implies "pertaining to life in an organised community; pertaining to welfare as such and generally dealing with shipboard matters outside the technical areas of work".

Relationship: State or mode of being related.

Multi-cultural, multi-culture: Differing cultures formed by the distinction of religion, locality, past history, educational system, country's administration, language, etc.

Crew: for this chapter includes all personnel on board. It refers to a number or set of personnel who have been brought together to manage and achieve the vision/ common goal/ objectives. It includes all ship staff at the management, operator or support level (as defined under STCW'95 amendments).

As the title implies, the subject deals with the management of personnel on board ship. It should be mentioned here that the selection and recruitment of crew by personnel ashore does affect management on board, but this falls outside the purview of this discussion.

Concepts of management, functions and organisation

Management has existed ever since man came on to this earth. In fact it starts from the day we are born. Seldom do we realise that most of our learning is borrowed. We have always been aping our predecessors, nature and experiences. We put two and two together and form a slightly different version of what we have experienced and then start claiming ownership. With good listening abilities, we add intuition or sixth sense to this and claim invention over

discovery. Thus starts creation by mankind. Until this stage all we have done is to imitate and borrow from one form or the other. Thus we have a conglomeration of "memes" (spoken/shared ideas/concepts/jingles), through which we perceive the world.

This is the way we may have generated different styles of management.

Figure 25.2

Functions and organisation

It is my belief that the concept of management of an organisation has also been borrowed. If we do determine where it is borrowed from, will we then come to an ideal form of management? My answer is YES.

The ideal form of organisation is within the human body. It is with this organisation that the body manages to perform the functions of command and control, respiration, circulation, digestion, locomotion, excretion and so on.

Man has aped organisation from the way the human body has organised itself. At the embryonic stage the functions required to run the human body have been decided. The organs then followed to take responsibility for carrying out the functions and we call this **organ**-i-sation.

Thus functions of the body takes precedence over the organs. These organs are designed to function in synergy. It is my conviction – that, in a nutshell, forms the ideal management, bereft of any "perceptions".

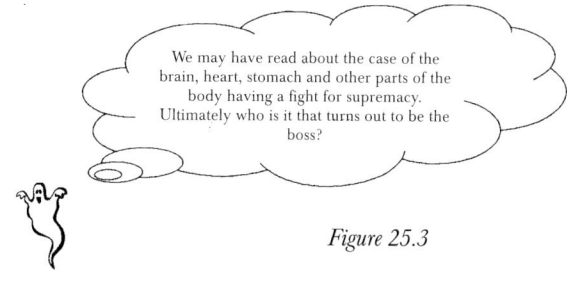

Figure 25.3

None can be called the boss. The way these functions are carried out by our very own body's organisation is the ideal scale of management efficiency. Thus we also restrict ourselves to a supposedly hierarchical style with one person on top,

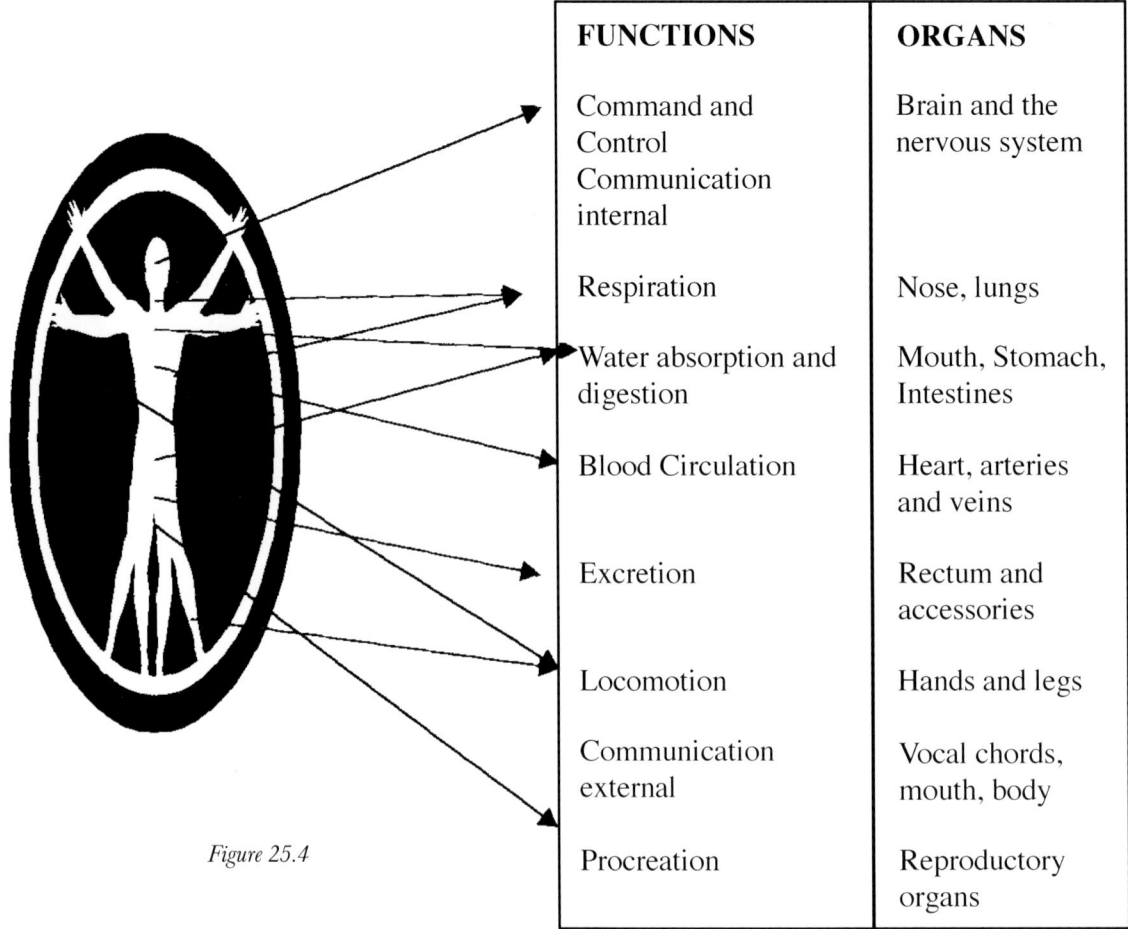

FUNCTIONS	ORGANS
Command and Control Communication internal	Brain and the nervous system
Respiration	Nose, lungs
Water absorption and digestion	Mouth, Stomach, Intestines
Blood Circulation	Heart, arteries and veins
Excretion	Rectum and accessories
Locomotion	Hands and legs
Communication external	Vocal chords, mouth, body
Procreation	Reproductory organs

Figure 25.4

as derived with the brain on top. The brain representing the top does not consider itself the boss. This responsibility is the function of "command and control" and considers itself equal to all other organs, as between the organs; there is supposedly no ego. This is where ego came in the way and got added to our borrowing from the human body.

Genesis of personnel management on board

In earlier times a ship belonged to one nation, was technically and commercially managed by the owner and was manned by one nationality, with one agenda. Communication was much easier, as the interaction was between people with similar perceptions.

These days shipping companies operate under diverse circumstances. Vessels may be financed by Japanese banks, built in Korea, for a company registered in Malta with the principals living in Italy. Ships may have commercial management from London, technical management from Singapore and personnel with Indians as management staff, Ukrainians at operator level and Filipinos as support staff, thus involving three or more crewing agencies.

The different entities involved in operating the vessel may never even know each other, let alone speak the same language. They may have different values and no common loyalty. Persons of unknown

compatibility with different levels of knowledge and intelligence, different social and religious beliefs, different eating habits, discipline and loyalty are brought together as a team on board.

These individuals, sometimes of widely different ethnic backgrounds, have varying values of community habits, probably as the result of limited civil liberties and class barriers which existed in the countries of their origin. At times it impacted their ability to take orders and restricted participation in informal social dialogue or expressions of conjecture and jest. Language barriers restricted the transfer of thoughts, exchange of knowledge, quality work and ability to learn. Differing body language complicated issues even further. A complex alliance sprouted as a result of essentially an economic wedlock.

In their flight to the developing countries for crew to manage and operate vessels, more traditional shipowners proceeded cautiously. Not surprisingly, in many cases, ties with former colonies were preferred over others of unknown and untried origin or familiarity.

All this may have eroded the shipboard culture. It is very important, under these circumstances, to have well defined personnel management, which must adapt to the cosmopolitan nature of the vessel's operation.

Figure 25.5

Navigation
Propulsion and power
Commercial/Cargo operations
Command and Control Systems
Planned Maintenance
Care of Persons on board
Mooring and Unmooring
Emergency preparedness

The functions of shipboard management need to be defined at this stage.

Functions of shipboard operations

As can be seen in the diagram above, these functions precede the persons responsible for carrying them out. Thus if a master is incapacitated, the chief officer, with the help of the chief engineer and the rest of the staff, would carry out the responsibilities of the master, thus completing the command and control and other associated functions.

An understanding of this is required to manage social relationships on board. Before that let us examine the seafarer's social responsibilities.

Social responsibilities of seafarers

Seafarer's social responsibilities can be classified as internal and external. Internally seafarers have responsibilities towards:

- Own vessel.
- Own shipmates.
- Safety of shore labour, officials, visitors and passengers.
- The flag they fly.
- The company.

Externally, seafarers have responsibilities towards:

- A cleaner environment.
- Other ships and seafarers outside their own ship.
- Ports and shipping facilities.

The avoidance of accidents, lower repair costs, reduced operational losses, lower insurance costs, improved company image and reputation are the benefits of keeping up to such social responsibilities. These can be achieved through:

1. Competent managers and operators
2. Professional cooperation and social attitudes such as:
   - Respect for other religions, languages, cultures, and races.
   - Interesting social and sports activities on board.
   - Help to the sick, depressed & distressed shipmates.

These are inherent for right functioning – the function of care of persons on board.

Seafarers' responsibilities towards the vessel and shipmates fall in the domain of social relationships with multi-cultural crews and thus the central domain of this paper.

National differences

National differences amongst a ship's staff have a direct bearing on social relationships on board. Doctor D.H. Moreby, in his paper presented to the international manning and training conference at Singapore in November 1989, has explained that:

"A significant difference between people from different countries is their attitude towards authority and rules. By investigating managers and workers in 40 different countries, Hofstede developed a Power Differential Index (PDI) which measures the hierarchical distance managers maintain from their subordinates and the distance workers perceive their managers to be removed. A high PDI shows that managers have a great deal of power over the workers and maintain a distance from them".

Another interesting turn to this came when Hofstede investigated the attitudes people held towards company rules. A high score on the Rule Orientation Index (ROI) is when people abide by the letter of the rules even when, under the circumstances, this is against the best interests of the company. A low ROI shows that workers use company rules as nothing more than general guidelines.

Thus emerged a matrix (see figure 25.6) of these combinations based on the works of Moreby and Hofstede. This matrix has critical implications for manning and ship management. A shipowner, ship manager or ship master employing crews from the same cluster (high PDI, high ROI, say), finds it relatively easy. However, one could well imagine the predicament if the master and management came from the high PDI, high ROI cluster and those at the support level were from the low PDI, low ROI cluster.

It should be appreciated that the above is based on a study of sections of populations at various points

	High PDI	Low PDI
High ROI	France, Italy, Greece, Spain, South America, India, Malaysia, Singapore	West Germany
Low ROI	Japan, Phillippines, West Africa, East Africa	USA, N.W. Europe, Scandinavia, Australia.

Figure 25.6

of time and may not hold true in all cases, all the time. Whilst agreeing with the works of Moreby and Hofstede a question has emerged:

"Isn't it possible to convert people from one cluster (high PDI, high ROI) to another cluster (low PDI, low ROI)"? The answer is Yes.

Problems in multi-culture – myth or reality – a case study

"Prescription without diagnosis is malpractice, whether it be in medicine or management" – Karl Albrecht, Organisation Development.

The author wishes to share the observations made through a 'case study' used as a learning aid to appreciate various factors contributing to human relationships on board.

The author acknowledges the 275 participants of the Vessel Resource Management course conducted by the School of Synergic Studies and 165 participants of the Master Revalidation/Upgradaing course, held between August and December 1998, at Lal Bahadur Shastri College of Advanced Maritime Studies and Research (LBSCAMSAR). The views of these participants are listed below.

A case study on personnel management with multi-cultural crews

MT YWCA was manned by Indian senior officers (master, chief engineer, chief officer, second engineer and radio officer) with the rest of the crew Filipino, except for a Polish fitter. The master joined with the bosun, pumpman, seven other crew members (all Filipinos) and a Polish fitter. The 11 other staff had already been on board for a month. The relieved master had not mentioned any untoward incident on board in his handover.

Within a fortnight the master realised that the chief officer, with a superior certificate, on a first promotion, was found wanting in many basics and required a lot of guidance. The master, who recognised that training of subordinates was a function required for the effective running of a vessel, decided to extend the guidance. There was also a tremendous shortage of chief officers.

One month later it was noticed by the master that the Filipino pumpman (a key post on oil tankers) on

the vessel was behaving arrogantly with the chief officer. On enquiring with the chief officer it was found that the pumpman had apparently written excessive hours in his overtime sheet and that this was a reaction based on the chief officer ticking him off.

The master called for the pumpman, whose version of the story was that he felt the chief officer incompetent as a tankerman and that there were quite a few times that clear instructions were not being handed over. He had therefore requested that his daily jobs to be carried out be given in writing. As about the overtime, he said, he followed the same norms as on his last vessel and if a different approach were to be taken he would abide by it. However, "I have come to work here and make money", he said.

Each participant was given the task of analysing the problem and stating it specifically to thus arrive at a possible solution. Their views are tabulated in figure 25.7 below:

As can be seen, the diagnoses are many. If each of them were a judge in the situation above, their diagnosis would have led them to prescribe accordingly. That is to say, if they considered the

Diagnosis/ problem as expressed by participants	% representation of participants views
Pumpman aggressive, arrogant	25
Pumpman wanted more money	7
Chief officer inefficient and incompetent	18
Overtime related problem	4
Pumpman taking advantage	6
Communication problem	6
Due to multi-cultural crew	14
Master's ineffective handling of the situation	8
Lack of command/control/monitor	2
Superior unwilling to learn from subordinate	1
Company selection procedure	5
Lack of procedures on board	3
Chief officer not giving written instructions	1

Figure 25.7

pumpman arrogant they would have disciplined him and expected the problem to be solved. If they considered that inadequate procedures were the cause they would have construed that additional procedures would have solved the problem and so on. What is alarming from the above is that each diagnosis has a different prescription.

If the root cause is restricted to on board the vessel then, of course, the chief officer's ineffectiveness or lack of competency is the problem. This can be ascertained by the fact that if the competency situation was corrected the possibility of such a situation arising is reduced to minimal. Moreover, this ineffectiveness was in spite of the fact that he was holding a superior certificate. Professionally he should have chosen to make himself competent at the time he got his mates certificate. It is this lacuna in the system that STCW'95 amendments to STCW'78 attempt to rectify. The problems, as we can see, are not multi-cultural in any way. This could have happened on ships with the same or differing nationalities and culture.

Looking beyond the scene on board we should review the procedures and role played by the employer during the selection process. Does the shore office have a responsibility for selection? Should we compromise on quality if there is a shortage? Should the ship's staff sympathise with the shore selection if there is no system for company training?

It is said that sympathy never corrects a situation. It is empathy that is required. That is seeking to understand before wanting to be understood. What is alarming is the small percentage of ship and shore personnel who accept this point of view! If the superior (in this case the chief officer) were inefficient, the subordinates would take advantage. This is a natural law. Through a further review the general consensus agreed was as follows:

In the final diagnosis, the chief officer had been exposed due to lack of competency, forcing him to oscillate between an aggressive and passive role. The aggression shown by the pumpman and his taking advantage of the situation is but a part of the natural law we live in.

The meaning of the term exposed

In a power hungry, hierarchical system it is most appropriate to empower authorities to pass and fail people – pass or fail students, pass or fail subordinates and pass or fail people in general. For example, 40 % and above is a pass, whereas below 40 % is declared 'fail'. The problem of failure arises only when the individual involved accepts failure.

In reality, people fail within themselves before they fail in the outside world. The positive way of encouraging a person who considers himself weak is to grade him.

Grade A = Excellent; B = Very good; C = Good; D = Fair and E = Exposed.

Grades A to D will be considered competent or passed, whilst grade E means exposed, or failed. Thus out of a group of 10 appearing for an examination, let us assume that two are with Grade E, i.e., Exposed. This means that when they are in the company of the others who have got Grade D and above, they would stand exposed to the latter's whims and fancies. Thus, in the case study discussed earlier, the chief officer has definitely been exposed due to lack of competence.

Human behavioural traits to understand multi-culture

This section deals with the relationship between aggression, assertiveness and passivity. The table in figure 25.8 is the author's concept of what leads to different behavioural tendencies and corresponding effectiveness. This should be considered when managing social relationships.

Assertiveness comes with having clear directions, understanding management and especially stress management.

How competence affects social relationships

We are a combination of mind, body and soul. This is why every habit or competence of ours is a combination of attitude (soul), skill (body) and knowledge (mind). Through various such imitations, acquirements and internalisation's, the present self is a permutation and combination of place of birth, parental influence, age, sex, language, religion, education, skills, environment, past experiences, etc., all of which reflect in our perception. Thus inequalities are caused. This inequality manifests itself as differences in culture, caste, religion, competence, language and nationalism.

	Technical	Competence of Management/ Human relationships	Degree of Understanding self	Effectiveness	
				Long term	Short term
AGGRESSIVE	High	Low	Low	Low	High
ASSERTIVE	High/medium	High/medium	High/medium	High	High

Figure 25.8

Such differences can affect social relationships. Many a time the competence of a person nullifies such differences. As we know, competence is subjective and as such affects social relationships.

Ratio of technical to managerial to social (T:M:S) skills

This calls for introspection into our educational system. As has been agreed by most of the professionals who attempted the case study, the ratio of competence required to perform functions on board vis-a-vis T:M:S should be 4:4:2 for the management level, whilst our formal system is designed for the ratio 8:1:1. This is a large mismatch and leaves most of our learning of managerial and social aspects to mimicking and borrowing from our superiors. This was our informal education. Anything informal, not documented, goes through a declining phase and that is what could have happened to shipboard/shore management. This is also due to the fact that of the three domains of our competence – attitude, skill and knowledge – attitude is the most difficult to document and hence the learning process of subordinates remains too subjective.

Standardised management cannot be passed down an informal system. Documentation is a necessity for standardisation. We can see that STCW'78 issued a certificate primarily on a knowledge based syllabus. STCW'95 looks at competence through knowledge and skills. However, it is the attitude which will determine whether the acquired knowledge and skill is put to good use. Welcome to STCW 2002 !!!, or should it be earlier?

Solutions

Until then the solution suggested to the above case study and, subsequently, to managing this so called "multi-cultural problem" is:

- Superiors should realise that the function of shipboard management is more important than the person.
- Superiors should self motivate, learn as a professional would and take a more assertive role.
- The chief officer should mend his relationship with the pumpman in the best interest of vessel and respect and utilise the pumpman's technical expertise. When we examine the T:M:S required on board for the pumpman, it would be in the ratio of 7:2:1. Hence a certain amount of aggression in a subordinate is to be expected, as he is not given formal management training. As we go higher in position, the requirement for our technical skills takes a secondary role compared to management skills.
- The company should review its selection procedures.
- Training institutions should review course syllabuses, based on a training need analysis, carried out with shipping company inputs and make effective changes.

- Multi-culture should not to be propagated as a problem, but as a strength. Shipboard personnel need to be aware and learn the ways different cultures manage their lives and organisation.
- Senior management both on board and ashore should be conversant with the peculiarities of various nationalities and learn to gain from their strengths. It is basically the responsibility of the person performing the superior functions to learn and understand the needs and peculiarities of the person performing the lesser functions.
- It would help if operator and support level personnel were aware of the multi-cultural differences of senior management.
- Awareness programmes in place about these differences, if any, should take a back seat, keeping the goals of the organisation in focus. It can be proved that these differences are internal barriers within the self.
- Flag states should make clear that they issue a certificate of qualification and not a certificate of competency. This would lead to people taking more interest in their own competency, rather than unknowingly submitting to believing that the certificate makes them competent.
- Promotion of a shipboard culture at an international level.

Shipboard culture

The points listed above would form the base for a shipboard culture. For safer ships, cleaner seas and profitability there is only one culture and that is shipboard culture. In this culture the functions of the vessel take precedence over the persons performing the functions.

The role of a master vis-a-vis shipboard culture

Ship masters used to be all in one, i.e., owner of the vessel, commercial manager, operations manager, personnel manager, insurance manager and average adjuster. They were responsible for various functions required to operate a vessel and, in fact, responsible for matters of safety and pollution prevention. Of course, pollution prevention may not have been a priority item in those days.

With the changing scenario the functions of owning and operating a vessel have shifted to shore based personnel, except for the master, who still has the overriding responsibility for matters of safety and pollution prevention. The ISM code recognises this and has made it mandatory to clarify the same under the Safety Management System.

The master and his team on board have the ultimate say in matters of safety and pollution prevention keeping in mind, of course, optimum profitability and that they have to exist in a safety culture. This aspect of shipboard social responsibility should be borne in mind at all times, to assist in proper decision making.

As commitment starts at the top, this is the first part of a shipboard culture required for bringing multi-cultural crew together. The message here should be made clear. Ships crew and superintendents have to leave aside their multi-cultural differences, if any, ashore before stepping on board.

Shipboard culture is presently influenced by the shore culture and, as per ISF, can be classed under three broad headings:

- Evasion culture caused by blame and punishment.
- Compliance culture caused by high rule orientation and power differential index.
- Safety culture brought about by self-introspection, understanding the self and by looking at the environment through a holistic approach.

Shipboard culture encompasses the safety culture and promotes assertiveness. We should remind ourselves here that the ideal form of organisation is within the human body. It is with this organisation that the body manages itself. However, the functions of the human body take precedence over the organs.

This is true of shipboard culture too. The functions of the vessel are supreme and of greater importance than the people (organs) carrying out the roles. If some specific function is not being carried out by one of the responsible persons, it is imperative that the others on board share the function, until that person redeems himself or is replaced.

Communications under shipboard culture

It would be most appropriate here to discuss effective communication under a shipboard culture. Let us do this with the help of a typical shipboard scenario.

MT MCCS is a crude oil tanker with a mixed crew consisting of Italian senior officers and Filipino junior officers and crew. The vessel has 15 cargo oil tanks (five across) and is preparing for dry docking. The tank cleaning operations are over and gas freeing is in progress. Regular gas readings of tanks are being taken. The two tanks being attended to are 2 centre (2C) and 3 centre (3C). The previous evening the gas reading showed 2C -12 per cent on the tankscope and 3C -60 per cent on the explosimeter. Accordingly, 2C was being purged with inert gas and 3C gas freed with fresh air blowers.

"Noel, take the gas readings of 2C and 3C before 6 a.m. and let me know", calls out the chief officer to the Filipino second officer. The second officer nods his head. The a.m. readings of the tanks being gas freed are nil, indicating that the tanks are gas free. The oxygen analyser reading shows 20 per cent oxygen. Based on this information the chief officer decides to make a man entry into 3C to verify its cleanliness. He, along with two crew members,

prepares to make an entry, carrying out the enclosed space entry procedures. Immediately on entry the chief officer suspects gas and comes out of the tank. He re-checks the gas content and finds 40% on the explosimeter.

The reaction, under pressure of work, could be an angry chief officer spilling his wrath on the second officer. Technically speaking, the wrong reading could be caused by the second officer using the explosimeter first in 2C tank, which had a very high content of hydrocarbons and where a tankscope should have been used. This would make the needle go to maximum and then come down to zero. If not noticed and the equipment was then used for the 3C tank, the needle would not indicate any gas content, leading to such errors in reading.

Training needs analysis, carried out by the chief officer on the second officer in the above case, would have revealed inadequacy in differentiating between an explosimeter and a tankscope. It was the responsibility of the chief officer to ensure that the subordinate knew the right use of equipment before instructing him to use it. A certificate of competence, under STCW '78, may not ensure full understanding of equipment.

Whenever we communicate with another if we first, to ourselves, define the purpose of our communication and that purpose has not been achieved, it is always prudent to self-introspect and find out where we could have done better. Some Filipinos are by nature submissive to authority and will not necessarily respond appropriately when being asked or told to do something they do not understand. Proper feedback and evaluation is a must when we communicate in a cross-cultural environment. In fact this is an intricate part of shipboard culture and applies to even single national crew and single cultures. Feedback is the breakfast of champions. To sum it up "effective communication is the responsibility of the sender".

Paving the path towards managing social responsibilities

- Have well defined aims and objectives.
- Remove internal communication barriers within ones self.
- Improve knowledge about representative cultures, including history and current economic environment, work ethic, religion, etc.
- Understand that differing economic conditions in each other's country creates differing priorities in individuals.
- Remove language barriers – by learning the other language or using one of the staff as interpreter.
- Use democratic leadership leading to participative management.
- Standardise work ethics.
- Improve listening skills. Understand the difference between listening and hearing.

- Keep an open mind.
- Use empathy instead of sympathy.
- Identify and discuss possibilities for inter-cultural adjustment.
- Know personnel by name.
- Be consistent, whoever the person in front of you.
- Most importantly – carry out a shipboard familiarisation for new joiners with respect to personnel interaction. In simple words, have an introduction to the rest of the ship's staff, maybe by having a get-together. Only the cynic would say – no time.

Well! Where there is a will, there is a way.

Conclusion

We all go through various stages of dependence, independence and interdependence. For any organisation, interdependence is the key to success. An effective shipboard organisation is a near absolute example of interdependence.

Many serious accidents and losses have been attributed to a sense of self centred, restrictive, independent thinking. At top management level it is possible that many of us think we can manage independently and we have been proved wrong repeatedly. The *Titanic*, *Torrey Canyon* and *Exxon Valdez* incidents are adequate proof of this.

Most importantly, only independent people can effectively choose interdependence. Feeling the necessity of interdependence is the key. Make interdependence the key to teamwork and multi-cultural problems will vanish from the ship. The question is "Why only from ships"?

Many shipboard multi-cultural problems usually sprout from the shore organisation, especially when there are different manning agencies with their own private agendas. This also has to be tackled prudently by management.

It's easier said than done and the question is "is it necessary"? My answer is that if "survival is compulsory" then:

- Banishing the myth called 'multi-cultural problem' is a necessity.
- Understanding social responsibilities should not to be left to subjective feelings.
- Inter-development is the key.

Inter-development is superior to interdependence and is the key to synergetic management. With a feeling of necessity, positive solutions to any problems are just around the corner.

Necessity is the mother of discovery. Ego converts discovery to invention.

Chapter 26

ON YOUR OWN

by Mr. C.J. Parker BSc FNI, Secretary, The Nautical Institute

Julian Parker obtained his Master's Foreign-Going Certificate in 1967, having served in cargo ships and tankers in various ranks. He then obtained a BSc in nautical science at Liverpool Polytechnic studying naval architecture, marine engineering and control systems. In 1970 he was appointed Administrative Staff Officer of the Ocean Group, Britain's second largest shipping company. During this appointment, Mr. Parker studied to become a qualified industrial training officer at the John Dalton College at Manchester Polytechnic. In 1972 he was appointed the first full time Secretary of the newly constituted Nautical Institute. In 1982 he was elected a Fellow.

Since then the membership has expanded from 1,500 to over 7,000 and continues to grow internationally. The Institute's primary aim is to promote high standards of knowledge, competence and qualification amongst those in control of seagoing craft. The Institute's journal SEAWAYS is recognised as the authoritative voice of the qualified mariner.

Introduction

Shipping is unusual when compared with other industries because masters are almost always promoted from experienced chief officers who have been at sea more than ten years and have had the opportunity to see and understudy a number of different masters. It is well known that managers ashore may be appointed from one division to another or even from outside the company and they clearly have to rely primarily on their management skills to be effective.

These are a few notes which have been found useful, they become obvious when you think about them but can make that initial transition less stressful.

The role of master carries expectations and with these expectations come the need for decisions. It is not a sign of weakness to ask advice from colleagues and agents. After all only the chief can tell you when the main engines will be available after an overhaul, but it is a weakness if having taken the advice a sensible time of sailing is not given. Bear in mind that being too rigid in situations where you effectively have no control is unwise. Be open to change if the circumstances demand it.

As master you are likely to have a bigger picture than the others on board. The agent may well say that a berth has been booked at the next port for a given time but points out that if it is not taken there could be a delay of two days. The mate wants more time to press up tanks or trim a stow, lash the containers before sailing and there is a classic dilemma.

First good masters learn to anticipate and plan ahead so that such a time constraint would have been established in advance and the cargo work planned accordingly - end of problem.

When there is a critical situation like crew who are still ashore, the aim should be to optimise the commercial viability of the voyage in accordance with adequate safety and practicality. Weigh up the implications, work out and roughly cost alternatives, establish limits e.g. tide. Discuss with others to see if they can give you information from previous experience, make a sensible decision and explain to heads of department and leading hands briefly why. Just as you would have supported the master when you were chief officer you will get their support too.

The master is expected to be the authority on board, it goes with the job and is woven into the fabric of maritime law. As such there is a particular interest in the new old man'. The importance of setting a good example cannot be emphasised too strongly.

Power and influence are difficult for the new shipmaster. On the one hand he has to demonstrate a presence and an authority, on the other hand he has to manage and to do this he must not be seen to be aloof so that nobody wants to speak to him. Different ships and different crews mean that the master should aim for a reasonable balance. Every manager in every enterprise lives with doubt about the right balance. The feed back comes from the company and from the crew if one is open to it.

An area where there can be no doubt is when controlling the ship from the bridge. It is essential to make sure that there is a proper procedure for taking and handing over the con. It is useful to remember that only one person can control a moving vehicle.

Communications

If ever there was a subject to turn off a class of masters' students communications did it. The subject demands quite a lot of concentration and of course was quite irrelevant! Looked at from a selfish point of view that is quite right. However, the whole purpose of communication is to inform somebody else of your intentions and it is worth spending a little time on this subject.

Compared to 'being there' communications is a pain. On the face of it, it is absurd that something we can see wholly before us has to be transmitted by a string of words which then have to be laboriously unravelled at the other end. The purpose of business communications is to make this process as quick, accurate and short as possible.

When writing a report, start off with the summary which provides the overview to the content. This will enable the receiver to know what it is about and thereby be able to read the report much more quickly or re-route it without reading it if it is not relevant. Secondly, always aim to provide numerical and when appropriate measured data. Think carefully what the report is going to be used for and check it out with the chief engineer or mate to see if it meets the requirements. Thirdly, keep reports and letters as short as possible. Generally they have to be read by several people in head office and it takes valuable time for them to do so. A shipmaster who cannot type should go home. Finally, it is always helpful to indicate what sort of response you are looking for and by what date. Avoid being rude, always justify your concern.

Whether Satcom, e-mail, fax and even telex you will be judged by the quality of your communications. The great opportunity for satellite links is that it can allow completely new management systems to evolve with the aid of computers. This is the subject of other chapters. Suffice it to say that computers make new demands which cannot be met entirely by traditional communications. A few notes on conducting interviews, running and chairing meetings are provided in the annex. These interpersonal skills are not always taught but guidance can be useful the first time a situation develops.

Taking over from a previous master

There is never enough time to take over as relieving master. To make the most of valuable handover time keep a note book and record all the items you would like to know about. These include ship condition, and defects, difficult operational limitations e.g. windlass efficiency, machinery, reliability and so on. Particular requirements concerning the cargo must be passed on, temperatures, ventilation, samples, dangerous goods etc. Surveys occupy a lot of time and the survey schedule and past survey results need to be well understood as you will have to manage the ship's time to fit them in.

The ISM has become a new master's responsibility, here it is important to sight the audit trail and establish how manuals, notices, circulars and technical and legal information is kept up-to-date. It is necessary to have an up-to-date crew list with crew changes, qualifications, passports and other documentation properly recorded. The company circular file should be sited and any cash items counted and the out going master should always insist on a signed statement of cash by you before leaving. Information about special features must be made known. Pilots find that some masters do not even know that their ships have shrouded propellers, others that the chart folio is hopelessly out of date.

Captain Eric Beetham writing about "*sub-standard ships – the master's dilemma*" observed that no relief master can assimilate everything that is important in a short handover. However, there is no substitute for carrying out a detailed inspection of the ship shortly after sailing, if possible with the mate and chief engineer to establish its order and condition and from which to develop the basis for work planning, cargo management and communications with the company.

The commercial business of the ship will be of special importance. You will need to see the charter party, where appropriate, know where the bills of lading are filed and certainly know about any clauses which have been inserted and for what reason. Notes of protest, the P&I Club handbook, the list of P&I correspondents and any other matter relevant to the cargo.

Planning

The Institute runs a management self-development programme to provide insight into useful management techniques. The books can be read or used as part of a study programme. For those not used to planning and setting objectives, which is not easy, there is useful advice.

- Define what needs to be done in action terms.
- Establish what resources are available.
- Estimate the time needed allowing for disruption e.g. port arrival.
- Decide if extra help is needed e.g. riding gang.
- Establish the results required.
- Monitor progress.

Involving the appropriate crew members in this process will achieve two major benefits.

(i) Clarity of purpose.
(ii) Improved motivation.

Contingencies

More than anybody else the master has to be ready for contingencies and increasingly emergency response is seen as an essential part of safety management.

Some useful advice can be derived from naval practices as naval officers have to be prepared for warfare. Firstly they recognise the value of training so drills, familiarisation and safety equipment use is essential including drills for man overboard.

Secondly it is recognised that small teams using equipment efficiently are the answer to most emergencies. To be effective the rapid response group need to know roles and relationships, how to respond in an emergency e.g. an injury, fire, asphyxiation, machinery breakdown or pollution. A junior officer may need to relieve the mate on the bridge or a junior engineer the second in the control room. This needs to be practised too. Why do navies adopt these strategies? The answer is because small teams acting quickly reduce the probability of a minor incident escalating into a major one in the most effective way with limited resources.

Problem solving

On every voyage there is usually something which happens which cannot easily be explained. Typically this happens when there is an engine failure, but it can equally well happen when the crew run a ships line to the tug when the intention was to take the tugs line and the tow line parts during a critical manoeuvre, or as Captain Jack Isbester observed in the previous edition when it became impossible to maintain a chill room at the desired temperature when all the cooling system was fully operational. It turned out after painstaking analysis of the problem that the extractor fan had been mounted back to front. Not untypically the ship had done several voyages in this connotation and no doubt the cargo temperature book had been flogged!

This advice comes from the Institute's book *Solving Problems and Making Decisions*:

- Recognise there is a problem.
- Find out relevant information facts, times, forces etc.
- Analyse the facts.
- Test for reasonableness.

Problem solving generally works by asking what, why, when, where? It generally fails when human nature intervenes and tries to put the facts to preconceived ideas – be warned!

Motivation

Section 5 of the ISM Code requires the master "to motivate the crew in the observation of the safety policy". Whoever drafted this section really had the wrong idea as it implies that the master can control motivation like the handling of the ship. It does not work that way. Motivation comes from within. Nearly everybody wants to do well and the trick is to provide the conditions and the encouragement. A moments reflection from ones own experience reveals that being given responsibility with helpful support is much more rewarding than being told what to do and being criticised if it goes wrong. Again, from the Institute's book *Leading and Motivating* the emphasis is not on the leader but on the individual.

"People need to achieve something worthwhile for their efforts to be motivated. They need to know how their effort fits into the overall scheme and how successful they have been. They need to feel a sense of responsibility for themselves and others, their work and their area of influence. They need people to talk to, to encourage them and value them".

An interesting psychological example of this occurred when one wise master was confronted by the crew of one ship complaining of the awful food. They were not complaining specifically about the cook, who worked hard. He just produced food which nobody liked.

The master asked everybody to produce their own menu for lunch and evening meal (even the cook couldn't spoil breakfast apparently). The master also gave anybody with an unusual recipe an hour of working time to help the cook prepare the meal. The result – of course – was satisfaction, more variety, less waste and a happy cook who could see a reward for his efforts.

Discipline

As authoritarian attitudes are changing and the industry embraces the principles of management and motivation, the need for old fashioned discipline and logging evaporates. Discipline is necessary in all enterprises, but it starts by those in authority informing the others about what is expected of them and why. There are two guiding principles for the safe operation of a moving ship.

(i) The ship must never be put into danger by the error or omission of one person. For this, every opportunity must be taken to check oneself and check others.

(ii) The ship and activities carried out on board must be conducted within controllable limits.

This does not mean to say that ships should not proceed into a tidal zone past a point of no return. It does mean that the ship can be navigated safely during the critical phase.

Of less consequence are crew who are late back after sailing, drunkenness and other self-inflicted behaviour. This has to be dealt with firmly and fairly. Loss of pay for loss of work is not unreasonable. Prohibiting shore leave is hardly a sanction today when shore leave is so difficult to achieve.

Mostly, with small crews, when one member does not pull his weight the others have to work harder. Inducing a sense of shame in the culprit is a very effective deterrent. In fishing vessels operating in the USA it is customary for all the crew to rattle their spoons at meal time if they disapprove of the conduct of one of their colleagues.

Crime

Crime is more serious. Violence, theft and drugs are perhaps the most usual but they are not common. In the Institute's book *Crime at Sea* the following advice is given:

"The Master himself is in a difficult position when a crime (if it can be defined) is committed on board. He has to be aware of the commercial consequences of delaying his ship against the social duty to maintain good law and order, a constraint which law enforcement agencies do not have.

The shipmaster has a number of options which are available when dealing with threats, violence, theft, drugs, sexual offences and unsociable behaviour. He can:

(i) Tell the individual or group to stop.
(ii) Formalise a caution with somebody else present as a witness.
(iii) Issue a formal warning which will be recorded.
(iv) Berate the individual or group and demonstrate authority supported by at least one person more than the people involved.
(v) Apply company disciplinary procedures if they exist.
(vi) Apply national disciplinary procedures if they exist (in most national fleets items v and vi will be similar).
(vii) Intervene physically (with care) to prevent further deterioration.
(viii) Discipline and/or fine the individuals concerned.
(ix) Seek advice from the company's P&I representative (this is advisable if there are commercial or liability issues involved).
(x) Consult with other senior crew members.
(xi) Record the facts – where possible these should be supported by witnesses.
(xii) Photographs and diagrams.
(xiii) Lock up and/or detain.
(xiv) Have the offender put ashore.

How then is the master to decide which course of action to take and why? There are five underlying guiding principles:

Firstly there is a moral duty to take all reasonable precautions to ensure the safety of the ship, including the safety of individuals and that the public is not exposed to danger.

Secondly there is an obligation to prevent the theft of property - cargo, ship fixtures and fittings, stores and personal effects.

Thirdly there is an obligation to maintain good law and order on board and to prevent occurrences such as violent drunken behaviour or at a different level the prevention of noisy radios disturbing the sleep of watchkeepers.

Fourthly the master has an obligation to comply with the law of the flag state and the law of the countries the ship visits. This has particular relevance for smuggling and stowaways.

Fifthly the master should be guided by a sense of fairness."

Media management

Should you be unfortunate enough to be involved in a major maritime incident it is likely that the media, press and television, will want to inform the public about what happened. Most companies prevent their employees from talking to the media, but this strategy can give the impression that the cause is being concealed.

Should you find that you cannot escape being interviewed, do some planning beforehand. First decide what you are not going to discuss. Because of liability issues it is acceptable to say what happened i.e. we were involved in a collision at 0620 this morning. It is not wise to try and explain what happened and why, however aggrieved you might feel. The answer to such questions is "This is a matter for the authorities who will examine all aspects of the incident."

The press needs information and if the incident is serious the public are entitled to know what is going on. The task of good media relations is to assure the public that everything possible is being done to mitigate the affects of the incident. In this context it is possible to turn a negative situation into a positive one.

"We immediately shut off the power" – "The bosun courageously took the line from the tug" – "We managed to disembark all the passengers without any accidents" – "The ship was listing and the crew did a magnificent job."

To end, either tip off an officer to say you are wanted after say five minutes or excuse yourself saying there is still much work to be done. Crew members are often interviewed without the master knowing. Like a company it is a good idea to carry out sensible public relations to ensure that the crew have the right facts.

The problem with the press is that they like a story and it is a better story if they can find a bogey to blame. A few good words "My ship was in excellent condition and we have an experienced crew" takes away the innuendo of rust buckets and flags of convenience. Make sure you get these comments in. Act with dignity, do not appear scruffy and remember you are representing your company in public.

Tanker companies, in particular, take press relations very seriously and if you have the opportunity to attend a course on presentation to the press and media my advice is to take it.

Conclusion

This contribution has been designed to demonstrate that there is frequently more than one way of looking at problems and that being 'absolutely right' gives way to the more mature 'exercise of judgement'.

There is no absolute security in the business world, only commitment to new enterprise. Now this is well appreciated with the bust up, flagging out or liquidation of traditional shipping companies and it is worth emphasising the quality of self-reliance which has to come more to the fore.

Management on board

Of course, a ship is an economic unit and the principles of using resources effectively apply equally to a ship as they do to a hospital or factory. A ship, though, is a self-contained unit and it is perhaps more helpful if those on board think in terms of optimising the use of resources.

It is often difficult to imagine from a ship the problems of running a shipping company in head office. There can be financial worries, problems in finding cargoes, personnel problems, claims, and a host of husbandry issues which need attention from a diminishing shore establishment. It is therefore worthwhile to reflect on your value to the company.

Here are some questions:

The present

Have I got my job in hand with the right information coming forward so that I can plan ahead and harmonise activities on board?

The future

Have I anticipated and planned for the future so that I can optimise the resources at my disposal?

Relationships with the company

Are my actions fully supporting the company's objectives? Do I need clarification on specific issues? Can I explain my value to the company?

Relationship with the crew

Do all on board know what is expected of them? Have I helped to create a good social atmosphere? Will officers and crew leave being able to make a more effective contribution to the ship both at work and socially than when they arrived? Do I avoid careless gossip, keep confidences, conduct myself professionally, keeping up to date and thereby contribute as a leader?

Finally

By its nature a new command brings forward a host of new ideas and possibly disturbing thoughts. "How can I possibly cope with all these?" The answer is methodically and in a relaxed frame of mind.

Humour is a great social lubricant – ultimately, self reliance is the name of the game for which there is no substitute for character.

Another way of preparing for command is to do The Nautical Institute's *Command Partnership Scheme*. This has been designed to help chief officers experience the tasks and responsibilities associated with Command. If you can encourage your chief mate to work through the programme which has been designed by those in command they will thank you when their time comes.

References

- *Setting Objectives and Planning* – The Nautical Institute open learning module
- *Solving Problems and Making Decisions* – The Nautical Institute open learning module
- *Leading and Motivating* – The Nautical Institute open learning module
- *Crime at Sea – A Practical Guide* – B.A.H. Parritt, The Nautical Institute 1996
- *The Practice of Management* – P. Drucker, William Heinemann 1996
- *The Nautical Institute Command Self-Development Programme 2000*

Annex I – Interviews

Just about every officer at sea has experienced an interview, whether it was recruitment, voyage out-turn or an oral examination. In each situation the personnel manager, superintendent or examiner had particular points they wished to establish. Their skill in asking questions and controlling the dialogue determined their effectiveness.

One thing is quite certain, that experience of being interviewed is not a very good guide when it comes to interviewing yourself. For a start the emotional balance feels wrong. Asking questions is different to answering them and responding is different to leading the discussion from a position of authority. The following, then, are some notes on techniques which can be useful when interviewing subordinates, discussing business affairs in head office and controlling the many face-to-face contacts with customs, agents and surveyors.

1. Establishing your authority

To control a situation somebody has to be in charge and it is important to establish in your own mind first, why the interview is being held, for what purpose, and what outcome is needed. In spite of 'modernism' communication is made more efficient by convention and it will help if you 'the captain' state your position and why the interviewee is brought before you.

For this reason, never undermine the company's authority with a statement like 'head office has asked me to interview you about this, but I do not really think it is a good idea'. If you do not think it is a good idea your discussion is with the company and not the subordinate. Unexpected visitors can be held in check by being told to wait a short time outside your cabin. When they enter you can adopt a formal position behind your desk. Invite them to sit down and then tell them that in 10 minutes or so you have another appointment. If you want to keep your independence maintain a distance. When the time is reached stand up shake their hand and ask them to leave.

2. When to formalise a meeting

It is useful to be clear in your own mind what you are trying to achieve:
- To improve performance of the ship or an individual.
- To test and/or improve morale.
- To obtain information or to impart information.
- To hear a grievance and enable a subordinate to let off steam.

- To analyse a situation, solve a problem or to make recommendations.
- To implement new policies and practices.
- To provide a formal method of feedback and accountability.
- To provide counsel.

3. Planning for an interview

Like navigation, effective communication needs to be planned for:

- Think through the interview, have a strategy to deal with possible snags.
- Have all the necessary information available. Be prepared to postpone or adjourn an interview until more data can be provided.
- Consider the probable length and plan the discussion.
- Make notes of the plan and refer to them.

4. Conducting the interview

To control an interview it is necessary to hold the initiative:

- Introduce the purpose and scope of the interview.
- Prepare questions to keep within the framework.
- Guide the discussion, confirming progress at intervals.
- Summarise and conclude the interview, making sure the interviewee fully understands the end result.
- Where there are irreconcilable differences, pick on some small point where agreement is common and plan another meeting after a cooling-off period.

5. Techniques and integrity

In any community those in authority must be seen to be fair, truthful and constructive. This engenders respect which is the best asset to a productive discussion. Interviews are controlled through questions and personal influence.

Questions can be posed:

- To relax or stiffen the interviewee.
- To draw out information and amplify points.
- To keep the discussion from rambling.
- To bring out distinctions and similarities.
- To encourage judgement.
- To exercise discipline.
- To bring the interviewee into line by asking limiting questions which have only one answer – i.e. Who? Where? When?
- To open up a discussion ask broadening questions like, Why? How? or What?

6. Personal influence

It is not often considered in conversation but there is considerable scope to relieve anxiety which is particularly important with ratings and junior officers; and scope to put across the seriousness of an incident to somebody who is irresponsible. Relaxers include:

- Being comfortable, relaxed approach, signs of understanding.
- Questions about family, other activities on board.

Stiffeners include:

- Seriousness of subject, formal colder relationship.
- Unpleasant consequences.

7. The emotional tangle of taking on somebody else's problems

It is possible to share problems and put forward helpful ideas. It is undesirable in the interests of the ship as a whole to become involved personally. Indeed, once you become emotionally involved you lose the objectivity to make original suggestions and a balanced sense of purpose. Concern yes; involvement no. The way to stay detached is to stick to the purpose of the meeting. If it is a compassionate case the objective of home leave or the consequences of not being able (physically or in monetary terms) to provide it should be thought through and dealt with sympathetically. Remember the Missions to Seafarers will usually be able to send a welfare officer to the home.

Fuller notes are provided by Fletcher[1], on selection interviewing, interviews within work like grievances, reprimands and counselling and a very valuable chapter on progress and appraisal interviewing. Here is how Mr. Fletcher sets out to conduct counselling and progress interviews.

Counselling interview

Aims
1. To help employees solve their problems concerning work or their private life.
2. To improve performance and working relationships by helping solve their problems.

Preparation
1. If possible, set aside so much time that the interview does not have to be cut short.
2. Ensure privacy.
3. Consider the person's background (education, home, work) and what problems he might have.
4. Consider what other persons or agencies (medical, social, legal, etc.) might help.
5. Consider how the person's work would be done if he or she had to have leave of absence.

Structure
1. Welcome and put at ease.
2. Let the person state his or her problem.
3. Redefine the problem, analysing it into different problems where necessary.
4. Take each problem separately. Use short questions to get him to expand.
5. Listen sympathetically.
6. Contribute your knowledge of the persons or agencies to whom he or she could turn for help.
7. Help the person to formulate a plan of action.

The interview at work
8. Assure the person of your help, and that his or her affairs will be kept secret.
9. Arrange a follow-up interview.

Check results
1. Hold the follow-up interview. This time five minutes may be enough.

Progress interview

Preparation
1. Study the job objectives.

2　Analyse the achievement of each objective.

3　Consider the person's potential; whether he or she is being fully 'stretched'; what changes could be made so that the job would use the person's full capacity.

4　Consider the forms of recognition and reward open to the person, apart from private congratulation at the interview: (a) financial; (b) promotion; (c) privileges; (d) extra responsibility or (e) training.

5　Plan the progress interview in relation to the person's long term development, and the development of the organisation.

6　Avoid holding the interview at a time of crisis.

7　Give the person at least a week's notice of the forthcoming interview, and invite him or her to prepare for it.

Structure

1　Put at ease.

2　State the nature of the interview.

3　Give an overall impression of the person's work and progress.

4　Outline the structure of the interview.

5　Get understanding of the purpose of the interview.

6　Get agreement on the main job objectives, and the achievement of each objective.

7　Discuss where improvement is possible and how – training?

8　Discuss strengths and points for congratulations.

9　Discuss the person's ambitions and enthusiasms.

10　Any questions?

11　Sum up (in a job-centred and impersonal way).

12　Get agreement on job objectives for the next six to twelve months.

13　Arrange the date of the next progress interview.

14　End on a note of confidence, trust, and satisfaction.

Check results

1　Watch the points raised for improvement, and congratulate if appropriate.

2　Check performance in the job generally.

3　Check relations and attitude.

4　Prepare for the next progress interview.

¹　For further reading consult *The Interview at Work*, by J. Fletcher, published by Duckworth, ISBN 0715607278. The style is clear, simple and uses good practical examples of difficult situations and how to avoid them.

Annex II – Running a meeting

A witty answer turneth away wrath

The role of the committee chairman

The role of the chairman will depend largely upon the type of committee, its function and purpose. If a committee has a clearly set function with a precise agenda for discussion, the chairman's role must be a dominant one, otherwise the business will not be settled according to schedule. Many committees, because of bad chairmanship, spend too much time on the earlier part of the agenda and not enough time is left to examine the other agenda topics in depth. If, on the other hand, there is no rigid agenda or timetable for a meeting, the chairman's role can be less dominant, the main function being that of keeping order and developing discussion.

Duties of the chairman

1.　He or she should make sure that the meeting over which he is about to preside has been properly convened.

2.　He should be fully conversant with the statutory rules, standing orders, or regulations of the organisation and that they are properly observed.

3.　When conducting the meeting he should keep to the order of items set out in the agenda.

4.　During a discussion he should ensure that sufficient opportunity is given to all present who wish to take part in the discussion. He should call upon each speaker by name when that individual indicates he wishes to speak. This procedure is essential in the early days of a new committee and enables members to get to know each other more quickly. It also assists the committee secretary in taking notes of the meeting which are then produced as 'minutes' at the succeeding meeting.

5.　He should not allow discussion of an issue unless there is a motion or proposition before the meeting on it. However, the chairman usually exercises some latitude, permitting discussion to take place if he thinks the issue is important.

6.　He must ensure that the discussion of any issue is kept within reasonable bounds and prevent the introduction of irrelevant matters.

Powers of the chairman

The ultimate power of control over a meeting and the maintenance of order is in the hands of the chairman.

1.　He has the power to adjourn a meeting when he considers that its business has been properly completed.

2.　He has the power to adjourn a meeting when a majority of members present decide that the remaining agenda items should be dealt with at another meeting.

3.　He has the power to adjourn a meeting when he finds it impossible to maintain reasonable order in the meeting. (This position would not often arise in a committee meeting but is more likely to happen at a general meeting of irate company shareholders.)

Running a discussion meeting

1. Outline subject clearly

State topic, problem or difficulty with which the meeting is to deal. Outline situation giving rise to topic, problem or difficulty. State purpose of the meeting, so that everyone knows what is appropriate for discussion and what is not. Define technical terms used. Outline the procedure to be followed (suggest a logical 'pathway' for the discussion and outline the time scale).

2. Guide the discussion

Assemble all necessary facts beforehand. Draw out information, viewpoints, experiences. Make sure that all contributions are understood. Keep discussion on the subject. Avoid purely personal arguments. Develop group participation.

3. Crystalise the discussion

Summarise the development of the discussion. Refer to any changes of opinion. State points of agreement and disagreement. State intermediate conclusions as reached. Make sure of understanding and acceptance of summaries.

4. Establish final conclusions reached

Give final summary of course of discussion. State conclusion(s) clearly. State the main points contributed at the meeting. State minor disagreement (if any) and the reasons for it. Check to be sure of a fair summary, and that members understand it.

5. Secure agreement on action

(where meeting warrants it)

Show that decisions are group decisions arising out of discussion. Show that decision is based on conviction, assent or reconciliation of views. Formulate the action.

Choice of committee officers

'A group is an enterprise in being'

It would be wrong to assume that the chairman runs a committee alone. Good committee work is teamwork. The secretary enables the group to be effective by recording the outcome and making sure that any action necessary is taken. The individual committee members contribute the substance of the meeting. However, in any group, certain guidelines are desirable: H. H. Taylor and A. G. Mears in '*On the Right Way to Conduct Meetings, Conferences and Discussions*' give the following:

Chairman
1. A calm and friendly disposition.
2. The ability to think clearly and objectively.
3. A sound knowledge of procedure.
4. A sense of humour and absolute control of temper .

Secretary
1. Good organisational ability.
2. Tidy and methodical.
3. Calm and clear-headed.
4. Tactful and friendly.

Chapter 27

PORT PROCEDURES

by Captain C.M.R. Lloyd FNI

Captain Lloyd attended HMS CONWAY as a cadet before joining P&O. He was chief officer and master with Offshore Marine and joined Arya National Line as master from 1973 to 1977. He then joined Worldwide Shipping where he has served as master on Very Large Bulk Carriers. He is a commissioned officer in the RNR, a Younger Brother of Trinity House and a Fellow of The Nautical Institute. Captain Lloyd has contributed many features to improve safety at sea, but above all he has campaigned to ensure that ships and seafarers are treated properly when they come to port.

Introduction

IT COULD WELL BE SAID that the port bureaucracy in many countries exists to engage ships' staff in hours of pointless paperwork, employing the maximum number of officials who have little else to do. All ports are not, of course, like that, but having recently visited Morocco and had the pleasure of 23 officials in my cabin, disposed of 40 crew lists, anything not tied down and all the cobwebs from the bond, I feel justified in making such statement. Those who have the added pleasures of transiting the Suez Canal might wish to add their own observations.

The reason that I opened the chapter with this comment is that the frustrations you will most certainly feel in dealing with ports and their officials during your time in command have been felt by us all.

There are two ways of viewing this. In the first, you allow your intelligence to use logic and fight the system. This leads to stress, even further frustration – because you will not win – and eventually alienation of the ship and port. You and the ship suffer, not the port. If you bear in mind that owners or managers pay you to get the ship through the port as quickly and smoothly as possible rather than engage in demonstrating your ability to run the port, you will see that they will not be amused.

The second is to accept that each country has differing ways and customs and that a port has the right to determine how it is managed, regardless of your opinions, and use your intelligence to prepare the ship for that port, to avoid, as much as possible, any problems. This way leads to long life, a prolonged career, and getting ashore far quicker than you would by following the first route.

Port planning

How you prepare your ship is entirely dependent on the trade, type of ship and staff you have available and port you are visiting. A ferry trading between two ports on a daily basis will be treated entirely differently by the ports from a foreign ship which has never visited the ports before. Regular visits to ports allow a relationship to develop with the port personnel and this, coupled with a familiarity with the port procedures, hopefully leads to trouble free visits.

Having recognised these contrasts, the safest path to follow is to presume the worst-case scenario, that of the large tanker or bulk carrier, which spends long periods of time between ports, with the ports often diverse and with the time in those ports measured in hours rather than days.

I have commented before, in other publications, on the problem of perception between the ship and port. To a ship such as described above, the port arrival is a major management event: to the port just another ship in a long line of ships. In other words, the port is not too interested in your problems. The terminal is only interested in getting the cargo in and out as quickly as possible and any other problem is a nuisance. The agency is such a variable factor in today's maritime industry that the reliance on it of yesteryear can no longer be guaranteed.

To achieve even orderly chaos, pre-planning is essential. Let us assume that you have a 'managed' ship. By that, I mean a ship where the master does not try to do everything, because he cannot, but where the officers all have some degrees of responsibilities. These officers all must be consulted as to their requirements and priorities established. If the port stay is short and the world and his dog are waiting for you, some form of port planning meeting is essential. From this meeting, not only will you develop a list of events but your officers will also know what is happening and that just might be a new development for some ships.

Let us presume that such meeting has been held and you now have a list to make up. A hypothetical list of requirements and officers responsibilities based on modern manning with no chief steward or radio officer could be as follows:

The Master
- Port formalities and paperwork.
- Agent.
- Mail in and out.
- Cash payments to various suppliers.
- Port victualling arrangements.

Chief Officer
- Cargo. Tonnage to load. Loading sequence. Deballasting time.

- Fresh water requirements.
- Essential safety programme to complete; for example, lowering lifeboats.
- Stores to load.
- Deck surveys.
- Essential work programme in port.

Chief Engineer
- Bunkers to load.
- Essential maintenance work.
- CSM or engine surveys.
- Spares to load or land.
- Shore technicians as required.

2nd Officer
- Port navigational requirements.
- Medical or dental treatments.

To the above list must now be added any special port requirements such as rat guards, brows, communications, signals, and port regulations, if they are known.

It is not suggested that only those officers listed deal with all the specified items above. On a well managed ship, with a modern company approach, all officers should have their individual responsibilities delegated and cross-departmental management should be in place. However, as we all know, we do not always sail with officers of management abilities or in companies that recognise shipboard management; and it is not unusual for the whole list to devolve to the master and chief engineer. Having established our list of requirements for the port, the next phase is forward preparation.

Forward preparation

In this phase we are trying to pave the way, as far as possible, for the ship and those who we will be dealing with in the port. The more work put in before you arrive, the less there will be to do on arrival.

Port papers

The crew list should always be sent ahead. In the case of the US a 'visa-ed' crew list is required to be sent ahead and this causes considerable problems, with these lists often arriving after the ship.

Some ports will accept computerised customs forms and crew lists in lieu of their own: unfortunately these are few and far between. Perhaps in some far-sighted time countries will issue their forms on disk. Or, even better, we will be able to 'sign on' at the first port with our own disk, which holds all the information required, and this will automatically pass with only the updated changes required. For the moment, though, the port papers must be prepared by hand in advance. In many cases, when you are going to a port for which you do not have the forms, these can be requested in advance or even possibly faxed to you if this is acceptable. If the port will accept any other forms being faxed, this will all help on the day.

Cargo documents

It is essential that the cargo stowage or discharge plan together with the ballasting arrangements are sent to the port as soon as possible. Then, should there be any dispute, the issues can be clarified prior to the ship arriving.

If any changes are requested and made, again send your changed plan. On your final plan you might consider stating that there will be no changes made to this final plan as they will inevitably be requested within hours of arrival.

The worst case will be when, having sent your plans, there is no reply from the terminal and, when you arrive, it then requires the whole plan to be changed. At least when this happens, and it will, the ship cannot be blamed for any delays incurred.

The agents

A word regarding agencies. The days when the agent visited the ship are gone, unless you are a cruise ship with a nice restaurant and female company. Now the ship will be visited by a boarding clerk whose experience will be variable.

The agency itself may not feel it is representing you anyway, as it could be the charterer's agent that your owner or management is using. It might be worthwhile to find out if your company is paying a proportion of the agency's costs as this will then allow you to refute this argument – which you will certainly hear some time in your career in command.

Next, the agency might be a division of the terminal which you are using and no other agency is allowed to compete.

The worst case scenario is that the agency is a division of the charterers and the charterers own the terminal. Here they can often behave as they please and there is not a lot that can be done about it.

The agency today, therefore, can be of such variable quantity that nothing can be taken for granted. It must not be assumed that they have all the information, either. Communications within the port organisation can vary greatly with the terminal often not advising the agency of changes or matters that may effect your ship. Equally, the fact that you have requested your company to arrange a surveyor or technician to attend on arrival is no guarantee that this has been done. In other words, regardless of what you may think has been arranged, presume the agency has no information

You should advise the agent as follows:

- Your requirements regarding presentation of manifests etc prior to discharge.
- Normally all dealings with the port/terminal are through the agent. However, if this is not the case, the agent should also be sent a copy of the crew list and cargo.

- Personnel leaving or joining, as well as any requiring medical or dental treatment.
- Fresh water requirements.
- Any technical assistance required or technicians that have been requested to attend. With this it is essential that the equipment is detailed together with the suspected problem or area of concern.
- Surveyors requested and what the surveys are.
- What cash is required, together with the denomination of the notes and exchange rates.
- Any stores or spares that have been sent to the port, preferably with the shipment number.
- Charts. Notice is required for the delivery of charts. If you do not have an appropriate chart for entering the port arrange, through the agent, for the pilot to bring such chart to the ship. The same applies to courtesy ensigns.
- Bunkers. Advise the agents what bunkers have been ordered. Remember that you are the customer. If time allows, specify when you want the bunkers to be delivered, otherwise you will get them whenever the bunkering company sees fit. If the ship arrives early in the morning and is sailing early morning the next day, you want the bunkers on arrival not during the night before sailing.
- For your port emergency listings, you will require the names and phone numbers of the pollution agencies. At the same time, find out what pollution protection, if any, the port provides.
- The disposal of waste continues to be a growing problem for the ships with many ports not able or unwilling to cope with this problem. Again, advance notice is suggested.
- Ask if the port regulations allow overside painting, lifeboats to be lowered and, most important, any port regulations regarding work on the main engine involving immobilisation.

Ship regulations

Most ports or terminals have regulations that you are often asked to sign when your ship arrives. These generally refer to safety matters and that particular terminal's requirements. Normally the master signs these as 'sighted' only.

There is no reason why the ship should not produce its own regulations for the terminal. Outline the requirements for protective equipment needed in the working areas of the ship, prohibited areas to shore personnel, accident reporting etc. This list should be sent ahead of the ship via the agent. Not only will this assist with the general safety and efficiency of the combined operations but it will help remind the terminal that the ship is also a factory, with its own particular problems, as well.

In many cases you will find the chandler the most useful man in the port and often the only man working for you. He will know what technical assistance is available and whether your crane is suitable for the berth. Even his estimate of when you are sailing will often be more accurate than the agent's. Properly used, the chandler can be invaluable.

This is not a comprehensive list but I hope it will provide the student with an insight into the possible normal requirements of a ship arriving at a port.

In the port

Without doubt, how the ship is treated depends considerably on first impressions. Clean, well prepared gangways, clean accommodation and uniformed officers show a well-ordered and disciplined ship. The port likes this. The fact that all the documentation is prepared further enhances the ship. In many countries the officials are in uniform and if you are as well you have an equal presence of authority.

With the reduced personnel of the modern manned ship, many of the niceties of old can no longer be offered. However, there is always room for courtesy and it is essential that politeness be maintained, especially with those who can assist the smooth passage of the ship through the port formalities.

It is important that all the required documents are correctly filled in and ready for the officials' arrival; also that personnel are standing by to assist with the port entry formalities. You know that customs will require to inspect the bond therefore someone is ready for this. Port health may wish to see the galley and store-rooms. Again, the cook should be ready.

Immigration may want the passports or seamen's documentation. If these are ready, the faster the port procedures will be over and you can begin the ship's business.

All too often, advice as to what documentation is required by the port is wrong or out of date. In general it is wise to have most forms ready and I follow with a typical list of port documentation required.

Port documentation
- Last port clearance. If any certificate is going to be mislaid, it is this one, mostly because it is brought by the agent at the last minute and left around in the ship's or master's office for days, or because it is often difficult to determine what it is, especially when written in a foreign language. It can easily get thrown away. If you do mislay this form, have a copy faxed from the agent of the previous port.
- Crew lists. Whatever the number of crew lists you think is required, double it. Also remember that if there is any change of crew, this list will have to be changed for departure.
- Passenger lists are often a problem because of the definition of what is a passenger. Some ports want the supernumeraries listed as crew, while others will want them on a separate passenger list. Check ahead with the agent.

- Customs forms. Read the requirements with care. Most ports find the entry 'personal effects' quite acceptable but there are those that require every single item belonging to the crew to be listed.
- Health forms. Few ports have their own form and any health form is generally acceptable.
- Vaccination lists. Very few ports still insist on this: generally you should make your own.
- Arms or ammunition. List or state none. Make your own list.
- General stores declaration. This is a peculiar form which seems – in some cases – to go back a couple of centuries, when you still required to list the cordage and tar carried on board When this is required, each country will have its' own list for completion.
- List of previous ports. Make your own list, which can be required to show ports visited up to three months previously.
- Drug list. Make your own and state where they are held.
- Stores or spares to be landed. List them ready for the agent and customs.
- Ship's certificates. These are the statutory trading certificates such as the safety certificate. In some ports they will be inspected 'in situ' by a number of agencies. In others the agent will take the certificates required ashore. Ensure a receipt for these is obtained.

I am sure that this list is not comprehensive, but it should cope with the majority of forms required by most ports.

Official visitors

Ashore, by which I mean in the normal world of business, it is customary to make appointments before visiting. Not so with a ship. The presumption is that everyone on board is instantly ready to deal with anyone who appears. Thus port state, customs, coastguard, and any other inspectorate body tend to appear out of the woodwork, usually at the worst times. They do not contact the agents or even the terminal. It does no harm to ask the agent if any of these organisations intend to visit the ship, to request that their visit be planned for a convenient time. It is, after all, your ship – another novel concept for many in the port organisation.

If there really is no one readily available to assist whoever has appeared, then explain the problem and ask for their patience. On the grounds of safety alone, visitors should not be allowed to wander around the ship alone.

Visitors to the ship should be 'signed in' in a visitors' book and they should sign an indemnity form, especially if they are spending some time in the working areas of the ship.

Conclusion

There is much wrong with the present relationship between ship and port, but it is not the aim of this chapter to debate this issue. The aim is to highlight the problem areas and guide the potential new master through these. Think of the three Cs – Communication, Calmness and Courtesy – as a guiding theme.

No port is the same; equally each country has regulations pertinent to it and its government. In some you are treated correctly and with courtesy, in others you are an upmarket able seaman.

Either way, your job is the same, to have the ship entered in and cargo work commenced as soon as possible, to respect that country's laws and comply with the port regulations during your ship's stay. If you can do this, then you have done your job as master.

Chapter 28

PICKING UP THE PILOT

by Captain R.M. Thorn FNI FRGS

Captain Thorn served his apprenticeship with the Anglo Saxon Petroleum Co. (Shell Tankers) from 1950 to 1954. He was third officer with the Rex Steamship Co. (tramp ships) from 1954 to 1955 and since 1956 has been in the Royal Fleet Auxiliary Service. He was selected for command in 1968 and has since commanded 10 RFAs of all classes as well as spending three years as an RFA marine superintendent (1977-1980). He has held exemptions for, and carried out pilotage in, several UK areas.

Introduction

ALTHOUGH THE HEADING of this chapter is 'Picking up the pilot', the term 'pilot transfer' will be used in context as dropping the pilot is a similar evolution. After the outgoing captain has left, the ship sailed and reached the end of pilotage waters, shiphandling to drop the pilot provides that first moment when the captain is on his own! It may be a simple procedure in daylight, calm weather, and open clear sea; however, the bizarre can also become a reality. Your pilot may depart by skidoo on to the icepack, a sailing boat or canoe rather than the traditional modern pilot boat. Sometimes helicopters are used, and, in at least one port, the pilot may opt to dive from the lower rungs of the ladder and swim ashore! In bad weather conditions, there may have to be a command decision to carry the pilot on to the next port of call.

Picking up the pilot is probably the most important seamanship task carried out by the captain for at least the three following reasons:

(i) The ship has to be manoeuvred to a safe transfer position, course and speed without external assistance.
(ii) By virtue of the need to pick up a pilot, the ship will be in, or approaching, an area of geographical difficulty and possible traffic density.
(iii) The act of picking up a pilot from a pilot boat may well be the only practical training available to a captain for that most difficult problem of rescue at sea – either launching a boat, or recovering people from a boat.

Sensibly, time must be allowed prior to sailing (and subsequent arrival) for planning, preparation, and checks

Planning

Area: Consider the area, possible traffic density, weather conditions and whether the transfer is to take place in daylight or not. Do remember that from heights to 50 ft and above from the water line, conditions alongside may seem much calmer than when viewed by the coxswain of a small boat trying to come alongside.

Shiphandling: How does the ship lie when stopped, should this be necessary? What is the stopping distance? What rate of drift should one expect in any given wind condition? At what speed does the ship cease to steer effectively? (Shiphandling is dealt with in another chapter; however, the above points provide the essence to carry out a safe pilot transfer.)

Positioning: The lee side for the transfer will be determined by the prevailing wind, weather and geographical location. Allow sufficient room within the transfer area to manoeuvre clear of any traffic, and at the pick up speed. Do allow sufficient time for the pilot to reach the bridge and have a verbal brief before his advice is required.

Publications: Check if possible, from the relevant pilot book and port guide, details of the pilotage service that you are about to use. Are there any special requirements from them?

It should now be possible to plan your track to the transfer position on the chart.

Contingency plan: Finally, do have a contingency plan. Traffic, weather, engine problems or just the idiosyncrasies of the pilot boat may dictate the requirements either to anchor or overshoot and put out into clear water – this could be difficult if your planning puts you within two cables of an obstruction and your ship has a five-cable turning circle.

Preparation

The brief: Those directly involved in all aspects of the transfer need to know what both the plan and contingency plan is. It should be possible to give exact timings so that any calls can be made in good time, and the captain can expect those involved to be at their posts and ready with the appropriate equipment in good working order and condition.

Standby: A pilot transfer is a standby situation.

Communication: The essence of all preparation is communication. Communication with the port of call giving the ship's ETA (or ETD) should include the pilot station and elicit any special requirements and details of local conditions; these are to be passed on at the brief. Internal communications from the command to each of the involved positions are vital for a safe operation (helmsman, engine control room, pilot ladder station and anchor party).

Checks

If at all possible it is no bad thing, on approaching the transfer area, to stop the main engines and check the astern movement. From this moment on, check the following:

- Engines are on standby, anchors cleared away and, if appropriate, stabilisers housed and bow thrust operational.
- Manpower is available, on duty and in communication.
- Pilot ladder checked.
- Access for transfer is equipped, lit, manned and provided with safety equipment.
- Communication with the pilot is established; position and time of transfer both clear and confirmed, including which side the transfer is to take place.

Having planned the transfer consulting charts and publications; prepared to carry out the plan with brief and communication; and checked the manning and operability of on-board systems, the safe conclusion of the transfer is governed by the ability to command and handle the ship and her systems to greatest effect in the prevailing conditions.

Duty of the master and crew during pilotage

The master of a ship must, among other things, ensure the safety of the ship, of all on board and of all who are threatened in any way by the proximity or operations of other ships. In the execution of his duties, he is entitled to the full cooperation and assistance from his officers and other members of his crew. All on board must go about their tasks in accordance with those ordinary practices of seamen that have been tried and tested over a very long period of time – i.e. the well understood standards of seamanship that safeguard against accident or error. It is the master's responsibility to ensure that the crew support the pilot in his duties and the master may delegate the authority for this to the officer of the watch or other appropriate officers.

When a pilot is on board, the general rule is that it is the responsibility of the master, officers and other members of the crew to pass on all relevant information, including defects and peculiarities, to the pilot and to keep a proper lookout. Such a duty has been interpreted by the courts to include the duty to report all material circumstances and facts which might influence the pilot's actions, even if the pilot is in a position where he ought to be able to see things clearly for himself.

Where, in the master's opinion, the situation developing is obviously dangerous, it is his duty to draw the pilot's attention to the risk and, if necessary in his judgement, take over the conduct of the vessel. The master is not justified in doing nothing.

Duty of the pilot

The duty of a pilot is to direct the navigation of the ship and to conduct it so far as the course of the ship is concerned. He has no other power on board. The common law relationship between master and pilot is such that, when the master hands over the conduct of the vessel to the pilot, the latter is legally responsible for his own actions and the master's right to interfere, without incurring his own liability, is restricted to circumstances where there is clear evidence of the pilot's inability or incompetence.

The legal position of the pilot on board a vessel is aptly summarised by the Canadian Royal Commission on Pilotage, Ottawa 1969, as follows:

. . . 'To conduct a ship' must not be confused with being 'in command of a ship'. The first expression refers to action, to a personal service being performed; the second to a power. The question whether a pilot has control of navigation is a question of fact and not of law. The fact that a pilot has been given control of the ship for navigational purposes does not mean that the pilot has superseded the master. The master is, and remains, in command; he is the authority aboard. He may, and does, delegate part of his authority to subordinates and to outside assistants who he employs to navigate his ship – i.e. pilots. A delegation of power is not an abandonment of authority, but one way of exercising authority.

Chapter 29

NAVIGATION IN PILOTAGE WATERS

by Captain F. Baillod FNI, Shipmaster

Captain Baillod started his seagoing career in 1963. After an early time with Scandinavian companies he joined Suisse Atlantique where he was promoted master in 1980. Captain Baillod is still serving as master and regularly contributes to industry forums. He is a member of The Nautical Institute Bulk Carrier Working Group and a Fellow and Council Member.

Introduction

CLOSE COOPERATION IS ESSENTIAL between master and pilot. By showing the shipmaster's view, I hope to highlight some problems and bring about better communications in this delicate and important relationship. The master and the pilot have a common goal – bringing the ship safely to her berth – but different priorities and viewpoints. The master is essentially protective about his ship. He is also under pressure, from both owners and charterers, to minimise delay and cut costs if possible. For the pilot, commercial pressures may differ a very great deal from one harbour/country to another. Some ports have a heavy schedule and they have to compete with others; some ports are short of tugs and others impose unnecessary tug services to increase their revenues. There are ports where pilots are well assisted in sound management, while in others there is hardly any organisation. Language is very often a barrier.

Many large ships are employed on tramp trade and it is very common nowadays for the master to call at a port for the first time. It is also common to call at a port built before the advent of large ships. Consequently, berths are too small, or the harbour has expanded offshore before extension of the breakwater, or the approach channel may not be properly dredged. In South America, the phrase 'safely aground' is used in many charter parties and its original context is often knowingly misinterpreted. Some pilots are reluctant to tell the master of the possible problems that he may encounter during his stay in port, for fear of prejudicing his employers, namely the harbour board. Others may exaggerate the hazards of a berth, so as to induce masters into lodging protests in order, indirectly, to achieve improvements they were unable to get by themselves.

During the past ten years I formed the impression that standards between various pilots have widened more than ever. We see very professional pilots dedicated to their jobs and keen on communicating with the master and the bridge team. At the other end of the scale we see those whose only preoccupation is to hurry through the operation of bringing the ship in or out, no matter how. The latter may be the result of undue pressure or fatigue, which is forgivable, but in other cases is simply a lack of care and professionalism.

In many cases the pilotage standard is directly linked to the quality of the port organisation, the pilot's working scheme and personal backgrounds.

The master usually has a pilot with local expertise handling his ship. There are, however, cases when the master has to handle the ship by himself, often in extreme weather conditions, when the pilot has to leave early or joins late. In other cases, the master may have to leave a port or a quay which is becoming unsafe, without being able to get a pilot and/or tug. There are occasions when particular features of a ship mean that the master has to have special knowledge to handle his own vessel, even in the presence of a pilot. It is, therefore, my opinion that it is important for the master to take a keen interest in shiphandling.

Communication between tug master and the ship should be standardised so as to allow a master to communicate efficiently in any country on leaving or entering a port in an emergency, without a pilot but with the help of a tug. Such a standardised vocabulary would also help the master, under normal circumstances, to understand the orders given by the pilot to the tugs during manoeuvring.

Standards of pilotage

Standards of pilotage can differ widely from country to country. To mention only a few examples, I have known river pilots in South America who knew nothing but sign language, with vague explanations in their native tongue. Once I had to berth a ship myself at a west African port I had never called at before because the pilot was intoxicated; and I realised it only when the ship was beyond the point of no return. I had to have a pilot escorted off the bridge in the Bosphorus for the same reason. In a middle east port a pilot feigned a heart attack after realising that the Mediterranean mooring operation was unsuccessful and, on entering a major Chinese port, a 22 year old pilot tried to cover up his mistake by misleading me into believing that an area had recently been dredged. I avoided grounding only by taking emergency action. In quite a few cases, I myself or the mate have observed pilots dozing.

On the other hand, pilots in most developed countries are very professional and dedicated. They honour their profession and I am sure they could give even more accounts of sub-standard crews and officers who are a disgrace to their profession. As much as we need to set crew standards, pilots' standards should be maintained on a world wide basis. Similarly, port facilities and safety margins should be recognised and reasonably standardised.

The pilot should advise the master of the possible risks of the berth. Of course, because the pilot is usually employed by the port, he may not be keen to suggest that a berth may not be safe. It should, however, be done honestly and without prejudice by the pilot and the port should take the view that the master should be warned in writing of any possible risks of the berth (eg in bad weather). With the growing number of inexperienced pilots appearing on the international scene, communication, mutual understanding and respect is more essential than ever. The pilot should brief the master of his intentions, calling his attention to any special characteristics of the port or berth. Likewise, the master should brief the pilot about his ship's expected characteristics. If the master knows the pilot's intentions well, he is far less likely to interfere.

The pilot expects the master to be able to comment on the ship's behaviour in various situations. Certainly this should include any peculiarity of which the pilot may be unaware and which may affect the ship's responses, such as critical speeds, engine notice, thrusters, special rudders propellers, engine type, etc. Comments should also include such information as reserved or forbidden areas for tugs to push and the type and number of mooring lines, which should be displayed next to the pilot card, speed table and manoeuvring board. Some pilots carry out a set of simple tests before commencing pilotage, to assess engine/rudder response, testing whistles, checking compass errors, the status of radars, echo sounders, speed logs and the VHF. Some may also watch the master and his officers carefully, in order to judge the amount of assistance they may get from them, whether bridge team management and procedures exist and whether the officers and crew are proficient.

Safely to proceed

Certain decisions ought to be taken together, such as crossing a bar in heavy weather. The underkeel clearance may not, for example, be sufficient to allow for the vessel's rolling and pitching motion. The master's own special knowledge of his ship should complement that of the pilot's local expertise. High sided ships, particularly at light draft, may encounter specific problems when manoeuvring within restricted waters in windy conditions. The amount of power and response, the availability of thrusters, variable pitch, propeller immersion and trim are among the factors that will be taken into consideration when deciding whether it is safe to proceed or not.

Many ports may have specific restrictions for such classes of ship. The final decision will, however, rest

upon both master and pilot. Mutual exchange of information prior to arrival can greatly help to reach a solution satisfying all parties. Ports are sometimes being built without enough consideration towards shiphandling. I have, as an example, seen a brand new car carrier terminal being built in northeast Asia, with all berths fully exposed and leading 90° to the prevalent winter monsoon winds.

Safe embarkation and disembarkation

Many masters such as myself feel concern about embarking or disembarking a pilot in rough seas. It is usually preferable to drop or pick up the pilot in sheltered waters. In some areas, distant pilotage takes place quite successfully. The means of disembarkation should be appropriate. The landing of a helicopter on the slippery hatch cover of a rolling bulk carrier can be very hazardous and options such as winching or simply over-carrying the pilot to a safer dropping area should be considered. In this case the master's opinion should be respected.

Passage planning in pilotage waters

The writer is aware that short manning and fatigue, in ever more demanding trades, regrettably often prevent master and officers preparing a well found passage plan in pilotage waters. Nevertheless, on a well manned ship, the master will probably have prepared a form of passage plan through an area of pilotage water with his officers. Such a plan would, however, be limited to the information available from various publications and the master's own particular experience in the area together with general experience to complement it. It may further be limited by a lack of up to date information. In many cases the berth may not be allocated until the last moment and in many areas of the world charts do not show the latest developments which may have taken place. The master has, at times, to rely only on information given by the charterers or his agents.

The following are some of the points which could be included in the ship's passage plan:

- Landmark identification.
- Margins of safety.
- Safe water.
- No-go areas.
- Points of no return.
- Contingency anchorage.
- Tidal window.
- Stream allowance.
- Wheel over points.
- Leading marks.
- Parallel indexing.
- Distance off.
- Reporting points.
- Traffic considerations.

The pilot's passage plan should, if possible, be faxed to the ship prior to her arrival and be updated, if need be, by the pilot on boarding (ie berth reallocation, possible delays, impediments etc.). It would complement the ship's passage plan and contain particular information which may not be available to the crew prior to arrival. A number of ships may not have a prepared passage plan so it should, therefore, also be self contained and include the above in a proper concise form, easy to absorb and giving the crew the necessary elements to update and correct their plan easily and rapidly. It would particularly mention such variables as dredged depths, tidal streams, the position of dredgers or other impediments, moving banks, navaids off station, the availability of tugs and local conditions such as wind, currents, ice, seasonal condition or any other anomalies.

It should complement the chart and especially inform the ship about any latest developments which may not figure on the charts or other publications commonly available on board.

Some of the available pilotage techniques may not be evident in the documentation available on board, and such should be included in the pilot's plan. Schematic diagrams of approaches to berths should include the disposition of tugs, sending of lines, mooring arrangements, planned swinging area with depth and available space, signals to tugs and possible delays, i.e. waiting for traffic clearance. It should also contain a preamble describing the general location, the general current and tidal stream circulation and strength and warn the mariner of any special hazards such as:

- Isolated dangers or shoals.
- Charts limitation and update.
- Surveys – quality and reliability.
- Strong currents.
- Unusual conditions.
- Prohibited areas.
- Emergency anchorage.

It would also include:

- Pilot's boarding arrangements and any special requirements or common underkeel allowance.
- Instructions with regard to his safe embarkation.
- Tidal and weather restrictions.
- Tug pick up points.
- Communication via VHF channels for:
    Passing agreements.
    Tugs.
    Pilot boat.
    Helicopter.
    VTS harbour control.
    Emergencies.

Bridge organisation

The bridge organisation should be such that on the pilot's arrival no break-up of procedures or communication occurs. The pilot should relieve the master at the con, after a short mutual briefing of the revised docking/passage plan and familiarisation with the location of bridge equipment, controls and status. An exchange of information would already have taken place well in advance via fax, so that both master and pilots are fairly briefed upon their initial meeting. The exchange of a few words, both technical and informal, should help them to reach the necessary human contact which I deem essential to achieve a degree of human relationship, and consequent mutual trust.

An important role is the ability of the master and officer to assist the pilot, particularly in the case of any abnormality such as the break-up of communication with tugs, VTS, meeting traffic, or machinery, gear failure (own or that of another meeting ship). There is a global need to improve the crucial efficiency of communication between the master/officers/crew and pilot. The master should be able to understand orders given to the tugs or dock master by the pilot. An improved standard marine vocabulary covering modern pilotage practices should be used. I have now, over the years, gained enough knowledge to understand commands in a variety of language. This is, however, not a solution and cannot be expected from all masters – it is sometimes safer to have no knowledge of a language than a little knowledge with chances of misunderstandings or confusion.

Some form of error control should be possible without offending the pilot. A master's interference during pilotage may, under certain circumstances, be premature and do more harm than good. In other cases, however, a lack of communication or action by the master can be a major factor leading towards an accident. The master must, therefore, balance very carefully between error control/ supervision on the one hand and avoidance of causing undue interference on the other. The application of good human relations and an open association with the pilot helps very much in this respect. Neither the pilot nor the master should become too self-imposed, and mutual consideration should prevail between the two.

As a master, I have observed pilots handling ships in a multitude of different styles. As such I have forged my own opinions and use every opportunity to do my own shiphandling. In many cases I try to use such experience to discuss matters with the pilot at the onset of the passage and we often gain mutual benefit in this way. The shiphandler must be patient and alert to noises and vibrations. Some of them prefer the old gyro repeaters clicking at every half degree to give them an idea of the rate of turn (the need to turn on to an analogue rate of turn indicator may distract his senses). Watching the ship's wake may also be the best indicator of the proximity to the bottom. In shallow and narrow canals, I have sometimes encountered pilots insisting on maintaining full rpm, resulting in heavy vibrations and poor steering, mainly due to increased interaction and substantial speed loss. After insisting on a reduction of engine speed, a striking improvement in ship handling characteristics and a damping of the vibrations could often be observed.

A master may view squat with a somewhat different eye from a pilot. Unlike a pilot, a master sees a variety of canals, rivers and bars where vessels behave very differently and the handling method may vary greatly. The master also concerns himself particularly about the resulting damage from any form of grounding. Even paint damage can bring serious consequences to the owners and this is often not fully appreciated by pilots. Underkeel clearance may become a rather superfluous word in areas such as the Orinoco, River Plate, Surinam River or the Amazon Northern Bar to name but a few areas where deep draft vessels feel strong vibrations, at times undergoing an alarming loss of speed and difficulty in steering, because of the extremely dense water layer on the bottom (floc), the echo sounder indicating zero underkeel clearance.

Such loss of speed may well not indicate grounding. It indicates that the vessel is navigating in denser muddy waters, the echo sounder being unable to detect the bottom. A heavy sounding rod would probably dig deeper than a lighter one. A reduction of engine speed by a few revolutions may often have the effect of reducing vibrations and improving steering.

When crossing a bar at the peak of the tide, planning and maintaining a safe speed is essential in order to cross it before the ebb catches up, thus avoiding becoming 'planted on a falling tide'. Charterers often seek protection under C/P terms as 'safely aground' to detach themselves from responsibility for the consequences of 'sailing in navigable mud or customary groundings'.

Master–pilot and VTS relationship

Basically, a VTS functions as an aid and assistance to the on board decision making process, monitoring progress and giving advance warning of potential danger. As such, a VTS operated by qualified and experienced mariners with the necessary tools at their disposal can greatly improve the efficiency of traffic flow, by keeping track of other ships and advising those ships under jurisdiction of local conditions, about hazards of various sorts and as an aid for confirmation of passing agreements. There are a great many VTS systems in operation. Their control of ships ranges from a purely informative overview of traffic with interference in emergencies or contravention of Collision Regulations only (such as Dover Strait), to almost full control of the ships (such as navigation in fog or remote pilotage in certain rivers and estuaries).

Accident prevention

Accidents in congested waters, particularly port approaches, are numerous. Very often they are caused by failure to understand another vessel's intentions.

VHF – which could be invaluable in such situations – is often misused. In fact, misunderstandings using this equipment have contributed to many mishaps or casualties. VTS systems are still non existent or not adequate in many parts of the world and the introduction of radar transponders would offer valuable help in this field.

Arrivals at busy pilot stations should be programmed in such a way that ships pick up their pilots in a given order. Although it is often more convenient for a group of pilots to board arriving vessels within quick succession, collision hazards should be taken into consideration. To avoid such problems, groups of arriving ships should be given sequence numbers to govern their arrival order. An experienced pilot or VTS controller should assign such numbers taking into account the position of various approaching and departing ships, possible tidal windows, their types and size, bearing in mind that a larger, deeper vessel will approach more slowly and will need additional sea-room. Such advice should be given sufficiently ahead of time and the VTS should help the masters of the ships concerned to identify each other by giving them their relative position. Such systems are customarily implemented very well in certain areas of the world. There are, however, still many regions where no such plans exist.

Manoeuvres to pick up or drop off a pilot are often the cause of misunderstandings and confusion to other ships. Unless efficient means of communication and identification exist, it is good practice to give a security call on the appropriate VHF channel, identifying the vessel and giving broad indications of intentions. For example – 'this is tanker 'Nonesuch' dropping off the pilot at 'Wherever', proceeding up channel and standing by on channels 16 and 13'. Some pilots are constrained by regulations to leave or join a ship at a designated station without allowance for weather conditions. When seas are heavy at the station, the pilot's life may be endangered and the master is sometimes obliged to make a wide turn to give a maximum lee when approaching shallow waters, or confusing other ships, thus jeopardising both pilot and ship, rather than dropping off the pilot earlier or picking him up (under circumstances) further inshore.

Passage planning with limited information

A practical example to highlight the need for local knowledge in certain areas, particularly rivers where huge changes can be expected:

Rivers, in particular their approaches, should be considered as 'living things', with a character and behaviour of their own, particularly such as the huge Amazon delta. The following account highlights the need for local knowledge and shows a particular side of a master's profession, where intuition and observation has to make good for a lack of local information.

In certain areas of the world the master may be left on his own, without the help of local pilots, when transiting an area where local knowledge is most needed, such as a river bar. This would not really be a problem for a master who has had previous experience in the area. But with the trend, nowadays, towards large numbers of tramp ships, increasing ports and frequent reliefs, it is quite common for a master to sail for the first time in a given area. As an example, deep draft vessels are often bound for upriver ports and have to negotiate the Amazon estuary where huge seasonal changes take place. There are normally no local pilots available and even the latest updated charts may not show the current channel. The agent sends the master a presumably updated position of various buoys marking the canal of Curua. A part of this area – a 22 miles stretch leading to the open sea – has to be negotiated. Tidal information may be scarce and sometimes appears contradictory to observations, as ships with 11·28m draft are required to pass through a 22 miles bar with charted depths ranging from about 8·9m to 9·6m at chart datum. Information regarding seasonal and meteorological interactions with the tidal level and streams is almost non-existent. The shifting of banks is so poorly documented that for a particular passage through the canal of Curua, the agent reported new buoyage positions passing over what appeared on up to date British charts to be drying banks. The latest Brazilian charts are impossible to get at short notice and many deep draft tramp ships going to the Amazon receive no prior notice of the intended voyage.

Corrected tidal levels based upon Brazilian publications, which relate only to a single point on the bar are, in my opinion, not accurate enough to cover seasonal and meteorological interaction. Gauges ought to be sited at strategic places and their level given by radio, to allow the master to time his transit through the bar. Local knowledge is essential in such an area and a well defined tidal window ought to be established using experience of the behaviour of such deep draft ships. This should take into account tidal levels, currents, meteorological conditions, squat and the usual response and behaviour of such ships, evaluating the optimum speed engine setting to avoid the risk of becoming planted on a falling tide or, on the other hand, damaging the bottom due to squat caused by excessive speed.

Critical spots and timing ought also to be properly established, taking into consideration seasonal and meteorological effects. The limiting draft may also need to be reviewed. Competent pilots ought to be made easily available, without unreasonable deviation. The Admiralty has suggested that pilots should board at Salinopolis (this – at the time of writing – is not normally done, as it involves a long additional passage through a poorly surveyed area at very high cost, which charterers are not willing to bear). Similar problems occur in other areas, particularly in South America: the Orinoco, Surinam River and Parana are other such examples.

Where information is insufficient it is prudent to leave an extra margin of safety. When proceeding it is advisable to maintain accurate depth records and positions on the chart. In the event of a dispute it is essential that the master can produce evidence of prudent navigation.

Conclusion

Good master-pilot relations are based upon a shared sense of purpose and this is best achieved through practical passage planning. Contingencies should be considered and my advice to masters is to have a competent feel for shiphandling so that you can take over the handling of the ship if the need arises.

References
- Rowe, R.W., *The Shiphandler's Guide*, The Nautical Institute, second edition 1999.
- *The Bridge Procedures Guide 1998*, International Chamber of Shipping.
- *Passage Planning – a nautical briefing*, The Nautical Institute, 1993.

Chapter 30

WHAT THE SALVAGE TUG WILL WANT TO KNOW IN THE EVENT OF DAMAGE

by Captain D. Hancox FNI, Consultant Salvage Master

David Hancox obtained his foreign-going master's certificate in 1969, taking command of a coastal tug immediately thereafter. Between 1971 and 1979 he was employed by Selco Salvage, becoming senior salvage master in 1977. He returned to Selco in 1981 as salvage and international towage manager and since mid-1984 has worked as a consultant salvage master, based in Australia. Captain Hancox is the author of Reed's Commercial Salvage Practice.

Introduction

VESSELS WHICH SUSTAIN a marine casualty of sufficient magnitude to require external aid usually find that such assistance is provided by professional marine salvage contractors. The salvor's principal representatives are either a senior salvage operations supervisor (known as a salvage master/salvage inspector or salvage superintendent) or the master of the salvage tug deployed to assist the casualty. The shipmaster unfortunate enough to require external salvage assistance should remember that three points are at the forefront of the salvors' minds:

1. To prevent the casualty and/or her cargo sustaining any further damage.
2. To prevent or reduce pollution of the sea and/or environment by either bunkers or cargo from the casualty.
3. To ensure that consequential damage to third parties or injuries to either crew or other persons are minimised.

Types of marine casualty

Prior to considering the information which the salvage master or the tugmaster may require, it may be useful to list briefly the principal types of marine casualties which usually require external assistance.

Casualty salvage afloat: Assisting vessels to stay afloat or to control a casualty arising from damage/leakage caused by stress of weather, collision, leakage, fire and/or explosion, breakdowns, navigational errors, hostile military action, or pollution control and abatement.

Stranded casualty salvage: The refloatation of stranded vessels which have driven ashore as a result of navigational error, enemy action, force of weather, intentional beaching, machinery breakdown, pollution control/abatement.

Oilfield salvage operations: Providing services to prevent the loss of, or reduce damage to, offshore drilling and/or oil production facilities arising from any of the following causes: fire-fighting, emergency stabilising services required as a result of fires, blowouts, collisions or weather incidents.

The salvors themselves will have a number of other sub categories for types of marine casualties, including such activities as refloating of sunken vessels, cargo salvage/recovery operations, special object recoveries, pollution control and abatement, wreck removal operations, offshore clearance and/or demolition. However, in the context of a vessel requiring immediate professional salvage assistance, only those categories listed under the three principal sub-headings need be considered.

In the paragraphs which follow, it has been assumed by the writer that all prospective ship masters, and indeed all practising masters, are familiar with ICS/OCIMF's publication, *Peril at Sea and Salvage – A Guide for Masters*. This was compiled with technical assistance from the International Salvage Union – the body which represents most professional salvage contractors. This publication contains much excellent practical advice to all ship masters who have the misfortune to require salvage assistance.

Casualty salvage afloat
Breakdown/loss of propulsive power

Assuming that the accident is a 'simple' case of 'engine failure', the casualty will require towage to a port or place of refuge and the tugmaster will normally require the following information:

(a) Time, date and geographical position of accident.
(b) Present position, weather, and drift rate.
(c) Heading of casualty and relative aspect to weather.
(d) Draft forward, aft and mean before accident.
(e) Present best estimated/calculated drafts and trim.
(f) Present displacement and list (if any).
(g) Whether deck/auxiliary power is available for heaving on board towing gear.
(h) Number of crew on board casualty.
(i) Type/nature and tonnage of cargo and/or quantity of ballast on board.
(j) Whether there is any loss of cargo/pollution.
(k) Is the casualty making any water/leaking.
(l) What radio (WT, SSB, and VHF) frequencies/channels will be guarded by casualty.
(m) Radio contact schedules.

From the answers provided in 'a' to 'm', the tugmaster will establish a mental picture of the casualty, and how he believes the vessel can best be towed. Where a point is unclear, the tugmaster will ask for clarification or further explanation as he develops the towage plan. Do not waste your own crew's time and energy by dragging out 'insurance wires' and devising elaborate towing methods without the full agreement of the tugmaster.

The professionally operated salvage tug requires *no* towing gear from the casualty, although the casualty master should advise the tugmaster if the vessel (being a tanker) is fitted with a special emergency pennant/ chafe chain system as specified under IMO Assembly Resolution A535 (13) or M. Notice 1147 promulgated 1984. (It should, however, be noted that even where a vessel complies with IMO A535 (13) – *Emergency Towing Requirements for Tankers* – the decision whether to use such equipment will rest with the chief mate/ master of the rescue tug, one of whom will normally board the casualty when towing gear is being connected.)

Finally, it is recommended that very regular radio contact is maintained with the approaching rescue tug, and preparations are made to rig a pilot ladder on the lee side, a long boat rope on lee side and have heaving lines and gantlines ready beside the pilot ladder to enable personnel from the tug to board the casualty safely and expeditiously. In benign weather conditions, the tugmaster himself may board by rubber boat for a brief inspection, but normally the boarding party comprises a deck officer, an engineer officer and one or two salvage hands.

Collision/leakage/stress of weather

In each of the above cases, it is assumed that the casualty has either sustained machinery damage, or has taken in water, rendering it impractical for her to proceed 'under command' by means of her own power. A collision in the engine room would generally presuppose the loss of main propulsion plant.

In addition to some or all of the questions asked by the tugmaster (breakdowns) earlier, the following questions will also probably be put to the shipmaster:

(n) Where does the leakage originate and how many spaces are flooded?
(o) Has any cargo shifted, or been lost overboard?
(p) Have any dangerous free-surface effects been produced by flooding of compartments?
(q) Has any distortion/damage to hatches, tank-lids, bulkheads and/or piping been observed?
(r) Is inter-compartment leakage/transfer of flood water taking place, and can it be controlled/ reduced?
(s) Has an estimate of the casualty's stability and hull shearing moments been made for the damaged condition?

(t) Are all crew members accounted for, or are any crew known to be trapped or missing?
(u) Can the casualty remain afloat, or must she be beached?

Again, immediately after arrival of the rescue tug, a boarding party will be despatched and a detailed examination of the casualty made to assess the situation in conjunction with the shipmaster and his staff. Where practical, the salvage tug will come alongside the casualty and transfer damage control/ salvage equipment to stabilise the situation prior to taking the casualty under tow.

Fire/explosion and/or hostile military action

In many cases, particularly on tankers and gas carriers, the situation rapidly develops to the point where partial or full temporary evacuation (or complete abandonment) of the casualty appears to be the most sensible course of action for the stricken ship's crew to adopt. Where communications with the approaching salvage tug are maintained by personnel remaining on board the casualty, the questions asked by the tugmaster will tend to follow those enumerated already, with the following more relevant points being queried:

(v) What tanks/spaces/bunkers are on fire?
(w) What is the cargo which is on fire?
(x) Is the emergency fire pump in operation?
(y) Is the fire encroaching into the cargo area?
(z) Is any of the cargo firing on the sea surface?

Under most circumstances of an engine room/ pump-room cargo fire on tankers and gas carriers, the first salvage tug attending the casualty will make a towing connection either forward or aft in such a position as will allow the tug to control the wind direction (relative to the fire front) across the front of the casualty. With the towing connection prepared, the tug will usually land firefighters and salvage/fire pumps on board the casualty to enable fire boundary controls to be established.

Unless the blaze is small, it is unlikely that the tug itself will make an all-out foam attack on the fire. Initially, a salvage crew aim to confine the blaze whilst additional salvage personnel and specialised equipment are transported to the casualty. It should be appreciated by shipmasters that, although salvage personnel do not necessarily look like professional shore-side firemen, the present generation of international salvage crews have extensive fire-fighting experience on ULCCs.

It should be noted that, on arrival off a casualty, particularly where towage services are required, the rescue tug will heave to, enabling the tugmaster to:
1. Observe and estimate for himself the drift of the casualty and relate drift and casualty behaviour to his previous ideas.
2. Determine the most effective position and heading

of the tug off the bow or stern of the casualty, consistent with where the towing gear will be connected.

3. Assess the total scope of the assignment and obtain any last minute information from the casualty's master.

Stranding salvage

In general terms, the information requested from a shipmaster whose vessel has stranded will be as follows:

(a) Time, date and geographical position of stranding.
(b) Has the casualty sustained any damage and/or are any tanks, holds or spaces leaking?
(c) How much of the vessel's length is in contact with the sea-bed?
(d) Is the casualty uniformly aground, or is it impaled on a single point and free to pivot?
(e) Drafts forward, aft and mean *before* stranding.
(f) Drafts actually observed, whilst aground – forward, amidships (port and starboard) and aft and time of observation.
(g) Quantity of cargo, fuel and ballast on board before stranding.
(h) Pre-stranding displacement, TCM/TPI, stability – GM and GZ.
(i) Whether any pollution has occurred.
(j) Is the casualty lying quietly and firmly aground or is the vessel moving on the strand?
(k) Are the main engine(s) and auxiliaries fully operational?
(l) What is prevailing wind direction and velocity and sea/swell height?
(m) Have detailed soundings been made around the casualty at high and low water?
(n) Any heel, excessive trim or shift of cargo as a result of stranding.

On receipt of this information, the tugmaster and/or salvage master will probably strongly caution/advise the casualty master in the following terms:

(i) To make detailed outboard soundings around the vessel.
(ii) To make detailed and comprehensive soundings of all internal bilges, spaces, tanks and voids.
(iii) To check that all watertight closures, stern gland(s) and access doors, etc., remain watertight.
(iv) To ballast all available tanks to harden the vessel down on her strand to reduce any wave or swell-induced damage.
(v) To satisfy himself personally of the stability of the vessel in conjunction with (ii) and (iv).

(iv) Not to jettison any cargo, bunkers or stores before being fully in possession of all material facts.
(vii) Not to attempt any refloating by his vessel's own means until all data in (i) through (vi) have been properly evaluated and tested.

Many shipmasters are suspicious of such advice, but it should be realised that the eventual fate of many casualties has often been determined by the actions of the master and his officers. The steps enumerated are some of those which can be taken to secure the casualty and prevent it from either sustaining further damage or being placed in greater danger.

Generally, only a few shipmasters' commands have the misfortune to require salvage assistance, thus, questions (often asked at long range) by the assisting tugmaster or a salvage master despatched by professional salvors are frequently irritating to the unfortunate master. However, difficult as it may sometimes be, these questions should be thoughtfully and comprehensively answered. What is hopefully a once-in-a-lifetime personal and professional misfortune for the shipmaster concerned is a relatively commonplace occurrence to the salvors contracted by either the shipmaster himself or by the owners/managers of the casualty.

The salvors, having agreed to provide the necessary services, must perform the salvage operations in the safest and most efficient manner, and they have legal obligations to use their best endeavours to render effective salvage assistance. The questions are part of a planning process which has been developed by salvage tug masters and salvage masters, due to their background and exposure to marine casualties, of which they have considerable experience.

References

1. *ICS/OCIMF/Peril at Sea and Salvage – A Guide for Masters*, 5th Edition, obtainable from Witherby & Co. Ltd., London. ISBN 0-900886 74 9.
2. *OCIMF Recommendations on Equipment for the Towing of Disabled Tankers*, July 1981, obtainable from Witherby & Co. Ltd., London. ISBN 0-900886 65 X.
3. *Admiralty Manual of Seamanship*, Volume 3 — Advanced Seamanship, 3rd Edition, Ministry of Defence/HMSO, London. ISBN 0- 11-771269-8.
4. *Shipboard Damage Control*, Bissell, Oertel and Livingstone, United States Naval Institute, Annapolis, Md. 1978, ISBN 0-87021-627-9.

Chapter 31

TOWING – RECEIVING THE TUG AND MAKING FAST

by Captain W.V. Hopper MNI,
formerly Towing and Operations Superintendent, United Towing Co. Ltd.

Captain Hopper served his time with the Roland and Marwood Steamship Company, obtaining his master's certificate in 1939 and sailing as chief officer with the same company. He joined United Towing in 1946 and has worldwide experience as an ocean tugmaster. In 1961 he was appointed assistant superintendent and served as superintendent and operations superintendent before retiring in 1978. In 1979 he was appointed to the board of Hull Trinity House and was elected Warden 1984-1985

Introduction

IF A VESSEL BECOMES DISABLED through main engine breakdown or loss of rudder or propeller and is in no immediate danger, the vessel's owner or underwriters' agent will put enquiries out to tug owners or tug brokers for a suitable tug within reasonable range. Terms of contract will be discussed between the two parties.

The contract could take one of many forms. Examples are: a lump sum to tow the vessel to a predetermined port of refuge; a daily rate to tow the vessel to a stated destination, with separate daily rates to cover the mobilisation and demobilisation of the tug; a daily rate with a lump-sum bonus on successful completion of the contract; or Lloyd's Open Form, where the parties agree to settle the award by submitting to arbitration should they not be able to come to an amicable agreement. The tug owner will want to protect himself by contract clauses to cover weather diversion, threat of pollution etc.

Lloyd's Open Form

Should a vessel be disabled and in immediate peril, there will not usually be much choice of salvage assistance, and the master will have to take the first available rescue vessel offered. In these circumstances, Lloyd's Open Form would be the safest contract. Should the first available vessel be underpowered to tow the casualty, then the master should not hesitate to contract another vessel, be it of the same company as the first or not. It does simplify final settlement and harmonious work if the rescue vessels are of the same company, but at the same time two or more contractors can each be engaged on separate contracts. It is possible for the initial contractor to engage other than his own vessels and to be the prime contractor in the final settlement.

Master's decision

None of these contractual arguments should preclude the decision of the master, who must surely be the best judge of the situation in saving his vessel and engaging on-the-spot assistance. The tug owner or tug master should detail the power and capability of assistance offered, in order to guide the shipowner or master in engaging further assistance should it be deemed necessary.

To help in settling salvage or assistance claims, the master should see that a very precise log of events, positions and weather is whenever possible strictly maintained, together with a log of all radio traffic between himself and the rescue vessels and coast stations. Weather forecasts should also be logged or recorded for his particular area.

Salvage contracts can, of course, be made verbally on the radio-telephone or by wireless telegraphy, and these contracts, if made by the master, should be passed on to the underwriters as soon as possible.

Propeller(s) trailing free

If the casualty's main engines are incapable of being used and it is not anticipated that they will be used before a port of refuge or repair is reached, the towing speed can be greatly aided by the propeller(s), shaft(s) being uncoupled forward of the thrust block and the propeller(s) left to trail free. The friction will be on the astern thrust and lubrication must be attended to throughout the shaft bearings and stern gland.

It is not easy to reconnect shaft couplings once the vessel is under tow unless shaft brakes are fitted. Therefore shaft uncoupling should be resorted to only when main engines are to be immobilised.

Connecting the tow

Once assistance has been accepted, preparations to connect and secure the tug should be made. As a guide, the following gear should be made ready and be to hand on the vessel's foredeck, assuming the vessel has not been in collision and suffered a heavily damaged bow. (In the latter case, if there is a risk of pressure on the collision bulkhead, the towing point would have to be at the stern.)

Check the line-throwing apparatus and leave on the bridge and have ready: three good long heaving lines; a handy billy tackle; boat hook; six rope stoppers, preferably manila or sisal; rope yarns; bundle of old canvas for parcelling; bucket of grease; deck axe; large bow shackle; good mooring wire, about three inches circumference and the usual bosun's tools – spike, knife etc.

Provided the casualty is not anchored, getting the tug's connection on board should not be too difficult.

A drifting vessel will invariably lie in the trough and beam to the wind, and the usual connecting approach is for the tug to steam across the bow down wind. If the weather conditions are very bad – too bad for a heaving line to reach the tug's after deck – the tug should shoot a rocket line across the foredeck of the casualty whilst he is still up wind, and once connection is established the tug crew should attach a messenger line to the rocket line or heaving line.

This will be followed by a heavier rope or wire to which will be attached the towing wire pennant. These towing wire pennants usually have a heavy thimble eye and the messenger is secured down the pennant splice and lashed at the eye.

As soon as the thimble eye reaches the towing lead the mooring wire should be shackled into the eye whilst it is still outboard and the mooring wire then worked as a preventer. This precaution should be taken to avoid losing the wire when the critical stage arises as the thimble is hove over or through the lead whilst the weight of a bight is outboard between the lead and the tug's stern.

Making the towing pennant fast

Some modern tugs are very powerful and heavy units, and their connections consist of a wire pennant attached to a short length of heavy stud link chain. The wire pennant is hove up until the chain – usually about three fathoms long – is laid in the lead or hawse pipe to take the chafing area. Due allowance must he made for the chain pulling out until the connection has been towed tight, and the wire pennant is to be belayed on bollards as near in line with the lead as possible. Two sets of bollards should be used, and the wire pennant can be backed up to the second set by reeving bights of mooring wire through the eye of the pennant back to the bollards. It is important to remember that it is a good seamanlike consideration to belay the tug in such a manner as to be able to release the connection quickly.

Assuming that the casualty has deck machinery power available, then choose a lead or hawse pipe where it is possible to use the warping drum of the windlass. An ideal lead for a tug's connection on a soft-nosed vessel would be a deep hawse pipe on the centre line – unfortunately not often fitted – but otherwise use a hawse pipe as near the centre line as possible after first ascertaining that the pipe will accept the pennant thimble. If no hawse pipe is available, then the open leads on the bow are all one can use, but the danger of an open lead is the possibility of the wire or chain jumping out of the lead when pitching deeply. Should an open lead be used, it is a good idea to wrack the wire or chain down inboard of the lead.

On a vessel with a bar stem, an extra precaution is to parcel the wire pennant well where it will lay across the stem when the vessel is on a sheer. If chain is used, make sure the chain covers the outboard area to the stem as well as the area in the lead.

Rope stoppers

When handling the tug's pennant use manila or sisal stoppers – never use chain stoppers, for a chain stopper jammed would ruin the wire. A rope stopper can easily be cut away, but a jammed chain stopper can be a danger to life. When messenger contact is made, pull up any slack rope rapidly by hand to avoid any slack rope bight washing under the tug's stern.

Once the connection has been established and the tug has stretched his gear, smother the wire or chain in the lead area with grease. When a chain is used, the first link outboard is continually sawing on the first link in the lead and these two links require frequent grease application. If a wire is used, a frequent check on the parcelling in the lead should be made and if any deterioration in the wire is seen, the tug must be advised. Should the circumstances permit, the tug will endeavour to take weight off the wire to allow a messenger to be put on the wire and an attempt made to heave inboard the chafed area till it is clear of the lead, at the same time taking in the slack on the bollards without risk of the wire slipping.

While under tow, contact between tug and tow must be maintained constantly; usually a VHF watch is maintained.

Should the casualty have lost or be unable to use her rudder, but be able to use her main engines, then main engines must be used only at the request of the tug master – if requested, it would be only at dead or slow speed. A violent sheer caused by the vessel using her own power could cause the tug to be girted and lose steerage way, even possibly turning the tug completely round. Tugs have been capsized by the gob rope (sometimes called the bridle rope) parting when the tug is girted. (The term 'girted' is used to describe the situation where the tug's stern is pulled across against the rudder by the towing wire leading too broad across the stern.)

Steering on the tug's stern

Use of the rudder is of great assistance. Unless the tug requires the vessel to hold a sheer, the casualty should steer directly on the tug's stern as near as possible. A following wind and sea often cause problems by inducing sheering of the tow and this occurs most if there is a lot of superstructure aft. If a following wind and sea is accompanied by a heavy swell, this can cause a dangerous situation, for the tug can run into the gear as the swell throws it forward. Should this occur as the tow drops back off a swell, the tow line becomes suddenly taut and may part.

In this dangerous situation progress is made by tacking. The weather is put about four points on the quarter and the engine revolutions are dropped till a comfortable speed is maintained, allowing the tug to steer and the tow, to hold a windward sheer – this is termed sailing. The tug master will decide how long to maintain one tack before changing on to the other tack and much, of course, depends on navigational hazards.

To enable a tow to have steering stability, trim is essential. An ideal trim would be at least a metre by the stern in the average vessel with about three or four metres as giving the better advantage. Pounding is very unlikely at towing speed.

Keeping a good lookout

While under tow, warnings to other shipping will be transmitted by the tug and at night a keen watch should be maintained from the tow, with visual signals being made to approaching vessels, especially from abaft the beam. The daylight signal lamp is very useful by day or night, to give warning to vessels on a closing course. The diamond shape must be hoisted and during poor visibility the fog signal is one long blast followed by three short blasts (which signal should follow the tug's signal).

When under tow in coastal waters, leeway allowances and tidal allowances may seem severe, but a tug master is used to navigating at very slow speeds with cumbersome tows and experience teaches him what allowances to make.

The catenary of the towing gear when on sea towing length is considered as important as the draft in order to avoid the wire touching the bottom. In shallow waters away from the swell it is the practice to shorten in the tow line so long as there is sufficient catenary to avoid the gear 'snatching'.

Fitting equipment

I feel the time has come when all the classification societies should encourage shipowners to fit, as standard, towing and mooring equipment – a towing hawse pipe, bollards and towing clench plate. By a towing hawse pipe, I mean a deep well-rounded hawse pipe on or near the centre line at the stem, a set of sturdy bollards abaft the hawse pipe and a towing clench plate abaft the bollards with the connecting area to one side of the after bollard post. The deck in way of these fittings should be suitably stiffened.

The hawse pipe and bollards would be in use throughout the vessel's life for docking and berthing and the clench plate would serve as back up to the bollards: so much time and effort could be saved if these units were fitted. I would not neglect the stern either: a centre-line sturdy hawse pipe or bull ring with bollards close by would also be useful during the vessel's working life.

As a further aid, the shipowner could fit a length of chain forward attached to the clench plate, the chain to be of sufficient length to reach outboard of the pipe to take any chafing.

When the destination or port of refuge is approached and the casualty is to be handed over to local tugs, I would advise the master not to be too hasty in dismissing the sea tug or bringing the contract to a conclusion, if there still remains a long river or channel passage to be made. He should make absolutely certain the local tugs are powerful enough to be able to deal with a dead ship. If in any doubt, he should have a word with the tug master, suggesting his tug remain connected or perhaps transfer from a sea towing connection to a harbour connection. The tug master would advise in this situation.

In conclusion, when accepting assistance, cooperation with the tug is essential to bring the tow to a successful conclusion of the contract. When taking the tug's connection on board, remember: many hands make light and quick work. It is not easy to hold a large ocean-going tug in one position, and the quicker the connection is made, the less risk of the tug getting into a difficult position.

Chapter 32

SHIPHANDLING AND BERTHING WITH TUGS

by Captain R.W. Rowe FNI

In 1958 the author, like many other young boys of the day, left home at the age of 15 to undergo a year of strict discipline and pre-sea training, before going on to serve four years as an apprentice in the hard school of a Scottish tramp ship company. Having served with several other companies in deep sea trades, up to the rank of first officer, he obtained his Masters Certificate (Foreign Going) in 1970 and thereafter continued a career in the demanding coastal waters of Europe. This was a diverse and interesting period with service as skipper on pilot cutters, master on ferries, from the age of 29, thence master of the sail training ships "Sir Winston Churchill" and "Malcolm Miller" and finally service as a sea pilot.

With this background in practical seamanship, he was employed by The Maritime Centre at Warsash in the south of England, where he developed a Manned Model Ship Handling facility and, in conjunction with Ship's Bridge Simulator training, ran specialised and unique ship handling courses for pilots and ship's masters. During this time he developed important skills as an instructor of senior personnel, whilst working closely with an enormous number of pilots and ships personnel, from a wide range of shipping companies and pilotage districts worldwide. This has also enabled him to keep up to date professionally, to create a more practical relationship between the Maritime Centre and personnel working afloat and to develop an enormous cross fertilisation in ship handling knowledge. He has recently used this experience to produce The Nautical Institute's very successful "Ship Handler's Guide" and was elected a Fellow of The Nautical Institute for this service to the industry.

Introduction

WHEN A CHIEF OFFICER is promoted to master a very important stage in the career structure is reached and with it comes the unforgettable experience of joining the first ship as master. There will be many things to consider, countless decisions to make and a learning curve, no matter what an individual's experience, that can be very steep indeed. Of all the important areas and responsibilities of command that are of concern to the master, it is often the case that ship handling is the least likely area to be considered for specialised training and yet, of all the things that can swiftly guarantee the end of a master's career, nothing is more certain than failure in some aspect of ship handling. In this respect, with the hindsight of past incidents and casualties, training has a tendency to evolve as a corrective measure which attempts to rectify past misjudgements or misconceptions. This is also reflected on those specialised training courses which are dedicated solely to ship handling where it is noticed over several years that certain areas of ship handling are persistently problematic.

It is not the purpose therefore, nor within the scope of this chapter, to make any attempt at instruction in ship handling, as this would be well beyond the limits of a single chapter in a large publication with a much wider over view, but instead to discuss those areas of ship handling that have habitually created difficulties in training and were also known to be the primary cause of certain incidents in the past involving collision or grounding.

Ship handling
General

It is not the intention to discuss in this chapter how a ship is berthed, or unberthed, at specific quays, docks and terminals, as this is entirely the concern of the individual master at the time. The sole objective of this section is to discuss some of the basic handling characteristics of a ship that have been known to be problematic. It is hoped that this will give masters a brief insight into how a ship is likely to behave and a means of assessing the difficulties and feasibility with respect any intended ship handling situation. The following will therefore be discussed briefly in this section:

a) The power to tonnage ratio.
b) The mismanagement of approaches.
c) The effect of the wind.
d) A failure to turn.
e) The influence of shallow water.

The power to tonnage ratio

When considering any manoeuvre at close quarters with another vessel, or within the confines of a pilotage district or harbour area, there is a point at which the size of the ship being driven dictates the need for a very different strategy, in terms of overall planning and thinking. This is a vague and difficult point to define but one which is greatly influenced by the power to tonnage ratio of individual ships. This can be illustrated with a few examples of typical new buildings (see figure 32.1).

Ship Type	Tonnes (dwt)	Draft (m)	Power (shp)
Break Bulk	20,000	10	17,000
Bulk Cargo	30,000	11	13,000
Tanker	80,000	12	17,000
Tanker	120,000	18	23,000
Tanker	250,000	21	31,000

Figure 32.1 Typical new buildings

This shows quite clearly that it is possible to go from a ship of 20,000 dwt to one of 80,000 dwt where the latter, although it is four times bigger, has only the same 17,000 shaft horse power (shp). This is progressive throughout the tonnage range, so that a 250,000 dwt ship, which is over twelve times the size of the 20,000 tonner, may merely have twice its shp! This is a very important factor when considering ship handling techniques across a wide range of tonnages.

Ships < 50,000 dwt

The ships in this range, because of their smaller tonnage and the lower kinetic energy created when they are making headway, tend to run off that headway fairly quickly when required. Their relatively good power to tonnage ratio, also means that they tend to have adequate stern power and can also be stopped quite smartly, when needed. This has the unfortunate tendency of encouraging higher speeds than are perhaps wise and when a ship is approaching its objective, a failure to reduce speed soon enough. It can also encourage over-confident attitudes in experienced ship handlers, to the extent that they sometimes adopt an unintentional, but somewhat 'cavalier' attitude towards excessive speed.

Ships > 50,000 dwt

The massive kinetic energy developed when making way through the water, by ships such as the Panamax, Cape and VLCC classes, invariably leads to problems with respect to:

a) Slowing and stopping.
b) Inadequate anchoring equipment.

Slowing and stopping

When attempting to slow down or stop, the massive amount of kinetic energy created by the larger ship results in its headway being carried for a considerable distance, before the propeller speed and ship speed are matched. To compound this situation the poor power to tonnage ratio will often mean inadequate stern power and their stopping distances are correspondingly large. For example, an emergency stop of 1·2 miles is not uncommon.

Anchoring equipment

Research has shown that the size of windlasses on ships of this tonnage is disproportionate to the size of the ship. In some cases a 100% increase in tonnage has only been matched with a 10% increase in windlass size. The kinetic energy generated, even at speed as low as 0·3 knot, is too much for the anchoring equipment to sustain and these ships must be handled with special considerations for this.

Masters moving up to larger tonnage ships

It is normal, for masters moving up to larger tonnage ships, initially to experience difficulties in establishing a more disciplined control of speed and a need to plan all manoeuvres much further ahead.

The prime cause of many incidents is excessive speed.

Mismanagement of approaches

With the exception of unusually difficult circumstances, the failure to stop a ship from hitting a berth, or running past its objective and sometimes even grounding, is usually the result of some misconception or misjudgement in ship handling. It has been observed, with consistent regularity, that the problems at the berth are usually created some considerable distance from it, during the approach. They are often the result of either poor management of the vessel's attitude of approach or, more frequently, an inability to establish and maintain 'slow speed control' of the ship during the approach.

Lack of slow speed control

When making an approach to any berth a ship will reach a certain position, depending upon its size, beyond which the position and speed of the ship are at all times critical to the ultimate berthing. Thereafter, whilst failure to keep the ship in the most suitable position can sometimes be rectified, this is not true if the master fails to achieve and maintain slow speed control of the ship throughout the approach. Of all the areas that can be problematic in ship handling it is in maintaining slow speed control that masters consistently appear to lack experience and therefore frequently require guidance.

Misconceptions

In many cases this is may be due to a misguided conception, for example:

a) "If I go too slow the ship will lose steerage way".
b) "I didn't want to slow down because I thought I would lose control in the wind".

These misconceptions generate a reluctance – entirely unfounded it should be said – to get the ship's way right off and even, if necessary, stopping the engine or propeller to do so. This fear of losing control simply illustrates a lack of experience in the very effective use of short bursts of moderate power, in conjunction with full rudder, with what are known as 'kicks ahead.'

Kicks ahead

In fact, the kick ahead is actually only effective with the ship at suitably low speeds anyway. Also, if the combination of rudder and propeller are not used correctly, the kick ahead cannot be utilised to keep control of the ship's heading nor, more importantly, to keep control of the ship's speed. The following errors are common:

a) Not having the rudder hard over during a kick ahead.
b) Using insufficient power for a kick ahead.
c) Keeping the power on for longer than is necessary.
d) Reducing rudder angle with too much power still on.

Checking headway

Having achieved slow speed control of the ship,

there is also a common failing to appreciate that the correct use of kicks ahead, no matter how careful, can cause the ship's headway to build up again, often in an insidious manner. It should be possible to check this headway with short periods of very limited stern power. If this is not possible then in all probability the approach speed has been allowed to become too high. It is usually the case, when long periods of high stern power are needed, that the master has not achieved slow speed control and has consequently not been unable to take full advantage of the effective use of kicks ahead! See figure 32.2.

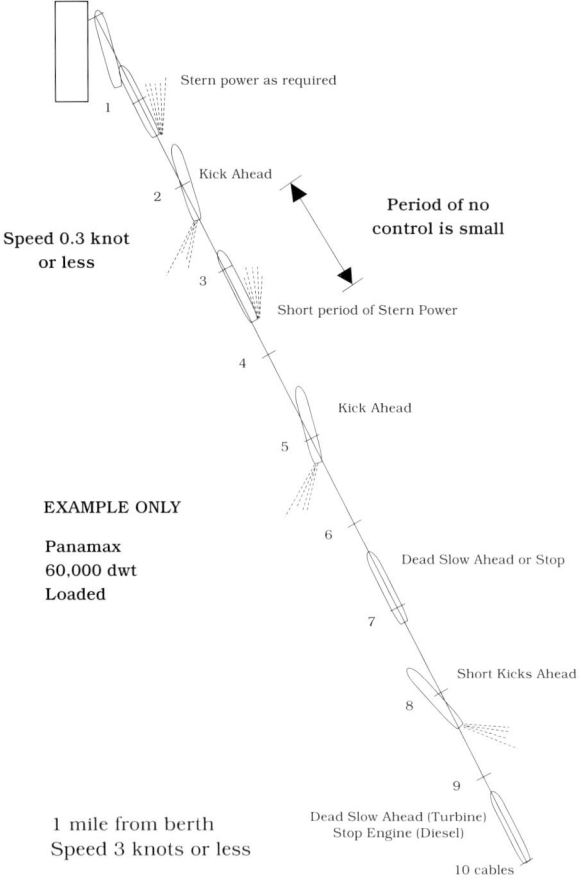

Figure 32.2 Maintaining slow speed control

The effect of wind

It is an unfortunate fact of life that, at the critical moment when a ship is slowing down in the final approach to a berth, the effect of the wind is at its worst and can often create major difficulties. The effect of the wind therefore needs to be thought out in advance, so that it can either be used to advantage, or the degree of difficulty anticipated. In some instances it may mean that tug assistance is required, or even that the objective is unattainable and should be aborted. Failure to do this has resulted in ships being placed in the most undesirable of situations, to the embarrassment of the master.

There is a strong correlation between the centre of effort of the wind (W) upon the ship and the under water area of the ship, represented by the pivotal point (P) about which the ship turns. See figure 32.3.

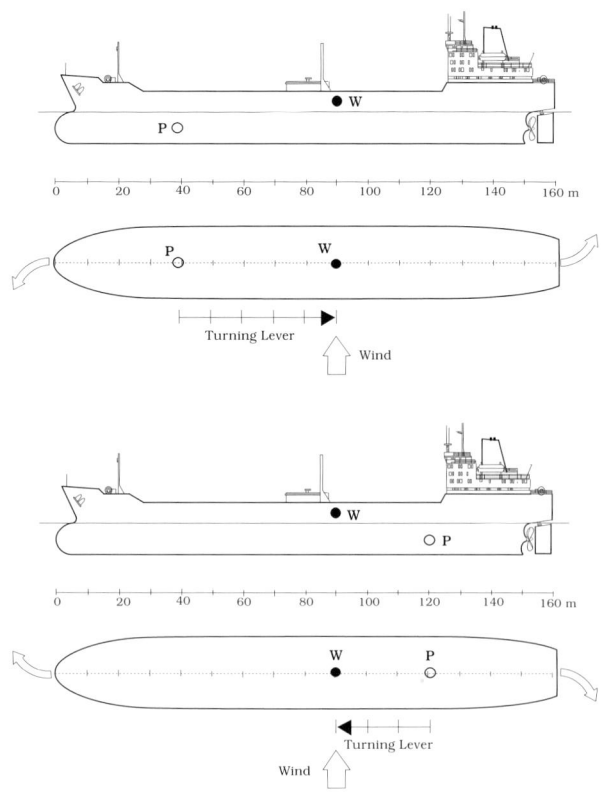

*Figure 32.3 The effect of wind –
top) with headway; bottom) with sternway*

In this example of a ship with the wind on the beam, the centre of effort of the wind is relatively static and remains where it is, but the pivot point moves forward or aft, according to whether the ship is making headway or sternway. Therefore, when the ship is making headway, it can create a strong turning moment into the wind, but as soon as the ship starts to make stern way, the bow may fall rapidly off the wind.

This effect of the wind upon the ship should always be taken into account, before committing the ship to any manoeuvre, in order to ascertain whether it will lead to problems, or can be used to advantage. In this respect it is often referred to as the poor man's tug!

A failure to turn

Slow speed control is also essential when positioning a ship for the approach to a difficult turn and there are numerous occasions when a ship needs to conduct such a turn, for example, at a pilot station, entering a buoyed channel, negotiating a bend in a channel, turning for a berth, or coming to an anchorage. It is absolutely crucial that the ship is set up correctly, in the right position and at the correct speed, before attempting any turn within limited space. It is then important to monitor the turn closely, increasing or decreasing the rate of turn as required but in exceptional circumstances, aborting the turn if necessary and feasible. It is clear in training and in the investigation of many incidents that the failure to conduct a turn satisfactorily can lead to collision or grounding. With the hindsight of monitoring officers negotiating thousands of turns in training, it is evident that the following errors are repetitive:

a) Neglecting to slow down prior to a turn.
b) Not maintaining slow speed control during the approach to a turn.
c) Failure to place the ship in the correct position before commencing the turn.
d) Not using full rudder to initiate the turn.
e) Not using enough power to initiate the turn.
f) Failure to take the power off, before easing the helm, thus allowing the speed to build up.

Spatial awareness

Any of the above errors can, individually or collectively, conspire towards failure successfully to negotiate a turn. Also, it has been apparent that some inexperienced masters can lack spatial awareness. In other words, they have attempted to turn in an area where there is insufficient space. This sometimes occurs when a master is tempted to bring a ship close inshore or venture into estuarial areas, for example, to land an injured crew member, pick up stores, or to embark a pilot when the pilot boat is off station. In these circumstances the inexperienced master is entering a high risk regime and should assess carefully beforehand the risk to the safety of the ship and his career.

Turning circles

It has been noted on numerous occasions that many masters, often those with considerable length of service, are totally unaware that the turning circles of a ship, when they are entered at any steady initial speed from Dead Slow Ahead or Full Ahead, remain relatively unchanged in terms of advance and transfer and the overall area they cover. See figure 32.4.

This is always rather surprising and in many ways alarming, because it encourages a misguided belief, with dire consequences in limited sea-room, that entering a turn at a high speed will make the turn smaller. In fact, all it actually achieves is the same turn in a shorter time! To make the standard turning circle tighter, it is absolutely essential to slow the ship right down beforehand and then use plenty of power to get the ship turning. However, this is only an initial effect and after approximately 90° of turn, with the ship's speed building up, it should be remembered that the ship will soon revert to its larger, standard turning circle again. See figure 32.5.

The effects of shallow water

There are various external forces which can have a considerable influence upon ship handling, for example, the effect of wind, tidal streams and shallow water. Of these three, the effect of shallow water is by far the most insidious. It has the ability to take a master completely by surprise with control of the ship lost in a very short space of time and with devastating consequences. It can be viewed in two broad categories:

a) Inadequate under-keel clearance.
b) Adjacent shallow water.

Inadequate under-keel clearance

If the under-keel clearance of a ship is poor it may result in a failure of that ship to follow its standard turning circle but, instead, to follow a turning circle which is alarmingly large. This can happen if the

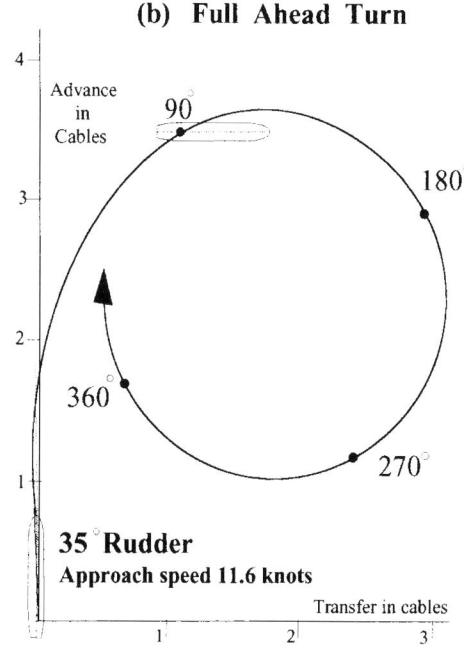

(a) Slow Ahead Turn

35° Rudder
Approach speed 5.8 knots

166m Tanker. Loaded in deep water

(b) Full Ahead Turn

35° Rudder
Approach speed 11.6 knots

Ship Handling Guide

Figure 32.4 Turning circles

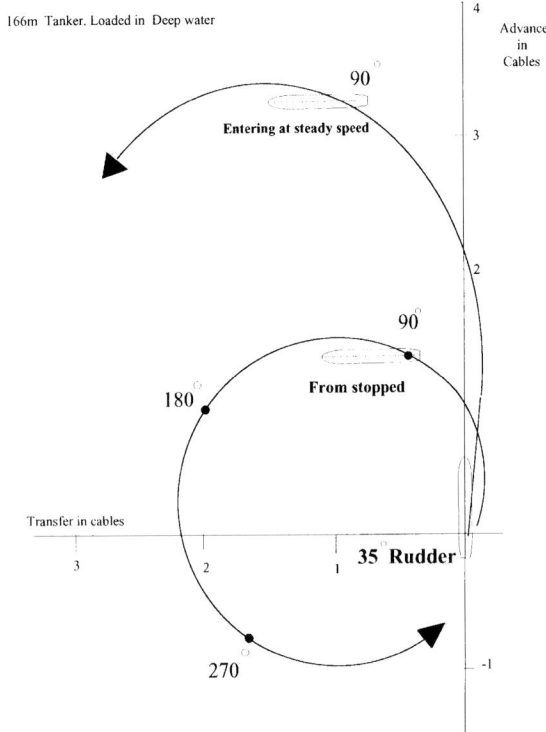

Figure 32.5 Standing turn from stopped

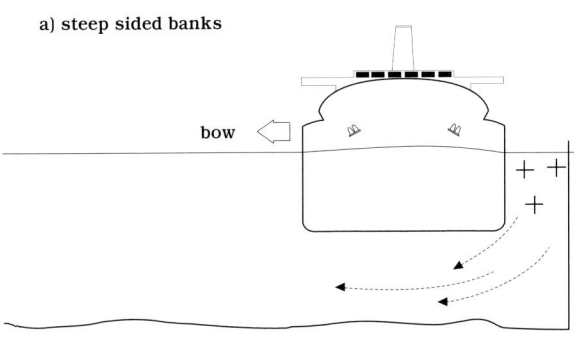

a) steep sided banks

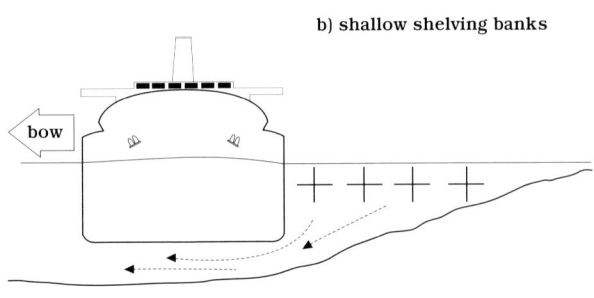

b) shallow shelving banks

Figure 32.7 Bank configuration

available depth of water is less than twice the draft, **but** incidents have occurred when the under-keel clearance was much larger due to excessive ship's speed. Those masters that have experienced the effect of shallow water on a turn will testify to watching the ship seemingly fail to turn, or respond to any power, and simply plough into another ship alongside or go heavily aground! See figure 32.6.

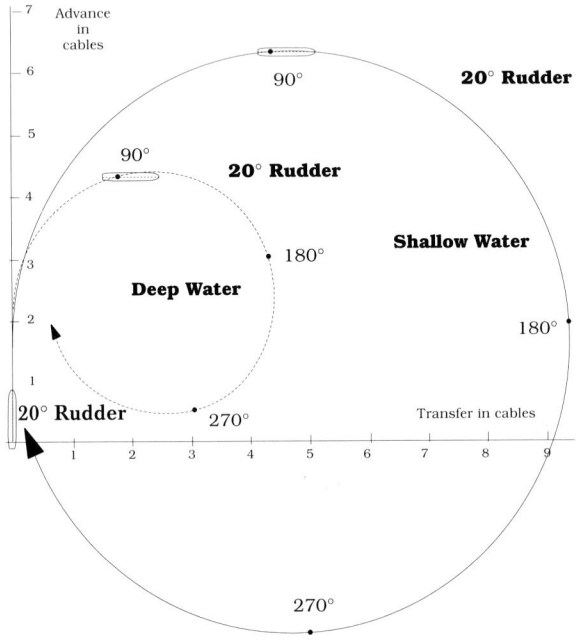

Figure 32.6 Turning in shallow water

Squat

This is an additional complication which can occur when a ship senses the close proximity of shallow water. It can be experienced at any time, regardless of whether the ship is turning and even in open water, if it is shallow enough. The bow may sink or squat and some masters have reported an increase in the forward draft of over one metre and, in the worst cases, the forward part of the hull has touched bottom. This can cause serious damage to the shell plating, even on a sandy sea bed.

Adjacent shallow water

If a ship is passing close by an adjacent area of shallow water, the resulting build up of pressure between the ship and the obstruction can unexpectedly create a violent shear of such force that any attempts to counteract it are useless. Incidents have occurred where the master has lost control of the ship, which has sheared rapidly from one side of the channel to the other, before grounding in a remarkably short space of time. In other incidents the ship has sheared across the bows of an oncoming ship, in some cases with appalling results. See figure 32.7.

Speed

In each of these situations it has often been the case that the master has passed through the area many times before without any problems. Then, unexpectedly, all the necessary components come together at once – the right trim, draft, under-keel clearance and speed.

Excessive speed in shallow water can lead to total loss of control of the ship!

Seeking tug assistance

It is clear from the foregoing resume that a master frequently may experience difficulties in ship handling, which in many cases can be anticipated with adequate training and experience. Having assessed the level of risk and the perceived threat to the safety of the ship, it may also be prudent, even in some cases mandatory, to seek tug assistance.

The use of tugs
General

Whilst tugs should never be perceived as an alternative to the correct handling of a ship, it is often clear that the degree of difficulty anticipated dictates the need for tug(s) assistance. This varies from the routine employment of tugs by large tonnage ships, for the obvious reason of size, to the occasional use by smaller vessels, even ferries, under stress of weather or in exceptionally difficult circumstances. They are available for a wide range of tasks:

a) Assisting with difficult channel turns.
b) Turning a ship off a berth.
c) Breasting and positioning onto a berth.
d) Lifting off a berth.
e) Dead ship moves.
f) Channel escort duties (tankers).
g) Attending emergencies.
h) Salvage.
i) Long distance towing.

The operation of tugs is, in itself therefore, a huge industry within an industry and the master of a ship may find himself, in some cases unexpectedly, on the periphery of this industry dealing with the additional dimension of a pilot and one or more tug skippers, all of whom may have their own ideas of how to handle the ship! In view of the extent of the industry it is unfair to expect the master of a ship to be an expert in the use of tugs. It is, however, very beneficial for the master to have a broad base of knowledge, so that he can monitor both pilots and tug skippers and communicate with them professionally. When contemplating the employment of a tug, there are several points that the master should determine:

a) What type of tug is it?
b) What is its bollard pull?
c) Where is it best to position the tug?

The type of tug

It is very important to be aware of the types of tug that are now commonly available, so that it is possible to understand their strengths and weaknesses. They may be grouped according to their working methods into the following broad categories:

a) Conventional tugs.
b) Combi tugs
c) Tractor tugs.
d) Azimuth stern drive tugs (ASD).

Conventional tugs

The conventional tug usually has a traditional single or twin screw propulsion unit *aft* and a towing hook *amidships*. Although a powerful and reliable workhorse of the industry for many years, this configuration seriously limits their manoeuvrability by today's standards in modern tug design.

Combi-tugs

Generally speaking these are older conventional tugs which have been retrofitted with some sort of bow thruster, or retractable azimuth thruster forward, to supplement their traditional propulsion unit. Their handling characteristics are improved accordingly, but they are not commonplace.

Limitations of conventional tugs

The limited manoeuvrability of conventional tugs is most evident when they are 'hooked up' to a ship that is making headway and this applies particularly to a conventional tug secured aft. They are also relatively slow at letting go and repositioning elsewhere around the ship. The biggest concern, however, is their vulnerability to the effect of interaction and the risk of girting.

Interaction

In very simple terms, a ship making way creates a zone of differing water pressures around its hull. In the vicinity of the bow there will be a positive pressure extending out from the ship, whilst along the ship's side and around the area of the stern, there exists a suction area.

The force of these pressure zones is increased when a ship is in shallow water and if the ship's speed is too high!

When conventional tugs enter any of these areas their handling characteristics are seriously affected because of their limited manoeuvrability and their safety is at great risk. In the worst case scenario a tug may be turned across the bow and capsized, with appalling rapidity and catastrophic consequences. See figure 32.8.

Girting a tug

With the towing line secure to a towing hook amidships, conventional tugs have always been vulnerable to a phenomenon know variously as girting, girthing, or girding, according to various sources around the world. It occurs when a tug is trapped with the tow line leading out on its beam, whilst being pulled bodily sideways by a ship, at a speed which prohibits the tug from doing anything about it. In many cases the tug is capsized with astonishing speed and quickly sinks. See figure 32.9. The prime cause of girthing may be due to any one of the following:

a) The ship turning away from the tug too quickly.
b) The ship proceeding at too high a speed.
c) Lack of cooperation between the ship's master and the tug skipper.
d) Poor communications with the tug skipper.

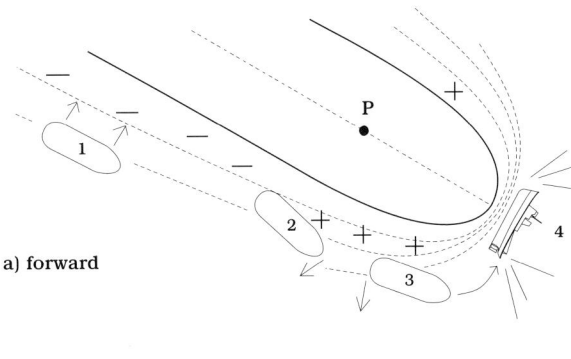

a) forward

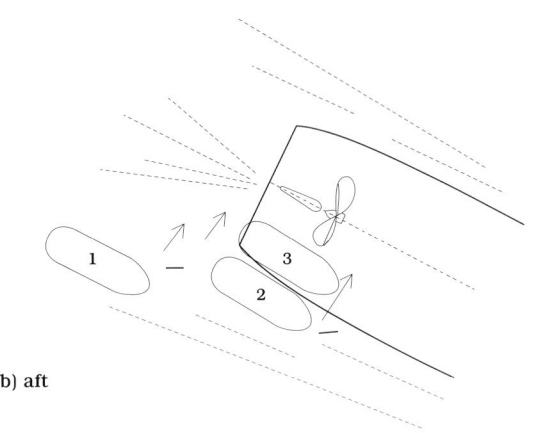

b) aft

Figure 32.8 Tug interaction

a) forward

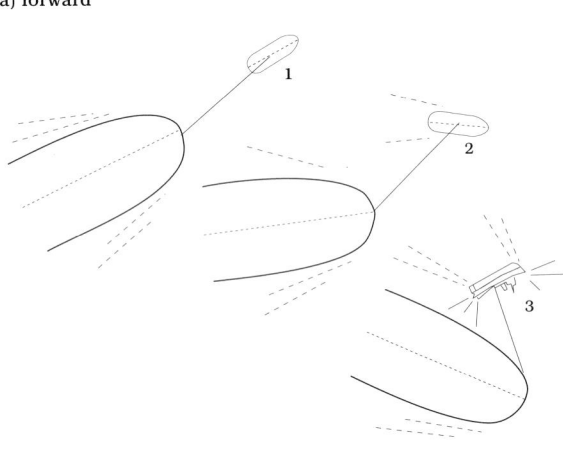

b) aft

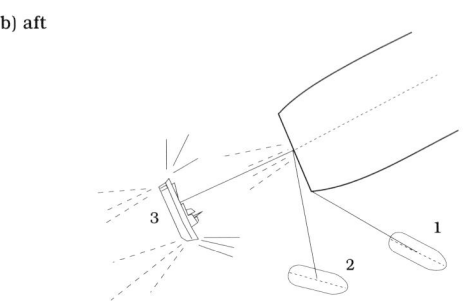

Figure 32.8 Girting a conventional tug

The sight of a tug being girted is an awesome and frightening sight. It usually happens too swiftly to activate quick release of the towline and leaves absolutely no time to evacuate the crew before the tug capsizes, often with a tragic loss of life.

Tractor tugs

The tractor tug differs completely in design to the conventional tug in that its tow hook is situated *aft*, whereas the tug's power is *forward* of the tow hook. The tug's propulsion comes from two multi-directional propeller units, sited athwartships, directly under the bridge. Tractor tugs are common throughout Europe, the most well known manufacturers being Voith Schneider and Schottel. They have outstanding manoeuvrability, can thrust through 360° and are able to work anywhere around the ship, repositioning quickly when required. They are consequently much less vulnerable to girthing and interaction.

Azimuth stern drive tugs (ASDs)

Although generally considered a tractor tug, the ASD is actually more of a compromise between a conventional tug and a tractor tug. Like the tractor tugs they also derive their power from twin multi-directional propulsion units, sited athwartships, but on the ASD these units are situated *aft*, in the same position as the propeller of the conventional tug. Also, again like the conventional tug, they have a tow hook *amidships*, but are better known for their exceptional versatility when commonly working *a tow line from the tug's bow winch*, by which means they are then effectively operating as a tractor tug. They were originally manufactured and widespread in Japan and are now, consequently, commonplace throughout the Pacific basin.

Mixed tug fleets

In many ports of the world there exist fleets of tugs which are a very mixed lot, in terms of design, type, age, horsepower, bollard pull and manoeuvrability. In this respect it is important that the master is able to make a modest evaluation of the tugs that are employed to assist the ship, in order to avoid directing a tug to a position where it is inadequate for the task intended. This is not particularly problematic for the master of a large vessel, working with several tugs on a regular basis and with the advice of a pilot. It can be problematic, however, for the master of a small ship, employing a single tug on rare occasions, to assist in exceptionally difficult circumstances, adverse weather conditions or emergencies. In these situations the master may unexpectedly be called upon to communicate coherently with a tug skipper and to make a value judgement as to where to position the tug for the particular manoeuvre or task intended.

Positioning a tug

When a tug is secured to a ship either alongside in a push-pull mode, or on a tow line forward or aft, it will exert a force in tonnes (bollard pull) that is working upon a turning lever within the ship.

It is most important to understand that this turning lever will be working upon a pivot point, the position of which moves according to whether the ship is either stopped, making headway, or making sternway. See figure 32.10.

In view of this and in order to make good use of a tug and achieve the best results, it is crucial to position it in the right place. It is therefore necessary to ask the following questions:

a) What type of tug is it?
b) What is the intended manoeuvre?
c) Will the ship be predominately making headway, backing, or swinging?
d) Where will the ship's pivot point be?

Whilst this may seem a little bewildering at first, these few basic concepts are simple to work with and also help to explain some of the important operational differences between the conventional tug and the tractor tug, particularly with regards to:

a) Tugs on long lines.
b) Tugs alongside.

Tugs on long lines

The effectiveness of tugs on long lines can be discussed with the simple example of a single tug, attending a ship during a channel or river transit. Also, it is in this role that the differing capabilities of the conventional tug and tractor tug are clearly illustrated. See figure 32.11.

Conventional tugs

In this situation the conventional tug's relatively poor manoeuvrability usually ensures that it is traditionally and quite correctly secured on a long line forward. This unfortunately results in the following:

a) With headway it is too close to the pivot point and is therefore working on a poor turning lever.
b) As the ship's speed increases it can only work effectively within a limited arc of operation.
c) It is vulnerable to girthing.
d) It cannot assist the ship to slow down, i.e. braking.
e) If required, it will be slow in repositioning.

In the light of these comments it is evident that the conventional tug cannot, in this position, effectively employ it's full potential in terms of total bollard pull and is therefore not particularly efficient. There is, however, no feasible operational alternative.

Tractor tugs

On the other hand a tractor tug, or an ASD tug, can be employed on a long line aft, with the following results:

a) It will be working a long way from the pivot point and creates an excellent turning moment.
b) It can paravane out, using just the weight of the tug on the tow line to assist the ship.
c) With it's manoeuvrability it is safe from girting.

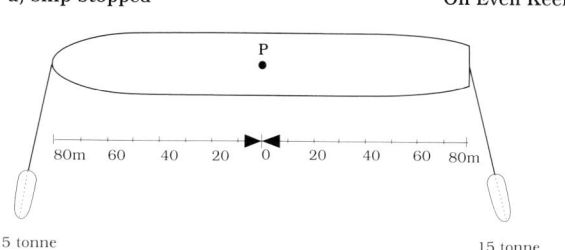

a) ship stopped

On Even Keel

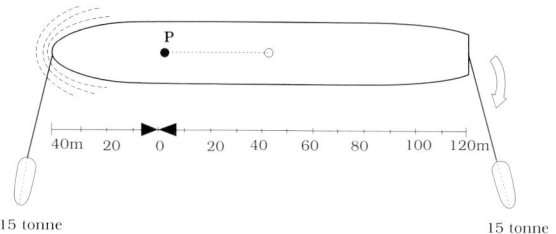

b) making headway

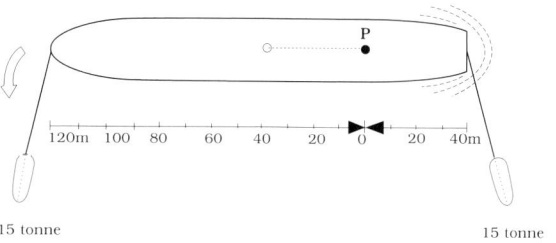

c) making sternway

Figure 32.10 Turning levers and moments

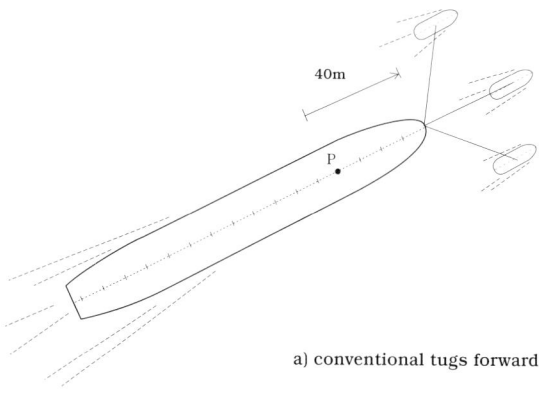

a) conventional tugs forward

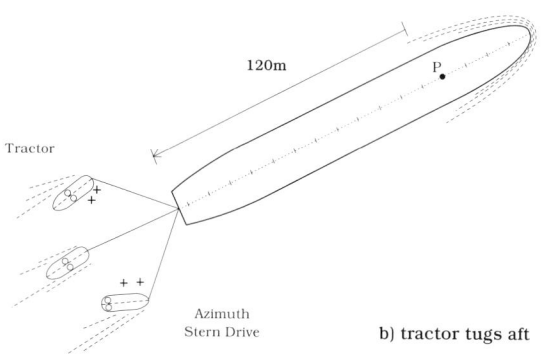

b) tractor tugs aft

Figure 32.11 Channel escort

d) It can assist the ship in braking and stopping.

e) It can quickly reposition alongside the ship when feasible.

f) The ASD tug is very effective in this role.

Tugs alongside

When a tug is positioned alongside it is still important to assess its position relative to the pivot point. If, for example, a tug is made fast in an area roughly adjacent to the pivot point, it will not be working upon a turning lever of any consequence, but will, instead, have a tendency to push the ship bodily sideways. This is very useful when employing one tug, because it can be used in much the same way as a bow thruster and will facilitate breasting onto a berth, or lifting off.

If, however, the tug is required to assist the ship with steering, it is preferable to position the tug as far aft as possible, so that it is some distance from the pivot point and working on a good turning lever. See figure 32.12. Alternatively, if the ship is making sternway, the roles are reversed. For example, when lifting off and backing away from a berth, it would be prudent to place the tug aft near the pivot point, to assist with lifting off, but as far forward as possible, to assist with steering when backing.

With their ability to thrust with full power in any direction, tractor tugs are particularly useful when working alongside, added to which their versatility

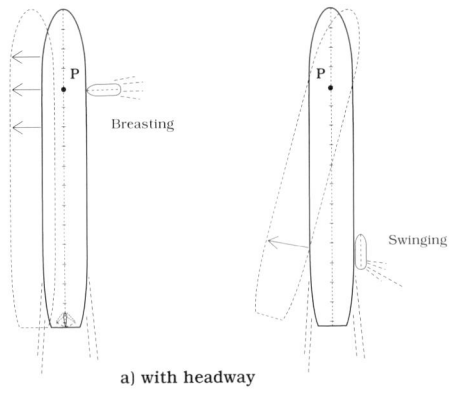

a) with headway

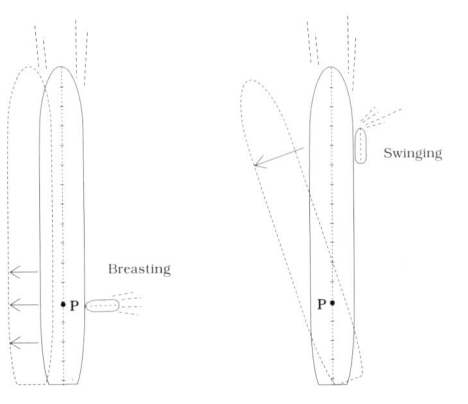

b) with sternway

Figure 32.12 Tugs alongside

enables them to reposition quickly and effectively, as required by the master. In comparison to the more ponderous conventional tug, the tractor tug is therefore well suited to attending a ship in a single tug capacity.

The use of tugs world wide is a vast and complex subject, that is well beyond the scope of this chapter. Consequently it has been necessary to oversimplify the subject. It is hoped, nevertheless, that these basic examples will serve the ship master with a simple method of assessing the optimum position for the most efficient use of a tug(s) and upon which to build practical experience, when observing tug operations in the future.

Training
General

The level of specialised training, dedicated solely to ship handling, has come a long way from pushing small wooden models around on a desk. There is now, world wide, a bewildering array of computer based training facilities, all of which purport to offer some sort of ship handling simulation. They range from low budget desk top systems to million pound, full mission, ship's bridge simulators. Although too numerous to discuss individually in detail, it is important to look briefly at their broad application in terms of ship handling and they have be categorised as follows:

a) Desk top computers
b) Radar simulators.
c) Ship's bridge simulators.
d) Manned models.

Caution

It is very important that officers are extremely cautious of computer programmes purporting to be a correct representation of ships' manoeuvring characteristics.

They may only be as accurate as the computer programmer thought they should be and may not have been validated by an experienced ship handler. It is, therefore, not unknown for them to contain serious errors! (See reference 3).

Desktop computers

Many manufacturers market desktop computers with a standard visual display unit (VDU) and a variety of ship handling programmes installed. They are low budget systems which are easy to install, both ashore and on board ship and can be programmed with a ship's individual manoeuvring data. Although some do offer excellent, high definition, VDU simulations of ship handling scenarios, it is difficult to raise the level of realism and credibility above that of a computer game. However, if they are viewed as an information reference source and retrieval system, they can be a valuable learning aid.

Radar simulators

It is a relatively inexpensive progression from a basic desk top computer to a computer which simulates a radar picture and has a passing resemblance, frequently poor, of a ship's bridge added to it. In many examples this will only consist of simple engine controls and basic navigational instruments, in a room that is very unrepresentative of a ship's bridge and with no visual scene! This type of system, therefore, offers little as a training facility for ship handling, but is very suitable for training officers in RADAR, ARPA and VTS operations, where familiarisation in blind pilotage is a major factor.

Ship's bridge simulators

There are now many ship's bridge simulators around the world which are constantly being upgraded, or replaced, with the very latest technology. They usually represent a multi-million pound investment programme and should offer a full scale bridge with daylight, night time, or twilight visual scenes, in a wide variety of ports and many differing types of ship. The degree of realism and credibility that they create is excellent and incorporates all of the inherent levels of psychological pressure that will be experienced on board a real ship.

Although many of them do specialise in dedicated ship handling courses, they are best suited to river and channel navigation, so the use of these simulators is frequently directed towards training in bridge resource management and passage planning. There is always, nevertheless, a strong ship handling input on such courses but, when handling a large ship in simulated 'real time', the ratio of actual time spent ship handling in comparison to the length of time on the course is limited.

Manned models

With experience in ship handling training, using everything from blackboards to small models on tables, desk top computers, full mission simulators and manned models, it is undoubtedly the latter that is the most successful of all. The manned models used are generally quite large, with an average length of eight metres. They weigh several tonnes and have sophisticated electronics on board to ensure the correct scaled times and responses of the anchor windlasses, bow thrusters, rudders and propellers.

Operating in open waters, they are influenced by all the same variable, unpredictable factors that influence a real ship, so that officers are able to develop that important 'feel' for handling a ship and experience the 'seat of the pants' element associated with it.

Also, because of their quicker, scaled, operating times, it is possible to practice and re-practice various aspects of ship handling repeatedly, thus gaining an enormous amount of experience in a short period of time.

Manned model facilities

The manned model is, therefore, an outstanding tool for training officers in ship handling. There are currently three manned model facilities in the world that run dedicated ship handling courses.:

a) Port Grenoble, Lyon, France.
b) The Warsash Maritime Centre, England.
c) Poland.

The first two, at Grenoble and Warsash, are well established, well known and highly successful, whilst the latter in Poland is relatively new. They each offer excellent training facilities and run similar, five day courses, with lectures and discussions, followed by practical 'hands on' experience in every important aspect of ship handling, for example:

Dedicated ship handling courses
a) Stopping.
b) Slow speed control.
c) Turning.
d) Effect of wind.
e) Bow thruster work.
f) Channel transits.
g) Berthing.
h) Interaction.
i) Anchor work (dredging).
j) The use of tugs.
k) Specialised operations i.e. SBM and FSU.

These facilities offer quality training in ship handling for any chief officer about to be promoted to master and also, in many instances, essential updating experience for serving masters.

Furthermore, as many pilots and masters will testify, this type of training does not stand alone, but is supportive of ship handling afloat with a real ship.

Nautical Institute publications

It has been the objective of this chapter to offer only a broad overview of some of those aspects of ship handling, including the use of tugs, which are of issue and importance to the ship master.

For more information and a more complete guide to these and many other aspects of ship handling, including the use of tugs, that it has not been possible to include in this chapter, the following Nautical Institute publications should be referred to:

References

1   Rowe, R.W., Captain FNI, *The Shiphandler's Guide for Masters and Navigating Officers, Pilots and Tug Masters*, The Nautical Institute, 1999.
2   Hensen, H., Captain FNI, *Tug Use in Port (A Practical Guide)*, The Nautical Institute, 1997.
3   Hensen, H., Captain FNI, *Ship Bridge Simulators – a project handbook*, The Nautical Institute, 1999.

Chapter 33

ANCHORING SYSTEMS – SOME INSIGHTS FOR MARINERS

by Captain A.O. Ojo and Professor J. King MSc FNI, UWIST Cardiff

Introduction

THE PRACTICE OF ANCHORING ships with a weighted line has been followed for centuries. Until recently, there has been little development in anchoring technology. As ships have become larger, anchors and cables have become heavier, windlasses stronger. But the standard stockless anchor commonly employed in merchant ships has been around almost unchanged for 100 years. In recent years, it has become increasingly clear that the capacity of conventional anchoring systems to serve large, modern vessels is now seriously in doubt.

Today, the anchor, cable and windlass of a ULCC or large bulk carrier must be regarded as an extremely fragile arrangement, for all that it may look massive when one is standing on the forecastle head. As ships have increased in size, anchors have become proportionately lighter, cables proportionately shorter, windlasses more vulnerable to shock loads. In consequence, the anchoring process must be conducted with extreme caution in such vessels lest the gear be carried away. The anchor, a monstrous weight often in excess of 25 tonnes, must be let go with the utmost delicacy, with the ship travelling over the ground at no more than a few centimetres per second. There is no margin for error. And in consequence the notion that the anchors can be deployed in emergency situations is no longer tenable. Indeed, even the 35-tonne anchors fitted in very large vessels are totally inadequate to secure them in anything but the gentlest conditions. As has been pointed out (in the discussion to reference 1), the anchors of a 542,000 dwt tanker are proportionately only one fifth as heavy as those of an 18,000 dwt vessel, and the cables proportionately only half as long.

Much experience has, of course, been gained in the offshore industry in recent years, where the securing of large fixed structures has presented challenging problems. Various new types of anchor have been designed and used with considerable success. There has, however, been little benefit to merchant shipping apart from these advances.

Unfortunately, merchant ships are supposed to be mobile most of the time. Being anchored is a temporary state. There, ease of deployment and retrieval is a crucial design consideration for their anchoring systems, to such an extent that weight and holding power may be sacrificed to achieve it.

Given their inadequacy, it is hardly surprising that anchoring systems should fail frequently. Anchors are lost or damaged, cables break, windlasses are unable to cope with the loads placed upon them. The extent of these failures has been highlighted by several recent studies [1, 2, 3, 4] which have shown, not only that the problem is a serious one, but that it is exacerbated by important technical and operational factors. There appear to be, for example, widely held misconceptions about the capabilities of anchoring systems and the operational procedures which should be adopted to meet them. There is, moreover, ample evidence of inadequate maintenance, poor design and perhaps most significant to us here, inadequate training.

Figure 33.1 summarises the major causes of anchoring system failures in VLCCs[1]. Although these categories of failures are very broad, it is clear that inadequacies of design and inadequacies of operation share almost equal responsibility for system failures.

There are several ways in which the present problem can be approached. We may attempt to design out weaknesses in the conventional system by better engineering; we may attempt to circumvent weaknesses by better operational procedures (remembering that seamanship has been defined as the art of overcoming poor design); or we may look for alternative ways to secure vessels. The first two of these are likely to be palliatives rather than solutions since it is becoming clear that for large vessels even the concept of anchoring in its traditional sense is unsound. The last alternative suggested above might be described as flying in the face of experience. Three thousand years of anchoring history must be telling us something.

However the problem is addressed, its solution will not be achieved without cost. Whether the failure of the system leads to the loss of an anchor or the loss of a ship, the costs involved are significant. There is now available sufficient information on such failures for their likelihood in any particular vessel to be assessed. This means that cost benefit analysis can be employed to help identify measures which might secure improvements in the operation of ships.

We are arguing here that there are grounds for concern that conventional anchoring systems are inadequate. But we are also conscious that these inadequacies only become unacceptable when there is sufficient pressure to do something about them. For individual ship operators, this point is reached when it appears that there is some net benefit to be gained from taking action. For the shipping community as a whole it comes when the rules that they all follow are

Background cause of failure	Per cent
Engineering design	38.1
Operational practice	33.3
Combination of design and operational practice	14.3
Inadequate maintenance	9.5
Others	4.8

Figure 33.1 Anchoring system failures

Operation	Component			
	Motor	Gearing	Brakes	Bearings
Letting go		X	X	
Weighing	X	X		X
At anchor			X	X

Figure 33.2 Anchoring system failures

changed. This probably means that, notwithstanding all the technical weaknesses of modern systems, relatively cheap relief such as might be brought about by better training is likely to be preferred to more radical measures.

What, then, are the areas to which attention might be given?

Improved engineering

Surveys ([1, 2]) published elsewhere have provided ample, detailed evidence of areas of weakness in the engineering of conventional anchoring systems. Anchors, cables, hawse pipes and stoppers all give cause for concern. But the most vulnerable part of the system from the purely engineering standpoint is the windlass. Both during the anchoring process and when lying at anchor, the windlass components are subject to substantial dynamic loads which, in practically every case, must be resisted by a windlass brake of startling crudity. Table 2 identifies the principal components at risk.

Windlasses have always been regarded as major items of safety equipment. This is reflected in, for example, the prohibition of lap and lead in windlass steam chests which goes back to the nineteenth century. But at the present time very little is done to measure the performance of a windlass, even though there is ample evidence to suggest that in many ships they are often operating very close to their practical limits. This is unfortunate, since the information gained from better performance monitoring would provide evidence not only of the current state of the equipment for assessing maintenance needs, but also for improving overall design.

Windlass control is an area of significant concern. Traditionally the deployment of the anchor and cable is under the control of a manually-operated windlass brake. While this was no doubt acceptable in relatively small vessels (and carpenters developed considerable 'feel' for the task) it is barely so today in large ships. The anchoring environment is dangerous, the operation extremely sensitive to unskilled hands and it is probably unrealistic to continue to be satisfied with manual control in such circumstances, especially when braking arrangements are themselves physically inadequate. It is remarkable that disc brakes are still rarely employed in windlasses, and automatic control of their application is still highly uncommon. The performance of windlass brakes is also sensitive to the content of the lining materials and the considerable amount of heat generated when they are applied. Some attempts have been made recently to monitor heat dissipation in brake drums.

There is clearly ample scope for improving the windlass and several new designs have been proposed, including one hydraulically operated type which is claimed to be capable of absorbing the loads likely to be experienced in emergency stopping manoeuvres.

Improving operational procedures

Ships are generally not provided with information concerning the operational capabilities of their anchoring systems. This means that anchoring operations depend for their success very much upon the experience of the master. There is some data now available on such things as brake liner efficiency, cable scope for a given depth/draught ratio, limiting cable tensions, windlass overloads and safe anchoring speeds, which could usefully assist masters, but at the present time these are not usually provided to ships.

In order to improve operational procedures there is a need for both better information on how the anchoring system actually performs in practice and for better training. Such monitoring of the system as is actually done at the moment is fairly rudimentary. At the very least, performance monitoring should include:

1. Measurement of cable length deployed.
White paint and seizing wire is the rough and ready system of cable marking which history has bequeathed to us. It hardly needs further comment. Very few vessels are fitted with cable meters.

2. Chain speed and acceleration.
In both manual and automatic operation this information is necessary if correct brake application rates are to be achieved. This is a vitally important aspect of anchoring, since correct brake application rates can reduce shock loads, and cable run away.

3. Brake liner temperature gradients.
It is common practice for the windlass brake to be applied frequently at short intervals. This practice can lead to serious risk of failure because of the high temperatures that it induces in the brake liners. Heat fading is a well documented

phenomenon. But without either the means to detect its onset or even an appreciation of its effects, operators are unlikely to apply the brake in the most effective way.

4. Windlass-bearing pressure.
Monitoring windlass-bearing pressure would allow the operator to assess the level of stresses within the anchoring system.

Many seafarers recognise that anchoring arrangements are inadequate in large ships, although the precise nature of the inadequacies are not always clearly understood. This, in part, may be due to the fact that few seafarers have received anything more than the most cursory training in anchoring practice. Many seamanship text books, for example, do no more than promote traditional practices which are quite inappropriate for larger modern vessels. And their recommendations on, for example, speed over the ground when anchoring, would be suicidal if followed in today's larger vessels.

Anchoring is a practical operation for which practical training is necessary but rarely given. Clearly this is easier said than done. There is no question of training on the job (although ad hoc learning by doing, which is not quite the same thing, has been the normal way to acquire most seamanship skills). This applies to much maritime training, of course, such as watchkeeping and shiphandling, and in recent years there has been growing use of simulation techniques to provide opportunities for practice. Anchoring is ideally suited to simulation training.

Computer-based simulation training[6] allows the anchoring system behaviour to be demonstrated. It provides a means for realistic practice to be undertaken in a variety of circumstances, without risk to either trainee or vessel, and it also provides a means for examining the skills of trainees.

The value of such training depends very much on the validity of the mathematical models upon which it is based. Several such models are available and attempts are being made at UWIST to produce the necessary software to form the basis of an anchoring package.

An initial survey of seafarers has revealed that the essential constituents of any anchor handling training course are:

1. Practical anchoring operations.
2. Anchoring forces.
3. Operational planning.
4. Cable deployment.
5. Communications.
6. Safety.

Alternatives to conventional anchoring systems

If the inadequacy of conventional anchoring systems is no longer acceptable, then alternatives have to be considered. Two alternatives suggest themselves.

One is to employ the dynamic positioning techniques now well established for vessels in the offshore industry. Another is to so manage the operation of large vessels that the need to anchor is reduced.

Dynamic positioning is expensive and has been installed to date in vessels which are substantially smaller than those which we are principally concerned with here. The technical problems associated with implementing such systems in large tankers are considerable. But that is not to say that considering them would not be rewarding.

Alternatively, solving the problem by avoiding it is a possibly fruitful approach for some trades, although it is not without cost. Since the present anchoring arrangements cannot be used for emergency operations, we need to be concerned only with planned anchoring. Good communications with some ingenuity might be exploited to plan voyages so that 'steaming-off' rather than anchoring is the usual way of waiting. The establishment of fixed, adequately-sized moorings at locations commonly used for anchorages would also help.

Both of these alternatives are more easily said than done. But after so many years of using anchors, no alternative which may be proposed is going to be simple – almost by definition. The inadequacy of anchors and cables for large ships will only become unacceptable, however, when there is sufficient discussion of the subject to generate the necessary concern.

Recommendations and observations

❍ In large ships, soon after brake release the rate of unrestricted descent of anchor and cable becomes excessive. Conventional band brakes operate at, or beyond, the limits of their capability in such circumstances.

❍ Repeated applications of the band brake after short lengths of cable have been paid out can keep the system under control, but overheating of the brake may still lead to a reduction in braking efficiency and subsequent loss of anchor and cable.

❍ Walking out the anchor can be recommended as a means of restricting velocities and loads in the system. Maximum benefit will be obtained if the anchor is walked out to the bottom or within a few fathoms of it. Attention must, however, be given to restricting the walkout speed so that damage to the windlass gearing and motor are avoided.

❍ Speed-limiting devices operating on the band brake help to relieve the windlass operator in the difficult task of controlling cable deployment, but undue reliance should not be placed on such systems.

❍ Even on windlasses fitted with auxiliary braking devices, or energy absorbers, it is advisable that the anchor should be walked out as recommended above.

○ Once the required scope of cable has been deployed, the vessel should be allowed to bring-up on the bow stopper. In any manoeuvring on the anchor, the stopper should normally be engaged.

○ The speed of the ship over the ground when the anchor is let go, and whilst the cable is being paid out, needs to be minimised. This requirement is more critical for larger ships, worsening weather conditions and decreasing water depth. The use of main engines may be required to achieve this. For a VLCC the permissible speed is of the order of 1/4 knot. Accurate determination of such low speeds over the ground is difficult.

○ The energy absorption ability of a range of anchor cables indicates that increasing scope should be used with decreasing water depth. Higher scopes are required in ballast conditions.

○ On large ships, conventional band brakes frequently operate at, or near, their limits of capability. More frequent failures are probably avoided by palliative measures taken by sea staff, for example, walking-out the anchor prior to brake release.

○ Designers of deck machinery are already considering, and in some cases have produced, alternative or auxiliary braking devices. At present, none of the devices considered is without some shortcomings, although disc brakes of one type or another appear to be the most promising for routine anchoring. Further development is needed.

○ At present, most operators have very little information as to system performance. Instrumentation which shows cable speed during free-running and walking-out, length of cable paid out and loads in the system would be helpful. Limits of windlass speed during walking-out should be clearly indicated to the operator.

○ On large ships the bow stopper should preferably be of the double-shearing type.

○ Liaison between the shipbuilder and the manufacturer of deck machinery is vital at an early stage if leads of cable and deck layout are to be acceptable.

○ Consideration should be given to suitable materials with which to coat the brake drum of the band brake to reduce efficiency losses caused by corrosion and contamination.

○ Consideration should be given to water-lubricated synthetic bearings. These would help to reduce the on-board maintenance by sea staff.

○ When brake liners are renewed, it is important that at least the minimum recommended number of screws securing the liner to the band are fitted. The performance of the brake will be seriously affected if the liner is not properly fitted.

○ The recommended mating surface for the brake lining should be maintained. Experience suggests that overlaid stainless steel will disintegrate after a few anchoring operations.

○ The thickness of the brake liner is not a good indicator of brake liner effectiveness. New liners can be ineffective due to heat level, wetness and corrosion.

○ New liners should be bedded-in before use.

○ Training in the anchoring of large vessels is recommended. This should underline the differences in procedure required on large vessels compared to smaller vessels.

○ Such training could be aided by computer simulation, but should also include supervised anchoring.

References

1. King, J. and Ojo, A.O., *Some Practical Aspects of Anchoring Large Ships*, Paper No 8, RINA Spring Meetings 1983.

2. Ojo A.O., Byrne, D. and Brook, A.J., *An Investigation of Ships' Anchoring Systems*, General Council of British Shipping, Technical Report TR/100, October 1982.

3. Brinkmeyer, H. and Russel, K., *Dynamic Behaviour of Anchor Windlasses*, Vol. 1 & 2, Shell International Marine Ltd., London, 1983.

4. Brook, A.J. and Byrne, D., *The Dynamic Behaviour of Single and Multiple Moored Vessels*, Papers No 9, RINA Spring Meetings, 1983.

5. Ojo A.O., *Survey of Anchoring Systems*, SEAWAYS, The Nautical Institute, Sept. 1983.

6. King, J., *Applications of Small Computers to Shipboard Training*, Paper No 7, RINA Spring Meetings, 1983.

Chapter 34

ANCHORING AND ANCHORAGE IN STRONG TIDES

by Captain S. Chaudhari FNI

Captain Somesh Chaudhari served his four years' apprenticeship leading to second mate, followed by mate and master, while with the India Steamship Co. from 1949 to 1958. He was assistant harbourmaster Calcutta Port 1958-1965, chief officer followed by 18 years as master with India Steamship Co. 1965-1984, executed small craft deliveries 1984-1985 and is now master OSV, Bombay Ocean Marine Agency.

Introduction

THE PORT OF BHAVNAGAR, in the Gulf of Cambay, has the strongest tidal streams in India. During neaps at half tide the tidal stream runs at over four knots. In springs it averages over seven knots. In equinoctial tides it is known to exceed nine knots.

The port has been used by power-driven vessels over half a century, to whom losing anchors in this area has been a fairly regular feature. 'Anchoring a vessel in a tidal way' and 'tending a vessel at anchor' appear in the syllabus for 'master's.' But it does not take into consideration the extreme tidal streams of Bhavnagar. The premises to begin with are:

- A cable rarely breaks under even strain, but invariably breaks when jerked with more than two to three shackles out.
- Anchoring with tide running is inviting trouble. Await slack water where possible.
- Be forearmed with knowledge of the approximate direction of ebb and flood, respectively.

Normal anchoring procedure consists of putting the engine astern and awaiting the propeller wash to reach just beyond the half length of the vessel. With the engines stopped, the anchor is dropped. The vessel at this stage is assumed to have no way on her or at best a feeble sternway. But supposing the vessel arrives at a time when the first of the tide has made, yet the stream is hard to discern in the absence of buoy or another vessel at anchor. Conventional anchoring could lead to burning-off the brake shoe or in the extreme, the cable parting.

Practical anchoring cases

Arrive at the anchorage with bare steerage way. Use a short burst of stern movement. When the wash just begins to catch up with the stern, let go the anchor. Hard brake it with one shackle in the water. It is impossible to part the cable or burn the lining at this stage.

The following possibilities will present themselves vis-a-vis the cable lead thereafter:

1. The cable lead remains up and down.

Inference: The vessel has no way upon her. Possibly it is near slack water.

Figure 34.1

Action: Pay out to required length, as the weight comes along.

2. The cable is leading astern and dragging; at the same time the stern is swinging round.

(Check the slack water time).

Inference: Headway exists; also the tide is making from the stern. The vessel is snubbing round.

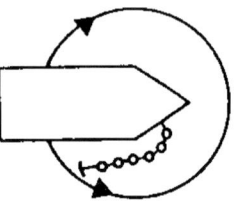

Figure 34.2

Action: Give a burst of stern movement while the cable leads between 4 and 8 o'clock. Stop engines thereafter. Let the vessel come round. When the cable starts dragging while leading between 10 and 2 o'clock, keep engines going ahead assisting with appropriate helm to swing, till the cable stops dragging. At this stage, the vessel has no way upon her. Stop engines and commence 'paying and checking' as the weight comes. In a strong tideway, depending on the strain on the cable, a 'kick on the engines' of short duration may be necessary before paying out the final length.

3. The cable is leading astern: dragging: vessel swinging but unlikely to turn due to decelerating swing.

(Check time for ascertaining flow.)

Inference: Headway exists. The vessel is stemming the tide.

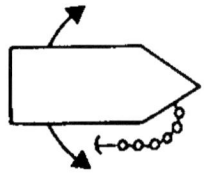

Figure 34.3

Action: Come astern on the engines. The moment the cable stops dragging, stop engines. The vessel now has no way upon her. Wait for the vessel to drift down, enabling the cable to lead ahead. 'Pay and check' using engines, and anchor as in figure 34.1.

4. *The cable leading ahead: dragging steady.*

Inference: The vessel is stemming the tide and has acquired sternway.

Action: Go ahead on the engines till the cable stops dragging. Then anchor as in figure 34.1.

5. *This is unlikely to happen but is a possibility.*

The cable is leading ahead: dragging: the stern is swinging acceleratedly.

Inference: The tide is from the stern and the vessel has acquired stern way.

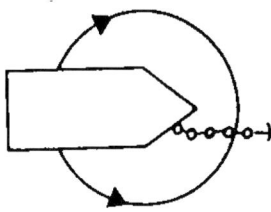

Figure 34.4

Action: Go ahead on the engines till the cable stops dragging. Then anchor her as in figure 34.2.

To summarise

a) In a tidal way, use an anchor with one shackle, or at most 'one and a half' in the water for guidance to vessel's way, vessel's speed, tide direction.

b) Always pay out little at a time (a couple of fathoms) and check. This may at worst make the anchor drag a bit. Eventually in Bhavnagar's anchoring ground, which is mud, the anchor will sink and hold the vessel with six shackles or more out.

Yawing

As the strength of the tide increases at the anchorage, the vessel grows listless – i.e. she yaws about. The cable leads – namely the hawse pipes – being 'off the centre line' the vessel's natural 'lie' becomes a 'cant' opposite to the anchor. In weak tides, this results in mild yawing. But when the tide is racing at four knots or more, the vessel becomes one giant pendulum. The inherent danger to such yaws is anchor dragging and, to a lesser extent, the cable parting.

The mechanism of this yaw is better understood if one observes a vessel drifting down 'stemming the tide' on the Hooghly. So long as she stems the tide, the drift rate is less. The stem slices the tide, and the water flows benignly past the bows. But let the vessel fall off, exposing one bow more to the tide than the other. The exposed bow becomes a tide catcher. The vessel swings merrily on till the bow loses its potency due to change of its angle to the tide. In this process, the drift rate of the vessel progressively increases, indicating greater pressure to the hull.

A vessel at anchor in a tide way running at over four knots behaves exactly in the same fashion except its drift limited by tensioning and easing of the cable finds expression in increasing yaw.

In figure 34.5, the configuration of '8' is an approximation of the path traced out by a starboard-anchored hawse. This is generated by the variation in pressure on the vessel's hull due to yaw: 'C' to 'A' represents the surge ahead brought about by extreme cable stretch combined with reduced hull pressure through reducing sheer; 'A' to 'X' represents increasing sheer and 'sheering over' stretching the cable. The rest is repetition of the cycle. If from the 'D' and 'E' position the vessel does not start breaking its sheer but continues to swing (increasing sheer), then arriving at 'C' and more likely at 'X', the cable will snap.

The asymmetry of the halves is a result of off-centring of the hawse pipe. In fact, as the hawse pipes are moved further aft, nearing the extreme breadth of a vessel, the asymmetry is extreme.

The 'drift' or fall back of the vessel in its travel from 'A' to 'X' is represented by the larger arrow 'O¹'. The smaller arrow 'O²' represents the drift as a result of travel from 'B' to 'C'. It is obvious that the jerk on the cable at its extreme stretch at 'X' is in excess of that at 'C'.

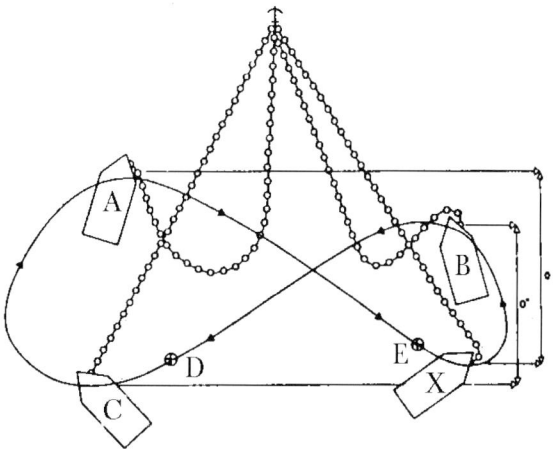

Figure 34.5

Snapping the cable

Cable breakages are sometimes brought about by heaving or shortening anchors with a substantial tide running. The moment the engine is put ahead to assist in heaving, or a powerful windlass manages to heave, surging the vessel ahead, the scope of the arrows marked 'O¹' and 'O²' thereby increases, increasing the jerk at 'X' and 'C'.

The standard remedy to arrest wild yaws is to drop the second anchor underfoot, with approximately two shackles on deck. This considerably dampens the configuration of '8'. Referring to figure 34.5, the ideal position to drop the second anchor would be 'C' and I should prefer there to be about three shackles on deck. The position 'C' ensures maximum distance between the anchors. Thus the vessel in dragging the short anchor about is unlikely to have a foul hawse.

When forced to heave-up with considerable tide running, as earlier stated, the anchor is vulnerable. How then should one go about heaving it up? No guarantees, of course, but ideally one should begin with the short anchor, heaving it short to one-and-a-half in the water. Having put the short anchor out of gear, commence heaving the riding anchor. In assisting the windlass with engines, endeavour to steer at all times a course reciprocal to the tide direction. Keep heaving till the cable is shortened to around three in the water. Now change over and heave the short anchor clear while the vessel rides or drags on three shackles. Even if the vessel now makes wild sheers, the vessel is unlikely to part but certainly drag. Now heave the riding anchor clear.

To summarise

a) In wild yawing, drop the second anchor with three shackles on deck. Referring to figure 34.5, position 'C' is the place to drop the anchor riding to the starboard anchor; position 'X', when riding to port anchor. This ensures maximum distance between anchors.

b) Heaving up assisted by main engines, endeavour to steer a course reciprocal to the tide direction.

c) Heave short the short anchor to one and a half in the water leaving it as dampener to yawing while the riding anchor is hove short to three shackles.

d) Heave clear the short anchor followed by the riding anchor.

Chapter 35

A NEW APPROACH TO ANCHORING LARGE VESSELS

by Captain C.A. McDowall MSc CEng MIMechE MRINA FNI

Captain Allan McDowall was educated at HMS Worcester and has a sea career spanning 45 years with 18 years in command, mainly of VLCCs and very large tankers. He spent 12 years ashore in engineering from a shop floor apprentice at Stothert & Pitt through the design office to R&D. He took HNC, endorsements and the IMechE direct examination to degree level, before being sent to Loughborough University by Stothert & Pitt to do a MTech in engineering design under the late Professor D.H. Chaddock CBE, of the Fighting Vehicles Research Establishment at Shrivenham.

Following R&D at Stothert & Pitt he was project leader with Rotork; development engineer, then chief design engineer with consultants Walters Engineers of Bath; then assistant works engineer at the Avon Rubber Company before returning to sea.

His MSc was in naval architecture (The behaviour of very large ship hulls) at the University of Bath in his spare time while at sea with Esso as second mate. He has done research into mechanisms (Studies of elastic joints) and also anchor performance, took out a patent on one anchor and a registered design on another.

Allan McDowall is Hon. Secretary of the Solent Branch of The Nautical Institute. Recently retired from deep sea, he sails an Evolution and flies a C152 in his spare time.

Note: This chapter comprises extracts from a Nautical Institute Monograph

Summary

ANCHORING SYSTEMS ON LARGE VESSELS are designed within the following general parameters. The anchor and cable are capable of holding a loaded vessel in a current of three knots and a wind of 28 knots, maximum. They are not designed to stop a vessel with way on, as this momentum exceeds the limit of the system.

There are generally 13 shackles on the starboard anchor and 12 shackles on the port anchor. The windlass motor is designed to lift three shackles vertically plus the weight of the anchor, with a 50% allowance on test when new. The cable stopper should be able to carry approximately twice the proof load of the cable and the windlass brake holding power is approximately half the breaking strength of the cable.

The usual way of anchoring a VLCC is to stem the wind and tide, stop the ship and put the engines astern. The anchor is walked out to just above the bottom, after which it is let go or walked out until the required length of cable is on the bottom. This approach to anchoring gives heavy wear to the anchor system and can take a long time. A better and more effective approach is to attempt to keep the cable leading at right angles to the bow so controlling the change in axial inertia rather than controlling ship momentum.

To achieve this the bow should be about 20° off the weather and moving sideways when the anchor is let go. This must occur at the end of a tightly executed turn of about 135°. To achieve this the anchorage is approached down weather at slow speed. On reaching the position abeam of where the bow is desired to be, the engine is put on dead slow ahead and the helm put hard over towards the anchoring position. As soon as the turn is initiated the engine is stopped. Let go the anchor (it may need walking out to free the cable) but control the speed of descent with the brake. Control the direction of the anchor cable at right angles to the bow until sideways motion has stopped and allow the vessel to rotate about the anchor until brought up. This chapter describes the principles behind this manoeuvre and discusses limitations in anchoring systems about which the prudent mariner should be aware.

Introduction

Anchoring by walking the anchor and cable back the whole way is permissible, providing the cable is kept up and down the whole time and providing the design speed of the windlass is not exceeded. Because putting 10 shackles out in this manner takes in excess of half an hour, it is exceedingly difficult to do in practice without damaging the windlass motor. However, the problem of speed control of the cable does not arise with this method as it does with the brake, which is why many people do it.

Alternatively, the brake designed for the purpose can and should be used with care, as described below. The brake has a rated static applicable force typically 10 to 12 times that sustainable by the motor. Dynamic force is reduced by a factor of about six, so the brake is about twice the available force of the motor. The problem with the brake method is that speed control and the force of brake application rest with the skill of the fo'c'sle crew. Maintenance of the brake in an as-new condition is also necessary.

Anchoring with the brake is a team skill on the part of the crew and the master. Despite the stories of accidents, these are mainly caused by human error of one kind or another – water too deep, only one man operating the brake, cable speed excessive, ship speed excessive, windlass brake not maintained, cable not kept abeam and failure of associated equipment also due to lack of maintenance. Occasionally equipment may fail unexpectedly, but this is really blaming the gear design rather than causal lack of maintenance. Using the brake rather than the motor has two main advantages:

1. In an emergency, having the skill to drop will save the day.
2. Using the motor rather than the brake and having an accident as a result could lead to problems of insurance, because the equipment is not being used for its designed purpose. The motor can only be used with the ship stopped over the ground and with power available, so walking back is not an emergency option. Habitually walking back, it has been found, only leads to an inability to drop the anchor at all due to the progressive seizure of parts.

Recommendation

The brake should be used with due care. Practice should be a minimum of monthly for each windlass. This will involve dropping both anchors at each voyage end, Arabian Gulf to Europe via the Cape. Less frequent practice is, in my opinion, inadequate.

Anchoring a VLCC

This skill is not taught in college and it is not taught at sea. People arrive on the bridge on their first command, having learned the habits of the people with whom they happen to have served. Due to lack of maintenance of anchor equipment and the increasing size of ships over the last forty years, more and more masters walk the anchor back all the way. This is not generally a good idea, for a number of reasons, as will be shown, though on occasions it may be unavoidable.

Masters act according to their perception

The general belief amongst ship's masters, particularly those who have little or no experience of anchoring a very large ship (VLCC) is that the anchor equipment has not in any way kept up with increases over the years of the mass of the loaded vessel. This is indeed so (reference OCIMF 'Anchoring procedures for large tankers'). Yet the actual tongue mooring stoppers provided on the fo'c'sle of tankers are all the same (78mm), because they limit the horizontal force that can be applied to the equipment of the oil terminal, the single buoy mooring (SBM), which force is sustained at the sea bed level. This safe working load (SWL) is a world standard of 400 tonnes (200 times two). This has been found to be quite satisfactory in winds up to 30 knots.

In some ports, the stoppers are used singly, not in pairs, to limit the force on the equipment at the sea bed to 200 tonnes instead of 400 tonnes. General experience has shown that this available strength is adequate, providing a tug is in attendance and/or the engines are on 10 minutes notice at all times. From the following data, it is clear that the anchoring equipment is well in excess of the strength of the SBM mooring stoppers.

A typical actual 150,000 tonne deadweight ship, a tanker, say, has anchor equipment rated approximately as follows, as calculated from the classification society rules:

Windlass brake holding force:	395 tonnes force
Cable stopper safe working load:	650 tonnes force
Ultimate tensile strength of cable:	600 tonnes force
Weight of one shackle of cable:	2·5 tonnes force
Weight of anchor:	10 tonnes force
Lifting power of anchor windlass*:	32 tonnes force

(This is based on the rule of 47·5 x diameter squared, newtons*. Divide by 10,000 to get tonnes.) Length of cable:

starboard 13 shackles, port 12 shackles. Two bow stoppers for SBMs, SWL: each 200 tonnes (78mm stud chain). It is immediately apparent that the cable stopper has twice the holding power of the brake, even when the brake is in the as-rated condition, without fade and the brake is twelve times stronger than the motor.

The International Association of Classification Societies (IACS) recommendation is that the maximum static pull on the brake should be 45% of the ultimate tensile strength (UTS) of the chain cable, the force at which the cable is designed and tested to fail. Proof strength of the cable is in the order of 86% of UTS, so it is apparent that the above brake is 70 tonnes over minimum recommended strength (see Appendix 6.8 for the IACS recommendations). The tendency, on this showing, is for brakes to be made stronger rather than weaker than the recommendation.

The reason for the deemed adequacy of strength of the anchoring equipment lies in the fact that the windlass motor is designed to lift three shackles (82 metres) of cable plus the anchor. There is an allowance of 50% over this for safety purposes on test, but not for in-service use. The brake, which is 12 times more powerful than the motor, is designed to control the mass of the cable in motion; not, absolutely not, the mass of the ship. Therefore persons who attempt to control the mass of the ship by means of the windlass brake or worse, the motor, are not using the equipment as it was designed to be used. They are liable to have an accident. Any weight coming on the cable is induced by the ship mass.

The situation as viewed by the classification societies

At present the standard, as stated, is three shackles/82 metres of water, cable up and down, whether hoisting or using the brake. In the case of the windlass motor, there is a proposal by the International Association of Classification

Figure 35.1 A modern windlass installation (150,000 dwt S.B.T. tanker) 200t S.B.M stopper in foreground. Pawl (guillotine stopped) 650t in background. Windlass behind.

Societies (IACS) that the windlass should be capable of lifting the anchor and cable in 100 metres of water, in a wind speed of 14 m/sec (28 knots), and a three knot current, at a speed of 0·15 m/sec (9 m/min). This proposal has not as yet been adopted. This would lift 10 shackles of cable in 30 minutes, which is approximately one and a half to twice the speed encountered in practice. Almost all ships are designed to the 82 metre rule.

There is no classification society rule for the testing of the brake. The brake is tested by the shipyard on trials. Some yards evade the full depth. However, test or no test, the designed strength remains the same, and provided the calculations are correct, the brake should operate as designed. The inference is that if the cable must be recovered in 82 metres of water, then presumably the brake must be capable of arresting the cable in that depth. This is the depth specified by the manufacturers.

The situation as viewed by the deck machinery manufacturers

Manufacturers state that the anchor should be dropped on the brake at some point from the hawse pipe to the sea bed, but that the cable must be kept vertical whilst the operation is by the brake, because of the risk of overload. Contrary to popular belief, it makes no difference to the speed of dropping whether the drop is made from the pipe or from sea bed level. This is because terminal velocity is √2gh, regardless of weight or density, water friction ignored. Dropping is made at sea bed level to protect the anchor (where g is 9·81 m/sec/sec, the acceleration due to gravity and h is the depth in metres). The manufacturers do not recommend walking back all the way, because of the difficulty of avoiding over-speed and/or overload of the windlass motor, which leads to internal damage. This practice was initiated without consulting them.

The pawl (guillotine or bar stopper) must be engaged and the motor declutched when the drop is finished, with the cable up and down. Windlasses are not designed to pull all the ship. They are designed to control the weight of the cable only at a reasonable speed (as slow as possible) in up to 82 metres of water maximum, with the cable up and down throughout the operation – not leading even short stay and certainly not long stay.

The usual method of anchoring can cause an accident, so is mistaken

This statement does not mean that we are all unwise. However, the solution to the perceived problem of using the believed-to-be inadequate brake of VLCC windlasses by using the motor to walk back the anchor all the way instead is itself also a problem, but a less obvious one. The usual method of anchoring a VLCC is to approach the position stemming the tide and wind, then to stop the ship, put the engine astern, possibly full astern. This is itself potentially damaging in the engine room due to the vibration induced, particularly on a steam turbine ship. The ship goes astern very slowly, at approximately 0·1–0·2 knots. This is 0·05–0·1 m/sec, 10 to 20 feet per minute – no more, over the sea bed and is exceedingly difficult to judge accurately without sophisticated navigation aids such as Doppler log, ground stabilised or GPS in an open anchorage.

The anchor is then walked out until just above the bottom or until it just touches the bottom, in which case the direction the cable starts to lead indicates the direction of drift of the bow. Then:

A. The anchor is then taken out of gear and let go, controlled by the brake.
B. Alternatively, the anchor is walked out all the way, not being taken out of gear at all, by means of the windlass motor. This is not recommended by the manufacturers of windlasses.

Failure to ensure that the ship is, in fact, going astern may cause a fouled anchor, because the cable is laid over the anchor, which itself lies on the bottom shank forward instead of aft. Therefore when the weight comes on the cable, the cable is liable to be pulled back over the anchor, with consequent possibility of fouling. Then the anchor has to be pulled round by 180°, either capsized or, worse, horizontally. This last has, on occasions, broken the shank of the anchor.

If the depth of water is in the order of 50 metres, two shackles being equal to 55 metres) and the final length of cable is 10 shackles, then the difference in horizontal movement of the ship from the moment that the cable is up and down to the moment that the cable is bar taut is, by Pythagoras, 49·3 metres. This is very nearly the width of the ship, which is usually between 50 and 60 metres (see figure 2).

If the depth is one shackle, say 27 metres, and the cable out five shackles, then there is only 25 metres before the cable becomes bar taut. The actual allowed distance is nil, because the cable is supposed to be maintained up and down and to do this when anchoring with the brake is quite easy (method A). However, to maintain the cable up and down whilst walking back is almost impossible (method B). The distance moved whilst maintaining the cable vertical depends on the speed of veering the cable with respect to the speed of drift of the ship. This is not difficult with the windlass brake, but is extremely difficult using the windlass motor.

It is absolutely necessary, therefore, to halt the ship's astern movement over the bottom before the cable becomes out of the vertical; and ships are very slippery in the fore and aft line: they are difficult to hold stationary, particularly where there is no reference point. Otherwise, the windlass brake or motor, designed to control the mass of the cable and anchor vertically only, will be being used to try to effect the deceleration of the mass of the hull. This is a so much a greater force than that for which the brake was designed that it is difficult to describe adequately. The motor is not designed to lower the cable in this manner at all.

Failure to achieve this halt to the ship's astern movement will result in a bar taut cable with no elasticity left by virtue of all the catenary having been used up – the astern movement being attempted to be arrested by the fo'c'sle crew with the brake. Long before this situation, the designed maximum forces, therefore stresses, in the brake or motor have been exceeded. Because the ship is proceeding astern, the full mass of the ship comes on to the brake, so the force being exerted is approximately one thousand times the maximum allowed force in practice.

Had the designer been asked to design a brake capable of arresting the mass of the ship, the scantlings would be of the order of the propeller shaft. The new stern towing brackets designed by Pusnes, for example, are massive. No mention of acceleration; solely steady state towing forces of 200 tonnes. If the reader is still not convinced, consider now that other operation that regularly takes place on the fo'c'sle, the securing of the 78mm chain in the tongue stopper for the SBM.

Securing the chain stopper of the nylon cable connecting the VLCC to a single buoy mooring (SBM)

The brake that is used here is the mooring brake, which has a rated holding power as tested of 47 tonnes, regardless of the size of the ship. The stopper is always put on with the nylon cable slack. Only when the chain tail is secure in the stopper, and the securing pin home, is the weight allowed to come on the nylon cable, very gently.

Yet people talk about swinging the ship about on the anchor brake or the motor, without the point of ground/sea bed reference that the SBM provides. There is only one component in the anchor handling equipment capable of sustaining the inertia of the ship, the pawl (guillotine stopper).

If the design forces are exceeded the cable will run out

In this case, before the cable can be halted, it has run out to the bitter end. Detachment of the bitter end from the cable locker then occurs and the cable is lost. If such brake failure takes place in a big way, centrifugal reaction causes the whole cable to rise up off the gypsy in a great arc about 10 metres high. When the bitter end is reached there is no discernible pause. The end comes out of the locker and flails forward on to the deck, where it may cause a split in the 20 mm deck plate, doing severe damage as it disappears from view. All this happens in about 12 seconds, with deafening noise and flames.

Fear of the above scenario

The practice of walking back the scope all the way on the windlass is largely caused by fear of the above scenario. The practice has other unpleasant surprises, too. The lifting power of the windlass motor is, typically, less than $1/12$th that of the brake holding force, as already seen. The motor, as already stated, is designed to lift the anchor and cable in a maximum of 82 metres of water, vertically.

Imagine for a moment that one was using an overhead gantry crane, but one where the wire and the gantry were greatly over-strength. Suppose that a load to be hoisted consisted of a large container. Imagine that this container was then progressively loaded until the weight in the container was ten times the original, safe, load. Now imagine what would happen to the motor and gear box if this overload was then lowered to the deck. Clearly, the components of the motor and gearbox would be grossly overloaded and damage would result. This is exactly what happens when the anchor and cable are walked back under load by the windlass motor, if the cable is not vertical.

The braking effect of the motor occurs because the mechanical advantage of an hydraulic motor plus gearing is more than 50:1. A gear ratio of 50:1 or more is not capable of running back on itself. In fact, a Sumitomo hydraulic motor alone has a reduction ratio in the order of 180:1, so there is no way it can be overrun. Instead, if the rated lifting power of the windlass motor is exceeded – which is very easy to do by allowing the cable to get out of the vertical so that part of the mass of the ship comes on to the motor – then what happens is that the casing of the hydraulic motor may become progressively over-pressurised, and so the allowable designed internal forces on the motor components also become excessive.

This always gives rise to metal particles in the hydraulic oil which, because filters on the pump are quite coarse, go through the pump, causing further similar damage. If you are a master who habitually walks his anchor back, it is suggested that you now ask your chief engineer to examine the filters in the anchor windlass hydraulic system. You will probably find metal fragments as described, for the reason given.

Two other adverse effects exist of walking back the cable all the way

The first is that the casing of the hydraulic motor may crack and, on occasion, does. This has the result that the anchor cannot be raised again. The cable has to be buoyed, disconnected and slipped, to be recovered later, if possible, at very considerable expense. The only reason that the casing does not crack more often is because of the huge extra strength that the designers have put into it, knowing that users will abuse it if they are able to do so, quite unintentionally. If your windlass is steam, then the stress that walking back puts on the valve gear, which is operated by an 'eccentric' disc, is colossal. Such an eccentric cannot be driven backwards. Failure of the eccentric is very common due to trying to rotate it by the valve gear and leads to difficult and time-consuming rectification by the ship's engineers, with the likelihood of reduced windlass power because of errors in resetting.

The second, more common and more dangerous happening is that the windlass clutch jumps out of engagement. This happens for a number of reasons, regrettably most often because the clutch lever securing pin has not been inserted or not secured. Added to this is the fact that the windlass clutch 'dogs' are manufactured straight crosscut, instead of slightly rebated, as would be most desirable. Because the clutch dogs are straight, most force comes on to the ends, with the result that they always wear slightly tapered. This in turn causes lifting torque on the shaft to result in a secondary parting force on the clutch, which is sometimes sufficiently strong to overcome the restraint of the operating lever securing pin, especially if the clutch dogs are well greased.

In addition to the above, the dog-clutch operating fork, which runs in an annular groove cut in the clutch sliding part, is a weak spot and has been known to deform and spring out of engagement owing to this parting force, caused by tapered wear of the dogs, as described. This accident has the same effect as releasing the clutch lever, as above. In both the above cases, the effect is to release the anchor suddenly with the brake off. It is very difficult to get the brake back on in time, because the crew are quite unprepared for this eventuality. To arrest the cable before the speed has built up too fast to stop takes very quick physical reactions – partly because the available length of cable in the locker is no longer there. This is a frequent mistake.

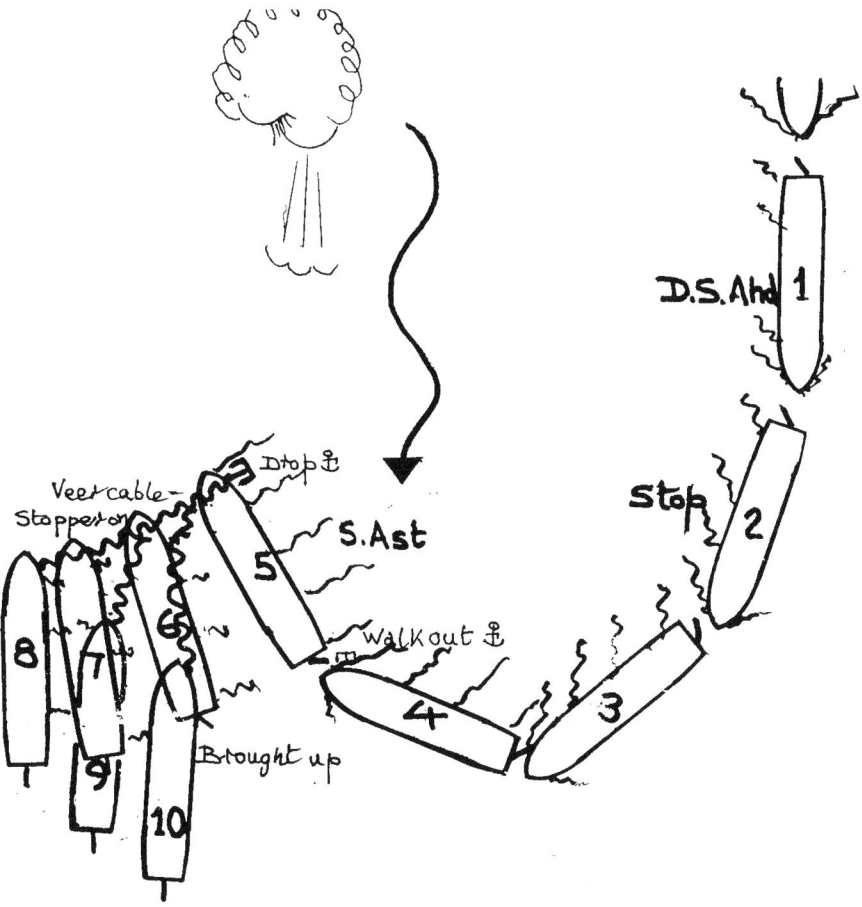

Figure 35.2 Turning in a strong tide and wind

Walking back the anchor and cable to full scope, all the way, itself can lead to accidents

Whilst the anchor is walking back, which may be very slow and on big VLCCs as slow as 7·5 cm/sec (15 ft/min) or even slower, the brake is normally off. This speed is slower than the speed at which the ship can normally be controlled. Walking back 10 shackles at this speed takes a long, long time – half an hour minimum, usually 45 minutes – so the tendency is for masters to use less cable than they should. This leads to dragging and consequent grounding – the writer is thinking of a particular recent case in Delaware Bay due to this.

Walking back, with stress coming on the anchor before there is sufficient cable to protect it, can also lead to over-stressing of the anchor itself with consequent fracture. This has happened on two occasions at Itaqui, on one occasion leading to the total loss of a very large bulk carrier on her maiden voyage. Her wreck is still there, a warning to others. The second occasion led to the fracture of the anchor at the join of the shank with the flukes. Who can possibly keep the bow of his ship under control for half an hour with the cable up and down, let alone one hour or more?

So care in keeping the cable fore and aft and walking back all the way can lead to the accident this procedure is designed to avoid

People have the kinds of mishap described above because they are being very, very careful, but operating the whole system in quite the wrong way, for wrong reasons.

There is another, safer method of getting the anchor and cable laid out on the sea bed

When our grandfathers in the navy anchored, they wanted to be secure in the knowledge that they could maybe have a pink gin, or possibly a huge party and know absolutely that the ship was not going to move. So what they did was to steam with the tide and or wind, whichever was stronger, put the helm hard over and just as the ship started to swing, let go the cable on the run on the inside of the turn. They then ran it out to the required length, set the stopper and allowed the anchor and cable to snub the ship round into the weather. This set the anchor and the whole operation was over in about four minutes. By today's standards this sounds deeply shocking.

The navy still anchor in a very similar way, except that they use the brake a bit, which is not the purpose for which it was designed, as already exhaustively described. This added 'caution' they caught from their merchant service colleagues, no doubt. This practice of 'running out' had its roots in the days of sail, where Admiralty pattern (Fisherman) anchors with stocks were used and the danger of fouling the flukes was a serious risk. The anchor absolutely had to set correctly first time – no engine to get you out of trouble, so no second chance.

Such an anchor must lie on the sea-bed in the correct direction, without any possibility of fouling. Therefore the hull movement had to be sufficiently brisk to ensure that the rope cable did not get entangled in the flukes or the stock. This happened naturally, because a sailing vessel's tendency when stopped with the sails aback is for the bow to fall off the wind, which gives the necessary sideways movement which is the secret of safe anchoring. The same thing applies today – it is fatal to get the cable fouling the anchor.

'One could not possibly do that in today's ships', you say. Certainly not deliberately, but one 250,000 tonne VLCC did just that by accident in the early 1970s. She was steaming towards Kharg Island, in ballast, at 19 knots when the starboard anchor was accidentally let go. Due to the great beam and the bluff hull form forward, the cable was deflected to the ship's side and the ship was turned by the cable 180° without the bitter end parting. How can this possibly happen? Is there a clue here in a safer way to anchor?

The secret lies in separating the momentum of the ship's hull from the forces necessary to control the movement of the cable

The reason is the difference between momentum of translation and momentum of rotation. This principle is seen in the operation of salvage tugs. When the load is taken up, it is observed that the tugmaster always aligns his tug at right angles to the fore and aft line of the ship towed. The ship is easily canted and the tug is then gradually aligned in the fore and aft line. This effect is well known. It avoids snatch of the tow wire.

To demonstrate this, you can take a walk into a marina and choose a small yacht. Push hard on the stern with your foot in the fore and aft line and the yacht will not move – you are trying to shove about five tonnes in a straight line. Now move round to the side and push at the end on the stern (or the bow) at right angles to the fore and aft line. The hull is easily deflected because the inertia, instead of being five tonnes, is now one tonne, with no friction and this can be moved quite easily.

The monograph continues by covering, in detail, many other aspects of anchoring large vessels and includes formulae for working out cable stresses, stopping distances, rotational inertia and so on. Cable management, anchoring procedures, maintenance and difficulties in recovering anchors are all covered extensively.

The monograph also has useful appendices concerning:

- Ship horizontal movement under various cable conditions.
- Derivation of coaxial force.
- Rotational inertia/axial inertia.
- Derivation of 2nd moment of area.
- Demonstration regarding 2nd moment of area.

The U-turn method

The U-turn method utilises the rotational inertia of the ship to control the tension in the cable. The full mathematical treatment is developed in more detail in the monograph.

To execute the U-turn method follow the steps outlined in the checklist on the pages following. The method is illustrated in figure 35.2.

The monograph
- McDowall, C.A., *A New Approach to Anchoring Large Vessels*, The Nautical Institute, 2000.

Bibliography
1. Green, W.G., *Theory of Machines*, Blackie Press, Glasgow.
2. *Steel Designers Handbook*, Dorman Long, Middlesbrough.
3. Roark, R.J., *Formulas for Stress and Strain*, McGraw-Hill.
4. den Hartog, J.P., *Strength of Materials*.
5. Merritt, W.E., *Gears*, C.U.P.
6. *Exponential Brake. On the Mathematics of the Band Brake*. Proceedings of Institution of Mechanical Engineers.
7. Manufacturers' data. Some prefer to remain anonymous.
8. Input from IACS., courtesy of American Bureau of Shipping.
9. Statistics of accidents taken from data base of Lloyds Register, by kind permission, with special thanks to Lloyds Register and Lloyds information service.
10. Actual ship data, Class NK. By kind permission.
11. Morton, A.J., Baines, B.H. and Ridgway, K., *On the stopping and anchoring of large ships — a feasibility study*. Proceedings of Institution of Marine Engineers.
12. Anchoring systems and procedures for large tankers. OCIMF 1982.

    13—18 taken from OCIMF:
13. Dove, H.L., MBE and Ferris, G.S., BSc, *Development of anchors*, RCNC. Proceedings of RINA, 23 March 1960.
14. *Improvements in mooring anchors*, Proceedings of INA, 31 March 1950.
15. Bruce, P., CEng FIMarE, *Inadequacy of anchors in large ships*, Transactions of IMarE, Vol. 92, paper C50, 1980.
16. Buckle, A.K, BSc CEng, *Ten year review of defects and failures in large ships anchoring and mooring equipment*, Transactions of IMarE, Vol. 92, paper C 46, 1980.
17. van den Haak, R., *Design of anchors, cables and mooring wires*, Transactions of IMarE , Vol. 92, paper C 51, 1980.
18. *The anatomy of the anchor*, Author, source unknown.

19. *Lloyds Rules for the Construction and Classification of steel ships.*

Anchoring checklist

	Yes	No
A. PRE-OP MAINTENANCE		
1. Has the windlass been tested within the last 30 days?	❏	❏
If NO, then extra care needs to be taken.		
2. Has maintenance been done as per the makers instruction book?	❏	❏
If there are NO instructions, do the following:		
a) Ensure the brake lining is 7mm or more.	❏	❏
b) Ensure the brake drum is smooth, with no build up of rust or resin.	❏	❏
(Use frequently, or use needle gun plus pneumatic wire brush)		
c) Ensure ALL bearings and joints are FULL of grease, with no grit or rust in.	❏	❏
d) Ensure that hydraulic oil is at the correct level (if applicable)	❏	❏
e) Ensure hydraulic filters are clean, with no metal particles in.	❏	❏
(Metal particles are an indication of past overload)		
f) Ensure the brake lead screw and nut are clean and greased.	❏	❏
3. Have the owners' managers' instructions been read?	❏	❏
4. These instructions should be in accordance with the maker's instructions. Are they?	❏	❏
5. Are the brake adjustments in the middle of the range?	❏	❏
If NO, then operation is near the edge of permissible limits.		
B. PRE-OP PLAN – ENVIRONMENT		
1. Is the depth less than 82 metres absolute maximum?	❏	❏
Unless your ship is specially equipped, this is the class limit.		
2. Is the depth less than the owners stipulated depth for using the brake?	❏	❏
If depth is more than 30 metres, then walk back, using the brake.		
Never walk back without using the brake at this depth.		
If no instructions, regard 60 metres as the limit for brake only.		
3. Is the nearest grounding line more than one mile away?	❏	❏
When allowing for low tide.		
4. Is the weather/tide onshore?	❏	❏
If the weather is onshore and anchorage close, special care is needed.		
5. Is the sea bed suitable? *Not rock or coral.*	❏	❏
6. Is there enough room to turn 180°/360°?	❏	❏
7. Is the wind less than 28 knots?	❏	❏
Is the current less than 3 knots?	❏	❏
These are Classification Society limits. You may trade wind for current:		
i.e. 1 knot current = 9 knots wind.		
8. Is the sea sufficiently calm? *Excess motion of the hull.*	❏	❏
C. PRE-OP PLAN – TRAINING		
1. Have the foc'stle crew had training and are they certificated through	❏	❏
the company's training scheme? *Windlass = primary lifting gear.*		
2. Has a pre-op briefing been held so that they understand that:		
a) There should be two men on the controls, particularly the brake.	❏	❏
b) One man to apply grease to gears when heaving.	❏	❏
c) The orders that will come from the bridge.	❏	❏
d) The cable will be walked back when at 2 knots to just above the bottom =	❏	❏
the DIRECT method by 'U'-turn,		

OR
    When stopped to just touch the bottom = the TENTATIVE method. ❏ ❏

e)   The cable will be veered in one go. *On the beam, 90° to the fore and aft line,* ❏ ❏
   because forces on the windlass are 20 times less this way,
   approximately 3·5 times for inertia and six times for added scope.

f)   The stopper will be put on and securing pin engaged whilst the cable ❏ ❏
   is still up and down.
   Because this is the windlass makers and class requirement.

D. THE APPROACH TO THE ANCHORAGE

1.   Are there any other ships at anchor to indicate tide/wind? ❏ ❏

2.   Is there a suitable anchoring space, not in the fairway? ❏ ❏

3.   Is there a clear, safe passage to the space? ❏ ❏

4.   Is the space clear of the fairway? ❏ ❏

5.   If the anchorage is empty with a strong current, do you know ❏ ❏
   the direction of the current?

6.   Is the chosen space accessible for bunker barges/launches/etc? ❏ ❏

E. THE ANCHORING OPERATION – AIDE MEMOIRE

1.   Choose a suitable speed of approach for the traffic/searoom. ❏ ❏

2.   If 'U' turn, approach at 180° to the final heading. ❏ ❏
   If 'tentative', approach at 20–90° to the final heading. In both cases, the aim is to ❏ ❏
   lead the cable at 90° to the ship.

The 'U' turn method

3(u) 'U' turn – start the turn when the bow is abreast of the planned bow final position, ❏ ❏
   full rudder. Speed is not important.

4(u) Once the turn is started, stop engine. ❏ ❏

5(u) When speed is two knots, start to walk the anchor out to above the sea bed. Use the ❏ ❏
   anchor on the inside of the turn.

6(u) When the ship has canted 135° she will be virtually stopped. Adjust the angle to ❏ ❏
   the weather to suit the strength of the tide and wind.

7(u) With the bow moving slowly sideways, let go/walk back with the brake to 3·5 to four ❏ ❏
   times the depth, five times if possible.

8(u) Put the stopper on and engage securing pin with the cable up and down. Do not ❏ ❏
   attempt to bring the ship on the brake or the motor – doing so is against the
   maker's and class limits.

9(u) Ensure the ship is brought up with the cable abeam before allowing the cable to ❏ ❏
   draw ahead.

The 'tentative' method

3(t) Approach the anchorage slowly, angling to the weather 20–90°. ❏ ❏

4(t) Start walk back at two knots, to avoid the anchor banging on the hull. Use the ❏ ❏
   anchor on the weather side, not the lee side.

5(t) When the ship is stopped, walk back the anchor to just touch the sea bed. The ❏ ❏
   fo'c'stle crew observe the lead, informing the bridge when leading out on the beam
   and clear of the hull.

6(t) When the cable is leading in the desired direction, let go/walk back to the required scope – 3·5 to four times the depth, five times if possible. ❑   ❑

7(t) Put the stopper on and engage the securing pin with the cable up and down. Do not attempt to bring the ship up on the brake or the motor – doing so is against the maker's and class limits. ❑   ❑

8(t) Ensure the ship is brought up with the cable abeam before allowing the cable to draw ahead, for inertia and scope reasons, the same as for the 'U' turn. ❑   ❑

In both cases, when the depth is shallow and the bottom is soft, practice letting go the anchor from the hawse pipe. In an emergency you will have to. It is surprising how few ships can do this. If you cannot, the necessary maintenance needs to be done. ❑   ❑

Chapter 36

MAN OVERBOARD – RESCUING SURVIVORS FROM THE SEA

by Captain M. Williams FNI

Captain Williams, who is a Younger Brother of Trinity House, has served 35 years at sea and is serving as master on diving support vessels. He is particularly interested in preserving life at sea.

Introduction

ONE OF THE MOST TRAUMATIC occurrences at sea for all concerned is the report of a man overboard. I assure you, this report is often met with incredulity by bridge staff and there can often be quite a delay before the fact is recognised and acted upon. I experienced this first hand in 1998 whilst my vessel was carrying out diving operations off the Indian coast. Fortunately the weather was calm at the time of the incident but a two-knot current was running and vessel was set up in DP stern to current.

A steward, who was afterwards diagnosed as suffering from severe depression, jumped off the boat deck into the water claiming afterwards that 'the voices in his head' had told him to swim to the stern of the vessel and re-board. He was swept away in the current and when it was reported to the bridge my immediate reaction after initial disbelief was to sound the alarm and then rush to the bridge wing to sight the man. Due to the helicopter deck obscuring my view I could not see him but a crew member on the helideck who had sight of him shouted to me that the steward had drifted clear of the bow thrusters. Others joined the crew member on the helideck and as dusk was approaching they continued to keep the man in view. Two lifebuoys were thrown from the bow to the man in the water. Fortunately he was able to swim to one of the lifebuoys.

The crash boat was prepared and launched by the crane. Obviously my vessel could not move as I had divers eighty metres below working on a pipeline. Also in the area where we were operating there were no other vessels nearby to assist. I therefore had to rely totally on my crash boat crew to recover the man and return him to the vessel. The crash boat in use had two seventy-five horse power outboard motors with wheel steering. I watched in amazement as the man drifted further and further from the bow of my ship and the crash boat steered at a tangent off to starboard. Apparently the steering control had become disconnected and eventually the crash boat crew had to manually steer the outboards to reach the casualty.

When the man was returned on board he was treated by the medic and as I had no way of getting him ashore that night, a guard was posted on his cabin after he had been sedated. The next day I managed to get him ashore by helicopter but had to send in another crew member to accompany him as the helicopter pilot, quite rightly, was not too keen on carrying a man suffering from severe depression.

From the time of the steward's departure overboard to getting him back was approximately thirty minutes. This was on a very well founded vessel, fully equipped with crash boats and a complement of ninety-five men. Think of a similar occurrence on a conventional vessel with a limited crew and only lifeboats available for man overboard recovery. Who do you allocate to man your crash boat/lifeboat? How do you get a person from the water into the boat? How often do you practise man overboard drills? Are you able to launch and recover the lifeboat in rough weather? Is your vessel's crew prepared in first aid to assist a person who has been immersed in a cold sea? What contingency do you have in place if your rescue craft breaks down during the recovery? Have you prepared a search routine to enable you to find a man in the water? Have you established who will man your GMDSS, transmit your Pan message and keep a log of events?

I suggest that the answers to all the above have not been fully addressed on most vessels. The only way they can be can be addressed is by carrying out realistic drills and from the lessons learnt, fine tuning your written bridge procedures. In addition to your written procedures that should be in place as part of the vessel's ISM, I would strongly advise a flip card system covering man overboard procedures for the lifeboat/rescue craft and the first aid teams.

Flip cards prepared

To aid our man overboard plan we have designed three flip cards, one for the crash lifeboat, one for the bridge and one for the sick bay. This assists the officers to follow a logical sequence and reminds them of the next duty. I am helped in the plan by having regular crews permanently attached to the ship. This way, the training falls into a standard pattern which officers can build upon. We can put the right person in the right job – i.e. some ratings have sharper eyesight and make better lookouts while others prefer to be boat's crew. This all helps to create team spirit, as well as practical experience, two important factors when searching for a survivor in the water, especially on a dark night or rough sea.

The flip-card for the crash lifeboat lists the following:

1. Extra searchlight at night, to make two portable lights.
2. Sleeping bag and spare life jackets from the 'immediate use locker' and nylon wrapping.
3. Crash boat should contain the man overboard net.
4. Second officer in charge of the crash boat carries the VHF handset for communications with the ship.
5. Warm waterproof clothing must be worn by all the lifeboat crew with lifejackets.
6. Box search plan to be followed after launch.
7. In the event of a VHF communications failure, general flag and whistle signals for search and recall.

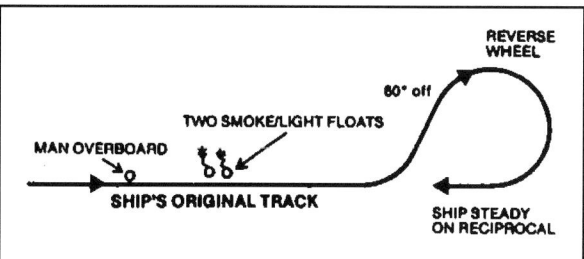

Figure 36.1 Williamson turn

Bridge procedure

For bridge use, the second flip card reminds the OOW of his immediate duties as soon as 'Man overboard' is shouted.

1. Log the time – this is most important, especially with the speed of modern vessels. (My ship travels 2,000 yards in four minutes).
2. Bridge smoke and light floats are both released.
3. Bridge lookout to search astern to try to locate the man in the water.
4. OOW sounds the alarm signal to summon all hands and place both engines on stand-by.
5. Ship reduces speed and starts a full-turn circle (Williamson turn) to bring the ship quickly back on to its original track.
6. Four bridge lookouts are posted, one for each quadrant, to carry out a set search pattern. First a general sweep through 90°, then a detailed layer search every 10° below the horizon, every two minutes. This needs to be taught at the practice drill. At night, the ship's two large searchlights would be manned and a similar layered search pattern followed.
7. Catering and motorman ratings would be spread out along the cargo deck to keep a similar search.
8. If the man in the water is not seen, the ship on completing her 180° turn will steam slowly past the two smoke/light floats – now established as

the datum, and steam back 1,000 yd from the smoke floats. The ship stops and will remain stationary in the water. The lifeboat is now launched.

9. The lifeboat commences a box search, 200 yards offset from the ship's track (see figure 36.2); the first box search is between the ship and the smoke floats. The smoke floats will be left in the water to check the drift of the water and mark the datum. This will be broadcast on all safety frequencies.

10. The survivor in the water would expect to be found in this first box, which is searched twice, once by the ship and once by the lifeboat. If the survivor is not found, a second box commences, with the ship moving along the track a further 1000 yd, and stopping whilst the lifeboat carries out a second offset box search using the ship as a reference point. A third and fourth box search can be continued in the same way.

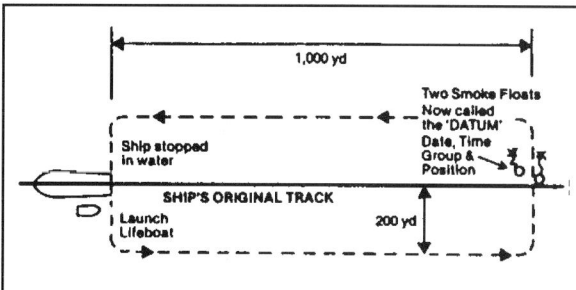

On completion of the first box search, the ship moves a further 1,000 yards along track and stops. The lifeboat carries out a second offset box search, using the ship as reference point.

Figure 36.2 First box search by lifeboat

Once sighted in the water, the ship will sound a long blast to indicate to the survivor in the sea that he has been seen. When picked up by the lifeboat he will be zipped up in the sleeping bag, covered with nylon sheeting and returned to the ship as quickly as possible.

The crash lifeboat has two 12ft manilla pendants, one spliced into each end of the boat for hooking on to the boat's falls. This is necessary in rough seas or heavy swells.

When we have the survivor on board, he is taken to the sick bay and given proper treatment for hypothermia and shock.

The third flip-card details the proper treatment to be followed. This is a critical time for a survivor, where loss of body heat, even by a small amount can be fatal. He needs to be kept in a warm room, have all wet clothes exchanged for dry ones and kept in bed. Hot water bottles wrapped in towels should be placed around his trunk. He should only be given hot sweet drinks and his temperature and pulse rate monitored every 30 minutes. If his arms and legs are very cold, they should not be allowed to draw off heat from his main trunk.

Danger of shock

Shock is also a real danger and can occur up to 48 hours after a fall overboard. The survivor should not be left on his own and, if possible, should be taken from the ship to a hospital.

Whoever is delegated to send the 'Pan' message by GMDSS should, as well as monitoring communications, be able to keep a log of events.

Recommendations

1. All the ship's company to take part in man overboard drills and not just a small part of the deck department.
2. All seafarers to complete a survival course every five years and be able to swim.
3. A systematic plan be prepared and practised for every ship (man overboard plan).
4. The old merchant navy expression 'If you fall in – you will die', be refuted at every drill.

Chapter 37

MASTER'S STANDING ORDERS

by Captain Eric Beetham FNI FRIN

Captain Eric Beetham served at sea for ten years prior to first sailing in command and spent 17 of the next 20 years in command, with three years as owner's marine superintendent. His 25 commands ranged from 500 grt to 300,000 dwt and included salvage ships, bulk and log carriers, fast reefer ships, tankers, VLCCs and OBOs. Each ship type presented different problems and circumstances.

The last 14 years have been spent as a surveyor carrying out casualty investigations, appearing as an expert witness or sitting as a nautical assessor in formal investigations or marine inquiries. In this work he sees the type of accident that occurs and the mistakes that cause them. He was a Vice President of The Nautical Institute for eight years and President from 1996 to 1998.

Introduction

VARIOUS CONVENTIONS, CODES AND GUIDES provide the framework within which officers' duties shall be performed in nearly all cases of routine and many extraordinary circumstances. Operational procedures will be based upon the owner's navigation policy and these should work without conflict within the safety management system. This will apply to every ship.

The master should provide his own standing orders – which will be supplemented on a daily basis by night orders – to spell out to his officers his own personal requirements. This may be with regard to the particular ship, her trade, the bridge team and their experience. These standing orders may reflect points that have caused him concern in the past and lessons he has learned and will set the standard that he requires from his watchkeepers.

Amongst the mass of written guidance on board, this is the opportunity for the master to set down quite simply the ground rules or exactly what he expects the officers to do in different circumstances, to reinforce practices that he expects to be followed and to create a relationship in which a mutual confidence is established. The officers will know when the master wants to be called and the master will know that they will do so.

It is advisable to consider carefully the special circumstances which exist every time a master takes over command. These will relate to the particular ship and to the officers and crew serving in her. There is a temptation to use just one set of tried and tested master's standing orders without any adjustment for each ship. This would be a mistake and a lost opportunity to address the special needs and the circumstances of each different command.

The purpose of good operational procedures is to ensure that a mistake – be it an error or an omission – by one person does not put the ship into danger. It is human to make mistakes and this applies as equally to the master as it does to everybody else on board. It is the duty of the officers to check their own work and to verify the work of others at hand-overs. When a

pilot is carried he must, equally, be told if you think he has made a mistake which might adversely affect the safety of the ship.

In port

1) Follow the instructions of the chief officer with regard to ballast, cargo being worked, repairs carried out etc. This supports the chief officer's authority with the ship in port.

2) Ensure that access to/from the ship is kept as safe as possible, well lighted and the gangway net properly rigged; make sure watchmen are on deck and shore people do not smoke in unauthorised places. The chief officer will see that the gangway and safety net are set up on arrival but it is then up to the OOW to keep it that way.

3) Keep the ship alongside and moorings tight; replace any ropes that break and call me if the ship starts ranging or weather becomes adverse. Some officers don't appreciate that mooring winches have much more holding power 'on the brake' than they do 'on heave' and if the ship comes off the berth in strong winds, it can make things worse by trying to heave her back alongside.

4) Never hesitate to call for shore assistance (tugs, pilots, fire brigade or ambulance) in any emergency and keep engineers advised. In practice the captain or chief officer will be aboard if cargo is being worked but make sure the OOW knows he has authority.

5) There are many thefts from ships in port and stowaways are a major problem. Try to check on people coming aboard, that they do have business on the ship and, if in doubt, take them to the person they wish to see or send the watchman with them. The cooperation of everybody on board is necessary to try to minimise thefts and stowaways but the example of a duty mate who takes this task seriously motivates others on duty.

Before arrival and sailing

1) Test all the bridge gear in accordance with the check list, switch on both steering motors, radars and check alignment of radars, gyro repeaters and course recorder. Prepare pilot information card.

2) Give the engine room 'one hour notice' meaning that at the end of the one hour on arrival we shall want to manoeuvre and likewise one hour before 'stand by' on departure. This is best defined to avoid confusion and of course the engine room has to be advised of this.

Log books

1) Entries must be clear and accurate; names of all persons involved in any incidents must be given fully and entries by the OOW or duty officer must be signed by him. This is invaluable a few years later if there are any claims made.

2) If the wind is force 7 or more, put the weather in every two hours and the barometer every hour if it is changing much, plus remarks on water coming aboard etc. In port, ensure that weather remarks continue to be made in the log book. In cyclone areas or adverse weather, further detail would be given in the night orders.

3) While the log book only needs the important times, keep a complete movement book with details of tugs, whose lines, moorings used, fendering of the quay, which side alongside and number of the berth. Routine again, but so often records are incomplete.

At anchor

1) Keep a good check on position of this ship and others close by – ships may drag soon after anchoring, when the tide changes, when the weather freshens or when the brake won't hold with a lot of yawing. The danger is not only of this ship dragging but of others drifting down to us. The bow stopper must always be in use when at anchor. In adverse weather it is helpful to paint a link on the aft side of the gypsy so it can easily be seen if the brake renders.

2) Normally full anchor watches will have to be kept but if cargo is being worked while at anchor the opportunity must be taken at regular intervals to check the ship's position. Always a problem but deck and bridge have both to be watched.

3) Ensure the lights/signals are correctly exhibited; usually a VHF watch will have to be kept and if you've been away from the bridge for a time, check with the shore station that they have not been calling us.

4) If another ship tries to anchor too close or starts to drag, try and get them on the VHF or flash them with the Aldis lamp.

5) At the moment of letting go the anchor, try to get a position on the chart and note the ship's heading – that way the swinging circle can best be worked out on the chart. If the scale of the chart is good enough, it gives a circle within which the ship should remain and is handy when weighing anchor in a crowded anchorage.

At sea

1) Make sure the navigation lights are on at night and that a good lookout is kept at all times. The seaman on watch is always available to the OOW and should be used as a lookout at night, in rain or in fog. Usually single seaman watches are kept at sea but the OOW must know that a man is available to him if required during daytime.

2) Comply fully with the regulations for preventing collisions with other ships and use sound signals when within two miles.

3) In an emergency do not hesitate to use the engines but, if at all possible, warn the duty engineer first and call me. Try to avoid close quarter situations by early and substantial course alterations and in open waters give all traffic plenty of room. Nothing is gained by passing too close. Running UMS, it is preferable to have the duty engineer in the engine room first if that is possible.

4) Respond to any requests from the engine room to reduce speed and, in the event of a blackout with other ships around, try to get maximum helm on quickly and switch on emergency NUC lights. Not always possible but, if it can be done, this is the best way of reducing travel as running the way off may take a long distance.

5) On taking over the watch, check the position, check the course to steer and the course actually being steered; check the distance to go to the next alteration, soundings or picking up land. In the night watches, please read and initial the night orders. The routine of using the night orders every night is preferred as it reduces the risk of something being missed if the book is sometimes used, sometimes not.

6) Compare magnetic and gyro compasses at least every hour and take azimuths every watch. This is not an outdated routine, but good navigational practice.

7) Change to hand steering and back each watch (tests both) and check the course recorder. Aim for the minimum use of rudder but don't fiddle with the settings unless you think you can improve the situation. Small alterations, of course, may be done on the autopilot but always change to hand steering for bigger alterations. When a helmsman is engaged in hand steering, keep a close watch on him until you are sure of his ability, both in steering and following helm orders. The ability of helmsmen, due to the small amount of experience they gain (both in general and in any particular ship), causes concern, particularly in canals and restricted channels.

8) Use the navigational aids fully (including the echo sounder) but as a backup to visual position fixing and do not rely on the aids to the point where common sense is ignored. Always check the chart details for WGS details when using GPS in coastal waters and in restricted waters always use visual bearings and radar distances. We passed through the era of 'radar assisted collisions' and may now be into that of 'GPS assisted strandings'. When a 'black box' (voyage data recorder) is fitted,

continue to fix positions on the chart, particularly in restricted waterways.

9) If not already running, always put the radar on in good time if there is rain around or visibility is doubtful. In open waters the best use of radar is in tracking ships from 12 miles so that their movement is assessed by 8 miles and there is then plenty of time to alter course if necessary and to make sure the alteration is having the desired effect. This clearly spells out the philosophy required by the master to avoid close quarter situations – the other ship may be fast, may not be keeping an efficient watch and may unexpectedly alter course.

10) Approaching heavy rain or fog, have a good look around, switch on radar, warn the engine room, call up the seaman for lookout, switch on the navigation lights, fix the position of the ship, switch on fog signal to automatic and call me. Extra manning or plotting routines will be arranged then, depending on the locality/situation. Specific arrangement for bridge manning in fog is wise for ships trading to the USA, and a lookout forward may be required.

11) Keep the ship on the course lines laid off on the chart and allow set as necessary to do so (and use GPS for this in open waters). In coastal waters bring the ship back to the course line and use set to keep her there, rather than simply laying off a new course line to the next way point. The passage planning notes should help with tides/currents. The whole point in laying off courses is that is the route we want to follow; laying off new ones when the ship has set inside can take her much closer to dangers than was the intention.

12) Fix positions regularly and continue to do so even when there is a pilot on board to ensure the pilot's route is safe. Ensure that pilot's instructions are correctly carried out by helmsmen and look after the pilot with coffee etc. We are still fully responsible for the navigation of the ship despite the presence of the pilot and position fixing and track monitoring continue in just the same way as without a pilot aboard. Language difficulties or unusual expressions sometimes confuse helmsmen. The ability of each helmsmen must be verified.

13) Never respond to calls on VHF to 'ship on my starboard bow' etc for any action unless you are positive of her identification (an Aldis lamp may be used for such identification at night). Even then, do not agree to any action that contradicts normal safe practices. This is a frightening habit in some ships but is better controlled rather than banned, as it is going to happen anyway.

14) All 'cancelled' charts will be removed from the chart room as they are replaced but there is a time lag in getting corrections/new editions. Do check and identify – lights and buoys can shift very easily – so try not to use them for position fixing without

using the land as well. In some overseas ports foreign charts are used for the channels and for these we may receive no corrections.

(15) The 'man overboard' response and manoeuvring data are posted on the bulkhead in the wheelhouse; you should be fully familiar with the former to respond immediately and be aware of the stopping distances and turning circles of this ship. The manoeuvring data is posted and available to pilots; the 'man overboard' response regarding release of the bridge wing 'man overboards' and Williamson turn should be detailed if they are not already available.

16) The OOW, particularly at sea, should be aware of the situation regarding cargo ventilation or work being carried out on deck. If weather worsens, the deck work may have to be suspended and a watch should be maintained to ensure the safety of those working on deck. Instructions will be specifically given with regard to cargo ventilation but the OOW should be directly aware of the work being carried out on deck (whether routine or of a specific nature) and must be aware that he is the one person able to keep an overview of such work and the safety of those doing it.

17) Rounds of the decks must be made after securing the anchors on any departure. These include ropes, forecastle doors, deckhouse and superstructure doors and lights, hold/tank access hatches, ventilators, any items stowed on deck being adequately secured and equipment left on deck being collected and secured. Rounds of the decks are to be made each evening at the end of the working day but before darkness and these are to be entered in the log. It is then a matter of naming who shall make the rounds; after sailing it will either be the chief officer or the officer on the forecastle for unmooring and at sea either the chief officer or the 1200–1600 OOW. It is a good practice to involve other officers in addition to the chief officer in these basic routines that are only too often neglected in many ships.

18) My presence on the bridge does not mean that I have taken over control from the OOW. My handover to the OOW or my takeover from the OOW will be made clear on each occasion.

General

1) All the deck officers should be familiar with the steering systems and changeover procedures, with all the bridge gear and with all the lifesaving/firefighting equipment, regardless of whose duty it is to look after them. All the publications – watchkeeping, passage planning, codes of practice and manuals etc – are there for your guidance. We may all think we've read them, but it is wise to look through them again from time to time. The background of the officers varies and ability to read pages of English may be limited; the deck officers are bridge watchkeepers firstly and

secondly have their individual duties and responsibilities.

2) If the weather gets bad and we may have to slow down or alter course, call me. Solid water washing aboard will damage deck fittings and ships do not slow themselves down in head seas (the power is being used to drive the ship into the seas rather than through the water). If we are losing more than 25 % of our speed (comparing rpm and log) it may well be time to do something about it. The safety of the ship, the crew and the cargo are always the first considerations and are all in your care while you are on watch. Remove the theory that ships slow themselves down. If the officers cannot sense when the ship is going too fast in heavy weather, give them a mathematical guideline to follow.

3) Call me any time, if in any doubt whatsoever – for navigation, traffic, weather, breakdowns, safety or anything else. I would rather be called many times, apparently unnecessarily, rather than just once too late.

Summary

Many of these 'standing orders' help the anticipation of the OOW and explain what is wanted – another master may have somewhat different ideas – but it helps the officers to know just what is expected from them by the master who is relying on them to manage but to call him if they are unsure of anything.

In the first night orders I would ask the officers to read and sign the standing orders if they are fully understood – and would go through them with the officers together explaining the 'whys' if there was any difficulty with English reading.

Night orders would give courses, rpm, manned/ UMS, clock changes (always at 0200 as far as the log book is concerned) and anything that was going on – fire pump under repair, cargo ventilation, gas-freeing, hatch lids or doors that are deliberately left open, etc.

A copy is normally sent to the owners for their retention.

The aim of providing these standing orders and night orders is to spell out the framework within which the OOW or duty officer is expected to work. It avoids any questions of 'but I wasn't told to do so' by the officers and for all of us in the bridge management team should remove any opportunity for anybody to suggest that we have been negligent in the conduct of our duties. Any such suggestion would be an affront to our individual professionalism!.

Chapter 38

WORKING WITH THE CHIEF ENGINEER

by Mr. M. Jerkovic CEng, Chief Engineer, Croatia

Miroslav Jerkovic, after technical school and two years work in Rijeka shipyard, finished High Maritime School for ship's engineers in 1955 and sailed as EO until 1967 when he was promoted to CEO – first class combined motor and steam. From 1969 to 1997 he sailed with different foreign companies as CEO. The longest service was with Kuwait Shipping Company and United Arab Shipping Company, mostly with British officers, which lasted for over 17 years. He has extensive experience of triple expansion steam engines, then with steam turbine propulsion and different types of diesel engines. He has also served on different types of ships, general cargo, container ships, chemical tankers and Panamax bulk carriers.

Introduction

THE RESPONSIBILITY OF THE Chief Engineer Officer (CEO) is to ensure the most cost effective and efficient function of all machinery on board. From this respect many CEOs can experience difficulties balancing the cost of running an efficient ship with its safety. Naturally, the equilibrium between these two sides depends very much on the owner's policy and standards. Nevertheless, the CEO must always take into consideration, as the first and essential task on board, **the safety of the ship**. From that point of view, it should be stressed that the first and most demanding duty of the CEO is the safety of the ship in its entirety and that also means safety of the seafarers.

Minimising the fire hazard

The right attitude of the seafarer is the first and most decisive factor in safety on board. Safety must be understood, emphasised and applied. Of course, the theoretical knowledge of the fundamentals of fire safety is by no means sufficient. Efficient training and a clear head will assure, in most cases, that initial fires will be extinguished before there is serious damage. Immediately after joining the ship the CEO should, as a first task, start building his own 'safety philosophy'. This should start with a most simple question: "what could go wrong?"

After that, solutions should be thought through; how to prevent and minimise consequences, how to secure recovery and what methods should be applied to enable the ship to reach port safely. Regarding the officers and crew, it is essential to create an atmosphere of mutual interdependence in work and safety. The CEO himself must take the role of a 'safety educator', because a well trained crew is almost never prone to panic and chaos. Drills and procedures are essential. If there is a fire it is very useful to take relevant notes, not only for the purpose of education but also for advancing safety and, if need be, to work on the eventual redesign of fire fighting systems for better prevention.

The International Convention for the Safety of Life at Sea requires all ships to comply with the general principles of safety. The master and CEO are responsible for applying these regulations. As the first 'safety factor' on board, the seafarer must be aware of and be instructed in the need to familiarise himself – immediately upon joining the ship – with escape routes from his cabin, accommodation or engine room in the event of fire. Nobody can ever tell if it could be his last opportunity!

Of course, the master and CEO are not in a position to select the crew. Nor can they teach the crew, if need be, immediately upon joining the ship about their correct duties, maintenance etc. This requires time and training. But what they have to do straight away is to organise and familiarise the crew with the position and use of fire extinguishers, fire hoses etc. and – most important – the way of safe escape, even after a long journey before joining the ship, when the crew is perhaps tired and tempted to go to sleep.

Statistics clearly show that three times as many lives are lost in fires in ships' accommodation compared to losses in the engine room and machinery spaces in general.

The chemistry of fire is well known. The most simple presentation is the triangle of thermal energy (heat), air (oxygen) and fuel. Removal of any of the three sides of the triangle will extinguish the fire – a point which I wish to emphasise. In other words, the hazard of fire is diminished when the crew is trained and aware of the danger of keeping, for example, cotton waste or oiled and paint splashed rags and boiler suits and similar away from pipes or anywhere close to a source of heat. Such old/used materials may cause fire, even through the slow oxidation of oily rags, where spontaneous heating causes ignition and combustion. The waste, therefore, should either be retained in airtight tins or disposed of ashore.

The causes of fire are endless. They include fire from a match or cigarette, electrical short circuits, oily cleaning rags, cotton waste, carelessly handling fuels, improper handling of inflammable materials, mixture of hydrogen and oxygen from batteries etc. It is perhaps worth mentioning that careless cleaning of fuel filters is a frequent cause of fire. In Japan, in a period of 12 years of fire investigation and an analysis of 6000 ships, it was established that **the biggest number of fires in engine rooms was due to inappropriate cleaning of fuel filters**. Frequent fires in engine rooms also come from bursting of uncovered high pressure pipes from fuel pumps to injectors, when the protective covers were forgotten. Many examples show that absent-mindedness can inevitably jeopardise the safety of a ship.

Regarding extinguishing media and installations they are standardised according to the International Maritime Organization. It is impossible here to cover all the systems for fighting fire on board. The most common and effective is carbon dioxide. It is generally designed to fill 40% of engine room space, which is in motor ships, for example, the greatest volume. 85% of the carbon dioxide should be discharged in less than two minutes. The alkaline powder system is more and more in use, especially in chemical tankers. It should be kept in mind that the engine room is a high risk space where, in case of a fire, the CEO must take direct command for fire fighting. Usually, the first step is to stop the fuel supply. Of course, if circumstances permit, it is desirable to change over from fuel oil to diesel, because fuel oil can cool and solidify in the system. With diesel, the engine can be restarted. If the extinguishing system is compressed carbon dioxide, the critical procedure is to check that everybody has abandoned the space where the fire should be extinguished before discharging into it. This is because of the very high risk of suffocation. On the other hand, prompt reaction diminishes the development of fire and reduces damage to machinery or cargo. It is clear how much more effective it is to have a well trained crew. Once again, therefore, it is stressed that the safety of the ship and lives on board depends in the first instance on the crew.

Main propulsion unit – introduction

Whoever sailed as an engineer with a steam reciprocating engine can only confirm that it was a reliable 'old work horse'. It was extremely simple, was reliable in operation and had full power available in ahead and astern movement which could be reached in a few seconds if emergency conditions arose. The engines are of robust and simple construction, inexpensive and with low maintenance. In spite of so many good characteristics their disadvantages are a very low ratio of power to weight and the high specific fuel consumption, making the steam reciprocating engine almost obsolete.

Next let us consider diesel, diesel-electric and gas turbine propulsion systems. As the specific cost of running a large ship by diesel engines is the most economic – the majority of modern ships are, for the time being, propelled by diesel. Regarding the steam turbine, it was reserved until recent times for large oil tankers, liquified gas carriers, third generation container ships and, naturally, for the great passenger ships. The gas turbine could be a very good choice in merchant shipping, as it is in naval ships and the air industry. Certainly the gas turbine offers remarkable savings in volume and weight, compared to diesel engines. And one further point – gas turbines produce approximately 30% less of nitrogen oxides than a diesel engine. In this way it fulfils anti-pollution requirements.

Diesel propulsion plant

The vast majority of merchant ships are propelled by diesel engines and are commonly named motor ships. Most modern seafarers have never sailed with any other type of ship propelling plant. It could, therefore, be of interest to describe briefly the essential parts and functions of such a design. Though the variations are endless, the basic design is more or less common for all diesel engines. In practice, each separate cylinder of an engine constitutes a power unit. If one engine has more units – which in marine diesel engines is general practice – each unit is an exact duplicate of the other. The ignition of the mixture of air (oxygen) and pulverised fuel causes the movement of the piston which moves, via other mechanical parts, the propeller shaft and propeller. In theory, an internal combustion engine, like the diesel engine and other types, is very simple. However, the application of the theory is not so. It has been necessary to employ generations of scientists, engineers, designers and others to develop these engines. In the end, what we have now are powerful, reliable and economic machines.

But let us consult the CEO and his work with, on and many times in, a diesel engine on board ship. What should be his basic care, routine work and responsibilities toward the main propelling diesel machine on board? The main aim, naturally, is to secure the movement of the ship and to prevent, as much as is humanly possible, breakdown of the propelling power. What the owner expects from the CEO is efficiency in the consumption of fuels and lubricating oil and care in the use of spare parts, stores, repairs – which can be carried out by the ship's staff etc. Regarding economy, the diesel engine is the best machine for fuel savings. This means the smallest heat losses (associated with the thermodynamic processes). For safe and efficient service this engine and, more or less, all combustion engines, require cleanliness of the different:

- Coolers
- Filters
- Superchargers.
- Fuel valves (injectors).
- Moving parts.

Very important for the safety and long life (durability) of an engine are clean and non-aggressive lubricants and cooling water. About the quality and influence of fuels, we shall have a word later.

What are the requirements of technology for the safety and longevity of an engine? This is one of the main questions or 'secrets of the trade'. To mention just one: what sort of metal should be used for a cylinder liner? or piston rings? – the components which undergo the most arduous of service conditions. As we all know, metallurgy of today can produce miracles. Still, for cylinder liners, almost without exception, it is 'good old cast iron' with chromium, vanadium, molybdenum alloys, etc. Cast iron possesses self lubricating properties, as opposed to steel, which does not. It is clear, therefore, that the life or durability of an engine depends on correct cylinder lubrication as well as compression and maximum pressure. In cases of lubrication failure it can produce damage, in quite a short period of time, to both pistons and cylinder liners. Bearings are even more sensitive. Very serious damage can occur in a few minutes. Of course, this will happen only during transit of the Suez or Panama canals, or in perils of bad weather! Protection systems must be fitted, but the main point is that care, knowledge and general professional qualities must be applied in the engine room at all times.

As regards different types and application of diesel engines on board, we should bear in mind that any strict classification of diesel engines is arguable. In spite of this, I would like to suggest a general classification for the ship's diesel engine, as slow and medium speed diesel engines. Both types are in use for main propulsion (engine) and for ancillary systems. These components are more or less common for all types of ship's diesel engines. Perhaps, at the head of such a list, we should put the lubricating oil pump and the whole system, of which essential parts are: filters and coolers, purifiers and safety gear. Next is the fresh water cooling system, generally called 'jacket water system', with pumps, coolers etc., also the fuel oil system with pumps, heaters, filters, purifiers etc.

On every diesel engine comes the fuel pump, of very special design, with gear and fuel valve(s) – 'injectors'. With a governor and all the above-mentioned essentials, a rudimentary diesel engine can work. Of course, for a modern diesel engine, many other parts are added. A very important unit is generally known as the supercharger, which utilises exhaust gas energy to provide an additional (supplementary) quantity of air, hence the name 'supercharger'. In this way engine efficiency is considerably increased. But this is not the end. Whatever energy is 'left over' after passing through the supercharger can be used to produce steam in an exhaust gas boiler. In this way, the efficiency of a marine diesel can be very much increased and we have not finished yet. Thermal energy from the main engine cooling water can be also utilised. Every modern ship has a 'fresh water generator', a distillation plant, which desalinizes sea water into high quality fresh water, of only approximately 2ppm (two parts of salt to a million).

However, we shouldn't get carried away with marine diesel engines. There are other power propulsion plants, which we must not neglect.

Marine steam turbine

Marine steam turbines are very reliable machines. This is of a great importance, especially for large ships, where penalties for 'downtime' are very high. Delays are very costly and it is sufficient enough to understand the pressure on the CEO. His attention is divided between boilers, turbines, steam and diesel alternators and many auxiliary plants and machines. The steam turbine, as one of the main components of the plant, gives a good feeling of safety and reliability. Therefore, without running into details, we can try to describe the ship's steam turbine plant; just a few essential parts.

The most basic marine steam turbine plant consists of a steam boiler(s) with accessories, turbines, condenser with extraction and feed pumps. From the condenser, condensed steam – as feed water – returns to the boiler. To improve efficiency after the high pressure turbine cylinder, the steam can be reheated, though the majority of turbines in service are of the so called 'non-reheat' types. The steam turbine, in most ships, operates with inlet steam pressure of 50 bar and a temperature of 510C.

Regarding the types of steam turbines, they are basically 'impulse' or 'reaction' types. The difference is in the way they convert the kinetic energy from steam into the torque. The superheated steam entering the turbine expands progressively through several 'stages' and turns the turbine's rotor. Superheated steam, after completion of expansion and finishing the work in the turbine, enters the condenser. By this way, an optimal proportion of energy is converted from steam to useful work. High vacuum created in the condenser is of great importance. It must be kept steady. Any fall of the vacuum value, for example of 25mm, creates an efficiency drop of 4% power. Engineers know this very well and also where to look for the cause and remedy. Generally speaking, to safeguard turbine efficiency and 'longevity' vacuum is of crucial importance. Utmost care must be given to prevent any humidity in the turbine casing and consequently water erosion, as well as thermal stress by sudden change of temperature. Other dangers are the vibrations and the critical revs, which must be avoided and resolved.

Because different turbine stages (high, low etc. pressure) develop from 3600 to 14000 rpm, it is necessary to reduce these revs, via gear reductors, down to the propeller speeds. They vary from 80 rpm (for full speed) for the fast container ships and up to 140 rpm for VLCCs and large bulk carriers.

Marine boiler

In operation at sea at the present time are three main types of marine steam boilers: bi-drum convection bank, bi-drum radiant and single drum boilers. All of them have superheaters, economisers, air heaters and sootblowers. Irrespective of design or construction, the first and the most important priority for any steam boiler is the cleanliness of all parts, especially the water side. It is very well known for example, that a scale of only 0·6 mm can increase the local temperature by an additional 215C, compared with a clean surface temperature. Scale, therefore, decreases not only the efficiency but the very 'life' of a boiler. Consequently, the chemical cleanliness of distilled water is of crucial importance.

In boiler management the operator (ship's engineer) is fully aware that boilers in general are exposed to extremely hazardous conditions. First of all a very high temperature, abrasive and chemically aggressive fuel constituents etc. Accordingly, vigilance is essential at all times and, because of this, it is necessary to underline that the prime consideration is cleanliness on both sides – gas and water.

One of the most important parameters is the, so-called, 'pH value' (alkalinity) of the feed water. It must be kept at 8·5 to 9·2 TBN (total basic number), preferably at 9·0 at all times. Very important also, is prevention of the penetration of oil from the returns from turbines, pumps and other machinery. Other problems, which are often present, are corrosion, loss of water, flame failure etc. One of the most dangerous occurrences is the hydrogen fire and, of course, the failure of the automation control system.

Maintenance of the feed system is relatively simple, but requires constant attention. It is, firstly, maintenance of the glands and joints of pumps and valves. Generally, steam and water leakage rectification is the most frequent and permanent job which requires attention. The boiler fuel system pumps, filters, purifiers, heaters and burners are also essential parts of the system, with a very important role and must always be kept in good working order. To ensure cleanliness and therefore a good heat transfer across the boiler tubes, not only inside the tube, but also outside the smoke surfaces, ship's boilers have 'sootblowers'. Heat losses in general must be dealt with rigorously, because of the direct influence on the efficiency of the boiler and the whole steam system.

Automation, in more or less every system and plant on board is progressing in new and old ships. It is a challenge which must be accepted and dealt with. Naturally, the CEO is not a superman and it would be wrong to expect him to be an 'expert' in everything. Maintenance and correct performance will be the responsibility of an engineer - specialist but it is the CEO who has the knowledge of processes and the overall performance of the boiler and systems. The CEO has the responsibility to identify and diagnose problems to ensure that the right level of maintenance is carried out and that the plant is operating efficiently. In particular, the CEO must know how to ensure the safety of the machinery.

Fuel oil quality

Far too often, seafarers can see waste oil and fuel sludge from ship's bilges, purifiers and settling tanks in open ocean waters. Discharge of pollutants on land, in the atmosphere and at sea have become alarming. Hopefully the MARPOL requirements should reduce the quantity of environmentally harmful emissions. It is becoming, at long last, a global task. IMO 2000 regulations will be a very serious challenge for shipowners and a very costly business too.

It is clear that residual fuels are not going to get better. Of course, though residual fuel is blended to meet standards, the CEO is never sure of its quality. Or, perhaps, he is almost sure that the blending means adding just enough good (distillate) fuel, to the leftovers after the refining processes! The CEO, therefore, is forced to keep samples of received fuel for at least as long as the 'bunkers' last. To analyse fuel on board thoroughly is practically not possible. The CEO cannot be sure of declared specified qualities, especially the declared percentage of sulphur, aluminium, silicon, vanadium, ash, water etc. Viscosity is critical and it is all very well if there is a viscosity control unit on board to control fuel temperature and to ensure its viscosity before reaching the fuel pumps and injectors. The viscosity should be in a range from 13 to 17 cSt – say generally around 15 cSt. If not, it will certainly lead to trouble.

Regarding the settling tank temperature, for reasons of safety fuel must be held at some temperature lower than the flash point, e.g 14° C (for British flagged ships!). As for separator efficiency, it can be considerably reduced by poor fuel quality or marginally or even completely seized. If the fuel received on board has a fresh water content of up to 3 or even 5% and a salt water up to 3%, the separator(s) and the settling tanks will be able to separate out the water. But it is not the end of the story.

There is always a problem of contaminated water and disposal of sludge. Another problem is high ash content and the very same with sulphur, aluminium, silicon etc. With carbon residue it is not any better and it is well known how injectors become fouled. Also, vanadium is the main contributing factor to the so called 'hot corrosion'. Unfortunately, vanadium is present in all residual fuels. Mexican and Venezuelan fuels, for example, are very well known as such. Many CEOs have nightmares receiving bunkers there. That is, unfortunately, a part of the job, but the CEO must do his very best to overcome problems and difficulties with fuels. So fuel testing has become an increasingly important routine. In my view, companies (shipowners) should perhaps provide the ship with proper (more sophisticated) fuel testing cabinets. This money would be very well invested, because the residual fuels are certainly not going to get any better.

Regarding harmful exhaust emissions, like nitrogen oxides (NOx), soot etc., relatively recently a unit has been launched named a 'fuel conditioner' for the production of water-in-fuel emulsion. Certainly it improves economy and at the same time ecology. Shipowners will most likely accept such a unit in order to respond to IMO requirements. The fuel conditioner is also accepted because of fuel oil sludge reduction, which is very welcomed, as well as NOx reduction for 30% and soot emissions too. Perhaps the so called 'eco-friendliness' will have a chance and the CEO will certainly accept such a plant for 'environmentally friendly propulsion', with great satisfaction.

Intelligent engines

The automation of ship's plant started in the early nineties. Probably the first full size low speed diesel engine without a camshaft was built in 1995. It was an engine with fully electronically controlled functions. These included cylinder lubrication, fuel injection, exhaust valve control and up to the engine start and stop, practically the full range of all mechanical systems, covering all engine functions. The project was named as the 'intelligent engine'. But this automation or 'mechatronic system' still requires a well trained - qualified crew. Engineers can't be replaced by a computer.

The whole technology still needs overall supervision, manoeuvring, maintenance etc. The system can give much better handling of engine functions. It can provide the CEO with good quality information. It can maintain and guarantee a greater flexibility and in general, better handling. In this way, a so called intelligent engine can advance safety and economy because it is crucial to have the ship running economically, whenever required, correctly and as much as possible with a minimum of harmful influences on the environment.

So, here we come again to the CEO, proper operation and professional maintenance. The reliability of components and systems, by which to trace the eventual deviations leading to stops or damages, must be improved. It must also be better than the crew, however well trained. It is necessary to keep in mind that proper operations, timely maintenance and the ability to trace defects and deviations – which all can lead to stops – depend on the human factor. Again, the main criteria are safety, efficiency, reliability and good maintenance. Once again the same conclusion: propulsion plants should be safe and simple. But they are definitely neither cheap nor maintenance free.

Fuel injection systems for the large diesel engine have evolved rapidly over recent years, driven by the need to satisfy emissions limits and therefore to satisfy legislation. Requirements for reduced fuel consumption means generally that the fuel spray into the cylinder must be controlled more precisely. Fuel quantity and the injection timing must be regulated by input from engine sensors and this inevitably leads to the introduction of an electronically controlled fuel system. Many new engines in service today have, for example, hydro-mechanically controlled 'jerk pumps' and injectors. They may have a hydro-mechanical governor which can be replaced with an electronic plus electric actuator. The whole system is much more flexible. In general, the electronic unit can provide the entire engine control and monitoring function. In the automobile industry such systems are already installed in over 100,000 similar units. The forecast is for a rapid application of such systems everywhere in shipping, perhaps in only five to six years.

Analysis clearly shows that the likelihood of technical errors are minimal compared with human in approximately the ratio of one to five or more (in favour of the technology!). Human errors usually occur because of deficiencies in knowledge and lack of experience, or perhaps because of inadequate leadership. But there are problems due to fatigue because of reduced manning. Simplicity of plants and mechanisms, by all means – we can accept this with greetings – but a crew of ten or even less could be a very tricky experiment and certainly could produce dangerous effects, especially if there is a need for firefighting. The times are past, alas, when the CEO knew his ship and engine inside out and tended it with loving care. These are days of tight schedules, short 'turn around time', drastically reduced crews and a decline in practical knowledge and standard of engine room crews. A certain standard of safety, therefore, must be created by the use of reliable materials, quality components, constant monitoring and intelligent design and construction.

Intelligent design means simplicity, achieved in a way that the irregularities are indicated to the operators (crew) clearly and on time. In this way reactions are prompt and the necessary work is carried out on time, relatively easily. The latest formulas: KISS and EEEE (Keeping it Simple for Seamen and Economy, Ecology, Environmental friendliness and Electronics) are very costly demands. How much is all of that close to reality? And how often will the CEO get his hands dirty? He should be watching the computer screen to get information about the work and the state of machinery and components. He should analyse the parameters, trends etc., then decide what will go ashore for maintenance or repairs. Perhaps there is nothing much more he can do with a crew of just a few people but how far can crew reduction go? Is our ability to intervene compromised with such sophisticated technology? The ISM code requires fully qualified and trained crew on board, especially for emergencies.

Simplification and advanced reliability of ship's machinery would be very beneficial. But can shipbuilders supply the shipping industry? Certainly they can, but at what price? The correct question should, perhaps, be: at how high a price?

Demands for the consumption of fuels with a low content of nitrogen and sulphur emissions, reliability and simplicity of the propulsion and other plants, eventually with a remote diagnoses etc. has a high price. Therefore automation should be environmentally friendly, user friendly (!) and perhaps owner friendly too.

Propellers

Perhaps the most simple, if not adequate classification would be to make a division between propellers of fixed and variable pitch. Both are very well known and I would prefer to point out some new, interesting designs, which have appeared very recently in the shipping industry. One is named as 'contracted and loaded tip' (CLT) and another is a part of a new concept of propulsors.

Interest in the CLT propeller is based on its efficiency and very good characteristics. The advantage over the classic propeller lies in four important points. The CLT propeller improves course stability, considerably reduces or eliminates hull vibrations, improves manoeuvrability and – very important for propulsion machines – fuel consumption is lower by up to 10%. Hopefully it will be reduced more with further development. The first ships furnished with such CLT propellers show the above-mentioned characteristics and, very important, this model of propeller could be applied to practically all types and designs of ships, from Panamax bulk carriers to fast feeder and container ships. Other good features are satisfactory cavitational behaviour and low vibrations of the ship's hull. Perhaps the so called 'intelligent engine' deserved a propeller of that type, as a crown to propulsion economy optimisation.

Another application of the ship's propeller is as a 'bow thruster'. The use of this plant is very popular in shipping today because of the much improved manoeuvrability in ports. The 'time is money' saying could be applied here very well. It is not necessary to remind you how good the bow thruster is for its 'ambient friendliness', but to remind you that the diesel engine or electric motor which drives the bow thruster has a considerably reduced exhaust contamination of the air in ports, as compared to tugs. Another type of propeller which deserves our attention is a very new propulsion system, where two propellers are driven by one synchronous electric motor, fitted in a submerged housing. The propellers are on the same shaft, one forward and one aft of the housing. Each propeller operates at 50% of total load. The advantage in efficiency is considerable. According to tests, the twin propeller unit shows an incredible 20% higher efficiency compared with the standard rudder propeller. It looks like the future has started!

Conclusion

At the end of this chapter, I would like to offer a word more about professional requirements and how I see it. Safety of the ship is the first and most important task and duty. To put it another way, I wish to repeat the following: fire fighting systems, emergency generator, emergency fire pump, lifeboat and lifeboat engines must always be in good working order and readiness. The seafarer cannot afford to be lulled into hoping that perils will not appear. As with the safety gear, so ship's staff must, in the first instance, always be prepared (trained!) to prevent conditions which might lead to eventual cases of emergency or fire hazard.

As for the ratings, irrespective of their nationality and irrespective of their training, it is essential to have a 'clear atmosphere' on board. Fair play is essential. All on board are members of a team and so should behave accordingly! And one point more; occasionally and very unfortunately, we could also have on board so-called 'trouble maker(s)'. Perhaps not the best, but the only approach, is to make a sincere attempt to understand and try to help, if possible. If not, with no hesitation, send them off from the ship, because very often it can easily develop into unpredictable difficulties.

It is not the job of senior officers to be psychologists but they have to be responsible for the whole ship first. Regarding the position and work of an Engineer Officer, he has to be a competent, self reliant operator, who must have a full understanding of the engine as a whole unit and all components and systems. Equally essential, he must be able to perform the necessary maintenance and to take action to prevent damage. In other words, he should be a professional and part of a professional team. As part of the ship's staff, he must be well trained to use his skill efficiently and always be ready to prevent conditions for any appearance of a fire hazard.

Regarding the old (and very often misused!) Latin proverb: 'Errare humanum est' (to err is human), it should be forgotten on board. Perhaps it should be translated as an idiotic approach, especially for younger officers. They should be encouraged to ask, for nobody on board is a superman! In turn, they should expect a patient reply and an explanation.

The old saying that oil and water don't mix has been proved to be very wrong even in fuel technology, never mind between people! Once, long ago, it was the approach to the two ship's departments – deck and engine. Can you imagine with twenty people or less (the idea of ten is already present!) that they should be divided, the master and CEO communicating only officially and only when forced to, or only by the engine/bridge telegraph? From my experience on board, I have realised how important are correct relations between the master and CEO. They should be friendly, but also with respect for mutual responsibilities. In the cabin, perhaps, it is fine to communicate with names or whatever fits. On the bridge or the engine room, however, only and exclusively by the position (title) so as to show all the respect given to each other's responsibilities, the psychological burden (pressure) of the job and by such behaviour to give support to each other also. This formal approach reduces stress and develops mutual trust and understanding. It is also of crucial value and importance to keep each other informed of everything that is going on, what action has been undertaken, or what plans are for maintenance, surveys etc.

Regarding the 'office' (company, owner), communications can sometimes be a 'sore' point. A cable: 'do your best', is not a great help. It would be much more welcome too if it asked for the situation or problem and offered alternative solutions. Communications nowadays are very advanced, but unfortunately misused also! It is easy to ask and give advice, to exchange opinions and perhaps to help just by talking, keeping the records and taking short notes. Some interesting or important details and remarks often come out to suggest eventual solutions.

A word more with regard to manning standards. From the owner's viewpoint, everything is based on cost and economy. Starting with the management and the crew's cost, there are the stores, maintenance and repairs, spare parts, fuels and lubes, insurance etc. The crew's cost today is everywhere under severe scrutiny. The tendency is to reduce the crew as much as possible. It immediately brings up the question of loyalty, training, continuity etc. I have a very strong impression, perhaps more than just an impression, that loyalty and continuity is being lost everywhere. Some Danish and Norwegian companies still successfully stick to this, with the benefits of continuity for the crew and profit to the owner. But in such an atmosphere and environment, all of a sudden, statistics show, as of all breakdowns and damages, that the human error becomes 5:1 and higher. A master and CEO over 55 years old cannot get a job, when their experience and emotional strength and stability are at their peak. The House of Lords Committee reflected critically on that policy where the depth of experience is reduced dramatically. Perhaps it could be fruitful to analyse the experience of the crew and the ship's reliability. Perhaps, when software and electronics become the most important element and when the concept of a truly 'intelligent engine' is more 'in', loyalty and continuity may be of less importance. It is difficult to be categoric, but perhaps the times when the CEO knew his ship inside out and tended the engine plants with loving care are over.

In closing this chapter, I wish to communicate to you, only how I have seen it, how I have lived it and how I have survived and retired, with reasonably good health and a reasonably clear head. I would like to point out, even more, that I wish to stress the need for a professional approach to the seamen's life. A life based not only on knowledge of thermodynamics, astronomy, flash points or stowage factors, but much more. A life which is founded perhaps on a kind of 'human bondage'. A bit of everything is involved, when I think and talk about it with you, gentle reader. So, if you have read these lines, thank you for your kind attention! In this way you have helped to share with me a bit of this fascination and experience.

Chapter 39

WORKING WITH THE CATERING DEPARTMENT

by the Committee of the Association of Marine Catering and Supply

Introduction

PROVISION OF A HIGH QUALITY of victualling, together with attention to personal health and welfare facilities, provides the right environment for good industrial relations, with efficient and safety-conscious crewing. Catering standards, departmental duties, and workload vary between individual ship managers, with the nationality of flag and complement and the differing requirements of deep sea, coastal and ferry trades.

The information which follows outlines in a generalised manner the what, why, where and how of shipboard catering.

Workload and complement: Determined by the crew manning regulations of the flag-State, particularly numbers of officers and ratings, and the ship manger's requirements on menu content and personal service standards.

Food preparation and meal service: Cooking, to destroy harmful bacteria and parasites, renders food more digestible in texture and also more receptive to the palate, by pleasing the eye and stimulating the digestive juices.

Housekeeping: An essential part of civilised living is the maintenance of a clean, pleasant and orderly environment. Protection of the investment in stores and equipment supplied for the vessel's continued operation demands consumption control with clean and orderly storeroom arrangements.

Administration and control: Supervision by an officer or senior rating in possession of recognised cookery, catering and supervisory qualifications. Knowledge and experience in health, immigration, customs and security procedures and the consequences of breaching these requirements.

Cost control: Estimates of average catering expenditure relative to daily operating costs, excluding fuel, shore administration and depreciation: victualling, between 3% and 4%; bond/bars/shop – usually sold at prices which are expected to cover handling and incidental costs; chandlery and furnishings 0·5%; shore laundry 0·5%; catering personnel 4%–5%.

Statutory requirements

Minimum standards are specified by the flag state and may be exceeded and enhanced by ship managers' own standards, values and requirements.

Victualling scales: Minimum quantities of staple food commodities usually stated as weight per man per week and embodied within articles of agreement. Ship managers may also publish their own scales. These exceed statutory minima, but form the basis for their daily cost allowances and include small goods (condiments, herbs, spices, sauces) and convenience foodstuffs which are usually outside statutory scales.

Medical scales: Recommended medicines, consumables and equipment for a specified complement size and voyage duration.

Fresh water: Requirements for the storage, treatment, purity, testing and uncontaminated supply of potable water for drinking and domestic consumption.

Articles of Agreement: Contractual agreement between seafarer and employer, itemising flag state statutory obligations and requirements. May also itemise minimum requirements for cabin fittings, carpeting, bedding, towels, soap, personal tableware and protective clothing issues.

Administration and control

Victualling: Selection, purchase, storage and preparation for consumption of foodstuffs to meet statutory victualling scales and ship managers' prescribed standards within expenditure guidelines. Special functions catering, for owners, managers, charterers, shippers etc.

Bond / bars / shop: Purchase, storage, sale and cash accounting arrangements for wines, spirits, beers, minerals, tobacco goods, toiletries and clothing.

Laundry work: Operation of ship's own laundry plant and/or use of shore contractors to maintain clean linen stocks.

Medical: Maintenance of medical stores in compliance with flag-state statutory scales and appropriate secure locked stowage for dangerous and controlled drugs. Provision of on-board first-aid and medical facilities to meet accidents and emergencies. Maintenance of ships' medical log of accidents, illnesses and treatments rendered. Liaison with port agents on medical, dental and vaccination facilities for personnel.

Equipment and chandlery: Purchase, storage and control of working consumables, crockery, galley utensils, housekeeping equipment and uniform stocks. Some managers also require the catering officer to coordinate the purchasing and control of general chandlery for the whole vessel.

Port entry documentation: Preparation of port papers, crew lists, special declarations for restricted or dutiable goods and stores.

Relationship with port authorities: Interpretation and compliance with international, national and port requirements and procedures relating to notifiable diseases, immigration controls and customs regulations, together with knowledge of requirements and procedures when security is breached – eg contagious diseases, illegal entry, stores theft, payment of duties and taxes.

Procedures and practice

Purchasing: Forward planning and relating ship managers' instructions to vessel's trading pattern. Anticipating consumption in relation to stocks held and the availability of produce in ports of call, at a price and quality to meet requirements, without incurring losses due to poor quality, overlong stowage or excessive quantity.

Stores orders should always be in writing and be countersigned by the master. Ship managers often give guidance on suitable ports for purchasing sea stock stores, including frozen, canned and dry provisions, also durable stores such as linen, crockery etc. Fresh fruit and vegetables must be purchased more frequently and quantity related to quality, price, voyage length, store capacity and the adequacy of substitutes available – eg frozen, canned or dried fruits and vegetables.

Where managers do not specify quality, pack size and style, purchases should be of a quality adequate for longer-term storage relative to intended consumption, with pack sizes appropriate to meal or daily consumption without wastage. Large cans and bulk sacks are wasteful for small complements. Woven sacks harbour insects and should not be accepted, as most bulk dry-provisions can be supplied in multi-ply paper sacks. As a general guideline on price and quality, UK and northern Europe remain the most cost-effective purchasing area for all stores.

Currency fluctuations obviously influence prices. A broad index of 100 for UK/Belgium/Holland during 1985/86 compared with:

120	France, Italy (north), Singapore
135	Greece, Australia, Chile, Brazil (South)
145/155	Italy (south), Spain, Morocco
175/190	Malta, Hong Kong, Saudi Arabia, Canada, USA (Atlantic)
200/235	Panama Canal, Uruguay, Japan, Gibraltar, USA (Gulf and Pacific)
250	Suez Canal

Ethnic commodities may not always be widely available, especially meat and poultry slaughtered to Mohammedan rites, and selective pre-planned purchasing is essential to meet requirements.

Storage: Foodstuffs are perishable products and require specialised storage to maintain fitness for consumption within a limited period. Any food item stocked in excess of five to six months is liable to progressive deterioration or infestation making it unfit for consumption.

Subject to good quality purchases, the usual storage temperatures are:

-10°/-18°C	*Deep frozen:*	meats, fish, ice cream, fruit, vegetables, some convenience foodstuffs.
0°/4°C	*Chilled:*	dairy produce, cheese, eggs, butter, fats, oils, fresh fruit and vegetables.
4°/8°C	*Handling room: (if available)*	potatoes, bananas.
10/15°C	*Air-conditioned:*	dry provisions: flour, sugar, cereals, also cleaning chemicals and products.
15°/20°C	*Ambient:*	utensils, durable chandlery, linen, crockery etc.

Refrigerated stores require good uninterrupted air circulation to prevent warm spots occurring, leading to thawing and putrefaction. All circulation must not be obstructed and neat, orderly stows give easy access for quantity and quality checks. All stores should be tidily stowed, labelled and capable of being read and counted from the aisles without further sorting and climbing. Wherever possible, stowage sequence should be similar to the ship managers' stocks records or account books, to facilitate checking and recording. All stows require securing against seaway movement.

Hygiene: Essential to have a systematic approach to the clearance of all refuse, empty cartons and wrappings wherever located. Storeroom decks require to be swept and kept clean on a regular basis. Stores racked with lowest levels stowed on boards clear of deck.

Fresh fruit and vegetables may be kept with other stores which can be served without prior cooking, such as cheeses and butter. It is essential to ensure that such produce is well wrapped and protected against earth and plant dust, carrying food poisoning bacteria, which is circulated by the cooling plant. Dairy produce also needs careful wrapping to protect it from acquiring the strong flavours of fruits, even though these will be segregated within the storeroom. Cold chamber scuppers need regular checking to ensure brine levels are maintained.

Shelf life dating: Primarily a retail facility, it provides a guide for the consumption sequence of ship's stores. Foodstuffs do not become 'unconsumable' overnight on the basis of date stamping and producers always allow a safety margin. Constant checking and care is required to avoid stock loss through over-stowage or unwise purchasing. The UK Department of Transport, Environment and the Regions (UKDTER) recommends that the period between production date and consumption date should be split one third for distribution and warehousing and two thirds for ship's use. The main determinant of consumability must remain physical condition and appearance of foodstuffs.

Rotation: All stocks should be consumed in rotation, with earliest supply being consumed first, unless this leads to potential losses from the rapid deterioration of newer purchases.

Health and hygiene in food handling

Ensure that:

1. Correct temperature control is maintained in all refrigerated and food stores.
2. Thawed produce is not re-frozen without prior cooking or rendering other preservative treatment.
3. Foodstuffs are not exposed to ambient temperatures for prolonged periods.
4. Food is not prepared too far in advance of meal times. It should be consumed very shortly after preparation and cooking.
5. Hot food is not frozen or refrigerated without first being allowed to cool to ambient temperature.
6. Correct cookery techniques, including temperatures, are used.
7. Frozen foods, especially meats and fish, are thoroughly thawed before processing and cooking.
8. Raw and cooked foods are never allowed to come into contact with each other, as this can lead to cross contamination with food poisoning bacteria. Similarly, knives, utensils, slicing machines, cutting boards and preparation surfaces must not be used for both raw and cooked foodstuffs without thorough intermediate cleaning.
9. Correct clothing is worn by all galley and food handling staff, both for personal protection and to prevent cross-contamination.
10. Infected personnel are kept away from food preparation and service areas. Coughs, sneezes and spittle can all transmit bacteria and it is incumbent on all concerned to maintain the highest possible level of good habits and hygiene in personal behaviour and at work.
11. 'No smoking' is strictly enforced in food storage, preparation and service areas.
12. Separate hand-wash facilities are provided in food preparation and service areas. Wash-up sinks must not be used for personal hygiene.
13. No person with open cuts, sores or skin eruptions is permitted to work in food handling areas. High visibility dressings or other suitable covering must be applied to these wounds before food is handled by the infected person.
14. An ample supply of clean linen or disposables is available for hand drying.
15. Spillages and waste matter on decks are cleared immediately and that decks of food preparation and service areas are cleaned after every meal service.

Pest control

Infestation is usually evidence of dirty conditions, inadequate cleaning and possibly the receipt of infested stores or packaging. Early eradication treatment is essential, either by use of shore contractors and/or a programme of treatment by ship's staff. New stock should not come into contact with old, infested stock. Prevention of infestation in the first place should be a prime consideration. Ensure that:

1. Food is not stored, processed or consumed outside of the designated storeroom, galley, pantry or saloon messroom areas.
2. Meals are not taken into cabins other than under controlled situations – eg medical cases. Soiled plates and discarded food attracts insects and flies which carry diseases.
3. Bulk foodstuffs are stowed in plastic food bins wherever possible, and all non-essential packaging, woven sacks and other wrappings are disposed of quickly.
4. There is a systematic procedure for the quick removal of food waste and refuse from food areas. When port regulations require special disposal, all waste and refuse should be removed to the designated and covered receptacles quickly and frequently.
5. There is a regular cleaning programme with close attention to corners beneath furniture and fittings, and other places which are difficult to reach.

Menu planning

Balanced and attractively presented meals provide variety and interest. Balanced menus which take nutritional values into account, contribute to good health, mental and physical efficiency. Seafarers require on average some 3,300 calories per day. Dietary and ethnic requirements as well as statutory scale allowances have to be taken into account. Special arrangements, such as additional rations or enlarged menu content, may apply for national or religious festivals. Consumption of popular items must be balanced with stockholdings and should include the less popular but often more nutritious items in the interests of healthy menu composition, variety and economy. A limited menu content can be dull and repetitive, leading to high consumption of the food available and it is therefore necessary to equate cooking capacity with demand. More extensive menus offering choices spread consumption and enable small quantities remaining from previous meals to be included, reducing preparation workload, wastage and costs.

The *current trend* is *away from* some traditional foods such as animal fats, whole milk, butter, full fat cheese, sugar and the undue use of salt *towards* whole cereals, lean meat, fish, poultry, fresh fruit and vegetables. Traditional British dietary habits have led to obesity related ailments – eg high blood pressure, diabetes and heart disease, with menus low in the dietary roughage necessary to help the bodily functions.

Meal service: There is a trend away from three full hot meals a day towards two meals with an informal buffet-style lunch. Self-service, buffet style presentation of meals is popular especially for cold courses, salads and lunches. Overall this can result in reduced steward workload for table service, but it is still necessary to clear soiled tableware and do the washing-up.

Safety

Statutory requirements of the flag state, eg the UKDTER's *Code of Safe Working Practice for Merchant Seamen*, and ship manager's additional requirements determine the safety standards to be met. It is incumbent on all to contribute to safe working on board by the application of care, common sense and cooperation. Ship safety, personal safety and job safety are inter-related. Ensure that:

1. Elements of safety already mentioned in this chapter are observed.
2. There is due consideration for others, as safe work practices relate closely to hygiene and good health.
3. Safety clothing and standard uniform dress is worn as appropriate in working areas.
4. There is a clear understanding of galley safety and action to take – eg deep fat fryer fire, turn pan handles inwards, keep gangways clear, wash knives with care, disconnect electrical equipment when cleaning or maintaining.

Work schedules: A planned programme should be followed to spread the workload as evenly as possible over the work period without excessive overtime. Specify the required hours of duty with rest and meal breaks, job description, areas to be covered and special duties. Indicate who directs the working arrangements.

Routine maintenance: Chandlery equipment and consumables should be used in a cost effective way to achieve good 'housekeeping' standards of cleanliness, safety and public health. A typical cleaning routine would include:

Galley and pantries

Food preparation utensils and machinery	– Wash after each use
Decks and working surfaces	– Wash after each meal service
Refuse removal	– After each meal
Refuse containers	– Wash daily
Fittings	– Wash twice weekly, or more frequently if necessary
Bulkheads, deckheads	– Wash weekly and conduct routine check for infestation evidence
Pantries	– Wash daily

Saloons and messrooms

Tables, chairs and vinyl decks	– Wash and clean dry after each meal. Thorough weekly cleaning
Carpets	– Vacuum after each meal
Storerooms	– Empty and re-stow every 2 to 6 weeks depending on stock levels, sweep daily, wash monthly *and* before each main storing.

Alleyways	– Sweep and wipe daily, deeper treatment as appropriate
Cabins	
Carpets and decks	– Sweep twice weekly
Furnishing	– Dust and polish weekly
Toilets and showers (cabin and public), bathrooms and laundries	
Decks, bulkheads, fittings and machinery	– Wash or wipe daily and check supply of disposables and soaps
Shower heads and flexible hoses	– Soak thoroughly every three months in chlorine solution
Tumble driers	– Clean filters after each use

All washing must be done using fresh potable water.

Training: An increasing number of non-UK catering ratings have only minimal craft training and seafaring experience. When ratings are willing to learn, properly structured on-the-job tuition can result in a better quality catering crew on subsequent appointments. If guidance and tuition is not attempted, there is unlikely to be much improvement in quality of personnel and, as it is impossible to stand still, there will be a lowering of standards.

Training in the following will contribute to the maintenance of safe working conditions and catering standards; managers' requirements, standards and job specification; health and hygiene practices.

Detailed accounting records

Invoices: These should be clearly signed by receiving officer and master with shortages, surpluses and breakages clearly marked. Invoices are usually settled by one of the following methods: as arranged by the ship managers; port agent as part of vessel's disbursements; master from vessel's cash float; ship manager's office direct with supplier; ship manager's office through an agent of the supplier.

Whichever method is adopted, the value of catering invoices is usually recorded in various books of account, and the master's cash records, if applicable.

Victualling: Account books show commodity, quantities stocked, purchased, remaining and stock valuation; invoice summary of purchases and value of the final remaining stock; comparison of actual consumption with scale allowances. Final analysis to show consumption value compared with budget allowance, usually on a cost per person/day and on a total cost per voyage day.

Bond/bar/shop: Account books show stock held, purchased and remaining on closure and selling prices applied; invoice summaries for purchases; cash receipts record; and subsequent payments to master or agents.

Inventory/equipment: Account books show stock held, purchased and remaining; invoice summary for purchases; stationery stocks and summary of invoices for shore laundry contractors; interior and soft furnishings maintenance and replacement may also be included within this category. Possibly includes statutory medical stores (excluding specific shore-administered treatments).

Maintenance: Record of painting and repairs with brief details of work completed and dates.

Files: Spare copies of port forms; spare copies of invoices and price quotations for comparison with other ports and use of relief personnel.

Storeroom operation
D. Sams, Managing Director, Garrets Ltd., UK

Physical Inventory should be taken:

- Before an order is placed.
- At the end of each month.
- When there is a change in chief steward/chief cook.

When possible, inventory counts should be carried out by two people, as this ensures a more accurate count. Items should be called as they are in the shelves, in the same order as they are stacked on the shelves to avoid miscounting.

Common errors which can occur when performing inventory counts:

- Miscounting, and organised storeroom should minimise this problem.
- Uncertainty about package size and weight can also lead to miscounting.
- All boxes and cartons should be checked if opened.
- Behind boxes and shelves should also be looked at: this could help locate missing items.
- Loose items should be weighed.

Chief Steward receiving checking list
- Quality, quantity and weight count of the invoice should be checked against the invoice.
- Inspect all cases or items that appear damaged.
- Expiry dates should be checked.
- Check that fruits and vegetables are fresh.
- Fresh fish (whole) is an extremely perishable item: if delivered attention should be taken in checking for firm flesh and no offensive odours. Fish eyes should be clear and bright and gills should be red/pink and free from any slime.
- Check all items for evidence of insect or rodent infestation or contamination.
- Check products for unusual or foul odours.

Returning unsatisfactory merchandise
Any damaged/spoiled items should be refused and either exchanged or deleted from the invoice, or covered by a separate credit note from the supplier.

Storeroom procedure
The purpose of any storeroom procedure is to ensure that the food received is available for processing when needed, without spoilage or deterioration.

Storerooms or storage place, refrigerators and freezers, should be kept clean, neat and organised so that items are easily located. There should be a place assigned for every item. Shelves should be labelled in the order of the inventory book listings Only authorised personnel should be permitted to enter the storeroom. When the chief steward is not in the area, doors should be kept locked and keys should be controlled.

One major rule in storeroom operations is '**first in, first out**'. Stock must be rotated to avoid being buried or forgotten. There is little extra work involved to move the old stock and place the new stock in the back or in the bottom. With this procedure you will avoid spoilage of food, which results in waste and loss and money.

Marking the date of arrival
on incoming items with a permanent marker on the boxes of meat, fish and perishable items is a must. It makes stock rotation much more easy to follow. Dairy products are dated by the dairy company, bakery products and rice should be tagged with their dates and all non-original containers *must be labelled* with the new product.

Expiration date
on all perishable food and beverage should be strictly observed. Food in danger of spoiling must be used quickly to avoid loss. Sometimes certain stock lies forgotten on shelves. Dead stock must be used or disposed of.

Catering management companies
Ships vary and with such a heavy demand for catering services aboard passenger ships it is inevitable that they have their own catering departments. The staff may be hired independently of the company, similarly ship storing may be subcontracted to specialist suppliers.

Increasingly masters on general cargo vessels are having to take a greater responsibility for catering supplies and voyage records can provide a useful insight into past practices and a guide for future ordering.

With further reduction in crews it is becoming economic to sub-contract catering supplies to a specialist company. They have specialist knowledge of ships and trades and can purchase in bulk and obtain discounts for this. Also there is a trade off in manpower which can tip the balance between management fee and company benefits.

Chapter 40

USING SHIPBOARD COMPUTER BASED MAINTENANCE SYSTEMS

by Captain Murdo Macleod FNI

Captain Macleod joined the Merchant Navy as an ordinary seaman in 1954. He joined United Baltic as third officer, being promoted to master in 1968. In 1973 he joined Salen UK in the Marine Services Division in 1979. In 1985 he set up Macleod Marine/Amos Systems and specialised in stock control and inventory management. He is a Fellow of The Nautical Institute.

The planned maintenance system concept

MAINTENANCE SYSTEMS should be graphical user interfaced (GUI) and highly visual, with features for inventory control and purchasing administration. They should be flexible and user-friendly. They should incorporate the following functions:

- Planned maintenance.
- Repairs, modification and docking work.
- Maintenance history.
- Spare parts transactions (usage/inventory).
- Import/export of data (linked to communications.
- Graphical interface (drawing/plans, etc.).
- Requisition of spare parts.
- Purchase of stock items.
- Quotation comparison.
- Budget.
- Transport documentation.
- Reports (any database information).

The maintenance system should present data in ways that are meaningful to the user. Functions are to be tightly linked with data, so that each operation is only a mouse click away.

This will be a marked improvement on the old systems: manual, con-cards, simple DOS, where no integration between maintenance and spare parts occurred. History was hardly ever written and, even if it was, with the passage of time it was very difficult to link to a specific incident or spares usage. Stock control was hardly ever exercised. It was, and still is, one of the most important aspects of a good maintenance system, with the result that the vessel's crew were never certain about which spares, or stock, they had on board, or where they were located. There was also a tendency to put wrongly ordered parts amongst the correct spares, later resulting in the crew being under a false sense of security. When these parts were then required urgently, the cost of shipping them to the vessel often exceeded the cost of the parts themselves (when you take into account the cost and freight of the wrongly ordered parts). It is for that, and many other reasons – integrated system, less breakdown, better maintained vessel, better communication between vessel and office – that

owners and managers decided on implementing these computer systems which have been proved to be successful.

There was also little or no continuity when one officer relieved another: time just did not allow it. As the vessel's system was not linked to the office, one individual, who did not use the system properly, could in as little as two months bring the system to a state of chaos. Because of that and other reasons, manual systems often fell into disuse and went out of favour.

The vessel's managers, in their offices, often had no clear picture of what was happening on board their vessels until it was too late, i.e. these systems never justified the expense of their setup, never had a definable saving and were never very successful. Other points to consider are: crew sizes have been reduced considerably since the advent of these systems and vessel turn round time, or time in port, has been reduced.

There are several components to a GUI (such as Windows) planned maintenance system:

- Platform (SQL Anywhere, Oracle etc.).
- Software (Spectec's A4W, MMS's Windows Systems etc.).
- Database (vessel's equipment, spares, jobs etc.).
- History (input information on maintenance, breakdown, spares usage, requisitions, purchase orders etc.).

The first three will usually be purchased and installed before the user ever sees them. The last item is all the information the user inserts as he uses the system and after he has proper training in its use. All the information and figures in this paper are based on SpecTec's Amos system.

Training in the proper use of these systems is vitally important in understanding, using and, for your employers, getting the financial return they should expect from such a system. The training should cover concept; maintenance; spares and stock control; purchasing, from requisition to receiving purchase order; import and export; backup procedures; and how to manage the system on board. This applies for whichever software you have on board your vessels.

Practical reasons for their use

There are many reasons for their use on board well-managed vessels today, especially so if the same systems are used by all vessels in the fleet:

1. Economic reasons.
2. Better management of the deck, engine and accommodation maintenance.
3. Better integration between maintenance, stock control and purchasing.
4. Better control of hull and engine classification requirements.
5. Better control of maintenance historical records for ISM requirements.
6. Easier assimilation for crew when transferring between vessels in the same fleet.

Terminology used

The terminology used in this paper will be as follows for the main items:

Component

A system or unit of equipment (such as tank; winches; safety equipment; pump; lifeboat; compressor; main engine or sub-system etc.), against which planned maintenance can be carried out.

Corrective maintenance

Maintenance which is irregularly planned for inclusion in the maintenance schedule (This can include repairs or services which are required some time in the future, such as port repairs or dry-dock work) which would usually be ordered from an outside contractor.

History

Usually, in planned maintenance, it is sufficient to report the work as done with date, time taken if required and parts used, if any used. History does not need to be written if you did the job as per specification, except when clearances or measurements are taken, or you did or noticed something which was not included in the job. When it is a classed component, then history should always be entered. History should ALWAYS be entered for unplanned maintenance (cause – effect – action) and for corrective maintenance.

Job code

The identification code and/or number, which usually includes a job heading.

Job description

A detailed description of a planned or corrective maintenance job, which should include full and clear details such as clearances or measurements required, with limits if appropriate.

Planned maintenance

Maintenance that is planned and carried out at regular intervals so as to prevent equipment breakdown (This can include hourly; weekly; monthly and yearly periods or multiples thereof. It also includes survey items and others, such as certificates, all required to be done at fixed period intervals).

Power tip

The icon in any GUI system which, when depressed, will give you access to whatever you want to work with or use, abbreviated as PT.

Stock item

Any item which can be used by the vessel such as spare parts; tools; charts; consumables (cleaning material, stationery, foodstuff, etc.); books and publications and which can be purchased by, or for, the vessel.

Unplanned maintenance

Maintenance which is carried out when a component breaks down or is damaged and the work is done to get it back into operation. Can be called unexpected.

The initial screen on a typical maintenance system should comprise:

- Component PT on far left.
- Stock.
- Jobs.
- Address.
- Functions.
- Rounds.
- Component hierarchy.
- Function hierarchy.
- Generate work order.
- Report work.
- WO detail.
- Planning.
- Requisition WO.
- Forms.
- Reports.
- Help.

See figure 40.1.

Numbering system

Any system used must have some sort of identification or numbering system. This is so that the user of the software can easily understand and handle the information. In Windows based software, the system generates another number when anything is created, so that the software can better handle the information. If the human interface number can be done in a logical way, it will be easier for the user to understand.

The numbering, as long as it is logical, can be virtually anything in a Windows based system. Obviously, if it is easier to understand by the user, e.g. ME – main engine; DG – diesel generators; LB – life boats & equipment; FW – fresh water; LO – lubricating oil systems; HH – hull etc., and all the components and stock items and spares for these items start with these two letters, so much the better. About forty of these two-letter headers would be sufficient for most vessels and about 60 for the largest passenger vessels. If this is followed by three numbers, e.g. ME-??? for components, this could allow you, if needed, to put 1,000 components under ME; or if stock items were ME-???,???, this would allow you to put 1,000,000 items of stock under ME, which would be far in excess of what you would ever need under any two-letter number.

Some numbering systems are very complex and date back to ancient accounting systems. Others can be such as SS.CC.NN.PPP or SSS.CC.NN.PPP, where SSS = system or location, CC = individual component, NN = sub-component and PPP = spare parts. Therefore, if SSS was life saving equipment; CC is lifeboat No. 1 and NN can be lifeboat No. 1 winch/davits/motor etc. so that you can have 100 (0 to 99) sub-components for lifeboat No. 1, against each of which you can have a thousand spare parts (0 to 999).

The numbers with which you identify a component or stock item are type numbers or reference numbers. They are the surest way for the manufacturer to identify a component or spare part. A name can be pronounced in many different ways and could easily be misunderstood, which means that a name without a number cannot be relied on. If you have a computerised system, you will have no problem, as you can have a combination of both and never print out the wrong number, as long as the correct numbers were originally entered.

An example of what some headers for a numbering system might look like, in alphanumeric order, is shown in figure 40.2.

Filters

All areas or screens which can be searched such as components; stock items; addresses etc. usually start with a filter screen, as shown in figure 40.3. If the 'Enter' key is pressed, when the screen is completely blank, all items in the defined area will be displayed (it will load it all into memory). If it has only the first two letters, as LP in this case, only the lifesaving and protection items will be displayed. When you are actually in any of these areas, the filter appears as a power tip on the second PT line, which can be pressed whenever another search is required. In other words, if you require anchor and mooring equipment, you would enter AM <CR>, and all that equipment would be displayed. If you require equipment such as pump, which could be anywhere in the 'name' field, you search for that with the % sign as follows: % pump in name line.

The filter point looks like this:

The resulting filter screen is not to be mistaken for data entering. You only enter new or changed data after passing through the filter in any working area.

Components

Figure 40.4 shows a component from the LP numbering – lifesaving and protection equipment with the free-fall lifeboat highlighted and all its information shown. On the second line of the power tips can be seen all the things which can be done or attached to this, or any other component: New; Save; Delete; Filter; Print; Cut; Copy; Paste; Details (technical description); Jobs (attached with all information such as period, last done etc.); Parts (attached); Counters; Images; Requisition Work and Report Work.

You will also notice that many of the power tips (the first eight) are quite standard in many Windows software programs today. Initially you will only be given access to what is considered necessary by the system manager, until you have proper training. In many companies only the chief engineer and the master are given system user access.

I also show a list of jobs attached to a component and the parts linked to the component. You will also note that the power tips on the second line always refer to the topmost screen – jobs (as in figure 40.4).

Stock items

Spares or stock items are vital for the management of any ship. The spare parts are for use during maintenance. Other stock items, from general chandlery items to stationery or provisions, are referred to in the following table as consumables:

- Stock item – any item consumed on board vessel.
- Stock used – spare part used for maintenance.
- Stock location – store room location of stock items.
- Stock inventory – match actual stock to system stock.
- Stock – consumables – stock item other than spare parts.
- Stock – consumables inventory – only way to use consumables in system.

The columns below show how you would expect to manage the stock in a planned maintenance system, and details on what you would achieve:

1. Wanted – stock you desire to purchase
2. Transactions – history of any or all stock item/s
3. In/Out of Stock – to use or add to stock items
4. Control – inventory control

Stock items do not need to be linked to a component in a Windows system unless it is a spare part belonging to that component. There are several things you can do with stock items:

1. While spares can be used doing maintenance, other stock items, such as consumables (cleaning material, stationery and foodstuff), will have to be 'consumed' by some other means, i.e. stock control: taking an inventory of your stock, by location, or for a specific section of these consumables, depending on how they were

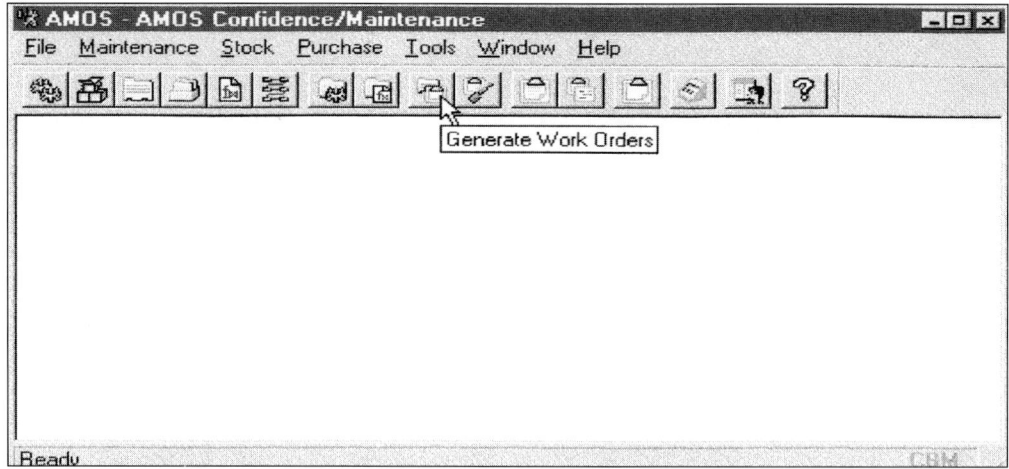

Figure 40.1 Initial screen on a computer maintenance system

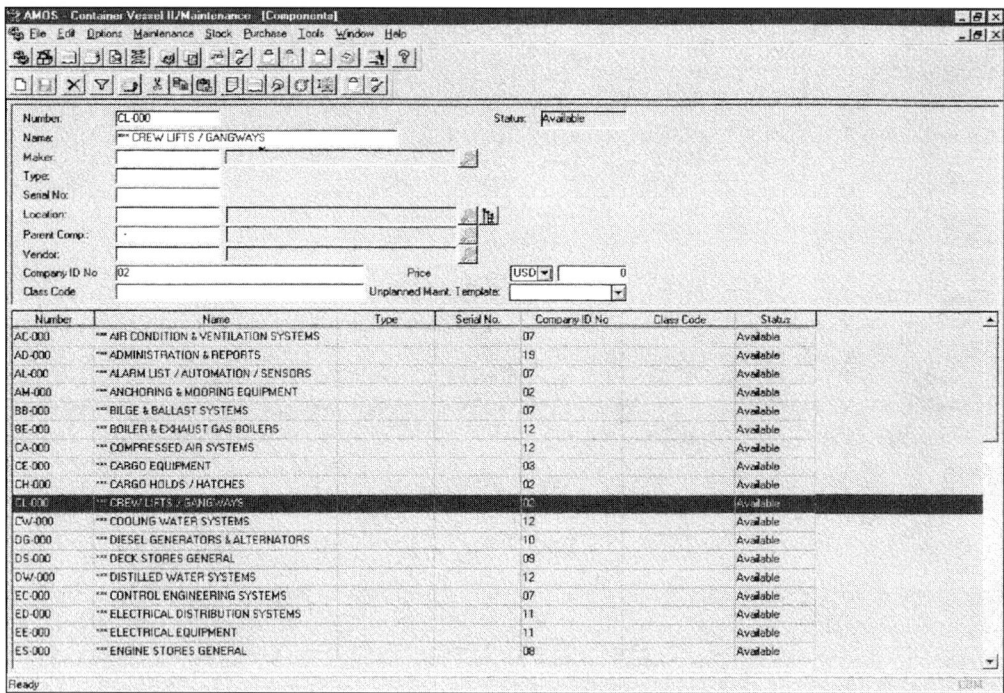

Figure 40.2 An example of what some headers for a numbering system might look like, in alphanumeric order

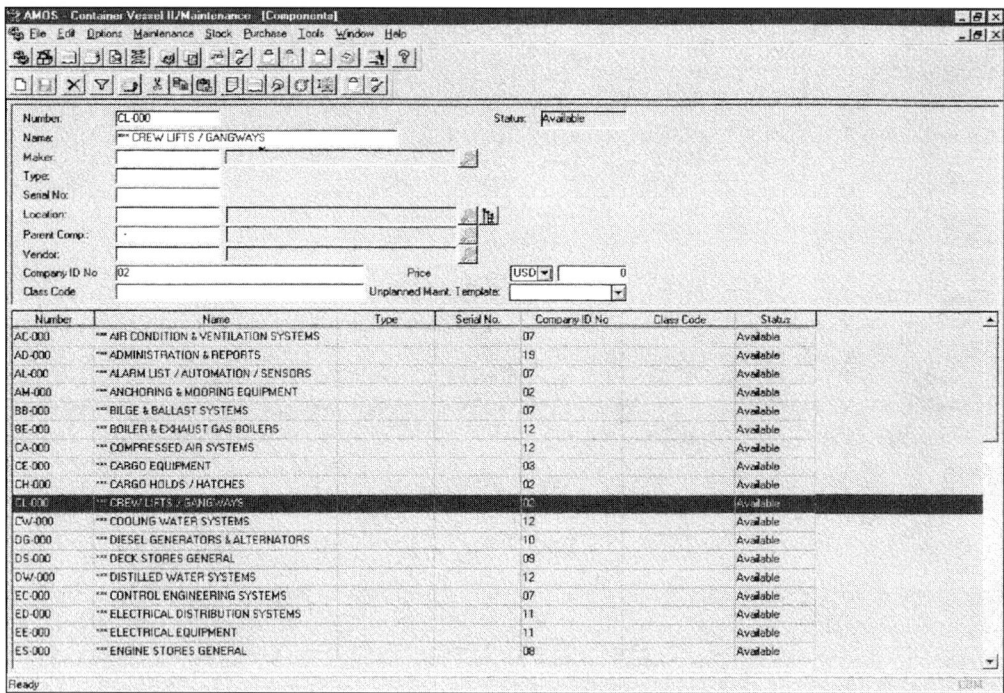

Figure 40.3 The 'filter' screen

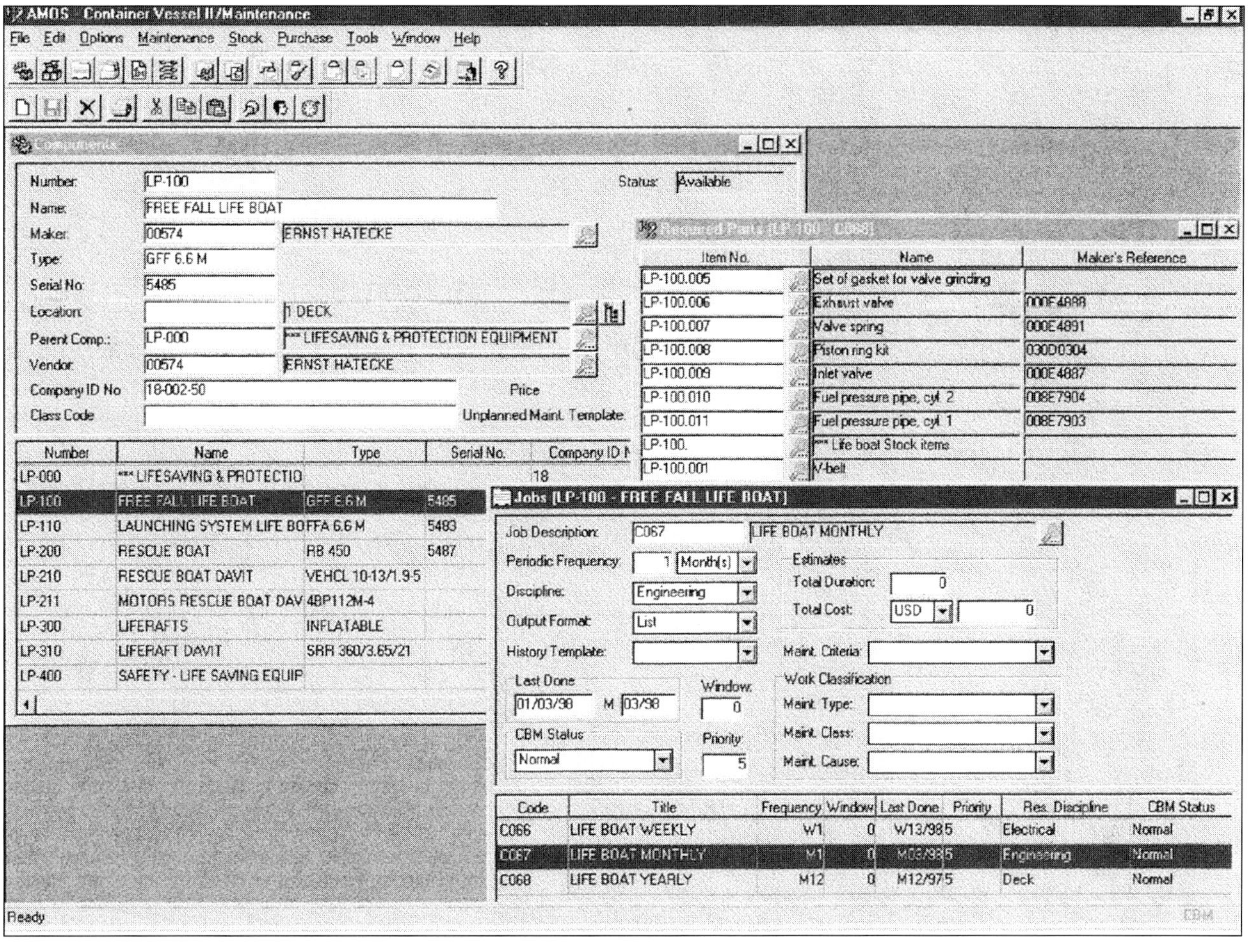

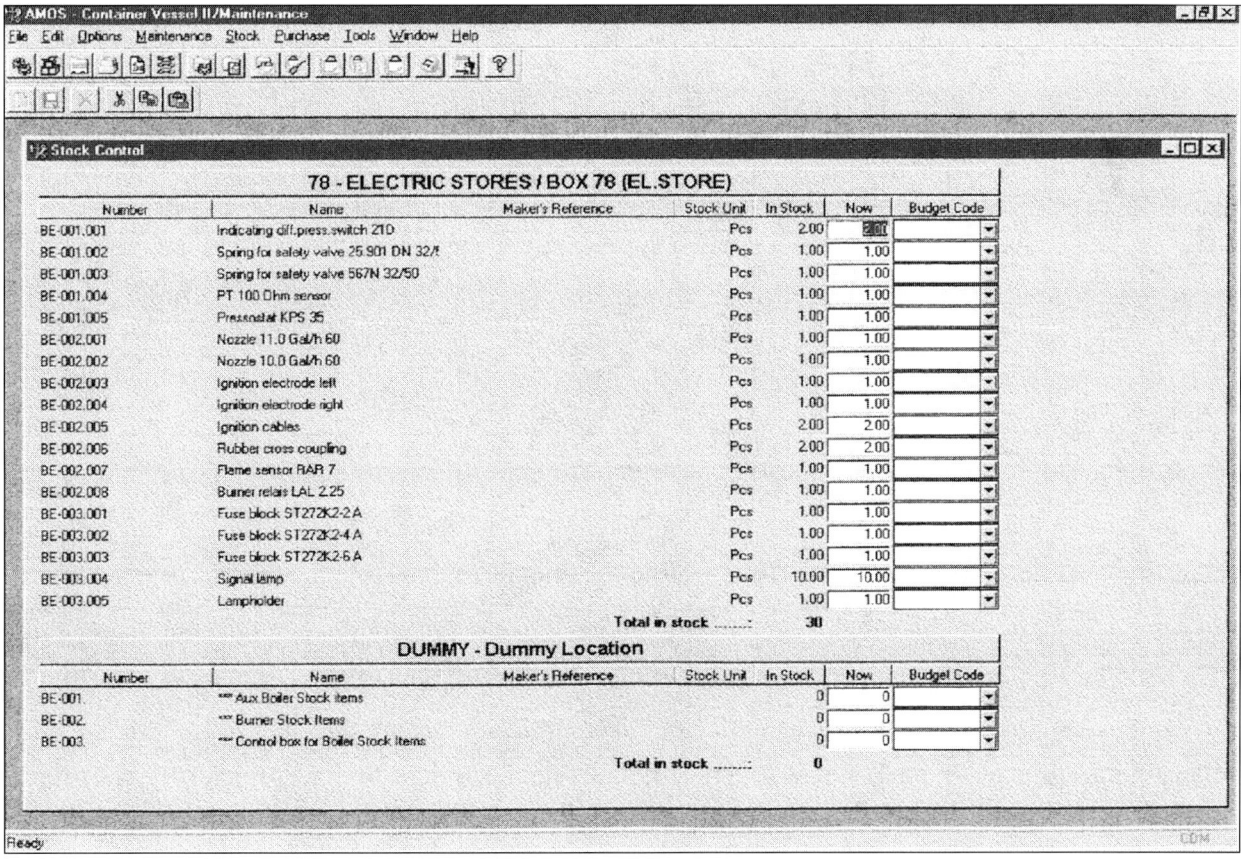

Figure 40.4 A component from the LP (Lifesaving & Protection equipment) numbering

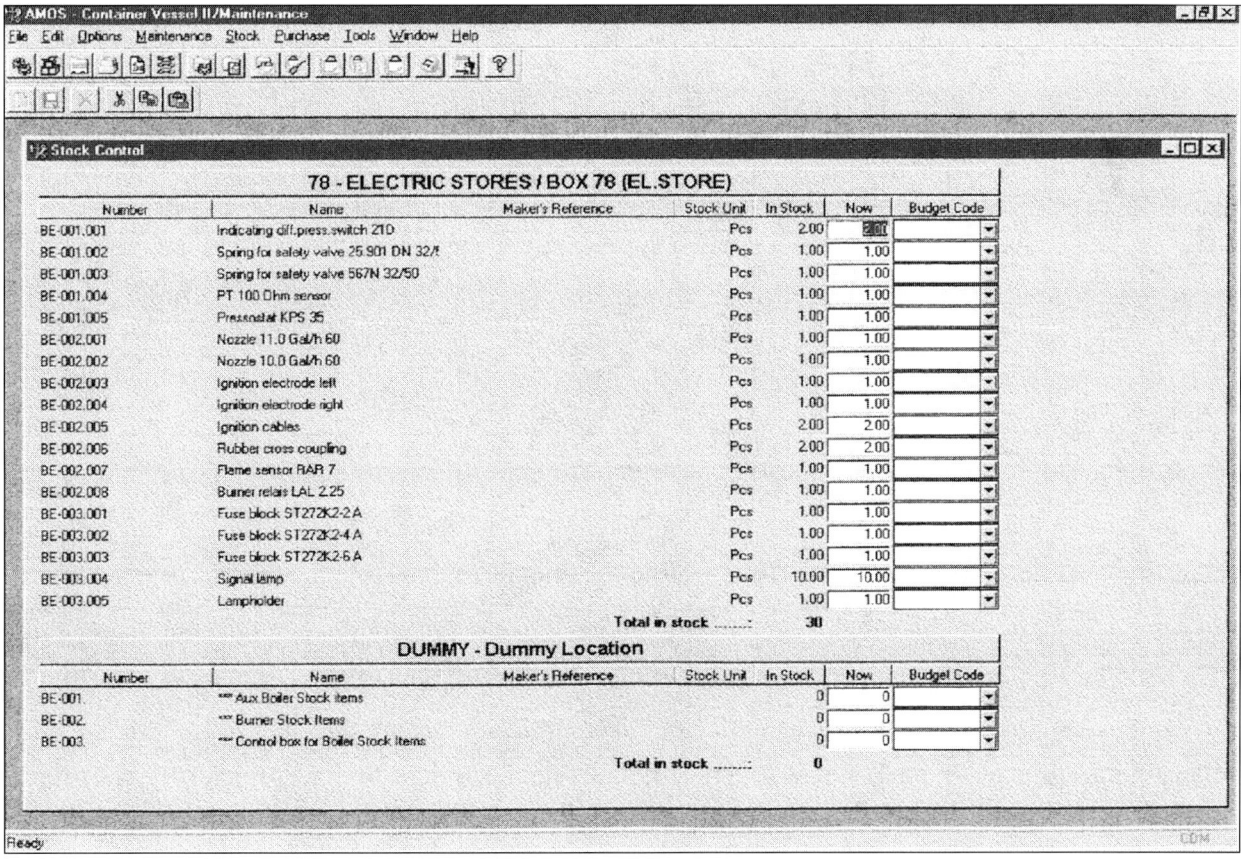

Figure 40.5 Stores in a particular location

numbered. For instance, cordage and wires could be prefixed by ROPE.???, and stationery STAT.??? etc., or the locations could be for cordage and wires BS00 to BS99 while the stationery could be stored in ST00 to ST49. Therefore you can do the whole cordage and wire by using ROPE, either doing them all at one go, or doing only one location at a time, such as BS14, or doing all BS by not putting any number. A stock check should always be done before a 'want or desire' to purchase is activated. To do a stock check, call up the location or the stock items section and then, when on screen, print out the list or fill in the now column with the correct number in stock. In figure 3.7 05 we see stock items starting with number BE in any location. As you can see, all of the items are stored in box 78 in the electrical store. To correct the stock quantity, the column marked Now would have to be updated (see figure 40.5).

2. 'Want' or 'have a desire' to purchase: this is where you indicate that you have a desire to requisition or purchase that particular stock item, and then the number you require. This can be done at any time you notice that you are getting short of the item. If it is a spare part item and you have set the stock levels: minimum, maximum, re-order level and quantity in stock, as soon as the stock quantity drops below the re-order level, the system will be triggered to 'want', whatever you have put in the re-order quantity. For instance, if you had one (1)

in each level, as soon as you used a spare carrying out maintenance, the system would consider that you have a need to requisition one replacement item (see figure 40.6).

3. Transactions: spare, lost, found or purchased are the only four transactions that can occur to any stock item.

Job description

Jobs are written with code, title, and class of job, followed by the details. These should be as detailed as possible; they should be precisely what you want done when this job is to be carried out, and if any measurements are to be taken. They should also be specified, with the normal range and limit clearly shown in the job. The period in days, weeks, months or hours are specified when the job is attached to a component, as well as stating when you want the job done next time, by entering the date when it was last done. You will notice that details (full description) and images (drawing) are available on the second power tip line. As can be seen in figure 40.7, the code is SAF025, the title of safety – fire fighting equipment and job class – safety job. Immediately underneath is the full description, or job specification.

Addresses

The address register should include all the addresses which a company would need including manufacturers, vendors, agents, etc. The address file

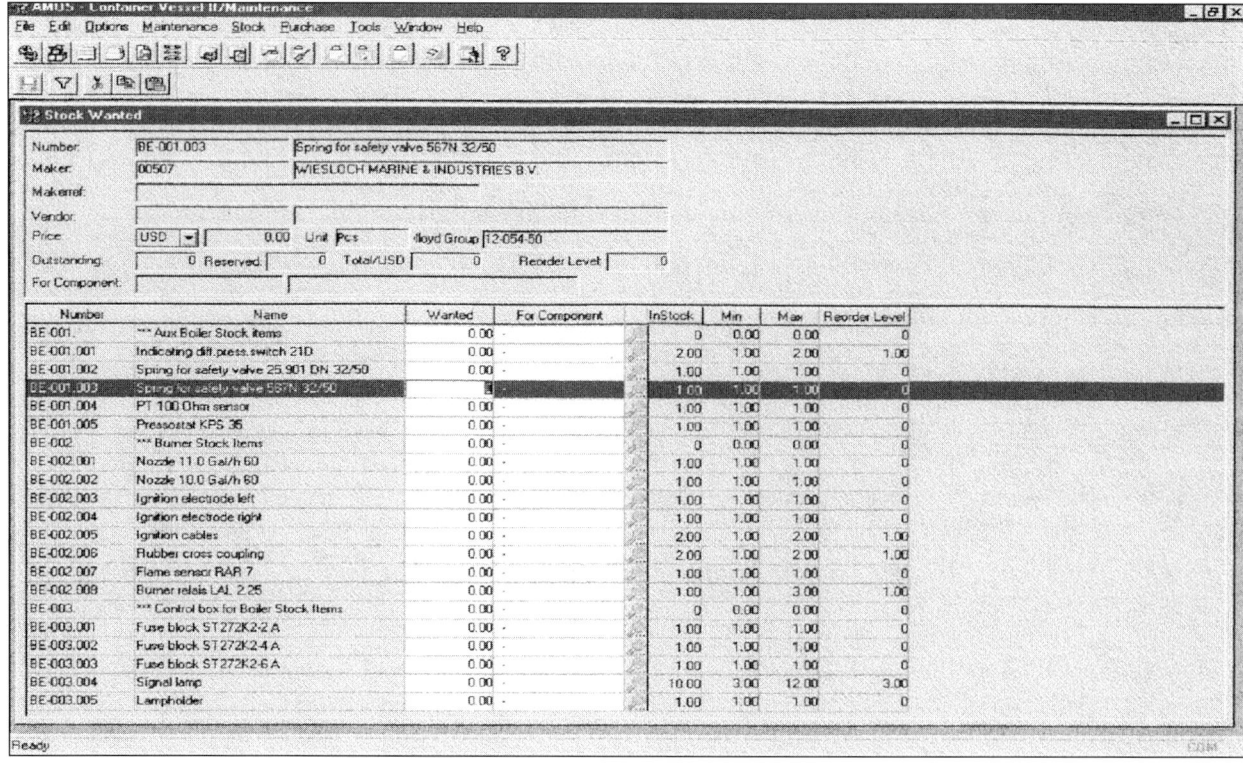

Figure 40.6 Transactions

should be common to the office and all the company vessels (see figure 40.8).

Database

Database construction is the 'difficult' (and often neglected) part of a good maintenance system. It requires vessel's manuals, planning, knowledge of shipboard systems, knowledge of maintenance, knowledge of the vessel's most critical equipment, knowing what must be included and what can be left out, choosing the correct spares from manuals, the ability to complete the system and testing the database.

All general items such as disciplines, counter types, currency codes, units, components, stock and job classes, QA grades and the various maintenance criteria – types, classes and causes, which will be common to all your vessel's databases – should be entered first. Then follow the four main items in any maintenance system – components, stock items, jobs and addresses. Then you have to link everything together and finally test the completed system before delivery.

A plea often voiced is for a simple software system. What would usually meet their aspirations would be a simple database. The software is vital for the proper operation of the whole system, but the database can be made simple, or overly complicated.

An experienced constructor would take from one to two months, depending on the amount of components and stock items a vessel would carry. For the inexperienced, the time could be from six to ten times that. One of their main problems is that they think it will be easy. They have no plan, they do not keep track of what has been completed and they get disheartened well before they can complete the database. It is not a simple job and it must be planned properly. The constructor must also have knowledge of engineering, electrical, safety and deck maintenance procedures. The system must also be completed and tested to the best ability of the constructor. The final testing will always take place in service, where minor inconsistencies can be corrected.

Some important aspects of a database are:

- Getting the stock locations organised.
- Giving an identity to those locations.
- Entering all that into the database.

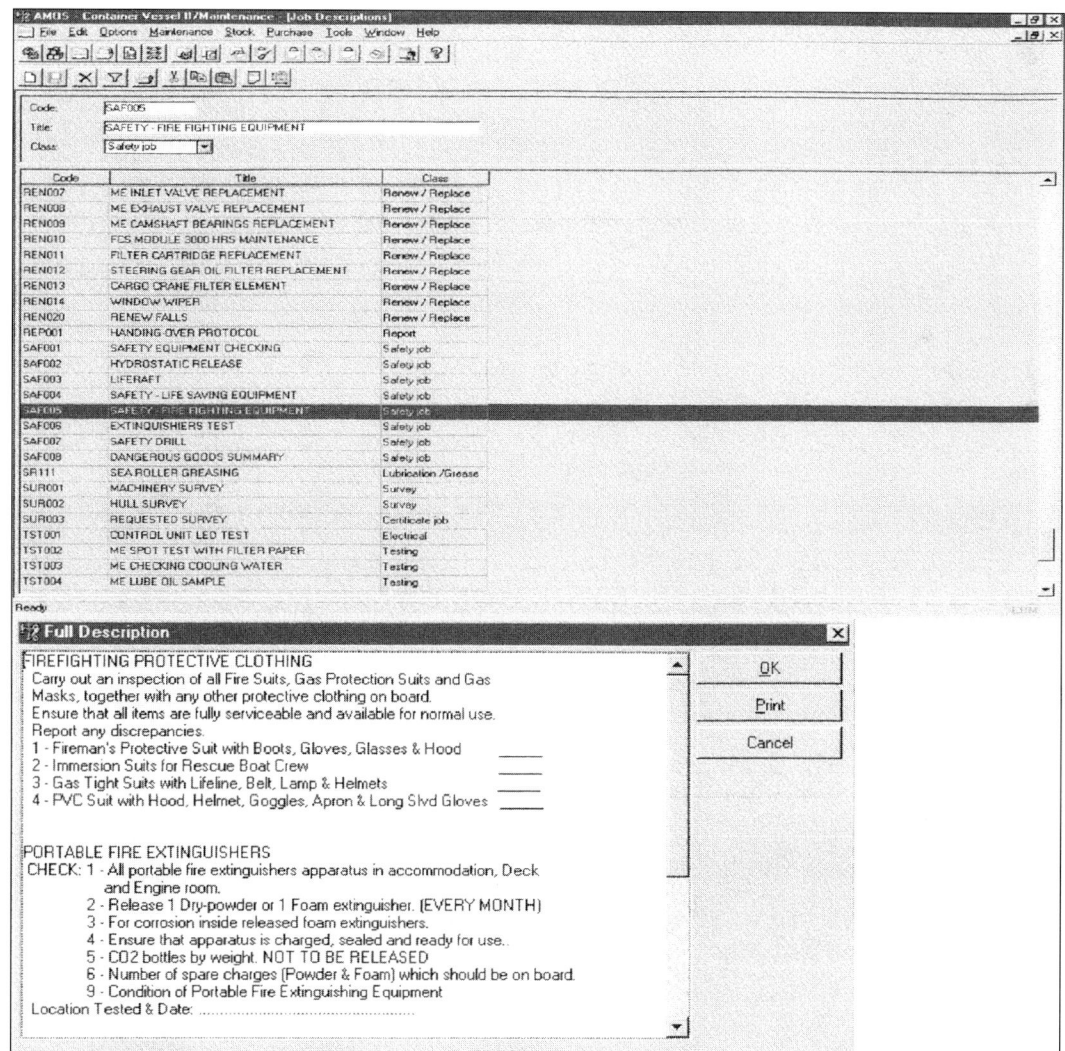

Figure 40.7 Job descriptions

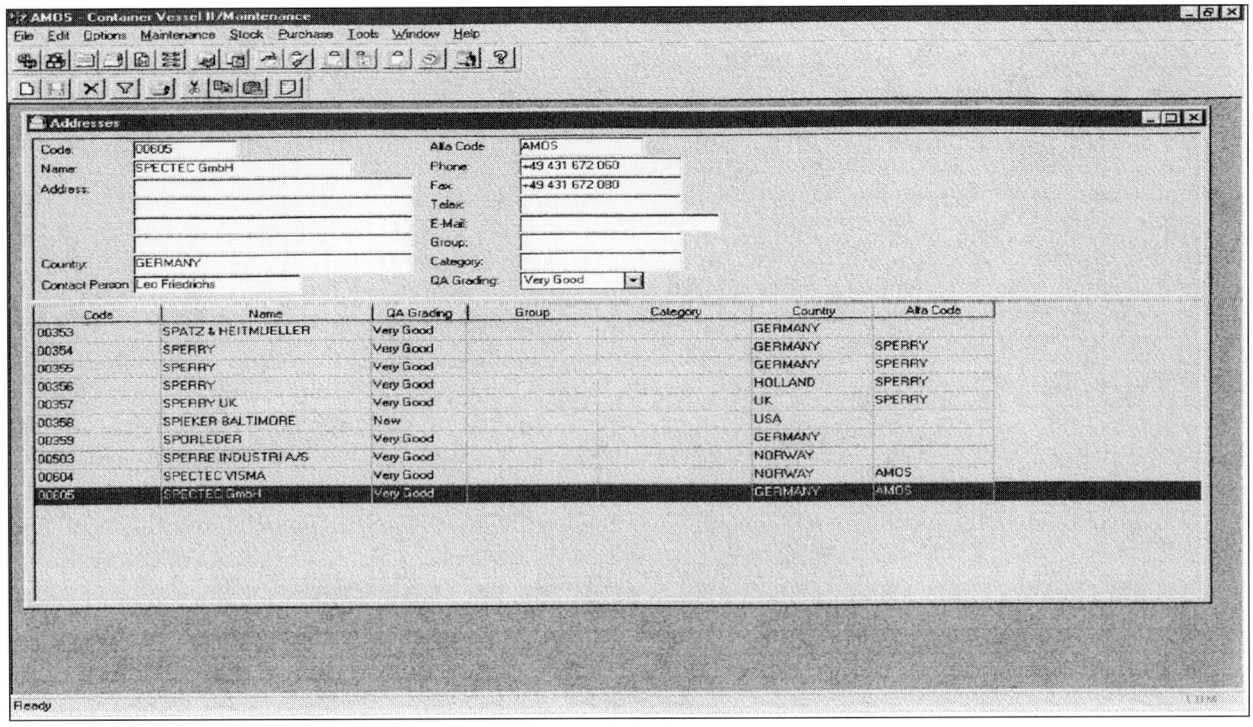

Figure 40.8 Address register

- Getting the labels printed and attached to the spares.

This is usually done at the time of installation and can take tow to four weeks. It is vital that all spare parts are at least given a location and the labels printed.

Maintenance

The maintenance system is composed of the following:

- Components and jobs (counters/time/date) – periodic maintenance (PM order).
- Counters – run time – voyages – starts.
- Maintenance – generating – planning – issuing.
- Reporting – report date done with time and spares.
- Work orders – unexpected – corrective – guarantee.
- History required always on above item WO – plus class items and measurement items.

Once the routine jobs have been attached to the component, the frequency entered, whether in days, weeks or months and the date when last done, then this triggers when the job is due for maintenance next. If a counter is attached to the component (hours, revolutions, starts, etc.), then the frequency (intervals between repetitions of jobs, 2500H or 100 starts) is entered and no further action is necessary under the component except to enter: discipline (department responsible for job); output format you want: listing or detailed; and if there is any history template, such as you would require for measurements to be taken, or a checklist.

When all the jobs have been written in detail, and then linked to the components, they must be generated

or converted into work orders; this only needs to be done once. When the work order is reported as done, it is then automatically generated again, ready for the next time it becomes due, whether in a week or in five years. If any new job is attached subsequently, it will also have to be generated once.

Before you start to plan, issue or print the maintenance for the next period, it is important to update any counters you might have attached to the system, as you would with the following example for hours counters (see figure 40.9 overleaf).

Any new jobs created and attached to a component will also have to be generated. This has to be done only once for a new database and once whenever a new job is created and attached. By reporting the routine maintenance job as done, the system automatically generates the next routine execution of the job. Pressing PT, as shown in figure 3.7 01, starts the generating process.

Once the work orders have been issued and printed they then have to be executed, by whichever department is responsible for doing so. This can only be done to work orders (whether PM or WO) that have been through the planning stage (see figure 40.10). Once the jobs are scheduled, which is done automatically, depending on time (days, weeks, months) or counters, if a condition based maintenance (CBM) module is fitted, then the action of the CBM monitoring system reaching a pre-defined condition would trigger a PM order being scheduled for that component. The next stage is that all the schedules orders go through the planning stage; these orders can be delayed or brought forward. Once the planning

Component No.	Name	Counter Type	Current Value
AC-210	A/C COMPRESSOR NO.1	Hours	2133.00
AC-220	A/C COMPRESSOR NO.2	Hours	1823.00
CA-010	STARTING AIR COMPRESSOR NO.1	Hours	1290.00
CA-020	STARTING AIR COMPRESSOR NO.2	Hours	1289.00
CA-030	TOPPING-UP AIR COMPRESSOR	Hours	802.00
CA-040	WORKING AIR COMPRESSOR	Hours	29.00
CE-100	CARGO CRANE NO.1	Hours	328.00
CE-200	CARGO CRANE NO.2	Hours	455.00
DG-100	AUX DIESEL GENERATOR No1	Hours	1680.00
DG-200	AUX DIESEL GENERATOR No2	Hours	1765.00
DG-300	AUX DIESEL GENERATOR No3	Hours	1748.00
DW-200	OSMOS UNIT (REVERSE OSMOSIS F.W.G.)	Hours	126.00
FO-300	FUEL BOOSTER MODULE (FCS)	Hours	1960.00
HS-100	SHAFT GENERATOR	Hours	2829.00
ME-100	ME MAIN ENGINE	Hours	2674.00
PV-110	PROVISION COMPRESSOR NO.1	Hours	1813.00
PV-120	PROVISION COMPRESSOR NO.2	Hours	934.00

Figure 40.9 Hours counters

stage has been gone through, the orders are then at the issuing stage and can be printed as required (see figure 40.11). These orders are then given to the appropriate departments to be carried out. When these orders have been completed (date done, time taken, spares used and comments written, if necessary) then reporting to the system has to be carried out (see figures 40.10 and 40.11).

If at any time you have unplanned maintenance and the work cannot be rectified on board, you will then need to create a work order for unexpected, corrective or guarantee (for new vessels) maintenance. They could be carried out at some future time or port, at the next dry-docking or the end of the guarantee period. The WO number will be generated automatically. You would give it a title (clear and precise), then link it to a component. Priority, due date (next port, dry-dock or guarantee), window (time before due date when you would want this job to be due), and discipline (shore contractor, dry-dock or builder) would then be entered.

All unplanned maintenance should list cause, class and type (what caused the breakdown, what effect did it have and what sort of maintenance does it require). The details should be written clearly and precisely (see figure 40.12).

The reporting can either be written on the order, or written to the maintenance system directly, the latter being the usual method after training. Once an order is reported to the system as done, it automatically generates the PM order ready for the next cycle. If the order was done as per job specification (PM orders), then there is no necessity to write any history

unless it is a class item. Below is a list of various maintenance orders and when history should be reported:

- PM order (as per specification) – NO – unless class item, then YES.
- PM order (with measurement taken) – always record measurements taken.
- PM order (problem noted) – always with details of problem.
- CMB maintenance work order- – always with detail.
- Corrective maintenance WO (dry dock, etc.) – always with detail.
- Breakdown maintenance order – always with cause/effect/action taken.
- Guarantee work order – always with cause/effect/action taken.

A reporting screen is shown for such a system (figure 40.13). In the reporting option, you tick the ones you want to report on. For instance, in our first item above, if we did not use spares none of the boxes would need to be ticked. The only part they would enter information into would be general information, with date done and duration in hours; then OK. If it had been a class item, you would also have the reporting option ticked and you would enter history description. By pressing history, a full description can be entered.

If you were reporting on unexpected maintenance, you would have the history and spares ticked and you would also fill in the work classification. If breakdown maintenance was classified in your company, history would always be filled, and usually stock used. If you

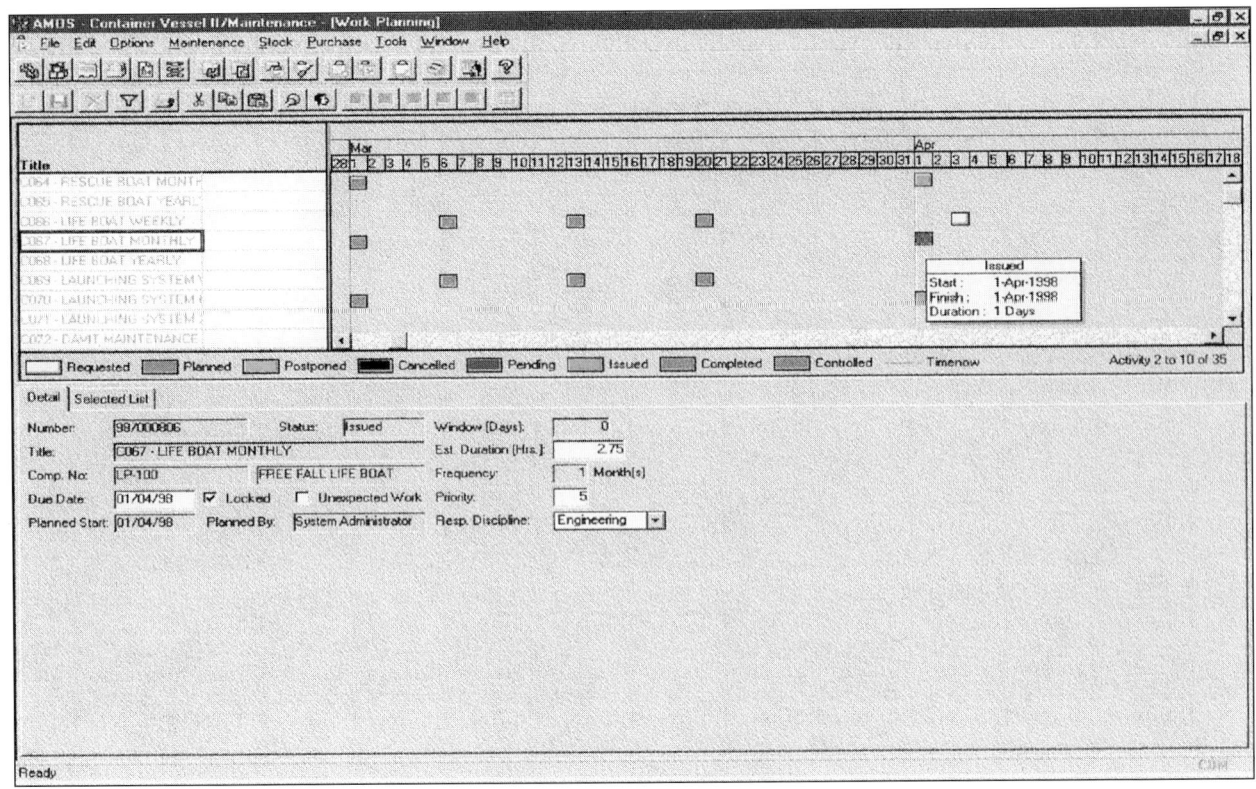

Figure 40.10 Work order, planning stage

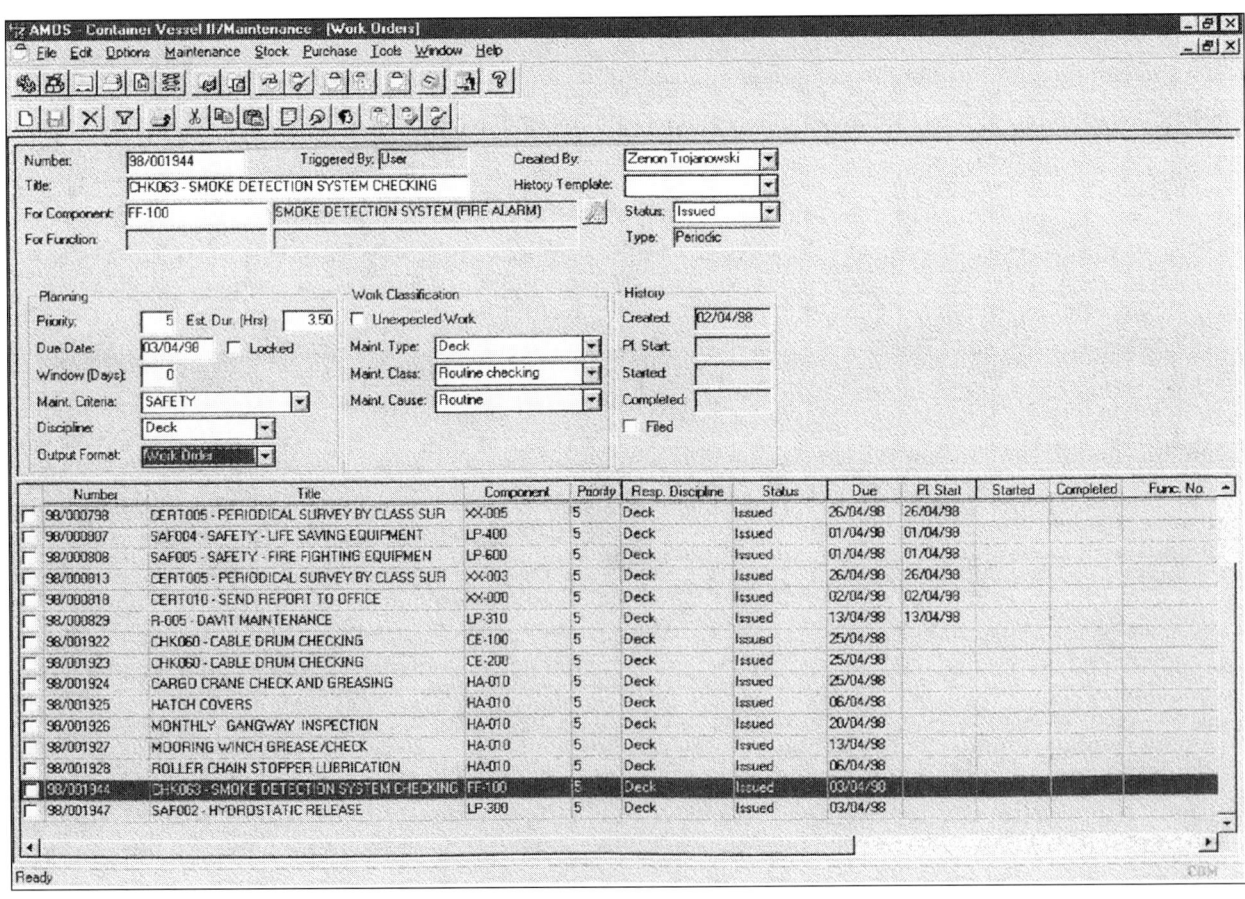

Figure 40.11 Order printing

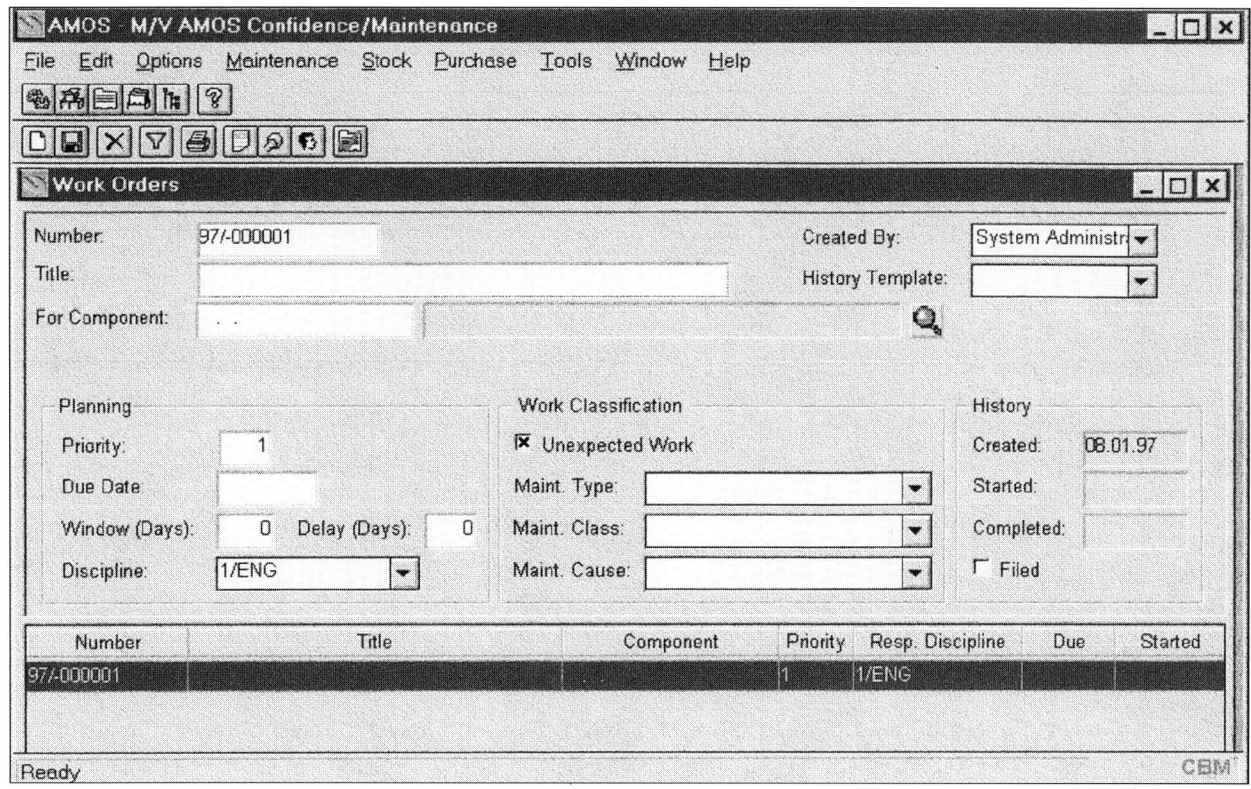

Figuere 40.12 A work order

Figure 40.13 A reporting screen

are carrying out any unexpected maintenance, which you would have done normally every 12 months, and which is due in three months time, then if you report this unexpected maintenance against this job, it will again become due in 12 months time and not in three months.

Purchasing

Everything that a vessel requires will involve purchasing. This will include the following: spares parts, consumables, corrective maintenance, and dry-docking repairs and services. Purchasing involves everything from the requisitioning, querying, ordering, delivery, to receiving and one step forward to the payment for the PO received.

Below is a list of these purchase form types, from requisition (when whoever created it gave it the number which will always identify it, through all its various stages), to purchase order and whatever could be happening to them:

- Requisition – created on board or in the office. It is a request for the purchaser to obtain some goods or services for you.
- Query – the purchaser is checking prices with one or a variety of vendors. You are waiting for that/ their quotation/s.
- Purchase order – the quotation has been received, the decision has been made to purchase and the purchase order has been issued. The requester/ purchaser is keeping track of the delivery, transport or receipt of the ordered goods.

During this process, any form of the above type could have a differing status as indicated in the following list:

- Active
  Being worked by either requester or purchaser. Active forms can be sorted or grouped according to the dates recorded in its various stages:
  * Approved for purchase.
  * Ordered by purchaser.
  * Confirmed by vendor.
  * Received by requester/or at final destination.
- Split
  This form exists, but all its original lines have been split off into other forms. It is not cancelled, as it is still useful for information purposes. It will still show all its original order lines, in ghost form and the number of the forms in which they are now located.
- Cancelled
  A form number no longer in use.
- Parked
  Either the requester or the purchaser feels this form is incomplete, or unnecessary at present and parks it in his local system. Amos normally transmits changed data from vessel to office and vice-versa. In the case of parked purchase orders, no information is exported until its parked status is changed.
- Filed
  A form on which all the goods or services have been received at the required installation. All filed forms can still be accessed, either for filling in the

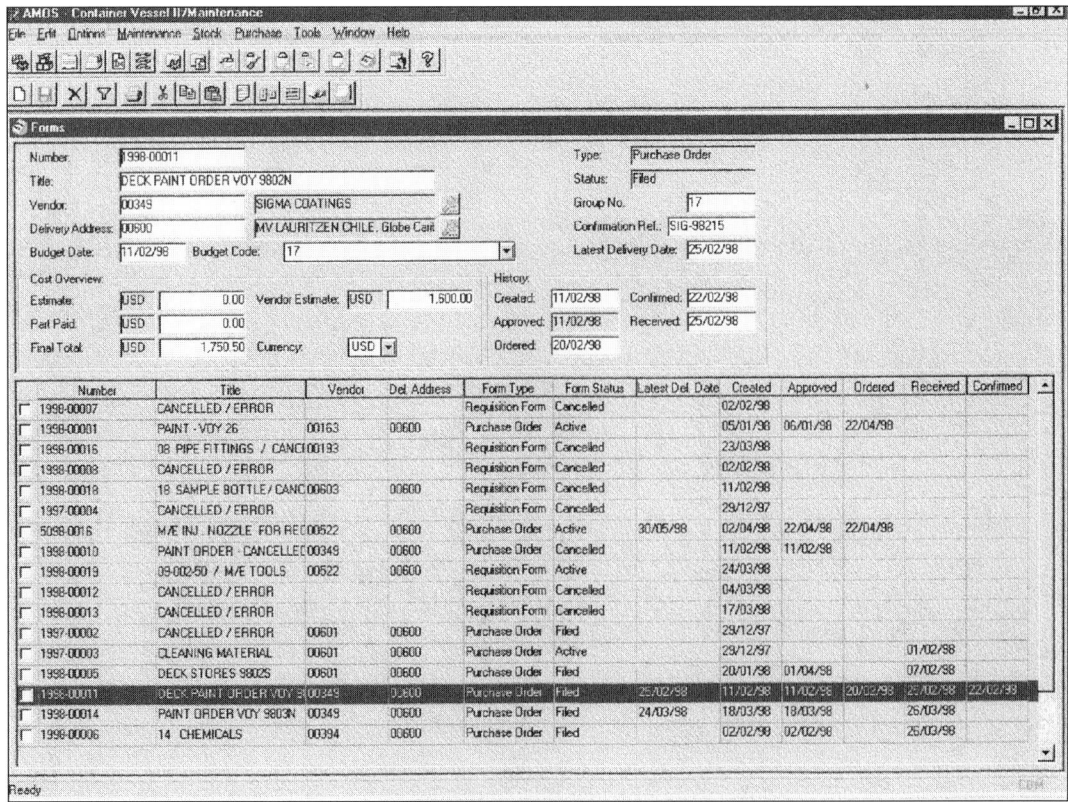

Figure 40.14 The form window

costs such as payments and final costs, or for further research.

All forms are in two sections – the form header and the order lines. They start from the form window. The form window usually consists of a header and the scrolling list of forms, or as many as can be seen on the lower part of screen (see figure 40.14). The top part will show the form header of whichever the scroll bar is on in the bottom half. The form number is generated by the system; In the one shown, the number has the year, a dash and a five figure running number.

Whenever you want to create a new form, you start from the form window. Requisition forms can be created automatically, or manually. If you want to do a form automatically you should, prior to that, have gone into wanted in stock and indicated your requirements. You then go to white page PT and a filter will appear. You indicate whether you want automatic or manual and whether you require purchase, requisition or query. On a vessel that has a central purchasing office it is usually always requisition, unless you were making a local purchase. If you have ticked off what you require in stock: wanted, then indicated 'automatic', the system will create the forms with order lines and all you have to do is fill in the form headers. When you choose 'manual' and the form header is available on the screen fill in the details, click on the order line PT and then, when it shows the order line screen (figure 40.15), go to new page PT for

each line and enter requirements: either from the stock list or write them out freehand (if what you required was not in the stock list). This could be done for such things as: 'boat hire to anchorage', 'repair deck rails' etc.

When the purchase order has been placed with a vendor, either locally or by the office, you wait for delivery. On the delivery of the purchase orders on board you must tell the system what you have received. You do this by going to the form window (see figure 40.16) and tag the POs you are receiving: you get a small option box. If you are receiving all the orders complete and if you want labels and the POs filed on completion, then tick off the boxes and press OK. By doing so, the orders will all be dated and marked 'received'. Stock items will be updated with the stock received and all the orders filed.

Filed orders are still available for editing; the office usually does this. The editing can take the form of either entering part or final payment or, if voucher handling is used (see figure 40.7), a form some companies use as a link to their accounts department, to link the purchasing to their accounting system. When final payment is made, the filed purchase orders are the only historical link with the whole process, and can be used for research.

Import/export

These systems usually have a mirror image in the office, so that if anything is changed in either system,

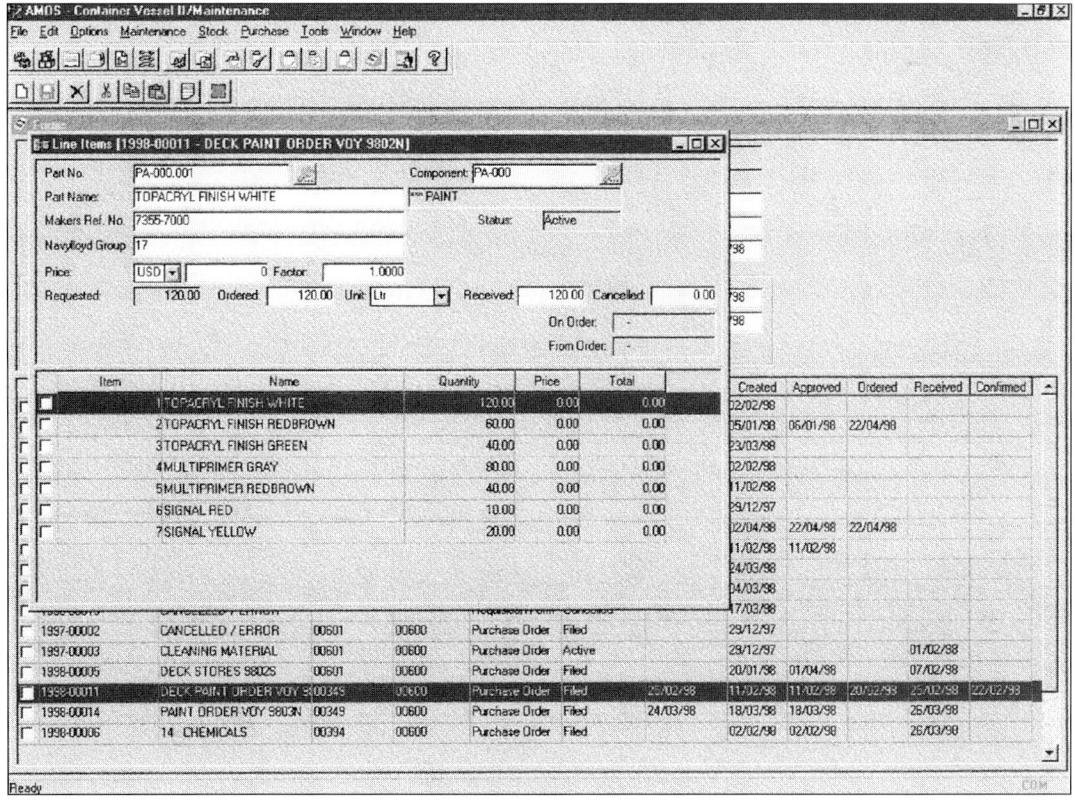

Figure 40.15 The order line screen

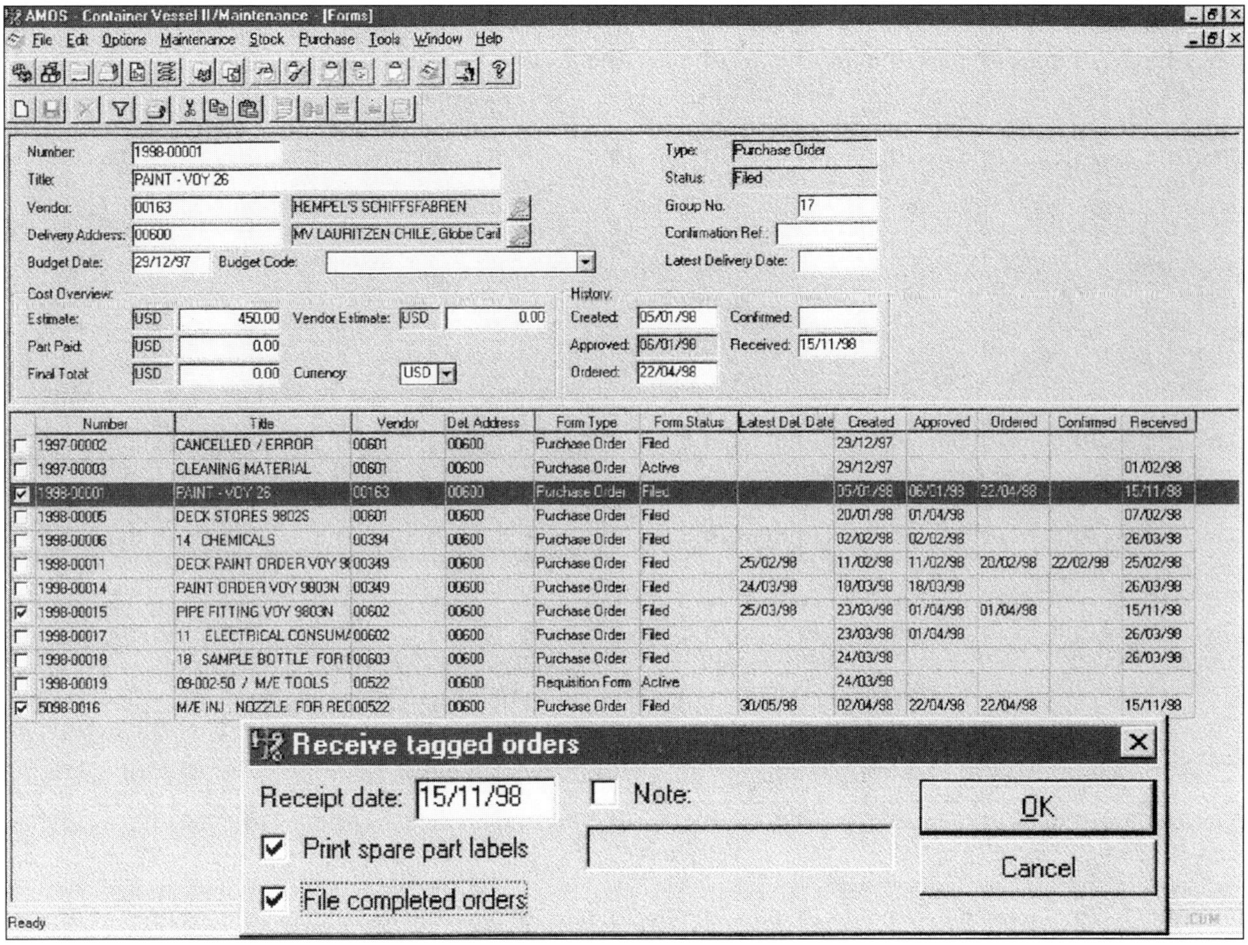

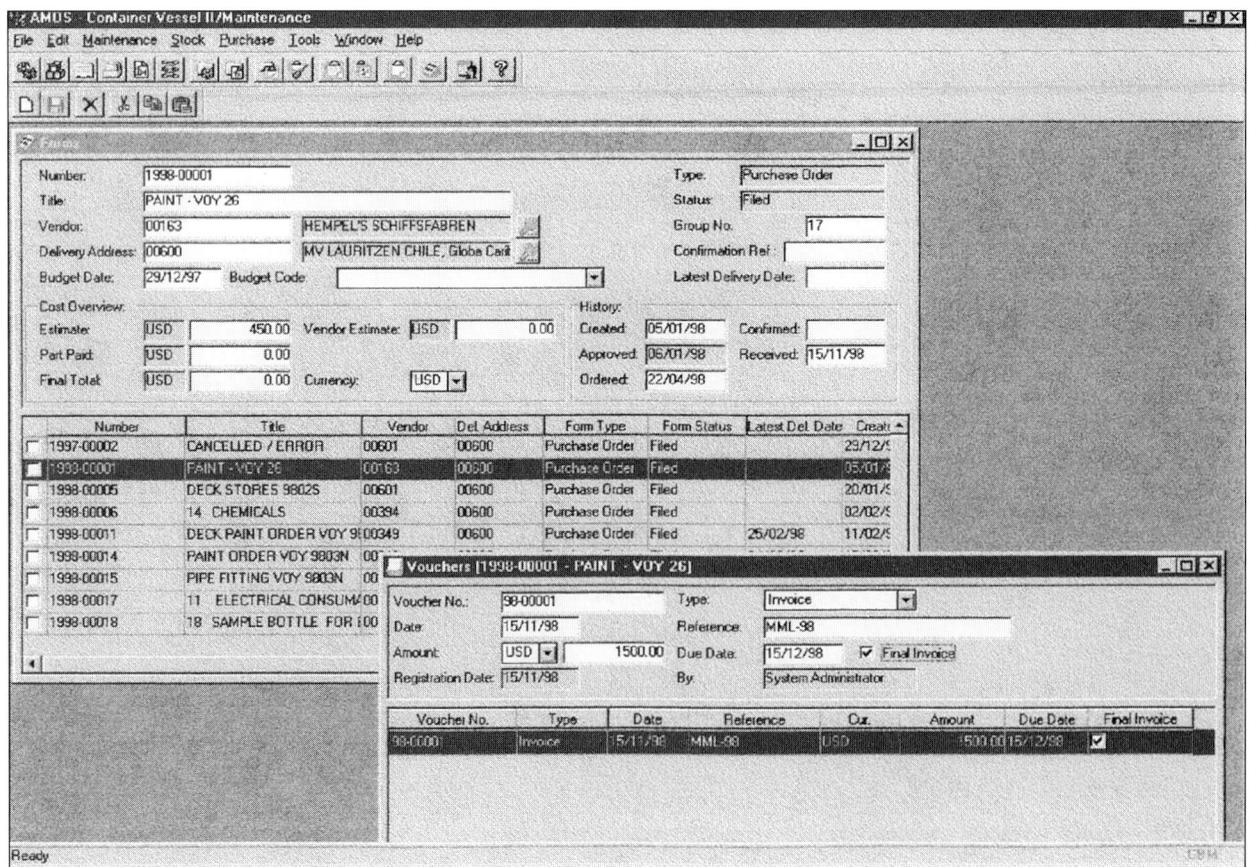

Figure 40.16 The form window

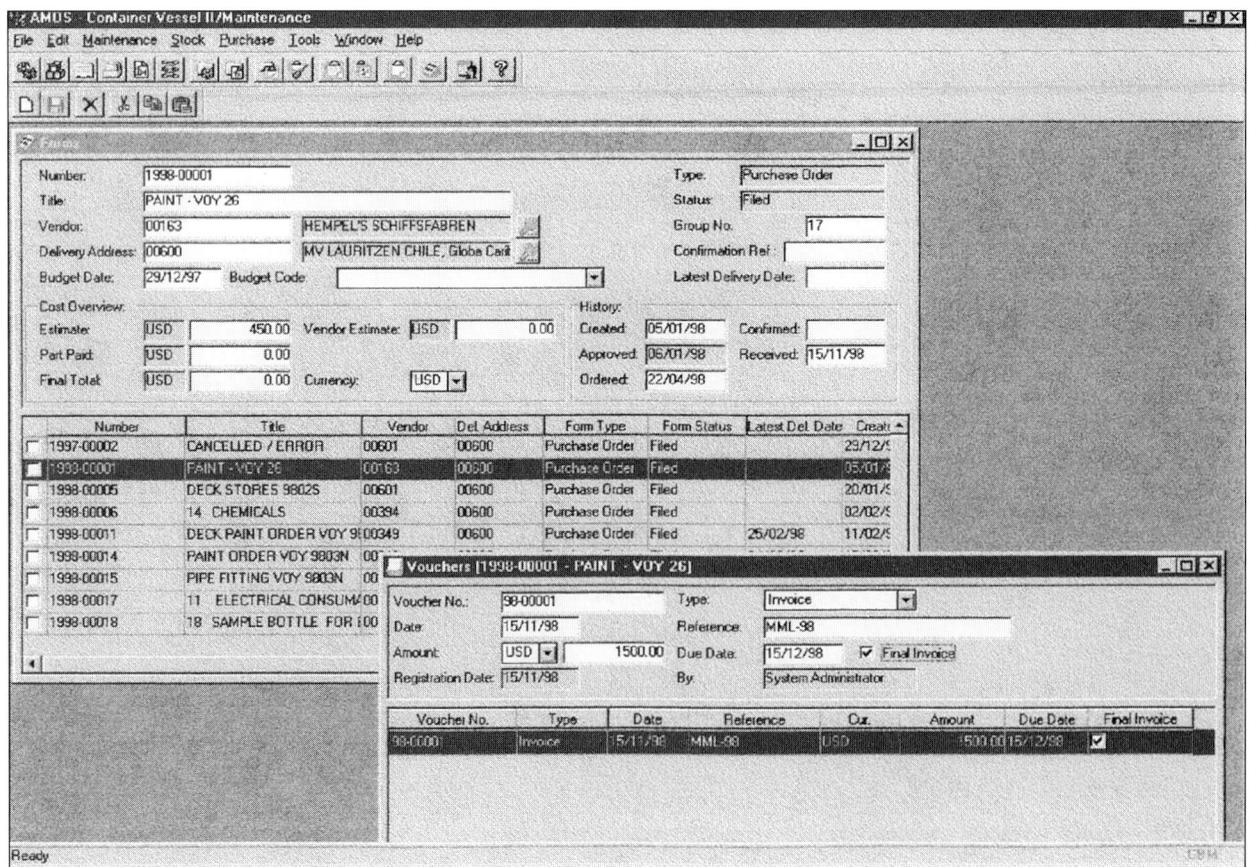

Figure 40.17 Voucher handling

especially with regards to purchasing, then it is known both on board the vessel and in the office. Other changed information that can be transferred includes maintenance, history, stock, and logs. In fact, it is easier to export all changed information. This can be done daily, weekly, or monthly, depending on your company's requirements. The most common interval is either daily or weekly, with the result that both you on board and those in the office always have the same information on hand.

Most software suppliers now can automate their systems to export information at predetermined times on a daily or weekly basis, using either selection files or generic tasks. This export (of changed data) can also be done manually, using selection files (files created to extract the required information). These then create export files, ready for transmission to the head office. By the same method, changed information from the office is imported from a data file into the system vessel system, using a selection file.

Communications

For any software system or vessel to be viable at sea nowadays, it must have good communications. All the exported information from your software must be exported, by some means, to your head office. This is usually done with some communication system, which usually can compress the files to be exported and then, via a modem and satellite, export the data at high speed to your head office.

Conclusion

Since I wrote this chapter 12 years ago, many things have changed at sea and in software systems used at sea. Back then, hardly anyone used computers at sea and maintenance systems were few and far between. GUIs such as Windows had not been heard of and gigabytes existed only on main-frame computers. Nowadays all modern vessels have a computer, usually several and seafarers know how to use them. Maintenance software is a useful tool if, like everything else, it is used properly. I hope that this chapter will help some in understanding some of its uses, and will be of assistance.

Chapter 41

ENTRY INTO ENCLOSED SPACES

by Captain F.G.M. Evans BA CertEd GradIFE FNI

Captain Evans is a master mariner and was, for many years, lecturer in charge of the fire and safety centre at the Warsash Maritime Centre, Southampton. He obtained a BA through the Open University and is a Graduate of the Institution of Fire Engineers. He has worked as an independent fire and safety consultant within the industry since 1989.

Summary

SINCE THE FIRST EDITION of this book, the ideas that this chapter embodies, that risks should be properly assessed and managed by the establishment of proper procedures, have become more widely accepted through the adoption of the International Safety Management (ISM) Code. Nevertheless, enclosed space incidents continue to happen. In one recent incident lives were lost for failing to follow procedures which were discussed the day before in the ship's management meeting. Education is a long psychological process and people do not learn just by being told.

In order to reduce further the numbers of enclosed space incidents, ships' masters must continue to ensure that sufficient information, instruction, training and supervision are constantly provided to keep awareness of the dangers of enclosed spaces and the need to follow proper procedures for safe entry at a high level. The risks described are definitely not confined to large tankships and respiratory accidents can and have occurred on all types of ship, large and small. The general principles of safe entry should be followed even entering a freight transport unit and after a spillage of certain cargoes an open deck space may become a dangerous space. In an emergency following a respiratory incident, human instinctive behaviour has often resulted in multiple casualties; therefore crews must be trained to make a conditioned response.

Introduction

Any enclosed space with limited ventilation may have an irrespirable atmosphere. An atmosphere may be irrespirable because it is:

1. *Oxygen deficient.* An atmosphere may be oxygen deficient due to:

- Oxidation of metals (rusting).
- Oxidation of oil residues in cargoes such as fish meal.
- The presence of any cargo which absorbs oxygen.
- The drying of paint films.
- The use of de-oxidant chemicals – e.g. in boilers.
- Substances which give off vapours which may displace oxygen.
- The presence of an inert gas or gases that have been leaked or discharged from firefighting or refrigerating equipment.
- Biological activity – e.g. rotting.

2. *Toxic, narcotic or intoxicant.* An atmosphere may be toxic due to:

- Toxic vapours given off from cargoes.
- The rotting or fermentation of cargoes such as grain, edible oil, meat or fruit.
- The decomposition of residues from chemical cargoes previously carried.
- The presence of vapours from solvents such as those used in paints.
- Products of combustion.

3. *Injurious* – i.e. corrosive, severely irritant, hot, or choking (dusts).

The toxic hazards of dangerous cargoes should be made known to those likely to come into contact with them; such information should be readily available to the emergency response party, perhaps on a clipboard. But toxic gases may be evolved from the residues of previous and otherwise harmless cargoes. Rotting or fermentation may produce carbon monoxide or hydrogen sulphide and dangerous concentrations may not be released until the residues are disturbed.

Gases that are narcotic or an intoxicant, which may include hydrocarbons and solvents, may cause the victim to fall and injure himself. Injurious atmospheres may occur when, for example, water is added to a strong alkali or acid, when boiling may cause a corrosive mist and fumes to form.

The problem with many of the gases causing respiratory accidents is that they give no warning – no visible indication, no smell – or in some cases the sense of smell may be anaesthetised at dangerous concentrations – and no taste.

The early symptoms of oxygen deficiency and many types of poisoning are similar and may be confused with drunkenness. The victim himself may not be aware because his senses have been dulled. The person at the entrance must be trained to look out for these symptoms and raise the alarm at the earliest signs of unusual behaviour.

With oxygen deficiency there are no feelings of suffocation. Such feelings are caused by an excess of carbon dioxide in the blood, operating sensors to tell the body to breathe out and in again. In an oxygen deficient atmosphere this carbon dioxide is breathed out normally but not enough oxygen is breathed in. If the brain is not receiving enough oxygen it cannot operate properly, it speeds up the blood supply so that the victim may die of heart strain, or he may feel that, instead of climbing this ladder, when he lets go he will float...

Why time weighted averages?

The effect of poisoning may be chronic or acute. With acute poisoning, the effect is immediate or delayed only a few hours. Chronic poisoning may be either where a dose received now may cause chronic illness in later years, or regular small doses may be accumulative or have an accumulative effect that will cause chronic illness.

The long term exposure limit (LTEL) expressed as a time weighted average (TWA) is the maximum concentration that can be worked in without harm, for an eight-hour day. Sets of published figures are available from the Health and Safety Executive (see *Code of Safe Working Practices*). A short-term exposure limit (STEL), is the maximum duration that can be endured for 10 minutes with one hour's rest between. Some substances have maximum exposure limits (MELs), which is an exposure limit which must never be exceeded and exposure must be kept as low as possible.

An atmosphere may be dangerous by reason of being flammable and in an enclosed space may form an explosive mixture with air. Flammable hydrogen may be formed by active cathodic protection.

This document is not meant to replace the various codes of safe practice (CSP) and should be read in conjunction with all the requirements of the codes which give information on the hazards of various cargoes, such as the IMDG code for packaged dangerous goods, the CSP for carriage of solid bulk cargoes and the international tanker safety guides. In particular reference should be made to chapter 17 of the *Code of Safe Working Practices for Merchant Seamen*. Couched in the officialese of nearly every paragraph, chapter 17 of the CSWP is a sad case history of death or injury involving needless waste of lives and skilled personnel and distress for bereaved relatives and friends.

Entry into dangerous spaces regulations

Every year a number of merchant seamen lose their lives through enclosed space incidents. This has prompted British legislators to produce a statutory instrument (SI) and a revision of chapter 17 of the *Code of Safe Practice for Merchant Seamen*. It puts responsibility on people, including the master or person in charge of the vessel, and lays down penalties for a contravention. Summaries of the main points are:

- Entrances to unattended dangerous spaces to be kept closed or secured.
- Safe entry procedures must be laid down.
- The master must ensure safe entry procedures are followed.
- The principles and guidance contained in the *Code of Safe Working Practices* Ch. 17 must be followed.
- An offence will have been incurred by any person entering an enclosed space not following the procedures or without authority.
- Drills to be carried out for rescue from enclosed spaces, at periods not exceeding two months on tankers over 500 tonnes or other ships over 2,000 tonnes (entry in official log).
- Oxygen meters and other appropriate test devices to be carried on vessels where entry into dangerous spaces may be required.
- Defences include taking all reasonable precautions and diligence to avoid the offence or that it was not reasonably practicable to comply.

Masters sailing on ships registered with maritime administrations that do not have such legislation in place should bear in mind that the contents of chapter 17 of the CSWP are just common sense and would represent no more than the normal duty of care required by a shipmaster. There is a maritime safety card giving a checklist and guidance for safe entry of enclosed spaces in the supplement to the IMDG Code at the end of the BC Code Section.

With amendment 29 of the IMDG Code, which came into force on 1st January 1999, a new appendix has been added to the BC Code in the supplement *Appendix F to the IBC Code – Recommendations for Entering Enclosed Spaces Aboard Ships*.

Prevention of enclosed space incidents

Rescue from an enclosed space is obviously very difficult and enclosed space incidents are best prevented. An enclosed or confined space should be the subject of a permit to work system as outlined in the CSWP. There was an incident in which an engineer entered an open-topped tank and a cleaning cycle was put into operation that opened steam drains to this space. Obviously such a space should be the subject of a permit to work, which would include the posting of a notice on the controls of the cleaning cycle.

Men doing hot work in an enclosed space where the only exit is upwards should avoid clothing of man-made fibre. Cotton or wool is preferable and will protect from flash fires but man-made fibres such as nylon may melt on to the skin and cause third-degree burns.

Any space which has been closed up or is poorly ventilated must be ventilated and have its atmosphere tested prior to entry. Thought should be given to providing additional ventilation in the form of portable fans and plastic air ducting when work is being done in an enclosed space.

Instruments for measuring flammable atmospheres should be calibrated before use. Remember, they are only calibrated for a particular gas. Oxygen meters will indicate a respirable atmosphere when there are toxic gases present which are toxic at low concentrations. Other gas detectors will only detect a specific gas so the hazard has to be known before it can be sampled.

The hazards associated with a particular cargo must be well known by all responsible persons. When persons are affected consult the *Ship Captain's Medical Guide* or the *IMO Medical First Aid Guide for use in accidents involving dangerous goods.*

Emergency procedures

Unfortunately, there is not only the danger of making an entry into enclosed spaces, but case history has shown that when an incident occurs, inept and unpractised emergency response leads to multiple casualties. It is up to the master to ensure that if there is an incident his crew will, through drills and positive instruction, do the right thing and will be acting as an efficient emergency team because they will be doing what they have been 'conditioned' to do by training.

A few realistic drills involving the rescue of a live-weight dummy from an enclosed space, involving movement through lightening holes and up ladders, will soon convince people how difficult this is and make them follow proper entry procedures to ensure that such an incident could not happen.

Drills are needed to ensure that the proper entry procedure is followed, even in an emergency. Many accidents which have occurred in enclosed spaces have been falls due to inadequate lighting, slippery surfaces, awkward access etc. and when a man falls in a tank, the instinctive thing may be to go and have a look at him. Such an incident could be reported as an injury which may set the emergency response off on the wrong foot if the fall was caused by a foul atmosphere.

In the event of an incident in an enclosed space the person standing by should raise the alarm and must not make an entry until other persons arrive and never make an entry without breathing apparatus. There should be one emergency signal, which takes people to their emergency stations, whether that emergency is following collision, stranding, fire or an enclosed space incident.

Command communication and control

The emergency response station for the master is the bridge or other prearranged control centre. As a general principle the master should stay in the control centre. The bridge or control centre should only be left if:

1. A responsible person can be left at the control centre.
2. He can be sure that all the crew have been accounted for – there was an incident in which two persons were rescued, and it was later discovered that a third person had made an unauthorised entry to the other end of the same space.
3. He has ascertained that the enclosed space incident is the only emergency occurring on board at that time.
4. Perhaps if he is receiving no communication.
5. There is no other responsible person available to take charge at the entrance.

The emergency response party is a small group of men whose muster point is at a place where the equipment necessary to deal with emergencies is stored. They should be communicating with the bridge, mustering and getting their gear ready all at the same time.

There should be one responsible person in charge of the incident at the entrance, with communications to the control centre (the bridge). If subsequent rescuers enter a space they come under the charge of this officer, even if they have come from a different party. There must be proper breathing apparatus (BA) control, with all entries logged. Backup relief rescuers will have to be made ready and enter to take over the rescue at about the time the first rescuers have to leave the space.

Priorities and training objectives

When there is an enclosed space incident, the first priority is to get air to the casualties. Second is first aid; removal of a casualty who has suffered a fall may be delayed to avoid compounding the injuries, but only if the atmosphere has been made safe or there is a limitless supply of air for victims and rescuers.

On-board training must ensure that, in the event of an enclosed space incident, nothing is done that is likely to produce more casualties. The multiple casualty situation gets more difficult and may go beyond the capability of the ship's resources to deal with it. This is why the CSWP suggests that only the minimum number of people necessary to do the job are sent into the space in the first place.

Without proper training, the instinctive thing to do is anything to save your shipmate. Lives have been lost:

- By removing a face mask to share his air with the casualty. Never remove a BA face mask in a suspect atmosphere.
- By would-be rescuers holding their breath and making a quick dash in to pull someone out or free a rescue line. Never enter a suspect atmosphere without breathing apparatus.
- By rescuers staying to make that last effort and running out of air. Leave with enough air supply to gain fresh air, remembering that it takes more air to climb a ladder than go down it.
- By rescuers hurriedly donning BA and not going

STRATEGY FOR SAFE ENTRY OF CONFINED SPACES

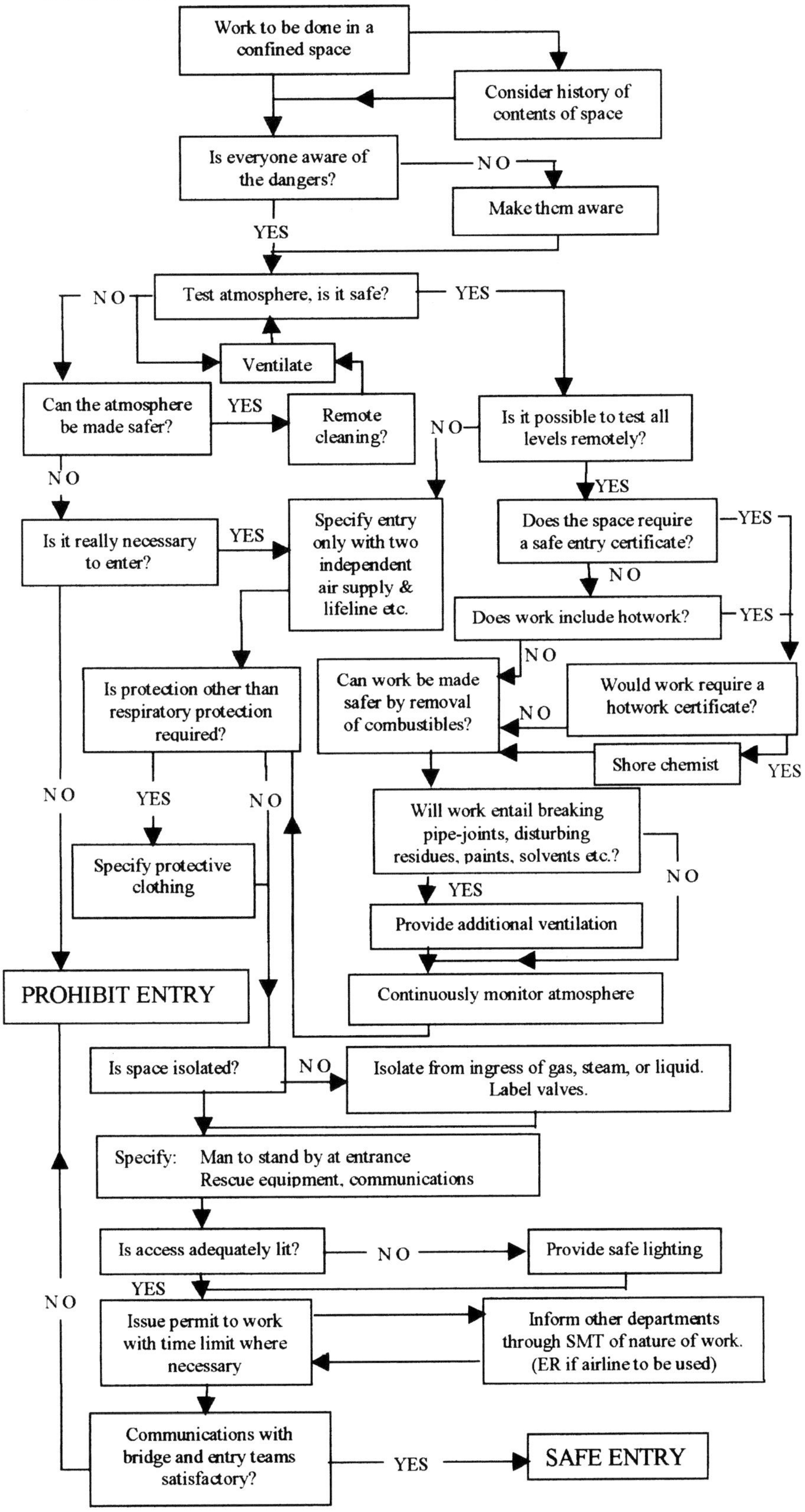

Figure 41.1 Strategy for safe etry of confined spaces

through the donning procedures and safety checks, or forgetting to switch to positive pressure. Every BA wearer, even in an emergency, must go through his safety checks and be checked by the control before entering a space. To do this quickly takes practice. A man who has stopped breathing needs to have his lungs ventilated within less than three to four minutes!

The above lays down the objectives of organisation and training of the crew for dealing with enclosed space incidents, plus the fact that rescuers need practise to be able to gain access to awkward spaces with a breathing apparatus on and to be able to move a dead-weight body through lightening holes or up ladder-ways. An effective training aid can be made from a plywood board with a hole in it of the same dimensions as a lightening hole. It can be used to develop the techniques for getting through with a BA set on.

The emergency response should see to it that air is got to the victim's lungs as quickly as possible. The rescuer must not enter the space without breathing apparatus, but equally he should not enter the space without an air supply for the victim or victims. Also, for a vertical rescue, a lifeline needs to be taken in to haul out an unconscious person.

Entry and evacuation from enclosed spaces
Procedures for rescue
Rescue equipment should be taken to the entrance when an enclosed space entry is to be made. The emergency response plan should be realistic and consider every eventuality in terms of what really may happen in an emergency. If a lot of equipment is taken up the foredeck, what happens if there is another emergency on board such as a fire and the equipment is not at the muster point? Certainly the one man at the entrance cannot carry it all back. There may be enough equipment on board for an attack to be made on a fire without needing the additional equipment except for backup. When giving instructions about taking equipment to the entry point, think where it should be taken from. Air line equipment is useful for rescue in that there is no limit on the duration of the air supply. As it is not likely to be needed for firefighting and is heavy and difficult to move quickly, it would be a good idea to have that standing by.

But it takes more time to bring into operation than a personal BA set so perhaps the initial rescue attempt should be made by BA wearers and the rescue taken over by men in air line equipment. Don't forget that the air line equipment should be plugged into a BA set and that the cylinder of the BA set should then be turned off so that the full contents of the BA cylinder remain if the air line fails. (Note: If an air line is given to an unconscious person watch the pressure carefully.)

The man standing-by at the entrance may don BA while he is waiting for someone else to arrive. He can then enter as soon as someone arrives and he has briefed him. Persons who arrive may be out of breath. The ship's management team may arrange to have others working nearby on radio call to assist. A rescue should be based on a prearranged plan and every ship will have its own individual problems, each of which may have a different rescue procedure.

It takes thought along the lines of the above to decide what are the best procedures in relation to manpower availability, equipment availability, size of space involved and ease or difficulty of access. When the procedure is decided upon, it should be practised as realistically as possible, making sure the space has been made safe. Afterwards the exercise should be debriefed and the procedures amended according to the lessons learned.

Some other points to be considered when laying down rescue procedures are:

- Rescue will be made easier if you have insisted that everyone entering a dangerous space was wearing a harness.
- Two men can handle an unconscious person better than one.
- Two men will be needed to move an unconscious person through a lightening hole.
- Going up a ladder, the men at the top do the lifting, the men below guide.
- Men in breathing apparatus may be needed to lift at a halfway stage.
- If there are two casualties in a space, air will have to be taken in for two.
- If there is no equipment available, concentrate on getting the men out as quickly as possible.
- Air shared is air halved; a device for sharing air from a self-contained breathing apparatus set must only be used for very short rescue routes.
- If bellows apparatus is being used, make sure the bellows is in fresh air. It might not be apparent in drills but there may be an irrespirable atmosphere outside a space, close to the entrance in a real incident.

Equipment
Members of the crew must be thoroughly familiar with all items of equipment. The best way of making sure that junior officers are familiar with equipment is: (a) arrange for them to give positive instruction to others, (b) see that they follow a planned maintenance schedule and (c) give them opportunities to use the equipment in drills.

- It may be necessary to provide a portable sheerlegs and tackle for rescue from tanks on large vessels.
- Some companies are providing guide lines, as used by fire brigades, to get relief rescuers quickly to the scene of the rescue (tape could be used), but remember lifelines should be worn where appropriate.
- Ordinary breathing apparatus cannot be used as a resuscitation apparatus, but the victim may not

have stopped breathing. If he has then the old 'Holge Neilsen' type resuscitation may be used to make him demand air.

- There are various types of resuscitation apparatus, some of which are not suitable for use in an irrespirable atmosphere as they use atmospheric air or oxygen enriched air. Some are switchable.

- If a resuscitator has a device which allows a recovering patient to breathe in atmospheric air when the machine is in an exhalation cycle then it should be fitted with a non-return valve when used in an enclosed space. (Sometimes supplied as an extra, on a ship it should be left in place.)

- There is a danger in taking oxygen into a flammable atmosphere, where this is likely to happen, it is better to put air in a resuscitator, medical oxygen will be available after rescue if necessary.

- Where a face mask is strapped in place ideally it should have a quick release mechanism as a patient who recovers his breathing will probably vomit.

- Escape apparatus of the type worn by persons entering, which would give enough air to enable escape to fresh air in the event of the atmosphere becoming irrespirable, offer some security, but the persons may be affected and may lose the will or ability to survive before they have time to don them.

Body-handling techniques

All the body-handling techniques described in the *Ship Captain's Medical Guide* should be practised, plus any other technique you may feel necessary to surmount problems of awkward access on your particular ship.

The way to get a casualty through a lightening hole is face down (don't break his back). One rescuer goes the other side of the hole after the casualty is in position – arms through first, then the body, turn him slightly when necessary.

What is a confined space?

When gases evolved are heavier than air, an irrespirable atmosphere may exist in an open hatchway. In one incident involving tapioca root, which respires to give off CO_2, two men entered the hold to attach the crane wires to a grab, which was sitting in a shallow depression in the surface of the cargo. They collapsed; two more went down to see what was wrong with them. Respiratory accidents have also occurred on the open deck where toxic fumes are coming from an opening to a dangerous space, or following dangerous cargo spillage.

Proper entry procedures and prearranged emergency response is the only answer to the continuing loss of life from enclosed space incidents – plus the fact that every opportunity should be taken to make crews more aware, so that accidents do not happen due to ignorance.

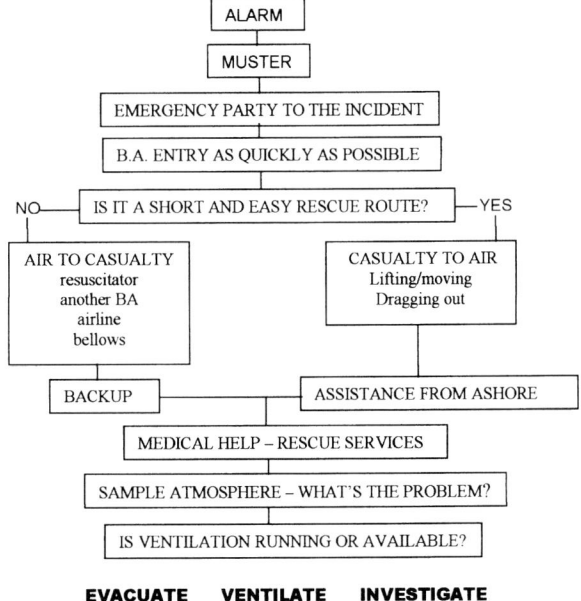

Figure 41.2 A strategy for emergency response

Chapter 42

SAFETY ON DECK IN ROUGH WEATHER

by Captain E.W.S. Gill FNI

This paper won joint first prize in The Nautical Institute's 1986 essay competition.

Introduction

UNLESS IT IS ABSOLUTELY NECESSARY, there is no reason at all to risk the lives of crew members on decks that under normal circumstances are difficult, if not impossible to make safe in times of bad weather. It is essential first to decide whether the risk is warranted, before exposing crew members to injury or death, especially on decks which are swept by heavy seas. The safety of property alone is seldom an adequate reason for such exposure.

For example, in 1947, a ship was travelling down the west coast of Central America, en route from Vancouver to Europe via the Panama Canal with a cargo of grain. Off the Gulf of Tehuantepec the ship was caught in a vicious sudden storm. It was a Sunday, a day of rest, with the crew taking things easy without overtime being worked. The ship laboured and rolled heavily, when a big sea came on board, breaking loose poorly secured drums of engine room lubricating oil.

The drums rolled about for some time before a young apprentice spotted them, by which time many of them had started leaking, making the deck a skating rink in every sense of the word. He reported the information to the bridge and the chief officer, reluctantly called from his siesta, organised a team to secure the drums. Initially, the apprentices alone were pressed into service (no overtime for them in those days). The chief officer and a young apprentice tried to move along the lee side of the deck by the side of the ship, but found that one section of shipside railing had already been carried away by the crashing drums. There was nothing to do but move towards the hatch coaming, despite the drums which continued to crash wildly about, and were even jumping over the hatch itself.

The chief officer let himself go, carefully judging the roll so that he would reach the hatch coaming safely before the ship started rolling in the opposite direction. He succeeded, but the young apprentice who did not possess the same degree of experience, failed and slid inevitably backwards with the roll towards the gap in the railings. The chief officer managed to grab the lad temporarily, but was forced to let go in order to keep his own balance. He yelled to the apprentice to catch hold of the margin plate at the side of the ship, which the apprentice did amidst the water and oil which was swilling around him. But he lost balance and was finally hanging onto the margin angle while being completely overside, drenched by lubricating oil, with oil drums smashing against the railings on each side of him. Mercifully he managed to swing himself in board again on the next roll and, badly shaken, crawled towards the accommodation. One of the lucky ones, and how needless it all was, if proper precautions had been taken earlier, and the mate had been less concerned about saving money in overtime.

That apprentice was myself and this experience has always made me appreciate how important planning and assessment of risk really is.

Summing up

There was a lack of preparation. No routine check was made of the ship from time to time. Insufficient crew members were available to carry out the work. A lack of leadership in enforcing areas of responsibility, as to whose job it was to secure the drums in the first place.

Ship characteristics

Every vessel has different problems confronting its personnel, in respect to heavy weather damage. On conventional break-bulk vessels, the problems are mainly structural damage, or damage to hatchways or deck cargo. As most ships of this type are relatively small, the vulnerability in a heavy sea is consequently greater.

With the passing of the break-bulk ships, and the greater use of container vessels, the problems on this type of tonnage, in addition to the above statements, are usually container lashings breaking loose, or slackening. But container vessels are vulnerable should the integrity of the containers themselves be broached by heavy seas, and a container collapses, destroying the tension of its lashings, and sometimes the integrity of the whole vertical cell. For this reason it is better to avoid exposure to heavy beam seas as much as possible. With container ships becoming larger, and also being jumboised, flexing of the ship in heavy seas can also cause container points or twist locks to shear, and containers to break adrift from their lashings.

Tankers have their own problems of low freeboard through deep-draught loading, and economies of size which exposes them to extreme stresses in bad weather.

Deck fittings are probably less vulnerable on tankers, as they are not so prominent. But the decks are more exposed should crew members be forced to work on them in bad weather.

Car carriers are more likely to have problems within the hull, rather than on exposed deck surfaces, as their high freeboard protects them in this respect. Rescuing people from small boats in heavy seas can pose a serious problem on these ships, owing to excessive freeboard and rapid leeway made by these ships. Crews are likely to be very vulnerable here.

Supply ships, by the very nature of their work and design, are very liable to damage, and crews working on these craft are subject to much stress, owing to schedules and weather slots. Their smallness also makes them very lively in heavy seas.

Likely emergencies

Surprising damage can be caused by loose equipment left lying on decks themselves. 1 recall an instance of dunnage having been left carelessly on deck when a heavy sea sent one piece smashing through a closed porthole to land on the desk of a chief steward. Fortunately, the man had recently left his desk at the time, so only damage to papers and property resulted, giving rise to malicious comments by some of 'the devil looks after his own'!

The most probable cause for crew members to be exposed on weather decks in bad weather is through something breaking adrift which requires re-securing before structural damage happens, or because the vessel has been damaged and requires to have its integrity restored. Anticipation of such incidents is difficult, but the only valid solution.

Sometimes it is a case of needing to give assistance to other vessels or people, when crew members are exposed to the elements by the very nature of the emergency. Careful handling of the ship to minimise heavy seas coming on board and good communication with the deck crew help to minimise the dangers here.

Whatever the cause, the crew members are in a place which normally is left exposed to the elements, and which is probably uneconomical and impractical to make entirely safe in all weathers. Therefore, the means of ensuring safety must be that of preparation, discipline, training, communication and correct equipment. It is too much to expect ships to be so designed that crews can operate in total safety.

Preparation, discipline and training

Bad weather should always be anticipated, but preferably avoided whenever possible. With all the technology that is available to the modern seafarer, there is really no excuse to be taken unawares.

With sufficient time to prepare, all normal precautions should be taken, such as securing of watertight doors, scuttles, loose equipment, and the crew members informed of the degree of intensity of the storm. The rigging of lifelines on exposed weather decks should never be neglected, or left until it is too late.

Most crew members, especially those who have had little experience of heavy seas, and operating in a hostile environment, underestimate the power of heavy seas coming on board. The first duty of the ship's officers is to ensure that no one goes on exposed decks without permission. Study of wave characteristics will help to ensure that crew members do not unwittingly wander out on the weather side of the ship.

People who know how to swim are usually better able to appreciate the dangers of waves, and the buoyant effect which waves can have on a body. Therefore, I believe that it is essential that all crew members should have this understanding. This knowledge should be supplemented by lectures or instruction as to the effects likely to be experienced by people caught up in heavy seas coming on board. From personal experience, the surprise at being bodily thrown up into the air with a wave is hardly a pleasant one, and the sheer helplessness of one's position seldom realised. The lucky ones remain on board their vessels, albeit chastened and possibly injured from their experience. But it is the unlucky ones who are washed overboard, and probably lost.

Bad weather is seldom conducive to rest, yet crew members should not be tired when called upon to meet an emergency. A tired man is a vulnerable one.

Communication

In these days of hand-held radios, there should be little trouble maintaining contact with the bridge, or other persons. The only difficulty is in ensuring that the radio is itself kept reasonably watertight or dry. I have seen many Japanese pilots using an ingenious transparent plastic cover for their radios, which seemed to be tailor-made for their sets. These are far more suitable, and I imagine cheaper, than the simulated leather covers normally supplied with this equipment.

Wherever possible, I believe that crew members should be within sight of someone on the bridge at all times. Otherwise, never lose sight of whoever has the means of communication, and never be alone.

It is self-understood, that damage control on the weather side of a ship means that the vessel will have to be turned away from the seas, so that crew members can gain access in reasonable safety to these parts. I have always been a firm believer in having the people with me on the bridge while manoeuvring, and prior to their venturing onto an exposed deck. In this way, 1 have ensured that over-eager (foolhardy?) people do not venture out before the deck is relatively safe. An overview of the situation can also possibly be made, and a discussion held as to the method of tackling it. 1 believe that wherever possible such work is best carried out during daylight hours, when people are more easily visible, and lighting no longer required.

For example, during a vicious storm in the Mediterranean Sea, the anchors were found to be slamming and possibly breaking loose. The chief officer with the bo's'n and two seamen hurried on to the forecastle without waiting for the captain to turn the ship away from the sea. The result was that a sea came on board, wrapping the chief officer around a bollard, which fractured his pelvis, while the bo's'n received cracked ribs, and one seaman a head injury. The vessel deviated to Malta to land the injured personnel. Was it all worth it, when a few minutes delay would have ensured safety?

Equipment and operations

1 believe that the time has come for a more suitable lifejacket to be supplied to ships. The present design has many faults, and appears designed more from a view of what can be made for a price, than to be really effective. The recent criticism that one can more easily drown in a DTp-approved lifejacket makes it imperative that a more appropriate type be designed. An inflatable type, which operates automatically by cylinder as many pilots are using today, is a better idea, especially whenever work is required to be carried out while wearing them. These would be used at least by those crew members whose need is to maintain mobility, for it is essential that mobility not be impaired when trying to avoid heavy seas. The fact that it would not give buoyancy immediately, but only at the command of the wearer, is important when caught in the seas themselves, for the reasons already stated.

Every seaman venturing out on deck should carry a knife, as well as being equipped with a safety harness which could be secured as necessary for greater safety. They should also be properly dressed, in adequate clothes appropriate to the temperature and conditions and which are not restricting. Self-reflecting strip stuck to these clothes is wonderful for making sure people are seen. Seaboots which afford a good grip of the deck must be used, for keeping one's balance in heavy seas can probably make the difference between living and dying, on decks that are tilting at all angles. Protected feet are also safer feet, rather than the popular 'thongs', beloved of seafarers.

Whatever the damage or duty, the essential means of dealing with this problem must also be anticipated and carried, to reduce time required to tackle the emergency. Prior to bad weather it is a good idea to have an emergency store of such items as rope, marline spikes, spanners, hammers and timber kept handily to the deck, possibly at deckhouse or accommodation entrances, to tackle an emergency that is likely.

Most ships have weak points, and it is the duty of prudent officers to anticipate them. On container vessels, the obvious problem is that of lashing bars and turnbuckles slackening off. It would be good to have the means of re-securing these at strategic points around the ship. Then, again, there is the ever present likelihood of something within these containers breaking loose, with disastrous results to the adjacent containers. For this emergency, it is essential to have timber and other items to secure them conveniently to hand. For it is invariably drums, or large coils of wire or sheet metal that break adrift in heavy weather, if they have been poorly secured in the first place.

Regular deck inspection, either physically, or by means of a careful inspection from any high position such as the bridge, can prevent many problems getting out of hand and becoming serious. An alert officer, appreciative to unusual sounds or noises, is invaluable to detecting problems in good time. I recall a case where, on a regular deck round, an officer detected the deep sound of something moving within a container. On opening it was discovered that 5-ton rolls of sheet steel had been improperly secured, and were smashing against the container side with the roll. Timely action prevented greater container damage, and minimised the risk to the crew who were immediately sent to obtain handily placed timber for bracing the cargo.

Conclusion

Finally, it should always be remembered that seagoing is a dangerous profession, and there are times when calculated risks must be taken in the interest of safety of life or ship. The risks themselves can be minimised only by good training, coordination of effort and experience. Unfortunately, the tendency these days is to emphasise the theoretical and technical knowledge of our career, while almost ignoring the essentially practical nature of seagoing.

Chapter 43

FIRE AND DAMAGE CONTROL

by Mr. G.B. Standring, Managing Director, Marine Safety Services Ltd.

Introduction

DAMAGE CONTROL IS A TERM that originated in the Royal Navy, referring to an on-board organisation designed to enable a warship to float, to move and to fight, after sustaining some form of damage. Ever since the days of Nelson, the ability of a warship to perform her designed function has been lost, or seriously impaired if the above capabilities are reduced to any great extent. This loss can be accomplished by various types of damage – fire and flooding being just two examples.

Damage of many kinds can occur in a ship at any time, as a result of a great variety of causes, ranging from spontaneous combustion to collision or explosion. The object here is to consider fire and damage control organisation in the merchant navy, bearing in mind that an organisation is required that will minimise the effects of damage, once it has occurred. It is not intended to discuss the way in which ships may be constructed so as to limit damage, nor the various materials now available to limit fire spread as these are adequately covered elsewhere.

It would be foolish to pretend that we will always do everything correctly or that machinery or materials will always perform or behave as we might anticipate. By the law of averages the unexpected will happen to some, if not all of us, and for this we must be prepared.

A damaged ship, even though she remains afloat and retains some mobility, is useless commercially unless she can load or discharge her cargo. Repair and salvage costs and time off hire are costly. It therefore behoves us all to ensure we limit damage by having an efficient emergency organisation – a term more appropriate in merchant ships than 'damage control organisation.' The task of such an organisation is:

1. To limit the extent of damage and injury to personnel by careful preparation and training.
2. To limit the spread of damage to the ship as it occurs, by effective countermeasures.
3. If possible, to effect the necessary emergency repairs.

How can all this be achieved in a merchant ship, where manpower is limited and the size of the ship may stretch lines of communication?

Clearly it is impracticable to have the sophisticated damage control parties that are part of Royal Navy ships. Indeed are such parties, trained in keeping warships afloat, practicable or necessary in merchant

ships? Warships are designed with small watertight compartments, where rapid shoring of damaged bulkheads can keep them floating and fighting. Although merchant ships are not constructed like warships there are aspects of the latter's damage control organisation that can be modified to deal with emergencies and limit damage.

Emergency organisation

To be truly effective in an emergency situation, the experience and skills of the individual have to be brought together within the ship's command and control structure. This is commonly referred to as emergency organisation. In designing such an emergency organisation, one has to take a number of factors into account:

a) The normal chain of responsibility
b) Individual skills and levels of training
c) The number of crew
d) Special circumstances, structural limitations, particular cargoes, passenger mustering, unmanned engine rooms or remotely controlled machinery, communication facilities etc.
e) Personnel who will have special duties in connection with any of the above
f) Equipment on board
g) The number of people who can physically get at the emergency
h) Flexibility

A further important consideration is that there should be an element of standardisation within a fleet, so that officers and crew will more readily integrate into the organisation on joining a new ship.

Figure 43.1 illustrates a typical emergency organisation derived from Royal Naval practice and first introduced into merchant ships a number of years ago. It can be adapted to suit almost any type of ship with only minor variations depending on circumstances and has gained acceptance within many shipping companies.

The central element of this organisation is the emergency team or squad which will be made up of certain key officers and ratings and which will deal with all types of ship emergencies. It will be backed up by the support squad which can provide extra manpower for such tasks as boundary cooling, fetching extra equipment, or even preparing lifeboats. The command will normally be from the bridge, whether at sea or in port, as this is the natural centre of decision and communication. Here, the master will be

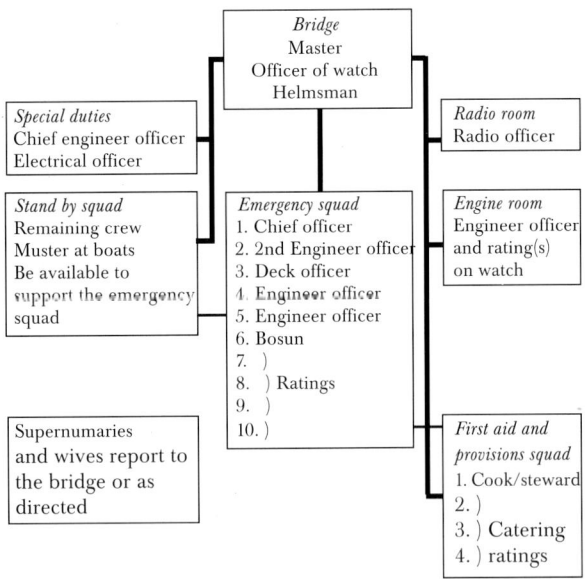

Figure 43.1 Typical emergency organisation

supported by possibly an officer and a rating and will also have easy contact with the radio officer in the radio room.

The chief engineer and certain other personnel are assigned special duties. In general, because of his particular responsibilities and knowledge of the ship, the chief engineer can be most effective if given a fairly free hand and not tied down to a specific duty. He will need to exercise overall control of the operation of machinery as well as providing the master with regular assessments of the situation and advising as necessary.

The first aid squad will stand-by to transport and care for any casualties. In most ships the cook/steward will be in charge of this squad which will usually comprise about four catering ratings. The first aid squad will also be responsible for taking blankets and extra provisions to the lifeboats if required.

This, then, is a basic description of a type of emergency organisation which has proved itself in a number of real emergencies and which has a good deal of flexibility.

Duties of the emergency organisation

There are three basic functions of the emergency organisation which may be listed as follows:

Identify and report the emergency

This may sound obvious, but there are situations – in smoke-filled accommodation, for example – when this may be difficult. Good communications and emergency reporting procedures can greatly assist the leader of the emergency squad in deciding how best to tackle a situation. Also, the initial actions in an emergency often dictate the success or otherwise of subsequent actions. A great many ships and lives have been lost because the person discovering the fire or other emergency did the wrong thing.

It is essential that everyone on board is trained and made to demonstrate clear confidence and understanding of the procedures in raising the alarm. Particular attention should be paid to junior members of the ship's company who might have inhibitions about breaking an alarm glass or pushing the button, perhaps preferring to try and avoid creating a disturbance or drawing attention to themselves. Some of the newer ones might not even know whom to call or where.

There are many cases on record where people tried to tackle the situation single-handed and unequipped. Many lives have been lost as a result of impulsive rescue attempts in tanks and pump rooms. In other cases people have tried to tackle fires with portable extinguishers and, only when it was too late, abandoned the attempt to raise the alarm, often leaving door open to allow the spread of flames. This is something hat affects everybody on board, and may mean the difference between ultimate success or failure.

Deal with the situation operating as a team

Certain emergencies are common to all types of ships and include fires in engine rooms, accommodation, galleys, store rooms and paint lockers, collision, grounding, man overboard, rescuing a victim from an enclosed space, or even assisting others in distress.

Quite frequently one emergency will trigger off a series of others, as in the case of a collision which causes an explosion or outbreak of fire and injury to personnel, as well as damaging the hull and affecting stability. Clearly, a ship's emergency organisation requires a good deal of training and realistic practice if it is expected successfully to tackle the various situations that may be encountered.

Communications

The emergency organisation can only function effectively if there is efficient means of communications. Most ships are now equipped with walkie-talkie radios which are generally ideal for this purpose.

Communication is obviously important from the beginning and throughout the emergency, as it provides the means of enabling the whole organisation to function as an effective entity, allowing the proper command and control structure to work. Fixed communications such as telephones and talk-back systems are useful, particularly in the early stages, but they could be knocked out by the emergency, particularly a fire or a collision and cannot, therefore, be relied on for all occasions.

Personnel should be trained in effective communication and should understand what information is important. Lengthy discussions and verbosity should be discouraged because they jam the system. Clarity of speech is essential.

Emergency headquarters

The emergency squad will require a suitable location at which to muster on the alarms being sounded and this position should contain such equipment as they will need, at least in the initial stages, and will include items such as breathing apparatus, protective clothing and some fire fighting and rescue equipment.

The selection of the emergency headquarters requires careful consideration. Ideally it should:

- Be readily accessible from open deck and in all weather.
- Be reasonably near to accommodation and engine room.
- Not be isolated by fire and smoke.
- Be large enough to hold the equipment stowed in a state of readiness and to allow accessibility by four or five men.
- Have communications with bridge and engine room.

If possible, it should also be reasonably near any emergency stops and controls and the operating positions of the major extinguishing systems. It should also contain the fire detection indicator panel. Of course, it is seldom possible to achieve all this in an existing ship and a degree of compromise is often necessary, but when designing new tonnage these features can usually be incorporated with minimum additional expenditure. Supplementary equipment stations will also be established adjacent to high risk areas and remote from the emergency headquarters where additional equipment will be available.

Leadership

Leadership is fundamental to the success of any emergency effort, and the leader of the emergency squad must be able to stand out from the remainder, issuing clear, concise and crisp orders. If personnel are to work together as a team, the leader must be identifiable as being the man in charge.

It was said of one famous military leader in action, that 'his men would follow him anywhere – if only out of curiosity'. This is perhaps an extreme case, but an emergency squad requires firm and definite leadership throughout an incident, particularly in the initial stages. Orders must be forthcoming to direct personnel to their duties and overcome the fear of the unknown that will exist in any emergency situation.

The command

The ultimate responsibility for the operation of the ship's emergency organisation rests with the master. In many situations he will rely on the advice of his chief engineer officer and these two must work in close cooperation to ensure the safety of personnel, the ship and her cargo, to see that the best possible action is taken by the emergency team.

Since the master is concerned with the safety of the ship as a whole, he must be kept in the picture concerning the overall situation at the emergency point. Without this flow of information, he will be unable to make essential and important decisions. For example, the master may, during the course of a serious engine room fire, decide from the information he has received that it is prudent to order all non-essential personnel off the ship, whilst leaving the emergency squad to continue fighting the fire, thus reducing the number of personnel exposed to the danger. He cannot possibly take this decision if he is not kept up-to-date with the situation in the engine room.

The master must decide if the situation is within the scope of his emergency squad, bearing in mind that personnel protection is vital. The master will require information from various sources, to assist him in deciding what his next step should be and in the worst situation he may decide that the saving of life is the only action the emergency squad can perform. The master can only take these decisions from his command post on the bridge and masters should not necessarily get themselves involved at the scene of an emergency.

Likewise, the chief engineer officer, during an engine room fire, must be in a position to decide when to use the fixed CO_2 flooding system, before the situation becomes so serious that it will be ineffective. As the main engine will then be out of action, it is clearly important for the master to be informed of this decision.

Training

The first training requirement is to draw up a realistic company safety policy, defining responsibilities, training and equipment requirements. It is then necessary to train sea staff:

(a) *To avoid accidents*
    This requires personnel to have a theoretical knowledge of why accidents occur.
(b) *To deal with emergency situations*
    Should the accident prevention part break down.

Shore-based courses teach the theory and practice of fire fighting, the use of equipment and, hopefully, an element of teamwork among the fire fighters. However, there will be a number of differences from the real shipboard situation, as there are limitations to the degree of simulation that is possible. The equipment used will possibly be quite different from that at sea and the command, control and communication structure normal in a ship will be absent.

Shipboard training, on the other hand, provides the vital catalyst between what is learnt ashore in the classroom, or on the fire training ground, and practical application on board. It relates directly to the ship and its equipment. The entire crew is trained to work together and within the normal framework of the ship's team, everyone benefits, even if they have not previously received training ashore. The best training policy will combine both programmes.

Realistic training drills are required to ensure that each member of the emergency organisation knows his duty. Substitution is important so that the full strength of the team can be maintained at all times. An element of surprise is required to test the efficiency of the organisation properly, although it is not necessary to hold drills in the middle of the night.

Conclusion

Training for emergencies is very much an ongoing process and should be conducted with imagination and as much realism as possible. There will inevitably be repetition if only for the sake of improving performance and ensuring a greater degree of understanding, but training should not be allowed to become an uninteresting chore. Lectures and discussion groups can provide a valuable alternative to drills, as can practical demonstrations in the use of specific equipment.

Masters should encourage officers and crew to think up new ideas for exercises and this in turn will help to generate enthusiasm. Drills should be developed to allow for the training of substitutes so that the emergency organisation will have in-depth capability and can thus overcome the problems created by the absence of personnel for whatever reason.

Exercises are often more beneficial if they are planned in advance and, if lessons are to be learned, they should be followed by a post-mortem discussion in which all crew members should be encouraged to participate. Above all, safety must come from the top and be seen to come from the top.

Chapter 44

BUNKERS – WHAT THE MASTER NEEDS TO KNOW

by Mr. D. Barrow MIBIA FInstPet AMNI

Doug Barrow is General Manager of Maxcom (UK) Ltd., global bunker traders with physical stocks being held by the parent company in Italy. He was the founder chairman of the Council of Management of the International Bunker Industry Association Ltd. (IBIA) and remains an active member of the Council. Initially at sea as a deck officer in the British merchant navy, he came ashore as a petroleum surveyor in Kuwait, prior to joining a leading Middle East marine fuel supplier in 1977 as Operations Manager and later as General Manager.

He left to head up the European fuel oil trading department of a major London based Japanese trading house for six years. A short spell followed in Singapore opening the office of a global American based marine fuel broking company before returning in 1990 to head the UK office of Maxcom Petroli S.r.l. He left in 1996 to spend a year opening the London office of a fuel supplier in Gibraltar and returned to Maxcom in January 1997.

A guest lecturer at Oxford University, he has also given many papers on IBIA and various aspects of bunkering at conferences around the world. His articles regularly appear in World Bunkering and other publications. As a supporting member of the London Maritime Arbitrators Association he has acted as expert witness and successfully advised in contractual disputes.

Introduction

A LOT HAS BEEN WRITTEN about bunkers in books, trade journals and inter-company memos. A lot has been said about bunkers in seminars, conferences and lecture theatres. There is a wealth of information available concerning the operational, commercial and technical aspects of bunkers so there is no reason for any ignorance on the subject. Unfortunately, there are knowledge gaps, especially amongst seafarers, and this chapter will try to cover some of the relevant information required by masters. It is appreciated that, while the master of a vessel is burdened with many issues, he is responsible for the vessel and accordingly must have some knowledge of what powers it. The first person that the master should turn to on bunker related matters would normally be the chief engineer. Unfortunately, even British certificates of competency do not cover all aspects of bunkering and it is not uncommon for seafarers to be unaware of particular facets of bunkering.

Since 1988 when the last edition of *Command* was published, there have been significant changes within the bunkering world. Refining technology has improved, leading to fuel quality changes and differing grade availability. Environmental pressures have also had an effect on product quality and fuel handling procedures. There has been a greater global awareness about bunkers that has led to the formation of the International Bunker Industry Association (IBIA), open to everybody within the industry – ashore and afloat. IBIA has taken the lead in bunker education since its formation in 1993. A requirement for increased standardisation has led to an international standard ISO 8217:1996(E), which covers the specifications of marine fuels and an international technical report ISO/TR 13739:1998(E) covering the practical procedures for the transfer of bunker fuels to ships. There has been a drive towards a standard bunker contract, which led to BIMCO developing

Fuelcon, but this did not find market acceptance although a revised version is being considered. Bunker prices have increased in volatility, probably more so than the crude oil from where the product originates.

Since bunkering can readily be sectioned into the three areas of interest described above – operations, commerce and technical – it is intended to cover the subject in those categories. There may be issues in each area that have an effect on one or both of the other areas, but the scope of this chapter is to provide an overview of the subject, allowing the reader to understand if further learning is required.

Delivery methods

There are three principal methods for delivery of bunkers. The most common method is by barge, which will be primarily considered below, but delivery can be made by road or rail truck and occasionally by shore pipeline.

Operations

The art of bunkering a ship is to transfer the fuel from the delivery facility to the vessel safely, efficiently and cost effectively. By paying attention to the first two points, the third will be achieved automatically. When the master is advised that bunkers have been arranged, he has little opportunity to influence the choice of supplier. There may be little comment that the master may make about the supplier anyway, unless the ship is a regular caller in the port. Accordingly, the onus for the safe and efficient receipt of the fuel lies with the ship. It is therefore of critical importance that there are proper fuel transfer procedures in place, that the concerned people are aware of those procedures and have been trained to carry out the procedures. Many shipping companies have developed their own bunker transfer checklists. Some P&I clubs have produced similar lists. In some ports, the local authorities have their own procedures that are mandatory for the supplier and receiver to follow.

Since the introduction of ISO/TR 13739:1998(E), it is hoped that this will become the standard for all bunker transfers which will greatly reduce the requirement for the multitude of various similar procedures found today. It should be pointed out that this document is not yet an international standard, so there is still opportunity for change, but it is anticipated that it will form the majority of a standard and should be read and referenced by all seagoing masters. The document covers definitions, pre-delivery requirements, post delivery requirements, bunker specifications, transfer procedures, quantity, sampling and dispute handling along with sample documents.

The key points to consider start with the provision of a safe berth for the barge to come alongside the vessel. Proper fendering and mooring facilities are required and vigilance must be maintained throughout bunkering to ensure the security of the barge and the vessel. If personnel are to move between facilities, then safe access will be required – not an unsecured plank, balanced between the bridge wing of the barge and the deck of the vessel, for the engineer to traverse like a tightrope walker, petrified with the thought that his next step may be his last – all for the sake of bunkers! Clear communication must be established between the crew of both vessels with special regard to emergency shut-off procedures. Crew should have the relevant protective clothing having regard to the fact that the thick black oily stuff to be transferred can be hazardous to health and may ultimately be carcinogenic if the body is in contact with it for long periods of time.

Having considered the security of the crew and the ship it remains to ensure the environment is not polluted. The first, foremost and never to be forgotten weapon in the fight against environmental pollution is the scupper plug. They come in various shapes, sizes and designs, but a failure to ensure that all scuppers are properly plugged before the commencement of bunkering may be considered criminal. The cost and effort are minimal, but the potential fines, claims and possible imprisonment that may befall the master are tremendous. You personally may be liable for oil spills from the vessel and, in many jurisdictions, the ship may be arrested and the master imprisoned until such time as adequate financial securities are in place. You have been warned.

Obviously it is important to ensure that there is adequate space in the bunker tanks to receive the nominated quantity, that the hoses are properly connected with bolts in every flange hole, save-alls are provided and hoses are properly drained prior to disconnection, but the scupper plug remains the king.

Commercial

At first sight, it may appear that the master's knowledge of the commercial aspects of bunkering need not be that great, but the implications of ignorance are great and it is important that the master is aware of some of the commercial practices.

The first point to acknowledge is that while fuel oil is often a nasty, black looking liquid, to be buried in the bowels of the ship from the moment it is loaded until it is consumed by the engines at the appropriate time, it is also a very expensive commodity. Depending on the type of vessel, the cost of bunkers may account for up to 60% of the running costs of the ship. It is normally the greatest single item on the ship's account, exceeding crew wages and insurance. There is no such thing as a standard price of bunkers, as the market is extremely volatile and its price depends also on location and local availability as well as the price of the crude oil from which it is produced. The price paid by the buyer will also include transportation to the ship as well as possible local taxes etc. but bunkers do not normally attract the levels of duty often paid on petrol for road transportation.

The buyer of the bunkers may be the owner of the vessel, the charterer or the manager. Bunkers are normally purchased under spot contracts, namely a one off purchase for the bunkers being supplied, but term contracts do exist in some cases.

Whoever has been responsible for purchasing the bunkers to be supplied will have entered into a contract with a seller. You may find it hard to believe, but in many cases the buyer will never have read the contract and be unaware of the exact terms and conditions of supply. Unfortunately, this is too often the case. As master, you should ask the buyer for the relevant clauses in the contract covering the point of transfer of title and risk, agreed sampling procedures and measurement methodology, who has responsibility for connection of hoses etc. etc. Due to a lack of a practical standard bunker contract, each supplier has their own terms and conditions and it may be impractical for you to get the details from the buyer, but you will alert the buyer to the fact that you are aware of potential areas of conflict.

Providing the bunkers are supplied at the agreed time and the correct grade and quantity are supplied, there should be few commercial problems. However, there is some significant documentation associated with bunkering and it is essential that such documents are properly completed and copies retained on board. While they may appear of little importance, they are critical pieces of evidence required in any dispute whatsoever. There should be a pre-delivery checklist. Ensure that this is completed conscientiously and answers given must be factual, not just a load of ticks in the boxes. It is usual that the supplier's measurements are those that determine the quantity delivered and accordingly it is essential that the opening as well as the closing gauges of the delivery facility are observed and recorded. As a mariner, be aware of draught changes of both receiving and delivering vessels and ensure those changes are reflected in the measurement calculations. Obviously, the chief engineer will monitor the quantity received on board but, under the terms and conditions of sale, the supplier's figures will usually take precedence unless some very convincing arguments can be given. This will need to be supported by documentary evidence.

Similarly with bunker sampling, ensure that the method used agrees with the contract, that it is followed precisely and that the proper documentation is completed. Sampling is one of the most important aspects of bunkering and proper sampling devices should be used. When considering the size of the sample versus the quantity of bunkers being supplied, it is of extreme importance to ensure that the sample is representative. Location of the point of sampling is often a cause for disagreement and it is important to be aware of where the point should be. If there is any concern that the sample has not been taken properly, then representation must be made immediately and a written record maintained. If the vessel is entered with a fuel testing service, it is important to ensure that the sample is despatched promptly to enable the results to be relayed back to the vessel prior to utilisation of the bunkers, if possible.

On completion of the delivery, the bunker receipt will require completion and signing. Do not allow the document to be signed prior to the delivery. If there is a dispute, you should make a remark to that effect on the bunker receipt. In some ports, the supplier does not allow this practice. If this is the case, it is important that a Note of Protest is issued immediately and the buyer notified.

Technical

This is an area where the chief engineer should be able to answer any questions you may have. Today, bunkers are normally sold that comply with one of the 15 grades of fuel oil or four grades of distillate fuel mentioned in ISO 8217:1996(E). Fuel is still commonly known by its viscosity, which seems illogical when it is really the energy content of the fuel that should be important! The most common grades of fuel oil are IFO 380 cSt, which is often to ISO-F-RMG 35, and IFO 180 cSt, usually to ISO-F-RME25. The common grades of distillate are Marine Gas Oil to ISO-F-DMA specification or Marine Diesel Oil to ISO-F-DMB or DMC specification.

The selection of which grade of bunkers is to be used may depend on some or all of the following:

- The engine manufacturer's warranties.
- The technical superintendent's opinion.
- The charter party.
- Local product availability.
- Product price.

The choice will not normally be the master's decision, but it is important to ensure that the product to be supplied is the product ordered. The initial way is to check the pre-delivery documentation to ensure it refers to the correct grade of oil. On board test kits have improved considerably and there are now some very efficient, portable and easy to use instruments that can monitor many of the main fuel qualities to give a good indication if the fuel being supplied is the same as nominated.

The common parameters to be checked would include:

- Density (defines the mass delivered, specific energy and CCAI).
- Viscosity (defines CCAI, determines fuel grade).
- CCAI (relates to combustion performance).
- Water (1% water = an energy loss of about 0.43 MJ/kg).
- Salt (salt-water causes fouling and corrosion).
- Pour point (of concern primarily on low temperatures).
- Flash point (storage is usually limited to < 60°C).
- Compatibility (if two parcels of incompatible bunkers are commingled it may lead to blocking of filters, pipes, heater and sludging in tanks).

As a master, when in doubt – ask.

Communications

Many of the problems associated with bunkering are as a result of lack of education and poor communications. It is important that you are able to facilitate communications between the buyer and the chief engineer, between the ship and the local agent and between that agent and the supplier. If the supplier does not receive the proper notices concerning the ETA of the vessel, don't be surprised if bunkers are not available on arrival. Similarly, if the supplier has not been notified of any impediments to bunkering, such as no night bunkering due to restrictions on crew overtime, or cargo operations likely to prevent access by the bunker barge etc., expect a complaint from the buyer when he or she receives an invoice for barge delay. Keep close communications with the buyer. If there is any problem, prompt notification to the buyer may allow action to be taken that would mitigate potential losses – failure to communicate could subsequently cost money. Ensure all communications are logged in case they are required as evidence to defend or support a claim.

Disputes

Disputes fall into four main categories – quantity, quality, delays and others. The first thing to remember is that disputes should be avoided and this can often be achieved by good procedures, careful planning and good communications. The master should ensure that losses are mitigated – namely any action taken should be to minimise the overall losses, not just those of the buyer. In the event of any dispute, it is the duty of the master to ensure there is proper evidence to demonstrate the actual chain of events so that a solution may be found at a later date. Too many genuine claims are lost due to lack of supporting documents. These include deck and engine logs, engineer's notebooks, copies of all relevant documentation and notes of protest.

Surveyors are sometimes used, especially in ports that have a significant claim history. Be sure of the terms of reference of the surveyor. For quantity surveys their function may be to check only the delivery facilities. At other times it may be to check the vessel's tanks and, on occasion, it may be to do both. If surveyors are used, it is important to give them every assistance and to remember that if they are supposed to be in attendance for the start of the bunkering, they have been notified.

In the case of a quantity dispute, it may be appropriate to employ a surveyor immediately to try and resolve the problem, but as they were not in attendance at the commencement of the bunkering, they will have to rely on existing documentation.

Conclusion

The foregoing only touches the surface of bunkering. It is not intended to be a finite text, but to give some pointers as to what may be relevant or of interest. Your involvement in bunkering will depend on the number and competence of the crew on board and the involvement and interest of the owners, charterers or managers.

The one point you should be clear about is your level of authority. If you suspect the bunkers to be of the incorrect grade, do you have the authority to reject them and on what basis? If a sample is provided at the conclusion of bunkering, with the barge master claiming it is a representative sample, but you have no knowledge of its provenance, what action should you take? If the chief engineer advises that the delivered figures are 50 tonnes more than he has loaded, do you have the authority to keep the vessel in port until it is resolved, even though cargo operations have finished?

Imagine it is 03:20. You are woken to be told that the bunker delivery hose has sprung a leak just inboard of the ship's rail. Despite the precautions taken, bunkers have spilt into the harbour and are drifting towards twenty white luxury yachts and a wildlife sanctuary – what do you do? It will be your decision. Unfortunately, these things usually occur just when the head office has closed for a long weekend, and the buyer has just gone on holiday. Be prepared – ensure you are not one of the uneducated.

You have already started your preparations by reading this chapter. Don't be complacent, but don't be too alarmed – most bunkers are supplied without problem. Most of the suppliers around the world today are responsible and they don't want to lose money or customers. If you would like to know more, do not hesitate to contact the International Bunker Industry Association – it is there to help.

References

- *IBIA On Board Test Kit Report*
- *IBIA Guide to Bunker Samplers*
- *IBIA Safety Cards for Vessel's crews*
- *Glossary of Bunker & Lubricating Oil Terminology*
  The International Bunker Industry Association
  The Baltic Exchange, St. Mary Axe, LONDON, EC3A 8BH, England
  ibia@globalnet.co.uk
- Leigh-Jones, C., *A Practical Guide to Marine Fuel Oil Handling*
  MEP Series, Volume 3, Part 19
  The Institute of Marine Engineers
  80 Coleman Street, LONDON, EC2R 5JB, England
  ljj@imare.org.uk
- Fisher, C. and Lux, J., *Bunkers – An analysis of the Practical, Technical & Legal Issues*
  Customer Services Department
  LLP Limited, Sheepen Place, Colchester, Essex, CO3 3LP, England
  enquiries@llplimited.com
- *Fuel & Lube Oil Training Manual*
  Kittiwake Developments Ltd.
  3 & 4 Thorgate Road, Littlehampton, West Sussex, BN17 7LU, England
  mail@kwdev.demon.uk
- *ISO 8217:1996 (E) & ISO/TR 13739:1998(E)*
  International Organization for Standardization
  Case postale 56, CH-1211 Genève 20, Switzerland
  iso@iso.ch

ANNEX

Example of a delivery checklist for spill prevention transfer procedures

A bunker transfer operation should not commence unless the following requirements are met and agreed upon by the cargo officer and vessel officer:

a) The mooring lines are adequate for all anticipated conditions.

b) Bunker hoses and/or loading arms are long enough for intended use.

c) Bunker hoses are adequtaely supported to prevent undue strain on the couplings.

d) The transfer system is properly lined up for discharging or recieving bunkers (additional checks should be performed each time a valve is repositioned.

e) All flange connections on the bunkering system not being used during the transfer operation are securely blanked or shut off.

f) The bunker hoses and/or loading arms are connected to the manifolds using gaskets and a bolt hole in every hole.

g) The overboard or sea suction valves are sealed or lashed in the closed position.

h) Adequate spill containments have been provided for couplings.

i) All scuppers or other overboard drains have been closed or plugged.

j) A communications system is provided between the supplier's delivery facility and the vessel.

k) The emergency shutdown system is available and operable.

l) Communication procedures are established and understood between the cargo officer and vessel officer.

m) Qualified and designated personnel are on duty at the supplier's delivery facility and vessel bunker stations.

n) The bunker hose(s) has been visually inspected to ensure that it (they) has (have) no loose covers, kinks, bulges, soft spots or gouges, cuts and slashes which penetrate the hose reinforcement, and that the hose(s) is (are) marked for identification and test data is maintained in a test log.

o) Adequate lighting of the manifold area is provided.

p) The cargo officer and vessel officer have met to ensure the mutual understanding of:

    1 The pre-delivery form.

    2 Starting, stripping, topping and shutdown.

    3 Emergency procedures including notification, containment and cleanup of oil spills.

    4 Watch and shift arrangements.

    5 Notification before leaving stations.

Chapter 45

ONBOARD TRAINING AND DEVELOPMENT

by Captain L.A. Holder ExC MPhil FRIN FNI

Len Holder served at sea from 1953 until 1963. He was then involved in Maritime Education and Training, at Liverpool Polytechnic, where he was Head of Department from 1977 to 1988 and then Director of the School of Engineering and Technology Management. Since 1989 he has been an independent consultant.

Len Holder completed a three-year term as President of the Nautical Institute in 1996 and since that time has been chairman of Videotel Marine International.

Synopsis

THIS CHAPTER IS ABOUT TRAINING and development on board. When you are in command, training is one of your many responsibilities. Your main objective must be to ensure that effective training is carried out in relation to safety and commercial efficiency on your current voyage. Your next responsibility for training is to support the long-term professional development and certification of all the seafarers on board. You also have a responsibility to keep yourself up to date and certificated to current professional standards, and to undergo refresher training as required.

Chances of success

There are various factors that will affect your chances of success in this part of your job. Some things depend upon other people, but more depend on you. The section which follows is a brief look at what you can expect from other people, and the rest of the chapter concentrates on what you can do. Factors that affect your success with training will include:

- The support you get from ashore.
- Whether you are set relevant and achievable objectives.
- The experience, motivation and ability of your trainees.
- The ability and motivation of senior sea staff as trainers.
- The time available for training on board.
- The resources, equipment and materials you are given for training.

Training can help to turn a group of individuals into a competent team. Like most activities, training requires organisation, knowledge, skills and practice. You may have little time for individual mentoring (coaching) of trainees, but you can motivate and organise others to achieve positive results.

Support from ashore: recruitment and selection

The first influence your shore management has on your shipboard training programme is at the recruitment and selection stage.

What is the minimum you can expect? The International Safety Management (ISM) Code requires, amongst many other provisions, that:

"...each ship is manned with qualified, certificated and medically fit seafarers in accordance with national and international requirements..."

Under the Standards of Training, Certification and Watchkeeping (STCW) Convention each crew member should hold an "appropriate certificate". This means:

- A national certificate of competence.
- An endorsement from the government issuing the national certificate attesting that it meets STCW standards.
- A separate flag state endorsement, if the original certificate was issued by another government.

Also under STCW, companies should ensure that company trainers and/or assessors are properly trained and qualified and that they are provided with adequate resources for their work.

Very few shipmasters have the chance to "pick their team" these days. So it is to be hoped that your company personnel managers ashore have been careful in selecting your crew members, checking their qualifications and previous sea service. If they have used selection tests, it would be helpful for you to have details of the results on board, as well as having access to the seafarers' certificates and records.

Many companies send their personnel on short courses ashore at colleges, in training centres or run in-house. The company should tell you what people have done. It is also helpful to know what is likely to be available in the future, so that you can make recommendations for others at the end of the voyage, or request a course to keep yourself up to date.

Relevant and achievable objectives
Legislation

The International Safety Management (ISM) Code requires that:

"the company should establish and maintain procedures for identifying any training which may be required in support of the Safety Management System (SMS) and ensure that such training is provided for all personnel concerned."

With ships that have ISM certification in place you should be building on and improving the procedures which already exist.

Other official documents that contain references or content appropriate to shipboard training include, as an absolute minimum, the up-to-date amended versions of:

1. International Convention on Standards of Training, Certification and Watchkeeping Convention (STCW).
2. International Convention for the Safety of Life at Sea (SOLAS).
3. International Convention for the Prevention of Pollution from ships (MARPOL).
4. Convention on the International Regulations for Preventing Collisions at Sea (COLREG).
5. ILO Convention 147 [Merchant Shipping (Minimum Standards) Convention].

Company policy

Company training policies are important. Your company may have a written policy which emphasises the commitment of the Board and Chief Executive to training, sets objectives, states who is responsible for what in training, allocates a budget for trainers and training, etc.

Whether or not you have such clear guidelines, you should, in your pre-voyage interview, phone calls and/ or correspondence, try to ascertain what your company's policy is, and what you are expected to achieve in your new appointment.

With that as background, you will need to set realistic training objectives for the current voyage.

Senior sea staff as trainers

Your major assets are the officers and senior ratings who are the face-to-face trainers you have to organise and supervise.

If your ship is a designated training ship, with a specialist trainer on board you have a valuable ally in making sure the training is done properly. Some masters and chief engineers like to designate one officer in each department to act as the "training coordinator". This will often be the 2nd Officer in the deck department, and the 3rd Engineer in the engine room.

In fact, training is the job of everyone on board,

other than the complete novice who does not know enough and has no one to pass it on to anyway. Designating an officer to have responsibility for training must not let other people think they have no further responsibility. However, training records would get in a mess if there were too many people involved in record keeping.

In the same way that you will need to know what the company expects from you, you will need to give a very clear brief to your trainers. Some people are natural teachers. Others find it difficult and have to work at it. Careful thought needs to be given to the allocation of responsibilities. The trainer needs to have the required qualifications, but must also be able to bridge language and cultural gaps, and gain the attention and respect of the trainees.

Trainees

Motivating trainees is the key to good training. When new crew members join, the company have a responsibility to familiarise them with the ship, particularly with safety features, such as firefighting and life-saving appliances and procedures. They need to know the part they must play in emergency procedures and be shown as well as told, where things

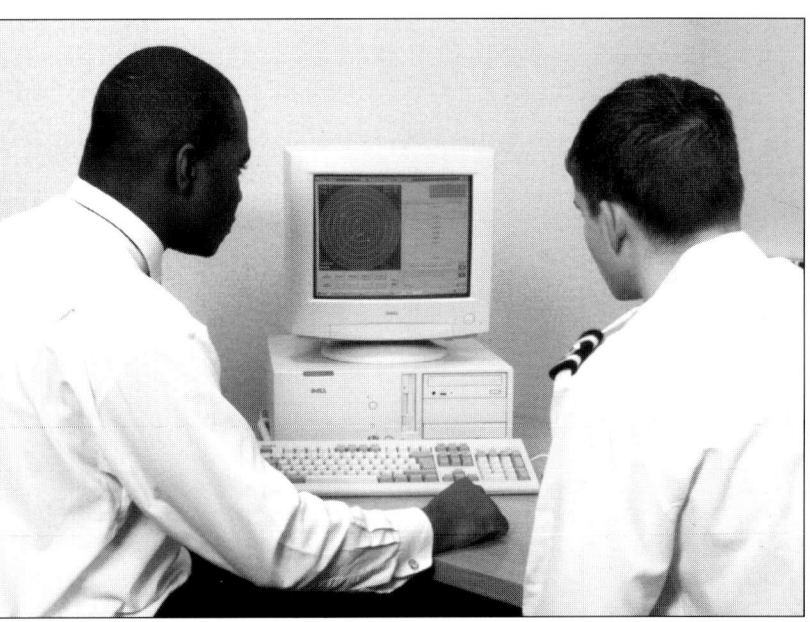

Figure 45.1 More use is being made of computer-based and multimedia training on board

are stowed and how they should be used. They also need to be instructed in the proper use of specialist equipment in their working areas. Some companies begin "familiarisation" with briefings in their own or the manning company' offices. Once crew members are on board, the responsibility for making sure the job is completed, rests with the Master. Familiarisation needs to be completed and "signed off" and suitable records kept.

Once your crew members are settled in on board,

you will get very little thanks for sending them back ashore as being not fully competent, other than in exceptional cases where a totally incompetent person has "slipped through the net" and cannot hold down their job on board. The first job in training is to sort out the shortcomings of the crew members you have been given and start making the best of things, through good management and through training where it is required. (See the Appendix to this chapter on Coaching Skills).

You are reliant upon the certificates, records of previous service, test results and initial observations and questions on board, to know whether each person has a background of sound knowledge to the required standard, and the practical aptitude to put their knowledge into practice.

There are statutory training exercises to be carried out and the day to day performance of individuals on board will soon start to show up any inadequacies. Above all, in these days of high pressure commerce and smaller crews, the only answer is for everyone on board to take some responsibility for their own training, finding out what they need to learn and meeting the trainer half way.

Organisation: priorities

There are four main areas of training to be considered:

1. Statutory safety training.
2. Technical training.
3. Training to improve commercial efficiency.
4. Career development training.

Statutory safety training

Senior officers need to liaise with company shore staff and help with the development and implementation of ISM Code and STCW Convention requirements. Particular importance will need to be placed upon standards in:

- Safety and pollution prevention.
- Shipboard familiarisation.
- Crew coordination and communication .
- Sea training requirements of certification.
- Assessment of competence and/or collection of evidence of satisfactory performance in the work place.

Safety training is the first priority, and needs to begin from the time crew members join.

Technical training

The operation and maintenance of the ship is probably the most important area of training. Legislation requires safety training to be carried out, but the company will expect the ship to be operated efficiently and properly maintained. Manuals and procedures may lay down the framework, but it is personal interest in trainees and properly planned training that will ensure satisfactory results.

Commercial training

The commercial efficiency of your company – and the future employment of everyone on board – will be determined in large part by the successful out-turn of your cargoes or the satisfaction of the passengers you carry. Each ship operator has experience and skills in one or more different trades. This experience is valuable and has usually been gained at a price. It needs to be passed on within the company, whether it is navigating high speed ferries, running high quality hotel services on a passenger ship, or loading, carrying and discharging special cargoes.

Career development training

Senior sea staff should assist trainees and junior staff in gaining skills and experience they require to do their present job more effectively and to prepare for their next certificate of competency. The Standards of Training, Certification and Watchkeeping (STCW) Convention places great emphasis on experience during sea service and the records of practical training are an important part of the certification process.

A few shipboard Training Officers may seek qualifications as specialist trainers or assessors, in which case they will need to be properly trained for their new role. Most ships' officers will simply be supervising training, evaluating candidate's performance and recording evidence in a prescribed format. The evidence collected on board will then be put with results from shore-based examinations and assessments, and used by qualified assessors to fulfil the requirements for issuing STCW certificates of competency.

In the past, officers have usually been required to sign cadet record books and to supervise and record experience for other certificates (such as steering and watchkeeping certificates). The new STCW

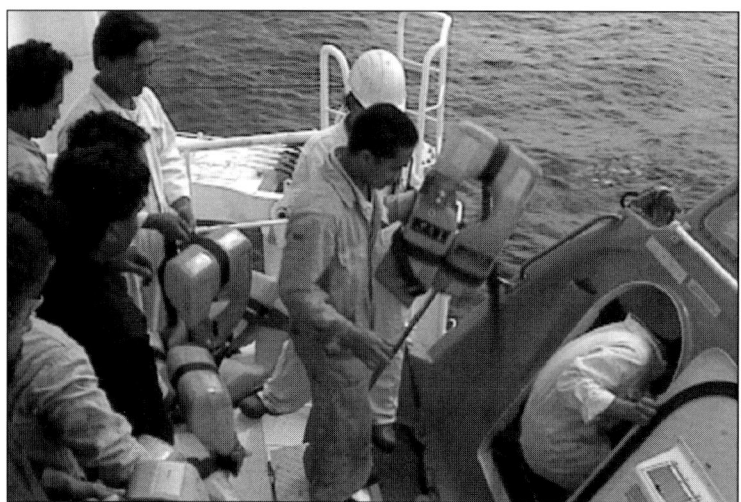

Figure 45.2 Drills form an important part of safety training

Code lays down clearer guidelines on the experience required and how candidates should demonstrate their competence. It is important that records to be used as part of STCW certification process are kept in a format that is approved by the certificate-issuing national administration.

The core of the Training Officer's role will still be in guiding and encouraging trainees, indicating what they should learn and what they can do to become better qualified.

Over and above basic STCW requirements, it will be appreciated if you take an interest in the personal career aspirations of your sea staff and point them in the direction of appropriate programmes. There are many opportunities available these days from general educational and recreational topics available through the Marine Society, through a wide range of college and commercial distance learning courses, to professional development for aspiring shipmasters, marine surveyors, pilots, harbourmasters or maritime lecturers through The Nautical Institute diploma schemes.

Resources

Your second most valuable training resource is your ship, its equipment and procedures. In addition, there are usually special aids to make the training more effective. These may include:
- Manuals and books.
- Videos.
- Computer-based training packages (using diskettes or CD-ROMs).
- Spare equipment provided for training purposes.

It is important to choose the right medium for each training task. Videos are excellent for group training sessions such as fire fighting or abandon ship drills, particularly when there is an experienced person leading the session and following it with a practical drill. Computer-based training (CBT) is well suited to the gaining of knowledge (e.g. learning rules or procedures that must be committed to memory). Most CBT packages allow the trainee to test him- or herself before applying for formal assessment. This makes sure the lessons are learned and saves time for supervisors.

Planning: making the best use of time
Your leadership role

The most important training at the start of the voyage is familiarisation and basic training in safety and departmental duties. It is particularly important to carry out drills with firefighting and life-saving appliances at the earliest opportunity so that everyone is prepared for emergencies. Contingency planning for other emergencies, such as oil spills, is also important these days. For these drills, you are the key person and must lead the planning, drills and debriefing

If you really want the training to be effective and not just an exercise resulting in a log entry, you should use your imagination and think out realistic scenarios in which fires occur in different parts of the ship, people must be rescued from enclosed spaces, someone has fallen overboard, life-saving appliances need to be launched under difficult conditions, an oil spill has occurred due to a bunker overflow etc. It is important that everyone learns from these exercises and gains confidence in dealing with emergencies. There are video and other programmes that can be used as part of an exercise, but people learn more from being active and involved in practical drills.

Delegation

You cannot do everything, but your attitude and commitment to training will affect those to whom you delegate and will also affect the trainees. When selecting people as trainers, their technical knowledge is important, but also bear in mind their ability as communicators, which depends upon personality and self-confidence and language differences and/or cultural relationships with trainees

Training on board can often be characterised by missed opportunities. "If only we had thought of it, we could have put a boat down when we arrived early". "It is a pity we did not get the cadets down in the shaft tunnel to observe the repair work", etc. To avoid these regrets and to make the best use of opportunities, it is necessary to think ahead and plan. Trainees should be encouraged to ask about training opportunities for themselves and their colleagues. They should point out the things they need to learn - after all, you cannot be expected to know that cadet ""x" or seaman "y" has never been on the fo'c'sle head when anchoring, or in the steering flat when testing the emergency steering. If you are successful, it may be possible to create a positive "training culture", with everyone participating.

Career development for yourself

It is important to take care of the professional and career development of crew members, but do not neglect your own requirements. Find out what your certification authority requires to keep your certificate of competency valid. Find out if there are courses that you need, to keep your endorsements valid, whether it is in oil and gas, chemicals, ro-ro, passenger ships or other specialist trades.

Keep up to date with professional developments and career opportunities through journals such as The Nautical Institute's *SEAWAYS*. These days you also have the Internet. The Nautical Institute world wide web site (http://www.nautinst.org) gives links to many other interesting maritime-related sites.

Your local maritime college is usually a good source of information on short courses, etc. but if you want to look further afield, Lloyds Ship Manager publishes an occasional supplement "Guide to Word Wide Maritime Training" which describes a large number of courses and gives contact numbers and addresses. The Marine Society in London is another good source of information.

As master you are a manager of people and a manager of resources. There are many good management training programmes you can follow, which will help you. A short course ashore allows you to share ideas with other managers, but there are distance learning courses as well.

Reporting back

On board, you should keep good records of training and drills and be ready to show them to properly authorised port or flag state inspectors, company P&I representatives, company auditors etc. Appropriate records should also be sent to the company and given to trainees. Finally, please do not forget to "close the management loop", and report back to your company on how the training has gone, what resources are needed for next voyage, who needs to go on refresher and updating courses, etc.

Conclusions

Despite the changes in legislation, there are no short cuts to competence. Companies that have good training schemes will be best prepared for the future. The normal methods of training, which include shore-based college or training centre courses, followed by practical training at sea will still be needed. And, you and your senior sea staff have an important part to play!

References

1 *Guidelines on the application of the IMO International Safety Management Code*, International Shipping Federation/International Chamber of Shipping, 1996.
2 *The Revised STCW Convention*, International Shipping Federation, 1995.
3 *On Board Training Record Book for Deck Cadets*, and *On Board Training Record Book for Engineer Cadets*, International Shipping Federation, 1996.
4 Holder, L.A., *Training and Assessment on Board*, Witherby & Co., London, 1997.
5 *Maritime Education and Training: A Practical Guide*, The Nautical Institute, London, 1997.
6 *Guide to Word Wide Maritime Training*, Lloyds Ship Manager Supplement, Lloyds of London Press.

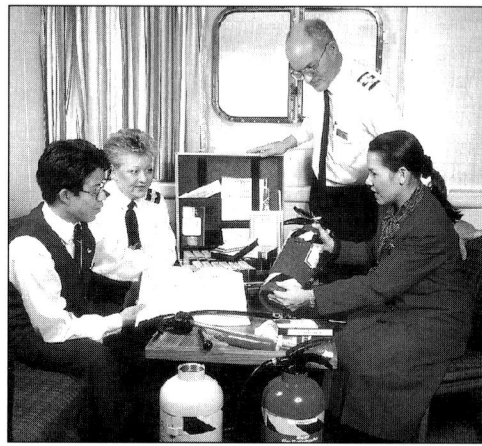

Figure 45.3 Demonstrations and "hands-on" practice are remembered longer than talks

Appendix to Section 3.10

Coaching/mentoring skills

Most shore-based training is through structured "off the job" courses. In contrast, training on board is mainly "on the job" training, **learning by doing**, and requires special management skills. These are referred to as **coaching** or **mentoring skills** and this appendix highlights some of the key points if this type of training is to be effective.

Coaching needs to be structured:

1 Determine the development needs of the trainee. These may be:
   a) short-term development for those who are not performing well in their present jobs
   b) medium term to prepare for changes and challenges in the job
   c) long term needs for promotion and career development

   Decide on the priorities

2 Choose appropriate learning strategies. These might include:
   a) "off the job" learning from books, videos or computer-based learning packages, or
   b) "on the job" learning by experience, with coaching.

   A combination of methods may be required.

The steps in coaching are as follows:

1) **Identify the gaps** in the trainee's knowledge and skills. Very often, junior staff on board know what needs to be done, but lack self-confidence. They may be unsure of their ability to plan and implement a certain procedure without direct supervision. Priorities can be determined by observation and by discussion with other officers and with trainees.

2) **Choose a suitable project or procedure**. Don't just delegate easy jobs: there should be an element of challenge, and it will probably involve some measure of risk. Don't make it too difficult. (For example, as master, you might let the second mate anchor the ship in an open anchorage in daylight, but not at night in poor visibility).

3) **Briefing**. Your management role is the key to good coaching. Brief the trainee well before hand, tell him or her the outcome you expect and any particular dangers to look out for. Help them to plan and let them ask questions.

4) **Carrying out the project or procedure**. Let them carry out the work without unnecessary interference. If possible let them "do it their way" and clear up their own mess. Of course, the safety of the ship and people remains paramount.

5) **Appraisal or debriefing**. Afterwards, talk through with the trainee how things went, what they have learned from the experience, and how they could do it better next time.

6) **What next**? Discuss with the trainee what the next step in their development should be. If it did not go well, perhaps trying a similar exercise again. If it went well, then it may be to try something more difficult next time.

Remember
- People learn from you all the time, by the example you set.
- People learn from their own mistakes.
- Don't blame people if they "screw up".

THE PERSON WHO NEVER MADE A MISTAKE, NEVER LEARNED ANYTHING!

Chapter 46

ALTERED COMMAND RESPONSIBILITIES
FOR PIRACY, STOWAWAYS, ILLEGAL DRUGS AND TERRORISM

by Brigadier (Ret'd) B.A.H. Parritt CBE, Companion
Chairman, International Maritime Security (IMS)

Brigadier (Ret'd) Brian Parritt served for 37 years in the British Army, culminating in five years as Director of the Intelligence Corps. Throughout his service he held a variety of senior intelligence and security appointments all over the world, including Hong Kong, Singapore, Malaysia, Borneo, Malta, Libya and Cyprus. He is a parachutist, was wounded and commended for bravery during the Korean War and was awarded the MBE during the Enosis campaign in Cyprus and the CBE in Northern Ireland.

A graduate of Hong Kong University in Chinese (Mandarin) and the Staff College, Camberley, he is a Freeman of the City of London and from 1981 to 1985 was an Aide de Camp to Her Majesty Queen Elizabeth II. In 1986 he participated in the series of International Maritime Organization (IMO) meetings, which resulted in the unanimous adoption by the United Nations of the policy document Guidelines to Prevent Illegal Acts at Sea.

Brigadier Parritt has also been an invited speaker at three seminars organised by the IMO to discuss methods by which the IMO Guidelines on the Prevention of Illegal Acts at Sea could be implemented. These were 1989 in Puerto Rico, 1990 in Greece and 1991 in Japan. In 1989 he was part of a delegation led by the Norwegian Ambassador, which toured the Caribbean to discuss with heads of State how to prevent the smuggling of illegal items.

He is now Chairman and Chief Executive of International Maritime Security (IMS) and has been a guest speaker at many maritime seminars which have discussed the problems of port and ship security. He was recognised by HM Customs & Excise for his contribution to the fight against illegal drugs and was elected a Companion of The Nautical Institute in 1994.

In 1991 he was asked by The Nautical Institute to write the book Security at Sea *which is a practical guide for masters to help them deal with terrorism, drugs and piracy. In 1992, following the success of this publication, The Nautical Institute commissioned Brigadier Parritt to compile another two authoritative books,* Stowaways by Sea *and* Crime at Sea. *These were followed by a further volume,* Illegal Drugs by Sea.

Introduction

ALTHOUGH THE THREATS FROM PIRACY, stowaways, illegal drugs and terrorism have always existed, in the last decade and particularly since 1st July 1998 with the introduction of the ISM Code, there has been a significant change in the command responsibilities of a master as regards security. He now has to demonstrate that he has taken every effort 'to establish safeguards against all identified risks'. (Management Objective Para 2.2).

In the past, an experienced master was able to deal with most acts of violence against his ship without public alarm or media attention. Maritime security law was non existent and the general view was that if a master could deal with a piracy or stowaway problem quickly and effectively, with the minimum of fuss or delay, this was the sensible thing to do.

Times have changed. Just as a master now has recognised responsibilities for safety, pollution and hygiene, so with maritime security he now has to conform to internationally accepted standards.

Traditional, robust, measures that masters could take in the past to solve security problems can now result in public disgrace, dismissal and even prison. This chapter deals with the current threats to the security of a vessel and the factors that now influence a master's command responsibilities.

Piracy

Piracy/armed robbery has always been part of a sailors life, the significant difference is that before, there was the combination of political will and naval power to deal with this type of maritime attack. Now, this is not the case.

All soldiers know that the best way to deal with an armed man is to confront him with a weapon of superior fire-power. The regular navies of the world, particularly the British and American navies, saw it as a legitimate part of their mission to flush out and destroy pirate craft. They were give extraordinary legal powers to punish pirates, including the right to hang those convicted so that they did not have the inconvenience of having to carry them back to their own countries. Special laws were enacted to allow them to pursue pirates, even into territorial waters.

Today we have a situation where, on the one hand pirates are becoming more numerous and sophisticated and on the other, regular navies are becoming smaller.

Naval vessels have, of course, improved their weapon capability and can go much faster, but most are designed to fight submarines or aircraft, to fire and avoid missiles, to transport troops. Very few are designed to capture or kill small fast canoes.

The biggest factor contributing to the growth in the capability of pirates is, however, not their deadly automatic weapons or their ability to acquire large twin outboard engines and craft with high speed low radar profile characteristics. It is the recent revolution in communications.

Many pirate gangs no longer put to sea just hoping to catch a rich prize. They have agents in the loading ports, they determine a ship's destination, they discover the nature of the cargo, they isolate the individual container that carries valuable items such as computers, TVs or Mercedes Benzes and they fax or e-mail this detail to their 'coordinating centre'.

Then, by the use of the ubiquitous mobile phone, the attacking craft can continually be guided and controlled both before and after the attack.

More significant, however, is that the major nations now feel positively inhibited about tasking their warships to 'search out and destroy pirates'. They would of course support any action on humanitarian grounds or, if they encountered an attack in progress would certainly try to stop it, but in an age of strong nationalistic awareness and extreme sensitivity over issues of sovereignty, there is a feeling of reluctance to instigate armed action in waters far from their own coast. This policy is generally welcomed by developing countries who, remembering the colonial era, feel uneasy about foreign naval vessels carrying out 'gunboat' type diplomacy.

There are also islands around the world whose ownership is bitterly in dispute, especially if there is the likelihood of the island producing oil. The competing countries, therefore, protest loudly if the warships of a rival approaches the disputed island. This results in a naval no-go area which can become a dream location for a pirate.

As it is now more and more unlikely, therefore, that a warship is going to be available to provide armed protection, the obvious solution would seem to be to arm the merchant ship? Paradoxically however, although there is considerable disagreement about how to provide protection for merchant ships on the high seas, there is almost universal agreement that merchant ships should not be armed.

As the UK government succinctly puts it – 'The carrying and use of firearms for personal protection or the protection of a ship, is strongly discouraged and will not be authorised by her Majesty's government'.

A letter written by a master and published recently in the press, highlighted this dilemma by asking: 'Why is it I am ordered not to carry a shotgun on my tanker loaded with oil going through the Malacca Straits, but when I come ashore I see elderly gentlemen carrying shotguns, sitting sleepily in the sun outside small jewellery shops?'

We thus have a situation which is so familiar to seafarers, where governments are very strong on advice about what a master can and cannot do, but are much less positive about their own responsibilities. It is left to the master to identify the risk and establish his own safeguards.

Pirates and armed robbers are thieves. They are not politically motivated to attack a specific ship or to kill specific people. The overwhelming evidence is that if these maritime thieves become convinced that their quarry is awake, vigilant and has protective measures in place, they will abort the attack.

Every master should therefore have a ship security plan designed to reduce the risk of a pirate attack. The plan should have the following phases:

The threat

It is not practical for a crew to maintain a high level of security for long periods. Security measures must conform to a known threat. In the first six months of 1998 there were 91 reported incidents of piracy – 32 in the South China Sea, 14 in the Indian Ocean, nine in West Africa and 19 in South America. While it is recognised that only one in three acts of piracy are reported, it is in these geographical areas that anti-piracy measures should be initiated.

In 1997 there were 250 reported incidents of piracy, 56% in territorial waters, 31% in ports and only 13% in international waters. Statistics also show that the majority of attacks take place between midnight and dawn and that most attacks come from aft rather than forward. The deduction is clear – when at anchor in dangerous waters, take extra care in the quiet hours, particularly aft.

The deterrent

Thieves dislike noise, lights and signs of activity. The ship security plan must, therefore, stimulate continual, irregular, physical movement.

Thieves do not like opposition when they are at their most vulnerable, i.e. when they are actually boarding. The plan must therefore include highly visible protective measures such as water hoses, anti-grappling weapons and objectionable additions to anchor chains, rat lines and railings.

The reaction force

Once on board the ship, the armed pirate has the initiative. The plan must, therefore, include the capability for the maximum number of crew to go to pre-planned defensive positions as soon as the approach of a suspect craft is identified.

Such action can be perceived as dangerous and outside the job description of the crew. An essential part of the plan, therefore, is to ensure that all crew are confident that this type of active response does provide a better protection than allowing themselves to be captured by the pirates. Probably the most important element of the ship security plan is the willingness of the crew to work together to prevent the pirate getting on board and the best way to achieve this is by repeated test exercises.

Firearms

A master who uses a firearm to defend his ship will certainly run the risk of having to explain his actions in court. Experience shows that using a firearm can lay him open to the charge of 'employing an inappropriate level force'. International law is not very clear on this point and each case would be reviewed on it's merits, but it would appear that a master using a Verey pistol or water hose which injured a pirate would not be under such heavy legal pressure as if he had used a firearm which is designed to kill.

The conclusion is, therefore, that although governments throughout the world have for various reasons decided that they cannot provide armed protection against acts of piracy/armed robbery, they still expect the master to take sensible precautions against the identified risk of maritime robbery.

A master should, therefore, prepare his ship security plan, which in addition to providing routine protection against theft, recognises that in certain areas of the world, particularly at night when at anchor, he must provide additional protection especially to the stern of his ship. The good news is that a highly visible display of vigilance does significantly prevent attacks. The negative side is that failure to take such protective measures will be seen to be a failure to establish sensible safeguards against an identified risk.

Stowaways

After leaving a South American port a stowaway was discovered on board. He proved to be aggressive and had to be secured and guarded. He demanded a particular diet and broke furniture. Before arrival at the next port, the master received a fax from the agent warning him of a 'severe stowaway problem at the port' and strongly recommending additional protective measures be taken. The agent requested confirmation of receipt of this fax.

The master told the chief officer to take extra precautions but made no budget provision for local security guards. In the event a stowaway did manage to board and hid himself in the bulk sugar cargo. Sadly he sank into the sugar and was asphyxiated.

On arrival in the USA his corpse was discovered and unloading was stopped. The ship was delayed until eventually the health authorities allowed it to be placed in a hygienic warehouse. The value of the sugar was dramatically reduced and a series of multi million dollar legal claims were initiated. The master and the chief officer found themselves accused of not 'establishing safeguards against an identified risk' especially as they already had a stowaway on board and had received a specific warning from the Agent.

Stowaway incidents are increasing. We now live in an era of mass migration. Whether it be for political reasons, economic reasons, natural disasters or wars, thousands of people are deciding each year to improve their lifestyle by moving country. A decade ago stowaways were perceived by the press as rather exciting figures, risking their lives to smuggle themselves on a ship. Now numbers have grown to such a volume that governments who previously showed great tolerance towards clandestine immigration, are now enacting legislation to punish the carriers.

In the United Kingdom a hefty flat fine is levied against every stowaway brought into the country. Other costs also rise – provisioning when on board, overtime of crew to guard stowaways, communications with owners, agents and club, attendance of special immigration officers and translators, transport to police court or jail, provisioning in jail, appointment of lawyers to obtain statements, visiting embassies, consulates, etc. to obtain travel documents, clothing, pocket money, flight expenses including escorts, hotel expenses in case there has to be a transit stop, payment of fines if the country of the port has financial clauses in their immigration legislation, expenses of agents, expenses of club correspondents and of course the cost of delay.

A further complication is the fact that governments make a moral distinction between an unauthorised stowaway defined as 'a person who, at any port or place in the vicinity thereof, secludes himself in a ship without the consent of the shipowner or the master or any other person in charge of the ship and who is on board after the ship has left that port or place', and a refugee who has a legitimate claim for political asylum and is defined as 'someone who, due to fear of prosecution for reasons of race, nationality, political beliefs or any other similar factors, is unable or does not want to stay in the country where he is and wishes to move to a new country'.

But however the stowaway is categorised, to the master he/she is a problem and generally an expensive problem. In the past the costs have often not been a great worry for the shipowner, as the P&I clubs have been willing to help. This is now changing and, given the escalating costs and complexity of stowaway legislation, the clubs are now demanding that the ship should establish improved safeguards against the identified risk of stowaways.

Illegal drugs

Every indication is that the movement of illegal drugs by sea is going to continue and will become an even bigger problem. The demand for drugs is increasing and large profits can be made by supplying this demand.

In 1998 Mr. Keith Hellawell, who has been appointed as the United Kingdom's first national anti drugs coordinator, made the following points:

1. A kilo of drugs in Pakistan costs £ 850; the same kilo in Felixstowe costs £ 7,200.
2. £ 186 million worth of drugs were seized in the UK in 1997.
3. One kilo caught equals two kilos not caught.

In the US, General Barry McCaffey, who is the Director of National Drug Control Policy, has declared a 'war on drugs' and in 1997 President Clinton allocated US $ 873 million to a revitalised anti-drug programme. Throughout the world governments are enacting more and more punitive legislation against shipowners and masters who, albeit inadvertently, are discovered to have transported illegal drugs. These punishments can range from whippings and hanging in the far east, to heavy fines and imprisonment in the west.

From the masters' point of view, this emphasis by governments on the carrier is unrealistic. Given the size of ships, the small numbers of crew and the frantic programme involved in loading hundreds of sealed containers in a limited period of time, it seems grossly unfair to expect the master to carry out a credible search for illegal drugs, particularly given the financial resources and ingenuity of the drug smuggler.

But given the perception of a 'war against drugs' countries, especially the US, see it as legitimate to say 'We don't want drugs here. You brought them. You, therefore, are guilty!'

Most countries do, however, want to be constructive in helping the master discover illegal drugs. The US sea carrier initiative programme, outlines those measures which, if put into force by the master, will be taken into account before a mandatory fine is imposed. In the UK there is a memorandum of understanding agreement which can be concluded between HM Customs and the shipowner which explains how the master can help detect illegal drugs.

Governments regard illegal drugs as one of the most dangerous threats to their social structure. Drugs bring crime, corruption, tragedy and despair. Governments expect masters to establish safeguards against this identified risk.

Terrorism

Although terrorism is perceived as a threat primarily against the passenger section of the maritime industry, stories of an oil tanker or ship carrying nuclear waste being taken over by terrorists and anchored in the narrow mouth of a busy port have already been published and are seen by many as a distinct possibility.

With so many acts of terrorism occurring all over the world, involving every type of transport, the public would not be the least surprised if a ship did become a terrorist target. They would naturally expect that, just as with the risk of oil pollution, ships were taking sensible precautions to prevent terrorists getting on

board with their weapons and explosives i.e. that the master had established credible safeguards against a clearly identified risk.

This, however, is usually not the case. Apart from the passenger industry, especially the cruise industry, if there were a terrorist incident on a cargo ship, it is safe to say that subsequent governmental and media enquiries would often reveal a standard of security which would now be considered inadequate even for the routine protection of a car or family home.

Acceptable safeguards

The good news for a master is that a ship is an identifiable entity with a hull and a limited number of accesses. It is not too difficult to put into effect a reasonable level of security which is able to reduce the risk from the composite threat of piracy, stowaways, illegal drugs and terrorism.

The way to do this was first agreed by the International Maritime Organization (IMO) in its document MSC/Circ. 443 dated 26 September 1986, which was published following the terrorist attack on the *Achille Lauro*, and then by the enactment of maritime security legislation by the US, UK and Canada.

Although these protective measures are primarily aimed at the cruise industry, the same principles apply and can be used by the non-passenger industry. They are simple: The appointment of a named individual responsible for security on shore and on board; and the production of a ship security plan which specifies how access control is to be maintained, how searching is to be carried out, which areas are to be denied to unauthorised persons and what reactive procedures are to be taken if the threat of violence escalates.

There is great flexibility in all these documents as to how these measures can be implemented and the final answer will depend on the type of ship and budget, but the most important factor is undoubtedly the motivation and training of the man on board who is responsible for security. If his attitude is not correct and he magnifies all the difficulties, then it is easy to find excuses not to make a credible defence. A ship security plan which makes use of all available resources and is supervised with intelligence and discipline can genuinely establish a realistic safeguard against attack.

Conclusion

In the past decade the actions of masters have been abruptly thrust into the public domain. With the unprecedented opportunities that citizens now have to put pressure on politicians, and the amazing development of media capability, actions that masters used take in the isolation of the open sea are now subject to detailed scrutiny, and have to be justified.

So it is with security. Piracy, stowaways, illegal drugs and terrorism are perceived by the public to be matters of concern to everyone, not just to those on the ship. They expect a master to have in place sensible, reasonable levels of protection.

The intangible problem for the master is what is 'reasonable'. Given the reality of cargo carrying and costs, how can he put in place a credible defence which will stand up to subsequent enquiry?

The answer lies in the ISM Code, which states that there should be a contingency plan which will 'establish safeguards against all identified risks'.

This means a ship security plan based on MSC/Circ 443 and the subsequent maritime security legislation, managed by an officer who is capable of ensuring that it is properly implemented.

Security has always been a function of command, the altered circumstances of the past few years now require that masters receive the correct training to carry out this function.

Useful references

Maritime terrorism
*   The International Maritime Organisation (IMO) Guidelines, *To prevent unlawful acts against Passengers and Crews on board Ships*.
    [MSC 53/24 annex 14 dated 26 September 1986].

*   The United States of America Maritime and Port Security Act 1986 for the Prevention of Terrorism at Sea.

*   The United States Coast Guard Proposals Rules issued by the Department of Transportation, concerning the Security for Passenger Vessels dated March 25th 1994.

*   The United States Federal Register Department of Transportation document, Coast Guard 33 CFR *"Security for Passenger Vessels and Passenger Terminals"* dated July 18th 1996 and November 13th 1998.

*   The United Kingdom Aviation & Maritime Security Act 1990.

*   Directions under the UK Aviation and Maritime Security Act 1990-1999.

*   Canadian Transportation Security Regulations 20 May 1997; Cruise Ship and Cruise Ship Facility Security Measures 1 August 1997; Memorandum of Understanding Cruise Ship Security 30 March 1998.

Piracy
*   IMO's Advice on Piracy *Guidelines to Shipowners and Ship Operators, Shipmasters and Crews on preventing and suppressing Acts of Piracy and Armed Robbery against Ships* (MSC/Circ. 623, 18 June 1993).

*   IMO *Guidelines for the use of Radio Signals by Ships under Attack or Threat of Attack from Pirates or Armed Robbers* (MSC/Circ. 805, 6 June 1997).

Stowaways
*   IMO's Advice on Stowaways *"Guidelines on the Allocation of Responsibilities to seek the successful Resolution of Stowaway Cases"* (A 20/Res. 871, 27 November 1997).

Illegal drugs and alcohol
*   IMO's Advice on Drug Smuggling *Guidelines for the Prevention and Suppression of the Smuggling of Drugs, Psychotropic Substances and Precursor Chemicals on Ships engaged in International Traffic* (A 20/Res. 872, 27 November 1997).

*   The Sea Carrier security manual US government document describing the Carrier Initiative Programme to improve cooperation between the US Custom Service and the Maritime Transportation Industry.

*   International Chamber of Shipping *Guidelines for Owners and Masters on Recognition and Detection of Drug Trafficking and Abuse*.

*   The Norwegian Chamber of Shipping *Guidelines for Owners and Masters on Recognition and Detection of Drug Trafficking and Abuse*.

*   US Coast Guard Regulations concerning Alcohol – describing US Coast Guard regulations on the testing of both nationals and foreign marine personnel.

Useful books
Four books published by The Nautical Institute and compiled by Brigadier (Ret'd) B.A.H. Parritt CBE:

*   *Security at Sea* – Terrorism Piracy and Drugs – A Practical Guide.

*   *Crime at Sea* – How could this affect you? – How can you protect yourself – a practical guide.

*   *Illegal Drugs by Sea* – A Nautical Institute study into the explosive growth of drug trafficking and its impact on mariners, companies and their liabilities.

*   *Stowaways by Sea* – illegal immigrants – refugees – asylum seekers. A guide for owners, managers, masters, agents, solicitors, immigration officials, correspondents, consuls and all those concerned with migrant problems.

Chapter 47

SEAFARERS AND WELFARE SUPPORT

by The Rev'd Canon K. Peters, Justice and Welfare Secretary, The Mission to Seafarers

Three years of Mother's Unions and Youth Clubs, etc., convinced Ken that parish ministry was not his scene. Having undertaken some training at The Missions to Seamen in Holland and Ireland as well as the Mersey Mssion to Seamen, after ordination he returned to Liverpool as port chaplain. The Far East became Ken's home whilst port chaplain in Kobe, Japan for seven years. After Japan, Ken was seconded to Liverpool once again until being invited by the Secretary General of the Missions to Seamen to join the Executive as Justice & Welfare Secretary (January 1994), since when he has become known as JAWS.

Ken's undergaduate studies were in theology and he obtained a post graduate Masters in Business Administration. Later he successfully completed the first year in MSc in Maritime Law before leaving Liverpool. Currently Ken is pursuing an MA in Maritime Policy at the University of Greenwich. Among other appointments Ken was an RNR Chaplain for twelve years.

Introduction

SEAFARERS ARE SUSCEPTIBLE TO STRESS and fatigue brought about by a working environment that imposes unnatural conditions. Multinational crewing has many problems brought about by language and communications difficulties, clashes of culture, religious differences and dietary requirements. All of these can be accentuated by living in close confines with people who do not share the same cultural climate, social structure and political positions. The taboos and mores of society are learned by immersion within a culture and by genetic inheritance. Balance of opinion is difficult to maintain within the ethnic diversity of ships crews particularly when they are 'thrown together' by a management that is not concerned with anything other than the best certification available at the lowest cost.

Good managers are aware of the hidden costs of such an employment policy. The isolation can be unbearable if crew members are unable to socialise with each other. The stress experienced by officers who are not confident that their orders have been understood, passed on accurately and acted upon, can be an immense weight. Crew who are expected to perform their duties efficiently and effectively can feel intimidated by the lack of clear precise instructions. The result is often disastrous. Even without any breaches in safety or a major incident, the cumulative effect is damaging to crew confidence and performance. A voyage can become a process of attrition. In these circumstances the relief of relaxation in the seafarers' centre is an essential element for the well-being of the crew. In these circumstances the listening ear of the chaplain is appreciated beyond measure. Especially so if the chaplain attends the ship during an all too brief time alongside when there is no opportunity for the crew to leave the vessel.

Seafarers' missions

Maritime missions have been a feature of the shipping industry for over one hundred and fifty years. Over that time welfare support for seafarers has proved to be a necessary resource for seafarers as they experience the difficulties of life at sea, separated from their loved ones, in an occupation that presents them with physical danger which is sometimes accompanied by various forms of exploitation and abuse. In efforts to ensure that seafarers do not remain 'out of sight and out of mind', the various missions established international networks of seafarers centres providing a warmth of welcome that is appreciated and has come to be expected by seafarers. Most widely known are The Apostleship of the Sea (Stella Maris) and The Mission to Seafarers (Flying Angel).

Port chaplains are regular ship visitors who, among the myriad of officials that climb the gangways, are the only people who want nothing from the seafarer but go, as a friend of all aboard, to listen, to bring news and to invite them to a run ashore at the seafarers' centre. There seafarers can relax in a convivial atmosphere away from the hassle and possible danger of night clubs and waterfront bars. They can telephone home, write the post card and e-mail their friends and family. They can socialise with local people as well as other seafarers and, perhaps with a drink, challenge others to games of pool or table tennis. The rest and relaxation offered at these centres is really appreciated by those who feel increasingly pressured and stressed by the demands of a fast turnaround with few opportunities to go ashore. With limited time for themselves seafarers often choose 'the mish' as their preferred place.

The missions have adapted to the dramatic changes within the shipping industry: containerisation with the consequent decrease in the length of time that a vessel is in port; automation and ever more sophisticated technological innovations that have reduced crew sizes; multinational crewing; flagging out with the remote management of ships; a plethora of legislation emanating from the International Maritime Organization and the International Labour Office; these have changed the face of shipping beyond all recognition. Shipping is no longer a homogenous industry, it is diversified and globalised.

Working together for more comprehensive care

The missions have recognised this and have themselves responded by entering into ecumenical partnerships to bring together many of the Christian denominations under the one roof of seafarers' centres. There are some notable examples of this development. In Hong Kong, the Mission to Seafarers invited the Roman Catholic Apostleship of the Sea (Stella Maris), and the Danish Seamen's Mission to work out of its premises. In Felixstowe, U.K., The Apostleship of the Sea, British & International Sailors Society, The German Seamen's Mission, Dutch Seamen's Mission and The Mission to Seafarers share a seafarers' centre. Similar collaborative partnerships exist in many ports throughout the world.

These partnerships are between Christian churches who see that in many ports the way to most effectively address the seafarers' needs is to join resources. In many cases there are partnerships with shipowners, unions, agents, port authorities, flag states and intergovernmental organisations. I believe that all these, as well as the Christian missions, have the responsibility of providing for and ensuring the welfare of seafarers. As shipping becomes increasingly globalised, with the expansion of second registers, open registers, or as they are more commonly known, flags of convenience, so the checks and balances that protected seafarers from some of the more dubious employment practices have become less and less effective. So it is that incidents of abandonment of crews, refusal to repatriate, failure to pay wages and other contractual difficulties have risen to unprecedented levels.

To support and empower seafarers, as well as to remind employers of their responsibilities, the missions are addressing these problems by offering more than a safe haven with its bar and recreational facilities. The port chaplain is often seen as the only person in whom the seafarer can place his confidence. When they seek help, the chaplain will often take up the seafarers' complaint with the company. If the company refuses to listen or even recognise that there is a problem, the chaplain may call upon the service of the harbourmaster, port state control or the International Transport Workers' Federation and the International Shipping Federation. It is in partnership with these institutions that the missions can provide a comprehensive system of care.

Speaking out for seafarers at an international level

Welfare work among seafarers is not only a reactive activity. The missions are very pro-active in their care. The ecumenical partnerships referred to earlier are assisted by the International Christian Maritime Association (ICMA), a free association of members that seeks to develop representation on an international scale. ICMA has consultative status at the International Labour Office (ILO) and its delegation attends the maritime sessions of the ILO. This advocacy role is in recognition that traditional pastoral work will always be a feature of the missions' activity unless the cause of the many problems can be addressed at source. The missions have developed their prophetic ministry in drawing to the attention of the industry any incident of illegal practice, exploitation and abuse of seafarers.

The Mission to Seafarers has developed its justice and welfare department to work in this area of advocacy. Tasked with liaison with the industry in its widest sense, including the regulatory bodies and political institutions, its secretary pursues the cause of seafarers' welfare, not only on the world's waterfronts but among ship owner representatives, union officials and politicians. The legitimate voice of the church in its care for seafarers is therefore heard in debates at various international bodies. Recent examples of ICMA participation have been at the joint IMO/ILO sessions on hours of work and manning and another joint session on human factors in casualties. In this context the missions are caring for all seafarers, unionised or not, contracted or not, coastal or deep sea, on commercial vessels, cruise ships or fishing smacks.

The success of ICMA is a great encouragement to its members. The missions, through ICMA, participate at grass roots level, as well as at the council and presidium of the International Committee for Seafarers' Welfare. This brings the missions into direct consultation with the ISF, ITF and governmental organisations who are all seeking to serve seafarers' welfare needs.

In this forum ICMA has expressed its support of programmes to encourage flag states and especially the labour supply countries, to sign up to international conventions that have the care of seafarers at their core. ILO 147, the Merchant Shipping (Minimum Standards) Convention 1976, is in a sense the flagship welfare instrument. Similarly, the missions would really like to see more nations sign ILO 163, the Seafarers' Welfare Convention 1987 and Recommendation 173. To enact enabling legislation for these conventions will do so much to acknowledge the basic rights of seafarers and assist the various missions and agencies to provide for seafarers' welfare. These instruments fit very well with the current emphasis on the human factors in shipping. The introduction of the ISM code and the heightened concern for safety at sea, the quality control and management of ISO and the STCW revisions, all contribute to a developing awareness of the salient importance of the seafarer. The recognition of seafarers not only as 'units of productivity' and the management of personnel not as a liability but as a company's most important asset, goes a long way to minimising the worst of employment practices.

Help with employment problems

Historically the missions pursued welfare for seafarers by speaking out against injustices such as crimping. Today there is still a multiplicity of needs. The blacklisting of 'troublemakers', the underpaying of 'double bookkeeping', the refusal to grant medical treatment, speak more to institutionalised exploitation than to problems presented by a job which demands physical fitness and mental alertness. No seafarer should object to the legitimate demands of such a hard life style but for companies to take advantage of the seafarer's particular vulnerability is unacceptable in days of such highly regulated employment legislation and practice. It is also unacceptable that, at the same time as the shipping industry is becoming more and more regulated, there is such a dramatic rise in incidents of exploitation and abuse.

The abandonment of crews is the worst possible indictment of a rogue ship owner. That the industry has to consider establishing a guarantee fund or make provisions within the insurance market to pay for such incidents points to the fundamental problem of substandard shipping. The juxtaposition of the IMO's effort to provide a comprehensive framework of legislation with an abandoned crew being forced to sell bits of the ship in order to purchase food is stark. When seafarers have to rely on the missions or unions for repatriation that is an indictment of the regulatory regime.

Keeping up-to-date

The traditional image of a seafarers' mission as an organisation offering low cost temporary accommodation is well out of date. It has been replaced by a strengthening of its ship visiting ministry and the transportation of seafarers. There is an array of activities such as bus tours for sightseeing, football matches, book and video library exchanges, and sports competitions. Seafarers' centres are fast becoming communications hubs where the tradition of writing post cards and letters is supported by access to the Internet and the benefits of least-cost routeing for their telephone calls.

Even the location of these centres often changes. The old docks system close to and sometimes in the heart of towns, as with many river berths, has given way to new dock developments far from communities. The sense of isolation that is very common among seafarers is reinforced by this. Tanker berths, scrap metal, coal and grain cargo handling are not environmentally friendly operations and are conducted as far away as possible so as not to impinge on local scenery and certainly not on luxury residential waterfront properties. All too often these out of town dock estates are not served by public transport and it falls to the missions to provide the essential lifeline to civilisation. Missions also have moved, either to where the ships berth or to where seafarers are drawn when

they do have the opportunity for a run ashore. They are either located close to, or actually within, the dock estate or are downtown in the entertainment district. The safety and security that they represent are also important aspects. The exchange of foreign currency at fair rates is in stark contrast to the 'rip off' that seafarers often experience. At least the evening begins with respect shown to the seafarers.

Ship visiting

This scenario is familiar to seafarers who welcome the chaplain on board and this ship visiting is of great benefit in these circumstances. When shore leave is denied by either the master of the vessel or the local authorities, the attendance of the chaplain is essential. This is not the place to list those countries that, for whatever reason, legitimate or otherwise, deny shore leave but it is to be emphasised that the close confinement of life on board ship is no longer the social existence it used to be. Long gone are the days when Friday evening was cinema night and the whole crew would gather together in one of the mess rooms and enjoy the latest MGM epic.

Now it is a case of watching a video alone in their cabins, squeezed in between watchkeeping and sleep. One Spanish speaking Honduran on board a ship alongside one Russian speaking Latvian, with the rest of the crew being Korean and Greek cannot make for a buzzing social life. The nationalities may change but if language divides then crews will not be either safe or productive. This situation is not helped by a cook who prepares fish and chips three days a week and steak pie and chips three days a week with pork chops and chips every seventh day when the crew are crying out for vegetarian curry and rice. If these issues go unresolved shipboard morale is seriously affected, attention to duty becomes lax and within a very short period of time the ship becomes substandard.

Practical and spiritual

With the tedium of life at sea, the temptation to seek a thrill ashore in the arms of a prostitute, or with the numbing effects of narcotics and/or alcohol, are all too present. Health risks are significant in seafarers' lives. Awareness of HIV and AIDS, other sexually transmitted diseases, the carcinogenic link with tobacco and the damage caused by excessive alcohol intake need to be raised. It is often left to the missions to distribute educational literature and counsel seafarers with such concerns. In addition to these very human concerns comes the spiritual well-being of seafarers. Central to every mission facility is the chapel. It is not an uncommon occurrence to see these chapels being used by seafarers who are clearly not Christian. They all recognise the chapel as a place set apart, a place of quiet contemplation and prayer. It is a place in which to give thanks to God for their safe passage and in which to remember those victims of maritime disasters. It is a place in which to think of family and friends at home and, in the dislocated world of seafaring, to keep in touch with the important things of life.

It is this word 'dislocated' that speaks so powerfully to a description of seafarers' lives and the need for the missions and other welfare organisations. When legislators fail to protect, when employers do not live up to their contractual obligations, seafarers suffer. It is because they are so dislocated from their home communities with their social structure that fits neatly with their cultural mores and a political and legal framework which recognises the primacy of their rights, that they are particularly vulnerable. This at a time when, far removed from their families, domestic life can be fraught. Tensions are set up within a family when a seafarer is away from home for month after month. Then when home leave comes the family dynamics are disturbed when the seafarer, usually the father, returns only to find that the family is functioning without him. The very thing that partners look forward to so much, and children love, having 'dad' home, develops into family arguments as each member tries to assert their position within the family whilst allowing the 'intruder' theirs. So it is that mission chaplains become involved with the domestic lives of seafarers. It is unfortunate when such intervention is needed especially when the home visit is to bring news of death of the seafarer. It is the least pleasant of all of the jobs of the chaplain to have to say, 'lost at sea, presumed dead'.

Care for all

There is a comprehensive system of care offered by the mission chaplain. This is freely given, regardless of race or creed. To be a seafarer or a member of a seafaring family is the only criterion for seeking help from the chaplain. The chaplains of ICMA members are in six hundred ports around the world, ever present to remind seafarers of God's grace. Shipping is an industry which, in large part, is seeking ways in which to uphold and remind seafarers of their worth, while unfortunately failing far too often to address the root causes of exploitation and abuse. The substantial growth in the number of seafarers seeking the help of chaplains for serious breaches of their rights represents the human cost of an industry which weaves an intricate web of corporate structure and tiptoes through breaches in international convention. The most important relationships for the missions are those with seafarers and ship owners. For both, the missions are here to serve.

Resources

The Mission To Seafarers is pleased and privileged to welcome seafarers into its centres in ports around the world. Its central office can be contacted with any welfare problem by:

e-mail to justice@missiontoseafarers.org

or
telephone +44-(0)20-7248 5202

or
fax +44-(0)20-7248 4761

or by writing to
The Justice & Welfare Secretary
The Mission to Seafarers
St. Michael Paternoster Royal
College Hill
London EC4R 2RL
England, UK.

Find out more by visiting our web site at
www.missiontoseafarers.org.

The International Christian Maritime Association (ICMA) has a web site at:
http://dspace.dial.pipex.com/icma/

The ICMA secretariat is at
2/3 Orchard Place
Southampton SO14 3BR
England, UK
e-mail icma@dial.pipex.com
telephone +44 1703 336 111
fax +44 1703 333 567

Chapter 48

MODERN COMMUNICATION SYSTEMS AND THE GMDSS

by Mr. I. Waugh, Mobile Radio & Satellite Communications Training & Consultancy

Ian Waugh has worked in marine radio/satellite communications for most of his adult life. As a Royal Navy radio operator, he was involved in SART operations both at sea and in Rescue Coordination Centres. He 'won' his Merchant Navy Radio Officer's ticket at Glasgow College of Nautical Studies and moved to work in Wick Radio – handling everything from distress cases to routine daily communications. He became BT's first Customer Service Manager for Inmarsat-B and Inmarsat-M services at their introduction in 1993. Ian now runs his own business – delivering GMDSS training – and is a GMDSS examiner.

Introduction

CHANGES TO INTERNATIONAL LEGISLATION to cater for the GMDSS (Global Maritime Distress and Safety System), which have resulted in many new 'distress and safety' communications tasks falling on deck officers, have come along at the same time as the rise in use of non-GMDSS and/or non-marine mobile-communications systems on board many vessels. The convergence of computing and mobile communications adds another perspective to the ever-changing world of marine communications. The modern deck officer must know what systems are for use within the GMDSS and which are not – and to know what should be included in the radio log and what can be left out.

This chapter will briefly explain GMDSS tasks – or 'functions' – and the marine radio/satcom equipment used for those tasks, together with alternative, non-marine/non-GMDSS equipment which might additionally be fitted on some vessels. Included (at figure 04.01.1) is a sample radio log for a fictitious voyage from Las Palmas de Gran Canaria to Reykjavik, Iceland, showing typical log entries for normal and emergency communications, and for regular equipment tests and checks.

To get the best from this chapter, it should be read in conjunction with Admiralty List of Radio Signals (ALRS) *Volumes 1, 5 and 6, which are referred to in the text.*

GMDSS functions and equipment

Vessels which have to comply with the GMDSS must fit particular radio and/or satellite communications (satcom) equipment to carry out a range of GMDSS functions – the equipment fitted being determined by their GMDSS sea area of operation. The type of functions which must be catered for are:

• Sending distress alerts from ship to shore; receiving distress alerts from shore and sending/receiving ship-to-ship distress alerts (in the GMDSS, the first priority for ships in distress is to get an alert to a shore-based rescue coordination centre (RCC) so that, if that was your only opportunity to communicate, the RCC will be able to coordinate the subsequent search and rescue (SAR) operation).

• Exchanging search and rescue coordinating communications with RCCs and on-scene communications between vessels in the area of the SAR operation.

• Sending locating signals when you are the one in distress and receiving locating signals from others in distress.

• Receiving maritime safety information (MSI) including weather and navigation warnings which, it is hoped, should help you keep out of trouble.

• Exchanging bridge-to-bridge communications, between ships in close proximity, for the safety of navigation.

• Exchanging general (routine day-to-day) radio communications with port authorities and vessel traffic services, pilot stations, other vessels; and with the office/home of owners, operators, charters, passengers and crew.

GMDSS equipment will cover all of the above tasks and should always be your first choice for all GMDSS distress and safety communications. In the general radio communications list, items such as telephone/telex calls and e-mail messages to homes and offices may additionally be catered for by using equipment outside of your GMDSS fit.

Where additional systems are fitted and may well prove, in some cases, to be more convenient to us – the GMDSS systems should still be used on a regular basis, for routine tasks, to ensure that personnel are familiar with the operation of the equipment which they might have to rely on in an emergency.

The basic equipment fit for all GMDSS vessels includes:

(i) Marine VHF radio with digital selective calling (DSC), used for distress (Mayday), urgency (Pan Pan), safety (Securite) and routine day-to-day communications between ships (including bridge-to-bridge communications for the safety of navigation) and between ship and shore in an 'A1' area (defined later).

(ii) A Navtex receiver (if operating in an area where the Navtex service is provided) – or an Inmarsat enhanced group call (EGC) receiver if operating in an area where Navtex is not provided. These two devices will provide automatic reception and printout of maritime safety information (MSI) – the GMDSS term for weather forecasts/warnings, navigation etc. warnings and initial distress alerts from shore-to-ship).

(iii) A (satellite) emergency position indicating radio beacon (EPIRB) for use as a secondary distress alerting device from ship-to-shore (when your VHF DSC or other primary system has failed to get the required attention) or as a position indicating device for the distressed vessel, a liferaft, or survivors in the water.

(iv) A search and rescue (radar) transponder (SART) used for locating a distressed vessel/liferaft using marine navigation radar operating in the 3-centimetre band.

(v) Marine VHF handheld radio for use in the liferaft after abandoning.

GMDSS sea areas of operation

The world according to the GMDSS is divided into four 'sea areas of operation', known as sea areas AI, A2, A3 and A4. The four GMDSS sea areas are defined by the ability of a ship to transmit a distress alert, using GMDSS equipment, to a shore authority. The sea areas are defined as:

Sea area A1:

'Within radiotelephone coverage of at least one VHF DSC shore station'. The above range of equipment would be appropriate to sea area A1, with the choice of NAVTEX or Inmarsat EGC receiver according to shore facilities for transmitting MSI in the particular region concerned.

Sea area A2:

An area outside of A1 but 'within radiotelephone coverage of at least one MF DSC shore station' – in which case a vessel would have to fit, in addition to the above basic list of equipment, a marine single sideband (SSB) radio operating in the medium frequency (MF) band and with DSC alerting facilities.

ALRS volume 5 List of Diagrams and Illustrations – *'DSC' shows sea areas A1 and A2, around the world.*

Sea area A3

An area, outside A1/A2, but 'within the global coverage of the Inmarsat geostationary satellite system' (considered to be consistently good for GMDSS purposes up to latitude 70°N and 70°S). In this area a vessel can fit either a marine SSB radio operating in the high frequency (HF) bands (which would normally be the same radio as the MF SSB radio fitted for A2 coverage) with DSC – or, as an alternative, Inmarsat-A, Inmarsat-B or Inmarsat-C equipment.

ALRS vol. 5 List of Diagrams – Inmarsat Satellite Coverage and Stations *shows the limits of sea area A3.*

Sea area A4:

'Any area not included in AI, A2 or A3' (and is considered to be the polar regions above latitude 70°N and 70°S) and in which, for the purposes of the number one GMDSS function – that of getting a distress alert from ship-to-shore – is covered only by marine SSB radio operating in the high frequency (HF) bands.

ALRS vol. 5 Diagrams HF DSC Coast Radio Stations, World Wide *is applicable here.*

Non-GMDSS marine equipment and non-marine equipment

All the distress and safety requirements and marine general radio communications requirements can be met with marine radio and satellite systems fitted for GMDSS purposes. Some requirements, particularly ship-to-shore and shore-to-ship telephone, fax and data calls, can additionally met by non-GMDSS (marine) equipment and/or non-marine systems. The most common *additional* systems which the modern mariner may find in regular use include:

- *Cellular radio:* either hand-held or fitted as a fixed unit/marine antenna. This provides telephone connection, including fax and limited data facilities, when within shore based cellular radio coverage. Where such systems are provided, the coverage is roughly the same as for marine VHF radio.

- *Mobile satellite services:* including Inmarsat-M and Inmarsat Mini-M (both being marine systems). It is also not unusual to find Inmarsat-A/Inmarsat-B equipment fitted for commercial communications but not included as part of the 'official' GMDSS fit.

- The newer *'polar orbiting' satellite systems* such as Iridium (which came into commercial service during 1999) and other systems which are projected to come into service during the year 2000 from Globalstar and from ICO global communications, are all projected to be 'dual cellular and satellite' services – which provide the connection through a cellular radio service as the first choice, and through the new mobile satellite services when out of cellular range.

Information about these new systems can be found in the Global Marine Communication Services *section of ALRS Volume 1.*

The radio log and regular equipment/ power supply checks

As well as operating the various communications systems, the officer on watch must keep a radio log as a record of communications. Regular equipment tests and power supply checks carried out must be recorded and the master must inspect and sign the log daily. The test routines are laid-down within the GMDSS regulations and include the following tasks:

Daily tests/checks

- DSC internal test, without radiating signals. All DSC equipment is provided with this 'self test' facility.

- State-of-charge of batteries should be confirmed using a hydrometer or a voltmeter. The level of electrolyte should be checked (liquid electrolyte batteries – normally about 1cm above the plates) and batteries should be brought up to full charge if required.
- Any Navtex receiver and any printers associated with GMDSS equipment (e.g. the EGC receiver) should be checked to ensure that there is enough paper to meet the expected requirement.

Weekly tests/checks
- A DSC test call should be exchanged with a coast station providing an MF DSC service. Radio regulations state that the 'DSC distress and safety frequencies should be avoided whenever possible' for testing. However, a number of coast stations are prepared to cooperate with testing on 2187·5kHz, as the test call is considered to be a safety category call. You should use the minimum power necessary to contact the station and a DSC acknowledgement should be received (and logged).

Note: you should always listen on the alerting frequency, making sure that there are no other transmissions, before hitting the 'send' button for a test call.

- The handheld VHF radio(s) for use in survival craft should be tested, using a working channel (i.e. not on Channel 16).
- Any reserve power supply other than batteries (e.g. a motor generator) should be tested to ensure starting/proper operation.

Monthly tests/checks
- All GMDSS EPIRBs should be tested using the self-test facility provided, without transmitting signals. The expiry date of the EPIRB battery and the expiry date of the hydrostatic release should also be checked. Make sure that some well meaning individual, in an attempt to prevent the loss of the EPIRB in heavy weather, has not used the lanyard to secure the EPIRB to the ship's rail.
- Search and rescue (radar) transponders (SARTs) should be tested against the ship's radar to ensure that it is being triggered by the radar when in the test position and that it displays the expected lights/sounds. Your own radar screen should display a series of concentric circles when the SART is activated. Only run the test for the few seconds necessary to ensure proper operation, or you may lead other vessels to believe that someone is in distress in their vicinity. SART battery expiry date should also be checked.
- Battery condition should be checked both externally and internally. External condition includes cleanliness and security, tightness of connections and integrity of wiring. Internal condition can be checked by a hydrometer (you should expect the same readings in each cell of a

liquid-electrolyte battery) or by using a load test where voltage readings off load and on-load are recorded in a separate log. Month-on-month, the voltage-drop on-load should not change if the internal condition of the batteries remains stable and all other relevant factors remain unchanged (i.e. no equipment additions/losses and all connections/cables remain in a good condition).
- Finally, a monthly check of all aerials/antennas, and their insulators, should be carried out. You are looking to see that the aerials have not been damaged in any way (particularly relevant to vertical VHF antennas and SSB whip antennas) and that connections remain tight. Insulators should be washed with fresh water as salt water merely replaces the dirty salt and carbon deposits with a fresh layer of salt. When physical contact with the antennas is likely (e.g. when cleaning insulators), all radio equipment should be switched off and, if necessary, disabled (by removing power fuses). Where there is a facility to earth or ground the antennas, that facility should be used to discharge any static build-up in the antenna wire. Even a light shock can cause a person to reverse quickly over the edge of the superstructure.

The log – Puerto de la Luz, Las Palmas de Gran Canaria to Reykjavik, Iceland

The ship's radio log shown in figure 48.1 might have been produced during the first few days of a voyage from an A1 area (the Islas Canarias) through an A2 area into the Atlantic ocean (a GMDSS A3 area) heading towards another A2 area around Iceland.

See ALRS Volume 5 – DSC station diagrams; Navtex diagrams and SafetyNET schedule for Navarea II and I – *which you will transit on this voyage.*

Equipment assumed
GMDSS fit: VHF with DSC; MF/HF SSB with DSC; Navtex; Inmarsat-C; EPIRB, SARTs and handheld VHF radios.

Additional fit: Inmarsat-B (including telex option); GSM cellular radio (which provides service in the Islas de Canarias, Madeira, the Azores, most of Europe and parts of Iceland, especially around Reykjavik)

Summary
Of necessity, this chapter has only scratched the surface of modern radio communications and the GMDSS. It is hoped that it will let the modem mariner see their communications role a bit clearer than before. The Nautical Institute has a new book in progress which will cover the full range of day-to-day communications tasks and procedures for both GMDSS and non-GMDSS functions – radio log keeping; looking after your antennas; computing and radio convergence; and how to prepare for your annual ship radio station survey.

GMDSS RADIO LOG BOOK

Vessel: S.S. ENTERPRISE
Callsign: GENT **MMSI:** 232999000

Date/Time UTC	Station To	Station From	Communications Summary, Tests, Remarks	Frequency Channel or Satellite
22/10/99			Alongside Puerto de la Luz, Las Palmas de Gtran Canaria	
0900			Daily tests: DSC internal OK; Navtex and printers OK	
			Batteries all fully charged J Uhuru (3 off)	
1550			Navtex programmed for Las Palmas (i)	
1600			Sat-C logged-in for Metarea II + Additional area I	AORE
1605			Sat-B acquired satellite	AORE
1725		Las Palmas	Weather forcast received (Master informed)	Navtex

The log should include

- *Your ship's position, at leats daily (when at sea – as we're sailing today it's shown here.*

- *Daily tests and checks for DSC equipment; batteries; Navtex and printers (to see that there's enough paper).*

- *A summary of Distress, Urgency and Safety communications.*

- *We've also set up Navtex and Sat-C SafetyNET in preparation for sialing – (Navtex station ID and Sat-C SafetyNET areas/ satellites from ALRS Vol. 5)*

Date/Time UTC	Station To	Station From	Communications Summary, Tests, Remarks	Frequency Channel or Satellite
1815-45	Port/pilots	GENT	(working harbourmaster/pilots)	Ch 12/14/16
1845			Departed Puerto de la Luz, bound Reykjavik	
1845			Set voice/DSC watch Sea Area A1	Ch 16/70VHF
1915			Sailing report to office (Sat-B telex)	AORE
2000			J Kirk (Master) J Uhuru (3 off)	
2015		Oostende	(traffic list – no traffic for GENT)	14179 kHz
2100			Set DSC watch Area A2	2187·5 kHz
2110		Meteo France	Wx Metarea II (Master informed)	Sat-C
2140		Bracknell	Wx Metarea I (Master informed)	Sat-C

- *Although there is no obligation to record 'routine' exchanges (port/pilot comms; traffic lists; messages to office, etc.) it does no harm and it can help others follow a routine when on watch – it also shows that you're using your GMDSS equipmentfor routine tasks.*

- *VHF channels for port/pilots forund in ALRS Volume 6.*

- *The log should be inspected and signed each day by the master and by the person nominated to handle emergency communications/ carry out the regular tests/checks.*

- *On entering an A2 area (see ALRS Vol. 5) add DSC 2187·5 kHz to the VHF watch.*

Date/Time UTC	Station To	Station From	Communications Summary, Tests, Remarks	Frequency Channel or Satellite
2240		234123455	DSC Distress Alert – 29°45'N 18°22'W undesignated J3E	2187·5 kHZ
2241			On watch J Uhuru	2182 kHz
2241		002241007	(DSC Distress Acknowledgement)	2187·5 kHz
2243	Mayday	Wizard/GWIZ	29°44'N 18°22'W – please cancel my false distress alert –	
		234123455	transmitted in error – MRCC Tenerife please acknowledge	
			(Tenerife Traffic acknowledged)	

Figure 48.1 Sample radio log

Chapter 49

MARINE PAINT TECHNOLOGY

by Mr. K.E.M. Haugland, Jotun-Henry Clark Ltd.

Mr. Haugland is a chemical engineer from Norway, having worked more than 30 years within Jotun Paints' worldwide organisation in a number of different countries. He started as a laboratory chemist and progressed via marine coatings inspector to become involved in all aspects of a paint company's operation. Presently he is Customer Services Manager for Jotun-Henry Clark Ltd., embracing technical support, training and education, customer relations, sales order administration and logistics.

Introduction

THE SINGLE MOST COMMON CAUSE for a vessel to be taken out of service is advanced corrosion. One of the most important factors influencing a vessel's operating costs is its friction while moving through the water. In both these important areas, paints or coatings play a crucial role.

While marine paints are the number one defence against both corrosion and fouling, they also provide the means to a pleasing appearance and identification of ownership. A nicely painted and maintained vessel has a greater effect on public image, and may instil more confidence with the general public, than the most sophisticated electronic equipment hidden behind its bulkheads.

Development of seagoing vessels is an ongoing process, where specialisation and new refinements replace old and tested solutions, and marine paints have to follow suit. Key words in this connection are life cycle cost evaluation (LCC), life cycle assessment (LCA), environmental / safety / health considerations, national and international legislation, industry standards etc.

With longer service life expectancy of a vessel, with less crew, faster operating speed, shorter time in port, longer docking intervals, and a fierce competition within the shipping industry, the requirements and expectations to the paint systems increases, as do the consequences in cases of paint failure. Surveys have shown that more than 95% of paint failures are caused by poor workmanship, unsatisfactory conditions during application, or wrong selection of coating system (not fit for purpose).

Following a suitable education, it takes years of experience to become an 'exper' in marine paints. Such experts, easiest found within the paint industry, should be consulted in crucial or complicated problems and decisions. However, a minimum knowledge of basic paint technology is without doubt beneficial to key personnel making decisions on paint specifications, supervising painting work or monitoring its cost efficiency. The following is intended as a basic introduction for such personnel to various aspects of protecting ships and vessels with paints and coatings.

Composition of paints

The ingredients included in a paint formulation can be grouped in four categories:

Resin (binder)

This is the ingredient in the paint that forms the film, binds the other ingredients together, and 'glues' the film to the substrate (provides adhesion). The resin is often referred to as the binder in a paint. A clear varnish is a good illustration of what a binder looks like.

Binders can either be naturally occurring or man-made. Examples of natural binders are linseed oil (boiled), coal tar, wood rosin, and bitumen. Synthetic binders include alkyd, epoxy, polyurethane, vinyl, acrylic, chlorinated rubber. One may frequently come across expressions such as epoxy paint, alkyd paint, acrylic paint etc. The most common way of classifying paints is thus by referring to its binder (or resin), often referred to as the generic types of paint.

As for most things, the different binders have their individual strengths and weaknesses. Properties like water resistance, chemical resistance, flexibility, hardness, mechanical strength etc. are primarily determined by the binder. It is thus important to select the type of paint that best can withstand the expected conditions and exposure.

Some paints contain more than one binder, often referred to as modified paints. Examples of such are coal tar epoxy, vinyl tar and acrylic modified polyurethane.

Thinner

Pure resin will vary in appearance from a sticky liquid, via a thick paste, to solid lumps. In order to be able to apply paint, one needs in most cases to incorporate thinner to the paint. The solid resins must be made into solution, the thick pastes must be made more liquid, and the sticky liquids perhaps made to flow more freely.

The primary reason for incorporating thinners in paint is to develop satisfactory application properties. Once the paint is applied, the thinners have carried out their mission and are no longer needed. They will disappear through evaporation. It is important that they leave the paint film before the drying/curing processes have advanced so far that the thinners are trapped in the film. Adequate ventilation in enclosed spaces is thus important not only for safety reasons, but also for the quality of the paint film.

The solubility of the different resins varies considerably, for which reason the solvent / solvent blends used to dilute them have to be carefully determined. Addition of the wrong thinner to paint can lead to reduced quality of the paint film. Gun wash and other unspecified thinners may possibly be useful for cleaning equipment, but should never be added to a paint.

Most paints are supplied from the manufacturer ready to be applied, i.e. addition of thinner will normally not be necessary prior to application. Only three situations may justify addition of thinner by the paint applicator:

1. Application on an extremely porous substrate (assists penetration).
2. Applications in very cold weather (the paint gets too thick).
3. Application in very hot weather (solvents evaporate too quickly for the paint to flow out).

Addition of thinner will increase the possibility of sagging during application. It will also reduce the solid content of the paint, altering the ratio between wet film and dry film thickness.

Most water-borne paints contain resin solutions that are dispersed in water. They use water as thinner. Solvent-borne paints use various types of hydrocarbons from the petrochemical industry as thinners. Common types are white spirit, solvent naphtha, xylene, isobutanol etc. They all have some degree of flammability.

Pigments

The term pigment is commonly used for a variety of powders used in paint manufacturing. They may be grouped as follows:

Colour pigments are powders which are added to paints in order to hide the substrate (provide opacity) and give the desired colour to the film. Most colours will be the result of mixing different colour pigments, and by altering this mixture one can adjust the resulting colour. Colour pigments may be natural or synthetic, organic or inorganic powders.

Extenders are naturally occurring mineral powders, which are added to the paint in order to improve the quality of the film. They may add volume to the paint, reinforce the film, increase abrasion resistance, reduce gloss etc.

Active or reactive pigments are present in paint for a specific purpose. Well known examples are anti-corrosion pigments such as red lead, zinc chromate, zinc phosphate and zinc dust. Other active pigments may have a biocidal effect, as is the case for cuprous oxide pigment in antifoulings. Other highly specialised active pigments may for example provide luminescence or conversion of rust stain.

Barrier pigments are flake-shaped and will both reinforce the film and make it less permeable to moisture (increase corrosion protection). The most common barrier pigments consist of aluminium flakes, micaceous iron oxide (MIO) flakes, or glass flakes. The two first are mostly found in primers and mid coats, while glass flakes also can be found in high abrasion resistant coatings.

Additives

A huge number of different chemicals are available for incorporation in paint's composition. These may speed up the production process, ensure storage stability, improve application properties, catalyse or accelerate the drying process, and enhance the quality of the resulting film.

Drying mechanisms

A number of different resins / resin combinations are used in modern paints. These generic types of paint have their strengths and weaknesses, something that may be a source of confusion to personnel only having a distant relationship to paints. A simpler way of assessing whether a particular paint is fit for purpose is to consider its drying mechanism.

Drying mechanisms can be divided into two main categories, each with their sub-groups:

Drying involving a chemical reaction

These paints come in two versions: single pack products and two (or multi-) pack products. The vast majority use organic solvents for thinners, but some water borne products will also fall into this category, as well as some solvent-free products. All chemical reactions are temperature sensitive. When the temperature increases, the speed of the chemical reaction increases as well (i.e. shorter drying time). At decreasing temperature the speed slows down and may even come to a stop. These paints will thus have a minimum temperature requirement, below which they should not be applied (curing reaction stops). Low-temp or 'wintergrade' versions may be available, curing at lower temperatures than the standard grades.

Two pack products

The resin will be in one of the packs and a curing agent/hardener will be in the other. Curing takes place through a chemical reaction between the two components. The reaction starts immediately after mixing, meaning application has to be completed within a given time (pot life). The resulting product is a new chemical compound that can not be reversed to its initial components. In general, these types of products will give the toughest films in terms of abrasion and chemical resistance. Some of the more common types are epoxy, polyurethane, two-pack acrylic, polyester.

Single pack products

These types of resin will react with a substance being present in the local environment. The most common type is alkyd resin (sometimes referred to as oil paint), which will react with oxygen in the air. If we prevent oxygen from reaching the paint, the drying process will stop.

The second most common group of resins in this category will react with humidity in the air. Moisture cured polyurethane resin and zinc silicates are typical representatives of this group. If the relative humidity is too low where these paints are applied, proper curing will not take place. After curing, their film can be comparable to that of two-pack paints. Storage time (shelf life) for these paints is normally restricted due to their sensitivity to moisture.

There are other single pack resins, but few of them are used for marine coatings. Certain silicone resins, used for heat resistant paints, require elevated temperature to cure completely (post curing).

Drying without a chemical reaction involved

These paints dry purely through a physical evaporation of thinners; no chemical reaction is involved. Their resins are solid in their pure state. During the paint production process they are dissolved in solvents, but once the thinners leave the film through evaporation, these resins will turn solid again. The evaporation process is considerably less temperature dependent than a chemical reaction.

Solvent borne

The solid resin is dissolved in suitable organic solvents, forming a solution. When the solvents evaporate, the resin becomes solid. If exposed to the same solvents again, the resin will re-dissolve. The dry film may thus have poor resistance against solvents. However, in a two coats system, solvents from the second coat will soften or slightly re-dissolve the surface of the first coat, resulting normally in excellent inter-coat adhesion. Common resins belonging to this category are chlorinated rubber, vinyl, acrylic, coal tar and bitumen.

Water borne

Resin is dispersed in water. A small amount of solvent is normally required to achieve this; so most water borne paints will contain some solvent as well. The drying mechanism consists of evaporation of the water, followed by evaporation of the co-solvent. After drying, these paints are not resoluble in water, nor in most solvents, but they tend to be less water resistant than solvent borne products. Useful temperature range is restricted by the presence of water. Common types of paints in this group are emulsions of alkyd, acrylic, PVA, PVAc.

Generic types

The most common way of classifying paints is to group them according to the binder(s) they contain. These groups are often referred to as generic types of paint. Even people outside the paint industry use this classification when they talk about epoxy-paint, alkyd-paint etc. The following is a list of the most common generic types used in marine coatings.

Acrylic paints, single pack

Based on synthetic solid resin, dissolved in solvents, physically drying through evaporation.

Acrylic paints, two pack

Based on acrylic resin that cures through a chemical reaction with a hardener, forming a topcoat with excellent outdoor durability. May have some restrictions on over-coating interval.

Alkyd paints

Based on chemically modified oils that dry through reaction with oxygen, sometimes referred to as oil paints or conventional paints. Have been used as general-purpose paints for a long time. Poor water resistance if submerged, limited chemical resistance, and the film may be spoiled by strong solvents and thinners (e.g. paint removers).

Bituminous paints

Based on solid to semi-solid residue from petroleum distillation, also found in asphalt. Physically drying through solvent evaporation. May cause discoloration of subsequent coats (bleeding).

Chlorinated rubber paints

Based on resin formed by the reaction of rubber with chlorine, forming a white powder that is dissolved in aromatic solvents. Physically drying through solvent evaporation.

Emulsion paints

Binder consists of resin dispersed in water (emulsified), such as polyvinyl acetate (PVA), polyvinyl acrylate (PVAc), also referred to as latex. Physically drying. Not resoluble.

Epoxy paints

Two-pack chemically curing paint with very good abrasion resistance, water resistance and resistance against chemicals. Require good pre-treatment.

Epoxy-mastic coatings

Based on two-pack epoxy binder, usually in combination with another binder (e.g. a hydrocarbon resin). This results in a much higher tolerance to surfaces not being blast-cleaned, a higher solid content of the paint, and the ability to apply high film thickness in each coat.

Epoxy tar paints (coal tar epoxy)

Based on two-pack epoxy binder that is modified with coal tar. This results in a higher tolerance to surfaces not being blast cleaned and an increased water resistance. Tar may be re-dissolved by subsequent coats and cause tar bleeding.

Polyester coatings

Coating in which the binder is unsaturated polyester. It needs peroxide for cross-linking. Most polyester coatings need glass-flakes for reinforcement. Chemically curing with very short pot-life. Extremely high abrasion resistance.

Polyurethane paints

Based on specially polymerised binder which is used in both one-component (moisture cured) and two-component (isocyanate cured) paints. Are hard-wearing and generally resistant to chemicals. Aliphatic types have good gloss, colour stability and weather resistance. Chemically curing.

Silicate paints

See zinc silicate paint.

Silicone paints

Mostly used for heat resistant paints. The resin is based on silicone instead of carbon.

Vinyl paints

Based on synthetic resins, often chlorinated, which are dissolved in strong solvents. Dries physically through solvent evaporation. Declining in use due to the need for high solvent content.

Vinylester coatings

Based on vinylester resin, which needs peroxide for cross-linking. Most vinylester coatings need glass-flakes for reinforcement. Chemically curing with very short pot-life. Very high resistance towards chemicals, particularly at elevated temperatures.

Vinyl tar paints

Contain both vinyl resin and coal tar as binder, both being physically drying (solvent evaporation).

Zinc silicate paints

Zinc dust filled paints based on an inorganic binder. Zinc silicates give very hard film, are resistant to solvents, have very high anti-corrosion properties and can tolerate high temperatures. Require very good pre-treatment. Ethyl-silicate need moisture for curing, alkali-silicate is water-soluble.

Wood – varnish

Wood comprises of hollow cellulose fibres held together by lignin. If left unprotected, water may penetrate the fibres (causing the wood to swell and crack), UV-light will decompose the lignin (causing discoloration and loose fibres), and fungi may attack the wood (causing rot and decay). The most common way of protecting wood against the elements is to apply a transparent barrier. This barrier may consist of wax, oil or varnish.

A varnish is a binder without any pigmentation. Most of the earlier described binders can be used as clear varnishes. A varnish with a certain degree of flexibility to cater for movements, e.g. oil or alkyd based, will best serve wood, being an organic material. A pigmented film will reflect or absorb UV-light, while a clear film may let it pass through. The result is that both the clear film itself and the wood may be in danger of degradation when exposed to strong sunlight for long periods. UV-absorber is sometimes added to exterior varnishes, but its effect is of limited duration.

Tropical hardwood (e.g. teak) often has a high content of rosin that may interfere with varnish, causing prolonged drying time, reduced adhesion, and affect its gloss. When varnishing such wood for the first time, clean its surface thoroughly with relatively strong thinner first, let it dry, and remove protruding fibres gently with fine sandpaper before applying the first coat of varnish.

Several coats of varnish are required to protect wood. Three coats should be the bare minimum, while five coats are preferable. Varnished wood, particularly when exposed outdoors, will require regular maintenance. Milky areas in the film may indicate loss of adhesion (uninflated blister), while pronounced discoloration of the wood suggests that the varnish film is no longer intact. Suggested maintenance procedure:

- Clean the wooden object with detergent and water to remove oil, salt and other surface contaminants.
- Remove all damaged varnish with a sharp paint scraper and/or careful abrading.
- Sandpaper bare wood to expose firm material, and feather the edges of intact varnish (smooth transition).
- Build up new film on exposed wood by spot-applying several coats of varnish.
- Abrade the entire surface with fine sandpaper and apply a full-coat of varnish.

Fouling – antifoulings
Introduction

It is estimated that some 4,000 to 5,000 species are involved in fouling. They can be classified into two groups based on the size of the fully-grown specimen:

Macrofouling: includes animals and plants.
Microfouling: generally referred to as slime, a complex mucilaginous mixture of bacteria and diatoms.

Some of these species are happy to swim or be carried about by currents. Many must however find a hard surface on which to attach in order to fulfil their life cycles. Every available space is contested, including ships' bottoms. The likelihood for fouling to settle on a ship's bottom will depend on a number of factors, such as:

- Geographical area
- Time of year
- Sea temperature

- Currents
- Pollutants in the sea
- Speed of vessel

Antifouling paints

The main purposes of antifouling paints are to prevent or reduce growth on micro-organisms on a ship's underwater hull, providing better fuel economy and avoiding growth penetration through the anti-corrosive coatings. This is achieved by incorporating biocides in the film. A biocide is a chemical substance that is released at very low rates and destroys or inhibits marine fouling from settling on the substrate it is released from. The most common antifouling biocide is cuprous oxide.

Conventional antifouling

The very old-fashioned antifouling, using cuprous oxide in a natural rosin binder. This rosin slowly dissolves in sea water, also known as 'soluble matrix'. Effective life is generally short, approximately 12 months.

Longlife antifouling

These are referred to as 'insoluble matrix' paints. The binder is insoluble in sea water, typically consisting of chlorinated rubber, vinyl or acrylic. When biocides are released into the water, the remaining part of the film will turn into a porous layer on the surface of the coating. As the thickness of the porous layer increases, the rate of biocide release reduces. This porous layer leaves a very weak substrate for any new coatings and a sealer coat would normally be required. Over the years this will lead to a build up of alternate sealer coat / antifouling coat (sandwich coating), which eventually will crack and loose its adhesion. Other biocides, like organo-tin (TBTO), often complement cuprous oxide. Effective service life is up to 24 months.

Self-polishing – tin containing

These coatings have organo-tin chemically incorporated in their binders, in addition to the usual cuprous oxide. When cuprous oxide is released, the binder will slowly decompose (hydrolyse) in sea water, releasing organo-tin as well. This hydrolysing will avoid build-up of a porous inactive layer, as is the case for longlife antifoulings. Biocide release is thus kept at a consistent level throughout its service life. The rate of hydrolysis can be adjusted to cater for vessels operating at various speeds. This type of antifouling has over the years proved to be the most efficient fouling preventing coatings, with their service life in principle only limited by external factors such as docking intervals and inspections by classification authorities.

Self-polishing – tin free

Environmental concerns about the release of organo-tin to the sea and its effect on marine life have steadily built up over the years. This has led to increasing restrictions for its use, and from January 2003 organo-tin containing antifoulings can no longer be applied to ships' bottoms. Early tin-free alternatives were based on 'ablative' or water sensitive physically deteriorating binders, in order to avoid the build-up of the inactive porous layer mentioned earlier. The challenge was to find a replacement for the organo-tin composition that was harmless to the environment and at the same time still being able to provide the hydrolysing abilities of the binder. At the time this is written, two different solutions are available in the market. Since organo-tin is not present in these products, other biocides may be incorporated in the film to act alongside the traditional cuprous oxide.

Other solutions

A number of more or less innovative solutions to the fouling problem for ships have been developed over the years, but few have had a commercial viability. One of the few is the 'non-stick' antifouling, where the surface of the coating has properties that make attachment difficult.

Corrosion – anti-corrosives
Theory

Iron, the main ingredient in steel, is found as iron ore (iron oxide) in its natural state. When the ore is processed to iron and steel, a considerable amount of energy is required (e.g. iron smelter). Iron is however most stable as iron oxide (the lowest energy level), and it will always try to revert to this form. The transition from metallic iron back to iron oxide is popularly called corrosion, and the end product is commonly referred to as rust. When we try to fight corrosion, we are thus actually fighting one of nature's laws. This is a battle we cannot win, but we can extend the battle for a considerable time.

Three conditions must be met in order for corrosion to take place:

- *Anode/cathode must be present*
  This simply means two different substances, or areas within the same substance, with differing electro-chemical potential. It can be two different metals, or two different parts of a piece of steel with slightly different chemical composition (a piece of steel will never be completely uniform throughout).
- *Presence of electrolyte (water/moisture)*
  Distilled water is a poor electrolyte, but any casual water will do. Sea water is an excellent electrolyte.
- *Presence of oxygen*
  Found not only in the atmosphere (air), but also dissolved in water/sea water.

If we can prevent any of the above three conditions, the corrosion process will not take place.

Barrier effect

All paint films will to some extent act as a barrier, preventing water and oxygen from reaching the steel surface, and thus preventing corrosion from taking place. The effectiveness of this barrier may vary from one paint to another, and may be enhanced by adding flake-shaped barrier-pigments (e.g. aluminium flakes, see section about pigments). The thickness of the paint film is of course crucial to the barrier effect as well.

Passivation

Certain pigments have the ability to passivate the steel surface under given conditions, such as zinc-chromate, zinc-phosphate and red-lead. Some primers contain these pigments and provide protection both through passivation and providing a barrier. Such primers are generally not recommended for use in submerged areas (may lead to blisters).

Galvanic protection

Galvanised steel will have a layer of metallic zinc on its surface. This protects against corrosion because the driving force that converts zinc to zinc oxide is greater than the driving force converting iron to iron oxide. When these two metals are (electrically) connected, the zinc will act as an anode and the steel will become a cathode. The result is that zinc will corrode while protecting the steel from corrosion.

Zinc-rich primers have a high content of zinc-dust. When such primers are applied directly onto bare and clean steel (electrical contact), they will protect the steel against corrosion along the same principles as galvanising. By applying subsequent mid-coats on top of the zinc-rich primer (or on top of galvanising), we slow down the corrosion of the zinc as well.

Aluminium/stainless steel

When certain metals start corroding, they form an even and relatively robust layer of oxide on its surface. This oxide layer may prevent further oxidation (corrosion) to take place, i.e. forming a protective oxide layer. Aluminium and stainless steel are typical examples of such metals. If however a damage is made in this oxide layer, both the metal-oxide and the metal itself are exposed to the elements. They will act as anode and cathode, and in the presence of oxygen and moisture, severe pit-corrosion may take place. This is the reason why such metals are often painted.

Cathodic protection (CP)
Principle

(See also the section on corrosion). When corrosion takes place, we will always find an anodic and a cathodic area. In the presence of an electrolyte (e.g. sea water), they will produce a flow of electrons (electrical current), moving from the anodic area towards the cathode. As a result the anode will slowly dissolve (corrode). This is often referred to as a corrosion cell. If we can suppress this flow of electrons, corrosion will not take place on the anodic steel area. This is what cathodic protection (CP) sets out to do. Although CP may be used as the sole corrosion protection measure, most commonly it is used in combination with paints. The paint film will provide the primary protection, with CP acting as a back up for weaknesses or damages in the film.

Sacrificial anodes (SACP)

We can interfere with a corrosion cell in such a way that electrons are supplied from a source outside the cell. This is arranged by connecting another metal electrically to the elements in the corrosion cell. If this other metal is less noble than steel, it will supply electrons to the original steel anode and become the anode in this new cell. The result is that the new (external) anode will slowly dissolve, preventing the steel from dissolving (corroding). This new anode is usually referred to as a sacrificial anode.

The majority of sacrificial anodes are made from zinc, but aluminium alloy is also used. The latter has a stronger driving force, so less metal is required to achieve the same effect as for zinc. These anodes appear as metal bars which are welded (or bolted) to the underwater hull area of vessels. They are also used inside tanks, e.g. ballast tanks, but will only be effective when they are submerged in sea water.

Impressed current (ICCP)

Instead of supplying electrons from a sacrificial anode, these can come directly from an electrical source, like a battery. Permanent anodes are built into the underwater hull of a vessel. These are connected to a source of current (power supply, transformer and rectifier) inside the ship. Using reference electrodes and electronic controls, a current is impressed on the underwater area, sufficient to prevent corrosion from taking place on exposed steel (damages in the coating system). Special coatings must be used in the area next to the permanent anodes.

Magnesium stripping

In normal sea water, the correct amount of zinc and aluminium anodes provide a current sufficient for preventing steel from corroding without damaging coatings of good quality. Anodes made from magnesium will supply a stronger current, so strong that poorly adhering paint and scales of rust will be forced away from the surface. This can be taken advantage of in connection with water ballast tank refurbishing. Coils of magnesium anodes are installed in the tanks two to three weeks prior to a scheduled docking. By the time the ship is docked, the anodes will be consumed and weak paint and cakes of rust loosened and will have fallen down to the bottom of the tank. After high pressure washing with fresh water and drying, the tank can be coated with a surface tolerant wbt-coating. Due to the formation of hydrogen gas during this stripping process, certain precautions must be taken during that two week period.

Coating systems
Primers

The first coat to be applied. Forms the foundation for the paint system and provides the adhesion to the substrate. Any active corrosion inhibiting pigments should be incorporated in this coat.

Mid-coats

Gives the main build (thickness) to the paint system, providing a good barrier effect. More than one mid-coat may be specified in a system.

Topcoats

Provides the decorative finish and the first-line defence against the elements.

Generic systems

If a primer, mid-coat and topcoat all have binders of the same generic type, it is not likely that there will be any problem in combining them in a paint system. Some care must though be taken if the manufacturer recommends different thinners for each of these products.

Hybrid systems

This term is used when paints of different generic types are combined in a paint system. It may also be used when a solvent-born paint is combined with a water-born paint, even if they both have the same generic type of binder.

The most common problem occurs when the solvents in the second coat are too strong for the first coat. Alkyd paint will 'lift' when subjected to strong solvents (as with a paint remover), while a physically drying paint will re-dissolve (see section 2: drying mechanisms).

Another possible problem may occur if a hard-drying paint (e.g. chemically curing) is applied over a thick layer of a relatively soft or thermoplastic film (e.g. physically drying). This may lead to cracking.

Discoloration may occur if the underlying coat contains easily soluble matters that may bleed into the following coat, e.g. coal tar, bitumen, dye etc.

Over-coating an unknown paint

It often happens that records of which paint was used previously are no longer available. This will cause difficulties in determining which type of paint to use for repainting at a later stage. Applying a test patch is the sensible way of approaching this situation.

A quick test to determine which main group of coatings the old paint belongs to is to perform a solvent-test. Make a scratch in the old paint and cover this with a rag soaked in a strong thinner, for instance an epoxy thinner. After 15 minutes remove the rag and examine the surface for any changes:

- If the old paint loose its adhesion, lifts and form blisters, it will be an oxidising type of paint (alkyd paint).
- If the old paint does not lift but is dissolved (soft, sticky, smears), it will be of a physically drying type (acrylic, chlorinated rubber, vinyl, bitumen etc.)
- If there is no change to the old film, it is likely to be a chemically curing paint (two-pack, epoxy, polyurethane, silicate etc.).

Surface preparation

Even the best paint in the world will only perform satisfactorily if the substrate has been prepared to the required standard.

Steel preparation

At the designing stage of a structure it is important that corrosion is taken into consideration. Corrosion traps should be avoided, like possibilities for stagnant water, inaccessible details, drain-holes that are too small to be painted.

During construction, faults in the steel (e.g. de-lamination and blowholes) must be repaired, rough welding-seams ground smooth and sharp edges rounded.

Cleaning

All contaminants must be removed from the substrate before pre-treatment starts. If not, they will be much more difficult to remove after being forced into pores and the profile of the steel. Oil, grease, dirt, welding smoke, etc. is best removed by an industrial detergent / degreaser, followed by fresh water cleaning to remove salt (the higher the pressure, the better result). Failure to remove contaminants is likely to result in subsequent paint failures, such as reduced adhesion (flaking) and blisters.

Pre-treatment

The best steel substrate for painting is bare metal with a certain roughness. The roughness (anchor pattern or surface profile) will ensure the best possible adhesion. Presence of mill-scale and rust will prevent the paint from being attached directly to the steel, leading to detachment. It may even promote continued corrosion under the paint film, resulting in rust penetration. Although hand tools may still have their uses, modern pre-treatment methods can broadly be divided in three groups:

Mechanical surface preparation

Needle-pickers and other impact tools may still be useful to remove cakes of rust, but they should only be used in combination with other suitable methods. Rotating wire-brushes and disks must be used with care to avoid polishing (burnishing) the surface or cutting too deep into the steel. Some more recent types of equipment are easier to work with, like flexible abrasive disks, abrasive pads, flap wheels and rotary peening tools. They may expose bare and clean metal combined with a certain surface roughness. The most common standards for mechanical pre-treatment are given as St2 and St3 (ISO 8501).

Blast cleaning

Blast cleaning has for a long time been considered as the most efficient method, producing the surface most suitable for paint application. A number of different blast media are available, giving varying surface roughness. The requirement for purity (particularly salt content) must be observed. Problems related to dust and air-born particles have imposed restrictions, which again have prompted some development within this field. Combining water with blast cleaning (shroud / wet / slurry –blasting) reduce the dust but cause flash-rust ('gingering'). New types of blast media are surfacing, but costs tend to limit their use to special applications. Examples of such media are sponge (with or without grit incorporated), solid carbon dioxide (dry ice) and baking soda. The widely accepted standards for blast cleaning are Sa1, Sa2, Sa2_, Sa3 (ISO8501).

UHPWJ

Ultra high pressure water jetting is defined by NACE as water jetting at pressures above 25,000 psi. UHPWJ is capable of removing old paint and corrosion products (rust), revealing a surface which initially correspond to Sa 2_. Due to the high humidity in the vicinity and fog created by cleaning adjoining areas, flash rust is usually encountered. UHPWJ does not create any surface roughness, but in cases of maintenance work it will reveal existing blast profile from under old paint.

Application

Before application starts, one must check that prevailing conditions are acceptable and the substrate suitably prepared. Observe that certain paints have temperature restrictions for application. While opening the tin, ensure that dirt from the lid does not fall inside the tin. Stir the contents before application starts. Two-pack paints must be mixed thoroughly, using a mechanical agitator.

- Addition of extra thinner to the paint prior to application is normally not recommended.
- Ensure that areas to be painted can be reached safely and that the operator can get close enough to the surface to carry out a satisfactory job.
- Strong wind and/or too long distance between a spray gun and the substrate will lead to dry-spraying and extra loss of paint (which eventually may settle on areas not intended to be painted).
- Confined spaces must have adequate ventilation.
- Edges, corners, notches, welding seams, bolt-heads, nuts and hard to reach areas should be stripe-coated, using a suitable brush (eventually airless spray).
- During application, wet film thickness readings should be carried out regularly to ensure the correct thickness is achieved.
- Brush application will force the paint into the profile of the substrate, but will result in a lower film thickness than spray application.
- Roller application tends not to force the paint into unevenness in the substrate and is not recommended for the first coat.
- Airless spray application is the fastest method and normally produces a higher film thickness than other application methods.

Inspection

Routines for inspections should be established before the work starts. Typical checkpoints would be:

- Steel preparation
- Surface cleanliness
- Pre-treatment
- Application equipment & paints
- During application
- Between coats
- After last coat

Daily reports/notes should be made, recording weather conditions, areas treated, products used, film thickness readings, drying times, general observations and any deviation from specification.

Failures

The majority of paint failures occur due to unfavourable conditions, use of incorrect product, faulty equipment or poor workmanship. A few of the common failures are:

Flaking. Caused by unsatisfactory adhesion. Often found to be due to application on a contaminated (oil, dust, water) substrate or due to incorrect over-coating interval.

Blisters. Caused by a pressure developing under the paint film. Submerged areas may suffer from osmotic pressure (painting over soluble salts), leading to water-filled blisters. Atmospheric areas may suffer from blisters created by solvents or impurities trapped within the film, which expands during increase in temperature (gas-filled blisters).

Cracking. May be caused by a hard-curing paint applied over a relatively soft substrate. In cases of many coats of paint accumulating on top of each other over the years, flexibility is reduced and cracking (often combined with flaking) may occur.

Drying. Lack of or extended drying times may be caused by too low temperature, addition of incorrect thinner, lack of or insufficient mixing of two-pack paints, inadequate ventilation.

Rust penetration. Many factors may contribute to rust penetrating a paint film, such as poor pre-treatment, low film thickness, lack of stripe coating, pinholes in the film, etc.

Health, safety and environment

The most commonly recognised hazard related to painting is the presence of solvent vapours. These will constitute fire or explosion hazard, a danger to health (inhalation and contact with eyes and skin), and environmental pollution (release to air). Other ingredients in paints may also have potentially negative effects, e.g. being harmful, toxic, carcinogenic, cause eczema, heritable genetic defects, etc. It is always important to use the recommended personal protective equipment (PPE), notably of approved quality. Information regarding PPE is found in individual products' material safety data sheet

(MSDS), issued by their manufacturer. MSDS will also contain other useful information, such as what to do in cases of fire, spillage, ingestion, storage, transportation, etc.

Painting newbuildings

With decreasing resources (manpower and time) available for routine maintenance work, it is important that the corrosion protection established at the newbuilding stage gives the best foundation for a continued anti-corrosion programme for the operative life of the vessel.

Life cycle cost (LCC) analysis

LCC is a tool that can assist in identifying the most beneficial paint system for a vessel. It should take into account costs of paint products, all costs related to paint-work during construction and subsequent maintenance (labour, scaffolding, pre-treatment etc.), maintenance intervals, interest and inflation rates, off-hire, and so on, for the entire expected service life of the vessel. Not surprisingly, choosing a better quality treatment during the construction period often proves to be by far the most economical solution when the whole service life of the vessel is taken into consideration.

Planning/specification

Discussions related to painting should be included in the negotiations with the building yard as early as possible. The painting programme must for instance accommodate requirements for climatic conditions and re-coating intervals in a realistic way. Most important is often the progress plan of paint application versus other types of work carried out. Repair of already painted areas due to damages inflicted by other trades is often the most frustrating aspect of a paint inspector's job.

Incorporating published standards into the paint specification during the negotiating process is by far much less painful than trying to achieve such standards in times of disputes during the construction period. The more detailed a paint specification for a new building is, the less disputes are likely to arise during the construction period.

Construction period

The most important aspects of paint-work during the construction phase is to have clearly identified and accepted responsibilities, authorisations, reporting lines / routines and communication channels. If these aspects are clear and the paint specification is sound, the foundation for a satisfactory result has been laid.

Dry-docking – paint perspective

Even after detailed planning of the work and considerable efforts having been put into establishing the most suitable specification, painting in connection with a docking often ends up with compromises. Condition of underwater hull area, weather conditions, time in dock, important unscheduled work, change of priorities, budget restraints, availability of material / equipment / manpower, and so on, may force the whole project to turn out differently from the initial intentions. Good communication between the parties involved and proper recording of work actually carried out (or not carried out) will be important in situations like that, as well as for the next docking. A few points worth bearing in mind for dockings:

- Seaweed, slime and other soft fouling will usually be removed easily by water jetting. Barnacle, mussel and other shell fouling may have to be removed by hand scraping. The barnacle bases that remain should be removed by sweep-blasting (or blast-cleaning). They should not be over-coated.
- Oil and grease must be removed from the surface with a suitable detergent while the vessel is being high pressure cleaned.
- Unless already used for water jetting, it is important to rinse the hull with freshwater to remove salt. Over-coating salt crystals is bound to give problems.
- Work should not be carried out on steel that is wet or moist from condensation. Air temperature changes faster than the temperature of steel, so both need to be monitored. Double-bottom tanks that are not empty may cause condensation on the outside hull, even if adjoining areas are dry.
- If spot-blasting is required on the hull, it is better to identify larger areas for a proper full-blast, than to have spots ("freckles") all over. Repairs in other areas can be carried out at the next docking, instead of spot-blasting the same areas at every docking. Weak areas will always be the transition between old and new coatings, as well as damages caused by over-blast. Treating larger areas will reduce the amount of such vulnerable transitions.
- Satisfactory access to work areas is crucial for good quality work. Too long a distance between water jetting or blasting nozzles and the substrate will cause reduction in effective pressure, which again will influence the productivity and/or the quality. Too long distance between a paint spray gun and the substrate will result in reduced coating film quality, dry spray and higher loss of paint.
- Drying times between coats, as well as drying time before flooding the dock, is often a bone of contention. One should bear in mind that manufacturers' recommendations are made to promote satisfactory results, and that deviation from these may have the opposite effect.

Training/qualifications

A number of training courses are available for personnel carrying out the tasks of a paint inspector. Some courses lead to widely recognised qualifications, while others are of a more general introductory type. Although quality control and inspection can do a lot to improve the outcome of a painting job, it is in the end the operators' efforts and skills which are decisive. One can not inspect quality into a job, merely reduce the number of apparent weaknesses. Training operators for pre-treatment and paint application, as well as their foremen, ought to receive at least the same, if not a higher, priority as for the paint inspector.

Personnel involved in deciding paint specifications, planning the work, and seeing it through, will also need certain qualifications. Experience gained over the years may in some cases be the predominant qualification as far as paint is concerned. One of the options ships' officers and superintendents have, is to receive updates and training from their paint suppliers. Jotun-Henry Clark arrange training courses and presentations at regular intervals (Jotun paint school) for personnel from various levels within their regular customers' organisations. An interactive CD-ROM disk is also available from the same company, from which individuals can learn about corrosion protection of steel at their own convenience, using a multimedia computer.

References

Informative and educational material is made available for further study from most paint manufacturers. Jotun Paints' *'Coating and Inspection Manual'* is an example of such literature. Various product manuals, working manuals and brochures related to different products and objects can also be a useful source of information, as can web sites (e.g. www.jotun.co.uk).

A considerable amount of literature is also available from sources other than paint manufacturers. Professional magazines related to the paint industry as well as to the shipping industry regularly feature marine coatings topics. A number of books related to paint technology are published, both of general nature and specific to the marine industry.

References

- Morgans, W.M., *Outlines of Paint Technology*, published by E Arnold, 1990.
- Berendsen, *Marine Painting Manual*, published by Graham & Trotman, 1989.
- *British Marine Technology*, published by British Marine Technology.
- *Recommended Practice for Protection & Painting of Ships*, 3rd edition, 1986.
- *Developments in Marine Corrosion*, Royal Society of Chemistry, 1998. (13 published papers from congress).

Web sites
- Paint Research Association (PRA) – www.pra.org.uk
- British Coating Federation (BCF) – www.coatings.org.uk

Chapter 50

STANDING BY A NEWBUILDING

by Mr. M.P. Cole IEng AMIMarE, Chief Officer (E) R.F.A.
MoD Integrated Logistic Support Manager

The author is a serving engineer officer with the Royal Fleet Auxiliary (R.F.A.) and has held a variety of positions both ashore and afloat. He is currently on secondment to the Ministry of Defence Procurement Executive (MoDPE) as the Auxiliary Oiler (AO) project Integrated Logistic Support Manager.

The MoDPE project team responsible for the procurement of AO class fast replenishment tankers are at the forefront of developing and using systematic analytical processes that enable inherent safety, operability and reliability characteristics of newbuilds to be optimised. The project team is an interdisciplinary group comprising career civil servants and operating personnel on secondment to the MoDPE from Commodore R.F.A's organisation. The vessels are being designed and built, within a Concurrent Engineering (CE) environment at Barrow-in-Furness by G.E.C Marine.

Special acknowledgement is given to John Moubray for the excellent advice and guidance contained in his book 'RCMII Reliability Centred Maintenance, Second Edition' published by Butterworth-Heinmann.

Introduction

IT IS POSSIBLE for potentially subjective requirements appertaining to safety, repairs and maintenance, human factors and husbandry to be qualified and quantified. However, as they seek to influence so many areas of ship design, it is not feasible to produce a build specification in which each applicable specific item of equipment or structure is allocated an individual set of requirements. Requirements in these areas therefore need to be actively managed during all stages of the design and build process. One way of achieving this is by the use of checklists, which can ensure that designers take due account of whole ship design requirements. The checklists may be used, in an iterative manner, to facilitate design reviews, plan approval (both 2D and 3D if applicable), build and acceptance. Examples of how these checklists may be compiled are given below.

Design and acceptance checklists

SHIP HUSBANDRY

Weather deck fittings

- Have non-corroding materials been fitted where possible?
- Have corrosion problems been addressed by insulating between dissimilar metals, providing protective coatings or covers?
- Have exposed surfaces been smooth finished with corners and sharp edges rounded to facilitate preservation?
- Have dirt and corrosion traps been avoided?
- If not, have areas been sealed by continuous welding and the structure behind effectively preserved?
- Has exposed equipment been protected against the ingress of water?
- If it is possible for water to enter, has adequate drainage been provided?
- Have water retaining ledges and pockets been avoided?
- Have overside ladders been sited clear of overboard discharges?

- Are overside ladders capable of being rigged safely and without damage to surrounding paintwork or fittings?
- Is lighting adequate over ladders?
- Have tread plates been fitted inside and outside adjacent to weather deck doors and hatches?

Accommodation and main superstructure

- Have furniture, equipment and fittings been carefully sited to allow access to ship's structure?
- Does compartment layout allow easy access into and within the compartment?
- Are ventilation grills and diffusers readily removable for cleaning and maintenance?
- Where systems are fitted behind linings, have suitable portable plates been provided for access and maintenance?
- Have suitable marker plates been provided to indicate important fittings located behind linings?
- Have non-watertight access doors been fitted with kick panels and finger plates?
- Have savealls been fitted under side scuttles to collect condensation?
- Does fixed furniture fit tightly against structure to alleviate dirt traps?
- Are passageways and lobbies as free as possible from extraneous items and fittings?

Machinery Space and Workshops

- Have savealls and drip trays been arranged to contain spillages, and under test taps and draw off cocks?
- Has equipment been arranged to allow all round access for survey, cleaning, preservation and maintenance?
- Are floor plates portable and sectionalised to allow lifting by two people?
- Has pipework been sited clear of structure, fittings and openings to facilitate cleaning and preservation?
- Is all equipment adequately illuminated for operation and maintenance?
- Are there any joints and valves on pipework

running through electrical compartments?

- Has all rotating machinery been fitted with guards and warning notices?

HUMAN FACTORS INTEGRATION

Ergonomics, operability and accessibility

- Can systems or equipment be operated?
- Are 'lines of sight' adequate:
  - With respect to specified operator populations and specific categories of controls and displays?
  - Where applicable, with respect to both internal and external (out of window) views?
- Are controls and displays situated for ease of use?
- Is there clear headroom adequate for the activities to be undertaken in the space:
  - With respect to specified operator populations?
  - With respect to specified tasks and activities?
- Is there adequate space around equipment for effective operation
- In particular are operating envelopes clear of obstruction:
  - With respect to specified operator populations?
  - With respect to specified tasks and operations?
- Is there adequate space for load handling on storage route, etc:
  - With respect to specified operator populations?
  - With respect to specified tasks and operations?
- Is there adequate clearance around equipment and systems for access to tasks:
  - With respect to specified operator populations?
  - With respect to specific equipment/system relationships?
- Have work stations been located to facilitate safe and effective traffic flow past the work station?
- Have footrests been supplied for personnel who cannot place feet flat on the floor when using the seat at the correct height for adequate sight lines?
- Do the work stations fully satisfy the ergonomic requirements of the defined user population in terms of anthropometric requirements?

Man machine interface (MMI)

- Has the MMI been designed to ensure commonality across work stations?
- Have controls and displays been grouped in accordance with ergonomic specifications in relation to functionality and spatial compatibility?
- Have controls and displays been grouped according to frequency of use and importance?
- Have controls and displays been satisfactorily located in accordance with line of sight requirements?
- Have controls and displays been satisfactorily located in accordance with reach envelope requirements?
- Have control types been designed to optimise task and activity requirements?
- Do dimensions of buttons and controls meet ergonomic specifications?
- Are modes of operation of controls acceptable from an ergonomics standpoint?
- Do displacement distances between controls meet ergonomic specifications?

Maintenance

- Is there sufficient space around equipment to allow access for maintenance without hindering other operations that are taking place?
- Has it been ensured that the installation of equipment in compartments does not compromise the necessary maintenance envelope?
- Where it has not been possible to avoid obstructions, has provision been made for local removal of obstructions to ensure that adequate maintenance envelopes can be achieved?
- Has consideration been given to the portability and ease of lifting equipment for maintenance?
- Has the effect of high or low temperatures and humidity been considered in relation to the ability of the maintainer to undertake the task?

Personnel movement and material handling

- Have passageways, doors, hatches, etc. along routes been designed in accordance with anthropometric population data÷
- Have passageways, doors, hatches etc. along routes been designed to accommodate personnel in full firefighting kit?
- Have compartments and spaces been functionally grouped to ensure that the internal movement of personnel within the vessel is minimised?
- Has adequate space been ensured to accommodate the carriage of injured personnel, specifically on stretchers?
- Have mechanical lifting/transporting arrangements been provided to minimise human handling efforts where heavy or bulk loads are required?
- Have direct access routes and sufficient handling space been provided for storing and cargo operations?

SAFETY AND HAZARDS

- Are 'emergency escape routes' identified and clear from obstruction?
- Are door sills and hatch coamings correctly sized?
- Are ladders of the correct type and free from obstruction?
- Is the escape and damage control equipment located for easy use and access under adverse conditions i.e. poor visibility and close to the associated equipment?
- Are there adequate hand holds for rough weather activities?
- Are there arrangements for safety harnesses?
- Are there guards around openings/dangerous equipment?
- Are there securing arrangements for loose equipment?
- Is lifesaving equipment readily accessible, including when the ship is heeled after damage?
- Is emergency equipment, including breathing apparatus, located where it may be required and that it is readily accessible by all personnel, including in damage situations such as smoke and heel?

- Have all areas of the ship in which potential hazards to personnel have been identified, been clearly delineated and labelled in accordance with the HSAW act?
- Has it been ensured that all drawers, lockers and loose furniture and equipment can be secured to minimise damage to walking and seated personnel, in all sea states?
- Have all safety related controls, alarms and warnings been designed to meet specific ergonomic requirements?
- Do warning signs satisfactorily meet the requirements of BS5378 and BS5499?
- Are safety related controls (such as emergency stops), alarms and warnings designed to a consistent specification?
- Are safety related controls (such as emergency stops), alarms and warnings easily operable by staff?
- Are safety related controls (such as emergency stops), alarms and warnings located in prominent, consistent, and easily reachable locations?

RELIABILITY AND MAINTAINABILITY

- Have all critical systems been identified?
- Are there any critical single point failures?
- Are there back up systems or equipment to maintain function in the event of failure?
- If so can the back up system or equipment be cross-connected quickly and with ease?
- Are equipment types, wherever possible, common and interchangeable?
- Is system design and equipment within the system, of existing and proven technology?
- Has the optimum use been made of condition monitoring and built in test techniques?
- Can all systems be accessed for maintenance?
- Can all equipment that is controlled remotely be operated locally?
- Has isolation of non-essential and essential services been addressed?
- Does current system design meet numerical targets for availability and reliability?
- Are portable sections in systems or adequate cable loops incorporated where required for withdrawal and maintenance routes ?
- Can equipment, where applicable, be removed from the ship?
- Has all lifting equipment been identified, or space envelope included?
- Is there adequate space for tools and parts to be set down during maintenance?
- Can equipment be maintained without climbing on other equipment or is protection provided for such activity?
- Are removal routes clear of obstruction, or where this is not possible, can obstructions be removed without unacceptable disruption?
- Have adequate lifting points and other facilities been provided to enable maintenance and removal?

- Have adequate special to type tools and test equipment been provided to enable maintenance and repair of machinery by ship's staff?
- Are equipments, where they have been identified, capable of being repaired by replacement?
- Have all critical workload drivers been identified?
- Do all electrical equipments have common test point access and identification design features?
- Is machinery contained in workshops adequate to allow maintenance and repair of equipment by ship's staff?

Appendix 1

Glossary of Terms

As low as reasonably practicable (ALARP)

The principle that safety risks should be reduced to a level as low as reasonably practical is central to much safety legislation. It means that not only must risks always be reduced to a tolerable level, but also that further reduction must be achieved, provided that the penalties are not disproportionate to the improvement gained. Reasonably practicable is defined as:

"So far as is reasonably practicable – qualifies the duty imposed by many health and safety (H&S) provisions. It implies that the risk must be weighed against the cost in money, time and trouble required to avert it. Only if there is a gross disproportion between them and the risk is insignificant in relation to the cost, can precautions be considered not to be reasonably practicable."

Failure effects analysis (FEA)

High level analysis carried out at system level to analyse the effects of major equipment failure on system functionality. Used to identify single point failures and determine redundancy requirements at major equipment level.

Failure modes and effects analysis (FMEA)

A lower level analysis identifying the individual ways (modes) in which an equipment can functionally fail and the effects of each failure mode. Used to identify maintenance tasks and, if applicable, allows redesign options to be evaluated.

Failure modes effects and criticality analysis (FMECA)

An extension of the FMEA in which account is taken of the severity criteria and conditional probability of failure.

Fault tree analysis (FTA)

Whereas FMEA techniques only identify a single failure mode and use a 'bottom up' technique to determine the effect of the failure mode, a fault tree is essentially the logical representation of the connections between a state of a system (a top event) and the primary events that lead to its occurrence. FTA is a deductive (top down) method concerned with the identification and analysis of conditions and factors that cause or contribute to the occurrence of a defined undesirable event. Thus the tree models the ways in which the system operates in order to produce the undesired top event.

All possible factors that can contribute to the top event are diagrammed in sequence and the branches of the 'tree' are continued until independent events are reached. Probabilities are determined for the independent events and, after simplifying the 'tree' both the probability of the undesired event and the most likely chain of events leading to it are computed. Fault tree analysis should consider:

- Component failures.
- Independent, dependent, and simultaneous hazardous events including failure of safety devices and common mode failure.
- Degradation of the safety of a subsystem or the total system from normal operation of another subsystem.
- Effects of defined human errors, including operator and maintenance errors.
- Environmental factors.
- Operational modes.

Hazard and operability study (HAZOPS)

To establish the hazardous states or conditions and their effects by means of a methodical examination of the system and its elements. The analysis should be carried out by a team with a broad knowledge of the system and its operation. Prior to the study being carried out agreed checklists containing guidewords relevant to the system should be compiled in order to provide a basis for the study. The degree of depth of the checklist should be dependant on the knowledge of the system at the time the study is carried out. This technique can therefore be applied at any stage of the project life cycle. In order to carry out a HAZOPS a system description is necessary. The HAZOPS can then be used to identify hazards which can subsequently be analysed further by hazard analysis techniques such as FMECA and FTA.

Investment appraisal (IA)

A means of comparing all proposals with financial implications with their alternatives. The technique can be used to:

- Assess competing tenders.
- Evaluate different development and production options (e.g. timescale, batches etc.).
- Evaluate payment scheme options.
- Assess financial options (e.g. leasing).
- Evaluate contracting out of services.
- Assess options for reorganisation/redeployment of work.

The depth of analysis required will vary from case to case and must be commensurate with the size of the investment decision being evaluated, the options available etc. The key is to ensure that the level of analysis is sufficient to enable a reasoned judgement.

The main steps involved in carrying out an IA are summarised below:

- Define the objectives
  These should be clearly defined and appropriate to the level of appraisal.
- List the options for meeting the objectives
  All possible options should be considered, including the 'do nothing' option.
- Sift the options
  Identify and eliminate options which perform worst against the objective. Make broad cost comparisons where appropriate to eliminate those options which are significantly more expensive. Ensure that reasons for rejecting options are recorded. Subject remaining options to full IA.
- Identify the costs, benefits, timing and uncertainties of each option
  Ensure that all costs are included in the assessment and that estimates are realistic. Only those costs that vary (in total or in timing) between options need be included. The primary objective is to reach a conclusion that provides value for money.
- Put those costs and benefits which can be valued in money terms onto a common basis (net present value - NPV) through the use of a discounted cash flow (DCF)
  Payments and receipts data used in a DCF should normally be expressed at the price base at the time of appraisal.
- Weigh up the uncertainties and risks
  Apply sensitivity analysis to the assumptions including timescale, cost etc. Three point costing should be used as the basis for sensitivity analysis.
- Assess other factors
  These may include environmental; health and safety; morale and other considerations which cannot always be valued in money terms.
- Present the results
  The main body of the submission of the analysis should contain an adequate summary of the results of the appraisal.

Net present value (NPV)

The value obtained by discounting all cash outflows and inflows attributable to capital investment by a chosen percentage e.g. the entity's weighted average cost of capital. The chosen percentage should take account of predicted inflation rates; cost of borrowing etc.

Note:
This chapter is an extract from *Improving Ship Operational Design*, The Nautical Institute, 1999.

Chapter 51

SHIP STRUCTURES INSPECTION AND MAINTENANCE

summarised from the IACS 1994 publication "Bulk Carriers – guidelines for surveys, assessment and repair of hull structure" by Lt. Cdr. J.A. Hepworth RN Ret'd, MIMgt MNI

The kind permission of IACS to include various quotations from their publication is acknowledged.

Tony Hepworth entered the Royal Navy as a cadet through Dartmouth Royal Naval College in 1953. Following training there, in several shore establishments and at sea he served aboard a variety of vessels, including time as a Commanding Officer. He travelled worldwide, including one circumnavigation of the globe aboard HMS KENT.

Retiring in 1969 as a Lieutenant Commander, Tony then worked chiefly overseas in the Middle East until 1982, in ports and airports in Bahrain, Saudi Arabia, Oman, Qatar, Kuwait and the United Arab Emirates. Tony returned to the UK in 1982 to set up his own business, which celebrated its 18th year in 1999.

Consultancy assignments have included work for the World Bank, Lloyds Register of Shipping, the UK Crown Agents, and the EU TACIS programme through the European Bank for Reconstruction and Development – in countries as diverse as Ethiopia, Malta, Trinidad, Jamaica, Pakistan and, more recently, in Kazakstan and Russia.

He has carried out a number of assignments for The Nautical Institute, including typesetting of books, some editing of publications and other work.

Acknowledgement

THE INTERNATIONAL ASSOCIATION of Classification Societies (IACS) published excellent guidelines in 1994, entitled *Bulk Carriers – Guidelines for Surveys, Assessment and Repair of Hull Structure*[1]. The publication acknowledged the significant contributions made to it by a variety of marine industry sources in the preparation of the text. It also acknowledged the kind contribution of Denholm Ship Management Ltd. in the development of selected graphic representation in that edition.

Introduction

Bulk Carriers – Guidelines for Surveys, Assessment and Repair of Hull Structure is one of an intended series of manuals with the intention of giving guidelines to assist surveyors of IACS Member Societies, and other interested parties involved in the survey, assessment and repair of hull structures for certain ship types. Interested parties will, of course, include masters.

It relates to a bulk carrier type ship which is constructed with a single deck, single skin, double bottom, hopper side tanks and topside tanks in cargo spaces, and is intended primarily to carry dry cargo, including ore, in bulk. Figure 04.04.1 shows a typical cargo hold structural configuration for a single skin bulk carrier.

The manual includes a review of survey preparation guidelines, including safety aspects, encompassing different main hull structural areas where damage has been recorded. An important feature which is included is a section illustrating examples of structural deterioration, what to look for and recommended repair methods.

Masters will also need to be aware of the "IACS Early Warning Scheme (EWS)", enabling statistical analysis of problems as they arise.

Survey requirements

The guidelines detail class and statutory requirements and other surveys. Class and statutory requirements include periodic classification surveys, damage surveys and statutory surveys. 'Other' include condition surveys and on-hire/off-hire surveys.

Technical background for surveys

Chapter 3 of the guidelines explains the purpose of periodical hull surveys, mentions the use of standard nomenclature and details structural damages and deterioration. This latter section includes:

* A general section.
* Material wastage/corrosion.
* Fractures.
* Buckling.
* Deformations.

The IACS Early Warning Scheme (EWS) for reporting of significant hull damages is explained.

Survey planning and preparation

Chapter 4 of the guidelines covers:

* Survey programme.
* Principles for planning document.
* Conditions for survey.
* Access arrangement and survey.
* Equipment and tools.
* Survey at sea or at anchorage.
* Documentation on board.

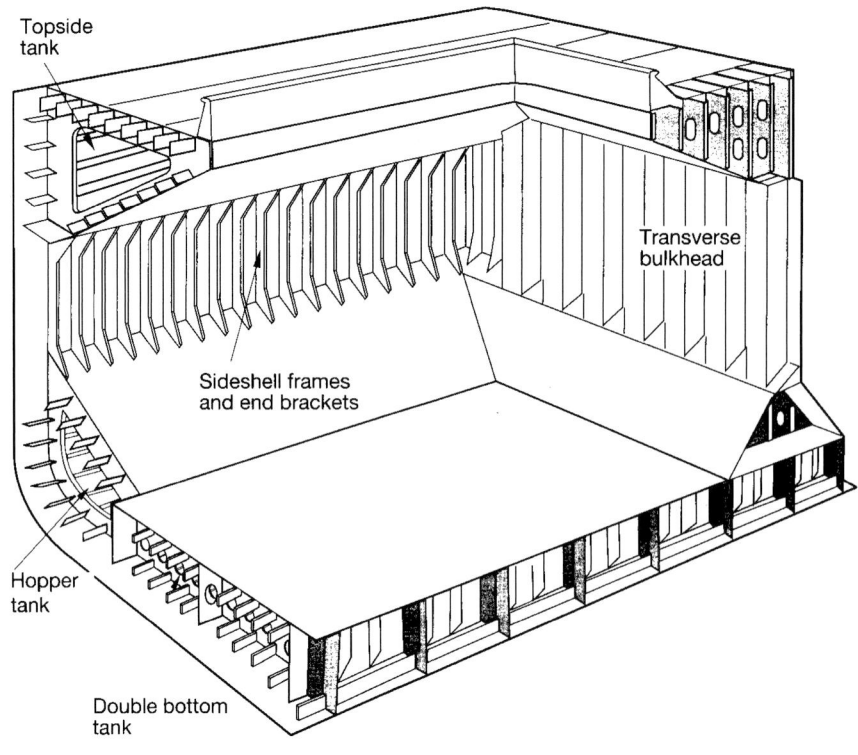

Figure 04.04.1 Typical cargo hold structural configuration for a single skin bulk carrier

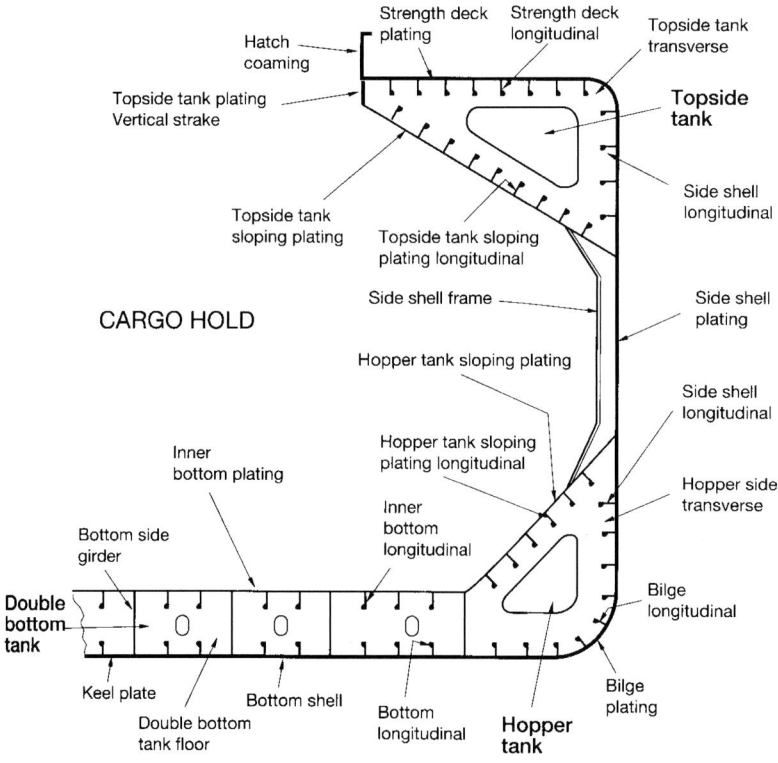

Figure 04.04.2 Nomenclature for typical transverse section in way of cargo hold

Survey execution

How the survey is conducted depends, naturally, on the type of survey to be carried out. Following a general section, chapter 5 of the guidelines lists definitions and considers thickness measurement and overall and close-up surveys.

Structural detail failures and repairs

Chapter 6 of the guidelines includes a catalogue of structural detail failures and repairs, collated from data obtained by the IACS Member Societies. It is intended to provide guidance when considering similar cases of damage and failure. The catalogue comprises:

Area 1   Shell plating, frames and end brackets.
Area 2   Transverse bulkheads and associated structure.
Area 3   Deck structure (including cross deck strips, main cargo hatchway corners, hatch covers and coamings and topside tanks).
Area 4   Double bottom structure including hopper.
Area 5   Transition regions in cargo spaces, fore and aft.
Area 6   Fore and aft peak structure.

Each area of the catalogue has a general introduction, explains what to look for and has general comments on repairs. A large number of clear, detailed diagrams are included to illustrate various points.

Conclusion

These excellent guidelines for surveys, assessment and repair of hull structure are aimed principally, of course, at surveyors of IACS Member Societies. However, some aspects will be of interest to the master when a vessel is due to be surveyed, assessed and repaired. In particular, the diagrams can be used, with technical staff, to explain what may be happening to a hull structure and what could be involved as a result.

Reference

[1]   *Bulk Carriers – Guidelines for Surveys, Assessment and Repair of Hull Structure*, IACS, 1994.
The publication and further information can be obtained from The Permanent Secretary, International Association of Classification Societies, 5 Old Queen Street, London SW1H 9JA, telephone 0171–976–0660, fax 0171–976–0440, telex 261720 IACS G.

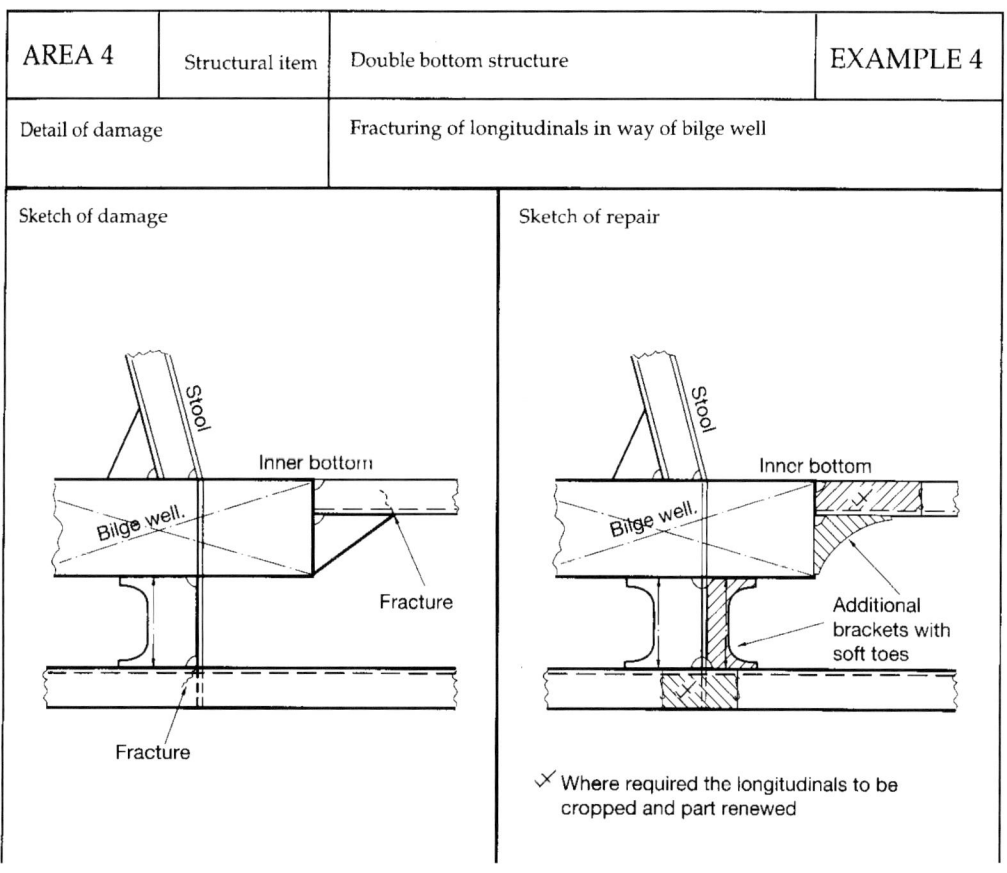

AREA 4	Structural item	Double bottom structure	EXAMPLE 4
Detail of damage		Fracturing of longitudinals in way of bilge well	

Figure 04.04.3 Example of double bottom structure damage and repair (part of diagram only)

Chapter 52

THE USE OF ELECTRONIC AIDS TO NAVIGATION

Marine Safety Agency Marine Guidance Note MGN 63 (M+F)

Notice to Owners, Masters, Skippers, Officers and Crews of Merchant Ships and Fishing Vessels

This Guidance Note supersedes Merchant Shipping Notice No. 1158

Summary

This note emphasises the need for correct use of navigational equipment by watchkeepers.

Key Points
- Be aware that each item of equipment is an _aid_ to navigation
- Be aware of the dangers of over-reliance on the output from and accuracy of a single navigational aid
- Recognise the importance of the correct use of navigational aids and knowledge of their limitations
- Appreciate the need to cross check position fixing information using other methods
- Be aware of the factors which affect the accuracy of position fixing systems

1. NAVIGATIONAL EQUIPMENT

Provision of Navigational Equipment on Ships

1.1 The Merchant Shipping (Navigational Equipment) Regulations 1993 (SI 1993 No 69) require certain ships to be provided with a magnetic compass installation and other specified ships to be fitted additionally with a direction finder, an echo sounder, a gyro compass, radar and ARPA installations, a speed and distance measuring installation and a rate of turn indicator.

1.2 Provision is also made in the Regulations in respect of siting and serviceability of the installations and, in the case of radar and ARPA installations, the qualifications of the radar observers.

1.3 A number of recent accidents have been caused by over-reliance on a single electronic navigational aid. Watchkeepers must always ensure that positional information is regularly cross-checked using other equipment, as well as visual aids to navigation.

1.4 Some radars are equipped with AutoTracking Aids (ATA) which enable targets to be acquired manually and automatically plotted. Such systems do not provide all the functions of ARPA. Radars for smaller vessels may be provided with Electronic Plotting Aids (EPA) which require the operator to plot each target manually. EPA provides the target calculations for each manual plot. Operators should be aware of the functional limitations of ATA and EPA.

2. THE USE OF RADAR AND PLOTTING AIDS

General

2.1 Collisions have been caused far too frequently by failure to make proper use of radar and ARPA in both restricted visibility and in clear weather. A common error has been altering course on insufficient information and by maintaining too high a speed, particularly when a close quarters situation is developing or is likely to develop. Information provided by radar and ARPA/ATA in clear weather conditions can assist the watchkeeper in maintaining a proper lookout in areas of high traffic density. It cannot be emphasised too strongly that navigation in restricted visibility is difficult and great care is needed even with all the information available from the radar and ARPA/ATA. Where continuous radar watchkeeping and plotting cannot be maintained even greater caution must be exercised. A "safe speed" should at all times reflect the prevailing circumstances.

Interpretation

2.2 It is essential for the observer to be aware of the current quality of performance of the radar (which can most easily be ascertained by the Performance Monitor) and to take account of the possibility that small vessels, small icebergs and other floating objects such as containers may not be detected. When video processing techniques are employed, caution should be exercised.

2.3 Echoes may be obscured by sea or rain clutter. Correct setting of clutter controls will help but will not completely remove this possibility. When plotting larger targets on a medium range scale, the display should be periodically switched to a shorter range, and the clutter controls adjusted, to check for less distinct targets.

2.4 The observer must be aware of the arcs of blind and shadow sectors on the display caused by masts and other on-board obstructions. They must be plotted on a diagram placed near the radar display which must be updated following any changes which affect the sectors.

Plotting

2.5   To estimate the degree of risk of collision with another vessel it is necessary to forecast the closest point of approach. Choice of appropriate avoiding action is facilitated by the knowledge of the other vessel's track. This can be obtained by manual plotting methods or using EPA, or automatically, using ATA or ARPA. The accuracy of the plot, however obtained, depends upon accurate measurement of own ship's track during the plotting interval. Observers should be aware that an inaccurate compass heading or speed input will greatly reduce the accuracy of true vectors when using ARPA or ATA, and should therefore treat the apparent precision of the digital display with caution. This is particularly important with targets on near-opposite courses where a slight error of own-ship's data can make the difference between a target apparently crossing ahead or passing clear.

Choice of range scale

2.6   Although the choice of range scales for observation and plotting is dependent upon several factors such as traffic density, speed of own ship and the frequency of observation, it is not generally advisable to commence plotting on a short range scale. Advance warning of the approach of other vessels, changes in traffic density, or proximity of the coastline, should be obtained by occasional use of longer range scales. This applies particularly when approaching areas of expected high traffic density when information obtained from the use of longer range scales may be an important factor in determining a safe speed.

Appreciation

2.7   A single observation of the range and bearing of an echo will give no indication of track of a vessel in relation to own ship. To estimate this, a succession of observations must be made over a known time interval. The longer the period of observation, the more accurate the result. This also applies to ARPA/ATA which requires adequate time to produce accurate information suitable for assessing collision risk and determining appropriate manoeuvres.

2.8   Estimation of the target's true track is only valid up to the time of the last observation and the situation must be kept constantly under review. The other vessel, which may not be keeping a radar watch or plotting, may alter its course and/or speed. This will take time to become apparent to the observer on own ship. Neither ARPA nor ATA will detect any alteration immediately and therefore should also be monitored constantly.

2.9   It should not be assumed that because the relative bearing of a target is changing, there is no risk of collision. Alteration of course and/or speed by own ship may alter the relative bearing. A changing compass bearing is more reliable. However, account should be taken of the target's range because, at close quarters, risk of collision can exist even with a changing compass bearing.

2.10   Radar should be used to complement visual observations in clear weather to assist assessment of whether risk of collision exists or is likely to develop. It also provides accurate determination of range to enable appropriate action to be taken in sufficient time to avoid collision, taking into account the manoeuvring capabilities of own ship.

Clear weather practice

2.11   It is important that all using radar and ARPA/ATA should obtain and maintain experience in its operation by practice at sea in clear weather. This allows radar observations and ARPA/ATA vectors to be checked visually. Thus misinterpretation of the radar display or false appreciation of the situation, which in restricted visibility could be potentially dangerous, is highlighted. By keeping themselves familiar with the process of systematic radar observation, and the relationship between radar and electronically plotted information and the actual situation, watchkeepers will be able to deal rapidly and competently with the problems which will confront them in restricted visibility.

Operation

2.12   The radar display should be kept on at all times when weather conditions indicate that visibility may deteriorate, and at night wherever fog banks, small craft or unlit obstructions such as icebergs are likely to be encountered. This is particularly important when there is a likelihood of occasional fog banks so that vessels can be detected before entering the fog. The life of components, and hence the reliability of the radar, will be far less affected by continuous running, than by frequent switching on and off.

Radar watchkeeping

2.13   In restricted visibility the radar display should be permanently on and observed. The frequency of observation will depend on the prevailing circumstances, such as own ship's speed and the type of craft or other floating objects likely to be encountered.

Parallel index techniques

2.14   Investigation of casualties where radar was being used as an aid to navigation prior to the vessel grounding have indicated that inadequate monitoring of the ship's position contributed to many of the accidents. Parallel index techniques provide valuable assistance to position monitoring in relation to a pre-determined passage plan, and would have helped to avoid these groundings. Parallel indexing should be practised in clear weather during straightforward passages, so that watchkeepers become thoroughly familiar with the technique before attempting it in confined difficult passages, or at night, or in restricted visibility.

2.15   The principles of parallel index plotting can be applied, using electronic index lines, to both relative and true motion displays. These index lines can be stored and called up when required on all modes of display. Electronic index lines also enable the operator to switch ranges. With such a facility, care must be taken during passage planning to ensure that the correct parallel index lines for the intended voyage are available for retrieval.

2.16   On a relative motion display, the echo of a fixed object will move across the display in a direction and at a speed which is the exact reciprocal of own ship's ground track. Parallel indexing uses this principle of relative motion, and reference is first made to the chart and the planned ground track. The index line is drawn parallel to the planned ground track with a perpendicular distance (cross index range or offset) equal to the planned passing distance off the object. Observation of the fixed object's echo moving along the index line will provide a continuous indication of whether the ship is maintaining the planned track. Any displacement of the echo from the index line will immediately indicate that own ship is not maintaining the desired ground track, enabling corrective action to be taken.

2.17   Electronic parallel index lines are drawn and used in the same way on true motion displays in both sea-stabilised and ground stabilised mode. Parallel index lines are fixed relative to the trace origin (i.e. to own ship), and will consequently move across the display at the same rate and in the same direction as own ship. Being drawn parallel to the planned charted track, and offset at the required passing distance off the selected fixed mark, the echo of the mark will move along the index line as long as the ship remains on track. Any displacement of the fixed mark's echo from the index line will indicate that the ship is off track enabling corrective action to be taken.

2.18   Parallel indexing is an aid to safe navigation and does not replace the requirement for position fixing at regular intervals using all appropriate methods available including visual checks.

2.19   When using radar for position fixing and monitoring, check:

(a)   the radar's overall performance,

(b)   the identity of fixed objects,

(c)   the gyro error and accuracy of the heading marker alignment,

(d)   the accuracy of the variable range marker, bearing cursor and fixed range rings,

(e)   that parallel index lines are correctly positioned on a suitable display.

2.20   Some older radars may still have reflection plotters. It is important to remember that parallel index lines drawn on reflection plotters apply to only one range scale. In addition to all other precautions necessary for the safe use of radar information, particular care must therefore be taken when changing range scales.

Regular operational checks

2.21   Frequent checks of the radar performance must be made to ensure that the quality of the display has not deteriorated.

2.22   The performance of the radar should be checked before sailing and at least every four hours whilst a radar watch is being maintained. This should be done using the performance monitor.

2.23   Mis-alignment of the heading marker, even if only slight, can lead to dangerously misleading interpretation of potential collision situations, particularly in restricted visibility when targets are approaching from ahead or fine on own ship's bow. It is therefore important that checks of the heading marker should be made periodically to ensure that correct alignment is maintained. If misalignment exists it should be corrected at the earliest opportunity. The following procedures are recommended:

(a)   Check that the heading marker is aligned with the compass heading of the ship.

(b)   Ensure that the heading marker line on the display is aligned with the fore-and-aft line of the ship. This is done by selecting a conspicuous but small object with a small and distinct echo which is clearly identifiable and lies as near as possible at the edge of the range scale in use. Measure simultaneously the relative visual bearing of this object and the relative bearing on the display. Any misalignment must be removed in accordance with the instructions in the equipment manual.

2.24   To avoid introducing serious bearing errors, adjustment of the heading marker should not be carried out by using the alignment of the berth on a ship which is alongside in harbour; nor should it be carried out using bearings of targets which are not distinct, close to the vessel or have not been identified with certainty both by radar and visually.

Electronic radar plotting aids (ARPA and ATA)

2.25   In addition to the advice given above and the instructions contained in the Operating Manual, users of ARPA /ATA should ensure that:

(a)   the test programmes are used to check the validity of the ARPA/ATA data,

(b)   the performance of the, radar is at its optimum,

(c)   the heading and speed inputs to the ARPA/ATA are satisfactory. Correct speed input, where provided by manual setting of the appropriate ARPA/ATA controls or by an external input, is vital for correct processing of ARPA/ATA data. Serious errors of output data can arise if heading and speed inputs to the ARPA/ATA are incorrect. Users should be aware of possible hazards of using ground stabilised mode with ARPA/ATA when assessing risk of collision with approaching vessels, particularly in areas where significant tidal streams and/or currents exist. When course and speed inputs are derived from electronic position fixing systems (e.g. LORAN, GPS and IDGPS) the display is ground~ stabilised. The output data of tracked targets will relate to their ground track and, although accurate, may be highly misleading when assessing target aspect and determining collision-avoidance manoeuvres. In cases of gyro failure when heading data is provided from a transmitting magnetic compass, watchkeepers should remember to determine and apply the errors of the magnetic compass.

2.26 The use of audible operational warnings and alarms to denote that a target has closed on a range, transits a user-selected zone or breaks a preset CPA or TCPA limit does not relieve the user from the duty to maintain a proper lookout by all available means. Such warnings and alarms, when the ARPA is in automatic acquisition mode, should be used with caution especially in the vicinity of small radar-inconspicuous targets. Users should familiarise themselves with the effects of error sources on the automatic tracking of targets by reference to the ARPA Operating Manual.

2.27 Information on detection and use of Search and Rescue Transponders (SARTs) is provided in Chapter 4 of Volume 5 of the Admiralty List of Radio Signals.

3. TERRESTRIAL HYPERBOLIC POSITIONING SYSTEMS

General

3.1 With world-wide coverage by satellite navigation systems, the use of hyperbolic positioning systems at sea is declining. The Omega system has ceased operation, and under present plans the Decca Navigator System will cease to operate in Europe around the year 2000. LORAN C, however, is to be retained for the time being in certain areas. It will be available to maritime users as the terrestrial electronic position fixing service to back-up global satellite systems.

3.2 The use of lattice charts with hyperbolic positioning systems has declined, because most receivers convert the readings to latitude and longitude. These receivers display positions referred to a particular horizontal datum (e.g. WGS 84). This may not be the datum of the chart in use. The user must still remember that hyperbolic systems have inherent errors, and that the apparent accuracy of the displayed positions should be treated with caution.

3.3 Some equipment processes data from several electronic positioning systems (e.g. Decca, LORAN and CPS) and computes the best possible position, so providing a valuable check of one system against another. The use of such equipment does not remove the responsibility of the navigator to check the position periodically using other means, including visual aids.

3.4 Users should be vigilant when receivers are capable of reverting to dead reckoning (DR) mode. Serious accidents have occurred when faults in sensors and antennae connections have caused the receiver to switch to DR mode undetected by the watchkeepers.

3.5 Some terrestrial hyperbolic navigation receivers give a numerical indication of positional accuracy in the form of values of Horizontal and Positional Dilution of Precision (HDOP and PDOP). Users should refer to the equipment manual, as the receiver will not necessarily allow for fixed or variable errors in the system.

3.6 Further information on hyperbolic position fixing systems as well as up to date details of their operational status and coverage can be found in the *Admiralty List of Radio Signals, Volume 2.*

The Decca Navigator System

3.7 Decca Marine Data Sheets give the fixed errors for geographical areas where these are known. Where no errors are given, it should not be assumed that no error exists. In areas where no fixed errors are given, Decca positions should be treated with caution, especially when near the coast and in restricted waters. Receivers which convert positional data to latitude and longitude may not take fixed errors into account.

3.8 Decca is also subject to variable errors which depend on the time of day, season and distance from the transmitters. The error in a given location is not constant, and the Decca Marine Data Sheets give diagrams and tables which can be used to predict an approximate error based on a 68% probability level, (i.e. they are not likely to be exceeded on more than one in three occasions).

Lane Slip

3.9 Particularly at night, there is a possibility of slipping lanes due to interference such as excessive Decca skywave signals, external radio interference and electric storms. The possibility of this happening is small at short range, but increases towards the edge of Decca coverage. Fouling of the Decca antenna and disruptions to the power supply can also cause lane slip. It can best be detected by plotting the ship's position at regular intervals and comparing with fixes obtained by other means.

The LORAN C system

3.10 LORAN C has a greater range than Decca and is based on the measurement of time difference between the reception of transmitted pulses. The ground-wave coverage is typically between 800 and 1200 miles, although the accuracy of positional information will depend upon the relative position of the transmitters.

3.11   When entering the coverage, or when passing close to transmitters on the coast, the receiver may have difficulty in identifying the correct ground-wave cycle to track. Care should be taken to ensure that it is tracking on the correct cycle.

3.12   The fixed errors of the LORAN C system are caused by variations in the velocity at which the pulses travel. Additional Secondary Factor (ASF) corrections are provided to allow for these errors. Account should be taken of ASF corrections which may be very significant in some areas. Some receivers automatically allow for calculated ASF values and display a corrected position.

4. GLOBAL POSITIONING SYSTEM (GPS)

4.1   The NAVSTAR GPS Standard Positioning Service (SPS) now provides a global positioning capability giving a 95% accuracy in the order of 100 metres. The system is capable of much greater accuracy, but the commercial service is deliberately degraded by Selective Availability (SA). Differential GPS (DGPS) is also becoming more widely available. DGPS receivers apply instantaneous corrections to raw GPS signals determined and transmitted by terrestrial monitoring stations. Positional accuracy of better than 5 metres may be possible.

4.2   The GLONASS system is fully operational and available to commercial users. The system is similar to GPS and also provides global positioning for 24 hours a day. Some receivers use both GPS and GLONASS signals to compute a more precise position. The repeatable accuracy of GLONASS is higher than GPS as there is no degrading of signals by SA. When navigating in confined waters, navigators must bear in mind that the displayed position from any satellite positioning system is that of the antenna.

4.3   Serious accidents have occurred because of over-reliance upon global satellite positioning equipment. In one case a passenger vessel grounded in clear weather because the watchkeepers had relied totally upon the GPS output which had switched to DR mode because of a detached antenna. The switch to DR mode was not detected by the watchkeepers. Checking the position using other means, including visual observations, would have prevented the accident.

Datums and Chart Accuracy

4.4   GPS positions are referenced to the global datum WGS 84. This may not be the same as the horizontal datum of the chart in use, meaning that the position when plotted may be in error. The receiver

may convert the position to other datums. In this case the observers must ensure that they are aware of the datum of the displayed position. Where the difference in datums is known, a note on the chart provides the offset to apply to positions referenced to WGS 84, but where this is not given the accuracy of the displayed position should be treated with caution. DGPS positions are normally referenced to WGS 84 though local datums may be used (e.g. NAD 83 in the USA). Also, when using DGPS, it is possible that the positioning of charted data may not be as accurate as the DGPS position. Mariners should therefore always allow a sensible safety margin to account for any such discrepancies.

4.5   From April 1998, a new Volume 8 of *The Admiralty List of Radio Signals*, entitled *Satellite Navigation Systems* will contain full descriptions of all satellite systems, including GPS and DGPS, as well as notes on their correct use and limitations. Also included will be descriptions and examples of over-reliance on GPS, together with the advantages and disadvantages of using DGPS, and a full account of the problems caused by differing horizontal datums. Mariners using satellite navigation systems are strongly advised to study the information and follow the advice contained in this publication.

5. ELECTRONIC CHARTS

5.1   A number of vessels now use electronic charts. Mariners should be aware that the only type of electronic chart system with performance standards adopted by IMO is the Electronic Chart Display and Information System (ECDIS). One requirement of an ECDIS is that it must only use official vector data produced by a national hydrographic office. At present, this Electronic Navigational Chart (ENC) data is not widely available and the use of ECDIS is limited. An ECDIS using official ENC data satisfies the SOLAS Chapter V requirement for vessels to carry up to date charts.

Vector charts

5.2   The ENC is a database of individual items of digitised chart data which can be displayed as a seamless chart. ENCs of appropriate detail are provided for different navigational purposes such as coastal navigation, harbour approach and berthing. The amount of detail displayed is automatically reduced when the scale of a particular ENC is reduced, in order to lessen clutter. Individual items of data can be selected and all relevant information will be displayed (for instance, all the available information relevant to a light or navigation mark.) ECDIS is therefore very much more than an electronic version of the paper, chart. With vector charts the data is "layered", enabling the user to de-select certain categories of data, such as a range of soundings, which are not required at the time. This facility, as well as reducing chart clutter, enables the user to select a depth contour so providing an electronic safety contour which may automatically warn the watchkeeper when approaching shallow water. Mariners should use the facility to de-select data with extreme caution as it is possible accidentally to remove data essential for the safe navigation of the vessel.

5.3   Unless using an ECDIS meeting the relevant international performance standards in an area where ENC data is available, navigation must be carried out on an up-to-date paper chart. A number of vector chart systems are available which use commercially produced data for which the manufacturers accept no liability. These systems vary in capability and are termed Electronic Chart Systems (ECS). Such systems have no IMO adopted standards. If an ECS is carried on board, the continuous use of paper charts is essential.

Raster charts

5.4   Another type of electronic chart system is the Raster Chart Display System (RCDS). This uses Raster Nautical Charts (RNCs), which are exact facsimiles of hydrographic office paper charts, for which hydrographic offices take the same liability as for their paper products. There are at present no IMO performance standards for RCDS and they too must only be used in conjunction with paper charts.

General

5.5   Electronic chart systems are integrated with an electronic position-fixing system (LORAN, CPS or DGPS) enabling the vessel's position to be continuously displayed. Problems may arise caused by the possible differences in horizontal datums referred to above. Electronic charts may also be integrated with the radar and electronically plotted data from ARPA, ATA or EPA, with part or all of the radar display overlaid or under-laid on the chart display. There is a danger that the combined display may become over-cluttered with data. The combining of target data on an electronic chart does not reduce the need for the targets to be observed on the radar display. Mariners should also exercise caution where target vectors based on the vessel's watertrack are overlaid on an electronic chart which displays the vessel's ground track.

5.6   Electronic charts will become an essential part of the navigation system of the modern bridge and contribute greatly to navigational safety. However such systems must be used prudently bearing in mind the proliferation of approved and unapproved equipment and the current scarcity of official vector data.

MSAS(A) Navigation & Communications
Marine Safety Agency
Spring Place
105 Commercial Road
SOUTHAMPTON
S015 1EG

Tel 01703 329138
Fax 01703 329204

February 1998

MNA 051/17/001

An executive agency of
THE DEPARTMENT OF THE ENVIRONMENT, TRANSPORT AND THE REGIONS

Chapter 53

WORKING ON SECONDMENT

by Captain R.F. Walker BSc MCIT MNI, Mobil Shipping and Transportation Company

Captain Robert Walker joined Mobil Shipping Co. Ltd. in October 1975 as a cadet and obtained 2nd mates license and an honours degree in Nautical Studies at Liverpool by the end of 1980. He progressed through the ranks within the company, serving in the tanker fleet and gained his master's license in 1988. As chief officer he was seconded to Mobil Shipping and Transportation in Fairfax USA in 1993 for 18 months in the traffic department.

Bob first sailed in command in 1995. As master in 1996 he spent eight months as marine advisor in Singapore before returning to Fairfax as supervisor in the dispatch department and as nautical advisor in the nautical services department. In mid 1997 he moved to Mobil Shipping Co Ltd. in London as supervisor fleet manning and training before returning to MOSAT Fairfax in October 1998 as nautical advisor. He was posted to Singapore in March 1999 as marine representative, Asia Pacific.

Captain Walker is a member of The Nautical Institute and a member of the Chartered Institute of Transport.

Introduction

WHEN I ARRIVED AT WASHINGTON Dulles International Airport in January 1993 I discovered that the terminal building was extremely busy. Crowds occupied every square inch of available floor space, the immigration lines snaked out for ever and when I finally made it through customs into the arrivals hall there appeared no way through to the exit. It was a Saturday and the world's press had arrived to witness the inauguration of President Bill Clinton's first term in Office, set for the following week. My arrival was also in preparation for a 'first term in office'. I was bound for a stint of duty at the company's headquarters located just outside Washington DC. I was then Chief Officer on secondment from the fleet for the first time. With eighteen years of sea going experience behind me I had temporarily swapped my uniform for a suit and was about to discover what it was like to work behind a desk that was not in continuous motion. With grim determination I managed to push my way through to the exit and strode my sea legs ashore for the first time.

The position was one of a number of shore based assignments currently held within the company for fleet officers. These assignments integrate seafaring knowledge and experience into the shore environment and also provide a learning opportunity for seafarers within the shore management structure. In essence a two way street in which an individual can look at the management system and life working ashore while at the same time provide managers with the opportunity of working with and getting to know sea staff better.

Six years later and my uniform has been replaced by a suit on a permanent basis. The several secondments that I experienced have proved very interesting and rewarding. Although there are periods when I miss being at sea I am content with the knowledge that I have been exposed to enough facts which have helped in my decision to pursue a career ashore. I also know that the knowledge and experience gained on these assignments would have been invaluable should I have decided to remain at sea in command.

In this chapter I will attempt to provide a summary of my personal experiences and views on secondment and describe some of the problems I encountered. I hope that this will be useful information to those considering similar opportunities.

Shore assignments

Since January 1993 I have undertaken five shore based assignments, both foreign and in the UK, in my capacity as chief officer and as master. The first assignment involved working as a member of the dispatch team in the company's Chartering and Traffic Department based in Corporate HQ in Fairfax, Virginia. This assignment understandably proved to be the one that required the greatest adjustment. Apart from moving to a shore based office environment, working in another country with a diverse work force was equally challenging.

The initial task was basically one of settling in as the new kid on the block and getting up to speed with the job requirements. Cargo scheduling, chartering, voyage orders, agencies, freight, demurrage and bunkering were the prime functions. Although some of the commercial considerations are to some extent covered by a sea going educational background it was quickly apparent that I still had a lot to learn – a daunting task for the proverbial fish out of water. My cargo handling experience at sea proved to be of great assistance and actually allowed me to contribute. This helped both the department and myself enormously. Although I was learning a new job I was also being asked about mine. This was indeed a two way street of exchange.

Explaining issues pertaining to the particular ships that I had sailed on in the fleet assisted the cargo schedulers and ship charterers a great deal. This included issues such as cargo quantities and stowage as they relate to stress and trim, cargo segregations and pumping sequences, tank cleaning and ballast change operations. My experiences relating to specific port calls and ship characteristics was also put to good use by the department.

A major adjustment I found was the difference in working schedule and vacation periods. Working around the clock for a number of months followed by an uninterrupted leave period is exchanged for a continuous working week. During sea leave periods it is not customary to bring the job home. I learned ashore however that it is not so easy to leave work at the office and often found it following me home. This may not necessarily bode well with the family and therefore they should be prepared to make adjustments as well. On a more positive note is the fact that you are always close at hand.

Domestic issues needed to be addressed prior to my undertaking the assignment. This included obtaining the correct working visas, arranging health care coverage and organising a place to live. To a large extent this was dealt with by the company on my behalf, but this may not necessarily be the case for all.

There are also financial implications, which need to be considered when accepting shore assignments. Most importantly one must recognise day to day living expenses will increase. At the same time disposable income may decrease when taxation considerations are factored in. Under the assignment scheme my company provided advice and assistance to address these issues but I caution this may not be the case for everybody.

Other complications arising from working overseas include on scene domestic issues such as opening a bank account, transferring funds, obtaining the appropriate driving license, driving on the 'wrong' side of the road and ensuring continued validity of the correct visas. In general, learning a new way of life can be both challenging and enjoyable.

Value of experience

The experienced I gained whilst working in the traffic department became extremely useful when I returned to sea in command following the assignment. There was a distinct advantage in understanding the problems experienced ashore and the different prioritisation of requirements. I was able to focus on aspects of shipboard operations that would directly impact commercial considerations. I well understood the complexities which arose in traffic department operations. Consequently a fifth change of cargo orders in as many hours taxed my patience less. Equally it was also comforting to know that shore staff were more aware of the problems experienced on board ship, since I had been able to pass on to them some of my knowledge.

My assignment ended in mid 1994. After eighteen months ashore becoming familiar with the new way of life it became quite a shock to find myself readjusting to life at sea once more. The boot was on the other foot and I was reversing the whole procedure. Once again I had to become used to being away from family and friends for a period of time and adjust to the routine of life at sea.

Once on board I quickly adjusted to the demands of life at sea. The need to make many decisions, often quickly and unaided, was in stark contrast to office life. Ashore, most decisions are made in conference or jointly and colleagues are readily available to assist. In January 1996 after an eighteen month period back in the fleet in command I was assigned to the Nautical Services department for my second shore based assignment. I would be working with the Marine Representative based in Singapore. This was a totally different job function and location from my previous assignment. My main responsibilities now lay in ship vetting and inspections, which has a high priority within the corporate Environment Health and Safety program. Having this service available in Singapore as well as Fairfax and London enables this program to be maintained on both a global and twenty four hour basis.

In addition the job included marine related matters associated with ports and terminals. Similarly new projects, terminal inspections, crisis response, incident investigations, overseeing tanker discharges and port turn-rounds were routine job requirements. Furthermore it was not unusual to find oneself assisting the company's Marine Superintendents during their attendance of ships in Singapore for repair and maintenance. The company has a Shipping Agency based in the Singapore Marine Office. Its running is the responsibility of the Marine Representative and consequently the assignment included involvement in agency work. Not unexpectedly, the performance of all these tasks required a certain amount of travel within the Far East region.

I found the transition from ship to shore was a little easier this time. Dealing with hands on marine related matters was much closer to sea life. The mix between being in an office environment and getting out into the field proved to be a good working balance. I was being made aware of another perspective of the marine industry which proved to be very interesting and educational.

Domestic issues

Just as with the initial assignment it was important to make the necessary arrangements prior to and during the assignment. Domestic issues again required close attention. This included maintaining a cultural awareness and an understanding of business and social etiquette. Acclimatising to the tropical conditions, adjusting to the relatively expensive standard of living and learning to commute on some very congested roads were examples of other adjustments I needed to make. Fortunately once again the company assisted me in obtaining work permits, driving license and housing arrangements which could be problematic without such help.

The assignment lasted for eight months and during that time I was able to apply my knowledge and experience gained at sea in a variety of ways. I also realised that the exposure to the different aspects of the marine industry received during this assignment increased my overall awareness and would serve me well in my next position in command.

The next two assignments followed directly on from the Singapore position in September of 1996 and were both back to back in two different departments based in the Fairfax, Virginia office. In this respect there was no real transition from ship to shore, rather an adjustment to environment and job requirements. I remember someone once told me that a change is as good as a rest and I can attest that this is true. Nevertheless, moving from the tropics of Singapore to winter in North America was a bit of a shock. I had spent eight months in short sleeved shirts and now had to find clothes to combat the rigours of winter.

Initially I was reassigned to the dispatch group, but in the more responsible position as supervisor. Having prior knowledge of the environment and work requirements I felt that the adjustment was a lot easier. I was able to focus more readily on the work and also found time to select different aspects of the business which I wanted to explore and learn more about. The business concept of chartering ships has always interested me and I found myself asking more questions and getting involved as much as possible. The responsibility of scheduling and purchasing the bunker fuels for the fleet was also an interesting addition with exposure to dealing on the open markets and hedging for best prices. Working in the corporate headquarters also gave me an insight into the non-marine aspects of the company. I was able to learn more about supply, trading and marketing functions of a major oil company.

After six months I was assigned to the Nautical Services Department as Nautical Advisor. It is here that the world-wide Nautical Services group is managed and includes the group I was a member of during my time in Singapore. My main responsibilities were to manage the global ship inspection program. This included scheduling inspections in the US region and screening ships for acceptability in company service. Travel was also a feature of this part of the assignment as I was required to inspect tankers in ports on the East and Gulf Coasts and visit proposed or new terminal sites throughout this region.

Office environment

By the time I had reached this stage in my career I was beginning to feel less like the proverbial fish out of water and was becoming more comfortable with the job requirements and surroundings. I was drawing more and more on the knowledge and experience I had gained at sea and it was being put to good use in the office environment.

In mid 1997 I was transferred to the UK and assigned to the Fleet Managers office in London as Supervisor, Fleet Manning and Training. It was my first assignment in the UK and my last assignment as a Fleet Officer.

The primary function was to oversee the scheduling of UK based officers and ratings to the fleet and to coordinate with the manning offices based in Bombay and Manila. Other responsibilities included officer and rating recruitment, shore based training for company and STCW'95 requirements, certification, cadet induction and training, disciplinary procedures, drug and alcohol policy, officer and rating appraisals, promotion assessments, financial budget control, pay awards and union negotiations.

Ship masters unwittingly find themselves as personnel managers because they too make daily decisions regarding personnel welfare, intervention in and resolution of personnel issues and the exercise of man management skills. In this respect I found my experience extremely useful. It was also reassuring for me to realise that I had been through the whole process of induction, training, certification and promotion myself and therefore had a good handle on what I was managing.

I quickly realised however, that keeping a fleet manned effectively and efficiently was rather more complex than I had originally envisaged. People are sometimes very unpredictable and the best plans were often laid to waste by individuals who for one reason or another were not able to follow the master plan.

The work proved extremely interesting and was not all office bound. I travelled extensively in the UK visiting nautical colleges, attending manning and training seminars and meeting with representatives of professional bodies. Visits to ships and overseas manning offices also involved a certain amount of foreign travel.

Although a UK citizen with no visa or work permit issues, adjusting to working in central London presented its own challenges. Since my home base was not within commuting distance, temporary residence had to be provided by the company. Living and working in a city is a trade off between price and commuting time. It is extremely important that to avoid undue stress in travelling to and from work careful consideration must be given to the selection of where one is going to live. In my case my commute was approximately one hour door to door. This worked fine for me, as the commuting life did not cause too many difficulties.

Issues arising during secondment

I have mentioned a number of fundamental issues, which need to be addressed and dealt with on temporary assignments. These issues are far ranging and varied but to assist may be summarised as follows:

Adapting to change in:
- Job specification and requirements.
- Work schedules and leave ratio.
- Working environment.
- Domestic situation.
- Financial circumstances.
- Housing.
- Transportation/commuting.

And consideration for:
- Family accompaniment.
- Bank accounts.
- Visas and work permits.
- Driving licenses.
- Social security numbers.
- Health care.
- Cultural awareness.

Conclusion

Secondments are clearly advantageous for both the seafarer and office staff since the broad knowledge and experience gained by both is invaluable. The experience is not without personal adjustment and sacrifice. Maintaining flexibility is extremely important and one must be willing to uproot and travel at a moment's notice. Family support is also a key issue and is essential if life on secondment is to prove a success. For example it is not easy to move children to different schools around the world at a moments notice and expect them to settle in quickly and readily.

It is a question of priorities and whether the personal sacrifices are offset sufficiently by the experience gained.

The company currently maintains about fifteen shore-based assignments for sea staff in various offices around the world for both deck and engineer officers. Apart from assignments mentioned thus far, other opportunities lie in technical operations and ship auditing.

These positions have been established over a period of time to meet the demand of the business and are varied to meet changes in requirements. As new ventures continue to be explored around the world the demand for quality nautical expertise is rising. Opportunities for masters and other sea going staff to work for periods of time on secondment are therefore becoming more and more frequent.

The decision to accept a shore-based assignment is not an easy decision to make. An individual who has spent all his working life pursuing a career path at sea is suddenly faced with a temporary shift in career priorities and a change in working environment. One may or may not have the inclination to do this or indeed be prepared to accept a disruption in personal domestic circumstances that may be required to fulfil the assignment.

Since that first time in 1993 I have passed through Washington Dulles airport on a number of occasions and it has never been quite as busy. The path through to the exit has become progressively easier. In the same way the knowledge and experience gained from each assignment has made the transition from sea to shore smoother. Throughout this process the personal adjustments I have made have undoubtedly been worth while.

Chapter 54

WASTE MANAGEMENT ON SHIPS

by Captain D.N.L. Yeomans BA FNI

Captain Yeomans started his career at sea with the Shell Tanker Company in 1955. In 1962 he joined the Royal Navy as an Observer in the Fleet Air Arm. In 1967 he joined the Royal Fleet Auxiliary and was appointed master in 1985. Captain Yeomans has made a special study of waste disposal on board ships and is a Fellow of The Nautical Institute.

Introduction

WASTE CAN BE DEFINED as materials and products that have ceased to be of use or commercial value to the purchaser or owner. The valuable raw materials that were used in the production in order to create the asset are now often heavily modified and occupy space needed for replacements. Their continued presence is unwelcome due to ancillary difficulties with health or toxicity and so disposal becomes increasingly more important. Shipboard waste starts to be produced and to become the problem of the master as soon as the ship itself is manned and commences its normal commercial role and it continues unremittingly until the ship is laid up or scrapping is completed.

The legislation concerning the disposal of shipboard garbage is clearly and succinctly laid down in Annex V of the International Convention for the Prevention of Pollution from Ships 1973 (MARPOL 73/78) and is mandatory for all vessels sailing under the flags of nations that are signatories of the International Convention. The aim of this chapter is to assist masters and their delegated representatives with the difficulties of the collection, segregation, stowage and disposal of ship generated waste, given the latest legislation that is now in force under MARPOL, UK law and forthcoming EU directives. The sources of waste will be highlighted, as will the factors that will tend to increase or diminish the total amounts.

Methods of segregation, securing, preventing its migration around the ship, mitigating its odour and pest attraction potential and the health and safety aspects in preventing it causing damage to ship or personnel will also be covered. Some ideas will be given which might assist in increasing the motivation and maximising cooperation of the personnel on board in the processing of their own shipboard waste.

The sources and possible volume reduction in waste input

Over 90% of ship's waste is the result of products or cargo brought on board. The only exceptions are parts of the ship's structure or machinery that have failed and that are now redundant. It follows, then, that if these imports can be reduced or their waste potential minimised, the result will be a reduction in the volume of waste requiring stowage for ultimate disposal. This is important because in most cases it is the volume of waste that creates the prime difficulty. The types and sources of shipboard waste are numerous and some are shown below. The exclusion of food and other biodegradable putrescibles from the waste stream is of vital importance on the grounds of health and habitability and their disposal in accordance with the regulations is assumed, though this is not as easily achieved as might be at first thought.

Waste that should be stowed intact under cover in original container (if possible)

Glass waste arises mainly from food packaging, with a small input from domestic breakage, with the residue being made up from glass liquor and cordial bottles. It is probably the most intractable type of waste to handle and treat. Intact in the original boxes it is bulky, heavy and if the boxes get wet and break down releasing their contents, extremely dangerous. Crushed, its volume is much reduced but it becomes potentially lethal to handle and the containers must be glass proof and not allowed to spill. However, if it is intended to dispose of this waste at sea, then crushed glass is to be preferred as it sinks instantly and does not constitute a hazard to marine life.

Heavy containers full of broken glass are not easy to land safely and without spillage to disposal facilities. In addition, if the colours of glass are mixed the glass "cullet" is valueless and cannot be reused to make glass. Glass crushing is also a hazard for the crusher operator during the crushing operation. Whole or cracked glass containers loose in garbage sacks are subject to breakage and liable to injure the sack handlers.

Wastes that should be washed (if necessary), compacted or crushed

Tin plated cans are normally residues of ships catering, with major additional inputs being used tins of various beers or cordials. (Disposal of beer cans outside Special Areas is made more difficult if they contain plastic "widgets" to condition the beer. In addition, these inserts make the cans heavier, more difficult to compact and uneconomical to recycle.)

Aluminium waste arises mainly from empty beer and soft drink cans. A very small additional amount might be created by aluminium foil food wrappings.

Wastes to be compressed and shredded

Paper, cardboard arising from food wrapping (soiled and clean), ship's stores packaging from food supplies, ship bars and recreation rooms, i.e. cardboard beer cases, old newspapers and magazines, redundant ship's/personal paperwork and correspondence and computer printouts. In this category, some of the most difficult types of waste to collect, control and store are packing materials such as straw and shredded paper.

Plastic films and pre-shrunk plastic wrappings form a major part of all waste. The latter are often found in close conjunction with cardboard as the retaining medium attached to a cardboard shell for bottles and cans of food or alcohol, etc. Hard and soft plastic/ PET bottles and plastic retaining rings for six pack beers are particularly dangerous environmentally if dumped, as they form potent and lethal traps for marine wildlife. The ubiquitous polystyrene packing chip is difficult to collect, control, compress and store and if allowed to escape forms an ideal agent for the blockage of pipes and strums.

Carbonaceous wood waste

Wood waste appears either in the form of redundant packing cases, wood shavings used as shock absorbent packing material, or the arisings from dunnage or other cargo related use. Wooden pallets, either damaged or intact, will frequently appear. These are useful for storage on board and in the landing of waste.

Potentially toxic or hazardous waste

Waste in 225 litre oil drums, empty or partly used paint tins of all sizes and drums (usually about 25 litres capacity) which have previously contained various toxic and non-toxic chemicals will appear regularly. Many of them will be of the hard plastic screw top variety, missing labels and COSHH designations and containing residues of their previous contents. From the 1st September 1996, items such as these require specialist disposal throughout the European Union under the Special Waste Regulations (1996).

It is very clear from the above, that the sources of the waste are primarily containers, packaging and paper. The waste hierarchy of Reduce, Re-use, Recycle and Dispose can be used to determine the Best Practical Economical Option (BPEO) for the shipboard waste problem.

Reduction

Reduction will require careful monitoring of the sources of stores. Heavily packaged and marketed goods normally have more waste than bulk supplies in paper sacks or plastic bags. Studies have shown that the order of merit for the least efficient packaging for a given amount of contents, is:

i.   Glass jars and bottles.
ii.   Tin plated cans.
iii. Aluminium cans.
iv.   Plastic bottles and tubs and jars.
v.   Cardboard, plastic and paper and woven containers.

Therefore, ship's supplies that arrive on board inside plastic, hessian, cardboard / paper containers or wrappings, all of which are easily shredded and/or compressed after use, mitigate the problem from the outset.

Re-use

Re-use is more difficult on board a ship but many uses have been and are found for oil drums and plastic containers. Some containers will be required initially as bins for collection of segregated materials i.e. glass cullet and, as they degrade, replacements will be required.

Recycling

Recycling will not be possible on board but if the waste stream of the vessel can be presented in its constituent elements it will avoid disposal difficulties with shore authorities, make the Garbage Book record keeping easier and possibly constitute a source of income for the ship or a local charity. Though difficult, this standard of waste presentation should be achievable given the available manpower and the command structure of shipboard life by instigating cleaning, sorting and segregation at source.

Studies have shown that each crew member on a normal well found and fed ship will generate from one to two kilograms of rubbish each day. As the level of affluence increases, the amount of waste generated per person increases. Each type of waste above has a value. For example, aluminium is now worth around £800 a tonne (about 33,333 tins of 30gms each!). Disposal is, of course, subject to the constraints of MARPOL and the current UK and EU legislation while the vessel is at sea, and in harbour to the facilities and control of the Nation State and the Harbour Authorities.

Possible methods of collection and segregation

Covered waste food bins must be located in every food preparing, serving and eating space, and be clearly labelled "For Food Waste Only". These must be regularly emptied and rinsed out. No food waste or other biodegradable putrescibles should be entering the waste output.

Ideally there should be differently coloured bags for each type of waste input; paper, cardboard, plastic film, plastic bottles, tins, glass etc., but it is unrealistic, both in terms of cost and organisation. The best possible economical option will probably be a number of triple bag sites around the ship. One for the collection of paper, cardboard, soft film plastics, plastic bottles and containers; one for tins and cans; and finally one for glass. These must all be clearly labelled for the desired inputs and also show a clear prohibition of food waste.

Paper, card and film plastics are readily compressible and a high density can be achieved using a specialist machine. The same thing can be said for plastic bottles and containers. With the latter, however, care must be taken to ensure that screw-tops and lids are removed prior to treatment to avoid dangerous explosions! For the purposes of recycling it is not important if tinplate and aluminium cans are held in the same bag. A normal plastic bag will reach its strength limit at about 20 kilograms of crushed cans and be only about 30% full at this point, whereas a full bag of uncrushed cans will only weigh about 3·5 kilograms. Cans should always be crushed, as opposed to shredded, to minimise the dangers to personnel handling the bags and to preserve bag integrity. In order to achieve any worthwhile results it will be necessary to provide some equipment capable of compressing and shredding the waste inputs. This must be user friendly, effective and kept serviceable at all times. Once the impetus is lost it is very hard to re-engender enthusiasm.

The main machinery must be sited in an area where the ambient temperature is comfortable and access safe in all weathers. Ideally it should be close to the area where the waste is stowed. All galleys, serving areas, recreation rooms and bars should be provided with can crushers capable of dealing with the type of tins used in that facility. It is essential that all food and drink tins are washed prior to crushing, to avoid smells and their becoming an attractant to insects and other vermin. Tins or other containers that held or still contain paints, solvents, chemicals etc., should not be crushed or damaged and where possible should be re-sealed and stowed carefully for disposal as hazardous waste. If possible, their COSHH labels should be preserved and on no account should their contents be allowed to enter the sea. Finally, once the waste has been segregated and its volume minimised, it must be stowed somewhere out of the weather until it can be landed. It must be secured carefully and covered so that it does not migrate around the ship in the wind and block scuppers, drains, strums and breather pipes. This also inhibits visitations of birds and insects.

In many cases it is possible to build a dump using redundant pallets or dunnage somewhere out of the weather and not too near to fan intakes or accommodation portholes or entrances and to keep it covered with tarpaulins when not in use. Ideally it should use pillars or ship's superstructure features to give it strength and, if necessary, should be wired around to stop it's collapse. It must not be in such a position that it can be broken up by boarding seas. The covering must be secured at night, in strong winds or heavy weather if the contents are not become saturated and prevent the containers being damaged

or bursting altogether. Re-collecting ship's garbage is not quick, pleasant or easy.

It must be remembered that quite heavy items will, from time to time, end up in the waste and their potential for damage is considerable. The *Braer* was lost because a length of pipework lashed on deck broke loose and removed air pipes to the bunker tanks allowing sea water to contaminate the fuel, resulting in total engine failure, and eventual grounding.

Achieving the end result

No matter how well the ship is provided with properly sited, well maintained and located equipment, the desired results will only be gained through the full participation and cooperation of all personnel on board. The fact that a well run ship is a small enclosed community with a fixed hierarchical structure should make it easier to motivate personnel to cooperate, but from personal experience it would appear that there is great sense of apathy and disinterest about what happens to items that are discarded. They immediately become somebody else's problem. Every beer can becomes an instant orphan as soon as it is empty.

It will be necessary to change the deep-seated ethos that the sea is there for the rubbish and that no one will know or be able to trace anything back. Despite years of publicity and continual inter-governmental legislative updating, campaigns by pressure groups, major television series and information broadcasts, the message does not appear to have reached its target. The problem could be exacerbated in multi-racial crews where environmental education may not be well established. However, good waste management is no longer optional and every ship which trades with the EU and the USA will soon have it's waste trail closely monitored and regulated and will eventually end up on a constantly updated database.

It therefore becomes important that all personnel are informed of the rationale behind the plans being implemented and that they are for the general well being of the entire crew in order to minimise the volume, the nuisance value and the effort in accounting and measuring the ship's retained waste.

The establishment of a rota for the operation of the waste treatment plant and, perhaps, a small reduction in working day might create an acceptance of the need to do this uncongenial job. It may also be necessary and helpful to state the possible penalties on the ship and crew if they do not comply fully with all the regulations. These will range from fines on the master and owner to detentions in port or, in extreme cases, exclusions from trading in EU ports. It is likely that the latter two would have greater persuasive power as arguments, as this would undoubtedly have an impact on jobs, pay and shore leave. So it would be very much in the crew's own interests to cooperate to the full.

It will be necessary to site clearly labelled receptacles well in advance of the start date and constantly publicise the desired response. It is unlikely that, at first, much waste will fall into its correct place in its desired condition. It is indeed probable that the first success will be with the waste food bins as these are easily recognised and become smelly if left for too long. Before long it becomes second nature to use them and then empty them. The next priority must then be the galley, where a large amount of metal and plastic containers, plastic wrapping and cardboard boxes are opened and emptied. If galley staff can be persuaded to wash out and crush all metal containers and rinse food contaminated plastics and glass prior to placement in the correct waste container, a major part of the ship's garbage input is under control.

The most intractable problem will be to achieve the crushing of recreational cans, i.e. beer and soft drinks and their separation from glass bottles used in the same recreation room/bar. It seems that despite the provision of can-crushers and every other facility, this is an aspect that needs constant monitoring and pressure to obtain a reasonable result. Paper and cardboard is not so difficult because it is not associated with food or communal recreation. It tends to collect naturally in piles in cabins and offices and stores so it is more easily collected. The big difficulty with much cardboard and paper packaging is that now it incorporates plastics, which, unless removed, makes the paper both undumpable outside Special Areas and un-recyclable when landed ashore.

The same difficulty is becoming common with glass bottles and containers which use a plastic cap with a locked on serrated neck sealing ring, making the bottle illegal to dump even outside Special Areas. Finally, if the ship's garbage is properly presented to the designated receiver (see below) and he can add segregated cans, glass, paper and plastic bottles to his stockpile for recycling, there may be a sum of money payable. This might be used, for example, to subsidise the purchase and operation of a ship's mobile phone or even to cover free supply of newspapers in port. These may be the kind of incentives needed to gain a greater acceptance of the need and purpose of a waste management scheme. Whatever happens it will be a constant challenge to obtain the cooperation of the personnel, especially on voyages with numerous officer and crew changes.

Conclusion

The job of achieving the desired result will not be easy and there will always be the mentality that thinks the sea is an anonymous and unlimited waste bin. Despite all efforts, rubbish will still enter the sea out of sight or at night. From the 1st of July l998 all ships over 400 tons gross or certified to carry 15 or more persons must keep a garbage book and full records regarding the dumping, incineration or destruction of its ship's waste. A detailed ship's garbage plan must be in force, with a responsible person designated to be in charge. There is also a requirement for all vessels over 12 metres in length to display placards indicating the correct regulations for disposal of waste in the native tongue of the Country of Registry and either English or French. All of these are subject to random inspection and failure to comply carries heavy potential penalties.

The garbage book and its trail has become as important as the oil record book. However, E.U. legislation in the pipeline is due soon to become ever more onerous and record intensive. The suggested model is the UK Environment Protection Act (1990) S.34(1), which will impose a "Duty Of Care" on the ship's master, necessitating a Waste Reception Facility Requirement Report at least 24 hours prior to arrival in an EU port. The arrival would entail the issue of a detailed waste consignment note to the receiver of the waste and all relevant shipboard paper work would be subject to inspection. There would be continuous tracking of the ship from one port to another if any waste (i.e. hazardous/ toxic/noxious) remained on board and was not landed.

It is immediately obvious that the COSHH legislation will play a big part in this consignment note and all substances taken on board which are subject to this legislation will have to be controlled very carefully and accounted for from the point of loading to the point of discharge. There is a lot more but it will be obvious that shipboard garbage is no longer something to be ignored or lightly discarded.

The master's constant problem will be to ensure that the entire ship's complement is aware of and fully cooperating with any garbage plan in force. There will be a need for constant monitoring of bag contents to ensure the absence of putresicibles, maintenance of segregation, volume minimisation, etc. The overseer of the Garbage Plan, Book and Logbook entries is bound to be called the Rubbish Officer, but it will be a name only, because he will require very considerable knowledge of regulations, patience, determination, persuasive and administrative skills and must be able to motivate the 'unthinking' and the 'uncaring'. He will more than earn his wages if he enables the ship to trade freely during his time on board without a single delay or fine imposed by government inspectors or harbour authorities incurred through default of ship's waste management or disposal arrangements.

References

1   Glen Plant, *Ship generated waste in the EU*, Proceedings of the Institute of Wastes Management, pp. 11–12.

2   MARPOL 73/78.

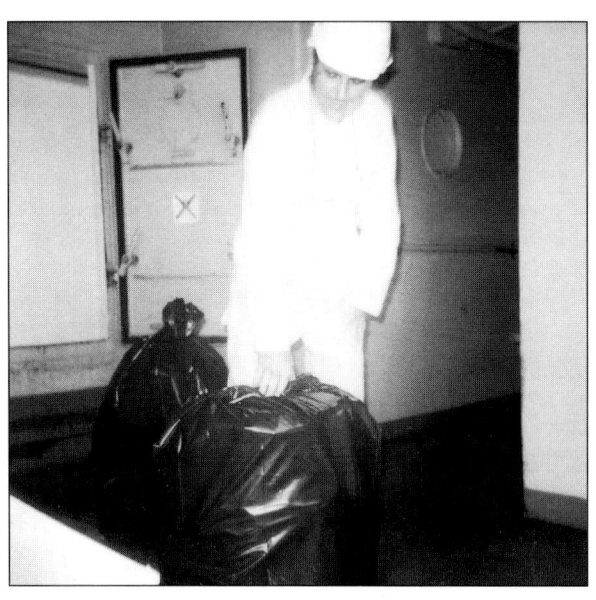

Figure 54.1
Two full bags of waste

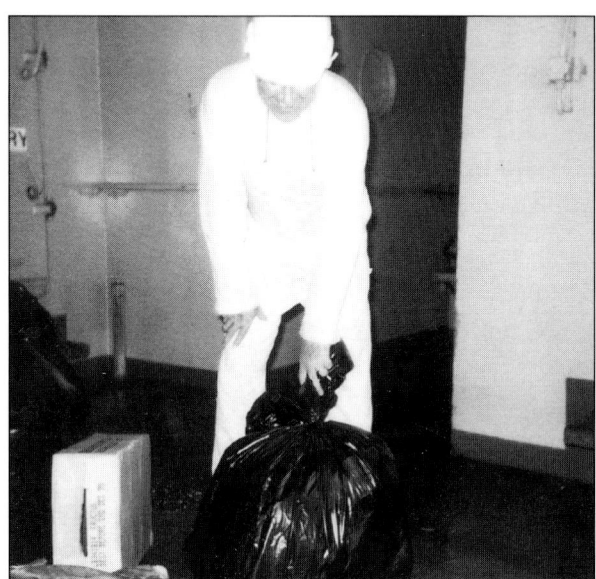

Figure 54.2
The same amount of waste as in figure 54.1, with the paper/plastic
and cardboard inside properly shredded and compacted

Chapter 55

BALLAST WATER ENVIRONMENTAL AND SAFETY ISSUES

Compiled by The Nautical Institute's Papers and Technical Committee
via Mr. D.J. Patraiko BSc MBA MNI, Project Manager for The Nautical Institute

David J. Patraiko graduated from the Massachusetts Maritime Academy (US) and sailed on a variety of international vessels in his twelve years in the Merchant Navy. He holds a Unlimited Master Mariner's licence and was awarded an MBA degree from Henley Management College (UK). After a brief period as an independent consultant

What's it all about?

Nobody likes to carry ballast, because nobody gets paid for it. Unfortunately, with today's trade patterns, carrying water for ballast is a way of life. To many, the practice of loading ballast water in one port and discharging it in another seems innocuous enough especially for those in the petroleum and chemical trades. However, as world trade has increased in volume and very large and ultra large bulk carriers (liquid and dry) transport millions of tons of water from one ecosystem to another around the world, adverse ecological effects are causing severe environmental and financial damage.

The root of the problem lies in the unfortunate coincidence that the environment in the port of loading quite often has the same characteristics, such as temperature and salinity, as that of the discharge port. This allows micro-organisms living in the ballast water to re-establish themselves in the discharge port. To combat this problem, national governments most affected by the import of ballast water have started to require ships to replace coastal ballast water with ocean ballast water, while at sea. The theory behind this is that any residual micro-organisms from brackish water will be killed off by the high salinity of sea water, and that any micro organisms loaded with the sea water will not survive when discharged back into brackish water.

This all sounds simple enough, but these procedures do impact on ship operations and can have fatal consequences to safety at sea. To begin with, the sheer exercise of swapping out ballast water (often in excess of 100,000 tones) consumes resources such as personnel, time and fuel oil and can double the wear and tear of associated equipment. Of primary importance though, are the effects the transfer can have on vessel safety. The vast majority of ships today, which are being required to exchange ballast at sea, were never designed for such operations. Using the flow through method of ballast exchange, a process by which ballast tanks are overfilled by pumping in additional water to dilute the original water, vessels are at risk of over or under pressurising tanks and causing a safety risk to the crew from large quantities of water on deck. Using the sequential method in which

ballast tanks are pumped out and then refilled with water, risks include poor stability, exceeded sheer, stress and bending forces and structural damage due to sloshing.

This situation is further exacerbated by there being no coordinating international regulations, thus leaving national administrations to set their own (often conflicting) requirements.

At the time of writing, Spring 1999, IMO have only been able to publish guidelines as a resolution (voluntary) and the industry is heatedly debating just about every aspect of the issue, from whether it should be an issue at all to highly complex alternatives to eliminating the offending micro-organisms.

It is a safe bet, however, that the issue of ballast water management will effect all ship masters on international voyages to some extent. An understanding of the potential dangers to his ship, and his planet's environment are therefore worthwhile.

Environmental issues

On the 27th of November 1997, the IMO adopted assembly resolution A.868(20) entitled 'Guidelines for the control and management of ships' ballast water to minimise the transfer of harmful aquatic organisms and pathogens'. But what exactly are these 'harmful aquatic organisms and pathogens' and how harmful can they be?

They are organisms that have moved beyond their natural geographical range of habitat. They represent all phyla, from micro-organisms to various plants and animals, both terrestrial and aquatic. Invasion of non-indigenous aquatic species, according to the 1995 National (US) Research Council's study "Understanding Marine Biodiversity: A Research Agenda for the Nation" is "one of the five most critical environmental issues facing the ocean's marine life".

What are the impacts of foreign introduction?

The impacts of introducing non-indigenous species can be divided into two areas: ecological and economic. These categories, however, are interdependent; an exotic species which has an ecological impact also has an economic one and vice versa. It is important to note that there are many species introduced each day which do not survive in their new environment and cause no damage whatsoever. But exotic species have the potential to cause far reaching economic and ecological impacts.

Ecological impacts

Every introduction of exotic species that become established results in changes to the receiving ecosystem. Unfortunately, most of the observed effects have been detrimental and irreparable by displacing native species and altering trophic level structure. Introduced species often prey on many parts of an already established food web or compete with indigenous species for resources such as food or space. Without any natural predators, invaders can threaten or even eliminate indigenous species. They also carry with them the threat of new diseases which can destroy vulnerable native inhabitants. In some areas, native species are on the brink of extinction due to the introduction of an exotic species.

Economic impacts

Introduced non-native species may cause widespread destruction by rapidly taking over an area and eliminating economically profitable native species. This can result in enormous spending by state and federal agencies as they attempt to eradicate pests and restore natural species. A study published by the US Congress, Office of Technology Assessment, *Harmful Non-Indigenous Species in the United States*, finds that the US alone spends hundreds of millions to perhaps billions of dollars trying to repair the damage of harmful exotic species. Numerous other economic sectors may be negatively affected, including agriculture, forestry, fisheries and water use, utilities, and natural areas. Exotic species may cause economic damage by (1) hybridizing with valuable species and producing worthless crossbreeds, (2) carrying or supporting harmful pests and (3) possibly reducing recreational prospects in an area. Another part of economic impact is one which has social and health consequences as well.

Not only may exotic species import diseases that affect related species, but humans as well. Often cures are costly. The threat of non-indigenous species is their unpredictability. They may be poisonous, serve as vectors for human disease, or create conditions for disease to spread. Invading species may also breed with native species, resulting in dangerous or poisonous hybrids, which humans may unknowingly consume. Again, any cures and preventions may be expensive and many people might suffer in the meantime.

Ballast water

Ballast tanks can hold millions of gallons of water containing any and all of the aquatic life found at a port; everything from bacteria and algae to worms and fish have been found in ballast water. As ships travel faster and world trade grows, species are better able to survive the journey and the threat of invasive species from ballast water increases. Around 150 million tonnes of ballast water are released in Australian coastal waters each year from international shipping and a further 34 million tonnes from coastal vessels. The US alone receives at least 21 billion gallons of ballast water each year from around the world, leading to problems like that of the well-known zebra mussels.

Eurasian zebra mussels, *Dreissena polymorpha (Pallas)*, were introduced via ballast to the Great Lakes in the mid 1980s. Originally from Europe, they now flourish, to say the least. 700,000 zebra mussels may occupy only one cubic yard. Able to thrive, the mussels spread throughout the Lakes, as well as the Mississippi and Hudson Rivers. The mussels have had a number of negative effects: because they rapidly reproduce, they have clogged up water and drain pipes at municipal water supplies and at industries. They are expected to cost the US $5 billion in control efforts and reparation. They have displaced native fresh water mussels of the area, and drastically altered the food web. The zebra mussel population continues to grow and no immediate end is foreseen.

Another example of an exotic species which has invaded an area after introduction via ballast water is the American comb jelly, *Mnemiopsus leidyi*. A comb jelly is a small, marine invertebrate superficially resembling a jellyfish. It is carnivorous, and preys on tiny aquatic animals, such as plankton. Transported in ballast possibly from New England, the American comb jelly invaded the Black and Azov Seas in Europe. The rapidly expanding population preyed so heavily on plankton that its biomass declined by as much as 90 per cent. Anchovies, which feed on plankton, sharply declined as well, causing local fisheries to suffer.

In Australia, Tasmanian authorities have been forced to implement expensive monitoring controls, and to close down shellfish harvesting in the Huon River several times in recent years due to the presence of toxic species of algae, known as dinoflagellates, in south-eastern Tasmanian waters. The dinoflagellates in question are taken into ships when ballast water is loaded and settle in a dormant stage in ballast tank sediment. When released with ballast on arrival in Australia the organisms settle on the sea floor until conditions are suitable for them to hatch; they then enter the water table and become part of the shellfish feeding cycle. They produce toxins which can then cause paralysis and sometimes death in humans who eat affected shellfish.

Ballast tanks are filled and emptied off the coastline, in estuaries and bays where fresh water and salt water meet. Thus species picked up during a filling are able to survive when emptied back into conditions similar to their native community. If, instead, ballast was emptied in the ocean and filled with marine water, species would be much less likely to survive in the foreign location.

Ballast regulation

In light of these problems, many governments are worried and concerned about the import of ballast water to their ports. Some governments and regional states have therefore issued restrictions for the discharge of ballast water under their jurisdiction. The countries most concerned have promulgated advice to ships for ballast management, together with a request for their cooperation in applying the techniques voluntarily. Standard procedures have been developed that will be accepted by quarantine authorities as achieving the level of acceptability desired by the port state.

At the time of writing (1999) these countries included Australia, Canada, Chile, Israel, New Zealand, USA and the regions of Buenos Aires in Argentina, the Orkney Islands in the United Kingdom, and Vancouver, Canada.

Unless applied carefully some of the measures being urged for ballast management can affect a ship's safety, either by creating forces within the hull that are greater than the design parameters, or by compromising the stability of the ship. It is because of concern about this that the IMO became involved in what would otherwise be a purely quarantine matter. It has been recognised by governments and the shipping industry that individual countries' needs should be harmonised with the greater need to ensure the safety of ships, their crews and passengers. While many parties are pressing for ballast discharge to be adopted as an annex (Code for Ballast Water Management) to the International Convention for the Prevention of Pollution from Ships, 1973, as modified by the Protocol of 1978 relating thereto (MARPOL 73/78), at the present time it has only been adopted as a resolution and is therefore voluntary. On the 27th of November 1997, the IMO adopted assembly resolution A.868(20) entitled 'Guidelines for the control and management of ships' ballast water to minimize the transfer of harmful aquatic organisms and pathogens'.

With this resolution IMO recommends that each ship should be provided with a Ballast Water Management Plan, detailing the way that the ship can comply with any measures demanded by a port state. Once it has been established that the management of ballast is necessary to meet the quarantine requirements of a port state, preparation for it should be treated with the same seriousness as preparation of a cargo plan. All concerned with the operation and safe passage of the ship can thereby be assured that they are both protecting the marine environment and ensuring the safety of the ship and crew.

In the introduction of Resolution A.868(20), it states that the potential for ballast water discharge to cause harm has been recognised not only by the IMO but also by the World Health Organization (WHO). The guidelines are not to be regarded as a certain solution to the problem. Rather, each part of them should be viewed as a tool which, if correctly applied, will help to minimise the risks associated with ballast water discharge.

The IMO guidelines cover issues of training and education, procedures for ships and port states, recording and reporting procedures, ships' operational procedures, port state considerations, enforcement and monitoring by port states, future considerations in relation to ballast water exchange and finally ballast system design. The guidelines come with annexes for a ballast water reporting form and guidelines on safety aspects of ballast water exchange at sea. To facilitate vessel compliance to these guidelines the International Chamber of Shipping (ICS) in cooperation with Intertanko have published an excellent book entitled *Model Ballast Water Management Plan* which comes complete containing a floppy disk with templates to incorporate into individual ships plans.

Shipboard operations

The voluntary guidelines put forth by the IMO call for all vessels to maintain a ballast management plan including a full and accurate ballast log. The plan will ensure procedures have been established taking into account all safety aspects and considerations for that particular ship. The log will demonstrate at the arrival port that the correct measures have been completed. Even if a ship is not trading in an area where ballast water information is required, it may later prove worthwhile to have a history of what water has been carried.

Water treatment methods

At the moment, although various methods of ballast water treatment are being examined, including dilution, heat treatment, exposure to ultra-violet light, filtering and chemical treatment, none as yet (with rare exceptions) seems to be practical or cost effective for general use by cargo ships and tankers. This leaves the only approved methods being retention on board (i.e. passenger ships and car carriers) or exchange at sea. The two methods of carrying out ballast water exchange at sea have been identified as the sequential method, in which ballast tanks are pumped out and refilled with sea water; and/or the flow-through method, in which ballast tanks are simultaneously filled and discharged by pumping in sea water.

When exchanging ballast at sea, guidance on safety aspects of ballast water exchange as mentioned later in this chapter should be taken into account. Furthermore, the IMO recommend the following practices:

- Where practicable, ships should conduct ballast exchange in deep water, in open ocean and as far as possible from shore. Where this is not possible, requirements developed within regional agreements may be in operation, particularly in areas within 200 nautical miles from shore. All the ballast water should be discharged until suction is lost, and stripping pumps or eductors should be used if possible.
- Where the flow through method is employed in open ocean by pumping ballast water into the tank or hold and allowing the water to overflow, at least three times the tank volume should be pumped through the tank;
- Where neither form of open ocean exchange is practicable, ballast exchange may be accepted by the port State in designated areas;
- Other ballast exchange options approved by the port state.

Safety precautions

Ships engaged in ballast water exchange at sea should be provided with procedures which account for the following, as applicable:

- Avoidance of over and under-pressurisation of ballast tanks.
- Free surface effects on stability and sloshing loads in tanks that may be slack at any one time.
- Admissible weather conditions.
- Weather routing in areas seasonally affected by cyclones, typhoons, hurricanes or heavy icing conditions.
- Maintenance of adequate intact stability in accordance with an approved trim and stability booklet.
- Permissible seagoing strength limits of shear forces and bending moments in accordance with an approved loading manual.
- Torsional forces, where relevant.
- Minimum/maximum forward and aft draughts.
- Wave-induced hull vibration.
- Documented records of ballasting and/or de-ballasting.
- Contingency procedures for situations which may affect the ballast water exchange at sea, including deteriorating weather conditions, pump failure, loss of power, etc.
- Time to complete the ballast water exchange or an appropriate sequence thereof, taking into account that the ballast water may represent 50 % of the total cargo capacity for some ships. and
- Monitoring and controlling the amount of ballast water.

If the flow through method is used, caution should be exercised, since:

- Air pipes are not designed for continuous ballast water overflow.
- Current research indicates that pumping of at least three full volumes of the tank capacity could be needed to be effective when filling clean water from the bottom and overflowing from the top, and
- Certain watertight and weathertight closures (e.g. manholes) which may be opened during ballast exchange, should be re-secured.

Ballast water exchange at sea should be avoided in freezing weather conditions. However, when it is deemed absolutely necessary, particular attention should be paid to the hazards associated with the freezing of overboard discharge arrangements, air pipes, ballast system valves together with their means of control, and the accretion of ice on deck.

Some ships may need the fitting of a loading instrument to perform calculations of shear forces and bending moments induced by ballast water exchange at sea and to compare with the permissible strength limits.

An evaluation should be made of the safety margins for stability and strength contained in allowable seagoing conditions specified in the approved trim and stability booklet and the loading manual, relevant to individual types of ships and loading conditions. In this regard particular account should be taken of the following requirements:

- Stability to be maintained at all times to values not less than those recommended by the organisation (or required by the administration).
- Longitudinal stress values not to exceed those permitted by the ship's classification society with regard to prevailing sea conditions. and
- Exchange of ballast in tanks or holds where significant structural loads may be generated by sloshing action in the partially filled tank or hold to be carried out in favourable sea and swell conditions so that the risk of structural damage is minimised.

The ballast water management plan should include a list of circumstances in which ballast water exchange should not be undertaken. These circumstances may result from critical situations of an exceptional nature, "force majeure" due to stress of weather, or any other circumstances in which human life or safety of the ship is threatened.

Duties of appointed ballast water management officer

According to the IMO recommendations, the ballast water management plan should include the nomination of key shipboard control personnel undertaking ballast water exchange at sea. Their duties will be established as part of the ship's operational procedures. Duties of the appointed officer in charge of ballast water management include:

- Ensure that the ballast water treatment or exchange follows procedures in the ballast water management plan.
- Inform the owner or operator by an agreed procedure when commencing ballast water exchange and when it is completed.
- Prepare the ballast water declaration form prior to arrival in port.
- Be available to assist the port state control or quarantine officers for any sampling that may need to be undertaken.
- Maintain the ballast water handling log.
- Other duties specified by the company.

Conclusion

This chapter has sought to outline some of the environmental problems caused by transferring harmful aquatic organisms and pathogens by ballast water, international and national regulations to minimise their effects and safety issues involved in vessel compliance to these regulations. It is not intended to be a guide to creating a ballast management plan. The ICS/Intertanko guide and IMO Res. A.868(20) are highly recommended for this purpose.

Most ships were never designed to exchange ballast at sea. Risks to the safety of the ship, her crew and ultimately the environment need to be carefully examined and planned for. The forces inherent in exchanging ballast at sea are very different from the same operation in port. The vessels motion in a seaway, even a gentle swell, can cause severe damage to internal structures due to sloshing effect and dynamic loads at sea can exceed permissible strength limits for shear force and bending moments.

Conditions which would make ballast water exchange at sea unsafe should be identified. Heavy weather is the most obvious, but there may be others, including crew availability and personal safety. The ICS recommends that a list be produced of circumstances under which ballast water exchange at sea should not be undertaken. This may include

specifying the sea state, whether the barometric pressure is rising or falling, the wind speed and other such criteria. Such information may prove to be the master's best defence if called upon to explain why he decided not to exchange ballast en route.

Nobody is sure what form of regulations will govern the discharge of ballast water in the future, but there is plenty of evidence that transferring certain aquatic organisms and pathogens can be extremely detrimental and is therefore taken seriously by national governments. Prudent ship operators should act to implement a ballast water management plan that protects their vessel, their business, the environment and is in accordance with port states in which they operate.

References

- The International Maritime Organization (IMO), 4 Albert Embankment, London, SE1 7SR, UK, Tel +44 171 7611, E-mail: info@imo.org, Web Site: www.imo.org. The IMO can provide up to date information on the state of international regulations covering ballast water. They also list, on their web site, links to other organisations involved with ballast water issues.
- International Chamber of Shipping (ICS)/ Intertanko publication '*Model Ballast Water Management Plan*', Contact: Marisec Publications, 12 Carthusian Street, London, EC1M 6EZ, UK, Tel: +44 (0)207 8844, Fax: +44 (0)207 8877.
- The Baltic and International Maritime Council (BIMCO) claim to keep up-to-date information on port state requirements on their web site (www.bimco.dk), but access is for members only.
- Aquatic Nuisance Species Task Force (ANSTF) web site: www.anstaskforce.gov.
- Massachusetts Institute of Technology Sea Grant College Web site: (http://massbay.mit.edu/exoticspecies/index.html).
- The Australian Quarantine and Inspection Service (AQIS) Web site (www.aqis.gov.au/docs/ballast/bpamphlet.htm).

Chapter 56

OIL POLLUTION PREVENTION AND EMERGENCY RESPONSE – THE SHIPMASTER'S RESPONSIBILITIES

by Captain C.J. Shill MNI, Chevron Shipping Company

Christopher Shill began his career as a deck cadet with Port Line in 1970. He also worked for Beta Maritime and Sanko Line before joining Chevron Shipping Co. LLC (CSC) as a chief officer in 1991. He came shoreside in April of 1997 to serve as technical expert for the Marine Manuals Update Project. This labour intensive project brought CSC's operation manuals into compliance with the ISM Code. He simultaneously served as demurrage analyst and upon completion of the manuals assignment worked as a voyage manager arranging voyage orders, communicating with agents, arranging bunkers and assisting with the safe and effective management of the CSC VLCC fleet.

Promoted to master in March of 1998, Chris Shill assumed command of a 35,000 tonne product carrier in May of that same year. Captain Shill is also the recipient of the 1997 Luddeke Prize for the Nautical Institute's Command Diploma Scheme.

Introduction

OIL POLLUTION PREVENTION and emergency response are but two of the ship master's responsibilities. These responsibilities encompass ensuring the safety of the vessel, preventing human injury or loss of life and avoiding damage to property and the environment.

To aid the shipmaster in the discharge of his responsibilities, the introduction of the International Safety Management (ISM) Code came into effect in July 1998 for oil tankers. Additionally, in compliance with the requirements of MARPOL 73/78 and the International Maritime Organisation (IMO) Resolution MEPC 54 (32), every oil tanker of 150 gross tons and above and every ship of 400 gross tons and above carries on board a Shipboard Oil Pollution Emergency Plan (SOPEP). The plan aids the shipmaster in responding to an oil spill or threat of oil spill, and in setting into motion the necessary actions to minimise or stop the discharge and mitigate its effects.

In addition to the SOPEP, tankers trading or intending to trade to the United States must carry a U.S. Coast Guard (USCG)-approved vessel response plan (VRP). This also applies to vessels conducting bulk cargo oil lightering operations within the exclusive economic zone of the U.S.

To assist Masters in the proper discharge of their responsibilities with regard to maritime safety and the protection of the marine environment, Chevron Shipping Company LLC (Chevron) complies with the requirements of the ISM Code by having a documented Operational Procedures System (OPS). The OPS contains interlocking procedures used to manage operations affecting safety and environmental performance. The Chevron VRP, in order to comply with the requirements of MARPOL and the USCG, incorporates the SOPEP into its VRP, making it an integral part of the OPS.

Purpose of the plan

The need for a predetermined and properly structured plan becomes clear when one considers the pressures and multiple tasks facing personnel when confronted with an emergency situation. In a time of crisis lack of planning often results in confusion, errors and failures to communicate. This can result in delays and a worsening situation. This in turn may result in the vessel and its personnel being exposed to increasing hazards or causing greater environmental damage.

For the purpose of the VRP, an 'oil spill' is an actual or probable discharge of oil. The body of the plan contains all information and operational instructions required by the SOPEP preparation guidelines. The appendices contain names, telephone numbers, telex numbers, etc., of all contacts referenced in the plan as well as other reference material. The plan includes:

- The reporting procedures to be followed by the master or other persons having charge of the ship at the time of an oil pollution incident.
- A detailed description of the actions to be taken immediately by persons on board to control and/or reduce the discharge of oil following the incident.
- The list of authorities or persons to be contacted in the event of an oil pollution incident.
- The procedures and shipboard point of contact for coordinating action with national and local authorities in combating oil pollution.

The master's role and responsibilities

The master is responsible for immediate notification and implementation of oil spill containment and clean-up activities.

Safety, the most important consideration when planning and conducting vessel operations, is never sacrificed for speed or economy.

Duty to report

The master involved in an incident reports the particulars of such incident to the fullest extent possible and without delay. This requirement is specified in accordance with MARPOL, Protocol 1, Provisions Concerning Reports on Incidents Involving Harmful Substances. Notifications are to be made:

- Whenever there is an actual discharge of oil resulting from damage to the ship or its equipment.
- For the purpose of securing the safety of the ship or saving life at sea.
- When there is an actual discharge of oil during the operation of the ship in excess of the quantity or instantaneous rate permitted under the present MARPOL convention.
- When there is a probability of a discharge of oil.

While it is impracticable to provide precise definitions of all types of situations involving an oil discharge, the general guidelines for making a report include cases of:

- Damage, mechanical failure or breakdown which affects the safety of the ship such as collision, grounding, fire, explosion, structural failure, flooding, or cargo shifting.
- Failure or breakdown of machinery or equipment which results in impairment of the safety of navigation such as failure or breakdown of steering gear, the propulsion system, the electrical generating system or other essential shipboard navigational aids.

Within Chevron, the responsibility for ensuring that these notifications are made is divided between the master and the Qualified Individual (QI). The QI is an English-speaking, shore-based Chevron representative who is familiar with implementation of Chevron's vessel response plan, is trained in their responsibilities under the plan and is available on a 24-hour basis.

The table below shows the notification sequence in the event of a spill.

Notification process

Any shipboard employee who witnesses an oil spill reports the spill to the watch officer or the master. The master then makes notifications as required by the SOPEP and coordinates shipboard activities with national and local authorities in combating an oil spill. The QI ensures that the master's notifications have been made and makes his or her own notifications as required by the SOPEP. These notifications include notifying vessel charterers, the cargo owner and company personnel and, within Chevron, activating the Oil Spill Response Organisation.

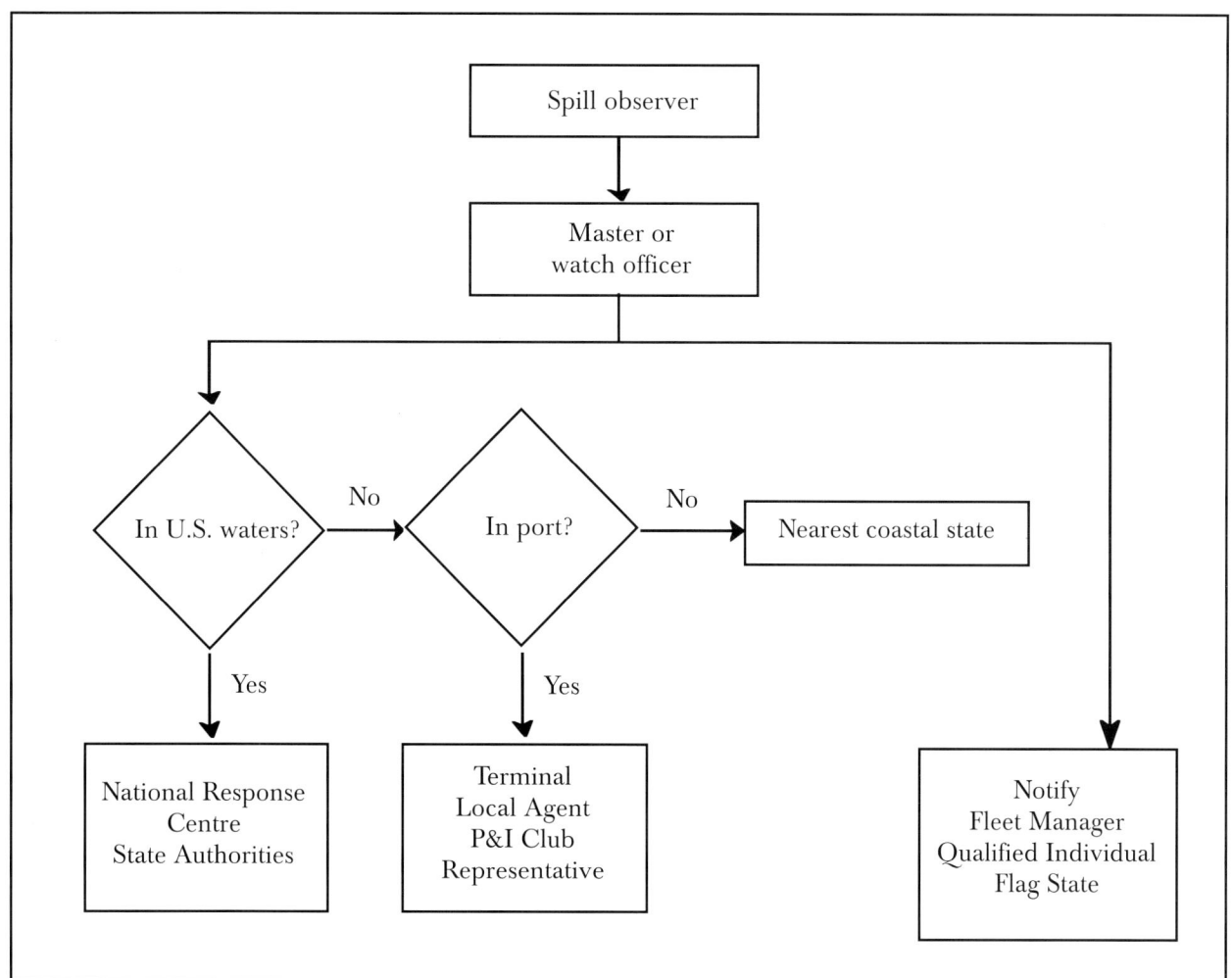

Figure 56.1 Notification sequence in the event of a spill

If the vessel is in port, the terminal and the local agent must be notified. From these two entities, the vessel requests the initiation of immediate containment and cleanup response using any available local equipment. The master, or designated person, notifies the fleet manager and the QI, provides details of the incident, describes the actions taken and the notifications made, identifies notifications yet to be made and requests the QI's assistance, as needed, in mobilising resources and making any additional notifications.

If the vessel is in U.S. waters, the National Response Centre and the state authority are notified. Additionally, a P&I Club representative is notified, provided with details of the incident and a request for assistance, if necessary, is made.

If the vessel is in open water, the master notifies the fleet manager and QI as above. The master also notifies the nearest coastal state, following the guidelines of IMO Resolution A 648 (16), General Principles for Ship Reporting Systems and Ship Reporting Requirements, using the report format defined in the SOPEP manual.

If in U.S. waters, the National Response Centre and the state authority is notified.

Methods of notification

In the event of an incident the master must report by radio whenever possible but in any case by the fastest channels available at the time the report is made. The primary notification method should be voice communication using the vessel's cellular phone, SATCOM, VHF and HF radios, or landline if available. The secondary notification method is by urgent telex, fax or electronic mail. Within Chevron, the telecommunications centre provides 24-hour routing of all vessel communications classified as "URGENT". Urgent communications are relayed by the telecommunications centre to the office-based manager's home fax machine and phone on weeknights, and to the weekend duty manager's home fax machine and phone on weekends and holidays. This ensures that a responsible person within the company is alerted as quickly as possible.

Reporting to flag state and local authorities

The master must ensure that all government-required reports are submitted, including those required by the country in whose waters an incident occurs. The master must also report to the country under whose flag the vessel is registered. With the help of the vessel agent, the master determines which local government agency has jurisdiction over oil pollution and what reports this agency requires. The format for notifying government authorities is stipulated by the IMO under Resolution A648 (16) and is required as an appendix to all SOPEP manuals. This appendix also includes the list of agencies or officials responsible for receiving and processing reports.

Advisory communications

Some countries require a radio advisory when a vessel near their coasts suffer casualties that impair the vessel's operating capabilities. By "advisory" it is meant that the communication is only to advise and alert government agencies of the possibility of a request for assistance.

It is possible that a vessel could suffer a casualty or an equipment failure such that it is not in any immediate danger or distress, but that the possibility still exists. The master should always err on the side of safety and immediately advise local authorities of the possibility of an oil spill; even if it is only a slight one.

Additional reporting and record keeping requirements

It is the responsibility of the master to ensure that an accurate written record is kept of events related to any spill, substantial threat of a spill or incident. Whenever possible, the record should include photographs or video footage. Only facts should be logged and speculation should be avoided. The written record includes at least, but is not limited to, the following:

- A description of the incident, including time and location.
- Actions taken by vessel personnel to respond to the spill or incident.
- If applicable, assistance received and the body or organisation that provided assistance.
- Transfer of authority from the master to the shoreside incident commander.
- Completed required notifications.

The master must also provide a written report of the incident. This report covers all aspects of the incident and should be supplemented by photographs and/or video evidence, whenever possible. This report should include at least the following:

- Note of protest.
- Statement of master, officers involved and any other vessel or terminal witnesses.
- Abstract of applicable logs – deck and/or engine.
- Copies of letters of responsibility served against or by the vessel.
- Copies of claims filed against the vessel.
- Copies of all reports made to local governments.
- Sketches or photographs, if available.
- Estimates of costs incurred by ship and/or shore.
- Survey reports.
- Reports to P&I Club.

In the event of an oil spill, the insurer will require a detailed account of how the incident occurred, what steps were taken to prevent it and what efforts were made to minimise damage. Such an account should be supported by the following items of evidence:

- A record of the quantity of the pollutant.
- The vessel's Oil Record Book.
- Video images of the extent of the spill, if possible.
- All relevant e-mail, telexes and other correspondence.
- Samples of the spilled oil, of any oil collected near the vessel and of on-board fuel and cargo.
- Accounts of the incident from all crew members involved.
- Evidence of previous oil pollution in berth or port area.
- The procedures followed during transfer of cargo or bunkers within the vessel.
- Rates and ullages, soundings of loading and/or discharging operations at the time of the spill.
- A copy of the terminal's cargo or bunker instructions concerning an acceptable loading rate.
- The name of the crew member in charge of transfer operations.
- Times and results of inspections of equipment used in cargo and bunkering operations.
- Instructions from the owner and/or the charterer.
- Methods of effecting emergency stops.
- Procedures governing use of equipment such as scupper plugs and drip trays.
- Broken parts of any on-board equipment whose failure contributed to the spill.

Evaluating the situation and prioritising responses

Should an incident occur, it is the responsibility of the master to prioritise required actions. The safety of shipboard personnel is always the first priority. The second priority is the stabilisation of the vessel in order to limit damages, with the ultimate goal being to prevent the loss of the vessel. The third priority is the summoning of firefighting, damage control, towing and spill response assistance from sources other than the vessel.

Incident Commander

The master serves as initial incident commander until being relieved by a shore-based incident commander. The incident commander is the responsible party's person in charge of the incident. It is imperative that the master, or other designated person, be clearly identified as the official and only point of contact on board for all matters related to the response and to the reported incident. These responsibilities include:

- Ensuring that personnel safety is accorded the highest priority in response operations.
- Ensuring the spill is contained, cleaned up and disposed of efficiently.
- Supervising the cleanup of spills confined to the vessels deck.
- Keeping shore-based management informed of all pertinent facts and the progress of the cleanup operation.

The master may delegate a responsible person as the only person of contact to deal specifically with communications.

After an oil spill, shipboard personnel take initial steps to stop the source; they notify Chevron, all applicable government agencies and monitor the oil spill. The shore-based personnel are responsible for handling the bulk of the response operations, including the development of strategic objectives that provide overall direction for the conduct of the safe and efficient control, containment, recovery and cleanup. The master informs the designated shore-based incident commander of the current spill status and response steps taken. The shore-based incident commander then assumes responsibility for subsequent actions, informing the full spill management team of incident status and response steps.

Responses

While it is also impracticable to provide the precise sequence of all types of responses for all spills, the following are general guidelines.

General initial response for all spills

1 Sound the general alarm and warn appropriate shore personnel of possible danger.
2 If applicable, stop oil transfer operations.
3 Secure any ignition sources and deploy firefighting equipment.
4 Ensure the safety and stability of the vessel.
5 Test the atmosphere for hydrocarbons and toxins.
6 Instruct crew to don appropriate personal protective equipment (PPE) before cleanup operations begin.
7 If possible, confine spilled material to vessel.
8 Commence cleanup operations.
9 Establish type and amount of oil spilled and estimate its potential impact on the surrounding area.

Internal cargo transfer in an emergency

In an emergency it may be necessary to transfer cargo internally, from a damaged tank to an undamaged one. If the vessel has power and its piping systems are intact, transfer cargo in the usual manner. If the vessel has no power and piping systems are not intact, use portable, submersible pumps, power packs, hoses and fittings to transfer cargo.

Ship-to-ship transfer in an emergency

Emergency lightering operations should be planned and conducted in accordance with the Oil Companies International Marine Forum (OCIMF) Ship to Ship Transfer Guide and the International Safety Guide for Oil Tankers and Terminals (ISGOTT). These two widely accepted publications detail industry standards in the area of ship-to-ship oil transfer operations. It should be recognised that, due to the emergency nature of the situation, actions taken may require deviations from these standards and guidelines.

Damage, stability and hull stress calculations

If the vessel is damaged or aground normal stress calculations may not apply. All relevant stability and hull stress parameters will need to be assessed prior to starting any movements of cargo or bunkers.

If necessary, additional damage stability and residual strength information can be obtained from the home office. This information provides the master with guidelines to plan the appropriate response.

Emergency towing

Under normal circumstances and time permitting, the home office or local agent, at the master's request, arranges towing services. If in the master's judgement the vessel is in danger, the master must immediately request assistance from any available source. Under these circumstances the preferred contract for services is Lloyd's Open Form. If the tug or vessel offering assistance declines Lloyd's Open Form, in order to ensure the safety of the ship, the master should accept whatever arrangement is insisted upon, under protest, record the fact and report the terms of the arrangement to the fleet manager as soon as possible.

Sampling

Safety permitting, any spilled oil should be sampled. Any oil observed on the water while the vessel is at anchor or at berth should be sampled if possible. Samples should be made in duplicate, properly marked with date and location and sealed. Samples will be most valuable if the sampling is authenticated by someone who is not part of the vessel's crew (e.g., a cargo surveyor, U.S. Coast Guard, Harbourmaster, or Terminal Representative).

Post incident drug and alcohol testing

It is important to carry out post incident drug and alcohol testing as soon as practicable after an incident. However, the master should never allow testing to interfere with critical operations generated by the incident. Actions such as stabilising the vessel, containing the spill, tending to injured personnel, firefighting, etc., must always take priority over regulatory-required testing.

The master or senior officer on board must determine who is to be tested. Tests should only be requested from those persons whose actions or decisions could have contributed to the incident. In most cases this means the officer in charge of the operation that led to the incident and those directly involved in the incident and watch-standers will have to be tested. Wherever possible advice should be sought from the home office.

Casualty procedures checklist

Due to the pressures and multiple tasks facing the master following an incident, a checklist will aid in carrying out duties and responsibilities.

Steering gear failure

When a steering gear failure occurs the master should consider the following actions:

- Switching to backup or manual emergency steering systems.
- Slowing the vessel to a safe minimum speed or stopping if necessary.
- Making the anchors ready for immediate use. The anchors should be made ready for use at the earliest opportunity. Deteriorating conditions may prevent or delay this action from being taken at a later time. In water too deep for an anchor to reach bottom lowering the anchor or anchors to about four shackles (60 fathoms) may help to reduce downwind drift. The anchor and cable may act as a drogue and may help to keep the ship's head into the weather. Recovering four shackles of cable and the anchor is within the design capabilities of most windlasses

Main propulsion failure

When a main propulsion failure occurs the master should consider the following actions:

- Steering the vessel away from any hazards.
- Establishing the vessel's position and determining set and drift.
- Making the anchors ready for deployment.
- Showing lights or day shapes for vessel not under command.
- Making ready for tug assistance if appropriate.

Making ready for tug assistance

Chevron vessels are fitted with emergency towing systems that meet the applicable regulatory requirements. Each vessel has a vessel-specific emergency towing arrangement instruction manual on board that includes a deck arrangement plan and describes the components, general safety instructions, deployment procedure and maintenance of the system. The prevailing weather and sea conditions, the nature and extent of vessel damage or distress, the type of towing arrangement on board the distressed vessel and the capabilities of the towing vessel determine whether the vessel is to be towed from the bow or the stern. Radio communications between the distressed vessel and the assisting vessel are established and maintained throughout the entire planning and execution of the towing operation. Once a plan has been agreed to and understood by both vessel crews, neither master takes any action in regard to navigation or engine manoeuvres without first informing the other master.

Collision or grounding

Following a collision or grounding, the master has to assess the situation to determine if prompt re-floating of the vessel is appropriate to reduce hull stress and decrease the chance that oil will leak from a ruptured tank. Re-floating may be inadvisable, however, due to the risk of further damage. To make this determination, the master should evaluate some of the following:

- Tides and currents.
- Weather (including wind, state of sea and swell) and any forecast changes.
- Characteristics of the bottom.
- Water depth around the ship, the calculated buoyancy needed to re-float and the draught and trim after re-floating.
- Hull stress status.

Explosion and fire

When explosion or fire occurs, the master should consider the following actions:

- Stopping all transfer operations.
- Fighting the fire with most effective means.
- Isolating the casualty area from cargo or bunkers by closing deck and tank valves.

Excessive list

Any list that is unplanned or greater than planned should be considered excessive. The master should consider the following actions:

- Stopping transfer operations.
- Checking all soundings/ullages in tanks.
- Determining the cause of the list.
- Checking hull stability and stress conditions.
- Correcting the list by transfer of cargo, bunkers or ballast.

Hull leakage

In the event of hull leakage the master should consider the following:

- Stopping all cargo transfer operations until the source is identified.

- Confirming that the leak is not from another source such as the stern tube or engine room overboard valves.
- Arranging for an underwater inspection as soon as possible. If the leak is identified a temporary underwater repair may be possible.
- Gauging tanks to check for previously unidentified cargo loss.
- Transferring cargo or bunkers out of the leaking tank.
- Once cargo level has reduced or the tank been emptied consider establishing a water bottom.

Summary

One of the most important tools that a master can have is a detailed response plan along with a thorough knowledge of that plan. This knowledge includes:

- The results of marine environmental pollution.
- The impact of oil on the marine environment.
- The penalties for spilling oil.
- The importance of preventing spills.
- The prevention of marine environmental pollution.
- The correct waste disposal procedures.
- On board crew response to incidents of marine pollution.
- Contingency plans for responding to an incident.
- Notification procedures in the event of a spill.

The master should ensure that, in the event of an incident, personnel are equipped with the organisational and technical skills required for efficient and effective rapid incident response.

Chapter 57

WEATHER ROUTEING AND VOYAGE PLANNING

by Captain F. Baillod FNI

Captain Baillod started his seagoing career in 1963. After an early time with Scandinavian companies he joined Suisse Atlantique where he was promoted master in 1980. Captain Baillod is still serving as master and regularly contributes to industry forums. He is a member of The Nautical Institute Bulk Carrier Working Group and a Fellow and Council Member.

Introduction

THE TWO ASPECTS OF WEATHER ROUTEING are safety and economy. The two are somewhat linked but do not necessarily come together. As an example, a short route in heavy following seas may appear attractive, but in case of engine breakdown or loss of steering control the vessel may come dangerously within the troughs, particularly if the GM is high and the cargo liable to shift. Generally speaking, however, it may be fair to say that a safe route is also an economic route, provided that the choice is reasonable. The prime factor for the success of weather routeing is the quality of the forecasts which, despite the improvement achieved in the past years, is still subject to many limitations. The accuracy of the storm tracks (particularly their latitude in cross-ocean passages) is an essential feature of the forecast data accuracy requirement, as it often plays an important part in the selection of a particular route.

Later in this chapter the steering principles will be described. Surface and contour charts are now available and their accuracy is sufficient to give the mariner a good assessment of the weather ahead. This can be accepted with confidence, provided the mariner understands the weather pattern by comparison with surface analysis, shorter term forecast and contour charts. This applies similarly to weather routeing computer data evaluation which may be available on board. The quality of the forecast is, naturally, inversely proportional to the extent of the forecast. A continuous update is necessary, therefore and the latest information has always to be preferred. The simulation ahead, of weather development with the help of computer data and software should include information to the user as to its value, i.e. the age and quality of the data upon which the forecast is computed. The clarity and conciseness that such tools afford should not deceive the user into a sense of false security or over-reliance.

Value of ship's reports

With the advent of increasing work loads affecting navigating officers, ship's weather observation reports are becoming more scarce. It is also a general belief that ship's reports are not needed any more. This is not really true. Present technology has greatly improved, but on-the-scene reports are still needed. For the common benefit, masters of ships not engaged in a weather observation program should report unusual weather occurrences for which there are no warnings being issued, whether compelled to do so by law or not. Significant weather patterns for which no warnings issued are still common nowadays, even in well covered areas such as the North Pacific. I have on several occasions reported sustained severe gale force winds for which no warnings were given. At the time of writing, certain areas such as the South East Pacific, South East Atlantic and Indian Ocean are still being poorly covered by weather charts and meteorological – ice warnings. Government budget cuts are often the cause for such shortcomings.

Weather maps: indication of probability

As an inexact science meteorology, particularly forecasting, is subject to the laws of probability. Some weather systems have a higher probability to develop than others. Their position, track and rate of development are also subject to various interacting physical laws. For example, in a pressure field resembling a saddle between two highs where pressure rises on two sides and falls in the other two directions, sudden storm formations are probable as a strong pressure flow quickly builds up, particularly downstream (in the direction of the upper flow). The degree of probability of storm formation in such areas will depend upon various factors as pressure differential, temperature inversion, velocity of upper stream, etc. It would be very useful to the mariner to be informed of such probabilities. Slower ships, in their routeing choice, tend to take more consideration of climatological statistical data than their faster counterparts. Climatological deviations from the norm, such as the forecasted persistence of a mid latitude blocking high in winter mid ocean, should be emphasised in weather warnings.

Numerous forecasting rules have been devised in the past. The science of marine meteorology has advanced a great deal. Today a 96 hours forecast is nearly as good as a 24 hours forecast was 20 years ago. Such rules are therefore now less actual, as animated satellite pictures linked with visualisation of the upper air stream and close tracking of the weather system offer better forecasting tools. Weather maps picturing past and future movements of relevant systems are available and computer technology is now offering animated ocean weather graphics along various projected routes.

Successful weather routeing can only be achieved by obtaining a regular update of synoptic and forecasting data. Such information can effectively be backed by observation of successive satellite pictures showing the size and following the development, persistence and trends of weather systems once they have been identified by comparison with synoptic charts. In order for the master to judge the value of computers, increasingly being used for weather routeing, it is essential for him to have a good understanding of the weather systems and deduce the reliability and quality of such aids by comparisons with own observations and the study of alternate weather maps.

The analyst communicates to the vessel via facsimile charts or by transmitting data to an on board computer. Important navigational decisions involving the safety of the ship may depend upon such information. Means of warning the mariner of the probability of sudden storm build ups way in advance, indicating its reliability, should be notified under circumstances of low probability. Alternative scenarios and their interactive effects could be proposed to the mariner.

When editing forecast charts or transmitting forecast data to computers, I feel that the degree of probability of a particular weather system to develop and become significant should be evaluated by the analyst. The reliability of the position, forecasted movement, speed and development could be quantified by a code indicating the confidence level of the information given. On weather charts a code or "confidence vector" could be added to indicate the reliability of the information given regarding the development, position, track and speed of a particular system. On a computer screen a particular colour could be used to indicate such information. Alternative scenarios and their probability could be made available in a separate window.

Various notions & weather routeing tips
Observations

When within range of a storm, constant observations can help the master to supplement very valuably the information he is receiving. Such information may quite well offer improved update and accuracy. The following are amongst the points to be considered:

• Obtain close observation of the wind direction and speed and compare them with the direction of isobars on synoptic charts to evaluate the angle of in-draught across isobars. This will help to apply

the Buys Ballot Law to assess the bearing of the storm. Note any shifts or tendencies.
• Observe the organisation and tendency of the storm using successive satellite pictures and compare to actual observations.
• Compare data from various sources (i.e. Japan, Hawaii and San Francisco or Halifax – DDK – NAM).
• Observe the sea and swell and take note of the various wave trains by checking their period and height.

By comparing the data available one can estimate, with reasonable confidence, the distance to the centre or the frontal trough where wind shifts occur. Steep swells with occasional breakers have probably not travelled a long way. They may just have achieved transition from swell to sea, whereas longer swell waves with rounded tops will have travelled a long way.

Close scrutiny of the barograph and the pressure differential rates will do much to assist in the assessment of distance to the storm. At night, observations of the sea are obviously far less effective. Changes of heading and a close watch on the ship's behaviour (rolling and/or pitching motion), noting the position of deck areas most subject to sprays or shipping water, can help. The use of searchlight and the observation of radar clutter may provide additional assistance. With experience, the wind constancy, precipitation, humidity levels and cloud formations will give further hints to the mariner.

Various notions

Some of the following statements are uniquely based upon my own observations and are not formally recognised. They must, therefore, be read with caution. Meteorology being an inexact science, an experienced master will draw up his own rules using his intuition as well as experience to complement data originating from weather maps and computer simulations.

• When passing by a slow or stationary cyclonic system, the wind shifts will more or less follow the Buys Ballot rules (subject to variations of in-draught angle across isobars). The shift of swell direction will, however, generally lag behind by approximately one half quadrant.
• Meeting a developing low eastbound (northern hemisphere). If you are unable to avoid being overtaken towards the south by a north east developing low, attempt to decrease latitude so as to meet it at a younger stage of development and benefit earlier from the west following wind shifts. (In the southern hemisphere read north for south and vice versa).
• Confused swells can create unwanted rolling and pitching motion, becoming very severe in certain areas and conditions. A constant watch with very frequent heading changes may be necessary

especially if the ship, due to the nature of her cargo, draft or stability is vulnerable to sea motion.

- Low powered ships, in general, lose proportionally more speed in moderate to rough seas and swells. At a certain point, the performance in rough seas depends upon the vessel's loaded condition, hull shape, strength and sea keeping qualities rather than power.

- In certain areas, particularly in the wake of a depression and despite experiencing favourable winds, cross swells may very significantly affect the performance and handling of a ship.

- Ships may differ significantly in their behaviour under various loaded conditions. Length, rolling period, block coefficient, freeboard, length to beam ratio, stability, reserve buoyancy and hull shape are amongst the many factors affecting ships, under various sea states. Control of heading and speed is a crucial factor governing the safety and performance of the ship.

- Light draft ships should, by all means possible, avoid areas of heavy swells – weather forecasting is usually less reliable on the west side of oceans where eastward travelling systems developing overland build up intensity and change behaviour as they meet the ocean. Ocean waters usually offer a favourable media for the development of frontal systems in particular. Some depressions, however, find favourable topographic features to develop over land prior to reaching the sea.

- Interacting lows. The weaker low will usually be absorbed by the more vigorous one.

- The merging of two lows may induce a temporary weakening of the system (although regeneration is consequently possible, particularly if there is a bordering steering high ridge). On the other hand, the merging of two highs often causes an intensification of the newly combined anticyclone.

- The advance speed of a young depression is usually proportional to its development rate. A developing low accelerates, whereas a filling low tends to slow down and stall. Older, slower moving systems may also regenerate. They may intensify and develop rapidly when meeting several blocking ridges as this has the effect of stopping their movement and feeding them. Such a slow moving and intensifying system may generate tremendous seas over an extended period within a particular area. Any ship caught in it may suffer very high seas and be unable to move out of it. The movement of such a system, if any, may be rather erratic and very hard to predict. A typical example of such a dangerous condition occurs in the north Pacific around 40°N/150°W, with bordering ridges to the northeast (Alaska High), southeast (California High) and northwest (Polar Ridge from the Bering Sea). It is not uncommon for 15m seas and swell to persist for more than a week.

- Close observation and records of consecutive contour and surface prognosis charts should be used to achieve an insight into the ocean weather pattern. The necessary information can be gathered by:
  - The 500mb Stream Lines.
  - The track, speed, tenacity and intensity of the large anticyclonic masses.
  - The building rate, speed and movement of the developing depressions on the ocean's west sides and their possible presence and development in mid ocean.

General storm tracks are often substantially affected after the passage of a large and intense storm. Consequent depressions may well follow similar tracks.

- The best avoiding action for heavy seas may sometimes be that of waiting for a storm system to pass by, particularly towards the beginning and end of ocean passages. The period of succession between troughs and ridges may hold fairly steady for a certain period. This knowledge should be used when choosing a coastal route prior to commencing the ocean passage, e.g. the Pentland Firth/English Channel and the Tsugaru Strait/South Kyushu. Careful consideration is needed when making such choices, weighing up the implications of extra mileage, the expected weather trend and the opportunity to revert, if unexpected conditions develop. Consideration for the safer route should far outweigh that of the extra mileage, especially during the winter season. As an example, having decided to go north about Japan when eastbound from the northwest Pacific via Tsugaru, out of Korean or West Japan Ports, much care is usually needed, as depressions build up very quickly in the area. Should the trend be for the high pressure ridge to precede the vessel in its eastward movement, a predominance for southerlies perhaps often reaching gale force winds (except in summer) can be expected. This would hinder attempts to move south of the depressions overtaking the vessel.

- Although climatological routeing has its value, particularly for slower ships in need of better strategic planning, the actual weather data must always be monitored closely. One must not neglect the fact that an unusual weather pattern may well occur. For example, prolonged and sometimes intense easterly gales may occasionally be felt where westerlies are normally very predominant. This may, as an example, happen in the North Pacific when high pressure predominates the mid 40s. South of the ridges along the upper 30s, easterly gales may be frequent and strong for some intermediate period.

- If possible avoid or be aware of the sector of a depression subject to the tightest gradient or deep troughs with heavy confused seas. Huge winter storms may build up fast. Severe gale to storm force winds with very high seas and swell may, in some cases, be felt 1500 to 2000 miles from the storm centre, particularly in the North Pacific. The whole North Atlantic, up to the upper 20s, may sometimes be affected by such systems.

- Cyclonic interaction: In practice, movement rules are often subject to interaction, particularly in complex systems. When two cyclonic systems approach within interacting distance their speed, track and behaviour are mutually affected, as the sectors featuring opposing winds meet the circulation and the tracks of both systems become subject to transformation. The intensity of circulation decreases, particularly at the bordering sectors and a deflection of their tracks takes place, usually inducing a mutual revolving cyclonic movement. After merging both systems often regenerate. A common example is that of a tropical revolving storm (TRS) becoming extra-tropical when nearing a sub-tropical low.

- Westerly swells generated by successive frontal systems principally affect the sea condition in middle latitudes. Winds are generally more consistent in their strength and duration along the warm sector of developing depressions, but high constancy and a prolonged wind path is also possible elsewhere, particularly along ridges.

- Heavy seas, particularly during winter months and west headings, are hard to avoid. Under these circumstances a sub-arctic route with better shelter, such as the Bering Sea, may lessen exposure to westerlies. East bound generally steer far to the Equator side of the depressions. As the systems are usually moving eastwards their effect is felt for longer periods and it is, therefore, important to attempt to avoid passing polewards of a depression. When west bound, if not impaired by ice or navigational restrictions, one may aim at sailing towards the polar side of depressions. Otherwise, sail as far towards the equator from the depression's track as possible and reasonable. Intensifying depressions in higher latitudes are often at a more developed stage (i.e. 30s versus 40s).

- Due to lesser wind constancy, one may observe less sea and swell originating from the polar side of a particular system than from its equator side. This may be particularly true if moving ahead of a depression. When eastbound, although the weather will generally be much closer to the bow, sea conditions may not be as bad as to the frontal side, provided the system moves quickly. On the other hand, be guarded when ahead of a northeast moving low (in the Northern Hemisphere). The decision to turn south to avoid head seas must be taken early, before the seas become too high. Southerly winds ahead of a depression may blow over an extended distance along a ridge and generate high seas and swells for a ship situated north of the system.

- Intensification (winds strengthening, pressure dropping) and development (size) of a low usually coincide in higher latitude in open seas. Intense storms of small diameter sometimes occur unexpectedly in certain coastal areas. Tropical revolving storms may also be very intense but small in diameter.

- Very heavy seas and swells can be encountered on any sector of depressions, particularly when they head across long ridges bordering a blocking high. This often occurs in the winter on the poleward side of depressions as they, on gaining latitude, meet a slowing sub-arctic high. When electing to sail a route with known heavy following seas it is essential to recognise the ship's condition and reliability. Although relatively little speed loss normally occurs in following seas, the presence of swell may seriously affect performance. The potential risks involved in case of losing power, or simply losing control of the ship due to steering difficulties, must be appreciated. This may become particularly dangerous if the ship is stiff and loaded with a cargo which may be liable to shift, or if her machinery is not fully reliable. The heavy load imposed upon the rudder and steering gear is another factor to be taken into account, particularly in ballast or light draft. If quarterly seas are becoming dangerous the master may have to consider heaving to. This should be done before the manoeuvre becomes too perilous.

- Deep frontal troughs may also be dangerous. The sudden passage of a cold front can bring very high and confused seas. If having to meet a low it is preferable to meet it in its early stage. This may be useful when travelling eastbound and observing the weather systems.

- In this respect it may be worth considering that due to lesser wind constancy one may observe less sea and swell originating from the polar side of a particular system than from its equator side. This may be particularly true if moving ahead of a depression. Although the weather will be generally closer to the bow, sea conditions may not be as bad as those on the frontal side, provided the system moves quickly. Very heavy seas and swells can be encountered on any sector, particularly when depressions steer across long ridges bordering a blocking high. This often occurs in the winter on the poleward side of depressions, when they meet the sub-arctic high as it slows down on gaining latitude.

- In higher latitudes the chances of encountering heavy seas are generally greater, particularly during winter months. When choosing a track in higher latitudes it is important to recognise that the chances of meeting extreme weather with confused seas may be greater than in temperate latitudes. In sub-arctic regions the frequent weather changes and low constancy in wind direction may result in a comparatively lesser build up of swell. In open oceans and higher latitudes, due to increased fetch length, high swells from the equatorial quadrants are usually more frequent than those of polar quadrants. The position, predominance, intensity, persistence and size of respective troughs and ridges are other factors affecting the predominance of swells and seas.

- Along the Norwegian west coast, heavy seas, swells and storms are very frequent, particularly in winter. This frequency generally decreases towards the northeast, between Haltenbank and the area southwest of Nord Kap.

- In areas such as the Bering sea, the ice limits to the north and the comparative shelter of the Aleutians may offer an attenuation of sea conditions. There are, on the other hand, exposed coastal areas where the sea and swell's interaction with coastal currents and abrupt depth changes generate abnormal and dangerous waves.

- The value of performance curves under given weather conditions is rather limited, particularly when the ship meets various wave trains under the interaction of sea waves, swells and wind speed.

- Cyclonic and anti-cyclonic track tendency. In the northern hemisphere the general track tendency is towards the northeast for cyclones and east southeast for anti-cyclones. This applies to high pressure cells with closed isobars but not to ridges of high pressure occurring between lows. The seasonal difference between tracks is that they are more southerly in winter. In winter, cyclones on the east coast of a continent sometimes follow a marked northerly track, those on the west coast a southerly track. In summer the reverse tendency occurs. This is due to the fact that continents are colder than the adjacent sea in the winter and warmer in the summer (substitute north for south and vice versa in the southern hemisphere).

Waves

Many empirical formulas have been evolved to estimate probable wave height for a given wind strength and may be useful for creating mathematical models and computer simulations. They may also be a guide to the mariner. In practice, however, wind seldom blows in a steady direction or at a steady strength. The appearance of the sea (the wave height and length) is influenced by a number of factors, which can be summarised as follows:

1. Wind speed and consistency of direction. Wave length and height are directly proportional to wind speed provided the direction remains steady. A "time saturation level" is reached, typically 24 to 48 hours, depending on actual wind strength. Beyond that time the generating waves will not grow any longer, although the significant swells thereby generated will travel longer distances.
2. Swell intrusion. In practice the sea is never really smooth. There is always an amount of disturbance interacting with the formation of waves as the wind blows over its surface.
3. Fetch (straight distance travelled over the surface), if typically less than 180 to 250 miles (depending upon the generating wind force) will restrict the development of waves.
4. Water depth. If depth is less than half the wave length the sea bottom will substantially slow the motion of the waves. The lower part of the wave nearest the bottom slows more than the top, thereby increasing the height and decreasing the length of the wave. When approaching shallower water, the effect will be amplified and the faster moving tops will cause instability in the form of breakers or surf. If approaching shallow water at an angle a change of direction of motion or refraction tending to become parallel to the depth curves takes place.
5. Current. An opposing current has the effect of increasing wave height and decreasing wave length, whereas a following current has the opposite effect – decreasing wave height and increasing its length.
6. Temperature differentials. A change of temperature gradient water/air, whereby the air becomes colder than the sea, tends to cause an increase in wave height, typically a 10 per cent increase in wave height for a one degree Centigrade change in temperature.

Tropical revolving storms

I do not propose to describe the rules of TRS avoidance nor their usual tracks. Those are well documented, fairly simple and available on the bridge of almost any ship. My object here is to comment on certain features of such storms and warn of the necessity to take early tactical action whenever possible.

TRS are being tracked very closely nowadays. Nevertheless, forecasting errors are still frequent and substantial. A master should not be lured by the apparent accuracy of computer generated forecasts but should always attempt to use alternate forecasting sources, such as Japan and Guam for the Pacific typhoons. Tropical storms can be very unpredictable. Sometimes their irregular path can be deduced by a close study of synoptic charts, such as the influence of a high pressure ridge for example, but in many cases the factors governing their movements are linked to the upper air structure and temperature inversions or other phenomena which may not be easily available or evaluated by the mariner. It is essential, therefore, to monitor very closely both the track and speed of a storm. A deceleration may be the precursory sign of a change of direction. Once this track change has taken place, re-acceleration is possible. Predicted positions can be a good help but a very wide margin for error must be allowed for.

When "TRS loops" occur it is usually at slow speed, when the storm "feels" resistance or attraction from different sides. A stationary or nearly stationary TRS must be treated with particular caution. Apart from its unpredictability, the seas generated can become enormous and with favourable upper air and high sea temperature the chances of further development are very good. Slow moving TRS, subject to various atmospheric interactions, are more likely to follow unusual tracks and, under certain circumstances, even a "looped path". A close record of the central pressure and radius of storm and gale force winds is also necessary in order to detect and appreciate its tendencies and to decide on the amount of safe distance keeping. I have recently witnessed a September typhoon almost stationary west of Luzon which, without warning, started moving east across Luzon then east southeast at 23 knots, before slowing down and turning northeast onto a more predictable track. I believe that a contributory cause for its irregular behaviour was the interaction of another typhoon at a higher latitude and a more advanced stage, creating an active flow in which that storm found a favourable breeding space.

Weather routeing climatology, the sea and weather routeing
Climatology and weather patterns
Initially, weather routeing was based on climatology without taking into account actual weather situations or trends. Today's technology is vastly improved and efficient weather surveillance analysis and prediction is available, its use being most effective in middle and high latitudes. Climatology is, nevertheless, still being used, particularly for slow vessels on long sea passages. Generalisations can be made with some conviction in certain areas. In the North Atlantic, for example, more severe sea wave activity takes place between latitudes 50° to 60° north in winter, with extensions of intense seas protruding into the Denmark Straits, the Norwegian Sea and along the south and east coast of North America. The many cyclones crossing this vast area in winter, particularly on their southern quadrants, induce the very hazardous wave conditions for ship operations, requiring large amounts of ship speed reduction.

The higher proportion of speed reductions and damage caused by heavy weather occur at lower latitudes during the winter than during the remaining seasons because of the more southerly trajectories and higher frequency of the majority of these migratory storms. Similar observations can be made in the North Pacific between Japan and the Gulf of Alaska. Less restrictive ice conditions permit western passages into the Bering Sea, north of the Aleutians, following easterlies. Due to reduced fetch, the sea conditions are more manageable than at similar latitudes in the North Atlantic. The southern oceans have similar seasonal characteristics but somewhat different patterns due to the absence of land masses.

Several areas are notorious for dangerous "freak waves", with a deep unusual trough. Such waves are usually generated by currents opposing winds and swells approaching shallow water. In particular, air/sea temperature differentials have also been known to contribute towards the generation of such abnormal waves. The writer has witnessed such waves on a few occasions. In one particular instance the impression of "free fall" was felt to such an extent as to raise grave concern to all on board. The vessel survived, but with important structural damage. Under certain conditions I recall having encountered abnormal waves or dangerous seas in the following areas: southeast Cape Africa (Aghulas current), East Taiwan, New Zealand waters, the southern tip of Kamtchatka, Cape Pilar northwest of Spain, areas northeast of Japan and southwest Norway.

Sometimes, on entering the ocean after the passage of certain straits, steep and dangerous swells are encountered, particularly when the ocean floor rises steeply into restricted waters, with tidal streams and eddies meeting the incoming ocean swells. Such swells are encountered with little warning. In a few instances I have had to reduce speed quite suddenly to avoid a severe pounding after passing through the following straits – Tsugaru, Lombok and Magellan (Cape Pilar). Similar swells may be encountered on passing numerous other straits, such as areas of Cook, Bass, Gibraltar, and so on.

Weather routeing
The master may have better knowledge of his ship and her response under the prevailing conditions and should, accordingly, have the last word regarding the choice of a route. He should also, however, never refuse advice if offered and should use the best means available to achieve the voyage safely.

One of the most challenging duties of the master remains that of choosing a safe and economical route for his vessel. The considerations are many. The master will try to keep his vessel clear of heavy seas but, depending on the area and the season, this may not be possible. In such cases he will seek a safe heading and speed for his ship, aiming to keep her under control, minimising sea impact and avoiding violent motion. The general route and tactical course, having due regard to expected weather developments and currents, will often be considered by a Weather Routeing Company (WRC), which has highly sophisticated long term forecasting methods and weather surveillance tools. Today's technology has greatly improved and an optimum route may be assessed with the help of computers with very good results. Whilst taking into account such recommendations from the WRC the master remains, nevertheless, fully responsible for his vessel and it would be foolish to minimise this attachment to the ship.

On the one hand, he may not have access to the wealth of information available to the WRC, but on the other hand is on the spot and far more conscious of safety considerations (i.e. cargo, ship condition and stability) and the ship's response and behaviour. Also, he will probably have a better on-scene appreciation of the sea conditions and therefore be best suited to adjust heading and engine power according to local conditions.

The WRC usually assumes that the master will be able to maintain the recommended course. In many cases this may not be possible due to slamming, heavy rolling or sea impact. For this reason, the WRC and the master should work closely together and try to understand each other's appreciation of the ship, her crew, her safety and her intended voyage.

- In most cases the WRC is hired by the charterers, who will have economics as their first priority, the safest route not always being the most economic. An economic route can only be accepted if it is safe for that particular vessel.
- In many instances, WRC are known to give initial recommendations for a shorter route towards a strategic position, based upon optimistic forecasts, with consequent re-routeing to avoid impending weather deterioration.
- Post-voyage analyses are usually carried out by the WRC at charterers' request. Such studies are based on numerous assumptions and have only a limited value. Computer Climatological Database is now available to the master giving him, together with up-to-date weather data analysis and forecast, access to an amount of information which could come close to that of the WRC.

On board computer systems are being installed on various vessels. Using these, the ship's response and resistance characteristics are being analysed and projected into a programme linked to the weather pattern and its predicted developments, regularly updated by satellite communication link. The information available from such a tool allows the master to have easy graphical access to all available elements in order to help him choose the optimum route for his vessel without outside interference.

Our intelligence analyses trends intuitively, whereas computers analyse them rationally according to a logic established by the programmers. Simulations are frequently used to establish trends which have been detected by the computer. The amount of trust put into the results of such experiments varies a great deal between humans. People familiar with computers or those who have witnessed their efficiency and those who understand the mathematical logic involved place more trust in them.

As an inexact science meteorology offers a very particular challenge for data analysis, processing and simulation. Nowadays, many of us mariners have

compared 96 hours forecast charts with forecast charts for 48 hours produced ten years ago and have noticed that the same or even better quality is possible today for a forecast period double the length. Computer models based on long term observations are established, data is simulated and compared with actual observations in order to establish any deviations from the norm, in such a way that trends can best be detected. Human intuition can be used to tailor a particular computer data analysis to suit local observations or own findings. The deviation between the computer and the human modified analysis can then be measured and compared with actual measurements to provide a useful human interface.

Weather routeing – some advice

1. Determine the vessel's operational limits, based on load line, Institute warranties and cargo characteristics.
2. Adjust routes to take into account navigational restrictions (including ice, load line, traffic and draft).
3. Consider alternative routes in order to seek advantage or minimise disadvantage from wind, sea, topographical or current conditions.
4. Start collecting surface, upper air (contour at 500Mb) and sea state prognosis charts, at least three to four days before commencing the passage, in order to get acquainted with the weather features, intensity of the systems and sea conditions.
5. Use upper air forecasts to locate the 5640 Mb contour which will give a good indication of the expected general direction and southern boundary of storm tracks. Watch for possible splits in the upper air flow as an indication of the formation of two storms tracking in opposite directions, typically north and south.
6. When nearing departure start collecting satellite pictures, if available.
7. Compare successive charts, particularly satellite pictures. Observe tendencies, organisation or a dissipation of respective systems.
8. Look ahead, plot the ship's approximate position well ahead of time and appreciate the situation on the planned track. Consider alternative routes and strategic positions, bearing in mind fetch and the ability to acquire some shelter from high sea and swell.
9. Bear in mind the limitations of your ship, her stability, condition and nature of the cargo.
10. Regardless of whether you are receiving WRC assistance, stay on top by monitoring the weather situation. Endeavour to keep officers fully involved and interested in the weather patterns and closely monitor winds, sea condition, pressure tendencies, precipitation, cloud formation and sea temperatures, comparing actual observations with the weather maps.
11. Endeavour to collect weather information from various sources.

12. Where applicable, collect ice charts and/or ice bulletins from various sources. Avoid the areas by as wide a margin as possible. Bear in mind uncertainties; be particularly aware in areas where shipping is scarce and information incomplete. Monitor sea temperatures as frequently as possible. Use all available means to detect ice, bearing in mind limitation of radar and other aids. If available use night imagery or infra red devices. Always bear in mind the possibility of ice drifting outside known limits. Beware of new ice formation, particularly in sheltered waters with calm and cold weather. Many ships have become seriously damaged when new ice was formed without warning in such areas as the Northern Baltic or the Bay of Bothnia.

We are all becoming aware of the climatological changes which have taken place in the past decade. Global warming is evident. We have also witnessed the El Nino phenomena and one of the worst hurricane seasons in the northwest Atlantic in 1998.

As a result, the mariner must make himself very aware of the consequences of such changes and be far more cautious when planning a passage. Today it is very frequent for well established seasonal weather patterns to become very disturbed.

References:

- *For the Safe Navigation in Japanese Coastal Waters*: Japan Maritime Safety Agency.
- *Geostrophic Wind Scale*, HMSO Metform 1258, North Atlantic Plotting Chart.
- Duxbury, K., *Seastate and Tides*, Stanford Maritime.
- *The American Practical Mariner*, Bowditch.
- *Mariners Weather Log*.
- *Tropical Revolving Storms*, The Nautical Institute, 19...
- *World Climate Research Programme*, World Meteorological Organisation, 1995.

Chapter 58

THE NAUTICAL INSTITUTE COMMAND PARTNERSHIP AND DIPLOMA SCHEME

Introduction

WHILE PREPARATION FOR COMMAND might be seen as a personal responsibility, appointment to command is a company responsibility. This scheme has, therefore, been drawn up as a partnership. It is important to note that The Nautical Institute Command Partnership Scheme is intended to complement, not supplant, company selection and training for those destined for command.

Having been selected as a candidate for command when the opportunity arises, the record book is designed to enable candidates to collect evidence to demonstrate your abilities to carry out most of the command functions.

The scheme cannot replace the need for training, which will have been identified during your selection interview. The scheme and record book will enable candidates to experience elements of command and help candidates define weaknesses in their knowledge and skills which can be discussed with their company. The record book is also offered to individuals who want to follow the scheme of their own volition.

The first part of the partnership scheme is designed to provide the guidance for understanding more clearly the purpose of the record book tasks and collection of evidence.

Command has a status of its own which is unique. The master is the ship's captain, the company manager, the custodian of cargo and a public authority.

The authority of command derives from two complementary sources: the public who empower governments through statutory law to bestow authority for safe ship operations through merchant shipping legislation and the company which assigns authority through appointment.

This authority cannot be transferred as it attaches to the position of master. The master discharges the responsibilities associated with command by delegating appropriate authority to the officers on board through their job descriptions, company instructions, master's standing orders supplemented by bridge orders and procedural arrangements.

It is not the master's role to do everything on board, but it is his responsibility to make provision for the safe and continuous operation of the ship through clearly understood delegated procedures.

In most cases there is no conflict of interest between charterer, company and marine administration, but every master will be able to give examples where they have had to make decisions based upon their best judgement.

Although there can be tensions and difficulties, all owners want, and indeed need to, ensure the inherent safety of the voyage because it is fundamental to the long term reputation of the company.

Whereas tasks as chief mate have been largely concerned with events within the ship, the position of command requires a wider sense of judgement. Very often masters are confronted with situations where there are no clear-cut right and wrong ways to decide the outcome.

The Nautical Institute, over the past twenty five years, has run a series of Command Seminars, from which it has been possible to derive some helpful limiting guidelines:

- Think ahead, anticipate and plan.
- Communicate well, keeping all involved – the crew, the company and the cargo owners – informed.
- Put in place procedures to ensure the ship is not put at risk through the error or omission of one person.
- Do not put the ship or people in a situation of uncontrollable risk.
- Care for the cargo.
- Seek to optimise the return to the company.
- When in doubt seek advice early.
- Act with integrity and set a good example.
- Be confident in good seamanship.
- Protect the marine environment.
- Strive for improvement.

Further information which contains the distilled wisdom of ship masters and other specialists is contained in this, the accompanying book, *The Nautical Institute on Command.* This is a practical book full of useful advice and should be read carefully because it will enhance the quality of the decisions you make. Good decisions in turn generate respect and respect translates into support and good management. Throughout the record book, references to relevant chapters are given.

These few introductory notes will be sufficient to demonstrate that the role of command cannot be separated from company management. Having been selected as a candidate for command it is very much in the company's best interests to develop a mutually agreed programme of preparation.

In the past this has usually been done through a series of interviews but there was growing evidence of the need for a more formal programme because the range and scope of issues to be covered are so broad that there is now a requirement to provide a well structured programme if all the subject areas where command decisions impact on the profitability of the company are to be covered.

In the guidance section there follow key points about what makes a good master and what makes a bad master. Undoubtedly the candidate will have their own views about this, because the aim of the scheme is to turn the negative influences into positive outcomes.

To do this there are two aspects. Firstly, the candidate may have to adapt to the role of command and secondly the company may need to provide training where this is seen as desirable.

Training needs can be identified at the selection interview by comparing the job description as mate with that of master, noting the training and seminars attended already and working out the areas for special attention. Some pointers are given in this section, but the subject cannot be generalised easily and the candidate should seek to strengthen any weaknesses.

Building upon that there should be a well structured visit to each of the principal managers concerned. The areas to be covered are too wide for a 'chat' approach. We recommend the use of a checklist in this section to cover all the key points.

With this background the candidate will be able to follow the task based scheme which covers a wide range of practical tasks relating to master's responsibilities.

For those who are able to undertake a special project, The Nautical Institute is providing the opportunity to obtain a prestigious diploma.

Full details of the Command Partnership Scheme can be obtained from The Nautical Institute, 202 Lambeth Road, London SE1 7LQ, or from the Institute's web site: www.nautinst.org.

Chapter 59

CASE STUDY – MAN OVERBOARD

Introduction

On 9 March 1978 in the late afternoon a cadet, Eric Hendry, fell overboard from a tanker close by the Tunisian coast.

There were three reports written to cover the incident, one by the master, one by the chief officer and one by another cadet, a girl, who happened to be working with Eric at the time. The reports speak for themselves. Here they are, direct from the original submissions.

Statement by the master

"At about 1610 hours 1 was summoned to the bridge by the ringing of the ship's general alarm bells. On the bridge were the OOW, the chief officer and the helmsman. The OOW who was standing in the vicinity of the radar informed me that there was a man overboard. The chief officer was standing outside the starboard wheelhouse door and was looking through binoculars in the direction of the starboard quarter. I noted that the vessel's helm indicator was at hard to starboard and that the vessel was swinging in that direction. I placed the telegraph to stand by and took a pair of binoculars to join the chief officer. I asked him if he had the man overboard in sight and he replied, 'Yes'. By noting the direction and angle of his binoculars I tried to locate the man. The chief officer informed me that the man had two lifebuoys in close proximity to him.

My first reaction was to reverse the wheel to hard to port in order to accomplish a Williamson turn but to bring the vessel to port would have meant blocking off the chief officer's field of vision as the vessel's funnel crossed the direction of the man overboard. As the man was in sight I decided to continue to turn to starboard.

At this time it registered in my mind that the man overboard smoke-light buoy had not been released. The only such buoy on the bridge at this time was situated on the port wing. The starboard buoy had been lost during heavy weather in the North Atlantic. A cable ordering a replacement man overboard was made to the vessel's owners subsequent to this loss. I returned to the wheelhouse and asked the OOW why he had not released the port side man overboard before the order to hard starboard wheel was given. He informed me that he had been told not to. When asked who had given the order not to release it he stated, 'I don't know.' I asked who had given the hard starboard order, he said, 'I did,' I again checked the direction and position of the binoculars being used by the chief officer and again asked him if the man was still in sight. He replied, 'Yes.'

In considering whether to release the man overboard at this time I estimated that the man was more than a mile from the vessel's position and with this distance and the fact that the vessel was on a hard

starboard turn I did not feel that the buoy would have cleared the ship's side. At about this time the radio officer was instructed to send the following message:

37° 23'N 09° 15'E Man overboard stop in sight we are proceeding all vessels keep clear.

As the vessel passed through a heading of about 225° the chief officer informed me that he had lost sight of the man and the buoys. At no time during the turn did I see either the man or the buoys. The time of the accident was estimated by the OOW to have been 1605. There was an accurate fix on the chart for 1600 with Cape Serrat being about nine miles distant. I brought the ship round to the 1605 position and at 1652, with the vessel accurately fixed in the 1605 position, I stopped the engines. At this time a round-the-ship lookout was underway with many officers and crew stationed around the vessel attempting to locate Cadet Hendry. Both motor lifeboats were in a state of readiness for lowering.

When the chief officer had lost sight of Cadet Hendry I instructed the radio officer to activate the auto alarm and transmit the following:

XXX Ref my man overboard now lost position all vessels in vicinity please assist.

This message was transmitted at 1636. The weather conditions prevailing were wind WxS force 5/6, moderate sea and swell. The sea was choppy and waves were breaking. The sky was overcast and visibility was getting poorer all the time. Sunset was at 1725 hours and by 1745 the vessel was searching the sea with searchlights (2) and the aldis lamp. At this time two other vessels were in the vicinity and assisting. At 1948 Tunis Radio Station repeated our XXX and continued to do so throughout the search. At about 2015 we were joined by two vessels. By 2045 six other vessels were assisting.

At about 2215 one informed us that he had seen something and the vessels turned to port. On investigation the sighting was false. By 2328 my concern for the cadet was grave. At 0030 the fourth engineer and the junior second officer reported sighting a floating object. A light was dropped and the vessel turned round. On investigation nothing was sighted but a piece of floating plastic and we resumed our easterly track pattern at 0110.

During the night vessels were assisting as they passed the area. PAN calls were made by myself on the VHF at regular intervals with the message:

Man overboard all vessels navigating in the vicinity between Cape Serrat and Cape Blanc please keep a sharp lookout. Man is with lifebuoys. All vessels please report any sighting.

At 0330 the vessel was positioned to the north east of Cape Blanc and I decided that the best hope lay in the fact that, with the inshore set being felt by the vessel and the wind, which had been veering during the night towards NW, the cadet could well have been carried inshore and I considered that the most profitable daylight searching would be made around the coastline. At 0608 I sent the following to 3VX:

Still searching urge you arrange helicopter assistance soonest.

At about 0630 a Tunisian naval patrol boat joined us and assisted by sweeping across our track. At about this time two aircraft were sighted but they were at too high an altitude to be of assistance. All the other vessels had left at this time.

By 1000 hours the vessel was three miles to the NW of Cape Serrat and I decided to look again at the overboard position. At 1040 the vessel had regained the position of the accident and after that tracked again on a course of 080°. At 1230 I was convinced of the futility of searching in this area and so again took the ship inshore and searched along the coast between Ras Dukara and Cape Blanc. At 1426 the vessel was off Cape Blanc and a course was shaped to regain the eastbound traffic lane off Cani Isle.

At 1530 the vessel had regained the course line and proceeded en route to Skaramanga. Sharp lookout was continued until nightfall but at 1845 there seemed no alternative but to abandon the search.

This statement represents a true statement of the incidents as I remember them."

Statement by the other cadet

"The chief officer told Eric and myself to drain out the port riser and remove the dry scale from the starboard riser and to throw this overboard. We took out some of the scale and put this on a large piece of folded sacking. We carried the sacking up a few steps to the height of the manifold grating. Eric then carried the sacking across the grating and dropped it to the deck below.

We were standing forward of a set of bitts. I suggested that we take off the gate but Eric said that it would be too dangerous. When saying this I saw that the pins were completely down. We then decided to swing the sacking over the top of the railings on the count of three. Eric and I took two corners each. At this time Eric was standing just forward and inboard of the set of bitts, also just in line with the gate. I was standing just forward of the gate. On the third swing I was looking down at the sacking so I did not see what actually took place but the next moment I saw Eric as a white flash but I could distinguish that he was falling feet first.

I started to run down the deck, shouting, 'Eric has fallen overboard', to where a few members of the crew and the chief officer were standing, which was around the manhole to the starboard slop tank. I then ran to the cargo control room telephone to the bridge to tell them what had happened. After this I went up to number one lifeboat but the chief officer shouted to me to go onto the bridge. He then asked me how it had happened. After this I stayed on lookout on the bridge."

Statement by the chief officer

"On the morning of 9 March I had the two cadets open up the inspection plate of the gas risers in the midships Sampson posts. On inspection the port one needed a few inches of water baled out from it and the starboard one needed about two feet of dry rust scale removed from it. I then told the two cadets to get on with that task after lunch. They first drained the water out of the port one and replaced the inspection cover. They then went across to the starboard one to remove the scale. I had told them to dump the scale over the side.

I was about halfway down the ladder from the lower boat deck to the main deck on the starboard side when I saw the female cadet running aft from the starboard manifold shouting, 'Eric has fallen overboard'. I turned and ran up the ladder to the after end of the boat deck shouting, 'Man overboard', hoping somebody on the bridge would hear. On reaching the after end of the boat deck I looked over the side and saw Eric Hendry floating past. He was sort of back paddling so as to keep clear of the vessel's propeller and looking up towards the ship. I picked up the nearest of the two lifebuoys positioned on the rail and threw it. It landed between five and ten yards from the cadet. I then saw a second lifebuoy land about 15 yards from him. Somebody had thrown it from the next deck down. I then ran up to the bridge going through the wheelhouse from the port side. The OOW was holding the telephone. I told him to give the 'three ring' signal on the alarm bells. I told the quartermaster to put the wheel hard to starboard and, grabbing a pair of binoculars, I ran to the after end of the bridge on the starboard side and tried to keep the cadet and lifebuoys in sight.

The sea was fairly choppy with white horses and after a while I lost sight of the cadet. I did not actually see him reach a lifebuoy but while I could see him he seemed to be swimming towards them. In the meantime the CPO and some men had started to get number one motor lifeboat swung out and lowered to the embarkation deck. I shouted down to him to also get number four motor boat ready. I then sent one of the crew to check that all the crew were out of the cargo tanks we had been cleaning. I then sent two sailors up to the bow to keep a lookout. Most of the crew were already at the ship's side looking out and boat crew were ready in lifejackets.

Once we realised it was going to be a long search I organised the lookout into watches of two hours each – two men on the bow, one at each manifold, one each side aft and one on the bridge; the chief engineer organised lookout watches for the engineers on the bridge. I spent the remainder of the search on the bridge with the master, leaving it occasionally to check on the lookouts posted around the ship."

This feature is published with the assistance of the Eric Hendry Memorial Trust, the purpose of which is to support measures to avoid similar tragedies from re-occurring.

Chapter 60

CASE STUDY –
THE GROUNDING OF PASSENGER VESSEL *HANSEATIC*

Extracts from a report by The Transportation Safety Board of Canada

MARINE OCCURRENCE REPORT

GROUNDING

PASSENGER VESSEL "HANSEATIC"
SIMPSON STRAIT, NORTHWEST TERRITORIES
29 AUGUST 1996

REPORT NUMBER M96H0016

Synopsis

While on passage from Gjoa Haven to Resolute Bay, the "HANSEATIC" ran aground in Simpson Strait. The weather was fine and clear and the vessel was being navigated visually, by reference to shore ranges, and by radar. The passage plan was disrupted when it was assumed that a buoy, which had been left in the strait from the previous navigation season, was marking a shoal. The buoy had been moved out of position by ice.

The Board determined that the "HANSEATIC" grounded because the bridge team did not strictly adhere to the plan that had been prepared for navigating the vessel through the strait. Relying on a navigation buoy left in the strait from the previous navigation season contributed to the grounding.

1.2 History of the Voyage

On 29 August 1996, the "HANSEATIC" (*a modern 8,378 gt passenger vessel*) was in the eleventh day of a Northwest Passage cruise which had started in Nome, Alaska, and was to have terminated in Greenland. The cruise had taken the vessel to several communities in Alaska, Yukon and the Northwest Territories.

On the morning of 29 August, the "HANSEATIC" made an eastbound passage in Simpson Strait to the village of Gjoa Haven where she was to anchor for part of the day, while passengers went ashore for a tour of the village. During the trip, several buoys were unexpectedly found in the strait. The master had not anticipated seeing any buoys in the strait because the Arctic Canada Traffic System (NORDREG CANADA) had advised him that the buoys for Simpson Strait were still on board the CCGS "SIR WILFRID LAURIER", as the ice breaker had not yet had an opportunity to position them. The majority of the range markers for the various legs of the inbound

passage were positioned ahead of the vessel and the passage was straightforward and uneventful. Little attention was paid to the buoys or whether they were in their charted positions.

The "HANSEATIC" left Gjoa Haven in the afternoon of 29 August for Resolute Bay. Initially, the voyage to Resolute required that the "HANSEATIC" retrace her morning passage through Simpson Strait, in a westerly direction. The route involves many alterations of course and, as on the inward passage, the master had the conduct of the vessel. With him on the bridge were a helmsman and the chief officer who assisted with the navigation. The ship, which has an operating speed of 14 knots, was making about 10 knots and no difficulty was experienced with the initial part of the transit. A position taken at 1738[3], confirmed that the vessel was proceeding parallel to, and approximately a cable south of, the 288° course line indicated on the chart for the ranges on Eta Island. The vessel was south of the charted course line to avoid a 6·1 metre shoal reported near the track. Once past the shoal, and approximately half way along this leg, the "HANSEATIC" was brought back towards the 288° course line. At 1745, a check of the ship's position by the chief officer showed the vessel abeam of the northwest extremity of Saatuq Island and almost exactly on the 288° course line. The vessel was at this point about half a mile from the next alter-course position, and the chief officer turned his attention to setting up the radar for the next leg.

Meanwhile, the master was monitoring the vessel's position relative to the 288° course line by reference to the Eta Island ranges. Because the ranges were

---

3 All times are CDT (Coordinated Universal Time minus five hours) unless otherwise noted.

astern of the vessel, and with the helm orders ranging from $290°$ to $293°$, the master had to frequently go out to the starboard wing of the bridge to check the ranges. The master was reportedly keeping the ship on a heading which was increasingly to starboard of the course line to counteract the effect on the vessel of the northwest wind.

As the "HANSEATIC" approached the alter-course position, the master was aware that the ship was north of the ranges, but the sight of a green buoy on the starboard side gave him confidence that she would pass clear of a shoal lying just to the north of the course line. However, the buoy had not been removed at the end of the previous navigation season and the winter ice had moved it about 200 metres to the northeast. Consequently, the "HANSEATIC" did not clear the shoal and ran aground in position $68° 33.75'$ N, $097° 32.2'$ W.

As the vessel was not considered to be in any danger, during the next few days, while awaiting assistance, passengers were afforded the opportunity to explore adjacent islands, using the ship's boats. On 05 September 1996, with the exception of a few who had requested to be flown home, the passengers were transferred to another vessel to carry on with their Northwest Passage cruise.

Following several unsuccessful attempts, the vessel was finally refloated on 08 September 1996, with the help of the tug "EDGAR KOTOKAK" and the coast guard cutter "NAHIDIK".

1.3 Injuries to Persons
No one was injured as a result of the grounding.

1.4 Damage
Damage was limited to the underwater hull between frames 77 and 126. The shell plating was holed and severely rippled on both sides of the centreline girder but there was no pollution as a result of the occurrence.

1.5 Certification
1.5.1 Vessel
The vessel was certificated, crewed and equipped in accordance with existing regulations.

1.5.2 Vessel's Navigation Personnel
Both the master and the chief officer held qualifications appropriate for the tonnage of the vessel on which they were serving and for the voyage being undertaken.

1.6 Personnel Experience
The master of the "HANSEATIC" had 26 years' experience as master on a wide variety of passenger vessels. Although he had sailed in the Canadian Arctic on several occasions, this was his first voyage through Simpson Strait.

The chief officer of the "HANSEATIC" had 25 years' seagoing experience, 10 as master. He had seven months' experience on board the "HANSEATIC" as chief officer.

1.7 Bridge Team
The master, chief officer and helmsman were on the bridge prior to, and at the time of, the grounding. Although an ice navigator was on board the "HANSEATIC", at this time of year the vessel was permitted to navigate in the Simpson Strait area without his aid, and he was not on the bridge during the passage.

The bridge team was well rested at the time of the occurrence.

1.8 Environmental Information
1.8.1 Weather
The weather was fine and clear with a northwesterly wind of 17 to 21 knots. The sea was calm in the sheltered waters of the strait and the visibility was reported to be about 5 miles. The air temperature was $7°C$; the sea temperature was $4°C$.

1.8.2 Tide and Tidal Stream
According to the *Sailing Directions - Arctic Canada, Volume I*, the average tidal range in Simpson Strait is about 0.6 m. The range for the tidal cycle during which the grounding occurred was calculated to be about 0.5 m. The grounding occurred about four hours after high water.

The *Sailing Directions* advise that "the tidal stream, from brief and broken observations, is rectilinear, running roughly parallel to the axis of the strait..." They also caution that "...tidal streams up to 4 knots, and up to 7 knots near Eta Island, have been experienced, with marked changes of direction, tide-rips and back eddies around the islets and shoals." On Canadian Hydrographic Service (CHS) chart No. 7735, tide rips are indicated in the area of the grounding.

From an analysis of the information available, the Institute of Marine Sciences in Sidney, B.C., formed the opinion that they "...would not expect there to be a strong deflection of the current from the along-channel direction in the vicinity of the range line..." They concluded that "...currents were unlikely to be a significant factor in carrying the *Hanseatic* off the range line."

1.9 Navigation of the Vessel
1.9.1 Navigation Equipment
The vessel's navigation equipment was reportedly in satisfactory condition. Two radar sets were being used in the navigation of the vessel and no deficiency was reported.

The Global Positioning System (GPS) was not being used. Positions obtained by GPS in Simpson Strait can be off by as much as one mile, when plotted on the chart. This lack of precision is due to the inaccuracy of geographical coordinates on charts of the area.

1.9.2 Charts and Publications

The marine chart being used by the vessel was the CHS chart No. 7735, Simpson Strait.

Many areas of the Arctic coast are either incompletely or inaccurately charted, or both. The geographical coordinates are not accurate on some charts (including chart No. 7735) but the shore lines and other features on chart No. 7735 are correctly depicted relative to each other. Positions obtained from the radar and by visual means will be accurately represented on the chart.

The *Sailing Directions – Arctic Canada, Volumes 1* and *3* are relevant to the area of the occurrence and these publications were on board the "HANSEATIC".

1.9.3 Aids to Navigation

The Sailing Directions advise that the channel through Simpson Strait is marked by beacons, beacon ranges and buoys. The Sailing Directions also advise that the buoys in Simpson Strait are seasonal. However, because the Canadian Coast Guard (CCG) policy is that the operational requirement for ice-breakers takes precedence over the removal of the buoys in the strait, the buoys are not always removed at the end of the shipping season. Each season, the CCC does not consider the strait to be buoyed until a Notice to Shipping is issued, specifically stating that the buoys for the area have been deployed. Such a Notice to Shipping had not been issued at the time of the occurrence. Although the buoys are built to be expendable, some of the buoys are not destroyed during the winter and remain afloat in the strait or grounded on adjacent beaches. Buoys that remain afloat are almost invariably displaced from their charted positions. While the buoy that marked the shoal on which the "HANSEATIC" grounded had been moved about 200 metres to the northeast, the buoy that marked the shoal on the other side of the channel was found some 1,300 metres to the west of its charted position.

A stretch of some 20 miles of the navigation channel depicted on CHS chart No. 7735 comprises eleven legs, eight of which are defined by a set of shore range markers. Persons experienced in navigating in the Arctic advise that, because some of the range markers are built on low islands, they may be pushed out of position by the ice and mariners must be cautious when using them. Six of the eight sets of range markers are ahead for an eastbound vessel.

The 108°-288° range markers on Eta Island were checked after the "HANSEATIC" grounding and were found to be in their correct positions.

All aids to navigation in Simpson Strait are unlit.

1.9.4 Cautionary Notes Regarding Buoyage

Canadian publications relevant to a passage through Simpson Strait contain several warnings against relying on buoys in the area.

A note on chart No. 7735 states that "the channel leading through Simpson Strait is marked by seasonal buoys which are liable to be displaced by ice." All *Sailing Directions* published by the Department of Fisheries and Oceans (DFO) advise that "mariners should not rely on buoys being in their charted positions at all times. Buoys should be regarded as warning markers and ... Masters should always navigate by bearings or angles on fixed shore objects." The *Sailing Directions – Arctic Canada, Volume 1* also warns that "buoys laid in Arctic waters must be regarded merely as temporary and very unreliable aids to navigation ... and they are always liable to be carried away by the movement of ice. . ." *The Sailing Directions - Arctic Canada, Volume 3* advises that "buoys in Simpson Strait are seasonal and consist of four oil drums welded together end-to-end and painted red or green. Some years, because of ice conditions, it is not possible to lay the buoys, and since buoys in these ice-strewn waters cannot be depended upon to remain in their correct positions for very long, little reliance can be placed on them."

1.10 Passage Planning and Bridge Resource Management

The master and the chief officer had been involved in the planning of the passage. The *Sailing Directions* describe the passage through Simpson Strait as probably "the greatest navigational hazard in the whole mainland passage... because of numerous shoals, narrow channels and strong tidal streams". This publication also states that "numerous dangerous shoals ... lie close to the channel and it is probable that these are altered considerably by ice action each season."

In describing the topography, the *Sailing Directions* advise that "on the north side of Simpson Strait, the ... coast presents a low, regular and rather featureless appearance, with no distinctive landmarks" while the south ". . . coast is somewhat higher than the north coast but its overall elevation is moderate gradually rising to distant hills ... The islands in Simpson Strait consist mainly of stones and large boulders, and ... tend to blend in with each other and with the adjacent shoreline."

For the passage in Simpson Strait, the master had the conduct of the ship and the chief officer was assisting by plotting the vessel's position. In the parts of the strait where the alignment of the channel is indicated by shore leading marks (ranges), any lateral displacement of the vessel from the alignment could be quickly detected by the master. To indicate the vessel's progress along the alignment of the channel, radar distances and bearings of the shore were to be obtained and plotted by the chief officer. No supplementary parallel indexing was being used when the vessel was on the Eta Island range markers, but parallel indexing was to be used on the next leg. With the vessel proceeding westbound on these two legs, the range markers were astern. When the vessel was proceeding on the Eta Island course, the radar distance ranges used varied with the application.

1.11 Ice Navigator

According to the Arctic Shipping Pollution Prevention Regulations, the "HANSEATIC' was not required to carry an ice navigator, although an ice navigator had been on board since the vessel departed Nome. The "HANSEATIC" was in open water at the time of the grounding and the ice navigator was not on the bridge-nor was he required to be.

1.14 Situational Awareness

Situational awareness can be defined as the accurate perception of the factors and conditions affecting the crew and the operations of the vessel during a specific period of time. This is developed by using "all the knowledge that is accessible and can be integrated into a coherent picture, when required, to assess and cope with a situation."[4]

A person performing a complex task such as ship navigation depends on situational awareness when making and carrying out plans throughout the operation. Situational awareness does not happen instantaneously, but develops on three different levels. First, the person has to perceive the situational elements from information displays, communication, or from external references. The person then integrates the information by using his/her experience and knowledge. Finally, the person projects the information into the future to make and modify plans as tasks are completed or delayed and new developments arise. In general, it can be expected that poor or unsuccessful performance will occur if there are problems at any one of these situational awareness levels.[5]

One of the ways that the integration of information can be erroneous is when a person is affected by confirmation bias. This is a tendency to seek information to confirm that which we already believe to be true. Information that is inconsistent with the chosen hypothesis is then ignored or discounted.

2.0 Analysis
2.1 The Tidal Stream

The Sailing Directions warn of the vagaries of the tidal stream in Simpson Strait but it was not possible to determine with any certainty what part, if any, the current played in the grounding of the "HANSEATIC".

---

4 N.B. Sarter and D.D. Woods (1991), Situation awareness: A critical but ill defined phenomenon. *The International Journal of Aviation Psychology*, 1 (1), 45-57.

5 M.R. Endsley, "Situational awareness in dynamic human decision making: Theory", in *Situational Awareness in Complex Systems*, Proceedings of a CAHFA Conference, Feb 1-3,1993, pp. 27-58 (Daytona Beach, Florida: Embry-Riddle Aeronautical University Press, 1994).

The radar had not been set up for parallel indexing on this leg and the only on-going means of promptly detecting lateral movement caused by the current would have been to keep the shore range markers in line. However, when the vessel was brought back to the course line, she was allowed to cross it and to continue with the range markers open. Range markers that are already open do not readily indicate to the observer that further, gradual deviation from the ranges is taking place.

The positions plotted by the chief officer at 1738 and 1745 show the vessel being brought back to the course line between these times. The 1745 position, taken from the radar some 2-3 minutes before the vessel grounded, showed the vessel to be slightly north of, but close to, the line of the ranges. This position suggests the possibility that the current contributed to the grounding of the "HANSEATIC". However, the direction and distance of the grounding position from the 1745 position, $308° \times 3^1/_2$ cables, calls into question the reliability of the 1745 position. The course required to be made good to keep the vessel on the line of the ranges was 288° and, with up to 5° leeway being allowed for the northwest wind, the vessel was steering 293°. A rectilinear tidal stream parallel to the axis of the strait would basically be in line with the 288° course. For the 1745 position to have been accurate there would need to have been an aberration in the rectilinear tidal stream. To sweep the vessel 20° off the course line (15° if she was not making the leeway), over the last $3^1/_2$ cables before the grounding, would have required an aberration in the tidal stream sufficient to produce a 3 knot component at right-angles to the line of the ranges. The analysis by the Institute of Ocean Sciences discounted such a cross-channel component, and observations from the stranded vessel did not detect any such anomaly on subsequent tides. Also, a dramatic deviation of this magnitude from the vessel's heading is not reflected in the actions of the master who, of those involved with the navigation, was the one constantly monitoring the range markers. The master did not detect a need for corrective action and, on the contrary, was increasing the leeway correction, to the opposite hand, just prior to the grounding. This would suggest that in plotting the 1745 position the distance off Saatuq Island was underestimated, and that the "HANSEATIC' was not making 5° leeway but was gradually deviating further from the line of the ranges.

2.2 Navigating on the Ranges

On the morning eastbound passage, most of the ranges had the markers ahead of the vessel and in that respect the afternoon westbound passage was less straightforward. Nevertheless, the plan that was prepared for the passage of the "HANSEATIC through Simpson Strait should have allowed the vessel to safely transit the area. Both the master and the chief officer were experienced navigators. However, by allowing the vessel to run north of the course line with the ranges open, the master lost the considerable contribution the ranges were making to keeping the vessel out of danger. Attempting to estimate how far a vessel is displaced from the course line by assessing the relative position of two "open" range markers provides, at best, imprecise results. As a vessel proceeds further away from the range markers, maintaining the same angular separation of the markers translates into a further displacement from the intended track. The degree of precision needed to safely navigate the "HANSEATIC' through Simpson Strait required that the vessel be kept on the line of the ranges; it would have been expedient to have promptly adjusted any allowance for leeway and/or set as soon as the ranges showed the vessel leaving the course line. This would be particularly appropriate when passing close to a shoal that the *Sailing Directions* warn could have been altered by ice action.

As there was the possibility that ice had displaced the range beacons, good seamanship suggests that parallel indexing should have been employed, to back up the ranges. And as it was likely that the gradually sloping terrain would have produced a less-well-defined radar image, it would have been prudent to have set up the parallel indexing using points on both sides of the channel, and to have checked the distance from land on both sides of the channel when taking positions from the radar display.

2.3 Plotting of Positions

As the passage was planned, the main purpose of the positions plotted by the chief officer was to allow him to monitor the vessel's progress along the course line, with lateral displacement from the course line being determined by reference to the ranges. When the vessel was on a leg without ranges or was intentionally running off the ranges, as when clearing the 6·1 metre shoal reported near the track, the positions plotted by the chief officer served to determine both progress along the intended course line and lateral deflection from it. This was also the case just before the grounding, when the master allowed the vessel to run north of the ranges. During this time the chief officer plotted a position, taken from the radar at 1745, some 2-3 minutes before the vessel grounded. This position showed the vessel to be slightly north of, but close to, the line of the ranges. Other evidence suggests that the 1745 position was not accurate. The chief officer who plotted the 1745 position was also monitoring the vessel's progress and, shortly before taking the position, had seen that the vessel was on the ranges. The 1745 position was, however, reportedly derived from a distance and bearing taken from the radar display. An accurate position at this point might have given the bridge team sufficient time to take action to avoid the shoal.

The position in which the vessel grounded is only about $1^1/_2$ cables outside the line of the ranges, and the 1745 position was plotted from a fix taken less than

three minutes before the vessel would have come up with the shoal. In such circumstances, where time and distance are critical, it is prudent to supplement manual plotting with parallel indexing, to allow the navigator to react quickly enough.

2.4 Composition of Bridge Team

It cannot be determined conclusively whether there would have been sufficient time for the bridge team to take corrective action had the 1745 position shown the vessel to be heading into danger. There was little time for the chief officer to resume monitoring the ranges after he had plotted the 1745 position. However, it should not have been necessary for the chief officer to divert his attention at such a critical time in order to set up the radar for parallel indexing on the next leg. More than one radar was available, and with the vessel only on the shorter legs for a few minutes, another, possibly junior, officer could have prepared a radar set for parallel indexing on the next course. Such an addition to the bridge team, by attending to supplementary detail, would have allowed the master and chief officer to concentrate fully on the navigation of the vessel, particularly critical in this most-demanding section of the strait.

2.5 The Role of Confirmation Bias in Course Selection

The master of the "HANSEATIC" was aware that the ship was north of the course line; he was also aware that there was a shoal just to the north of the course line, in the last half mile before the alter-course position. However, he believed that the vessel was still in the channel. Contributing to this assessment was the influence of confirmation bias. The two most obvious cues available to the bridge team with respect to the vessel's position were the open range markers and the green buoy. The open range markers in themselves were not easy to interpret and required supplementary input before a decision on corrective action could be made. Previous exposure to warnings against relying on buoys during navigation did not overcome the reassuring sight of the green buoy (on the starboard bow, where it was expected to be). In addition, a lack of conflicting information from the chief officer's radar plot reinforced his incorrect assessment of the vessel's position, and no other action was taken to verify that position.

Consideration was given to the possibility that a left-right reversal error could have accounted for the erroneous heading. This is one of the more common errors to occur in situations such as that faced by the master, in which the range markers are astern of the vessel. However, this type of error – the master calling for a starboard heading adjustment when he meant a port adjustment – is usually recognized immediately, and then corrected. It should have been readily apparent that the ranges were continuing to widen and the vessel's head was moving to starboard. That the master repeatedly called for further starboard heading

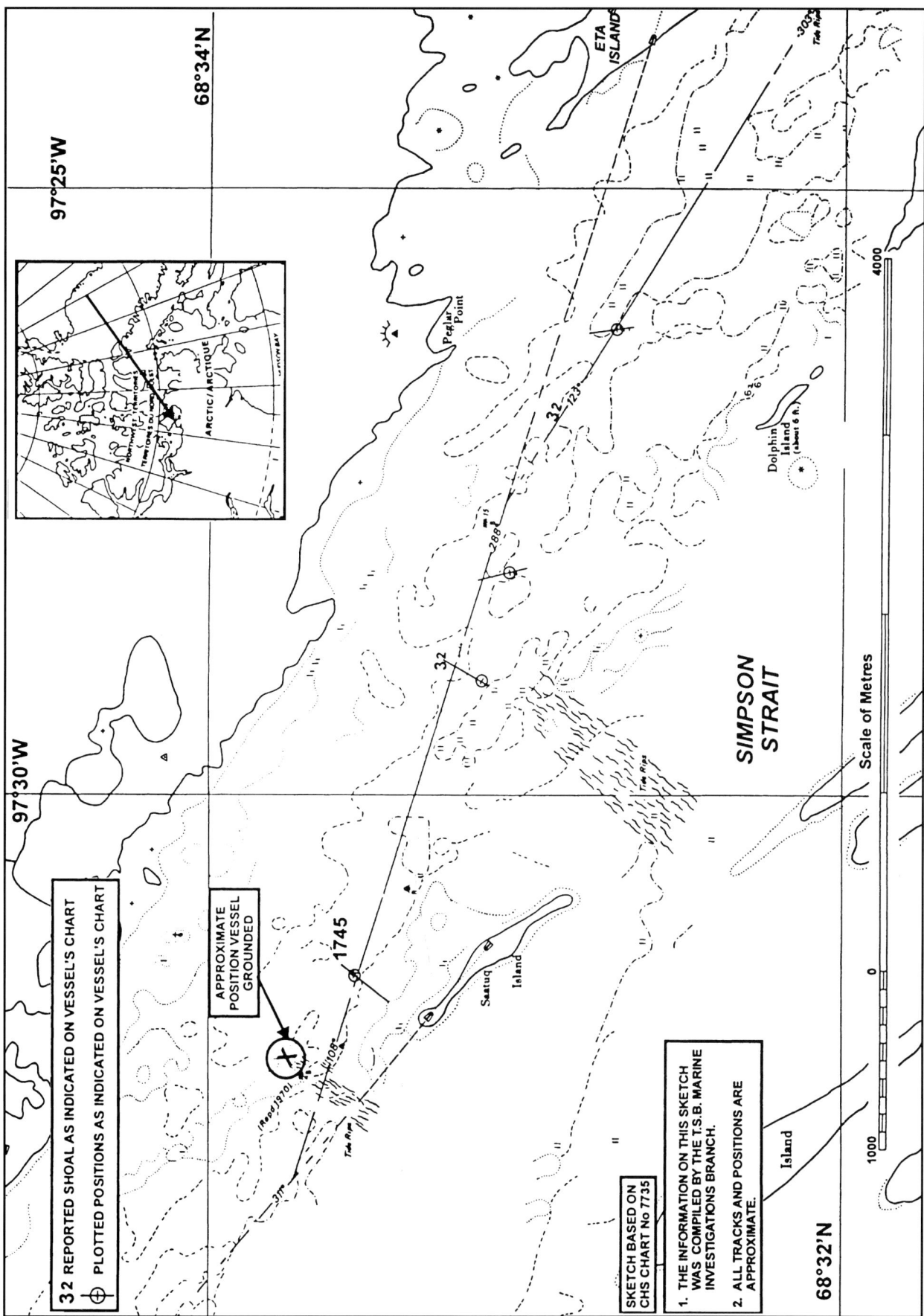

Figure 60.1 Sketch of Area of Grounding

adjustments does not support the hypothesis that left-right reversal error accounted for his behaviour.

3.0 Conclusions

3.1 Findings

1. A passage plan was prepared for Simpson Strait which employed the navigational experience of the master and the chief officer.
2. The passage plan made use of the range markers in the area and positions derived from the radar display.
3. Parallel indexing was not used to supplement the passage plan on all course legs.
4. The vessel was allowed to proceed off the ranges when this was not necessary to avoid a navigational hazard.
5. Buoys had not been removed from Simpson Strait at the end of the previous navigation season.
6. Some buoys were not destroyed by the winter ice and a critical buoy was displaced only about a cable from its charted position.
7. Despite warnings in the relevant navigational publications, the displaced buoy was used as a navigation mark.
8. The vessel grounded on the shoal that the buoy had been positioned to mark during the previous navigation season.

9. During the inbound passage the bridge team did not determine if the buoys unexpectedly found in the strait were in their charted positions.
10. A position plotted on the chart some 2-3 minutes before the grounding was probably inaccurate.

3.2 Causes

The "HANSEATIC" grounded because the bridge team did not strictly adhere to the plan that had been prepared for navigating the vessel through the strait. Reliance upon a navigation buoy left in the strait from the previous navigation season contributed to the grounding.

4.0 Safety Action

The Board has no marine safety recommendations to issue at this time.

This report concludes the Transportation Safety Board's investigation into this occurrence. Consequently, the Board, consisting of Chairperson Benoît Bouchard, and members Maurice Harquail, Charles Simpson and W.A. Tadros, authorized the release of this report on 14 May 1998.

Note: The term 'ranges' refers to leading lines.

Index of chapters

CONTENTS IN ALPHABETICAL ORDER

Chapter	Subject	page

Command notes:

Command notes:

Command notes:

Command notes:

Command notes:

Command notes: